43D CONGRESS, 1st Session. } SENATE. { REPORT 307, Part 1.

REPORT

OF THE

SELECT COMMITTEE ON TRANSPORTATION-ROUTES TO THE SEABOARD,

WITH

APPENDIX AND EVIDENCE.

APRIL 24, 1874.—Ordered to be printed.

WASHINGTON:
GOVERNMENT PRINTING OFFICE.
1874.

CONTENTS.

TRANSPORTATION-ROUTES TO THE SEABOARD.

Mr. WINDOM, from the Select Committee on Transportation-Routes to the Seaboard, submitted the following

REPORT:

The Select Committee appointed "to investigate and report upon the subject of transportation between the interior and the seaboard," submit the following report:

On the 16th of December, 1872, the Senate of the United States adopted the following preamble and resolution:

"Whereas the productions of our country have increased much more rapidly than the means of transportation, and the growth of population and products will in the near future demand additional facilities, and cheaper ones, to reach tide-water; and

"Whereas in his recent message the President of the United States invites the attention of Congress to the fact that 'it will be called upon at its present session to consider various enterprises for the more certain and cheaper transportation of the constantly increasing Western and Southern products to the Atlantic seaboard,' and further says 'the subject is one that will force itself upon the legislative branch of the Government sooner or later, and I suggest, therefore, that immediate steps be taken to gain all available information to insure equitable and just legislation; * * * I would therefore suggest either a committee or a commission to be authorized to consider this whole question, and to report to Congress at some future day, for its better guidance in legislating on this important subject;' therefore

"*Resolved*, That a committee of seven be appointed, to whom shall be referred that part of the President's message relating to transportation-routes to the seaboard."

And on the 26th day of March, 1872, the following resolution was passed by the Senate.

"*Resolved*, That the Select Committee on Transportation-Routes to the Seaboard be authorized to sit at such places as they may designate during the recess, and to investigate and report upon the subject of transportation between the interior and the seaboard; that they have power to employ a clerk and stenographer, and to send for persons and papers; and that the actual and necessary expenses attending such investigation be paid out of the contingent fund of the Senate upon vouchers approved by the chairman of said committee."

On the same day two members were added to the committee.

In entering upon the investigation directed by the above resolutions, the committee were impressed with the important and difficult nature of the duty assigned to them. Though they have assiduously devoted themselves to its discharge, they are conscious that the information herewith submitted is by no means as complete as could be desired. It is perhaps unnecessary to say that an investigation covering a field so broad, embracing interests so vast and complex, and involving an examination of details almost infinite in number and variety, required more than a single vacation of the Senate; and that the pressure of business during the session has afforded but little opportunity for the preparation of a report commensurate with the importance of the questions involved.

The absence of systematized statistics, with regard to the course and magnitude of the internal commerce of the country, has added largely to the labors of your committee. Perhaps the most extraordinary feature of our governmental policy touching the vast internal trade of the nation, is the apparent indifference and neglect with which it has been treated. While detailed information has been obtained by the Government, under customs and revenue laws, in relation to commerce with foreign countries, no means have been provided for collecting accurate statistics concerning the vastly more important interests of internal commerce. No officer of the Government has ever been charged with the duty of collecting information on this subject, and the legislator who desires to inform himself concerning the nature, extent, value, or necessities of our immense internal trade, or of its relations to foreign commerce, must patiently grope his way through the statistics furnished by boards of trade, chambers of commerce, and transportation companies. Even the census reports, which purport to contain an inventory of the property and business pursuits of the people, and which in some matters descend to the minutest details, are silent with regard to the billions of dollars represented by railways and other instruments of internal transportation, and to the much greater values of commodities annually moved by them.

We have no means of measuring accurately the magnitude of this trade; but its colossal proportions may be inferred from two or three known facts. The value of commodities moved by the railroads in 1872 is estimated at over $10,000,000,000, and their gross receipts reached the enormous sum of $473,241,055. The commerce of the cities of the Ohio River alone has been carefully estimated at over $1,600,000,000 per annum. Some conception of the immense trade carried on upon the northern lakes may be formed from the fact, that during the entire season of navigation, in 1872, an average of one vessel every nine minutes, day and night, passed Fort Gratiot light-house, near Port Huron. The value of our internal commerce is many times greater than our trade with all foreign nations, and the amount annually paid for transportation is more than double the entire revenues of the Government.

Finding that whatever information was to be obtained on this subject must be sought for mainly from original sources, your committee have addressed themselves to the inquiry as thoroughly as the time and means at their command would permit.

The following is a brief *résumé* of the principal subjects which have especially commanded the attention of the committee, and which, with others, are embraced in this report:

First. The annual average price of wheat and corn during the five years, 1868 to 1872, inclusive, at Chicago and Milwaukee, and at points west of these cities; at Buffalo, Montreal, New York, Saint Louis, New Orleans, and Liverpool.

Second. The quantity of grain received and shipped from all the lake-ports; ports on the Ohio and Mississippi Rivers; and ports on the Atlantic and Gulf coasts.

Third. The total shipments of grain to the States on the Atlantic seaboard; the quantity distributed between the western and eastern borders of these States; the total quantity consumed in the New England States; the Atlantic States south of New England; and the total quanty exported; also the quantity of grain shipped to the Gulf States, and the quantity exported from those States; the quantity exported to Canada; and also from the Pacific coast to foreign countries.

Fourth. The shipments of grain from the West by the lakes and Saint Lawrence River; by the lakes, Erie Canal, and Hudson River; by the lakes to the east end of Lake Erie; thence by rail toward the seaboard; and by the "all-rail" lines from lake-ports and interior points in the West, to the East and to the South; and the quantity shipped southward by the Mississippi River.

Fifth. The average annual freight-charges from point to point are presented as follows: From points on the Mississippi River to Chicago and Milwaukee; Chicago to Buffalo; Chicago to Montreal by lake and Saint Lawrence River, and by rail; Chicago to New York by lake and canal, by lake and rail, and by all rail; Saint Louis to New Orleans; New Orleans to Liverpool, New York to Liverpool, and Montreal to Liverpool. These averages have been deduced from computations based upon the quantity shipped and the average rates which prevailed each month.

Sixth. Great Britain being the principal grain-importing country, very full information in regard to the sources of her supply, the quantity received from each country for thirteen years, the rates of freight from each country to England for a period of ten years, and the average prices in the English markets of wheat and corn imported from each country during a period of thirteen years. This information has been obtained from the British reports on trade and navigation, and from data furnished especially for the committee by the British Board of Trade through the United States consuls at London and Liverpool.

Seventh. Some general facts are presented in regard to the commerce of the Pacific coast.

One of the most important branches of the work commanding the attention of the committee has been that of the improvement and construction of water-lines of transport. The lines which the committee have personally examined and most carefully investigated are—

First. The proposed Caughnawaga and Lake Champlain route, from the river Saint Lawrence to New York.

Second. The Oswego and Oneida Canal route, from Oswego to New York.

Third. The Erie Canal route, from Buffalo to New York.

Fourth. The James River and Kanawha Canal, or central water-line, from Richmond to the Ohio River.

Fifth. The Atlantic and Great Western Canal, from the Tennessee River to Savannah Ga.

Sixth. The proposed ship-canal across the peninsula of Florida.

Seventh. The improvement of the Ohio River.

Eighth. The improvement of the Mississippi above the Falls of Saint Anthony; between Saint Paul and Saint Louis; and between Saint Louis and New Orleans.

Ninth. The Fort Saint Philip Canal, and other plans for improving the mouth of the Mississippi River.

Tenth. The Wisconsin and Fox Rivers improvement.

Eleventh. The Illinois and Hennepin Canal.

Twelfth. The Niagara Ship-Canal.

It is believed that the information contained in the report is as full and accurate in regard to all of these lines as can be obtained without further official surveys.

In addition to these routes the committee have obtained information in regard to the canals of Pennsylvania and the Chesapeake and Ohio Canal.

The inquiries of the committee in regard to railroads have embraced among other subjects the following:

Combinations between different lines; the consolidation or amalgamation of lines; fast-freight lines; the issuing of stock not representing money paid in for construction, a device commonly known as "stock-watering" or capitalization of surplus earnings; competition between railroads and water-lines; the relative cost of the various methods of transportation; the regulation or control of existing railroads by States and by the national Government, involving the questions as to the limitation of the powers of Congress under the commercial clause of the Constitution; the construction of one or more double-track freight-railroads by the Government, to be operated by it or leased to parties who shall operate such road or roads subject to governmental control; and the chartering of freight-railroads to be constructed and managed by private corporations, such roads to receive aid from the Government and to submit to governmental regulation with regard to their rates of freight and the facilities which they shall afford.

A thorough elucidation of these topics involves a study of railway abuses in all their various phases, and the whole question of the economy of transport by rail and by water. The committee do not pretend to have exhausted the subject, but they may be permitted to express the hope that the facts submitted will stimulate further inquiry and enable Congress to inaugurate measures which will be productive of great benefits to the country.

PRODUCTION—HOME CONSUMPTION AND FOREIGN EXPORTATION, FREIGHTS AND PRICES, THE COURSE OF TRADE, AND FOREIGN MARKETS.

PRODUCTION OF CEREALS IN THE UNITED STATES.

The production of cereals in the United States during the years 1840, 1850, 1860, and 1870, is presented in the following table, compiled from the census reports for those years. In the same table are presented the exports of cereals and the home-consumption during the same years:

Production, home-consumption, and exports of cereals from 1840 *to* 1870.

Year.	Production of cereals.	Home-consumption.	Export of cereals.	Exports, what per cent. of production.
	Bushels.	*Bushels.*	*Bushels.*	
1840	615, 525, 302	602, 326, 353	13, 199, 049	2. 1
1850	867, 453, 967	851, 502, 312	15, 951, 655	1. 9
1860	1, 239, 039, 945	1, 216, 084, 810	22, 955, 135	1. 8
1870	1, 629, 027, 600	1, 571, 737, 179	57, 290, 521	3. 5

From this table it appears that the exports of grain to foreign coun tries were only 2.1 per cent. of the entire product in 1840, 1.9 per cent. in 1850, 1.8 per cent. in 1860, and 3.5 per cent. in 1870.

The following table indicates the fact that our annual home-consumption of grain increased 969,410,826 bushels from 1840 to 1870, while the increase of exports to foreign countries during the same period was only 44,091,472 bushels, the increase of foreign exports having been but 4½ per cent. of the increase of home-consumption.

Increase of production as compared with increase of exports.

Years from and to.	Increase of production.	Increase of exports.	Increase of home-consumption.
	Bushels.	*Bushels.*	*Bushels.*
1840 to 1850	251, 928, 665	2, 752, 606	249, 176, 059
1850 to 1860	371, 585, 978	7, 003, 480	364, 582, 498
1860 to 1870	389, 987, 655	34, 335, 386	355, 652, 269
Total	1, 013, 502, 298	44, 091, 472	969, 410, 826

On page 199 of the Appendix may be found a valuable table, which gives the estimated yield of cereals in each State of the Union during the year 1872; also, the total yield in each of eight geographical divisions of the country. This table was prepared for the committee by Mr. J. R. Dodge, statistician of the Agricultural Department.

The total production of cereals in the United States during the year 1872 is estimated at 1,656,198,100 bushels.

It is unnecessary for the committee to enter upon any discussion in relation to the production of grain in all these divisions. It is sufficient in this connection to refer to the production of the States of the first division, viz, Ohio, Michigan, Indiana, Illinois, Wisconsin, Minnesota, Iowa, Missouri, Kansas, and Nebraska.

The following was the estimated yield in those States during the year 1872:

	Bushels.
Wheat	156, 228, 000
Corn	693, 625, 000
Rye	5, 563, 300
Oats	163, 479, 000
Barley	10, 092, 000
Total	1, 028, 987, 300

It appears from the above statement that the total product of wheat in these States during the year 1872 was 156,228,000 bushels. The Agricultural Department also estimates that the consumption of wheat in these States was 5 bushels per capita, and that 1½ bushels per acre were used for seed.

The total consumption of wheat in the States of the first division appears, therefore, to have been as follows:

	Bushels.
Population, 13,000,000 × 5 (bushels per capita)	65, 000, 000
Acres, 13,811,008 × 1½ (bushels of seed per acre)	20, 716, 512
Total home consumption	85, 716, 512

This amount being subtracted from the total production shows the amount exported to home and foreign markets to have been 70,511,488 bushels.

From the data in regard to the eastward movement of wheat from the West to the sea-board we find that the total shipments from the above-mentioned States to have been as follows:

	Bushels.
Shipped to the Atlantic States	55,248,046
Shipped to the Gulf States	11,281,328
Shipped to Canada	7,566,639
Total quantity shipped from the Northwestern States	*74,096,013

The substantial agreement of this result with the results arrived at by the Department of Agriculture—the difference of 3,584,525 bushels being only 2⅓ per cent. of the total product of wheat in the year 1872—

* This amount includes the wheat consumed in the Atlantic and Gulf States and in foreign countries.

is a proof of the correctness of each result for the purpose of any general discussion of questions relating to the production and exportation of grain.

The enormous quantity of corn produced in the States of the first division (nearly 700,000,000 bushels) is largely fed to animals, and is converted into spirits, in which form it constitutes a very large surplus product of the West. The quantity shipped to other States in the form of grain represents but a part of the actual surplus corn-product.

Oats are also very largely fed to animals at the West, and contribute to the surplus products of those States in animals and their products.

The principal part of the rye and barley produced is consumed in the Western States.

The following statement exhibits the amount of grain produced in the States of Ohio, Michigan, Indiana, Illinois, Wisconsin, Missouri, Kansas, Nebraska, Iowa, and Minnesota, the quantity consumed in those States and in the Atlantic and Gulf States, and the quantities exported to foreign countries:

		Bushels.
Consumed in the States in which produced		815,955,574
Consumed in the Atlantic States	104,877,122	
Consumed in the Gulf States	33,783,526	
Consumed in foreign countries	74,360,778	
		213,021,426
Production of the States named		1,028,987,000

The amount of grain consumed in the States above mentioned (815,955,574 bushels) includes not only the quantity consumed as human food, but the total quantity consumed there, and exported to other States and to foreign countries, in the forms of spirits, and of animals and their products.

HOME CONSUMPTION AND FOREIGN EXPORTATION.

In our home-markets, producers of grain in this country meet only the competition of grain imported from Canada. The official returns of the foreign commerce of the United States show that during the year ending June 30, 1873, we imported from Canada 6,701,001 bushels of grain,* as follows:

	Bushels.
Barley	4,513,409
Corn	226
Oats	207,590
Rye	213,598
Wheat and wheat-flour	1,766,178
Total	6,701,001

* The imports during the year ending June 30, 1873, consisted almost entirely of the crop of 1872.

The wheat received from Canada consisted entirely of the higher grades, and was imported chiefly at the ports of Buffalo and Oswego. The average value of all the wheat imported was $1.58 per bushel, as against $1.40 per bushel, the value of American No. 2 spring wheat at Buffalo.*

The total imports of grain from Canada were, however, only half of one per cent. of the entire production of grain in the United States in the year 1872, and only 4 per cent. of the entire shipments of grain from the Western States to home and foreign markets.

The markets to which grain produced in the Western and Northwestern States is shipped:

Home-markets:

	Bushels.
The New England States	41,132,225
The Atlantic States south of New England	63,744,897
The Atlantic States	104,877,122
The Gulf States	33,783,526
Total to home-markets	138,660,648
Exported to and consumed in foreign countries	74,360,778
†Total quantity shipped to home and foreign markets	213,021,426

Specific information in regard to shipments to home-markets by rail and by lake, canal, and river, and also as to exports from the various ports of the United States, and the quantities exported to each country, may be found in other parts of this report.

FREIGHTS AND PRICES.

Commerce among the States of the Union has assumed vast proportions and varied conditions. Any treatise upon this great subject in all its bearings would far transcend the limits of this report. The inquiries of this committee have, therefore, been confined chiefly to the transportation of the surplus products of the Western States to the sea-board, and to foreign countries. These inquiries have incidentally involved a consideration of the general conditions affecting the movements of trade between the interior and the Atlantic and Gulf States, and between the United States and foreign countries. Tables may be found in the Ap-

* The duties on grain imported into the United States are as follows:

Wheat	20 cents per bushel.
Wheat-flour	20 per cent. ad valorem.
Corn	10 cents per bushel.
Corn-meal	10 per cent. ad valorem.
Rye	15 cents per bushel.
Rye-flour	10 per cent. ad valorem.
Oats	10 cents per bushel.
Barley	1 cent per pound.
Barley, pulverized	20 per cent. ad valorem.

†The exports to foreign countries in the above table include only grain produced east of the Rocky Mountains.

pendix which show the tonnage of the leading articles of commerce shipped from the principal cities of the interior to the sea-board, and the quantities of the same commodities which have been exported.

It is estimated that 90 per cent. of the freights shipped eastward from Chicago by the lakes consists of breadstuffs.

The proportion of the principal and other articles shipped east from Chicago by the four main-trunk-railway lines during the year 1873 was as follows:

Articles.	Tons.	Per cent.
Grain, flour, seeds, and feed	904, 284	44. 10
Animals and their products	796, 241	38. 70
Lumber, shingles, laths, staves, and headings	72, 941	3. 56
Alcohol, high wines, liquors, ale, and beer	22, 481	1. 14
All other articles	258, 469. 7	12. 50
Total	2, 054, 416. 7	100

As the principal part of the lumber, shingles, laths, staves, headings, and general merchandise was shipped to points in the Western States, it may be inferred that about 50 per cent. of all the freight shipped from Chicago to the Atlantic States consisted of cereals, and that about 45 per cent. consisted of animals and their products. An elaborate table may be found on page 230 of the Appendix, which gives in detail the facts here stated.

The transportation of freights westward has also a very important bearing upon the cost of transporting the cereal products of the West to the sea-board. Upon those lines which have a large amount of return-freights the cost of transporting grain and flour to the East is, of course, less than upon lines which depend mainly or entirely upon eastward-bound freights.

In prosecuting this branch of their investigations the committee have confined their attention to the prices of grain at the principal markets in this country and in Europe, and to the means and cost of transporting such products to home and foreign markets. The data in regard to freights is confined chiefly to wheat and corn.

For the purpose of instituting accurate comparisons, prices have been obtained of the grade of wheat known as "No. 2 spring," and of the grade of corn known as "Western mixed." A large amount of such information has been collected, which may be found in the Appendix.

From this data the average annual prices at each point have been carefully computed for the years 1868, 1869, 1870, 1871, and 1872. The average annual freight-charges, by various lines of transport, have also been computed for the same years. The information is embraced in the following statements, in which both prices and freight-charges are stated in currency at the average rate of premium on gold:

Statement showing the average rates of freight per bushel on wheat from ports here mentioned during the years 1868, 1869, 1870, 1871, *and* 1872.

From—	To—	How transported.	Year. 1868.	1869.	1870.	1871.	1872.
			Cts. m.	*Cts. m.*	*Cts. m.*	*Cts. m.*	*Cts. m.*
Chicago	Buffalo	Lake	08 3	7 1	06 0	08 5	12 7
Do	New York	Rail	42 6	35 1	33 3	31 0	*33 5
Do	....do	Lake and rail				22 3	28 8
Do	....do	Lake and canal	25 3	24 1	17 5	21 6	26 6
Do	Montreal	Lake and Saint Lawrence		17 2	16 6	18 8	24 1
Buffalo	New York	Rail				18 3	18 0
Do	....do	Canal	17 0	17 0	11 5	13 1	13 9
New York	Liverpool	Steam				20 1	19 2
Do	....do	Sail				16 3	16 5
Montreal	....do	Steam	26 2	28 4	19 7	25 1	25 7
Do	....do	Sail		27 4	17 4	22 3	24 8
Saint Louis	New Orleans	River					13 9
New Orleans	Liverpool						27 0

* The all-rail rate from Chicago to New York during the season of navigation of 1872 was 32.7 cents per bushel.

Statement showing the average rate of freight per bushel on corn from ports here mentioned during the years 1868, 1869, 1870, 1871, *and* 1872.

From—	To—	How transported.	Year. 1868.	1869.	1870.	1871.	1872.
			Cts. m.	*Cts. m.*	*Cts. m.*	*Cts. m.*	*Cts. m.*
Chicago	Buffalo	Lake	6 0	6 0	5 1½	6 3	10 1
Do	New York	Rail	38 7	31 7	31 0	30 3	*30 7
Do	....do	Lake and canal	18 3	20 2	15 2	17 8	21 6
Do	Montreal	Lake and Saint Lawrence.					20 4
New York	Liverpool	Steam				19 0	17 0
Do	....do	Sail				16 9	16 4
Montreal	....do	Steam	20 5	20 8		23 5	20 6
Do	....do	Sail	17 5	18 7		20 9	20 3
Saint Louis	New Orleans						13 0
New Orleans	Liverpool						25 0

* The average all-rail rate from Chicago to New York during the season of navigation of 1872 was 28 cents and 4 mills per bushel.

Statement showing the average price of No. 2 spring-wheat at Chicago, Milwaukee, Buffalo, New York, Montreal, Liverpool, and Saint Louis, during the years 1868, 1869, 1870, 1871, *and* 1872.

Port.	Year. 1868.	1869.	1870.	1871.	1872.
	Dolls. cts. m.	*Dolls. cts. m.*	*Dolls. cts. m.*	*Dolls. cts. m.*	*Dolls. cts. m.*
Chicago	1 55 7	1 12 2	1 01 2	1 19 8	1 22 6
Milwaukee	1 56 4		1 03 5	1 21 2	1 22 0
Buffalo	1 63 8	1 26 0	1 14 4	1 34 7	1 40 3
New York			1 26 8	1 49 1	1 58 2
Saint Louis					1 27 0
Montreal	1 81 7	1 40 8	1 25 7	1 43 8	1 52 5
Liverpool	2 38 9	1 76 1	1 44 8	1 74 3	1 86 9

Statement showing the average price of western mixed corn at Chicago, Buffalo, New York, Saint Louis, Montreal, and Liverpool, during the years 1868, 1869, 1870, 1871, *and* 1872.

Port.	Year.														
	1868.			1869.			1870.			1871.			1872.		
	Dolls.	*cts.*	*m.*	*Dolls.*	*cts.*	*m.*	*Dolls.*	*cts.*	*m.*	*Dolls.*	*cts.*	*m.*	*Dolls.*	*cts.*	*m.*
Chicago	0	87	2	0	72	4	0	74	7	0	49	2	0	40	2
Buffalo	1	01	5	0	83	7	0	83	7	0	60	4	0	52	7
New York	1	17	8	1	01	7	0	99	5	0	73	6	0	65	7
Saint Louis													0	41	7
Montreal	1	14	2				0	93	1	0	71	0	0	63	3
Liverpool	1	53	9	1	15	4				1	02	8	0	90	1

Besides freight-charges there are certain terminal or incidental charges incurred in passing through the various ports, which go to make up the entire cost of transportation. These consist of commissions, elevator-charges, insurance, weighing, and inspection.

The following statements, however, include only the actual transfer-charges. These transfer-charges at the various ports are as follows: Chicago, 2 cents; Buffalo, 1¼ cents; Montreal, 1 cent; Saint Louis, 2 cents; New Orleans 1 cent; New York, 1½ cents.

In addition to these charges, the insurance by water is to be taken into account. The following table gives the average rates for the various routes:

From—	To—	Average rate of marine insurance.
Chicago	Buffalo	1 per cent.
Do	Montreal	1½ per cent.
Buffalo	New York	¼ per cent.
New York	Liverpool	Sailing-vessels, 1¼ per cent.; steam-vessels, 1 per cent.
Montreal	do	Sailing-vessels, 2¼ per cent.; steam-vessels, 1¼ per cent.
Saint Louis	New Orleans	1 per cent.
New Orleans	Liverpool	1½ per cent.

For the purpose of comparing the cost of transportation by the principal competing lines and routes, the following statements are presented. They refer to the data for the year 1872, and *include transfer charges and insurance.*

(*a.*) *Cost of transporting wheat from Chicago to New York and to Montreal.*

	Aveage cost of transportation per bushel of 60 pounds, including transfer charges and marine insurance.
From Chicago to New York, (rail)	35.5 cents.
(all water)	31.7 cents.
From Chicago to Montreal, (water)	27.9 cents.
From Saint Louis to New Orleans, (river)	17.2 cents.

(*b.*) *Cost of transporting wheat from Chicago to Liverpool, via New York and via Montreal, and from Saint Louis to Liverpool, via New Orleans the water rates being taken in each case.*

	Average cost of transportation per bushel of 60 pounds, including transfer charges and marine insurance.
Chicago to Liverpool, via New York, (sail)	51. 7 cents.
(steam)	53. 7 cents.
* Chicago to Liverpool, via Montreal, (sail)	57. 1 cents.
(steam)	56. 5 cents.
Saint Louis to Liverpool, via Mississippi River	47. 3 cents.

The following statements have been compiled from the foregoing data for the year 1872. They indicate the differences between the prices of wheat at various ports; the actual cost of transportation between such ports, including transfer charges and insurance, and the differences between the cost of transportation and the difference of prices, or the profits realized above the actual and necessary cost of transportation.

(*a.*) *No. 2 spring wheat; Chicago to Buffalo by lake*, 1872.

Average price of No. 2 spring wheat at Chicago	$1 22. 6
Average price of No. 2 spring wheat at Buffalo	1 40. 3
Difference between these prices	17. 7
Total cost of transportation, including transfers and insurance	15. 9
Difference between prices in excess of cost of transportation	1. 8

The difference between the average prices of No. 2 spring wheat at Chicago and Buffalo appears to have been composed of—

Cost of transportation	90 per cent.
Difference of prices in excess of cost of transportation	10 per cent.

(*b.*) *No. 2 spring wheat; Chicago to New York by lake and Erie Canal*, 1872.

Average price of No. 2 spring wheat at Chicago	$1 22. 6
Average price of No. 2 spring wheat at New York	1 58. 2
Difference between these prices	35. 6
Cost of transportation, including transfers and insurance	31. 4
Difference between prices in excess of cost of transportation	4. 2

* The marine insurance on sailing-vessels from Montreal to Europe during the latter part of the season of navigation is very much greater than the rates on steam-vessels; hence the average cost of transportation for the entire season is greater in sailing-vessels than in steam-vessels.

The difference between the average prices of No. 2 spring wheat at Chicago and New York appears to have been composed of—

Cost of transportation	88 per cent
Difference between prices in excess of cost of transportation	12 per cent.

(*c.*) *No.* 2 *spring wheat; Chicago to Montreal by lake and Saint Lawrence,* 1872.

Average price of No. 2 spring wheat at Chicago	$1 22.6
Average price of No. 2 spring wheat at Montreal	1 52.5
Difference between these prices	29.9
Cost of transportation, including transfers and insurance	27.9
Difference between prices in excess of transportation	2.0

The difference between the prices of No. 2 spring wheat at Chicago and at Montreal appears to have been composed of—

Cost of transportation	93⅓ per cent.
Difference between prices in excess of cost of transportation	6⅔ per cent.

(*d.*) *No.* 2 *spring wheat; Chicago to Liverpool, transport via New York by ocean steamer,* 1872.

Average price of No. 2 spring wheat at Chicago	$1 22.6
Average price of No. 2 spring wheat at Liverpool	1 86.9
Difference between these prices	64.3
Cost of transportation, including transfer and insurance, (steam)	53.7
Difference between prices in excess of cost of transportation	10.6

The difference between the average prices of No. 2 spring wheat at Chicago and Liverpool appears to have been composed of—

Cost of transportation	84 per cent.
Difference between prices in excess of cost of transportation	16 per cent.

(*e.*) *No.* 2 *spring wheat; Chicago to Liverpool, transport via Montreal by ocean steamer,* 1872.

Average price of No. 2 spring wheat at Chicago, year 1872	$1 22.6
Average price of No. 2 spring wheat at Liverpool, year 1872	1 86.9
Difference between these prices	64.3
Cost of transportation, including transfer and insurance, (steam)	56.5
Difference between prices in excess of cost of transportation	7.8

The difference between the average prices of No. 2 spring wheat at Chicago and at Liverpool appears to have been composed of—

Cost of transportation	88 per cent.
Difference between prices in excess of cost of transportation	12 per cent.

(*f*.) *No. 2 spring wheat; Saint Louis to Liverpool, transport via Mississippi River and ocean steamer*, 1872.

Average price of No. 2 spring wheat at Saint Louis, year 1872	$1 27. 0
Average price of No. 2 spring wheat at Liverpool, year 1872	1 86. 9
Difference between these prices	59. 9
Cost of transportation, including transfers and insurance	47. 3
Difference between prices in excess of cost of transportation	12. 6

The difference between the average prices of No. 2 spring wheat at Saint Louis and Liverpool during the year 1872 appears to be composed of—

Cost of transportation	79 per cent.
Difference between prices in excess of cost of transportation	21 per cent.

The facts presented in the preceding statements in regard to wheat are based upon data relating to the direct shipment of grain from point to point, without expenses attending sale or storage longer than may be necessary to transfer from one vessel to another. The transfer charges in each case refer to handling in bulk, and do not include the expenses of bagging when shipped in that way.

When wheat is sold at intermediate points, or is held in store at such points for a longer period than is necessary to transfer from one vehicle to another, the incidental charges are of course greater.

No comparative statements can be made to illustrate such cases, as the charges incurred are variable, depending upon the time during which it is held in store, and the ever-changing conditions of the markets.

The foregoing facts are presented in a condensed form in the following table, and relate to prices and freight charges which prevailed during the year 1872:

No. 2 spring wheat.

From—	To—	Difference between prices.	Cost of transportation, including transfer and insurance.	Profits.	Cost of transportation, per cent.	Profit, per cent.	How transported on the ocean.
		Cts. m.	*Cts. m.*	*Cts. m.*			
Chicago	Buffalo	17 7	15 9	01 8	90	10	
Do	New York	35 6	31 4	04 2	88	12	
Do	Liverpool via New York.	64 3	53 7	10 6	84	16	Steam.
			51 4	12 9	80	20	Sail.
Do	Liverpool via Montreal.	64 3	56 5	07 8	88	12	Steam.
			57 1	07 2	89	11	Sail.
Do	Montreal	29 9	27 9	02 0	93	7	
New York	Liverpool	28 7	22 3	06 4	78	22	Steam.
			20 0	08 7	70	30	Sail.
Montreal	do	34 4	28 6	05 8	83	17	Steam.
			29 2	05 2	85	15	Sail.
*Saint Louis	do	59 9	47 3	12 6	79	21	

* The barge rates are taken from Saint Louis to New Orleans, and the average of the sail and steam rates from New Orleans to Liverpool.

Western mixed corn.

From—	To—	Difference between prices.	Cost of transportation, including transfers and insurance.	Profits.	Cost of transportation, per cent.	Profit, per cent.	How transported on the ocean.
		Cts. m.	*Cts. m.*	*Cts. m.*			
Chicago	Buffalo	12 5	12 5	....	100	0	
Chicago	New York	25 5	25 4	00 1	99.6	0.4	
Chicago	Montreal	23 1	23 0	00 1	99.6	0.4	
New York	Liverpool	24 4	19 2	05 2	79	21	Steam.
			18 7	05 7	77	23	Sail.
Montreal	Liverpool	26 8	22 4	04 4	84	16	Steam.
			22 7	04 1	85	15	Sail.
Chicago	Liverpool, via New York.	49 9	44 5	05 4	89	11	Steam.
			44 1	05 8	88	12	Sail.
Chicago	Liverpool, via Montreal.	49 9	45 4	04 5	91	9	Steam.
			45 7	04 2	92	8	Sail.
*Saint Louis	Liverpool	48 4	42 2	06 2	87	13	Barges, St. Louis to N. O.

* The barge rates are taken from Saint Louis to New Orleans, and the average of the sail and steam rates from New Orleans to Liverpool. The column entitled "profits" in the above tables refers to the excess of the differeuce between prices above the total cost of transportation.

Many other comparative statements may be formed from the statistics hereinbefore given in regard to freights and prices. The committee have only presented those which seemed to have the most important commercial bearing.

The cost of transporting wheat from points west of Chicago on the Mississippi River to Chicago averages about 17 cents per bushel, and the cost of transporting corn about 15.9 cents.

Subtracting these sums respectively from the prices of wheat and corn at Chicago during the year 1872, and we find the value of No. 2

spring wheat at the Mississippi River to be $1.056 per bushel, and the value of western mixed corn 24.3 cents per bushel.

Referring to the foregoing statistics in regard to the value of No. 2 spring wheat during the year 1872, at the various points mentioned, it appears that the value of one bushel of wheat at Liverpool was equal to the value of $1\frac{12}{100}$ bushels at New York, $1\frac{22}{100}$ bushels at Montreal, $1\frac{33}{100}$ bushels at Buffalo, $1\frac{52}{100}$ bushels at Chicago, $1\frac{8}{10}$ bushels at the Mississippi River directly west of Chicago, and $1\frac{47}{100}$ bushels at Saint Louis, and $1\frac{32}{100}$ bushels at New Orleans.

In like manner it appears that during the year 1872 the value of one bushel of corn at Liverpool was equal to the value of $1\frac{37}{100}$ bushels at New York, $1\frac{42}{100}$ bushels at Montreal, $1\frac{71}{100}$ bushels at Buffalo, $2\frac{24}{100}$ bushels at Chicago, $3\frac{71}{100}$ bushels at the Mississippi River directly west of Chicago, $2\frac{16}{100}$ bushels at Saint Louis, and $1\frac{65}{100}$ bushels at New Orleans. The following tables exhibit data of this sort for five years.

Statement showing the number of bushels of wheat at New York, at Montreal, at Buffalo, at Chicago, at the Mississippi River west of Chicago, at Saint Louis, and at New Orleans, worth one bushel at Liverpool, during the years 1868, 1869, 1870, 1871, *and* 1872.

One bushel of wheat at Liverpool, worth at—	Years.				
	1868.	1869.	1870.	1871.	1872.
	Bushels.	*Bushels.*	*Bushels.*	*Bushels.*	*Bushels.*
New York	....	....	1.14	1.17	1.12
Montreal	1.31	1.22	1.15	1.21	1.22
Buffalo	1.45	1.40	1.30	1.29	1.33
Chicago	1.53	1.57	1.42	1.45	1.52
Mississippi River	....	....	....	....	1.77
Saint Louis	....	....	....	....	1.47
New Orleans	....	....	....	....	1.32

Statement showing the number of bushels of corn at New York, at Montreal, at Buffalo, at Chicago, at the Mississippi River west of Chicago, at Saint Louis, and at New Orleans, which were worth one bushel of corn at Liverpool, during the years 1868, 1869, 1870, 1871, *and* 1872.

One bushel of corn at Liverpool, worth at—	Years.				
	1868.	1869.	1870.	1871.	1872.
	Bushels.	*Bushels.*	*Bushels.*	*Bushels.*	*Bushels.*
New York	1.31	1.13	....	1.4	1.37
Montreal	....	....	....	1.45	1.42
Buffalo	1.52	1.38	....	1.7	1.71
Chicago	1.76	1.6	....	2.09	2.24
Mississippi River	....	....	....	....	2.71
Saint Louis	....	....	....	....	2.16
New Orleans	....	....	....	....	1.65

In order to prevent erroneous conclusions in regard to the value of the various routes from the West to the sea-board and thence to foreign countries, it must be remembered that there are other commercial facts which determine the amount of grain which can be profitably shipped from the interior to the sea-board and from American ports to foreign countries, besides the actual freight-charges which may prevail upon such routes. These facts may be summarized in the expression that the extent of the shipments on the various internal lines of transport depends mainly upon the amount of return-freights on such lines, and that the extent of the exportation of grain from any American port to foreign countries depends mainly upon the available supply of tonnage for foreign shipments at such port. These circumstances point to the explanation of the following facts in regard to the actual amount of wheat and corn exported from New York, New Orleans, and Montreal during the year 1872, as follows:

Wheat exported from New York	17,889,037
Wheat exported from New Orleans	None reported.
Wheat exported from Montreal	3,818,450
Corn exported from New York	18,331,147
Corn exported from New Orleans	790,959
Corn exported from Montreal	7,546,390

The point here referred to is, however, more fully discussed in other parts of this report in treating of particular routes.

THE COURSE OF TRADE.

The general movement of grain from the West to the seaboard.

In tracing the course of the grain-trade of the Western and Northwestern States, the first inquiry which suggests itself relates to the movement of grain to the States of the Atlantic sea-board, and to the Gulf States, or, in other words, the *eastward* and *southward* movements. The general conditions governing these movements will also be treated of, so far as the limits of this report will permit.

The relative eastward and southward movements of grain from the States north and west of Indiana is approximately indicated by the receipts and shipments at Chicago and Milwaukee, the chief depots of the grain-trade on the lakes, and at Saint Louis, the chief depot of the same trade on the Mississippi River.

The following statements are based upon such data for the year 1872:

Receipts.

	Bushels.
Receipts of grain at Chicago and Milwaukee during the year 1872	111,478,245
Receipts at Saint Louis	28,365,945
Shipped east.	
From Chicago and Milwaukee	102,695,975
From Saint Louis	6,597,126
Total shipped east	109,293,101

Shipped south.

	Bushels.
From Chicago and Milwaukee	738, 665
From Saint Louis	15, 750, 202
Total shipped South	17, 267, 767

The proportion of eastern to southern shipments from these cities appear to be as 100 to 16.

Until about the year 1856, almost the entire surplus grain product of the Western States was transported to eastern markets by the lakes and the Erie Canal, and to southern markets by the Mississippi River and its tributaries. New York was almost the sole distributing port at the East and New Orleans at the South. At the present time about 67 per cent. of the grain shipped east is transported on the main trunk railroads.

The extension of the railroad system throughout the Western and Northwestern States has effected radical changes in the conditions of transportation. By means of combinations of roads, and by the organization of through freight-lines, grain is transported from interior ports at the West to the local and exporting ports of the East without breaking bulk, thus saving the terminal or incidental charges at the shipping and receiving ports on the lakes. Active competition has sprung up in many directions, between railroads and the water-lines, with different results according as the conditions have been more favorable to the one mode of transport or the other.

Practically the railroad interests control the transport of grain from all that part of the States of Illinois and Indiana situated south of a latitudinal line sixty miles south of Lake Michigan. This section embraces the principal part of the great corn-producing area of Illinois, as may be seen by referring to the crop-map at the end of the appendix to this report. In order to illustrate the manner in which the control over the transport of grain by rail is exercised, the following facts are presented from data furnished to the committee by Mr. J. D. Hayes, general manager of the Blue Line, under date of January 31, 1874. Mr. Hayes says: "The through all-rail rates from Vandalia, Centralia, and Sandoval to New York will average about 60 cents (at present 65 cents) per 100 pounds, equal to 36 cents per bushel on wheat.

	Per 100 pounds.
Local rates from Vandalia to Chicago	$26 35
Local rates from Centralia to Chicago	26 05
Local rates from Sandoval to Chicago	26 30

The rate from all competing points to Boston 5 cents per 100 pounds *over* New York."

The distance from Vandalia, Centralia, and Sandoval to New York, by rail, may be stated at 1,040 miles. At 65 cents per hundred pounds, the freight-rate is 1¼ cents per ton per mile. The distances and the freight-rate, per hundred pounds, and per ton per mile, from those points to Chicago, are as follows:

From—	Distance.	Rate per 100 pounds.	Rate per ton per mile.
	Miles.	*Cents.*	*Cents.*
Vandalia to Chicago	230	26. 35	2. 3
Sandoval to Chicago	250	26. 30	2. 1
Centralia to Chicago	253	26. 05	2. 1

The rate per ton per mile from these three points to Chicago appears to be very nearly twice the rate to New York. In view of the facts presented in this report in regard to the wide differences in the actual cost of transportation on different railroads caused by differences as to the amount of business, return-freights, distances transported, &c., the committee are not prepared, with the information before them, to declare that the differences in freight-rates just noted are in the nature of unjust discriminations. They merely present the above facts as illustrating one of the conditions which seem to determine the course of internal commerce.

In order to illustrate the economy of transport by rail from interior points at the West to the markets of the Atlantic States, let us compare the cost of transporting a bushel of wheat from Sandoval to New York by the direct all-rail line, and by the route via Chicago, the lakes, Erie Canal, and Hudson River, to New York, taking in each case the average annual rate. The cost of transport per bushel from Sandoval by the way of Chicago may be stated as follows:

	Cents.	Mills.
Sandoval to Chicago, rail	15	8
Transfer at Chicago	2	0
Chicago to New York, lake and canal	26	6
Buffalo transfer	1	3
Lake insurance	1	2
Canal and Hudson River insurance	0	4
Rate via Chicago and the water-route	47	3

Mr. Hayes states that the average "all-rail" rate is 36 cents per bushel. This shows the all-rail rate to be $11\frac{3}{10}$ cents, or 15 per cent. less than cost of transport by the lake and canal route, including transfer charges and marine insurance, but not including commissions, which would amount to about 2 cents per bushel. Even if the rail rate from Sandoval to Chicago were no greater than the rail-rate from Sandoval to New York, the entire cost of transporting grain via Chicago and the lakes and canal would be about $3\frac{9}{10}$ cents less by the former route than by the all-rail route. Many other cases of this sort could be instanced, but the one stated is sufficient to illustrate the general fact, that grain can be transported from a large part of the Western States to eastern and southern markets by the all-rail lines at less cost than by the lakes and Erie Canal.

It is believed that higher rates are charged from points east of Sandoval to New York than from that point to New York. Discriminations as against points where there is no competition from rival railway lines, or from water-lines, are common throughout the country. Persons interested in the management or proceeds of railroads, attempt to justify such discriminating or differential charges upon the ground of sound business principles; but whatever may be the merits of particular cases, the committee are unhesitatingly of the opinion that, in very many cases, charges of this sort are totally unjustifiable, and in defiance of those principles of equity and of right which should characterize the management of every public highway. In view of the great importance of this subject, the committee regret that they have not been able to devote to it as much time as was necessary in order to arrive at definite conclusions. With this notice the subject has been deferred to a supplementary report.

The distance from Sandoval to New York is 1,040 miles, and the average rail charge is 36 cents. The average lake and canal charge from Chicago to New York, during the year 1872, was 26.6 cents per bushel, and the average all-rail charge 33.5 cents per bushel, the rail distance being 922 miles.

By applying this distance to the rates from Chicago to New York by rail and by water, we have, in connection with the data in regard to the all-rail shipment from Sandoval, the following comparative statements:

	Average charge per ton per mile.
Chicago to New York, water-route	$9\frac{6}{10}$ mills.
Chicago to New York, all rail	$12\frac{1}{10}$ mills.
Sandoval to New York, all rail	$11\frac{5}{10}$ mills.

It appears that for the same distance as from Chicago to New York the rate from Sandoval is $5\frac{3}{10}$ cents per bushel, or 20 per cent. higher than the lake and canal rate from Chicago.

From all that part of the country lying west and northwest of Lake Michigan, and from which the railways do not necessarily make a large detour, as from Sandoval, in order to reach a lake port, it is evident that the cost of transport by the lakes is cheaper than by rail, even at those points where competition between water-transport and rival railway lines operates to its fullest extent.

The amount of grain transported from interior points at the West to the Atlantic States, without passing through any lake port, amounted in the year 1872 to 25,515,000 bushels, or 14 per cent. of the total quantity transported.

Besides the actual and incidental charges connected with the transport of grain from the West to the sea-board, there are commercial causes which will always maintain great grain-markets on Lake Michigan and on the Mississippi River. Each of the grain-crops comes to maturity within the space of two or three weeks, but a year passes before the entire product of a season reaches the consumers.

In the mean time a very large part of a crop must be held by the producers, or by purchasers of grain, who desire to hold it in store at the West, or at other points between the West and the East, according to the demands of home and foreign markets. Such grain will be held by grain-buyers for advances in the markets, either in ordinary commercial transactions or for speculative purposes, where all the artifices are employed for causing fictitious inflations of prices.

It is evident, therefore, that the single question as to the relative cost of transport by rail and by water does not alone determine the course of the grain trade of the West.

The development of the railway system of the country, in connection with the formation of "through freight lines," and the use of the telegraph in commercial transactions, undoubtedly tend to promote direct shipments from interior points at the West to the distributing points in the Atlantic and Gulf States, and thus in a measure to eliminate the profits of middle-men from the cost of transport between the producer and the consumer.

A very effective means of cheapening the cost of transport by rail has yet to be provided, viz, the establishment of adequate terminal facilities at the chief exporting ports. It is only within the last five years that the most important railway companies have regarded the grain-traffic as a source of sufficient profit to warrant them in establishing it as a distinct branch of their business, by setting apart the requisite number of cars specially adapted to the carriage of grain in bulk, together with the necessary terminal facilities. Such facilities embrace extensive water-fronts, in or adjacent to the large ports, with commodious structures built upon piers or bulkheads, and provided with the necessary machinery for unloading railroad-cars and for loading sea-going vessels.

It is believed that the Baltimore and Ohio Railroad Company is the only one which has already provided adequate facilities of this nature. Other companies, however, are now taking steps toward securing like facilities.

In relation to this subject, the general freight-agent of the Baltimore and Ohio Railroad states that previous to January, 1872, all grain shipped to Baltimore "in bulk" was unloaded by hand, at an expense of from 4 to 5 cents per bushel. At that time the company completed an elevator of 600,000 bushels capacity, and reduced the charge for receiving, weighing, wharfage, delivery to vessels, and storage for ten days, to 1¾ cents per bushel, by which means also the detention to vessels in loading was reduced from five or ten days to as many hours. This is a fair index of the saving effected by proper terminal facilities.

This company is now building an elevator of 1,250,000 bushels capacity, in order to accommodate its rapidly-increasing grain business.

The freight-agent of the Grand Trunk Railway, at Portland, Me., states that, previous to the burning of their elevator, in August last, the charge for elevating and ten days' storage was 1 cent per bushel.

Mr. Edwin D. Worcester, secretary of the New York Central and Hudson River Railroad, states that his company has an elevator at Buffalo of 600,000 bushels capacity. He also states that within the last year negotiations have been entered into to secure a large plat of ground, situated upon the water-front at New York, on which to erect capacious elevators, yards, and all the appendages to a complete freight establishment. These arrangements are to be carried into effect at the earliest practicable moment.

It is understood that since this statement was made the New York Central Railroad Company has completed the arrangements referred to, and that the erection of the required structures will proceed at once. The Pennsylvania Railroad has an elevator at tide-water in the city of Philadelphia of 480,000 bushels, and another elevator of 800,000 bushels capacity is in course of construction. The same company is also making preparations for the construction of an elevator on the Hudson River, opposite the city of New York, of between 3,000,000 and 4,000,000 bushels capacity. The Erie Railroad Company is also making efforts in the same direction.

The general movements of grain from the States of Ohio, Michigan, Indiana, Illinois, Minnesota, Iowa, Wisconsin, Kansas, and Nebraska, and the general conditions affecting such movements are indicated by statistics furnished to this committee by boards of trade and by the various railroad companies. These statistics may be found in the Appendix. The eastward and southward movements of grain will be treated of separately.

The eastward movement of grain by the various lines of transport.

The following tabulated statement has been compiled from statistics of the movement of grain on the Erie Canal, and on the various trunk railway lines connecting the Western States with the States of the Atlantic sea-board.

Statement showing the quantity of flour and grain shipped from the Western States to the States of the Atlantic sea-board during the year 1872, by the Erie Canal and by the several trunk railroads.

	Wheat.	Wheat flour.	Corn.	Rye.	Oats.	Barley.
	Bushels.	*Barrels.*	*Bushels.*	*Bushels.*	*Bushels.*	*Bushels.*
Erie Canal, Buffalo	11, 001, 069	5, 172	30, 934, 606	210, 705	4, 598, 237	1, 729, 972
Erie Canal, Oswego	1, 928, 850	44, 202	969, 587	241, 125	42, 750	2, 590, 500
	12, 929, 919	49, 374	31, 004, 193	451, 840	4, 640, 987	4, 320, 472
Central Vermont Railroad	1, 074, 756	327, 200	3, 179, 500	1, 786	880, 100	431, 810
Rome, Watertown, and Ogdensburgh Railroad.	289, 229	148, 882	290, 801	5, 476	37, 183	87, 960
New York Central and Hudson River Railroad.	2, 244, 634	2, 234, 115	15, 036, 400	52, 684	8, 081, 786	642, 469
Erie Railway	1, 990, 676	1, 371, 256	6, 777, 826	12, 360	4, 638, 330	450, 185
*Pennsylvania Railway	2, 344, 489	1, 180, 012	11, 483, 211	35, 885	5, 808, 890	690, 787
Baltimore and Ohio Railroad	458, 447	920, 264	4, 952, 449	25, 176	1, 609, 770	33, 733
Grand Trunk Railway	328, 519	583, 319	961, 098	....	391, 235	71, 660
By rail from Oswego	261, 147	591, 407	357, 581	5, 820	28, 283	180, 625
Total by rail	8, 991, 897	7, 356, 455	43, 038, 866	139, 185	21, 475, 577	2, 589, 229
Total by rail and canal	21, 921, 816	7, 405, 829	74, 043, 059	591, 027	26, 116, 564	6, 909, 701

Total, Erie Canal, 53,569,594 bushels; total, by rail, 109,338,803 bushels; total, by rail and canal, 162,908,397 bushels.

* The statement furnished by the Pennsylvania Railroad Company gives *grain* and flour. The grain has been stated in the proportion carried by the other roads.

In addition to the quantity of grain moved from the West to the Atlantic sea-board, stated in the above table, the total quantity of western grain shipped to Canada amounted to 15,113,029 bushels. The total eastward movement of grain may therefore be approximately stated as follows:

		Bushels.
Shipped to Montreal		15, 113, 029
Shipped to Atlantic States:		
By Erie Canal		53, 569, 594
By railroads:		
Central Vermont Railroad	7, 040, 352	
Rome, Watertown and Ogdensburgh Railroad	1, 380, 618	
New York Central and Hudson River Railroad	36, 111, 490	
Erie Railway	20, 041, 032	
Pennsylvania Railway	25, 672, 316	
Baltimore and Ohio Railway	11, 220, 761	
Grand Trunk Railway	4, 377, 447	
Rail from Oswego	3, 494, 787	
		109, 338, 803
Total shipped to Atlantic States		162, 908, 397
Total eastward movement of grain to Canada and to Atlantic States		178, 021, 426

It appears, therefore, that of the total eastward movement of grain, amounting to 178,021,426 bushels, 8½ per cent. was shipped to Montreal and 91½ per cent. to Atlantic ports of the United States.*

*About 95 per cent. of the shipments to Montreal are by the lakes and the Saint Lawrence River.

It appears that of the total eastward movement of grain from the West to the Atlantic States, amounting to 162,908,397 bushels, 53,569,594 bushels were shipped by the Erie Canal and 109,338,803 bushels by the railways extending from the lower lakes or crossing the Alleghany range to the sea-board. This immense direct transport of the cereals by rail has sprung up within the last fifteen years. It has increased about 100 per cent. within the last five years, and is still rapidly increasing. The quantity and percentage of wheat, wheat-flour, corn, rye, oats, and barley shipped to the Atlantic States by canal and by rail during the year 1872 was as follows:

Shipped east by canal and by rail—1872.

	Quantity shipped by rail.	Quantity shipped by canal.	Per cent. shipped by rail.	Per cent. shipped by canal.
	Bushels.	*Bushels.*		
Wheat	8, 991, 897	12, 929, 919	41. 0	59. 0
Wheat-flour	33, 104, 047	222, 183	99. 3	0. 7
Corn	43, 038, 866	31, 004, 193	58. 2	41. 8
Rye	139, 187	451, 840	23. 5	76. 5
Oats	21, 475, 577	4, 640, 987	82. 3	17. 7
Barley	2, 589, 229	4, 320, 472	37. 4	62. 6
Total	109, 338, 803	53, 569, 594	67*	33*

* Average.

Of the entire quantity of grain transported to the Atlantic States, 67 per cent. was transported by rail, and 33 per cent. by the Erie Canal. The fact that 59 per cent. of the wheat and only 41.8 per cent. of the corn was transported by the canal is readily explained by referring to the crop-maps at the end of the appendix. The principal part of the eastward shipments of wheat are from Wisconsin, Iowa, and Minnesota. Wheat, therefore, naturally seeks the markets on Lake Michigan and Lake Superior. The great surplus of *corn*, however, is produced in the State of Illinois. By means of the combinations and fast freight lines already referred to, the great trunk railroads are able to control the direct shipment east of a very large proportion of this grain. The manner and extent of this control over the transport of grain produced south of Chicago has been explained. Grain shipped from interior points south of and remote from the lakes can be transported to the local markets of the east at less cost by rail than by lake and canal, the transfer and terminal charges, together with marine insurance by the latter route, amounting to more than the excess of rail-rates of freight over the rates which prevail at the water-line.

As already stated, the total eastward movement of grain to Canada and the Atlantic States amounted, during the year 1872, to 178,021,426 bushels. Of this quantity, 152,506,182 bushels were shipped from lake ports, showing that the quantity of grain shipped by rail directly from interior points at the West to the East amounted to 25,515,244 bushels, or 14 per cent. of the entire eastward movement.* Of this quantity, 17,600,000 bushels was corn.

A striking instance of the effect of the establishment of the through-freight lines from the West to the East, without breaking bulk, is seen in the change in the course of the grain trade to Boston. Formerly grain was shipped by the way of the lakes and Erie Canal to New York, and thence by coastwise vessels to Boston and other ports of New England. At the present time, however, the great bulk of grain reaches Boston directly from the West in through-cars. This change in the mode of shipments is clearly shown by the following table:

	RECEIPTS OF GRAIN AT BOSTON.							
	Flour.		Corn.		Oats.		Barley.	
	Coastwise.	By rail from the West.	Coastwise.	By rail from the West.	Coastwise.	By rail from the West.	Coastwise.	By rail from the West.
1868	701, 727	733, 955	1, 847, 159	483, 875	656, 037	606, 033	64, 039	197, 951
1869	506, 458	818, 827	1, 055, 676	1, 384, 284	338, 756	1, 076, 675	118, 173	122, 713
1870	658, 714	995, 950	945, 981	1, 370, 421	423, 853	1, 676, 108	106, 536	254, 370
1871	569, 303	1, 052, 042	481, 303	3, 156, 800	179, 807	2, 244, 086	84, 559	228, 811
1872	493, 258	988, 491	320, 755	5, 119, 749	82, 767	2, 384, 699	85, 408	288, 488

The oats shipped from the West to the Atlantic States are produced chiefly in Ohio, Michigan, Indiana, and Illinois, and for the reason just stated in regard to corn, are shipped east largely by the all-rail, fast-freight lines.

The interior distribution of grain between the western borders of the Atlantic States and the seaboard.

One of the special advantages pertaining to the transport of grain by the railroad lines consists in the facilities which they afford for shipment directly from the producing areas of the West to the local markets in

* The shipments eastward from lake ports during the year 1872 appear to have been as follows:

Lake ports.	Bushels.
Duluth	1, 279, 217
Milwaukee	21, 157, 792
Chicago, (east)	78, 565, 060
Detroit	8, 000, 000
Cleveland	16, 800, 000
Sandusky	1, 730, 000
Toledo	20, 226, 202
Port Huron	4, 747, 911
Total from lake ports	152, 506, 182

the Atlantic States without breaking bulk. The total quantity of grain received at each of the eastern termini of the lines of transport between the western boundaries of the Atlantic States and the sea-board during the year 1872 is shown by the following statement:

	Bushels.
Received at Portland	3, 741, 413
Received at Boston	12, 241, 145
Received at New York	86, 032, 450
Received at Philadelphia	14, 317, 584
Received at Baltimore	9, 590, 399
Total received	125. 922, 991
Received by rail	76, 051, 240
Received by canal	49, 871, 751

NOTE.—The total receipts of grain at Portland are taken from a table furnished by the Grand Trunk Railway; the quantity received at Boston is taken from a table presented by the board of railway commissioners of Massachusetts, and includes only grain received directly from the West by rail; the receipts at New York are taken from the last report of the New York produce exchange, and include receipts by rail and Hudson River boats; the receipts at Philadelphia are from a table prepared for this committee by the Pennsylvania Railroad Company; and the receipts at Baltimore are taken from a like table furnished by the Baltimore and Ohio Railroad Company.

It appears that the total quantity of grain shipped east by the Erie Canal and the railroads during the year 1872 amounted to 162,908,397 bushels, and the total quantity received at the sea-ports above mentioned by the same lines amounted to 125,922,991 bushels, or 77 per cent. of the total shipment to those States.

The interior distribution by the railroads and the canal appears to have been as follows:

	Shipped east.	Delivered at tide-water.	Distributed between the western boundary of the Atlantic States and the sea-board.
	Bushels.	*Bushels.*	*Bushels.*
By the Erie Canal	53, 569, 594	49, 871, 757	3, 697, 837
By the railroads	109, 338, 803	76, 051, 240	33, 287. 563
Total	162, 908, 397	125, 922, 997	36, 985, 400

It appears from this statement that the quantity of grain distributed between the interior boundary of the Atlantic States and the sea-board was—

	Bushels.
By canal	3, 697, 837
By rail	33, 287, 563
Total	36, 985, 400

The quantity distributed by canal at interior points amounted to 7 per cent. of the canal shipments, and the quantity thus distributed by rail amounted to 30 per cent. of the rail shipments.

It is evident, therefore, that the railroads do a very large business in the way of internal distribution which cannot be done by the canals, and in which the competition of canal transport is not much felt. In this interior distribution the railroads possess decided advantages over the water-line, both in regard to distance and in the saving of expenses incident to transshipments.

The shipment of grain from the Western States to Montreal and to New York.

From the time of the opening of the Erie and of the Canadian canals, the tendency of the shipments of western grain, as between these two routes, has been a subject of great public interest. It is not practicable to enter here upon any detailed history of that competition between New York and Montreal for the trade of the West. A few general facts will, however, suffice for this report.

Prior to the year 1855, grain and flour received at New York from the Western States was transported almost exclusively on the Erie Canal. At about that time transport by rail began. The completion of the Welland Canal in the year 1848 formed a navigable passage around the falls of Niagara, and, in connection with the Saint Lawrence canals around the rapids in that river, opened a continuous line of water transport from the upper lakes to Montreal, at the head of ship-navigation on the Saint Lawrence River.

In the year 1867 grain was first shipped from the West by lake to ports on Lake Huron, and thence by Grand Trunk Railway to Montreal. The amount of such shipments is, however, quite limited. A small amount of grain is also shipped from the West to Montreal by all-rail lines, such shipments being confined to the months when lake navigation is closed, and to shipments under exceptional circumstances during the summer season, when rail-rates are much below the average rate for the entire year.

Wheat, wheat-flour, and corn are the only cereal products of the West which are imported from the United States at Montreal in any considerable quantities.

Canada produces about as much wheat as is consumed within her own territory, together with the quantity annually exported to the United States, which consists almost entirely of the higher grades. She, however, produces very little corn. It is stated by Mr. William Patterson, secretary of the Montreal Board of Trade, that the total exports of wheat at that port are about equal to the receipts of wheat from our Western States, and that all the corn received and shipped is exclusively of American growth. The statistics of export of corn from the United States and of shipments from Montreal show that the consumption of American corn in Canada amounts to about 1,160,000 bushels annually.

It may therefore be assumed that the great bulk of American wheat and corn transported via the Saint Lawrence route is destined to foreign markets beyond Canada. Almost all the grain transported from Montreal is sent to Great Britain. The Saint Lawrence route lies almost exactly in the direction from the Western States to England, and, as has already been shown, possesses advantages which constitute it a sharply competing route for western trade with the Erie Canal and with the railroads in the United States extending from Lake Erie to the Atlantic sea-board. In the markets of the West Indies and South America, however, which take about 15 per cent. of the entire foreign exports of grain from the United States, the Canadian route is not to any considerable extent a competing line, the distance to those countries by the Montreal route being about fourteen hundred miles greater than by way of New York; and besides, there is generally an abundant supply of tonnage for those ports at New York, and very little at Montreal.

In the transportation of western products to the Atlantic States the Montreal route is debarred from all competition with American lines on account of the import-duties which are required to be paid upon the re-exportation of American grain into the United States. Upon this point the Hon. Hugh McLennan, president of the Montreal Board of Trade, in a letter to the chairman of this committee, dated November 1, 1873, states as follows:

"The privilege of selling grain or flour, the products of the Western States, to New England without hinderance or charge, would, even with our present canal facilities, enable us to import largely from the West; not only to obtain that additional trade, but with that as an alternative for surplus, our export trade by sea would assume larger proportions. The vessel, owned or chartered, now acts with caution, fearing that the tonnage may exceed the volume of freight offering. The grain-operator, if he now orders in excess of the tonnage, has no alternative but to store until relieved by additional arrival of vessels."

Mr. McLennan further states that in 1872 there was a surplus of over a million bushels held at Montreal, in consequence of the lack of ocean tonnage to transport it abroad, and that in 1873, in consequence of the caution of traders, a million bushels more could have been exported at Montreal than were actually received. It is true that this amount is very small in comparison with the great bulk moved east. But it would doubtless be largely increased by the remission of duties on re-exportations, whereby an alternative would be afforded to the Montreal purchaser which would enable him to compete in the New England markets, and thus secure himself against loss in the event of a lack of tonnage to ship his surplus to Great Britain. This would prove of great benefit both to the western producer and the New England consumer: to the producer because it would largely increase competition in the carrying-trade of the lakes, and thereby tend to prevent the extravagant charges made by vessel-owners during the pressure of traffic which always occurs in the fall months. It would also contribute toward the overthrow of the railway monopoly, which, as we have seen, has substantially taken possession of steam-navigation on the lakes. The freedom of transporting western products via Montreal would be an advantage to the New England consumer, because it would give him the benefits of cheap water-transportation for a large part of the distance from the West, and of reduced railway charges by reason of such water competition. This subject will again be referred to in another connection.

The exports of oats and barley from the United States to Canada are very small, as Canada produces a large surplus of both these grains. Rye is not mentioned in the commercial statistics of Montreal. We therefore assume the shipments of wheat, wheat-flour, and corn from Montreal to represent the total shipment of grain from the western States by that route. The following table gives the quantity of western grain received at Montreal and at New York for 10 years:

Year.	Western grain received at New York.	Western grain received at Montreal.
	Bushels.	*Bushels.*
1863	65, 320, 158	6, 151, 521
1864	53, 323, 903	6, 289, 824
1865	52, 918, 983	5, 388, 291
1866	55, 289, 763	4, 541, 892
1867	47, 484, 262	4, 928, 830
1868	58, 125, 725	4, 980, 709
1869	62, 174, 663	10, 050, 651
1870	65, 781, 264	10, 368, 899
1871	86, 131, 705	14, 641, 630
1872	87, 381, 040	15, 213, 029
Total	633, 931, 466	82, 555, 276

This table includes grain received at New York by coastwise vessels.

It appears from this statement, that during the period of ten years (1863 to 1872 inclusive) the receipts of western grain at Montreal and at New York were as follows:

	Bushels.
Received at New York	633,931,466
Received at Montreal	82,555,276

Of the total receipts at the two cites 87 per cent. was received at New York and 13 per cent. at Montreal. The quantity received at the two ports during the first five years of the period (1863 to 1867) amounted to 301,637,427 bushels, of which 91 per cent. was received at New York and 9 per cent. at Montreal, and the total quantity received at the two ports during the last five years of the period mentioned amounted to 414,849,315 bushels, of which 86.7 per cent. was received at

New York and 13.3 per cent. at Montreal, showing that the relative amount of the receipts of western grain at the two ports had remained nearly the same. By comparing the total receipts at New York and at Montreal during the two periods of five years mentioned, it appears that the increased receipts at New York amounted to 85,257,328 bushels, and the increased receipts at Montreal to 27,954,560 bushels. A table may be found on page 56 of the appendix which gives in detail the shipments of wheat, wheat-flour, and corn at New York and at Montreal for eleven years.

It is also a matter of interest to note the relative proportion of receipts at New York and at Montreal by water and by rail. The statistics of movement are exhibited in the following table, the shipments to Montreal including wheat, wheat-flour, and corn, and the shipments to New York including wheat, flour, corn, rye, oats, and barley:

Receipts of western grain at New York and at Montreal by water and by rail.

Year.	Received at—			
	New York.		Montreal.	
	Water.	Rail.	Water.	Rail.
	Bushels.	*Bushels.*	*Bushels.*	*Bushels.*
1870	33, 633, 694	29, 728, 190	8, 857, 669	2, 509, 709
1871	51, 818, 172	32, 100, 675	12, 383, 212	3, 296, 046
1872	49, 871, 757	35, 474, 465	13, 203, 910	3, 266, 699
Total	135, 323, 623	97, 303, 330	34, 444, 791	9, 072, 454

It appears that during these years, 1870, 1871, and 1872, the receipts at New York were by rail 97,303,330 bushels, and by canal and Hudson River 135,323,623 bushels, or 41.8 per cent. by rail and 58.2 per cent. by canal and Hudson River. During the same period the receipts at Montreal were by rail 9,072,454 bushels, and by canal 34,444,791 bushels, or 79.2 per cent. by canal and 20.8 by rail.

It is impossible to state separately the quantity of wheat and wheat-flour received at Montreal from the Western States and from the province of Ontario. It may be assumed that almost all the wheat and wheat-flour and corn received at Montreal via the Saint Lawrence River comes from the United States. But a very large portion of the receipts of wheat and wheat-flour by the Grand Trunk Railway are undoubtedly the production of Canada. This is evident from the following statement:

Receipts of wheat, wheat-flour, and corn at Montreal during the year 1872.

	Received by Grand Trunk Railroad.	Received by Saint Lawrence River.
Wheat, bushels	528, 764	4, 136, 550
Wheat-flour, barrels	607, 319	314, 649
Corn, bushels	5, 000	7, 651, 440

All the corn received at Montreal is imported from the United States, yet less than one per cent. of the receipts were by rail.

It is probable, therefore, that only a small part of the wheat and wheat-flour received at Montreal by rail is the product of the Western States.*

The comparative statements as to the receipts of western grain at New York and at Montreal are somewhat more favorable to Montreal than they would be if only western grain were included. Still the difference is so small that, for the purposes of such general comparisons as as those here instituted, the results arrived at are substantially correct.

Grain and flour received at Montreal from the Western States by rail is principally shipped from Chicago and Milwaukee to ports on Lake Huron, and thence to Montreal by the Grand Trunk Railway. The average all-rail rate from Chicago to Montreal during the year 1872 was 9½ cents per bushel higher than the average water-rate. This fact, of course, prevents all-rail shipments except during the months when navigation is closed, and, under exceptional circumstances, during the summer season, when the all-rail rates are much below the average for the year.

The relative quantities of wheat, wheat-flour, and corn exported from Montreal and from New York to foreign countries are shown by the following table:

Statement showing the quantity of wheat, wheat-flour, and corn, in bushels, exported from New York and from Montreal each year from 1856 to 1872, inclusive.

Year.	Exported from—		Year.	Exported from—	
	New York.	Montreal.		New York.	Montreal.
1856	16,492,538	1,817,690	1865	13,864,147	4,389,291
1857	21,011,750	1,965,397	1866	....	4,541,892
1858	10,706,395	1,574,047	1867	14,240,247	4,818,830
1859	6,263,722	537,898	1868	19,579,536	4,940,709
1860	8,803,327	2,918,647	1869	17,224,452	10,050,651
1861	40,189,883	9,758,580	1870	29,011,391	10,368,899
1862	56,943,942	10,963,988	1871	31,941,546	14,641,630
1863	49,567,522	7,151,521	1872	41,341,341	15,113,029
1864	30,618,158	6,289,824			

It appears that during the first five years of this period there were exported from New York 63,277,732 bushels, and from Montreal 8,813,679 bushels. During the last five years there were exported from New York 139,098,266 bushels, and from Montreal 55,114,918 bushels.

During the first period of the total exports at the two ports 88 per cent. was from New York and 12 per cent. from Montreal, while during the last period 72 per cent. was from New York and 28 per cent. from Montreal. Comparing the exports at each of the two ports during the periods of five years mentioned, it appears that the increased exports at New York amounted to 75,820,534 bushels, and the increased exports at Montreal to 46,301,239 bushels.

* The board of trade reports of Montreal do not observe the distinction of American and Canadian grain in their statements of receipts and shipments.

Almost the entire exports of breadstuffs from Canada are shipped to Great Britain, and, as stated, consist almost exclusively of the cereal products of the United States.

About 80 per cent. of the foreign exports of breadstuffs from the United States are shipped to Great Britain, either through ports of the United States or through Montreal. The exportation of cereals from the Western States to foreign markets, therefore, depends almost entirely upon the British markets.

But Great Britain draws her supply of breadstuffs, not only from the United States, but from Russia, Turkey, Austria, Germany, Chili, Australia, and other countries.*

Now there are various causes, such as the scarcity or abundance of crops in one or more of these countries, the ruling rate of ocean freights, or a general reduction of prices which may, during any one season, cause the supply from a particular country to drop out of the British market entirely, and that without effecting the aggregate importation of breadstuffs into Great Britain. In consequence of this fact we find that the shipment of grain to Great Britain is a very fluctuating, and, consequently, a very uncertain business. This is shown by the shipments of wheat from Montreal during certain years; in 1862, 6,500,000 bushels; in 1866, 83,278 bushels; in 1867, 1,576,528 bushels; in 1871, 7,680,000 bushels, and in 1872, 3,818,000 bushels.

The quantity of corn exported from Montreal each year during the last ten years has varied from 6,043 bushels to 7,546,000 bushels.

The exports of grain from ports of the United States to Great Britain show corresponding fluctuations. Within the last ten years the exports of wheat to Great Britain have varied from 2,582,000 bushels to 33,138,000 bushels, and the exports of corn from 66,000 bushels to 25,786,000 bushels.

These fluctuations in the export-trade to Great Britain are of course prejudicial to the interests of trade, and affect the cost of transport of grain via the Montreal route to a very considerable extent. The transportation of grain eastward by the Erie Canal and by railroads in the United States depends, however, mainly upon the demands of our home market, which are quite constant, and exceed by fully 75 per cent. the entire exports of grain from the United States to foreign countries.

The fluctuations in the shipment of grain to Montreal, in connection with the fact that Canadian vessels are not allowed to engage in trade between American ports, give to American vessels a very decided advantage over Canadian vessels in the commerce of the lakes. It is stated upon reliable authority that fully three-fourths of the grain shipped from lake ports to Kingston, at the lower end of Lake Ontario, is carried in American vessels.

---

* Tables may be found on page 74 and 75 of the Appendix which give the quantity of wheat and corn imported into Great Britain from various countries.

Comparative cost of transportation by the two routes.

By referring to the table on page 16 it will be seen that the average freight charges on wheat by lake, canal, and Saint Lawrence River to Montreal, and by lake, Erie Canal, and Hudson River to New York, during the years 1871 and 1872, were as follows:

Freight charges on wheat from—	Rate per bushel.	
	1871.	1872.
	Cents.	*Cents.*
Chicago to New York	21.6	26.6
Chicago to Montreal	18.8	24.1
Less to Montreal	2.8	2.5

The average ocean freights on wheat by steam-vessels from Montreal to Liverpool and from New York to Liverpool during the years 1871 and 1872 appear to have been as follows:

Freight charges on wheat from—	Rate per bushel.	
	1871.	1872.
	Cents.	*Cents.*
Montreal to Liverpool, (ocean steamers)	25.1	25.7
New York to Liverpool, (ocean steamers)	20.1	19.2
Less from New York to Liverpool	5.0	6.5

The through-freight charges from Chicago to Liverpool via Montreal and via New York appear to have been as follows:

Freight charges on wheat from—	Average rate Chicago to Liverpool.	
	1871.	1872.
	Cents.	*Cents.*
Chicago to Liverpool, via Montreal	43.9	49.8
Chicago to Liverpool, via New York	41.7	45.8
Montreal route in excess of New York route	2.2	4.0

It appears that the average freight-charges by the water-route from Chicago to Montreal are less than the average freight-charges by the water-route from Chicago to New York, but that the average ocean freight-charges from New York to Liverpool are less than the average ocean freight-charges from Montreal to Liverpool, although the distance from New York is 200 miles greater than the distance from Montreal.

The total freight-charges from Chicago to Liverpool were 2.2 cents greater by the Montreal route than by the New York route in 1871, and 4 cents greater by the Montreal route than by the New York route in 1872.

If we add the incidental charges of transferring from one vessel to another, and marine insurance, to the freight-charges, we shall obtain the following comparative statement as to the cost of transporting wheat and corn from Chicago to Liverpool during the year 1872:

Total cost of transporting wheat from Chicago to Liverpool in 1872, including transfer charges and insurance.

	Wheat.	Corn.
	Cents.	*Cents.*
By steamer from New York	53. 7	44. 5
By steamer from Montreal	56. 5	45. 1
Greater by Montreal route	2. 5	0. 6

	Wheat.	Corn.
	Cents.	*Cents.*
By sailing-vessels from New York	51. 4	44. 1
By sailing-vessels from Montreal	57. 1	45. 7
Greater by Montreal route	5. 7	1. 6

The above statements indicate that the entire cost of transport from Chicago to Liverpool via Montreal is in each case less by the New York route than by the Montreal route.

The fact that the average ocean-rates from New York to Liverpool are so much less than the average ocean-rates from Montreal to Liverpool, although the distance from New York is greater, is chiefly due to the following causes:

1st. The commerce of Montreal is suspended by ice about five months each year, whereas the harbor of New York is never closed. A constant and reliable channel is one of the most important conditions of a large and prosperous commerce.

2d. The dangers and difficulties of navigation by the Montreal route, on account of fogs and ice during several weeks after the opening and before the closing of navigation, also add to the cost of transport by that route, Montreal being situated 986 miles from the ocean by the way of the straits of Belle Isle.

The average annual difference in the rates of insurance from New York to Liverpool and from Montreal to Liverpool are as follows:

	Average rate for the year.	
	Sailing-vesels.	Steam-vessels.
New York to Liverpool	1¼ per cent.	1 per cent.
Montreal to Liverpool	2¼ per cent.	1¼ per cent.
In favor of New York route	1 per cent.	¼ per cent.

The difference of one per cent. on wheat transported in sailing-vessels during the year 1872 amounted to 1½ cents per bushel, and the difference of $\frac{1}{4}$ per cent., when transported in steam-vessels, amounted to $\frac{4}{10}$ of a cent per bushel. This accounts for the fact before stated, that the difference in the freights in sailing-vessels between New York and Liverpool and between Montreal and Liverpool is greater than the same difference in steam-vessels. The rate of insurance on grain carried in sailing-vessels rises to 6½ per cent. in the month of November, but is never greater than 3½ per cent. on grain shipped in steamers.

A statement showing the average rates of insurance between Montreal and Liverpool may be found on page 52 of the appendix. This statement was furnished to the committee by Hon. Hugh McLennan, president of Board of Trade of Montreal.

3d. There is a larger and much more constant supply of tonnage seeking freights at New York than at Montreal. This is due to the immense ocean commerce at New York. The comparative tonnage entered at these two ports in the year 1872 was as follows:

Entered at the port of New York....................	3, 969, 339 tons.
Entered at the port of Montreal.....................	391, 926 tons.

The tonnage entered at Montreal was only 10 per cent. of the tonnage entered at New York.

On page 79 of the Appendix may be found a table giving the tonnage entered, imports and exports at Montreal and at New York for the twenty years, 1852 to 1872, inclusive.

Vessels arriving at New York in ballast, or with partial cargoes, are much more likely to secure remunerative outward cargoes than vessels entering at Montreal in like case.

The actual charges for transporting grain by any particular route do not alone determine the amount of grain which may be shipped by that route. Such charges depend very much upon the general commerce of the port. This fact has been very clearly stated by the Hon. Hugh McLennan, president of the Montreal Board of Trade, in a letter addressed to the chairman of this committee, dated November 1, 1873. (See appendix, page 171.) "No one port can increase its grain-trade largely out of proportion to the other business of the port. Any large increase enhances the cost of ocean-freights and other charges to a point that will give some rival port the next opportunity."

* * * * * * *

"The ocean tonnage which could be secured for the grain-trade of the Saint Lawrence has, therefore, been the measure of our imports of grain in the past."

In other words, the available amount of tonnage at Montreal for the transport of grain is confined to those vessels which arrive at that port either with full or partial cargoes, as the ruling grain freights do not pay the expenses of a round voyage. This is equally applicable to the grain-trade of ports of the United States.

The total eastward movement of grain from the Western States during the year 1872 amounted to 178,021,426 bushels, of which 15,113,029 bushels were shipped to Canada, and 162,908,397 bushels were shipped to the Atlantic States.

It appears, therefore, that the Montreal route can be considered a competitor for only about 8 per cent. of the entire eastward shipments of grain from our Western and Northwestern States, and this amount as stated represents almost exclusively shipments to Great Britain. This fact seems to limit the magnitude of the possible shipments of American wheat and corn from Montreal.

While, therefore, the shipment of grain to Great Britain via the Montreal route can only increase with the increase of the total business of that port, it is evident that even if the charges for internal transport be nearly the same, the great bulk of the eastward shipments of grain for export to Great Britain and other foreign countries must for many years be made from the Atlantic and Gulf ports of the United States, and that, under the present system of duties, almost the entire transportation of grain from the West to our home markets must be over rail and water routes in our own country.

The movement of grain from the Western States to the Gulf States.

The committee have not been able to procure as satisfactory data in regard to the southern movement of grain as in regard to the eastern movement.

The shipments from Cincinnati and Saint Louis have been furnished by the boards of trade of these cities. Mr. John Newell, president of the Illinois Central Railroad, has furnished the data as to the amount of grain delivered by that road at Cairo, and Mr. Albert Fink, vice-president and general superintendent Louisville, Nashville and Great Southern Railroad, has given the quantity shipped south at Nashville, the chief distributing point for rail shipments through the States of Kentucky and Tennessee.

This data affords but a partial view of the entire southern shipments. The committee have not been able to procure data as to the shipments by river at the small towns and landing-places on the Ohio and Mississippi.

The southern shipments during the year 1872, according to the data obtained, were approximately as follows:

	Bushels.
From Saint Louis	15, 750, 202
From Cincinnati	2, 784, 127
From Cairo	4, 964, 890
From Nashville	5, 356, 184
	28, 855, 403

The shipments from Saint Louis were—

	Bushels.
By river	12, 134, 598
By railroad	3, 615, 604

The returns of the board of trade of Cincinnati do not indicate the amounts shipped by river and by railroad. It is believed, however, that the shipments were chiefly by river.

The shipments from Cairo by rail and by river are not known. It is estimated that about 30 per cent. of the entire southern shipments were by rail, and 70 per cent. by river.

From all the information which can be obtained, the southern movement in the year 1872 is estimated at 35,000,000 bushels.

The total movement of grain from the Western States during the year 1872 appears, therefore, to have been as follows:

	Bushels.
Eastward	178, 021, 426
Southern	35, 000, 000
Total	213, 021, 426

The facts stated in regard to the economy of rail transport from the West to the East apply, in a more marked degree, to rail shipments from the West to the South. Owing to the greater extent of territory in the Gulf States, through-freight lines by means of combinations and running connections between the West and the South afford correspondingly greater advantages for internal distribution, on account of the shorter distances and the saving of transfer-charges, than existing or possible water-lines.

The development of southern markets for the grain of the Northwest is believed to be a subject of very great commercial importance. The States of South Carolina, Georgia, Alabama, Tennessee, Mississippi, Arkansas, Louisiana and Texas, constitute, beyond doubt, the largest and most valuable cotton-growing area on the surface of the globe. The soil and climate of a large part of these States are, however, unfavorable to the profitable culture of cereals. The States of Ohio, Indiana, Illinois, Michigan, Arkansas, Wisconsin, Minnesota, Iowa, Nebraska, Missouri and Kansas, on the other hand, embrace the most extensive, and by far the richest, grain-producing area in the world. Owing to the cost of transport of the cereals of the West to the South Atlantic and Gulf States, the demand for breadstuffs causes thousands of acres of land to be diverted to the unprofitable culture of wheat and corn, where cotton might be much more profitably cultivated, if cheap breadstuffs could be procured elsewhere. With cheap and direct transportation provided between the grain States and the cotton States the interests both of the producers of cotton and of grain would be subserved.

This saving in the cost of transportation would accrue to producer and consumer alike. The distance from the center of the grain-producing area in the Western States to England is about 4,500 miles, and the distance from the central line of production of the grain-producing States to the central line of the cotton belt is about 800 miles. If the entire quantity of grain now shipped to Great Britain could be sent to the cotton States, and the withdrawal of our foreign exports of grain be supplemented by an increased exportation of cotton, a vast saving would be effected in the aggregate cost of transporting those two products from the producer to the consumer. This may be illustrated as follows:

The value of cotton in England in 1872 averaged $18.44 (gold) per 100 pounds, the value of wheat $3.10 per 100 pounds, and the value of corn $1.61 pér 100 pounds. Assuming that the cost of transportation from the point of production of both grain and cotton to Great Baitain to be 90 cents per 100 pounds, the cost of transporting these three commodities would bear the following proportions to the value of each in Great Britain. The values here stated are in gold:

Commodities.	Value per 100 lbs. in Great Britian.	Cost of transportation.	Difference betw'en value of, in England, and cost of transportation.	Percentage which cost of transport is of value in Great Britain.
Cotton	$18 44	$0 90	$17 54	5 per ct.
Wheat	3 10	90	2 20	29 per ct.
Corn	1 61	90	71	50 per ct.

While the cost of transportation is only 5 per cent. of the value of cotton at Liverpool, it is 29 per cent. of the value of wheat and 50 per cent. of the value of corn at Liverpool.

The value of cotton at New Orleans during the same year was $19.28 per hundred pounds in currency; the value of wheat at Chicago was $1 22.6 per bushel, and the value of corn 40.2 cents per bushel. The cost of transporting to Liverpool at the average rates of freight during the year 1872 was 6 per cent. of the home value of cotton, 44 per cent. of the home value of wheat, and 111 per cent. of the home value of corn. If, however, the producers of wheat and corn could send the products of their labor to home markets in the Southern States at only one-third of the cost of its transport to Great Britain, and the withdrawal of American grain in the British markets be supplemented by increased exports of cotton, it is evident that the cost of transporting our aggregate surplus products of grain and cotton would be very much less than at the present time.

If the additional facilities so much needed for securing cheap transportation between the grain-producing and cotton-producing States are provided, we may expect to see a very large increase in the shipment of cereals from the Western States to the Gulf States, and also a large increase in the production of cotton in the Gulf States.

That the Southern States can supply to foreign countries a very much larger quantity of cotton than is now exported is evident from the following facts:

During the year 1860 the imports of cotton into Great Britain from the United States amounted to 1,115,890,608 pounds, and from all other countries 275,048,144 pounds; whereas, during the year 1872, the imports from the United States were 625,600,080 pounds, and from all other countries 783,237,392 pounds, showing that the imports from the United States had fallen off 490,290,528 pounds, while the imports from all other countries had increased 508,189,248 pounds. The imports of cotton into Great Britain from the United States in 1860 were 80 per cent. of the total imports, and in 1872 only 44½ per cent. of the total imports.

Another disadvantage to producers of wheat and corn in the United States incident to the foreign exportation of these products arises from the fact that in all commercial dealings in this country prices are regulated almost absolutely by the ruling prices in Liverpool and London; and this fact exists, although our total foreign exports of wheat and corn are not more than 3 per cent. of the entire annual production of those cereals in the United States. Since the telegraph has become so potent an agent in commercial transactions, the daily fluctuations of wheat and corn at the great grain markets of England cause corresponding fluctuations at Montreal, at New York, at Buffalo, at Chicago, and at every market in the United States. If we could provide home markets for our entire products of wheat and corn, prices would be regulated under the laws of supply and demand, by the rates of wages which prevail in this country instead of those which prevail in Europe. As the rates of wages in this country are uniformly higher than in Europe, it is evident that if home markets could be developed for our entire products the prices realized by the producers would be higher than could be expected in the markets of Europe.

The exportation of grain from ports of the United States to foreign countries.

The following tables indicate the cause of trade, in so far as relates to the exportation of grain from the various ports of the United States to foreign countries:

Wheat (including wheat-flour) exported at the principal, and other ports of the United States, during the year ending June 30, 1873.

Ports.	Bushels.
New York	21, 221, 254
San Francisco	17, 156, 104
Lake ports	6, 595, 786
Baltimore	1, 651, 411
Astoria and Portland, Oreg	1, 079, 604
Philadelphia	984, 017
Boston	948, 633
New Orleans	243, 027
Portland, Me	39, 394
All other ports	814, 442
Total	50, 733, 672

Corn exported at the principal, and other ports of the United States, during the year ending June 30, 1873.

Ports.	Bushels.
New York	20,211,512
Baltimore	5,869,519
Boston	947,584
Philadelphia	2,909,150
New Orleans	946,457
Lake ports	7,408,706
All other ports	249,002
Total	38,541,930

The exports of wheat and corn during the year 1872 amounted to 89,275,602 bushels. The total exports of cereals amounted to 93,080,400 bushels. The total exports of wheat and corn were, therefore, 96 per cent. of the total exports of grain.

The foregoing tables need no explanation; they clearly indicate the course of the exports of grain from the interior to foreign countries.

Attention is called to the fact that the exports of wheat from San Francisco, Portland, and Astoria, Oreg., amounted to 18,235,708 bushels. This quantity comprised the entire exportation of wheat from the Pacific coast, and amounted to 35 per cent. of the total exports of wheat from the United States to foreign countries. It is estimated that the exports of wheat from the State of Oregon during the year ending June 30, 1874, will amount to nearly five million bushels, an increase of nearly four million bushels since 1872. On page 59 of the appendix may be found a table showing the exports of wheat and corn from Portland, Me., Boston, New York, Philadelphia, Baltimore, and New Orleans each year from 1856 to 1873, inclusive. This table, of course, shows only the exportation of wheat and corn produced in the States east of the Rocky Mountains. It appears that during the first five years of the period mentioned the exports from New York amounted to 63,277,732 bushels, and the exports from all the other ports mentioned amounted to 42,649,690 bushels. Also that during the last five years (1869 to 1873) the exports from New York amounted to 160,951,496 bushels, and that the exports from all the other ports amounted to 48,184,210 bushels. Comparing these results for the two periods of five years, it appears that the increased exports at New York amounted to 97,673,764 bushels, and that the increased exports of all the other ports amounted to 5,534,520 bushels.

FOREIGN MARKETS.

The value of the total exports of breadstuffs from the United States during the fiscal year ending June 20, 1873, amounted to $83,683,815, and the value of wheat and corn exported amounted to $82,070,108. Wheat and corn appear, therefore, to have constituted 98 per cent. of our entire foreign exports of breadstuffs. Our principal foreign markets are Great Britain, Canada, the West Indies, Central American States, Brazil, China, France, Belgium, and Portugal. The relative importance of these markets is exhibited by the amount of the exports of wheat and corn to each country during the year ending June 30, 1872, as shown in the following tables:

Statement showing the number of bushels of wheat, including wheat-flour, exported from the United States to foreign countries during the fiscal year ending June 30, 1872.

Countries.	Bushels.	Per cent. to each country.
Great Britain and Ireland	20, 495, 859	54
Canada and other British possessions in North America	6, 096, 938	16
West Indies and Central American States	3, 773, 858	10
Brazil	1, 719, 972	5
China	688, 309	2
France	1, 430, 799	4
Belgium	1, 294, 635	3. 3
Portugal	447, 800	1. 1
All other countries	1, 790, 317	4. 6
Total exports	37, 738, 487	100

NOTE.—The exports to Canada are properly exports to Great Britain via Montreal.

Statement showing the number of bushels of corn exported from the United States to foreign countries during the fiscal year ending June 30, 1872.

Countries.	Bushels.	Per cent. to each country.
Great Britain and Ireland	25, 786, 359	72. 2
Canada and other British possessions in North America	7, 913, 582	22. 2
West Indies and Central America	834, 094	2. 4
Germany	737, 014	2
France	161, 520	. 5
All other countries	294, 421	. 7
Total	35, 726, 990	100

Statement showing the number of bushels of wheat and corn exported from the United States to foreign countries during the fiscal year ending June 30, 1872.

Countries.	Bushels.	Per cent. to each country.
Great Britain and Ireland	46, 282, 218	63
Canada and other British possessions in North America	14, 010, 520	19. 2
West Indies and Central American States	4, 607, 952	6. 3
Brazil	1, 719, 972	2. 3
France	1, 592, 319	2. 2
Belgium	1, 294, 635	1. 7
Germany	737, 014	1
China	688, 309	. 9
Portugal	447, 800	. 6
All other countries	2, 084, 738	2. 8
Total	73, 465, 477	100

In foreign markets American grain comes into competition with the grain products of all other grain-exporting countries. Our exports of cereals to foreign countries on this continent consist chiefly of wheat-flour. In these markets we enjoy decided advantages on account of their proximity to us.

The following statement shows the total exports of grain from the United States to Great Britain, the West Indies, and South America, and to all other countries:

Wheat, wheat-flour, corn, rye, oats, and barley exported from the United States in 1873.

Countries to which exported.	Bushels.	Per cent.
Great Britain*	78, 313, 335	84. 1
West Indies, Central and South America	8, 596, 968	9. 3
All other countries	6, 170, 710	6. 6
Total	93, 080, 413	100

* Exports to Canada are included in exports to Great Britain, as the exports of grain from the West to Canada are almost entirely exported to that country.

In the markets of Great Britain, however, to which we send about 84 per cent. of our entire foreign exports of grain, we meet the competition of every other grain-exporting country, and upon conditions not particularly favorable to us with respect to the cost of transportation. The United Kingdom of Great Britain and Ireland imports more grain from foreign countries than do all other countries combined. A large proportion of the wheat, oats, and barley consumed is produced within her own territory, but almost all the Indian corn consumed is imported from abroad. The imports of grain into Great Britain appear to be steadily increasing. During the five years, 1860 to 1864, she imported from other countries 97,386,181 bushels of corn and 332,132,745 bushels of wheat.

During the five years, 1868 to 1872, she imported 174,559,362 bushels of corn and 391,592,114 bushels of wheat, the increased importation of wheat amounting to 59,459,369 bushels, and the increased importation of corn amounting to 77,173,181 bushels. (See statements, on pages 72 of the Appendix.)

It was estimated that during the 5 years, 1862 to 1866, the average annual consumption of wheat in the United Kingdom amounted to 184,000,000 bushels. Her average imports during the same period amounted to 61,325,253 bushels, or 33⅓ per cent. of her total consumption. But her total imports of wheat during the year 1872 amounted to 88,877,406 bushels, or 48 per cent. of her estimated annual consumption.

Our principal competitors in the wheat markets of Great Britain are Russia, Germany, Egypt, Turkey, Wallachia and Moldavia, Chili, Australia, Denmark, France and Austria. (See appendix, page 74.

The imports of wheat and corn into Great Britain from each country during the thirteen years—1860 to 1872 inclusive—and the proportion from each country, are shown in the following tables:

Summary statement of wheat (including wheat-flour) imported into the United Kingdom from 1860 to 1872, inclusive.

Countries whence imported.	Bushels.	Percentage of total imported from each country.
United States	257, 852, 380	28. 555
Russia	224, 035, 760	24. 785
Germany	154, 761, 283	17. 205
France	70, 166, 789	7. 705
British North America	55, 440, 657	6. 665
Egypt	32, 232, 606	3. 485
Turkey	25, 636, 830	2. 855
Denmark	16, 905, 758	1. 825
Chili	15, 854, 994	1. 765
Wallachia and Moldavia	11, 048, 665	1. 225
Austria	9, 673, 485	1. 075
Spain	7, 905, 813	. 785
Australia	4, 728, 839	. 525
Italy	3, 110, 929	. 345
India	1, 004, 721	. 115
Holland	691, 942	. 075
Sweden	570, 646	. 065
Belgium	526, 461	. 065
Brazil	116, 496	. 015
Portugal	101, 800	. 015
Syria and Palestine	98, 136	. 015
Italy and Greece	70, 477	. 013
Argentine Confederation	46, 567	. 012
Other countries	7, 266, 574	. 81
Total	899, 848, 608	100

Summary statement of corn (including meal) imported into the United Kingdom from 1860 to 1872, inclusive.

Countries whence imported.	Bushels.	Percentage of total imported from each country.
United States	123, 273, 007	37. 32
Turkey	107, 581, 577	32. 85
Wallachia and Moldavia	30, 035, 171	9. 25
Russia	25, 380, 477	7. 74
British North America	17, 777, 509	5. 42
France	6, 231, 208	1. 92
Egypt	4, 425, 151	1. 34
Italy	4, 585, 566	1. 39
Morocco	2, 640, 861	. 95
Austria	2, 044, 595	. 62
Germany	797, 032	. 24
Portugal	481, 722	. 14
Azores	167, 771	. 05
Denmark	103, 192	. 04
Other countries	2, 395, 219	. 73
Total	327, 920, 058	100

During the thirteen years from 1860 to 1872, inclusive, 35⅕ per cent. of the wheat imported into Great Britain came from the United States, and 24¾ per cent. from Russia, the imports from Canada being included in imports from the United States, as they consist almost exclusively of wheat produced in the United States. The average value of wheat imported from all countries into the United Kingdom during the thirteen years from 1860 to 1872, inclusive, was $1.47½ per bushel. During that period the average value of wheat imported from the United States was $1.54½ per bushel, and the average value of wheat imported from Russia $1.49½ per bushel, showing that the value of wheat imported from the United States was 7 cents per bushel above the average value of all the wheat imported; that the value of the wheat imported from Russia was only 2 cents above the average of all the wheat imported, and 5 cents below the average value of the wheat imported from the United States. During the five years, 1860 to 1864, inclusive, the imports of wheat into the United Kingdom from the United States amounted to 127,047,126 bushels, and the quantity imported from Russia amounted to 47,376,809 bushels; but during the last five years, 1868 to 1872, the imports from the United States amounted to only 116,462,380 bushels, and the imports from Russia amounted to 117,967,022 bushels, showing that the imports from the United States to Great Britain had not only decreased relatively with respect to the imports from Russia, but also that they had actually fallen off 10,584,746 bushels during the last five years, while the imports from Russia had increased 70,590,213 bushels. This great increase in the imports from Russia is mainly due to improvements in the means of transporting grain from the interior to the great shipping ports on the Black Sea.

The consumption of corn in Great Britain is rapidly increasing, and the United States is her chief source of supply. The total quantity of corn imported into Great Britain during the thirteen years, 1860 to 1872, amounted to 327,920,058 bushels, of which 141,050,516 bushels, or 43 per cent., was imported from the United States. (See statement on page 75 of Appendix.) The imports of corn from British North America are included in the above statement as to imports from the United States, as the entire exports of corn from Canada to Great Britain are produced in our Western States and exported by the way of Montreal.

The exportation of corn from this country appears to be a very fluctuating trade. The cost of transporting corn from the Western States to Great Britain leaves so small a margin of profit to the producer that a trifling change in the rates of freight, or a reduction of the price in England, caused by unusually large crops in other countries, or short crops in the United States, causes almost an entire suspension of the exportation of corn from this country. Referring to statement on page 75 of the Appendix, it appears that the annual import of corn into Great Britain from the United States (including Canadian exports) has ranged from 82,000 bushels to 41,000,000 bushels. The other countries from which England chiefly imports corn are Turkey, Russia, Moldavia, and Wallachia, Austria, France, and Egypt.

While abundance or scarcity in the crops of these several countries and the relative cost of transportation must always have a marked effect upon our exports of both wheat and corn to Great Britain, the actual falling off in the quantity of wheat exported from the United States is undoubtedly due to the greatly increased demands of our home markets, caused by the development of manufacturing industries in this country, the re-establishment of the agricultural interests of the South, where the staple products are cotton, tobacco, sugar, and rice, together with the greatly improved facilities which have been afforded within the last eight years for the transport of wheat and corn from the Western States to the South Atlantic and Gulf States by means of the new and economic system of rail transport afforded by through freight lines which take grain from the points of production to the various local markets at the South without breaking bulk.

On pages 58 and 59 of the Appendix may be found tables giving detailed information in regard to the exportation of breadstuffs from the United States.

ACTUAL COMPETITION BETWEEN WATER AND RAIL TRANSPORT.

In the discussion of the comparative merits of these two systems of transport, we shall rely for information upon those statistics which are the expressions of practical experience in the navigation of the natural and artificial water-ways, and in the operation of the railroads which form actual competing lines between the West and the East. The comparisons instituted between rail and water lines will, of course, refer to parallel routes between competing points. Therefore we take Chicago and Milwaukee, the great grain-markets of the Northwest, and New York City, the chief grain-market of the Atlantic coast, and confine ourselves to the two principal cereals, wheat and corn. In treating of this subject we shall endeavor to illustrate, first—

COMPETITION BETWEEN TRANSPORT BY THE LAKES AND RAILROADS.

Products of the West are transported from Chicago and Milwaukee to the Atlantic seaboard by three modes of conveyance, as follows: 1st. "All water," or the lake, Erie Canal, and Hudson River route; 2d. "All rail;" and 3d. "Lake and rail," or the lines of transport composed of propellers from Chicago and Milwaukee to Erie, Pa., and to Buffalo, N. Y., and from thence by the various railroads which run in connection with those propeller lines and prorate with them upon the general basis hereinafter stated.

The following table gives the average freight-rates from Chicago to New York for five years by the three modes of transport, and illustrates the comparative cost of each.

Average monthly freight charges per bushel on wheat from Chicago to New York by water (lakes, Erie Canal, and Hudson River,) by lake and rail, (lake to Buffalo and thence rail to New York,) and by all rail, 1868 to 1872, inclusive.

Month.	Year—														
	1868.			1869.			1870.			1871.			1872.		
	All water.	Lake and rail.	All rail.	All water.	Lake and rail.	All rail.	All water.	Lake and rail.	All rail.	All water.	Lake and rail.	All rail.	All water.	Lake and rail.	All rail.
	Cts.	*Cts.*	*Cts.*	*Cts.*	*Cts.*	*Cts.*	*Cts.*	*Cts.*	*Cts.*	*Cts.*	*Cts.*	*Ct.*	*Cts.*	*Cts.*	*Cts.*
January....	......	....	51	......	....	42	......	....	42	......	......	39	......	......	39
February...	......	....	51	......	....	39	......	...	42	......	......	39	......	......	39
March......	......	....	48	......	....	30	......	....	36	......	......	30	......	......	36
April.......	......	28	42	......	26	30	......	22	30	......	22	27	......	.....	30
May........	20	26	36	19	25	30	16	20	27	16	21	27	18	25	27
June	19	25	30	21	25	27	16	21	27	16	21	24	21	23	27
July........	18	25	33	18	23	27	15	20	27	16	22	27	23	23	27
August.....	22	26	36	19	20	30	15	20	27	18	24	30	22	23	27
September..	25	33	39	22	22	39	15	23	30	23	28	33	27	32	33
October	27	34	42	29	27	39	21	25	36	27	32	39	31	37	39
November..	28	35	45	32	36	42	20	29	39	25	32	39	28	38	39
December ..	......	....	45	......	....	42	......	....	39	......	......	39	......	......	39
Average..	25.3	....	42.6	24.1	....	35.1	17.5	...	33.3	21.6	22.3	31.0	26.6	28.8	33.5

Elaborate data upon this subject may be found upon pages 29, 30, and 35 of the appendix; also a statistical chart at the end of the Appendix. The average rates by the three modes of transport appear to have been as follows:

During the year 1872 the "all-rail" rates were 24.5 per cent. higher than the "all-water" rates, the "lake and rail" rates were 7 per cent. higher than the "all-water" rates, and the "all-rail" rates were 16.3 per cent. higher than the "lake and rail" rates.

The average summer rail rate for 1872 (May, June, July, August, September, October, and November) was $31\frac{2}{7}$ cents, and the average winter rail rates in 1872 (December, January, February, March, and April) was $36\frac{3}{8}$ cents, the average winter rate being 16 per cent. higher than the average summer rate. By comparing the all-rail rates for the months of June, July, and August with the all-rail rates for December, January, and February we obtain a more accurate expression of the effect of ample water facilities in competition with equally ample rail facilities. The average all-rail rate during the three summer months just named was 27 cents, and the average of the winter months was 39 cents, the winter average being 44.4 per cent. higher than the summer average, when the competition of water transport was in full force. It may be supposed that the increase in the rail rates during the winter months is caused by the increased cost of transport during that season of the year, but this is true only to a very limited extent. The chief cause is the absence of competition by lake and canal. This is evident from the fact that although the cost of transportation by rail is not greater in October and November than in June and July, yet the average of the rates during the former months is 44.4 per cent. higher than the average of the rates during the latter months. The pressure of traffic during the months of October and November, when the facilities for transport by water are limited, in connection with the fact that the Erie Canal is at that time taxed to its utmost capacity, causes an advance in the rates on the lake and on the canal, and the rail rates at once go up to about the average for the winter months. It appears that in this case the increased charges by rail are due solely to the increase in the rates on the lake and on the canal. This fact was clearly stated before the committee by Mr. J. M. Walker, president of the Chicago, Burlington and Quincy Railway, (evidence, page 266,) a road which does not compete with any water-line. Mr. Walker states that the winter and summer rates are the same on his road, and he thinks that "this is the rule with the western roads generally." He states, also, that he believes that those roads which run in competition with transport on the Mississippi River make such changes in their freight-tariffs.

It is generally true that the roads which increase their rates during the winter months are those which run in competition with the water lines during the summer months, and it is quite probable, therefore, that but for such water competition the winter-rates would be maintained throughout the year.

It is unnecessary here to state the relative rates by rail and by water from Milwaukee to New York, as they are almost precisely the same as the rates from Chicago to New York.

The commercial statistics of lake shipments at Chicago and Milwaukee include shipments by lake and rail, as well as by all water, (or lake and canal.) The following table, compiled from such statistics, indicates simply the effect of competition between the lake and railroads upon the movement of wheat by each mode of transport.

Statement showing the number of bushels of wheat shipped from Chicago and Milwaukee by rail and by lake for ten years—1863 to 1872, inclusive.

Year.	By rail.	By lake.	Total.
	Bushels.	*Bushels.*	*Bushels.*
1863	91, 617	23, 479, 396	23, 571, 013
1864	185, 271	18, 964, 167	19, 149, 438
1865	1, 178, 762	16, 669, 568	17, 848, 330
1866	4, 811, 661	16, 774, 237	21, 585, 898
1867	2, 251, 383	17, 798, 543	20, 049, 926
1868	1, 869, 027	18, 308, 542	20, 177, 569
1869	2, 228, 246	25, 220, 877	27, 449, 123
1870	3, 264, 091	29, 204, 889	32, 468, 980
1871	1, 011, 093	25, 203, 883	26, 214, 976
1872	3, 975, 766	19, 547, 835	23, 523, 601
Total	20, 866, 917	211, 171, 937	232, 038, 854

It appears that during the first five years of this period the shipments by lake amounted to 93,685,911 bushels, and the shipments by rail to 8,518,694 bushels, or 8 per cent. by rail and 92 per cent. by water. It also appears that during the last five years of that period the shipments by lake amounted to 117,486,026 bushels, and the shipments by rail to 12,348,223 bushels, or 9½ per cent. by rail and 90½ per cent. by lake, the shipments by rail having increased only from 8 per cent. to 9½ per cent. of total shipments.

The following table illustrates the same subject in regard to the transportation of corn from Chicago. The shipments from Milwaukee are not included, as in the case of the former table, for the reason that the shipments of corn from that port are very small.

Statement showing the number of bushels of corn shipped from Chicago, by lake and by rail, for ten years, (1863 to 1872, inclusive.)

Year.	By rail.	By lake.	Total.
	Bushels.	*Bushels.*	*Bushels.*
1863	302, 050	24, 749, 400	25, 051, 450
1864	193, 217	11, 993, 475	12, 186, 692
1865	902, 369	24, 421, 600	25, 323, 969
1866	1, 369, 771	31, 257, 855	32, 627, 626
1867	1, 285, 428	19, 940, 172	21, 225, 600
Total	4, 052, 835	112, 415, 337	116, 415, 337
1868	2, 978, 388	21, 671, 071	24, 649, 459
1869	4, 501, 481	17, 019, 940	21, 521, 421
1870	4, 108, 942	13, 598, 387	17, 707, 329
1871	2, 515, 154	34, 200, 876	36, 716, 030
1872	5, 424, 044	41, 589, 508	47, 013, 552
Total	19, 528, 009	128, 079, 782	147, 607, 791

It appears that during the first five years of the period embraced in the table 96.6 per cent. of the corn was shipped by lake, and 3.4 by rail, and that during the last five years of the period 87 per cent. was shipped by lake, and 13 per cent. by rail, the quantity shipped by rail having increased from 3.4 per cent. to 13 per cent. of the total shipments.

The increase in the transportation of wheat and corn by rail is due chiefly to the organization of through-freight lines from all the principal points at the West to interior points in the New England States, and in other States of the Atlantic seaboard, such transport being practicable, notwithstanding the greater cost of movement per mile by rail, from the fact that grain thus carried is distributed directly to the consumers, and also because it thus avoids the terminal charges at Buffalo and at New York, formerly the chief distributing point of western wheat and corn consumed in New England.

It appears that 90½ per cent. of the wheat and 87½ per cent. of the corn shipped east from Chicago and Milwaukee is transported by lake-vessels. When in connection with these facts we consider that lake navigation continues only about seven months each year, while rail transport continues throughout the year, we shall clearly appreciate the superiority of water-transport, in comparison with the best facilities afforded by railway-lines, between Chicago and the Atlantic seaboard, which, with respect to their grades, amount of business, and the skill with which they are managed, are perhaps in a condition to transport freights cheaper than any other railway-lines in this country.

The following table gives the shipments of wheat from Chicago and Milwaukee, and of corn from Chicago, by lake and by rail, during each month of the year 1872:

Shipments of wheat from Chicago and Milwaukee, and shipments of corn from Chicago, by lake and by rail, during each month of the year 1872.

Month.	Shipments of wheat from Chicago and Milwaukee.		Shipments of corn from Chicago.	
	By lake.	By rail.	By lake.	By rail.
	Bushels.	*Bushels.*	*Bushels.*	*Bushels.*
January	....	43, 394	22	725, 856
February	....	75, 408	....	534, 097
March	....	167, 198	1, 000	442, 952
April	131, 175	462, 570	1, 445, 606	1, 018, 271
May	974, 964	477, 469	2, 568, 080	694, 000
June	1, 986, 342	170, 138	6, 850, 326	369 036
July	1, 629, 923	107, 726	7, 574, 131	265, 458
August	3, 312, 378	419, 216	7, 829, 558	323, 947
September	3, 520, 423	574, 647	6, 264, 918	444, 015
October	5, 053, 449	455, 254	6, 819, 201	329, 991
November	2, 939, 181	517, 260	2, 214, 145	184, 107
December	....	505, 486	22, 521	92, 314
Total	19, 547, 835	3, 975, 766	41, 589, 508	5, 424, 044

The shipments of wheat from Chicago and Milwaukee during the months when navigation was closed, (December to March, inclusive,) and during the months when navigation was open, (April to November, inclusive,) appear to have been as follows:

	Bushels.
Total quantity shipped by rail during the four months when navigation was closed	791, 486
Total quantity shipped by lake and rail during the eight months when navigation was open	22, 732, 115
Total shipped by rail during the year	3, 975, 766
Total shipped by lake during the year	19, 547, 835

The average monthly rail-shipments amounted to 197,871 bushels when navigation was closed, and to 398,035 bushels when navigation was open. The total rail-shipments during the months when navigation was closed, were only 24.9 per cent. of the rail-shipments when navigation was open, only 20 per cent. of the total rail-shipments, and only 3½ per cent. of the total shipments by lake and rail during the year

It also appears that the shipments of corn by rail during the months when navigation was closed were 33.1 per cent. of the total rail-shipments, and 4.3 per cent. of the total lake-shipments.

The comparatively small amount of wheat and corn transported from Chicago and Milwaukee to eastern markets by rail during the winter months, taken in connection with the facts that the average winter rail-freights during the last five years have been about 24 per cent. higher than the average summer rates, prove the inability or indisposition of existing railroads to meet the demand for the cheap and constant transportation of grain during the months when lake-navigation is closed It might be supposed that this is due to the fact that the producers of the West send to Chicago and Milwaukee during the summer and autumn only so much grain as can obtain transport during the period of open navigation, when rail-freights are lowest. That this is not the case is proved by the following facts: On the 1st of January, 1872, there were in store in Chicago and Milwaukee 2,516,697 bushels of wheat, and during the months of January, February, and March, there were received at those ports 1,578,790 bushels. Of this total quantity in store and received, amounting to 4,095,487 bushels, only 286,000 bushels, or about 7 per cent., was shipped by rail from the 1st of January to the 1st of April, the remaining 93 per cent. being held in store until after lake-navigation opened. It also appears that the quantity of corn in store January 1, 1872, and received at Chicago during the months of January, February, and March, amounted to 8,898,236 bushels, of which only 1,702,905, or 19 per cent. was shipped by rail during those months, the remaining 81 per cent. being held in store until after lake-navigation opened.

In the month of April, the approach of open navigation caused a reduction of 6 cents per bushel on the all-rail rates from Chicago to New York, as will be seen by reference to the table on page 52, and this reduction of charges caused 462,570 bushels of wheat to go forward by rail during that month as against a total by rail of 286,000 bushels during the three preceding months. The effect of this reduction of rates on the movement of corn was to send forward, by rail, in April, 1,018,271 bushels as against an aggregate of 1,702,905 bushels shipped during the months of January, February, and March.

COMPETITION BETWEEN THE ERIE CANAL AND PARALLEL RAILWAYS.

Having indicated the practical results of competition between lake and rail, we proceed to state the relative conditions of transport between the Erie Canal and Hudson River and competing railroads.

One general fact in regard to the economy of water and rail transportation should be noted, as it affords an explanation to some facts apparently paradoxical. There is no practical limit to the carrying capacity of natural navigable waters, whereas the capacity of both canals and railways is limited; railroads by the frequency with which trains may be run and by the limits of inadequate terminal facilities; and canals by the number of boats that can pass through a single lock in a given time. The effect of a pressure upon the capacity of the Erie Canal causing an inefficiency in its competition, will be observed in the increase of rates during the autumn months.

The railroads which compete with the Erie Canal are the New York Central and the Erie, all having their termini at Buffalo and New York. The length of each of these three avenues of commerce is as follows:

		Miles.
Erie Canal and Hudson River,	Erie Canal..... 345; Hudson River.. 150	495
Erie Railway		422
New York Central and Hudson River Railroad		440

Both of these railways are thoroughly equipped and ably managed.

The canal is owned by the State, and hence is incapable of entering into combination with the railroads.

The tonnage annually moved on each of these lines from 1856 to 1872, inclusive is shown by the following table:

Total tonnage moved each year on the Erie Canal, on the Erie Railway, and on the New York Central and Hudson River Railway, A. D. 1856 *to A. D.* 1872, *inclusive.*

Year.	Tons moved on the—		
	New York Central and Hudson River Railway.	Erie Railway.	Erie Canal.
1856	776, 112	943, 215	2, 107, 678
1857	838, 791	978, 066	1, 566, 624
1858	765, 407	816, 954	1, 767, 004
1859	834, 319	868, 073	1, 753, 954
1860	1, 028, 183	1, 139, 554	2, 253, 533
1861	1, 167, 302	1, 253, 418	2, 500, 782
1862	1, 387, 433	1, 632, 955	3, 204, 277
1863	1, 449, 604	1, 815, 096	2, 955, 302
1864	1, 557, 148	2, 170, 798	2, 535, 792
1865	1, 275, 299	2, 234, 350	2, 523, 490
1866	1, 602, 197	3, 242, 792	2, 896, 027
1867	1, 667, 926	3 484, 546	2, 920, 578
1868	1, 846, 599	3, 908, 243	3, 346, 986
1869	2, 281, 885	4, 312, 209	2, 845, 072
1870	4, 122, 000	4, 852, 505	3, 083, 132
1871	4, 532, 056	4, 844, 208	3, 580, 922
1872	4, 393, 965	5, 564, 274	3, 562, 560

From this table it appears that the tonnage movement by rail has increased very much faster than by the Erie Canal. The New York Central Railroad tonnage increased from 776,112 tons in 1856 to 4,393,965 tons in 1872, and the Erie Railway tonnage increased from 943,215 tons in 1856 to 5,564,274 tons in 1872, while the Erie Canal tonnage increased from 2,107,678 tons in 1856 to 3,562,560 tons in 1872.

During the first five years of the period mentioned, (1856 to 1860, inclusive,) the tonnage moved on the canal exceeded the tonnage moved on these two railroads by 460,125 tons, but during the last five years the tonnage moved on the two railroads exceeded that on the canal by 24,239,272 tons. Of the total tonnage moved on these three lines during the first five years, 51.2 per cent. was transported on the canal, and 48.8 per cent. on the railroads; while during the last five years only

28.8 per cent. was transported on the canal, and 71.2 per cent. on the railroads.

This large increase of railway-tonnage over that of the canals has been supposed to measure the relative merits of the two systems of transportation, and to prove that canals are gradually becoming unpopular and falling into disuse. This fact must, however, be considered in connection with the circumstances which have led to its existence. First. The tonnage of the railways is given for the entire length of their lines, which have increased very much since 1856. The New York Central now includes the Hudson River Road, about one hundred and fifty miles in length, which has largely increased the tonnage of the line. Second. The last twenty years have constituted a period of railway improvement, in which the inventive genius and business talent of the country have been devoted to the newer and more rapid means of transport, while the artificial water-ways have been comparatively neglected. But by far the most efficient cause of the relative increase of railway-tonnage is to be found in the administrative organizations of the railway companies, and in their combinations against the water-line—the two railways competing with the canal having their traffic arrangements with lines of steamers on the lakes, carrying from all the principal western ports. There are now but few, if any, lake-steamers that do not constitute a part of some through-line by water and rail to New York. The Erie Canal has no such connections. Consequently, when western products are once on board steamers at Chicago, Milwaukee, and other ports of the upper lakes, they are substantially under the control of the railways leading from Buffalo, Erie, and Dunkirk to New York, and it is not difficult to understand how they are prevented from being carried on the canal, although the charges by canal are less than by rail. The object of the organization of mixed lines, consisting of lake-steamers and railroads, is to direct the traffic over the railways after it reaches the eastern lake-termini.

These mixed lines are constituted as follows:

The Northern Transportation Company connects with the Central Vermont Railway at Ogdensburgh, and is managed by the officers of that road.

The Grand Trunk or Sarnia line of steamers runs in connection with the Grand Trunk Railroad, receiving freight at Chicago and delivering it to the railway at Sarnia.

The Western Transportation line of steamers connects with the New York Central Railway at Buffalo, where its freights, if not otherwise consigned, are delivered to that road.

The vessels of the Union Steamboat Company run from Chicago to Buffalo, where they connect with the Erie Railway.

The boats of the Anchor line of propellers run from Chicago to Erie and Buffalo, where they connect with the Empire Fast Freight Line, on the Pennsylvania and Erie Railways.

The above facts regarding lake and rail connections are stated upon the authority of Mr. R. Diefendorf, agent of the Northern Transportation Company, who also states that a few years ago the steamers upon the lake were generally engaged in free competition, the same as sailing-vessels, carrying freight to the railroads or to the canals, as the circumstances of trade might determine. Now, however, there are very few propellers "running wild"—that is, not having prorating arrangements with some railroad. These prorating arrangements give to the steamers so employed a very decided advantage over other steamers which have no running arrangements with any of the railroad companies. This undoubtedly furnishes an explanation of the rapid increase in the transport of grain by railway from Buffalo.

But there is still another cause for such increase.

The area of the greatest cereal-production has moved rapidly westward until its center is now far west of the lakes. Within a few years "fast freight-lines" have been organized, which extend into the interior of the Western States far beyond Chicago and other lake-ports. They form through-lines, and offer through-rates to the eastern cities, and to the consumers in the Atlantic States. These freight-lines have their agents in nearly all the local markets of the West who solicit traffic for them, and as the local rates to lake-ports are much greater per mile than the through-rates by such lines to the East, a large traffic is thus diverted from the lake and canal line. The Erie Canal has no such agencies. It receives only such traffic as seeks it in consequence of lower rates. It is not difficult so to adjust rates to the nearest lake-ports from points west of these ports as to prevent the traffic from being diverted to the water-line. There are also other circumstances which have caused large shipments to be made by rail during the season of navigation, at rates higher than those which prevail on the canal, viz: 1st. The fact that railway-transportation is preferred for grain in bad condition, since it sustains less injury when shipped in that way than by canal. 2d. The fact that grain is at times required to be delivered in New York in order to meet contracts for ocean-shipment, sooner than it can be transported by canal.

But the chief cause of the shipments of so large a quantity by rail during the summer-months at rates higher than those charged on the canal is found in the fact that a large portion of the grain transported from western points is destined for interior towns in New York and in the New England States. By such direct-rail shipments the cost of transportation from Buffalo, even at the rail-rates stated, is less than the cost of transport by the water-line to New York City, where terminal charges are incurred, together with the additional freight-charges from New York to the points of consumption. The amount of this interior distribution by rail is shown by comparing the shipments of grain during the year 1872 from Buffalo, Suspension Bridge, and Salamanca, the western receiving-points of the New York Central and Erie Railways, with the quantity delivered by the same roads at New York City:

*Grain shipped by New York Central and Erie Railways from Buffalo, Suspension Bridge, and Salamanca	56,135,522
Grain delivered by the same roads at New York	26,129,043
Distributed to interior points	30,006,479

The quantity delivered at New York appears to have been but 46 per cent. of the shipments from the western points mentioned.

The receipts of wheat, wheat-flour, and corn at New York *by canal* were, during the same year, (1872,) 91 *per cent.* of the shipments from Buffalo and Oswego, as appears from the following table:

1872.	Shipped by canal from Buffalo and Oswego, from western points.	Delivered at New York.
	Bushels.	*Bushels.*
Flour, (reduced to bushels)*	222,183	532,822
Wheat	12,929,919	10,916,497
Corn	31,904,193	29,968,026
Total wheat, wheat-flour, and corn	45,056,295	41,417,345

*A large amount of the wheat shipped from Oswego and Buffalo was converted into flour at milling points between those cities and New York.

From this brief review of the causes which have led to the relative increase of railway-tonnage as against that of the canal, it will be seen that the fact of such increase affords a very unsafe rule by which to measure the respective merits of these two modes of transport.

It is stated by Mr. E. H. Walker, statistician of the New York Produce Exchange, in his report for the year 1873, that "the receipts at New York, flour included, in 1872, were 90,481,912 bushels, of which 33,142,889 bushels were by railroad against 53,711,100 bushels received at tide-water by the Erie and Champlain Canals:" or 38 per cent. by rail and 62 per cent by canal.

The foreign exportation of grain at New York depends chiefly upon receipts at that port by canal and Hudson River.

It may be stated in this connection, that of the total quantity of grain shipped East on the New York Central Railroad from Buffalo and Suspension Bridge during the year 1872, amounting to 36,111,490 bushels, 24,809,428 bushels, or 66 per cent., were sent directly to the New England States by rail from Albany and Schenectady.

The following table exhibits the average freight-charges per ton for the transportation of all classes of commodities from 1856 to 1872,

* The shipments of grain by rail from Buffalo and Suspension Bridge include imports of grain from Canada, and a very large quantity of grain from interior points in the United States delivered to the New York Central and Erie Railroads at the points above mentioned, and never reported at any lake-port.

inclusive, on the New York Central Railroad, the Erie Railway, and the New York State canals:

Cost of transportation per ton per mile on the Erie Canal, on the Erie Railway, and on the New York Central and Hudson River Railway, from 1856 to 1872, inclusive.

Year.	Rate per ton per mile on the—					
	New York Central and Hudson River Railway.		Erie Railway.		State Canals.	
	Cents.	*Mills.*	*Cents.*	*Mills.*	*Cents.*	*Mills.*
1856	3	0	2	5	1	1
1857	3	1	2	5	0	8
1858	2	6	3	3	0	8
1859	2	1	2	1	0	7
1860	2	1	1	8	1	0
1861	2	0	1	7	1	1
1862	2	2	1	9	0	9½
1863	2	4	2	1	0	9
1864	2	7	2	3	1	1
1865	3	3	2	7	1	1
1866	2	9	2	4	1	0
1867	2	5	2	0	0	9
1868	2	6	1	9	0	9
1869	2	2	1	6	0	9
1870	1	9	1	4	0	8
1871	1	6	1	5	1	0
1872	1	7	1	5	1	0

N. B.—The cost by canal in this table includes both freight and tolls.

It is to be observed that the average cost per ton per mile on *all the canals of the State of New York is given in the above table.* The cost of movement on the lateral canals being much greater than on the Erie, the cost per ton per mile on the Erie Canal is considerably less than the rates given in the table. It appears from this statement that the cost of transport on the canals is now, and always has been, less than the cost of transport by rail; but on account of the immense increase in the business of transporting grain from the West to the seaboard, and the fact that the canal is taxed to its utmost capacity during the latter part of each season, the average cost of transport by canal for the entire season is greater than it would be with larger canal facilities. Comparing the cost of movement on the canals during the first five years with the average cost of movement on the two railroads during the same period, it appears that the cost of movement on the canal was only 35 per cent. of the cost of movement on the railroads, and that during the last five years mentioned (1868 to 1872, inclusive) the cost of movement on the canals was only 51 per cent. of the cost of movement on the railroads, the increased pressure of business on the canal having led to the advance of canal-rates. It is believed that the enlargement of the canal and the application of steam as a motive power will reduce the canal-charges as much below the present rail-rates, as they were during the first five years of the period above named, again compeling the railways to improve and cheapen their facilities in order to maintain successful competition.

In this connection it is interesting to note the change in the nature of the traffic on the canals, which has taken place in consequence of the competition of railroads. There appears to have been in the very beginning of rail competition a falling off in the carriage on the canals of light and valuable articles requiring quick movement, while the carriage of grosser freights, in which the chief element incidental to commercial exchange is the actual freight-charges imposed, exhibits a steady and regular increase.

The following table shows the effect of rail-competition from 1861 to 1872 on the carriage of flour and grain on the canal:

Statement showing the movement of flour, wheat, corn, and oats on all the New York State canals from 1861 *to* 1872, *inclusive.*

Year.	Barrels of flour.	Bushels of wheat.	Bushels of corn.	Bushels of oats.
1861	1, 667, 416	33, 171, 900	25, 024, 643	6, 105, 313
1862	2, 102, 574	37, 579, 967	27, 225, 643	6, 550, 187
1863	1, 930, 731	26, 577, 166	22, 287, 036	16, 040, 937
1864	1, 474, 582	19, 932, 067	11, 086, 536	15, 122, 937
1865	1, 271, 129	14, 423, 566	20, 689, 500	11, 973, 939
1866	751, 870	10, 989, 800	28, 904, 143	12, 138, 250
1867	569, 334	13, 630, 300	17, 930, 500	10, 476, 000
1868	575, 900	14, 425, 567	18, 437, 100	11, 927, 250
1869	657, 870	22, 351, 133	9, 159, 643	5, 769, 312
1870	509, 055	21, 950, 800	6, 893, 893	7, 371, 312
1871	381, 583	23, 951, 633	24, 002, 035	8, 118, 187
1872	190, 129	13, 463, 433	32, 241, 179	5, 809, 938

The movements shown by this table seem to illustrate a principle which governs to a great extent the traffic by canals and railways, viz: that, in proportion as the value of the commodity increases relatively to its weight and bulk, it seeks the rail in preference to the canal.

The transportation of flour—the most valuable article—has fallen off about 88 per cent., and wheat, next in value, 60 per cent., while the quantity of corn transported has increased 28 per cent.

The transport upon the canals of grosser freight, requiring the lowest freight-charge, has, however, increased, as appears from the following statement:

Transported on all the canals.	1866.	1872.
	Tons.	*Tons.*
Coal	1, 136, 613	1, 462, 590
Iron-ore	183, 937	377, 592
Stone, lime, and clay	235, 101	398, 188

The total tonnage moved on the Erie Canal, although somewhat fluctuating, exhibits a gradual increase.

The average monthly freight-charges for transporting wheat and corn from Buffalo to New York by rail and by canal can be stated only for the last two years.

This is shown in the following table:

Statement showing the average monthly rates per bushel by rail and canal for the transport of wheat and corn from Buffalo to New York during the years 1871 and 1872.

Months.	1871.				1872.			
	Rail.		Canal.		Rail.		Canal.	
	Wheat.	Corn.	Wheat.	Corn.	Wheat.	Corn.	Wheat.	Corn.
January	$0 18.0	$0 16.8	....	....	$0 21.0	$0 19.6	....	....
February	21.0	19.6	....	....	21.0	19.6	....	....
March	18.9	17.7	....	....	21.0	19.6	....	....
April	18.0	16.8	....	....	18.5	17.2	....	....
May	18.0	16.8	$0 11.6	$0 10.6	18.0	16.8	$0 09.9	$0 09.0
June	18.0	16.8	10.2	9.2	18.0	16.8	12.3	11.1
July	18.0	16.8	11.1	10.1	15.8	14.7	14.5	10.5
August	18.0	16.8	11.7	10.7	15.0	14.0	12.1	11.2
September	18.0	16.8	13.6	12.6	17.1	17.0	12.3	11.1
October	....	16.8	13.9	12.9	19.4	18.1	14.5	12.9
November	21.0	19.6	16.1	14.5	21.0	19.6	16.0	14.0
December	21.0	19.6	....	....	21.0	19.6	....	....
*Average	18.3	17.3	13.1	11.3	18.0	16.0	13.9	11.3½

*These averages are computed from the total quantity transported each month in connection with the average rate of freight each month.

Computing the average cost of transport of wheat and corn per bushel, from Buffalo to New York, during the years 1871 and 1872, upon the basis of freight-charges and the quantities moved, we obtain the following comparisons:

Average rail and canal charges for the years 1871 and 1872.

	1871.			1872.		
	Rail. Cts. M.	Canal. Cts. M.	Less by canal per cent.	Rail. Cts. M.	Canal. Cts. M.	Less by canal per cent.
	18.3	13.1	28.4	17.98	13.9	23
	17.3	11.29	34.6	15.89	11.3½	28.5

Table on page 37 of the Appendix, exhibits the monthly shipments of wheat and corn from Buffalo during the year 1871 and 1872, from which it appears that of the 46,155,884 bushels shipped in 1871, 6,956,221 bushels were sent by railroad and 39,199,663 bushels by canal; and of the 49,766,935 bushels shipped in 1872, 5,392,711 bushels were shipped by rail and 44,374,224 bushels by canal. From this it may be seen that the Erie Canal is yet a very important member of the transportation-routes between the interior and the seaboard, and that it is the means of preventing a great increase in the rail-charges upon the transport of western cereals. If the canal had not been in existence the railway charges would doubtless have been much higher then they were during the years mentioned.

If the quantities transported by canal had been carried at the actual average railway rates, the enhanced cost of movement in 1872 would have amounted to $2,196,000.

It appears from the table (Appendix, page 37) that the shipments of wheat and corn from Buffalo by rail during the winter months of the year 1872 were only 19.2 per cent. of the entire rail-shipments during the year, and only 2 per cent. of the total shipments during the year by canal and rail. The average monthly shipments by rail and canal during the summer months appear to have been 6,973,507 bushels, and the average monthly shipments during the winter months only 206,477 bushels. The smaller amount of wheat and corn shipped by rail during the winter months than during the summer months, taken in connection with the fact that the average winter rail-freights were 10.8 per cent. higher than the average summer rates, point to the same conclusions as to the rail-shipments from Chicago and Milwaukee, viz: the present inability or unwillingness of the railroads to meet the full demands of commerce during those months when navigation on the Erie Canal and Hudson River is closed. The very limited amount of grain shipped by rail during the winter months was not due to the fact that there was not a large amount of grain at Buffalo awaiting shipment. This is proved by the following facts: On the 1st of January, 1872, there were in store at Buffalo 1,451,231 bushels of wheat and corn, but during the months of January, February, March, and April, (prior to the opening of navigation,) only 432,382 bushels were shipped by rail, or but 30 per cent. of the quantity in store on the 1st of January, the remaining 70 per cent. being held in store at Buffalo until after the opening of navigation, when it was shipped either by canal, or by the railways at the reduced rates of rail transportation which prevail during the summer months.

Referring to the great disparity between rail shipments at Buffalo during the summer and winter months of the year 1872, namely, 4,440,327 bushels from May to November, inclusive, and 1,032,384 bushels from December to April, inclusive, we have a forcible illustration of the effect of railway and lake-propeller combinations. In the winter season 70 per cent. of the grain in store awaits the opening of the canal, but during the season of navigation a very large portion of the grain which reaches Buffalo by lake is shipped thence by rail, in consequence of the combination just mentioned.

On referring to the tables of monthly rates and monthly shipments by canal, it will be observed that during the months of September, October, and November there is a pressure upon its capacity, accompanied by an increase of rates on both canal and railways, indicating the necessity for enlarged facilities by the water-line. The financial results achieved by the Erie Canal are stated elsewhere. The benefits which it has conferred upon the country at large, and particularly upon the city of New York and the great interior of the continent, are beyond computation. These results emphasize the policy of free water-lines, under the control of a State or of the nation, and point to the expediency of continuing and extending a system from which such valuable fruits have been gathered.

Another result of water-lines may be briefly noted here, namely, the incidental increase in the traffic by rail. Perhaps the most successful and prosperous railway in the United States is that which extends for nearly five hundred miles along the Erie Canal and Hudson River. The business developed by the water-line, creates a traffic in articles which require speedy transport, and which can bear rail-rates. In like manner, the railway passenger traffic is largely increased. While, therefore, the whole county is benefited by the water-lines, the railways themselves share in the general prosperity. Instead of there being any antagonism between water-lines and railways, they are really helpful of each other.

Having thus traced somewhat elaborately the extent and effects of actual competition between the great northern water-route and the railways parallel with it, we proceed to consider the

RELATIVE COST OF TRANSPORT BY WATER AND BY RAIL IN VARIOUS PARTS OF THE COUNTRY AND UNDER DIFFERENT CONDITIONS OF WATER-CARRIAGE.

On this subject the committee rely wholly upon facts drawn from practical operations. The verdict of commerce itself, pronounced upon various routes and under diverse circumstances, is recorded in the following facts:

On the through-line from the Ohio River to Boston, composed of the Baltimore and Ohio Railroad and the Boston Steamship Company, the railroad received 68 per cent. of the earnings and the steamship company 32 per cent., making, for the actual distances operated by each, 4 to 1 in favor of water-transport. On the line between Baltimore and New York, consisting of mixed navigation, canal and open-water, and involving payment of tolls on the canal, the prorating arrangement with the Baltimore and Ohio Railroad Company allowed the vessels only one hundred and twenty-five miles for an actual distance of two hundred and thirty miles, being nearly 2 to 1 in favor of water-transport.

The Erie company now has an arrangement by which its rates from Buffalo to Boston by the outside steamers from New York are so divided as to allow the steamers 28 per cent. of the rate which, on five hundred miles, would be equivalent to one hundred and forty miles of rail for about four hundred and fifty miles of actual water transportation, or about 3 to 1 in favor of water.

Between Parkersburgh and Cincinnati the arrangement between the railway and the river steamers allows the latter for two hundred and fifty miles by water the same as for one hundred and twenty-five miles by rail, being 2 to 1 in favor of the river.

The arrangements between the Erie Railway Company and the lake steamers is, that the railway shall furnish terminal facilities at Buffalo and Dunkirk, and the steamer lines terminal facilities at Milwaukee and Chicago; and the actual distance of one thousand miles is prorated at two hundred and twelve miles, making nearly 5 to 1 in favor of the lake. (G. R. Blanchard, second vice-president Erie Railway· Evidence, page 366.)

The Central Vermont Railway and the Northern Transportation Company (steamer line) constitute a through line from Chicago to Boston and other places in New England. The distance by water is one thousand three hundred and sixty-five miles, and the distances by rail average about five hundred miles. The earnings are divided equally, being nearly 3 to 1 in favor of water. This comparison is the more valuable because the officers of the railway company own a controlling interest in the stock of the steamship company, and hence may be supposed to divide according to actual cost of service. Mr. Deifendorf, agent of the steamboat company, testifies that this division of earnings "is predicated upon the cost of transportation." (Evidence, page 228.)

The Chesapeake and Ohio Railway prorates with vessels on the Ohio River upon the basis of two to one in favor of the river. (Mr. Wickham, president Chesapeake and Ohio Railway; evidence, page 440.)

The gross earnings on the through line from Chicago to New Orleans, via the Illinois Central Railway to Cairo, (three hundred and sixty-five miles,) and thence by the Mississippi River to New Orleans, (one thousand and fifty miles,) are so divided as to give three-fifths to the railroad and two-fifths to the river; making, on the charge of $7 per ton, from New Orleans to Chicago, 2.7 mills per ton per mile for the river, and 11.5 mills per ton per mile by the railroad, or over five to one in favor of the Mississippi River, against the current. (Evidence of James F. Tucker, pp. 898, 899.)

From the Kanawha coal-mines to Huntington, W. Va., the distance by rail is sixty-seven miles, and the minimum charge for transporting coal is 75 cents per ton. From the same coal-mines to Cincinnati, by the Ohio River, the distance is two hundred and seventy-five miles, and the charge per ton for coal-transportation is 50 cents; being at the rate of nearly 2 mills per ton per mile by river, and 11.2 mills per ton per mile by rail, nearly six to one in favor of the river. The river-rates include the cost of returning the boats to the coal-mines. (Evidence of W. H. Edwards, of Coalsburgh, W. Va., p. 461.)

From Pittsburgh to New Orleans, via the Ohio and Mississippi Rivers, two thousand four hundred miles, coal is transported during good stages of water for $1.60 per ton, or at the rate of two-thirds of one mill per ton per mile. This is done in barges, and in very large quantities. (Evidence of Mr. Coyle, p. 890.)

Hon. Abraham Murdock, president of the Mobile and Ohio Railroad, thus describes the competition of the Mississippi River:

"Question. Are you not in competition with the river-lines?

"Answer. All the time.

"Question. Which do you find the most active and difficult competitor?

"Answer. The river-line is the hardest thing to fight; the Mississippi is the hardest thing to fight that was ever struck yet, I reckon.

"Question. You find that a much more active and dangerous competitor than the other route?

"Answer. Yes, sir; in good weather, when the river is up; but when we catch them with low water, or an ice-gorge, we turn the tables on them."

The New Orleans Chamber of Commerce furnished to the committee a detailed statement of the actual expenses of a tow-boat with five barges, (each barge of 1,500 tons capacity,) from Saint Louis to New Orleans, (one thousand two hundred and fifty miles,) from which it appears that the expense per ton per mile was .7 of one mill, or at the rate of 5¼ mills per bushel of wheat for the entire distance. (Evidence, p. 851.) Also the actual expenses of the steamer John F. Tolle, 1,650 tons capacity, value $65,000, showing a cost per ton per mile of 3.47 mills, or at the rate of 1⅕ cents per bushel of wheat for the whole distance. (Evidence, p. 851.) Neither of the last two cases include any profit to the carrier nor interest on the cost of vessels.

Many other illustrations on this point may be found in the evidence submitted by your committee, but these taken from various parts of the country and from all kinds of water-carriage—by ocean, lake, river, and canal—will suffice to show the relative economy of the two modes of transportation for heavy and cheap commodities.

Perhaps the most unsatisfactory and defective kind of navigation known is that of the Ohio canals. Arguments based upon the results of these canals have been adduced against artificial waterways. But even the Ohio canals, only 40 feet wide, 4 feet deep, partially filled with mud, and capable of passing vessels of only 65 tons burden, are by no means an entire failure. True, they do not compensate the lessees who operate them, nor do they pay dividends to the State; but they do, to a very considerable extent, hold the railways in check, and regulate their charges. Hon. Benjamin Eggleston, who has been connected with those canals in various ways for thirty years, testified before the committee that even the opening of those very inefficient canals reduces railway rates from 25 to 15 cents per hundred between Cincinnati and Toledo. He adds that the canals would long since have been controlled by the railways but for the fact that they belong to the State of Ohio, and by law the lessees are prohibited from increasing tolls. (Evidence, p. 538.) The practical effect of nearly all the canals in this country, however small and defective, has been to reduce railway charges. Where they are susceptible of being worked at all, they exercise a potential competition which always prevents exorbitant rail-charges, and thereby indirectly confer upon the public the benefits of reduced cost of transport.

The superior advantages afforded by artificial water-lines for the transport of commodities requiring the lowest possible freight-charges is clearly shown by the relative amount of tonnage transported by rail and by canal when the two modes of transport come into direct competition.

Between the cities of New York and Philadelphia there is a railroad and an interior water-line, both of which are controlled and operated by the Pennsylvania Railroad Company.

The Philadelphia, Wilmington and Baltimore Railroad and the Chesapeake and Delaware Canal, in common with the Chesapeake and Delaware River, form competing lines of transport between the cities of Philadelphia and Baltimore, the two railroads mentioned extending from New York to Baltimore, and most favorably situated for the cheap transportation of freights. They have double tracks for nearly their entire length, low grades, a large and uniform business, and they connect important commercial cities. They are also managed by practical railway men of marked ability and long experience in their profession. The water-lines are also favorably situated. They consist of canal and natural navigable waters, the canals being of large dimensions, and having a small amount of lockage.

The actual result of the competition between these rival rail and water lines, (both the water-lines being, by virtue of their charters, free commercial highways,) is shown by the relative amount of freights transported upon them, as follows:

Freights moved between New York and Philadelphia during the year 1872.

By railroad	206,398 tons.
By water-line	1,258,732 tons.

Tonnage moved between Philadelphia and Baltimore during the year 1872.

By railroad	838,568 tons.
By water-line	2,837,532 tons.

These figures show that 85 per cent. of the tonnage moved between New York and Philadelphia, and 77 per cent. of the tonnage moved between Philadelphia and Baltimore, is transported by the water-lines.

The commodities transported almost exclusively by water, are coal, timber, grain, flour, iron ore, pig-iron and refined iron, oysters, lime, and other weighty articles. Groceries, dry goods, and general merchandise are transported both by the water-line and by the railroads. During the year 1872 the total tonnage of what is known to transporters as merchandise, amounting to 185,153 tons, was transported between Philadelphia and Baltimore by water. While the railroad does not attempt to compete for the carriage of the grosser articles mentioned, they do compete sharply for the carriage of "merchandise." A compromise has finally been entered into between the Philadelphia, Wilmington and Baltimore Railroad and the Chesapeake and Delaware Canal Company, the railroad company being allowed to make all the rates on merchandise, and the canal company agreeing to carry at the same rates.

This fact also serves to illustrate the tendency of all railway management to form combinations in opposition to the principle of competition, which always determines the rates of freight upon free highways of commerce.

In refutation of the erroneous supposition that railroads have superseded or are likely to supersede the use of natural and artificial waterlines, it may be mentioned that the Pennsylvania Railroad Company, probably the weathiest and one of the most skillfully-managed railway corporations in this country, now controls four hundred and twenty-seven miles of canal navigation, (360 miles in the State of Pennsylvania and 67 miles in the State of New Jersey,) which it has gained possesssion of by purchase and by lease.

The canals in the State of Pennsylvania controlled, by this company, have, since they came into its possession, been greatly enlarged and improved, and they are now being operated very profitably. It is also worthy of note that these canals generally run parallel with the railroads owned and operated by the same company. This company finds that iron, coal, and other minerals, and certain other grosser freights, can be transported cheaper by canal than by rail. The Pennsylvania Railroad Company can hardly be accused of the blunder of attempting to sustain an effete mode of transportation. The Philadelphia and Reading Railroad Company transports freight (principally iron, coal, and other minerals) at less cost per ton per mile than any other railroad in the United States, yet this company also operates two canals: the Susquehanna Canal, forty-five miles long, on which there were delivered at tide-water, during the year 1871, 480,075 tons of freight; and the Schuylkill Canal, one hundred and eight and a quarter miles long, by which there were delivered at tide-water, during the year 1872, 907,223 tons of freight, principally coal.

It is true that canals of small size, canals which do not connect natural navigable waters, canals which have an excessive amount of lockage, and canals which have not the facilities for transporting a larger amount of heavy freights, have failed to be remunerative to their owners. A few canals badly located have been abandoned. But, on the other hand, hundreds of miles of unremunerative railroads have been built in this country, and millions of dollars have been lost to those who embarked in their construction.

The following extract from a letter addressed to the chairman of this committee by Gen. J. J. Wistar, president of the Pennsylvania Canal Company, contains valuable facts in regard to the economy of transport by rail and by canal:

"As you are considering the subject of great trunk-lines of canal, I will add that the cost of proper facilities for 'handling,' that is, loading and unloading, is not greater for grain in bulk than for coal, and that the toll-rates above given for coal would be very remunerative for grain, viz, 4.08 and 5.38 mills per gross ton of 2,240 pounds per mile.

A trunk-line with a heavy tonnage could maintain and operate a canal properly constructed, of capacity for 300-ton cargoes, at very much reduced rates, especially on long distances, where the terminal and fixed expenses are arranged upon a greater number of miles. I should say that 1½ or 2 mills per ton per mile would be highly satisfactory on such a canal between the Ohio River and tide-water, with reasonable gradients or lockage, and the heavier the tonnage the lower the tolls, since the expense of maintaining and operating the canal is practically the same for 100,000 tons as for 10,000,000 tons, water being abundant.

"In other words, every ton transported on a railroad is the cause of an appreciable wear and tear, while on a canal, after you have once transported tonnage enough to meet the expense of maintaining and operating the canal, any additional quantity of tonnage costs nothing appreciable, and whatever tolls can be got for it is clear net profit, always assuming the supply of water to be ample."

The committee also take pleasure in referring to a letter addressed to the chairman by General Wistar, which may be found on page 90 of the appendix.

The experience of other nations accords with our own upon the relative economy of water and rail transportation and the effective competition between them. In England various parliamentary committees, after seeking in vain for means of securing competition among railways, report that they can find no practical means of securing that end, and that the only effectual and reliable competition which can be expected is that between railways and artificial water-lines. In France, where competition has always been discountenanced, it has been found necessary, in some cases, in order to prevent it, to authorize the railways to purchase the canals. Throughout the commercial world the unvarying testimony of practical experience is that water-routes are the surest competitors and the only effective regulators of railroads.

In view of the facts above mentioned, in regard to the beneficial results produced by the competition afforded by the great northern water-line; the the verdict of commerce itself as expressed in the prorating arrangements between railways and water-lines; and of the reduced rates caused by even the most inefficient artificial water-channels, (such as the Ohio canals,) the conclusion of the committee is that for all coarse, cheap, and heavy commodities natural water-routes and canals favorably located with respect both to geographical position and amount of lockage, and sustained by a sufficient amount of business, will continue to afford much the cheapest known means of transport; and that for long distances, in which a large proportion of the value of a commodity is consumed by the cost of transport, water-channels will always be an element of prime importance in any successful solution of the transportation question. This brings us to the consideration of the third subdivision above mentioned, namely:

DEFECTS AND ABUSES OF EXISTING SYSTEMS OF TRANSPORTATION.

Concisely stated, the defects and abuses alleged against the existing systems of transportation are insufficient facilities, unfair discriminations, and extortionate charges.

With reference to the matter of facilities; it is believed that the improvements of natural water-ways and the construction of additional channels of water communication have been wholly inadequate to the growing demands of trade; and by reason of this neglect on the part of the Government, the commerce of the country has been compelled to accept the more expensive methods afforded by railroads. That railway companies, having thus secured a substantial monopoly of the business of transportation, have failed to recognize their responsibilities to the public, or to meet the just demands of the rapidly-increasing commerce between the interior and the seaboard.

Discriminating and extortionate charges, however, constitute the chief grounds of complaint. The principal causes which are supposed to produce such charges, and which have aggravated and intensified the public discontent, may be summarized as follows:

1. "*Stock-watering,*" a well-known process by which the capital stock of a company is largely increased, for purely speculative purposes, without any corresponding expenditure on the part of its recipients.

2. *Capitalization of surplus earnings.* By this process the net profits, over and above the amount paid on interest and dividends are supposed to be expended in permanent improvements, and charged up to capital account, for which additional stock is issued, and increased charges rendered necessary to meet the increased dividends required. It is insisted that this is a double form of taxation: first, in the exorbitant charges from which such surplus profits are derived; and, second, in the conversion of such surplus into capital-stock, thereby compelling the business of the country to pay increased charges on all future transactions, in order to provide dividends on capital thus unjustly obtained. It is argued, with great force, that as all the legitimate claims of railroad companies are met by the public, when it has paid a fair and reasonable return for the capital invested and services rendered, any surplus earnings expended in improvements should inure to its benefit, instead of being made the basis for future exactions. In brief, the people believe that by this process they are first robbed, and then compelled to pay interest on their own money.

3. The introduction of intermediate agencies, such as car-companies, fast-freight lines, &c.

4. "Construction rings" and other means by which the managers are supposed to make large profits in the building of railways, which are charged up to the cost of the road.

5. Unfair adjustments of through and local rates, and unjust discriminations against certain localities, whereby one community is compelled to pay unreasonable charges in order that another more favored may pay less than the services are worth. This will be fully considered hereafter, in the discussion of "equal mileage rates."

6. General extravagance and corruption in railway management, whereby favorites are enriched and the public impoverished.

7. Combinations and consolidations of railway companies, by which free competition is destroyed, and the producing and commercial interests of the country handed over to the control of monopolies, who are thereby enabled to enforce upon the public the exorbitant rates rendered necessary by the causes above named.

8. The system of operating fast and slow trains on the same road, whereby the cost of freight movement is believed to be largely increased. This is perhaps the misfortune rather than the fault of railway companies. It is doubtless a necessity, growing out of the conditions under which our railway system has been developed.

Of the defects and abuses above enumerated, perhaps none have contributed so much to the general discontent and indignation as the increase of railway capital by "*stock-watering*," and *capitalization of surplus earnings*. It is freely conceded that a fair and even liberal remuneration should be paid for capital actually invested, but that the industry of the country should be taxed for all time to meet dividends on *paper*-capital, is indignantly denied.

To what extent the nominal railway capital of the country is represented by fictitious stock is not easy to determine. The manner in which railway accounts are usually kept renders it very difficult for the managers themselves to state what proportion of the entire cost of a given road was paid by the stockholders, and what part from the surplus earnings. Replacements and improvements are constantly being made, and paid for out of current receipts It was quite impossible for the committee to obtain accurate information on this point, without going into a detailed investigation of the accounts of the several companies extending over a long series of years, and involving in many cases, the cross-examination of reluctant witnesses, which would have consumed the entire time of the committee, to the exclusion of all other matters.

Enough is known of the extent and vicious effects of such stock manipulations to justify the adoption of prompt and efficient means for their prevention in the future. The conclusions at which the committee have arrived in regard to the practical measures of relief to be recommended to Congress, render it unnecessary to enter upon a detailed examination of such stock transactions by the several railways engaged in transportation between the interior and the seaboard. A very few facts may serve to illustrate the nature and extent of this abuse.

The capital of the New York Central and Hudson River Railways, as represented by stock and bonds, amounts to $105,925,487, and the capital of the Lake Shore and Michigan Southern Railway to $84,262,650, making a grand total for the through line from New York to Chicago of $190,188,137.

The cost of the main stem of the Erie Railway, from New York to Dunkirk, (459 miles,) is represented by a capital stock of $108,807,687.26.* The cost of its branches and leased roads makes the entire stock and bonded indebtedness $118,265,979.38. The manner in which the stock of this road was manipulated by its former managers is too well known to bear repetition in this report.

The capital stock and bonds of the Pennsylvania Railway amount to $88,000,000. Of this sum the cost of the road, equipment, shops, stations, &c., stands on the books of the company at $42,437,859, and the balance of $45,562,141 appears to have been invested in connecting railroads, in the purchase of the Pennsylvania canals, and in various other ways. The cost of the Pittsburgh, Fort Wayne and Chicago Railroad, as represented by stock, bonds, and floating debt, is $35,852,515, making for the entire line, from Philadelphia to Chicago, $78,290,374; in addition to which the road from Philadelphia to Pittsburgh is incumbered by a debt of $45,562,141, which has been invested, as before stated, in various other enterprises, and for which interest must be provided.

The cost, to the stock and bond holders, of the Baltimore and Ohio line, from Baltimore to Chicago, when finished and equipped for the whole distance, (795 miles,) will, as the committee are informed by, the officers of that road, be represented by a capital, including stock scrip and bonds, of not exceeding $57,000,000.

The actual cost of the Baltimore and Ohio line, on which no "watered stock" has been issued, and on which the surplus earnings amounting to $29,033,131.18, after paying interest and dividends, have been charged to "profit and loss," and used in the construction of connecting roads, may serve as the best guide we are able to furnish on estimating the probable cost of the other lines above mentioned. If the actual expenditures of the stock and bond holders have not exceeded $57,000,000 on the construction and equipment of a line from Baltimore to Chicago, involving the heavy and expensive work over the Alleghany Mountains, it is fair to presume that if no "watered stock" had been issued, and if no surplus earnings had been charged to capital account, the actual cost of the New York Central line to Chicago, which traverses a level country nearly the entire distance, did not exceed, in its present condition, $75,000,000, that of the Pennsylvania line $67,000,000, and the Erie, from New York to Dunkirk, $40,000,000. Assuming these estimates to

* See Poore's Manual, p. 648.

be approximately correct, we have an excess of capital over actual cost on these three lines as follows:

Name of line.	Present capital in stock and bonds.	Probable actual cost.	Excess of capital over actual cost.
Erie line, New York to Dunkirk, 459 miles	$108, 807, 000	$40, 000, 000	$68, 807, 000
New York Central line to Chicago, 980 miles	190, 188, 137	75, 000, 000	115, 188, 137
Pennsylvania line, from Philadelphia to Chicago, 890 miles	78, 290, 374	67, 000, 000	11, 290, 374
Totals	376, 285, 511	182, 000, 000	195, 285, 511

Making a total of over $195,000,000, on which, to pay a dividend of 10 per cent. per annum, the commerce between the West and the East must annually contribute over $19,000,000. In the presence of such facts as these, and with no assurance that the evils of stock-inflation are to be restrained in the future, it is not surprising that the murmurs of discontent have swollen into a storm of popular indignation, which will only be appeased by a thorough and radical reform, or by opening up new channels of commerce which shall relieve the public from absolute dependence upon those, which by reason of stock-speculations, are rendered incapable of performing the service required at reasonable rates.

It is but fair, however, to state the answer of the railway managers on this point. The evidence of Mr. Edwin D. Worcester, secretary of the New York Central Railway, on pages 138 to 156, presents the railroad view of this subject. He insists that "the amount of capital has nothing whatever to do with charges; that the amount taken is one thing, a thing by itself, and what the business will bear," having reference to the largest development of traffic, quite another thing. He adds: "Rates cannot be put up beyond a certain point—business will not bear it. Beyond that point combinations can effect nothing." * * * "There never was such a thing heard of as a company that increased its capital stock as an excuse or occasion for putting up rates. It could just as well put up rates if the business would bear it without increasing the capital, and, if able, pay double the rate of dividend." * * * "When the prosperity is considerable there is an inducement to increase the capital." * * * "A question of disposition to charge would be one thing, the question of ability to charge would be another. The ability to charge depends upon what property will bear in view of its moving to market, in view of the development and magnitude of the business, and considerations of that kind. With a doubled capital stock, there might be an inducement to a road to increase its rates, if those rates would bear an increase; it would be found, however, in every case I ever knew of, that rates were already as high as the business would bear in view of all the circumstances, and of the principle of the maximum amount of business of which I spoke. When it has been found in some cases that these already existing rates produced more than a certain percentage of revenue there has been a capitalization, but this has been an effect, not a cause."

He further says, "it is a fact well known to all railroad people, that the companies having the largest capital, and that watered the most, as it is called, are doing the work cheaper all over." (Evidence p. 142.) And on page 151 of the evidence he submits a table of charges on the New York Central Railway from 1862 to 1871 inclusive, showing a constant reduction of rates since 1865, notwithstanding the increase of capital stock. He also states that "from 1853 down to 1868, when the Vanderbilt people came in, the average dividends paid was a little less than 7 per cent. That was on what was called the old stock, not increased by any operation whatever. During all that time, however, the rates of freight were considerably higher than they have since been In 1865, the last year that Mr. Richmond managed the road, the average per ton per mile, including all classes of freight, was 3.26 cents. In 1866, the year that Mr. Keep managed it, it was 2.87 cents. The dividends during the two years of Mr. Keep's and Mr. Richmond's control were 6 per cent. In 1871, when all were paying on a larger capital, the average rate per ton per mile was 1.49 cents." This result is accounted for by Mr. Worcester on the ground that the larger profits from the smaller charges, are due to the greater economy now practiced by the managers of the road. (Evidence, p. 150.) Much credit is also claimed by railway men generally, because on the through trunk lines between the West and East great reductions have been made in charges since 1865, and in nearly all the statements on that subject presented to your committee, the present charges are compared with those of that year. Now, it happens that in 1865 the effects of the war and of our depreciated currency had caused railway rates to reach the highest point ever known, since this system of transportation came into general use. Perhaps a more instructive comparison may be made between the years 1860 and 1872. By reference to page 35 of the Appendix it will be observed that the average charges on fourth-class freights (such as wheat and corn) from Chicago to New York was as in 1860, 31.3 cents per bushel of 60 pounds; and in 1872, reduced to a gold standard, the average charges were 30 cents per bushel. The tonnage moved on the New York Central Railway in 1860 was 1,028,182 tons, and in 1872 it was 4,393,965 tons. As we shall hereafter see, the cost of movement diminishes in proportion to the increase of tonnage. But while the tonnage has increased 327 per cent., the charges have been reduced only 4 per cent. But for the additional dividends rendered necessary by the increase of *paper* capital, the charges could have been reduced somewhat in proportion to the increase of business. It is admitted that economical and able management should afford, to some extent, the measure of compensation; but railways are *public highways*, and as such are authorized to take private property for *public uses*, which involves the corresponding duty on their part to render the public the best and cheapest service in their power, consistent with a fair and reasonable compensation to themselves. If, by reason of increased business, they are able to pay dividends on a doubled capital, it would seem to afford a reason for reduction of rates one-half, rather than for an additional issue of stock. The principle upon which the State grants to a railway a portion of her soverignty, whereby it is enabled to appropriate private property to a *public* use, is not that the corporation shall tax the public the highest rates for transportation that the "property will bear in view of its moving to market," but that the service shall be rendered for the smallest compensation that will pay a reasonable, and even liberal, return for the capital invested and service performed.

If, by the exercise of economy, the company can pay, at a given rate of charges, a dividend that will justify an increase of stock, the public is entitled to a reduction of the rates, because the exercise of economy and administrative ability is one of the implied conditions on which a monopoly of the line is granted to the corporation. And if by reason of a large increase of business furnished by the public, the cost of carriage is diminished, those who furnish such increase should have at least a portion of the benefits accruing from it.

Your committee are of the opinion that stock inflation is wholly indefensible; that it necessarily produces increased charges, and promotes corrupt speculations, and hence should be prohibited. It would of course be difficult, if not impossible, to cure existing evils by legislation, because such inflations have been in nearly all cases authorized by State legislatures, and hence have the sanction of law; and because a large proportion of such stock has passed out of the hands of the original holders, and is now owned by innocent persons who have paid full consideration for it. The remedy for this abuse seems to fall peculiarly within the jurisdiction of the States who have created the corporations from which such practices proceed, but your committee believe the evil to be of such magnitude as to justify and require for its prevention the co-operation of both Congress and the States.

The third of the above enumerated causes of high rates, namely "the introduction of intermediate agencies, such as car companies, fast-freight lines," &c., has been the subject of some misapprehension. These agencies are not always an unmixed evil. On the contrary, they are often productive of beneficial results, both to the companies and to the public. We will briefly refer to some of their good and evil characteristics and results. The hiring of cars at the rates they are furnished by car companies, namely 1½ to 2 cents per mile run, is doubtless a very expensive operation, and evidently profitable to the car company, but to a road that is unable to supply itself with sufficient rolling stock to meet the demands of business at certain seasons of the year, it is a necessity. When this is done to supply a real necessity, and not for purposes of speculation by the managers of the road in collusion with such car company, we are unable to discover in it anything to condemn.

Fast-freight lines.—There are several kinds of fast-freight organizations, the history and description of which are given by Mr. G. R. Blanchard, second vice-president of the Erie Railway, on pages 361 to 368 of the evidence. These organizations are divided into two general classes: 1st, *co-operative*, and 2d, *non-co-operative*. The co-operative organizations are nothing more than arrangements and combinations between railways for forwarding freight over their respective lines. They are formed by each company contributing a *pro rata* of cars based upon mileage, or upon the amount of business done by each. The mileage balances are settled upon the clearing-house principle, at the rate of a cent and a half per mile. By this co-operative plan railway companies receive all the profits from the business transacted, and the public receives the benefit of greater efficiency and economy of service. These lines are also enabled to reach the small interior points of supply, and without transshipment or intermediate expenses, to distribute freights at the points of consumption; thus avoiding the expenses of transshipment and the charges of middle-men. The adoption of this system, and of carrying in bulk, has, as we shall hereafter see, contributed more than anything else to the large increase of grain transportation by rail which has taken place within the last five years. A full discription of the operation and effect of these lines will be found on pages 74 to 81 of the evidence.

With the exception of the tendency to bring about a general combination of railways, as hereinafter mentioned, the committee are unable to find any serious objection to the *co-operative* lines. On the other hand, there is much to commend them to public favor.

Non-co-operative freight-line organizations embrace such as are not owned by the railways over which they are operated, but by corporations or individuals whose interests are not identical with the interests of the railway companies, and who stand between them and the public. The various forms of this class of freight-lines, and their influence upon the cost of transportation, are fully explained on pages 361 to 364 of the evidence, from which it appears that they are in many, if not in all cases, a fraud both upon the stockholders of the railway, and upon the public. Mr. J. M. Walker, president of the Chicago, Burlington and Quincy Railroad, denounces them as "parasites that should not be tolerated in any railroad management," and as "unjust to the railroad, to the shipper, and to everybody else, because all the profits that come from these freight-lines should go into the railroad treasury; if the railroads receive all the profits there is from transportation, they can reduce their charges to that extent." (Evidence, p. 259.)

The inducements on the part of railway companies to contract with such companies are ostensibly to secure the large aggregate of traffic they claim to control, but in a great many cases a division of profits between the officers of the railway company and the persons entering into these contracts is effected by a judicious distribution of their stock. (Evidence, p. 365.) Mr. Blanchard expresses the opinion that the introduction of middlemen between the interests of the railways and the public "has had a great deal to do with the system of peculation and fraud which has crept into the railway management of this country." He illustrates these effects upon the cost of transportation as follows:

"We have here on our own line parallel cases, which show how much more just the co-operative form is, to both the owners of the property and the public, than perhaps any other that could be drawn. Under the contract made by Mr. Gould for the Great Western Dispatch Company, which is the second form I have spoken of—a commission line—we have paid to them 15 per cent. upon the first three classes west-bound, and 10 and 8 upon the fourth and special classes west-bound. We have also paid 10 per cent. upon the upper classes east-bound, and 8 per cent upon the lower classes east-bound, although a portion of the receipts were returnable to the railways in dividends. Running parallel to that line to Chicago, the Erie and North Shore Line was organized two years ago this fall, upon the completion of the Niagara Falls branch of the Erie Railway. Mr. Joy, the president of the Michigan Central Road, being an economical and fair manager, and having the interests of his stockholders and the public much more at heart than Mr. Gould is ever regarded to have had, demanded that the co-operative form of line should be made, and the Erie and North Shore Line has, during the year which I have been immediately supervising the freight-traffic of the Erie Company, been running parallel to the Great Western Dispatch. The average which the Great Western Dispatch has deducted from the Erie Railway earnings has been in the neighborhood of 9 per cent., (although we do share ultimately in a dividend,) while the North Shore Line costs less than 3 per cent."

This practical illustration shows that 6 per cent. of the cost of trans, portation was due to the agency of the non-co-operative organization- and also affords an explanation of the reason why certain roads, which do a large business at high rates, fail to pay dividends to their stockholders. In short, this system of freight lines constitutes one of the most efficient instrumentalities by which railway officers sometimes grow rich, while the public pays high rates, and stockholders wait in vain for dividends. It is gratifying to state, however, that this abuse prevails to a less extent now than formerly. Stockholders are beginning to understand its effect upon their profits, and hence non-co-operative freight-lines are being changed to the co-operative systems.

The committee are of the opinion that great good would result from the passage of State laws prohibiting officers of railway companies from owning or holding, directly or indirectly, any interest in any non-co-operative freight-line operated upon the railroad with which they are connected in such official capacity.

The committee will consider the other "defects and abuses" above enumerated in connection with the remedies which have been suggested.

The discussion of these measures involves the consideration of, first:

THE CONSTITUTIONAL POWER OF CONGRESS TO REGULATE COMMERCE AMONG THE SFVERAL STATES.

In discussing the constitutional power of Congress over this subject, we shall intentionally omit all consideration of the dangers of its exercise. Whatever those dangers may be, they address themselves to the sound discretion of Congress, in view of its responsibility to the people, but do not, in the slightest degree, affect the inquiry as to the existence of the power itself. To argue that because a power may be abused it therefore does not exist, is to contradict facts patent in the constitution of every civilized nation. It would in fact be impossible to construct a government that could maintain its own existence, without giving it powers which may be used to the injury of its subjects, and even to its own ruin. Take, for instance, the war-powers of our own Government. Congress may to-morrow, without any cause whatever, declare war against all the nations of the earth, and yet no one will argue that because of this liability to abuse, the power to declare war does not exist. The power to lay and collect taxes may be used to the injury of the people in many ways, but no one doubts its existence. So of many of the other acknowledged powers of the Government. The wise and illustrious men who embodied in our Constitution the element of free government, were careful to delegate to Congress all the powers essential to the existence and progress of a great nation, but at the same time they provided an ample safeguard against the abuse of such powers, by making those to whom they were intrusted directly responsible to the people. In fact the theory upon which they constructed our Government was, that the people themselves exercise the powers granted, through their special agents appointed for that purpose; and this being not only the theory but the practical effect of our constitution, there was less danger in conferring power on Congress than there would be upon the legislature of any other nation.

"Where there is a doubt as to whether a certain power has been granted, the inquiry very naturally and properly arises, is it unusual in its character, and unknown in other governments?" If so, the keenest scrutiny will be invited, and the most satisfactory demonstration of its existence will be required. "But if, on the contrary, it be a power which every government in Christendom is admitted to possess, which has always been exercised by every government hitherto existing, a power essential to the progress of civilization, without which agriculture must languish and labor be unrewarded, commerce and trade must be impeded and intercourse obstructed, then the inquirer will approach the investigation in a different spirit. While he will still require satisfactory evidence, he will be prepared to give a favorable ear to what may be adduced to establish the fact of such a power having been granted." There can be no doubt to which class of powers the one under discussion belongs.

It being conceded that certain powers over inter-State commerce are delegated to Congress by the Constitution, the inquiry to which we shall address ourselves, is not what powers *ought* to have been granted, but *what is the nature, extent, and application of the powers actually delegated?*

In the discussion of this question we shall endeavor to maintain the following propositions:

First. That the powers of Congress, whatever they may be, are derived *directly* from *the people* of the several States, and *not from the states themselves.*

Second. That prior to the adoption of the Constitution, the powers now possessed by the General Government constituted a part of the *supreme sovereignty* which resided *in the people* of the several States; and that the sovereignty of the people of the States over commerce was absolute, excepting only as it was limited by the articles of confederation.

Third. That whatever *elements* and *attributes* of *sovereignty* appertained to these powers when they existed *in the people of the several States, were transferred* to the General Government *with the powers themselves*, by the Constitution; and that they now exist in Congress as fully and completely as they formerly did in the people of the States, subject only to the express limitations of the Constitution.

Fourth. That the grant of powers to Congress is an investment of power, for the general advantage, in the hands of agents selected for that purpose, and hence they are not to be construed strictly, and against the grantee, but according to the natural and obvious meaning of the language of the Constitution, taken in connection with the purposes for which they were conferred.

Fifth. That every important word in the clauses which confer the "*power to regulate commerce among the several States*," and to "make all laws which shall be necessary and proper for carrying it into execution," has received judicial construction by the Supreme Court of the United States, and that under such construction the power of Congress to regulate inter-State transportation by railroads, and to *aid* and *facilitate* commerce, is clearly established.

Sixth. That in the exercise of its delegated powers, Congress is authorized, under the grant of auxiliary powers, to employ such *means* as are *appropriate* and plainly *adapted* to their execution, and is not confined to means which are *indispensably necessary;* and that the courts will not inquire into the degree of *necessity* of any particular means which may be adopted.

Seventh. In the selection of *means* by which inter-State commerce shall be regulated, Congress in its discretion, and under its responsibility to the people, may, *first*, prescribe the rules by which the *instruments, vehicles*, and *agents* engaged in *transporting* commodities from one State into or through another shall be governed, whether such transportation is by land or by water, on railroads or in steamboats. Second. That it may appropriate money for the construction of railways or canals, when the same shall be necessary for the regulation of commerce. Third. That it may incorporate a company with authority to construct them. Fourth. That it may exercise the right of eminent domain within a State, in order to provide for the construction of such railways or canals; or, fifth, it may, in the exercise of the right of eminent domain, take for the public use, paying just compensation therefor, any existing railway or canal owned by private persons or corporations.

THE POWERS OF THE NATIONAL GOVERNMENT ARE DERIVED DIRECTLY FROM THE PEOPLE.

In the case of McCulloch *vs.* Maryland, the counsel for the defendant in error insisted that in the construction of the Constitution it was important to consider that instrument not as emanating from the people, but as the act of sovereign and independent States. The powers of the General Government, it was argued, "are delegated by the *States*, who alone are truly sovereign, and must be exercised in subordination to the States, who alone possess supreme dominion." The court, by Marshall, C. J., in reply, says: "It would be difficult to sustain this proposition. The convention which framed the Constitution was indeed elected by the State legislatures; but the instrument, when it came from their hands, was a mere proposal, without obligation or pretensions to it." It was reported to the then existing Congress of the United States, with a request that it might "be submitted to a convention of delegates chosen in each State by the people thereof, under the recommendation of its legislature, for their assent and ratification." This mode of proceeding was adopted, and by the convention, by Congress, and by the State legislatures the instrument was submitted to *the people.* They acted upon it in the only manner in which they can act safely, effectively, and wisely on such a subject, by assembling in convention. It is true they assembled in their several States—and where else should they have assembled? No political dreamer was ever wild enough to think of breaking down the lines which separate the States, and of compounding the people into one common mass. Of consequence, when they act, they act in their States. But the measures they adopt do not, on that account, cease to be the measures of the people themselves, or become the measures of the State governments. From these conventions the Constitution derives its whole authority. *The Government proceeds directly from the people, is "ordained and established" in the name of the people,* and is declared to be ordained "in order to form a more perfect Union, establish justice, insure domestic tranquillity, and secure the blessings of liberty to themselves and to their posterity." The assent of the States in their sovereign capacity is implied in calling a convention, and thus submitting that instrument to the people. *But the people were at perfect liberty to accept or reject it; and their act was final. It required not the affirmance, and could not be negatived by the State govern-*

ment. The Constitution, when thus adopted, was of complete obligation, and bound the State sovereignties.

"It has been said that the people had already surrendered all their powers to the State sovereignties, and had nothing more to give. But surely the question whether they may assume and modify the powers granted to the Government does not remain to be settled in this country. *Much more might the legitimacy of the Government be doubted had it been created by the States.* The powers delegated to the State sovereignties *were to be exercised by themselves, not* by a distinct and independent sovereignty, *created by* themselves. To the formation of a league, such as was the Confederation, the State sovereignties were certainly competent. But when, 'in order to form a more perfect union,' it was deemed necessary to change this alliance into an effective government, possessing great and sovereign powers, and acting directly on the people, *the necessity of referring it to the people, and of deriving its powers directly from them, was felt and acknowledged by all. The Government of the Union, then, is emphatically, and truly, a government of the people. In form and substance it emanates from them. Its powers are granted by them, and are to be exercised directly on them, and for their benefit.*" (4 Wheaton, 403, 404.)

WHAT IS THE NATURE AND EXTENT OF THE POWERS THUS GRANTED BY THE PEOPLE TO CONGRESS?

The powers of the National Government, though limited in their objects, are, in their sphere of action, absolute, sovereign, supreme. "The power existing in every body-politic is an *absolute despotism;* in constituting a government it distributes that power as it pleases, and in the quantity it pleases, and imposes what checks it pleases upon its public functionaries." (Livingston *vs.* Moore, 7 Peters, 546.)

From the Declaration of Independence, in 1776, to the establishment of the Confederation, in 1781, this "absolute sovereignty" existed in the body-politic of each of the several States, then separate and completely independent sovereignties.

By the articles of confederation, a portion of these sovereign powers were conceded *by the several States* to the United States, each State retaining "its sovereignty, freedom, and independence, and every power, jurisdiction, and right which is not by this Confederation *expressly* delegated to the United States in Congress assembled." When experience had very soon demonstrated the weakness and defects of the Confederation, "*The people of the United States*" resumed all the powers of sovereignty which had previously existed in each independent body-politic, and by a Constitution of their own creation established a new Government; and in constituting it, distributed the plenary and absolute powers residing in themselves, in accordance with their own supreme will and pleasure. To the Congress of the United States they delegated certain powers, enumerated and implied, together with the auxiliary powers to carry them into execution. To the States, certain powers were prohibited. "And the powers not delegated to the United States by the Constitution, nor prohibited by it to the States, are reserved to the States respectively, or to the people." These powers, thus delegated to Congress, are, therefore, a part of the absolute sovereignty of the people, and are the same in quality, and as absolute and unlimited as were the same powers when they previously existed in the people of the separate and independent States, unless some limitation upon them can be found in the instrument by which they were delegated. Why should they not be? They are derived directly from the source of absolute power—the people. They constitute a part of their sovereignty, held in trust by the nation for the people, to be exercised for their benefit, and under such restrictions only as they have been pleased to impose. All the limitations and safeguards which they deemed necessary, or intended to put upon the exercise of those powers, are expressed in the Constitution. Hence, where no limitations or restrictions are imposed, by that instrument, upon the powers delegated to Congress, they are, within their sphere of action, and as to the objects for which they were granted, absolute and supreme. In the words of Marshall, C. J, (4 Wheaton, 405,) "*If any one proposition could command the universal assent of mankind, we might expect it would be this: that the Government of the Union, though limited in its powers, is supreme within its sphere of action.*"

Speaking of the power conferred on Congress by the terms "to regulate commerce," Mr. Calhoun, in submitting the report of a select committee June 26, 1846, said: "They (the committee) are of the opinion, after due reflection, that they confer on Congress all the powers which, by a fair interpretation, belonged to the States, as fully as the States themselves possessed it, except such, if there be any, as may be prohibited by the Constitution from being exercised either expressly or impliedly. That they confer on Congress all the power to regulate commerce with each other, with that exception, would seem to be so clear as hardly to admit of doubt, as the words by which it is delegated are used without qualification or condition. But if there should be room for doubt, it would be removed by adverting to the reasons for delegating the power. It was not to limit or prohibit it as a power of a dangerous character, and which on that account ought to be restricted or prohibited. On the contrary, it was regarded as one of the utmost utility, and on the proper control of which the prosperity of the States essentially depended, and it was accordingly for the purpose of obtaining such control, as well as to prevent collisions among the States, and not to restrict or prohibit it, that it was delegated to the Federal Government as their common representative and organ in their external relations with each other and with foreign nations." But in order to silence forever all doubts as to the sovereignty of the Union within the sphere of its delegated powers, the Constitution expressly provides that "this Constitution, and the laws of the United States which shall be made in pursuance thereof, shall be the supreme law of the land, anything in the constitution or laws of any State to the contrary notwithstanding."

RULE OF CONSTRUCTION.

The rule by which the powers delegated to Congress are to be construed is thus laid down by the Supreme Court of the United States, in Gibbon *vs.* Ogden, 9 Wheaton, 187: "This instrument contains an enumeration of powers expressly granted by the people to their Government. It has been said that these powers ought to be construed strictly. But why ought they to be so construed? Is there one sentence in the Constitution which gives countenance to this rule? In the last of the enumerated powers—that which grants expressly the means for carrying all the others into execution—Congress is authorized 'to make all laws which shall be necessary and proper' for the purpose. But this limitation on the *means* which may be used *is not extended to the powers which are conferred*, nor is there one sentence in the Constitution which has been pointed out by the gentlemen of the bar, or which we have been able to discover, that prescribes this rule. We do not, therefore, think ourselves justified in adopting it. * * * As men whose intentions require no concealment generally employ words which most directly and aptly express the ideas they intend to convey, the enlightened patriots who framed our Constitution, and the people who adopted it, must be understood to have employed words in their natural sense, and to have intended what they said. * * * The grant does not convey power which might be beneficial to the grantor, if retained by himself, or which can inure solely to the benefit of the grantee; but is an investment of power, for the general advantage, in the hands of agents selected for that purpose; which power can never be exercised by the people themselves, but must be placed in the hands of agents or lie dormant. We know of no rule for construing the extent of such powers other than is given by the language of the instrument which confers them, taken in connection with the purposes for which they were conferred."

This general view of the origin, nature, and extent of the powers of Congress, and the clear and authoritative rule for their construction laid down by the highest judicial authority, brings us to the consideration of the power conferred by the eighth section of the first article of the Constitution, and its application to the subject of inter-State commerce as carried on by railroads passing from one State into another:

"Congress shall have power * * * *to regulate commerce with foreign nations, and among the several States*, and with the Indian tribes;" and the auxiliary power "*to make all laws which shall be necessary and proper for carrying into execution the foregoing powers*, and all other powers vested by this Constitution in the Government of the United States, or in any department or officer thereof."

The rule of construction above quoted will apply with peculiar force to this clause. It is a fact, as well known as any other in the early history of our Government, that the necessities of commerce constituted the chief cause for the formation of the Constitution. Under the Confederation each State exercised the power to regulate commerce for itself, which resulted in unequal, unjust, discordant legislation; interfered with the public revenues; deprived certain States of a fair and equal participation in the benefits of the Government; involved the country in the most serious difficulties and embarrassments, and threatened the gravest consequences to the nation. In no other respect were the defects of the Confederation so apparent as this. "In the history of the times," says Mr. Webster, "it was found that the great topic, urged on all occasions as showing the necessity of a new and different government, was the state of trade and commerce. * * * The leading State papers of the time are full of this topic. The New Jersey resolutions complain that the regulation of trade was in the power of the several States, within their special jurisdiction in such a degree as to involve many difficulties and embarrassments; and they express the earnest opinion that the *sole and exclusive power* of regulating trade with foreign states ought to be in Congress. Mr. Witherspoon's motion in Congress in 1781 is of the same general character; and the report of a committee of that body in 1785 is still more emphatic. It declares that Congress ought to possess the *sole and exclusive* power of regulating trade, as well with foreign nations as between the States. The resolutions of Virginia, in January, 1786, *which were the immediate cause of the convention*, put forth the same great object. Indeed, it is the *only* object stated in those resolutions. There is not another idea in the whole document. *The entire purpose for which the delegates assembled at Annapolis was to devise means for the uniform regulation of trade.* They found no means but in a general government, and they recommended a convention to accomplish that purpose. Over whatever other interests of the country this Government may diffuse its benefits and its blessings, it will always be true, as matter of historical fact, that *it had its origin in the necessities of commerce*, and for its immediate object the relief of those necessities, by removing their causes and by establishing a *uniform* and steady system."

It is fair to presume, then, that the convention was not unmindful of the vital importance of this subject, and that when the framers of the Constitution inserted the provision granting power to regulate commerce, they gave to it that careful consideration that would naturally be demanded by a matter which was "the immediate cause of the convention," and in which the Constitution itself "had its origin." If, therefore, in any part of that instrument, singularly conspicuous for its plain, simple, precise, and comprehensive language, we should expect to find the intention of its authors expressed in unequivocal words, it would be in this clause. If any limitations, qualifications, or conditions were intended to be placed upon the sovereign power delegated by it, we might expect them to be as clearly and unequivocally expressed as is the grant of power itself. We, therefore, know of no safer way of arriving at its intent than by the natural and obvious meaning of its language. Fortunately we are not compelled to rely on our own construction. Every important word in it has, on several occasions, received judicial construction by the highest court in the nation.

JUDICIAL CONSTRUCTION.

Says Chief Justice Marshall, in Gibbons *vs.* Ogden, 9 Wheat., 189 and 194: "The subject to be regulated is *commerce*, and our Constitution being, as was aptly said at the bar, one of enumeration, and not of definition, to ascertain the *extent* of the power, it becomes necessary to settle the meaning of the word. The counsel for the appellee would limit it to traffic, to buying and selling, or the interchange of commodities, and do not admit that it comprehends navigation. This would restrict a general term, applicable to many objects, to one of its significations. Commerce undoubtedly is traffic, but it is something more; *it is intercourse.* It describes the commercial intercourse between nations and parts of nations *in all its branches.* * * * *Commerce, as the word is used in the Constitution, is a unit, every part of which is indicated by the term.* If this be the admitted meaning of the word, in its application to foreign nations, it must carry the same meaning throughout the sentence, and remain a unit, unless there be some plain, intelligible cause which alters it."

In the same case, Mr. Justice Johnson, concurring in the opinion delivered by the Chief Justice, says: "Commerce, in its simplest signification, means an exchange of goods; but in the advancement of society, labor, *transportation*, intelligence, care, and the various mediums of exchange, become commodities, and enter into commerce; the *subject*, the *vehicle*, the *agent*, and their *various operations*, become the *objects* of *commercial regulation. Ship-building*, the *carrying-trade*, and the propagation of seamen are such vital agents of commercial prosperity that the nation which could not legislate over those subjects would not possess power to regulate commerce." (4 Wheaton, 229.)

In the Passenger cases, 7 Howard, 416, it was said by the court: "Commerce consists in selling the superfluity; in purchasing articles of necessity, as well productions as manufactures; in buying from one nation and selling to another, or in *transporting the merchandise* from the seller to the buyer to gain the freight."

And again, in a very recent case, the Philadelphia and Reading Railroad *vs.* Pennsylvania, decided at the December term, 1872, the Supreme Court says: "Beyond all question the *transportation of freights* or of the subjects of commerce for the purposes of exchange or sale *is a constituent of commerce itself.* This has never been doubted, and probably *the transportation of articles of trade from one State to another was the prominent idea in the minds of the framers of the Constitution when to Congress was committed the power to regulate commerce among the several States.* * * * It would be absurd to suppose that the transmission of the subjects of trade from the seller to the buyer, or from the place of production to market, was not contemplated, for without that there could be no consummated trade with foreign nations or among the States."

In the same case the court says, "To *regulate* commerce means to *prescribe the rules by which commerce is to be governed.*"

As defined by Webster, to "regulate" means "to adjust by rule or by method; to subject to a prescribed course; to direct; to rule; to conduct."

Construing the words "*power to regulate*," Chief Justice Marshall, in Gibbons *vs.* Ogden, 9 Wheaton, 196, says, "*This power*, like all others vested in Congress, *is complete in itself, may be exercised to its utmost extent, and acknowledges no limitations* other than are prescribed in the Constitution."

Defining the Federal "power to regulate commerce," Mr. Justice Johnson, in the same case, argues that it is the *same power that previously existed in the States*, and that the power of a sovereign State over commerce "is the power to limit and restrain it at pleasure." If this great interest of the people may be limited and restrained at pleasure, upon what principle shall we deny the power to aid and encourage to the same extent? The power was granted for beneficial purposes, not to cripple and destroy the commercial interest of the country.

The power to regulate commerce among the several States does not stop at State lines, but may be exercised within the territorial jurisdiction of a State.

"The word '*among*' means *intermingled* with. A thing which is *among* others, is intermingled with them. *Commerce among the States cannot stop at the boundary-line of each State, but may be introduced into the interior.* It is not intended to say that these words comprehend that commerce which is completely internal, which is carried on between man and man in a State, or between different parts of the same State, and which does not extend to and or affect other States. Such a power would be inconvenient, and is certainly unnecessary. Comprehensive as the word 'among' is, it may very properly be restricted to that commerce which concerns more States than one." * * * *

"But in regulating commerce with foreign nations, the power of Congress *does not stop at the jurisdictional lines of the several States. It would be a very useless power if it could not pass those lines.* The commerce of the United States with foreign nations is that of the whole United States. Every district has the right to participate in it. The deep streams, which penetrate our country in every direction, pass through the interior of almost every State in the Union, and furnish the means of exercising that right. *If Congress has the power to regulate it, that power must be exercised wherever the subject exists.* If it exists within the States, if a foreign voyage may commence or terminate at a port within a State, then the power of Congress may be exercised within a State. *This principle is, if possible, still more clear when applied to commerce 'among the several States.'* * * * *The power of Congress, then, whatever it may be, must be exercised within the territorial jurisdiction of* *the several States.* The sense of the nation on the subject is unequivocally manifested by the provisions made in the laws for *transporting goods* by land between Baltimore and Providence, between New York and Philadelphia, and between Philadelphia and Baltimore." (Gibbons *vs.* Ogden, 9 Wheaton, 194, 195, and 196.)

THIS POWER EXTENDS TO LAND AS WELL AS TO WATER.

Is there any distinction between the power of Congress over commerce on water and on land? If so, on what principle is such distinction founded? Is the National Government, which is so potential over foreign and inter-State commerce when conducted on water, suddenly smitten with impotence when that same commerce touches the land? Is it possible that the Constitution places the commerce of some insignificant stream, capable of floating a schooner of ten or twenty tons burden, under the protecting power of the nation, while it excludes from such protection and care the many thousands of miles of railroad, extending from ocean to ocean, traversing half the States of the Union, conducting a traffic probably twenty times more valuable than the entire commerce of the nation when the Constitution was framed, and destined, at no distant day, to become the great channels of commercial intercourse between the continents of Asia and Europe? In the words of another, "Does the constitutional power of Congress over inter-State commerce depend upon a question in chemistry? Is it so that if commerce rides from State to State on *water*, Congress may regulate it fully; but if it rides on *iron*, then the power ceases? This chemical test of what is good constitutional law once and long had advocates, who held that the way to decide whether Congress could improve a river was to taste the water and find whether it was salt; and if salt, then Congress could pass the law for improvement; and if not, not. But this school of chemical constitutional lawyers is extinct, but will need to be revived before the Constitution will be made to read that "Congress shall have power to regulate commerce when it goes on water, but not when it goes on land."

The courts have not left this question in doubt. In the United States *vs.* Coombs, (12 Peters, page 78,) Mr. Justice Story, in delivering the opinion of the court, says, "The power to regulate commerce includes the power to regulate navigation, as connected with the commerce of foreign nations, and among the States. It does not stop at the mere boundary-line of a State; *nor is it confined to acts done on the water*, or in the necessary course of navigation thereof. It *extends to such acts done on land* which interfere with, obstruct, or prevent the due exercise of the power to regulate commerce and navigation."

In delivering the opinion of the court in the Genesee Chief *vs.* Fitzhugh, (12 Howard U. S., 244,) Chief Justice Taney, arguing that the admiralty jurisdiction could not be made co-extensive with the power to regulate commerce, says, "*This power* [the commercial power] *is as extensive upon land as upon water. The Constitution makes no distinction in that respect.* And if the admiralty jurisdiction in matters of contract and tort which the courts of the United States may lawfully exercise on the high seas can be extended to the lakes, under the power to regulate commerce, it can with the same propriety, and on the same construction, be extended to contracts and torts on land where the commerce is between different States, *and it may also embrace the vehicles and persons engaged in carrying it on.*"

In further illustration of the unreasonableness of holding the admiralty jurisdiction to be co-extensive with the power of Congress over commerce, the learned judge says: "It would [in that case] be in the power of Congress to confer admiralty jurisdiction upon its courts over the cars engaged in transporting passengers or merchandise from one State to another, and over the persons engaged in conducting them."

Could there have been any doubt in the minds of the judges who concurred in that opinion, or of the able and experienced Chief Justice who delivered it, as to whether the power of Congress to regulate commerce extended to railroads, over which freights are transported from one State to another? It is true the direct question before the court was not as to the extent of the commercial power, but the court assumes the principle above stated to be so clear that it may be used in illustration of the argument against a doubtful construction of another power. This opinion is the more valuable because it comes from a judge always jealous of any infringement of State-rights, and never suspected of an undue leaning toward the enlargement of Federal powers.

Again, in the recent case of the Philadelphia and Reading Railroad *vs.* Pennsylvania, decided at the last December term, the direct question before the court was as to whether a certain statute of Pennsylvania which imposed a tax on freights carried by rail from another State into or through the State of Pennsylvania was in conflict with the power of Congress to regulate commerce among the States. The court held, as we have already seen, in the reference made to this case, that, "*beyond all question, the transportation of freight, or of the subjects of commerce, for the purpose of exchange or sale, is a constituent of commerce itself.*" And *because* such *transportation by rail* through, into, or out of the State of Pennsylvania constituted commerce among the States, the court decided that a tax upon it was a regulation of inter-State commerce, and hence in conflict with that clause of the Federal Constitution which gives to Congress the exclusive power to regulate commerce among the States. If, therefore, a State cannot impose a tonnage-tax on commodities carried from one State to another by rail because such tax interferes with the power of Congress to regulate commerce among the States, does not the conclusion follow irresistibly that *transportation of freights by rail from one State to another* is commerce among the States, within the meaning of the Constitution, and within the regulating power of Congress? This decision of the Supreme Court establishes the following propositions:

1st. That the power of Congress over inter-State commerce extends to the land as well as to water.

2d. That *transportation by rail* from one State into or through another is a *constituent of inter-State commerce itself.*

3d. That being a constituent of inter-State commerce, such transportation by rail is under the exclusive control of Congress, by virtue of the power to regulate commerce among the States.

In deciding that inter-State *transportation by rail is commerce among the States,* the court, we insist, has established a principle from which the conclusion is irresistible that such commerce or intercourse, in all its parts, is subject to the full scope and extent of the operation of that congressional power by which commerce is to be regulated.

This brings us to the consideration of—

1st. The *extent* to which this national power over commerce may be exercised; and,

2d. The *means* which may be employed to carry the power into execution.

The first proposition has been pretty fully considered in the general remarks already submitted upon the origin, nature, extent, and rule for the construction of Federal powers, and need not be repeated. We have seen that both upon principle and by the repeated decisions of the Supreme Court of the United States, this, like all other Federal powers, is derived directly from the people, and is a part of their sovereignty, held in trust by Congress, to be exercised for their benefit; that it is the same power in quality and extent which previously existed in the people of the States; that when it existed in the people of the States it was unquestionably supreme and absolute; that when it was transferred by the Constitution from the people of the States to the nation it was complete and perfect in all its parts, and that it is subject to no restrictions except those expressly imposed by the Constitution.

What, then, are the limitations prescribed by the Constitution? They are all very clearly expressed, and do not in the remotest degree affect the question under discussion.

1. "No tax or duty shall be laid on articles exported from any State."

2. "No preference shall be given by any regulation of commerce or revenue to the ports of one State over those of another; nor shall vessels bound to, or from, one State, be obliged to enter, clear, or pay duties in another." Another limitation is contained in the clause itself. The words commerce *among* the *several States* imply that it must be a commerce that affects more than one State, and hence the power does not extend to that traffic, intercourse, or transportation of commodities which is totally internal—which begins and ends within the boundaries of a State. Subject, therefore, to these limitations, this power is unrestricted and supreme. The scope of its operation extends to every

phase and element of international and inter-State commerce. "*Traffic*," "*intercourse*," "*transportation*;" the "*vehicles*," "*agents*," and "*instruments*," and all the multifarious means and appliances by which foreign or inter-State commerce is carried on, come within the wide sweep of its operation.

THE "POWER TO REGULATE" INCLUDES THE POWER TO FACILITATE, AS WELL AS TO DISBURDEN COMMERCE.

It has been claimed that this power is merely *negative*, and can be constitutionally exercised only in *disburdening* commerce, by preventing duties and imposts on the trade between the States, and by forbidding all local reactions and restrictions. It might be a sufficient answer to this argument to say that no clause, or word, can be found in the Constitution to support it. No decision of the Supreme Court, we believe, has ever countenanced it; but, on the other hand, the principles of constitutional law expressed in the opinions of the court, pronounced by the eminent judges from whom we have quoted, expressly refute it. If this be the meaning of the clause as applied to commerce among the States, the same must be its meaning when applied to foreign nations. The power is precisely the same in both cases, expressed in the same sentence, and in the same words. Unless some plain and intelligible reason can be given why its construction should be more restricted in the one case than in the other, the meaning must remain the same throughout the sentence. No such reason is apparent. Hence, if the power to regulate commerce among the States means nothing more than the negative power to *disburden* commerce, it means the same thing in regard to foreign commerce. But, in that view of the case, what becomes of the numerous acts of Congress in aid and encouragement of commerce, both with foreign nations and among the States? Congress has passed statutes defining how steamboats shall be constructed and equipped, prescribing the number of officers and crew, how much freight they may carry, the space to be allotted to each passenger, the kind and quantity of food that shall be provided, the signals that shall be displayed, and, in short, an elaborate code for the regulation of vessels engaged in commerce. Light-houses, beacons, buoys, and public piers have been established under the same power.

The first Congress was largely composed of able statesmen and learned lawyers who had participated in the discussions which preceded the formation of the Constitution, and who had been members of the constitutional convention. On the 7th of April, 1789, just a month after the commencement of the Government, an act was passed and signed by George Washington entitled "An act for the establishment of lighthouses, buoys, beacons and public piers." "These provisions," says Mr. Calhoun, in the report before referred to, "furnish conclusive proof that the object of the power was the increased safety and *facility* of commerce along the coast." It may be added that at almost every session of Congress since the formation of the Government, acts have been passed for the purpose of *aiding* and *facilitating* commerce in some form. "The practice," says President Jackson, "of defraying out of the Treasury of the United States the expenses incurred by the establishment and support of light-houses, beacons, buoys, and public piers within the bays, inlets, and harbors, and ports of the United States, to render the navigation thereof safe and *easy*, is co-eval with the adoption of the Constitution and has been continued without interruption or dispute."

It will not be seriously argued that light-houses, buoys, piers, &c., are themselves commerce. They are nothing more nor less than *facilities* or *aids* to commerce. But if it be admitted that Congress may *aid* or *facilitate* commerce at all, we ask where shall the line of limitation on such power be drawn?

If we may appropriate money for *any facilities* such as those mentioned, does not the authority of Congress extend to the whole subject, and is there any limit to such power except the sound discretion of Congress under its responsibility to the people, or in the express restrictions of the Constitution?

ACTS OF CONGRESS REGULATING RAILWAYS.

The legislative and executive departments of the Government have in two instances distinctly asserted the power of Congress to regulate the conduct of railways carrying freights from one State to another.

The act of July 15, 1866, passed at the instance of the railroads themselves, authorized railroad companies chartered by the States to "carry passengers, freights," &c., "on their way from any State to another State, and to receive compensation therefor, and to connect with roads of other States so as to form continuous lines for transportation of the same to the place of destination."

Again, by an act which went into effect October 1, 1873, Congress declared that "no railway within the United States whose road forms any part of a line or road over which cattle, sheep, swine, or other animals shall be conveyed from one State to another, or the owners or masters of steam, sailing, or other vessels carrying or transporting cattle, sheep, swine, or other animals from one State to another, shall confine the same in *cars*, boats, or vessels of any description for a longer period than twenty-eight consecutive hours, without unloading the same for water, rest, and feeding for a period of at least five consecutive hours, unless prevented from so unloading by storm or accidental causes;" and provided a penalty of from $100 to $500 for non-compliance with the provisions of the act, which penalty may be recovered by a civil action in the name of the United States, in the circuit or district courts of the United States, and making it the duty of the United States marshals, their deputies and subordinates, to prosecute all violations of the law which shall come to their notice.

In these two acts we find, from the legislative and executive departments, a construction of the extent of the power over inter-State commerce and transportation as decided and unequivocal as that we have quoted from the judicial department of the Government. If Congress has the power to say under what circumstances roads chartered by State governments shall connect and form continuous lines, and carry freight and passengers and receive compensation therefor; if Congress may prescribe rules fixing the times when, and how long, a train shall be stopped, under what circumstances the cars shall be unloaded, and authorize the United States courts to inflict a penalty for disobedience to such rules, it can hardly be doubted that the same power can regulate transportation in other particulars, including the tariff on freights, and the manner of conducting the business of such roads. It is true the constitutionality of these acts has never been affirmed by the Supreme Court, but that fact would seem to indicate that it has never been seriously questioned.

STATE CHARTERS DO NOT INTERFERE WITH THE EXERCISE OF THIS POWER.

It is said that Congress may not regulate the acts of companies created by State authority, because their charters are in the nature of contracts, which, under the Constitution, are inviolable. Whatever may be the power of the States in this regard, it is not now our province to discuss, but it is very clear that no constitutional inhibition restricts the power of Congress—

1st. Because "the prohibition against the passage of laws in violation of the obligation of contracts does not apply to Congress." (Evans *vs* Eaton, Pet. C. C., 322.) The words of the Constitution are: "No *State* shall pass any law impairing the obligation of a contract."

2d. Because the arrangements between the companies, by which their lines extend through different States, are their own voluntary acts, with which the States have nothing to do.

3d. Because the States must have granted, and the companies accepted, their charters with the full knowledge and understanding that when connections should be formed at State boundaries, making continuous lines through more than one State, and thereby becoming the channels over which inter-State commerce should flow, they would pass under the paramount power of the General Government. In other words, all such grants were made and taken subject to such future commercial regulations as Congress might lawfully prescribe.

Is it not, therefore, fair to assume that whatever is contained in such charters that is in the nature of a contract, was made and accepted subject to the controlling power of the United States, whenever Congress should see fit to exercise it? Hence the exercise of the regulating power of Congress cannot be, in any sense, a violation of the chartered rights of such companies as have by their own voluntary arrangements and connections brought themselves within the sphere of its operation.

If, as will be readily admitted, a State cannot levy a tax or impost on the commerce of another State passing through her jurisdiction, which shall be beyond the control of Congress, surely she cannot, by an act of incorporation, authorize one of her creatures to do so. She may not do by indirection what she cannot do directly. To hold otherwise would be to clothe the States with power to nullify this provision of the Constitution, and to remand the Union back to all the difficulties, embarrassments, and dangers of the Confederation.

To illustrate this proposition, for five months in the year there is practically no means of transportation for a large section of the country but by railroads. Illinois and Kentucky extend from the lakes on the north around to the Alleghany Mountains at the east, thus rendering it impossible for the products of those States lying west and south of them to reach a market without passing through their limits.

Now, suppose those two States have granted to all the railroad companies within their jurisdiction the right to construct railroads and to charge such rates as they please for transportation, and that those roads have become parts of the great through lines of transportation between the States to the west of them and the Atlantic sea-board. Suppose, further, that in a season of short crops at the East and in Europe, the managers of those roads combine, purchase a large quantity of breadstuffs, ship them to the East, and, having them safely stored in New York and other eastern cities, put up the tariff for transportation so high as to prevent the products of other States from going forward. Can any one doubt that, in such a case, it would be, not only the right, but the sacred duty of Congress to interfere, by prescribing needful rules and regulations for the conduct of this traffic through those States? If the power does not reside in Congress it is nowhere. The aggrieved States could do nothing, and the people of one-half the Union might starve, while the other half, with overflowing granaries, would be denied the privilege of feeding them. It is true, this is a strong case, but its circumstances would change no principle of the Constitution; its hardships and aggravations would create no new powers. If the power be in the Constitution it exists at all times. If it exist for the purpose of relieving the people of the States in the aggravated case supposed, it exists for all purposes connected with inter-State commerce. The circumstances do not call it into life, though they may demonstrate the necessity for its existence and the policy of its exercise.

Again, if a State can by an act of incorporation enter into a contract with a railroad company which will defeat the exercise of the national power to regulate commerce, it is in the power of the State of New York, extending as she does from Canada to the ocean, to authorize her railways to impose such charges as will virtually place an embargo upon the trade between New England and the West. That she probably will not do so is no answer to the argument. States have been known to be unfriendly to their sister States, and some of them would have gladly excluded New England if they could. The question is not, what will the

State of New York *permit* in this regard, but what are the commercial *rights* of the States, and by what power are those rights guaranteed? Were the illustrious men who framed our Constitution so incompetent to their high duty as to have created an instrument which leaves it in the power of any one State to cripple and destroy the commerce of another? Is it conceivable that such a blunder could have been committed in view of the fact that "the *design* and *object* of *that power* (the power to regulate commerce) as evinced in the history of the constitution *was to establish a perfect equality among the several States as to commercial rights, and to prevent unjust and invidious distinctions, which local jealousies or local and partial interests might be disposed to introduce and maintain?*" (14, Howard's Rep., p. 574.) But if the power to prevent unjust and invidious distinctions exist, how is it to be exercised if any one State may create corporations with unlimited powers to levy tribute at pleasure and without control upon the commerce of other States?

THE GRANT OF AUXILIARY POWERS CONFERS UPON CONGRESS A CHOICE OF MEANS, AND DOES NOT CONFINE IT TO SUCH MEANS AS ARE INDISPENSABLY NECESSARY.

The words of the grant are: "Congress shall have power to make all laws which shall be necessary and proper for carrying into execution the foregoing, and all other powers vested by this Constitution in the Government of the United States."

When the tenth amendment to the Constitution was under consideration, it was proposed to amend it by inserting the word "expressly" before "delegated," so as to reserve to the States and to the people all "powers not *expressly* delegated," but it was perceived that this would strip the General Government of some of its most essential powers, and the amendment was rejected. Hence, unless a particular means be expressly prohibited, it is involved in the sphere of the specified powers.

The Constitution does not indicate the particular means by which its enumerated powers may be executed. This was unnecessary, if not impossible. Instead of prescribing the particular *means* to be employed in each case, the grant of powers in the eighth section of the first article concludes with the sweeping grant of the auxiliary "power to make all laws which shall be *necessary* and *proper* for carrying into execution the foregoing powers."

It has been doubted, however, whether this clause conferred any additional power on Congress, for the reason that it is difficult to conceive of a grant of power to do a thing which does not include a grant or the necessary and proper means of doing it. But in order to guard against a too strict construction, which might dwarf and cripple the General Government, the authors of the Constitution expressly authorized the use of all needful and proper means for carrying into beneficial execution its delegated powers.

In the case of McCullough *vs.* Maryland, (4 Wheaton, 316,) it was gravely insisted by the counsel that this clause should be construed as a limitation on the preceding enumerated powers, and that "it was inserted for the purpose of conferring on Congress the power of *making laws.*" Marshall, C. J., ridiculed the idea that it could be necessary to say that a legislature should exercise legislative powers in the shape of legislation; that, "after allowing each house to prescribe its own course of proceeding, after describing the manner in which a bill should become a law," it could "have entered the mind of a single member of the convention that an express power to make laws was necessary to enable the legislature to make them. That a legislature, endowed with legislative powers, can legislate, is (says the learned judge) a proposition too self-evident to have been questioned." (4 Wheaton, 412.)

The word "necessary" in this clause means "needful," "appropriate," "adapted to the end." It was also claimed in the case last cited that this clause is restrictive, because by limiting the action of Congress to such laws as are "*necessary* and *proper*" it excluded a *choice of means*, and confined Congress to those means only which were indispensable, and without which the power would be nugatory; that the word "necessary" should be construed as "*absolutely* necessary," *indispensable.* The court (Chief Justice Marshall delivering the opinion) held that no such restriction was intended; that "the word *necessary* admits of all degrees of comparison, and is often connected with other words which increase or diminish the impression the mind receives from the urgency it imparts. A thing may be necessary, very necessary, absolutely or indispensably necessary," and "to no mind would the same idea be conveyed by the several phrases." To illustrate this comment, the learned Chief Justice compared the clause which declares that "no State shall, without consent of Congress, lay any impost or duties on imports or exports except what may be *absolutely* necessary for executing its inspection laws," with that which authorizes Congress "to make all laws which shall be necessary and proper," and insisted that "the convention understood itself to change materially the meaning of the word "necessary" by prefixing the word "absolutely." "It must have been the intention (continues the court) of those who gave these powers to insure, as far as human prudence could insure, their beneficial execution. This could not be done by confining the choice of means to such narrow limits as not to leave it in the power of Congress to adopt any which might be *appropriate* and *conducive* to the end. This provision is made in a Constitution intended to endure for ages to come, and consequently to be adapted to the various crises of human affairs To have prescribed the *means* by which Government should, in all future time, execute its powers, would have been to change entirely the character of the instrument, and give it the properties of a legal code." * * * "To have declared that the *best* means shall not be used, but those alone without which the power would be nugatory, would have been to deprive the legislature of the capacity to avail itself of experience, to exercise its reason, and to accommodate its legislation to circumstances. If we apply this construction to any of the powers of the Government, we shall find it so pernicious in its operation that we shall be compelled to discard it."

Further illustrating the argument by reference to the *implied power of punishment*, the court adds, "it is a means of carrying into execution all sovereign powers, and *may be used although not indispensably necessary.* It is a *right incidental to the power*, and conducive to its beneficial exercise. If this limited construction of the word "necessary" is to be abandoned *in order to punish*, whence is derived the rule that would re-instate it when the Government would carry its powers into execution by means not vindictive in their nature? If the word "necessary" means "needful," "requisite," "essential," "conducive to," in order to let in the *power of punishment* for the infraction of law, why is it not equally comprehensive when required to authorize the use of means which facilitate the execution of the powers of Government without the infliction of punishment?" After a thorough and exhaustive discussion of this subject, the court concludes: "The result of the most careful and attentive consideration bestowed upon this clause is, that if it does not enlarge, it cannot be construed to restrain, the powers of Congress, or to impair the right of the legislature *to exercise its best judgment in the selection of measures* to carry into execution the constitutional powers of the Government." * * * "*Let the end be legitimate, let it be within the scope of the Constitution, and all the means which are appropriate, which are plainly adapted to that end, which are not prohibited, but consist with the letter and spirit of the Constitution, are constitutional.*" (4 Wheaton, 414, 18, 21.)

In United States *vs.* Fisher, 2 Cranch, 358, the court decides that "the power to make all laws necessary and proper for carrying into execution the powers granted, confers on Congress a *choice* of *means*, and *does not confine it to what is indispensably necessary.*"

In the case of Dickey *vs.* The Maysville Turnpike Company, (7 Dana, Ky. Rep., 113,) this point was most fully and ably discussed by Kentucky's eminent jurist—Chief Justice Robertson—who says: "All admit that there are *implied* powers to adapt *any means* that are necessary and proper for effecting the end of any express power." * * "But if power to adopt a particular means for attaining the end of some express power should not be implied, unless that means be indispensable—that is, unless the express power cannot be otherwise executed, then it is demonstrable that there can be no implied power; for it is evident that suitable or effectual means for executing every express grant or power are various and of almost infinite modification, and therefore no single means can be deemed indispensable, because the power may be exercised by some other means. But, although no one means alone can be deemed indispensable, yet as no end can be accomplished without some means, *all the means which are adapted to an* *end, and will effectuate it, are necessary, and each is equally and in the same sense necessary;* and, therefore, if any one of them be constitutional, any other of them must be equally so, unless it be prohibited by the Constitution, or be subversive of some fundamental principle, and therefore would not be proper as well as necessary. And of course in choosing between proper means, thus equally necessary in the political sense, the question is one of expediency only, and not of power."

THE DEGREE OF NECESSITY FOR THE EMPLOYMENT OF ANY PARTICULAR MEANS WILL NOT BE INQUIRED INTO BY THE COURTS, BUT MUST BE LEFT TO THE DISCRETION OF CONGRESS.

On this point the Supreme Court, in McCulloch *vs.* Maryland, (4 Wheaton, 423,) held that, "where the law is not prohibitive, and is really calculated to effect any of the objects intrusted to the Government, to undertake here to inquire into the *degree* of its *necessity* would be to pass the line which circumscribes the judicial department, and to tread on legislative ground. This court disclaims all pretensions to such power."

From these decisions we think the following conclusions may fairly be drawn:

1st. That in the exercise of the power to regulate commerce, Congress is not restricted to the use of such *means* as are *indispensable* or *absolutely* necessary; but that *all means* are authorized which are *appropriate*, and *plainly adapted* to facilitate the execution of that power, and which are not prohibited in the Constitution or in violation of some fundamental principle.

2d. That a *choice* of *means* is confided to the wisdom and discretion of Congress; and the courts will not inquire into the *degree* of necessity that will justify a resort to any particular means.

Guided by the light of these expositions of the language and principles of the Constitution, we are now prepared to inquire—

First. May Congress, in the execution of its power to regulate commerce among the States, if in its discretion the means be appropriate and most conducive to the end, appropriate money to construct a railroad or canal?

Second. May it incorporate a company with authority to construct them?

Third. May it, in exercise of the right of eminent domain, authorize to be taken for the public use, paying just compensation therefor, private property within a State for the right of way for such railroad or canal?

Fourth. May it, upon paying just compensation therefor, authorize to be taken for the public use any existing railroad or canal owned by private persons or corporations?

We think the answer to these questions will depend upon another: Is the appropriation of money, or the incorporation of a company, or the exercise of the right of eminent domain, for the purposes indicated, prohibited by the Constitution, or in violation of any of its fundamental principles? If either be so prohibited, or in conflict with the principles of our Government, of course it is not a "proper" means; but if not, it is proper, and may be employed under the auxiliary powers of Congress.

THE POWER TO APPROPRIATE MONEY FOR INTERNAL IMPROVEMENTS.

The power to appropriate money for purposes of internal improvement has been so often affirmed by every Department of the Government, and exercised without question in so great a variety of ways, that it is no longer a debatable question.

POWER TO INCORPORATE A COMPANY FOR THE PURPOSE OF CONSTRUCTING A RAILWAY OR CANAL.

The power of Congress to incorporate a company with authority to construct a railroad or canal, is, in the judgment of your committee, equally clear, though it is possible there may be those who entertain a different opinion. There is no provision in the Constitution which expressly authorizes an act of incorporation, as an *end*, but the statutes of the United States abound with acts of incorporation as the *means* of carrying its express powers into execution. One of the earliest cases of the exercise of this power was the incorporation of a bank by the first Congress, in 1791. Numerous acts of succeeding Congresses assumed this power, and, in 1816, Congress again incorporated the Bank of the United States. Thereupon the State of Maryland, through the act of her legislature, raised the question of its constitutionality. The best legal talent of the country was employed on both sides, and the question was ably and elaborately argued before the Supreme Court of the United States. It was insisted by counsel for the State of Maryland that, as the power to establish corporations is not delegated to the United States, nor prohibited to the individual States, it is, therefore, reserved to the States or to the people; that the power of laying and collecting taxes implied the power of regulating the *mode* of assessment and collection, and of appointing revenue officers, but that it did not imply the power of establishing a great banking corporation, branching out into every part of the country, and inundating it with a flood of paper money. The court held that, though the *express* power to create a corporation was not found in the Constitution, yet, "no sufficient reason is perceived why it may not pass as incidental to those powers which are expressly given, if it be a direct mode of executing them." "The Government, which has the right to do an act, and has imposed on it the duty of performing that act, must, according to the dictates of reason, *be allowed to select the means*; and those who contend that it may not select any appropriate means—that one particular mode of effecting the object is excepted—take upon themselves the burden of establishing that exception." (McCulloch *vs.* Maryland, 4 Wheaton, 410.)

The counsel for the State of Maryland also argued that, as State banks were then in existence, the Government could conduct its financial operations through their agency, and hence the establishment of a United States bank could not be *necessary*; therefore it was not constitutional. Just as it is now claimed that, because the States have chartered railroads, which can conduct the commerce of the country, it is unnecessary, and hence unconstitutional, for the Government to exercise this power in aid or regulation of commerce. To this position the Supreme Court replied: "It can scarcely be necessary to say that the existence of State banks can have no possible influence on the question. *No trace can be found in the Constitution of an intention to create a dependence of the Government of the Union on those of the States for the execution of the great powers assigned to it.* Its means are adequate to its ends; and on those means alone was it expected to rely for the accomplishment of its ends. To impose on it the necessity of resorting to means which it cannot control, which another government may furnish or withhold, would render its course precarious, the result of its measures uncertain, and create a dependence on other governments which would disappoint its most important designs, and is incompatible with the language of the Constitution. But, were it otherwise, the *choice* of *means* implies a right to choose a national bank in preference to State banks, and Congress alone can make the election." (Ibid., 144.) So we claim that the *choice* of *means* for the execution of the power to regulate commerce implies the right to choose national means in preference to those which may or may not be furnished by the States.

In illustration of this position, take again, if you please, the case of a State, lying in the pathway of commerce between the West and the East, which may have granted to a single corporation the exclusive right to construct a railroad across a territory which may be totally inadequate to perform the service required; and that such corporation exerts an influence over the legislature which enables it to prevent the construction of any additional means of transportation, thereby practically excluding the products of one State from the markets of another, or of the world; or suppose the four great trunk-lines leading from the West to the Atlantic seaboard (which are chartered by State authority) should combine to exact tariffs so exorbitant as to practically produce the same result, (a supposition by no means unreasonable;) would it be insisted, under such circumstances, that, without the consent of the State, Congress is impotent to aid the commerce of the country or to relieve the people from the intolerable burdens and exactions of chartered monopolies? If so, the Union is dependent on the States for the means of executing its powers; and a single State may exert a power over the internal commerce of the country which cannot be exercised by all the people of all the other States, through their chosen and delegated agent, the General Government. Nay, more, the industry and commerce of a dozen States would be completely at the mercy and under the control of an irresponsible creature of a single State. Such a doctrine, by exposing the commerce among the States to the whims, the caprice, and the selfishness of any individual State or to the cupidity of one of her creatures, would strip the Constitution of one of its most vital powers—the very one, in fact, which led to its formation.

Take another case. Suppose the State of Indiana had always persistently refused to grant the right of way for, or authorize the construction of, railroads across her territory, thereby excluding the great States lying west of her from a fair participation in the internal or foreign commerce of the country, and causing a delay of many days in the transmission of the mails between the seat of Government and the people of the Northwestern States. Would it be argued, in such a case, that neither the "power to regulate commerce among the States" nor the "power to establish post-roads" could be invoked to open channels of communication through her borders? We think not. And yet if the power exists for such an exigency, it exists at all times, and the question as to its exercise is one of expediency only, and not of constitutional right. To hold that the power would exist if the State of Indiana had so refused to act, but that it does not exist because she has authorized the construction of railroads, would be to say that a single State may enlarge or diminish the powers of the Government, and thereby change the Constitution.

NATIONAL RIGHT OF EMINENT DOMAIN WITHIN A STATE.

It must be admitted, however, that Congress cannot construct nor authorize the construction of such roads and canals, unless it can exercise the right of eminent domain. It remains, therefore, to consider the question: May the General Government, in the execution of its power over commerce, or in the execution of any other power, authorize the taking of private property for public use, within the limits of a State?

We believe it may. It is true the Constitution does not in express words grant this right to Congress, though it does, as we shall hereafter see, expressly recognize it. Without such recognition, we think its existence clearly demonstrable, on the ground that *it is an inherent and essential element of sovereignty*, without which some of the acknowledged vital powers of government could not be exercised. President Monroe (a strict constructionist) said, "The great office of the Constitution, by incorporating the people of the several States into one community, and enabling it to act directly on the people, was to annul the powers of the State governments to that extent, except in cases where they are concurrent, and to preclude their agency in giving effect to those of the General Government."

In Gibbons *vs.* Ogden, (9 Wheaton, 197,) the court says: "If, as has always been understood, the sovereignty of Congress, though limited to specified objects, is plenary as to those objects, the *power over commerce* with foreign nations, and among the several States, *is vested in Congress as absolutely as it would be in a single government* having in its constitution the same restrictions as to the exercise of power as are contained in the Constitution of the United States."

We have seen that the delegated powers of the United States are independent powers, coming directly from the people, acting directly upon the people, directly responsible to the people, in no sense dependent upon the States for their means of execution; that for all the purposes and objects for which they were granted they are *absolute* and *supreme;* that they are *complete in themselves, may be exercised to their utmost extent, and acknowledge no limitation* other than are prescribed in the Constitution, and that the rights of the Government as sovereign, and its prerogatives as such, are co-extensive with the functions of government committed to it.

If these premises be correct, we hold that the following decisions apply with as full force to the sovereign powers of the Union as to the powers of a single State:

"*The right of eminent domain is a part of the sovereign power.*" (4 Cr. C. C., 75.)

"The right to take private property for public purposes is an *incident to all governments.*" (Baldwin, 205.)

"The right of eminent domain *is an inherent and essential element of sovereignty.* It results from the social compact, and hence would exist without any express provisions of the organic law upon the subject." (4 Miss., 349.)

"The right to take private property, for public purposes, does not depend on any express provisions of the charter of Government, *but it is an inherent attribute of sovereignty existing in every independent State.*" (Haywood *vs.* New York, 3 Seldon, 324.)

To deny the application of these principles to the sovereign powers of the Union, is to deny that the United States constitute an independent Government. It will not do to say that because the General Government is not sovereign and supreme for *all* purposes, therefore rights which are essential attributes of State sovereignty do not pertain to the acknowledged powers of the Union. This argument would apply with equal force to the States, for they too are limited in their powers, both by their own constitutions and by the Constitution of the United States.

That the sovereignty of Congress, within the scope of its delegated powers, is the *same in kind,* and *possessed of all the elements* and *attributes* of sovereign State powers, is clearly asserted by Mr. Justice Johnson, in 9 Wheaton, 227: "The power to regulate commerce, here meant to be granted," says the learned judge, "*was that power to regulate commerce which previously existed in the States.* But what was that power? The States were unquestionably supreme; and each possessed that power over commerce which is acknowledged to reside in every sovereign

State." Therefore, as we have already seen, whatever elements and attributes of sovereignty appertained to this power when it existed in the States, have been transferred with it, to the Federal Government.*

The right of eminent domain is clearly implied as incidental to the enumerated powers, because it is a necessary and proper means of executing them, as, for instance, the "power to establish post-offices and post-roads," and the power "to regulate commerce." It was impossible, as already stated, for the authors of the Constitution to specify for the long future, all the means that might become necessary to the full and beneficial exercise of the power delegated, both on account of the endless detail it would have involved, and the infinite variety of circumstances which could not be foreseen. Hence the necessity for the incidental or auxiliary powers which are so liberally provided. The statutes of the United States abound with acts based upon powers derived wholly from implication.

Congress is empowered "to establish post-offices and post-roads," from which comes the implied power to carry the mails from one office to another, and from this again the implied authority to *punish* mail-robbers. Under the power "to collect duties and imposts" Congress has the implied right to *punish smuggling*. The power to "coin money and regulate the value thereof," and "to provide for the punishment of *counterfeiting* the *securities* and *current coin* of the United States," implies the power to make laws punishing the offense of *altering* and *passing* the coin or securities thus counterfeited.

The power "to dispose of and make all needful rules and regulations respecting the territory and other property of the United States," involves the unquestioned power to incorporate a territorial government. The power "to regulate commerce" has always been held to involve the auxiliary power to erect wharves, buoys, beacons, and light-houses in aid and encouragement of commerce. The power to "lay and collect taxes," &c., includes the incidental power to incorporate a national bank, with branches and authority to issue paper money.

If, therefore, all the acknowledged incidental powers to which we have just referred are constitutional, upon what principle shall the rule of construction be so changed as to exclude the right to take private property for public use whenever the exercise of such right is conducive and appropriate to the execution of an express power? In the instances just cited, the power of *punishment* is not among the enumerated powers of Congress, and yet all admit that it is incidental to them. "The good sense of the public has pronounced, without hesitation, that the *power of punishment* appertains to sovereignty, and may be exercised whenever the sovereign has a right to act, *as incidental to his sovereign power.*" (Chief Justice Marshall in McCulloch *vs.* Maryland.)

Can an American citizen be immured in prison under an incidental

* The same doctrine was maintained, as we have seen, by Mr. Calhoun in 1846, in his report upon the memorial of the Memphis convention. (Senate Doc., 1st session 29th Congress, vol. 8, p. 410.)

power of Congress, while his property cannot be taken for a public use, though just compensation be paid therefor? Will it be claimed that Congress may enter the limits of a State, and, by virtue of its incidental powers, fine one of her citizens, and even imprison him for life, and yet that his property cannot be taken when demanded by the exigencies of the public service? Is personal liberty less sacred than private property? If to take private property for a public use, paying just compensation therefor, be to encroach upon the rights of the States, is it not a much greater encroachment to take the liberty of one of her citizens? True, the punishment is inflicted because of his willful violations of law, but the crimes of a citizen cannot add a new power, and thereby change the Constitution.

But we have said that the Constitution expressly recognizes the existence of the right of eminent domain. The fifth article of the amendments declares that "private property shall not *be taken for public use without just compensation.*"

In Barron *vs.* Baltimore, (7 Peters, 250,) the Supreme Court, adverting to this clause of the Constitution, says: "The powers they [the people] conferred on this Government are to be exercised by itself; and the limitations on its power, if expressed in general terms, are naturally, and, we think, necessarily, applicable to the government created by the instrument. They are limitations of power granted by the instrument itself."

And, again, in Withers *vs.* Buckley, (20 Howard, 89,) the court held that the first ten amendments to the Constitution "were designed to be modifications of the powers vested in the Federal Government, and their language is susceptible of no other rational, literal, or verbal acceptation." *It is therefore clear that this clause limits a power existing in the Constitution, for if no such power exists there, why prescribe the conditions of its exercise?*

But it is argued that inasmuch as Congress is expressly empowered to exercise exclusive jurisdiction over the ten-miles square, which should become the seat of government, this condition may properly apply to that District, and hence that the clause recognizes no existing right to take private property elsewhere. It undoubtedly does apply to the District of Columbia; but we submit, it can hardly be seriously contended that it is to be confined within such narrow limits. After the adoption of the Constitution it was feared by many that the *rights of the States* might be invaded by the General Government, and hence the first ten amendments were adopted as a sort of bill of rights for the protection of the people of the States. In the case from 20 Howard, 89, just cited, the court, in commenting on the clause in question, said: "To every person acquainted with the history of the Federal Government, it is familiarly known that the ten amendments first ingrafted upon the Constitution had their origin in the apprehension that in the investment of powers made by that instrument in the Federal Government *the safety of the States and their citizens had not been sufficiently guarded.*"

"That in order to remove the cause of this apprehension, and *to effect that security* which it was feared the original instrument had failed to accomplish, twelve articles of amendment were proposed at the first session of the first Congress, and the first ten articles in the existing series of amendments were adopted and ratified by Congress and by the States, two of the amendments having been rejected."

And, again, in the case from 7 Peters, 250, the court, referring to the causes which led to the adoption of the amendments to the Constitution, remarks: "In almost every convention in which the Constitution was adopted, amendments to guard against abuse of power were recommended. These amendments demanded security against the encroachments of the General Government; not against those of the local governments."

The conclusions clearly expressed in both of these opinions are, that the first ten amendments were intended to restrict the powers of the Federal Government in order to make the *States* more secure against its possible encroachments, and that the provision requiring just compensation to be paid was designed to be a limitation upon an existing national power which could be exercised within a State. The forced construction that would confine the operation of this clause to the District of Columbia would restrict within the same narrow limits the operation of seven of the ten amendments. It can hardly be conceived that the people of the States had suddenly become so extremely solicitous about the rights of this District as such a construction would indicate. It is therefore very apparent, from the discussions of the times, as well as from the amendments themselves and the construction given them by the Supreme Court, that they were intended as restrictions on the exercise of the powers of the General Government within the States, and that in the execution of the enumerated powers of Congress *it was understood that the right of eminent domain could be exercised within the limits of a State;* and hence the amendment proposed only to regulate this "attribute of sovereignty" by requiring that when so exerted it should always be upon the condition of paying just compensation.

But it is said that the Constitution grants specifically the exclusive right of *legislation* * * * "over all places *purchased* by *consent* of *the legislature* of the State in which the same shall be, for the erection of forts, magazines, arsenals, dock-yards, and other needful buildings," and, therefore, as one specific mode of acquiring rights in the soil within a State for a public use is named, for certain purposes, all other modes, and all other purposes, are necessarily excluded, and hence the exercise of the right of eminent domain is inadmissible. Stated in other words, the argument is, Congress may *purchase*, by *consent* of the *legislature*, certain places for forts, magazines, arsenals, dock-yards, and other needful buildings, but such "places" can be acquired in no other way; and therefore if it should become necessary to erect a fort for the protection of the nation against a foreign enemy, Congress is utterly impotent to make such provision for the common defense, no matter how great the peril, nor how urgent the necessity, so long as the *consent* of the legislature to the *purchase* is withheld, or the citizen refuses to sell. And, of course, if it happen that the State is in sympathy with the enemy, or the citizen owning the land be unfriendly, the Government must remain defenseless. If a light-house be imperatively demanded for the security of the lives and property of American citizens engaged in commerce, the Government would, under this construction, be entirely dependent upon the State for the means of exercising one of its unquestioned powers. So, too, if a State should be unfriendly, the Government would be powerless to establish a post-office within her limits though expressly empowered by the Constitution to do so.

We submit, therefore, that a construction of the Constitution which thus robs the Government of its independence, strips it of its vital powers, and renders it impotent to provide even for its own defense, can hardly be the true one.

But the argument that because one specific mode of acquiring rights in the soil is mentioned, therefore all other modes are excluded, may be further tested by some of the *acknowledged incidental* powers of Congress. And we will again take the one which affects the dearest and most sacred right of the citizen, the power of punishment.

If the argument be sound when applied to the national right of eminent domain within a State, it is surely so, and for a much stronger reason, when applied to a power that may deprive a citizen of his liberty. In three cases *specifically mentioned* Congress is empowered to punish, namely: "To provide for the punishment of counterfeiting the securities and current coin of the United States," and "to define and punish piracies and felonies committed on the high seas and offenses against the law of nations;" also, "to declare the punishment of treason." These three provisions comprise, we believe, all the cases in which the Constitution expressly confers on Congress the power to inflict penalties for an infraction of its laws.

Might it not be argued with far greater plausibility that because the power of punishment is specifically mentioned in these cases, that therefore it is excluded from all others? And yet we know it is not so excluded. The power of the Government to punish any infraction of its laws is unquestioned. Mail-robbery and smuggling are not in the remotest degree related to any of the specified powers of punishment, but no one doubts the constitutionality of the laws which provide penalties for these offenses.

The weakness of the argument, based upon the clause in question, will be apparent by a reference to its real object, which was not to grant any new powers for the erection of buildings or for obtaining rights in the soil of a State, but simply to confer on Congress *exclusive legislative jurisdiction* over such places as should be purchased *with consent of the State.* This view is fully sustained by the Supreme Court of the United

States in 3 Wheaton, 388, where it was held that Congress may purchase land for a fort or light-house *without the consent* of the State, but where such consent has not been obtained the *jurisdiction* remains in the State. It will be perceived that this clause does not attempt to prescribe the manner in which rights may be acquired under Federal authority to any part of the soil in a State, but rather that it affords a fair inference that the framers of the Constitution understood that such power already existed, and that the sole object of the clause under consideration was to provide that, when such rights should be acquired by *cession*, the *exclusive legislative jurisdiction* over the place ceded should pass to the Federal Government.

The Government of the United States has, on more than one occasion, distinctly asserted the right of eminent domain within a State. In 1864 an act was passed entitled "An act in addition to an act for the establishment of certain arsenals," the preamble to which reads: "Whereas it is necessary that the Government of the United States should, at an early day, for the purposes of the arsenal at Rock Island, *in the State of Illinois, obtain* the *possession of* and *title to certain lands*, now the *property* of *private persons*, upon which to locate the said arsenal, with the grounds and buildings needful for, and to make a part of same." It was enacted that the Secretary of War should be empowered to *take and hold full, complete, and permanent possession of all the land* and shores of the island of Rock Island, in the *State of Illinois*, for the purposes aforesaid; and in case the Secretary should be unable to agree with the owners of the land thus taken upon the price to be paid, it was further provided that a *commission*, consisting of three persons, *should be appointed by the President of the United States*, with power to decide "what compensation for the taking of the land is due to the claimants." From the decision of said commission an appeal was allowed to the courts. This act, from beginning to end, is a direct and unequivocal assertion of the right of eminent domain, by the United States, within the State of Illinois.

The act of Congress authorizing the construction of the national road involved the exercise of the national right of eminent domain. The land upon which the road was located was not taken under a State law; it is true the States assented that it should be taken under a law of the United States, but such assent could confer no power on Congress which it did not possess without it. If the Constitution gave Congress power to pass the act, it did not need the assent of the States. If the Constitution did not grant such power to Congress the States could not supplement it. No new powers can be delegated, except in the manner and by the number of States prescribed in the Constitution.

The right of eminent domain is conceded to be in the States, but this, like every other right, is subject to whatever qualifications may be necessary to the exercise of the powers granted by the Constitution of the United States. If it be necessary, in the exercise of the national power to regulate commerce, or to "establish post-offices and roads," that a railroad should be constructed through a State, the auxiliary power also exists to employ the necessary and proper means for its construction. It is difficult to distinguish between the exercise of such a power and the conceded one to improve the navigation of rivers running through two or more States. In both cases it is for the purpose of *facilitating* commerce, or of *creating* it if none existed before, and in both cases a portion of the soil of the State must be appropriated.

It seems unnecessary to discuss the question whether the right to take the property of a private corporation for public use does not exist to the same extent as to take the property of an individual. It will hardly be insisted that the rights of a corporation are any higher or more sacred than the rights of a natural person. If a railway company may lawfully enter upon the homestead of the citizen, or the burial-place of the dead, and appropriate them for public use, there would seem to be no good reason why the railway itself may not be taken for the same purpose and upon the same condition.

The direct question as to the power of Congress to regulate rates and fares on railroads, and to construct railways or canals through States, has never been decided by the Supreme Court; but we submit that the enunciation of principles, and the construction of the Constitution to which we have referred, leave no room to doubt how those questions will be decided when brought before that court.

Mr. Justice Miller, of the Supreme Court, after a full discussion of the power of Congress to regulate commerce, thus expresses his conclusions: "*For myself I must say that I have no doubt of the right of Congress to prescribe all needful and proper regulations for the conduct of this immense traffic over any railroad which has voluntarily become a part of one of those lines of inter-State communication, or to authorize the creation of such roads* when the purposes of inter-State transportation of persons and property justify and require it." (American Law Reporter for January, 1868.)

The committee proceed next to consider the expediency and practi-ability of the various remedies proposed, as follows:

First. Competition between railways, and its promotion by additional lines without regulation.

Second. Direct congressional regulation of railway transportation, under the power to regulate commerce among the several States.

Third. Indirect regulation, and promotion of competition, through the agency of one or more lines of railway, to be owned or controlled by the Government.

Fourth. The improvement of natural water-ways, and the construction of artificial channels of water-communication.

1.—COMPETITION BETWEEN RAILWAYS, AND ITS PROMOTION BY THE CONSTRUCTION OF ADDITIONAL LINES.

The nature and value of railway competition may be best understood by a brief reference to its history in other countries as well as in the United States.

COMPETITION IN OTHER COUNTRIES.

France.

In France the system of independent corporate management was tried and proved unsuccessful. The independent companies failed, and the progress of railway development was slow and unsatisfactory.

It was found necessary, as early as 1842, to change the policy to one of government guarantees and surveillance, which, being better adapted to the French people, restored confidence, and largely stimulated railway construction. Under this policy the Government undertook to construct the earthwork, masonry, and stations, and to pay one-third the cost of the land. The other two-thirds was to be paid for by the departments. The companies were to bear the expense of the iron, rolling-stock, maintenance, &c., it being the intention that two-fifths of the total cost should be borne by the companies, and the other three-fifths by the State and the departments. This system of copartnership existed from 1842 to 1859.

In the latter year the Emperor, dissatisfied with the slow progress and feeble management of the railways of the empire, took them in hand, and adapting his policy to the genius of the French people, launched out upon a bold system of railway development. Capital, rendered cautious by experience, shrank from shares without a guarantee, and he guaranteed $4\frac{65}{100}$ per cent. on the new lines. The French people preferred debentures to shares, and an enormous issue of debentures was authorized. The companies complained that their concessions were too short, and he extended them to ninety-nine years. At the same time a rigid system of regulation and audit was instituted for the protection of the interests of the state. Discarding all idea of competition, and believing that small companies were inexpedient, he consolidated them into six great companies, and assigned to each a distinct territory.

This financial partnership between the state and the companies made it the interest of the former to sustain those lines on which she was guarantor, and hence competition was discouraged by the government. The fact that the whole empire has been subdivided into six great districts, and handed over to the exclusive control of the company to which each is respectively assigned, renders competition impossible Certain modifications were introduced by the law of 1865, which may give rise to slight competition in certain localities. By that act, which is said to have been a concession to the principles of self-government, the departments and communes within their jurisdiction were authorized to undertake the construction of railways themselves, or to sanction their construction by private individuals, subject to the approval of the government. The object of this law was to facilitate the construction of feeders and branches to the main lines, but under it an effort has been made, through charters procured from contiguous departments, to form continuous and competing lines. Neither the government nor the companies regard this movement with favor. The companies insist that it is in violation of the spirit of the law of 1865, by which they claim only local or branch lines were to be constructed, and the government, looking to the interests of its guaranteed lines, has not been disposed to assent to new projects which might become competitors. The result is that only about one hundred and fifty miles have been constructed under the law. It is very apparent, therefore, that competition among railways is unknown in France. The principle upon which they have been constructed, and the policy of the government on the subject, alike preclude it. Canals and rivers afford the only actual competition ever known in the country. But even this has been discouraged, and in some cases the railways have been authorized to purchase the canals for the express and avowed purpose of suppressing competition.

Prussia.

The Prussian government has freely contributed to aid the construction of railways. Almost every form of financial partnership with the companies has obtained, guarantees of interest on stock and bonds have been freely given, and subsidies have been liberally granted. In some cases the state is a stockholder in the companies, and in others the owner and operator of the roads. In 1870 the state owned nine lines, and worked three others belonging to private parties, aggregating 3,264 English miles, against twenty-four lines owned and operated by private companies and aggregating 3,595 English miles.

The original policy of the state was adverse to competition, possibly on account of an interest in the roads as just stated. Section 44 of the Prussian railway act expressly prohibited competing lines, as follows:

"No second railroad running in the same direction as the first one, and touching the same principal points, shall be allowed to be constructed by undertakers, other than the undertakers of the first railway, within a space of thirty years from the opening of such railway, provided that improvements of the communication between these points, and in the same direction by other means, shall not be interfered with hereby."

This act proved a great impediment to railway development, and from time to time arrangements were made with the companies entitled to the benefit of it, so that at present, notwithstanding the early renunciation of the principle of competition, there are several lines opened between competing points. Article 41 of the constitution of the empire repeals the act interdicting the construction of parallel or competing roads.

The policy of the government has been changed, but the natural laws which govern railway competition have not. Since the state has permitted the construction of competing lines the companies have taken the matter into their own hands, and by agreements as to rates have substantially destroyed competition. It matters but little what may be the policy of government on this subject, the policy and practices of railway corporations, being governed by self-interest, are always and everywhere the same. They are necessarily, from the very laws of their being, monopolies, and if left to the regulation of those laws will always remain so.

Belgium.

The railway policy of Belgium differs in several important particulars from that of any other country, and, as we shall hereafter see, its results in affording cheap transportation are exceptionally satisfactory. Railway development began in 1833, shortly after the Belgian revolution, when on account of the general financial prostration, private enterprise was unable to undertake railway construction, and hence the government assumed the task. Having occupied the most important and remunerative lines through the central portions of the country, the state suspended for a time the active work of construction, and permitted private companies to continue it by building branch lines and extensions. The success of railway enterprises in England and elsewhere stimulated the independent companies, and in 1850 about three hundred and forty miles were owned and operated by the state, and one hundred and ninety miles by the companies. During the succeeding ten years the mileage owned by private corporations gained rapidly on the state lines, so that in 1860 there were of the former seven hundred and twenty-six miles, and of the latter three hundred and forty-five miles. In granting these concessions the state pursued the opposite policy from that which always prevailed in France, and which obtained at the commencement of the system in Prussia. Railways seem to have been regarded from the first as the servants of the public, and the principle of competition was expressly recognized and rigidly enforced through the practical working of the state lines by the government.

The plan of districting was never adopted. The right of the government to construct branch lines connecting with those of the companies, and to authorize the construction of competing lines, was expressly reserved in the concessions. This reserved right was freely exercised by the government, and competing lines were liberally granted. With one exception the concessions were for short and separate roads. In 1860 the average length of lines, worked by twenty-one companies, was only about forty-three miles each. About that time the results of these numerous concessions became apparent. The small and detached companies consolidated their strength, formed through trunk-lines, and having thus become powerful associations, boldly challenged competition with the government itself. For a time the state, backed by the public treasury, worked its roads at a heavy loss. The money with which the state roads were built was borrowed, under an arrangement for its gradual redemption by periodical payments from their net revenue, and until they became profitable the funds necessary for the redemption of the debt were advanced by the treasury. And for the years in which the expenditures exceeded the receipts, the amount was added to the losses, and carried forward as a charge against the railways.

It will be seen that in Belgium, as elsewhere, the increase of private lines, which for the time stimulated competition, in the end led to combination among themselves for self-protection. The subsequent history of railways in that country furnishes a most remarkable illustration of the fact that competition between railways ends in combination. After the consolidation of the small companies, competition between themselves and the government became very sharp. The state acted as the richest and most powerful company, against private companies who were not much its inferiors in power, and who were dealing on equal terms with it.

"One effect of this," says Mr. W. R. Malcolm in a paper submitted to the parliamentary committee, "was that when the government was pressed by the competition of its rivals, its first resource was to seek for traffic as they did. It began to work upon *commercial principles.* It made *special contracts* and *special tariffs* in order to get business on its lines, and it ran a severe competition between the most profitable sources of traffic; *the result of which was in some cases at least an agreement with its adversary and a joint-purse arrangement.**

It is stated in the same able paper that this period is now passed, and the question of competition, both in the matter of tariffs and of routes, has been pretty well settled. Rates are now mutually agreed upon between the companies themselves and between themselves and the state, and in one case it was arranged between a private company and a competing state line, that by whichever route the traffic went, the line that carried it should take a certain percentage of the gross receipts and pay over the balance to the other.

Though the results of state management have proved satisfactory to the public in securing cheap rates and efficient service, it is clear that there is no longer actual and efficient competition even between the state and private railways.

Great Britain.

The history of parliamentary action and inquiry in Great Britain shows that the predominant idea in the minds of English statesmen has always been, that competition which is so powerful a regulator in

*Paper of W. R. Malcolm, submitted to the joint committee of the British Parliament on railway amalgamation.

most commercial affairs, would also suffice to regulate railways; while by a slow and gradual process of experiment, one form after another has proved to be inadequate.* It was at first supposed that railways like canal companies would be merely the owners of the way, receiving tolls for the use of it and that among the carriers using their own carriages and locomotives on the lines there would be ample room for competition. The companies were therefore bound by their acts to admit the cars and engines of other persons on their lines at a certain rate of toll, and in many cases they were limited, if acting as carriers themselves, to certain maximum rates specified in their acts. But in 1840 a committee of Parliament, which included among its members Sir R. Peel, reported in the strongest terms that this form of competition was both "impracticable and undesirable," and that monopoly upon the same line, at all events as regards passengers, was inevitable. And as the railway companies were not bound to furnish any accommodation except the right of way, and as a single management was necessary, that kind of competition never went into effect.

In 1844 the great development of railway speculation brought prominently into view another form of competition, which was at first hardly contemplated, viz., between different railway companies. Another strong committee, of which Mr. Gladstone was chairman, was appointed to consider the whole subject. Their second report contemplates competition both between existing and future railways, and recommends the appointment of private bill committees to consider competing schemes.

The favor shown by Parliament to competing enterprises stimulated a large number of speculative schemes, causing what was known as the railway mania, which culminated disastrously about the year 1847. The reaction caused many schemes to be abandoned, and disclosed results exactly the opposite of what had been anticipated. Instead of cheapening rates and preventing combinations, the over-competition of the numerous companies caused them to seek self-protection by means of combination, and brought about a rapid consolidation of competing lines. Thus the very means by which the committee of that year and the Parliament sought to insure competition had the effect to defeat their object and greatly to accelerate the progress of amalgamation. In their third report the same committee expressed the opinion that, "though the effect of monopoly both on the public directly and indirectly on the railway companies was to be dreaded and guarded against, yet that competition would do more harm to the railways than good to the public."

In 1844 a board was constituted, under and within the Board of Trade, the chief duty of which was to report upon new railway schemes and bills, with especial reference to the questions of extension, amalgamation, and competition.

* In preparing this review of competition and combination in England, the committee has consulted the recent report of the select committee on railway amalgamation, and, wherever practible, has adopted the language of that report.

Other parliamentary committees were appointed in 1846, 1853, and 1865, all of whom gave special attention to the matter of competition, and presented elaborate reports deprecating the progress of amalgamation, and recommended measures for its prevention, and for the regulation and reduction of charges.

Lastly, in 1872, a joint select committee of the House of Lords and the House of Commons was appointed, and specially charged to inquire concerning railway amalgamations. That committee, after an investigation covering nearly a thousand pages of evidence, and a thorough review of the struggle against combination extending through forty years, admit that the general recommendations and resolutions of committees, commissions, and government departments, have had little influence upon the action of private-bill committees, and have not staid the progress of union and amalgamation; "and while committees and commissions carefully chosen have, for the last thirty years, clung to one form of competition after another, it has nevertheless, become more and more evident that competition must fail to do for railways what it does for ordinary trade; and that no means have yet been devised by which competition can be permanently maintained." And that "in spite of the recommendations of these authorities, combination and amalgamation have proceeded at the instance of the companies, without check and almost without regulation." "Nor is there any reason to suppose that the progress of combination has ceased, or that it will cease, until Great Britain is divided between a small number of great companies."

They further say, that on different occasions there has been effectua competition between railway companies in the matter of charges, and it is probable that charges now made still bear the traces of that competition, "but it may be taken as a general rule that there is now no active competition between different railways in the matter of rates and fares. Wherever different companies run between the same places they arrange their prices." * * "And if a new railway should ever be started with the promise of lower rates, it is sure, after a short time, to arrange with its original rivals a system of equal charges."

They close their review of the whole subject of competition with an expression of opinion that the only real and effective competition is between railways and water-transport, and recommend that the harbors should be kept out of the hands of the railway companies, and that every effort be made to keep up and develop the system of inland water-navigation.

This, it must be admitted, is a melancholy tone with which to close the history of a forty-years' struggle between a Parliament of unlimited powers and the forces of self-interest working out their results through combination. The actual effects of railway competition, even while it existed, and the greater combinations and more powerful monopolies which it ultimately induced, have disheartened those who regarded competition as the panacea for railway abuses, and it is said that the present tendency of the public is toward state ownership as the only effectual remedy.

We have thus passed hastily in review the railway systems of France, Prussia, Belgium, and England, in order to see to what extent competition prevails, and we find that however diverse the principles under which they have grown up, or the government regulations which have been imposed, actual and permanent competition between railways in the matter of rates and charges does not exist. In France it is, of course, impossible. In Prussia it is defeated by agreement among the companies. In Belgium, though the influence of former competition between the state and the companies is still shown in rates much lower than in any other country, yet the state has been compelled to make an agreement as to charges with the companies, and in some cases has even adopted the most objectionable form of combination, viz, "a joint purse," or pooling of earnings. In England, Parliament with unlimited powers having struggled in vain for forty years against amalgamation, has ceased to look for relief competition.

COMPETITION IN THE UNITED STATES.

Let us now inquire to what extent railway competition exists in our own country, and how far its permanence may be relied upon to regulate and cheapen transportation.

The theory here has always been, as in England, that the transportation business, like other commercial affairs, would regulate itself on the principle of competition. On this theory our railroad system has attained its present gigantic proportions. Believing that additional lines would create and stimulate competition, and thereby reduce rates, towns, cities, counties, and States have made haste to burthen themselves with debt in order to secure the coveted boon. The General Government having never interfered, and, until recently, the States having made but little effort to control or direct it, the system has developed itself under the influence of the natural laws which govern that kind of business. Hence the tendencies and results evolved by the operation of those laws, if carefully studied by the light of the experience of other countries, will enable us to form an opinion as to what may be anticipated from railway competition in the future if left to regulate itself by the ordinary laws of trade. That there is effective competition in the matter of charges at many points cannot be doubted, but that the same natural laws which have destroyed it in other countries are vigorously at work here, and will ultimately produce the same results is also obvious. The history of railway combinations in Europe, and especially in Great Britain, discloses the fact that during the period of development, and while each corporation was struggling to appropriate to its exclusive control as large a district of country as possible, competition was very sharp. When, by the consolidation of separate links, through trunk-lines were formed between the principal centers of population and trade, competition at once sprung up between those points. But self-interest very soon suggested to the competing companies that as the traffic must be divided, it was desirable to divide its profits between themselves rather than with the public. The result was an agreement as to rates and an end of competition. Having become strong and rich, the trunk-lines began the work of extending their power by the construction of branches and the absorption of weaker lines extending into the adjacent districts. Then followed a great struggle for territorial dominion, during which sharp and active competition re-appeared at numerous points in the contested districts. Its duration and vigor were measured chiefly by the relative strength of the giants contending for the prize, but the ultimate result was seldom long delayed and never doubtful. By purchase, lease, arrangement of rates, or some other of the numerous forms of combination and consolidation, one point after another disappeared from the competing list, and finally the disputed territory passed under the exclusive control of one of the contestants.

The same motives and influences which operated in Great Britain are rapidly producing similar results in this country. The existing competition, whatever may be its extent and value, is gradually disappearing from the trunk-lines, and is found mainly at points in the outlying districts from which these roads draw their support. The contest between the great companies for territorial dominion is still progressing in our country, and the struggle for control of the trade at some of the common termini and points of intersection of branch lines and feeders owned and operated by them, is apparent in the reduced charges which prevail at those places. The number of such competing points is, however, constantly diminishing, as each of the great corporations absorbs one after another, the inferior lines which have served as allies to its rival. Thus every additional absorption defines with constantly increasing precision, the boundaries of the territory which is certainly and rapidly passing under its exclusive domination. The wide extent of our country, and the colossal proportions of our railway system, (equaling one-half of the railway mileage of the globe,) requires a longer time for complete development than in some of the states of Europe, and hence the influences which induce competition will extend through a longer period, but the ultimate result will probably be the same. And when the natural tendencies of corporate power working through railway organization shall have wrought out their inevitable conclusions, the magnitude of our combinations will probably be in proportion to the extent of the field in which they operate.

In illustration of the statement that competition has already substantially disappeared from the main trunk-lines, take those which center in Chicago from the east—the Pennsylvania line, running to New York and Philadelphia; the Lake Shore and Michigan Southern, running in connection with the Erie and New York Central; and the Michigan Central Railway, in connection with the last two, and also the

Grand Trunk. These lines all have agents at Chicago who meet together and agree on prices for east-bound freight; and the prices established by such agreement bind the eastern roads. Mr. Homer E. Sargent, general superintendent of the Michigan Central line, when asked upon what principle their rates are fixed, answered, "The rates from there east-bound are fixed somewhat according to the demand for transportation. The Western men generally meet together and agree upon prices. The managers of the Eastern roads meet together at New York and arrange matters."

Mr. C. M. Gray, assistant general freight agent of the Lake Shore and Michigan Southern Line, said, "We meet together, and if we deem it proper to advance, we do so, and the same is usual in the way of reduction. *We are governed by the quantity moving and the price of freight on the lake.* The lake craft take the lead in reducing rates, and they also have a very decided influence in the advance of rates when it comes toward winter. If they are carrying very high, so that it comes near to the railway, we immediately advance a little, and keep a little above them all the time." (Evidence, page 278.)

Mr. E. D. Worcester, secretary of New York Central Railroad, testified that in fixing rates, "*the only question is what will the property bear*, keeping always in view the future development of the business, and the elements of public prosperity involved in such development." (Evidence, page 133.)

Mr. Joseph D. Potts, president of the Empire Transportation Company, says, "The method of fixing the rates is about this: The various freight representatives of the different roads going eastward from Chicago usually fix unitedly upon the rates which are to govern all shipments out of Chicago by each of the lines, their own roads and the lines running over them." (Evidence, page 33.)

Mr. Hayes, general manager of Blue Line, testified, "That the rates eastward are made by the general freight agents of western roads centering in Chicago. *They get together and find what the water communications are doing, their rates, &c., and base their rates upon that as a competing rate.*"—(Evidence page 7.)

The tariffs on all freights moving eastward over these lines are thus fixed by agreement between the western agents; and the charges on westward-bound freight by agents with like powers at the eastern termini. It is obvious from these statements, that there is no competition between these lines in the matter of charges, and that the principle upon which they are adjusted is not what are the services worth, but *how much will the article bear, and what is the extent of water competition?* This combination for the establishment of charges does not formally include the Baltimore and Ohio line. Mr. Homer E. Sargent testified that he did not know whether the agents of that line were always present at the meetings, "but they adopt the same prices that the other roads make;" and that any road that should reduce fares without consulting with the other agents would be regarded as 'cutting.'" (Evidence, page

274.) "Cutting" is considered dishonorable among railway men, and at once gives rise to what are well known as "railway fights," which tem porarily reduce charges below a paying rate at points of competition, accompanied generally by an increase at the non-competing points, and when the "war" is over, by enhanced rates on the entire line in order to make good the losses.

The two great companies which largely control the traffic of Wisconsin and Minnesota—the Chicago and Northwestern, and the Milwaukee and Saint Paul—afford another illustration of the value and and extent of railway competition when regulated by its own laws. Towns and cities favored with a line belonging to, or controlled by, one of these companies eagerly contributed to aid in the construction of a second, which should be in the interest of the other company. For several years, while those great corporations have been extending their branches and absorbing weaker lines, competition has at times been active at certain places, but the territory which each can hope to control being now pretty well defined, an agreement as to rates has been made, and the people are alarmed by rumors, but too well founded, of a contemplated arrangement for pooling receipts. Thus the people of the great wheat-growing region of the continent, after having hoped and struggled for years for reduced rates through competition, and after having in many cases imposed upon themselves grievous burdens of taxation for that purpose, now find that instead of bringing into the field a competitor, they have not only doubled the power with which they have to contend, but that they have quartered upon themselves a new and expensive organization which must be supported from the products of their toil.

Very suggestive illustrations of the progress of combination and centralization of power are readily found in the history of the great trunk lines having their base at Boston, New York, Philadelphia, and Baltimore. But a quarter of a century ago there was no connection by rail between the great lakes and any of the eastern cities, or between Boston and New York. When subsequently the connection was formed between Albany and Buffalo it was composed of ten distinct links, each owned by a separate company. In 1850 the Pennsylvania Company was endeavoring to find its way over the mountains, which, by means of an inclined plane and stationary engine, it accomplished in 1851. In 1853 the Baltimore and Ohio united the Chesapeake Bay with the Ohio River. In 1850 there were but ten miles of road westward from Chicago, and three years thereafter that city was first connected by rail with the Atlantic Ocean. At that time not more than one company in the United States owned over two hundred continuous miles of road, and but few had half that number. Consolidations proceeded slowly, until about ten years ago, when a spirit of railway aggrandizement took possession of the stronger companies, since which the work of centralization and absorption has progressed without a parallel in the railway history of the world.

But it is not our purpose to multiply illustrations of this subject. The same forces which have produced the colossal combinations now in existence are still at work everywhere, and in our opinion will not cease to operate, if uncontrolled by legislative power, until railway competition shall have substantially disappeared from the country.

Combination assumes various forms, which, commencing with the simplest and most common, may be described as follows, viz:

1. An agreement as to rates and fares between competing points.

2. An arrangement to forward traffic over one another's lines, each company receiving all the profits earned on its own line.

3. An arrangement which permits each company to run its cars over the line of the other, the profits being divided in certain fixed proportions.

4. An agreement to "pool earnings," or, as it is called in England, a "joint-purse," by which it is agreed that by whichever route the traffic goes, the line that carries it shall retain a certain proportion of the gross receipts, and pay over the balance to the other.

5. Lease of one road by another, under which a certain fixed sum is annually paid by the lessee, or an annual interest on the stock of the leased road.

6. A form of combination very similar to the last is where one company agrees to operate and maintain the line of another, paying over a certain proportion of the earnings.

7. Consolidation, as where one company purchases the stock of another, or where each road is valued and stock issued, and divided in proportion to the respective values of each.

A new form of combination, recently introduced, threatens to greatly accelerate the work of combination. We refer to the "fast freight-lines," the nature and advantages of which are discussed elsewhere in this report. At present we have to do only with their influence in bringing about a general combination of railway interests, and in placing under the control of a very few individuals the immense traffic of the country.

These lines are formed by each road contributing its *pro rata* of cars, and hence, as there is necessarily a unity of interest, it is not likely that their harmony will be disturbed by competition. The number of cars owned by the fast-freight lines, running in connection with the New York Central, is as follows:

	Cars.
Blue Line	3,287
White Line	3,247
Red Line	3,489
Merchants' Dispatch	1,500
International Line	1,000
Total	12,523

(Evidence p. 131.)

Each of these lines occupies a different district of country, and has its own alliances with the roads which furnish their quota of cars. The Blue Line combination includes twenty different roads, though its cars run over a much greater number.*

In the month of November, 1872, the Blue Line run its cars over one hundred and twenty-four different roads.

If the combinations of each of the other lines include an equal number in proportion to the number of its cars, we may assume that the unity of interests thus affected extends to more than one hundred roads. Now, if we remember that the New York Central owns about one-third of all the cars run by each of these fast freight-lines, we may form some conception of the power wielded by that company over the transportation interests of the country; and also of the irresistible influence these organizations may exert in suppressing troublesome competition in the vast districts through which they operate.

Fast freight-line organizations similar in character and magnitude, connected with the Pennsylvania and other trunk-roads at the North, are extending their ramifications into all parts of the country, and rapidly bringing the vast districts in which they work under the harmonizing influence of the systems which they respectively represent. In the South there are several of these organizations, of which the "Green Line" is the chief, and which substantially controls the inter-State traffic of Tennessee, Georgia, South Carolina, North Carolina, Florida, and Alabama, and also a large part of the freights which reach those States from the West and North. This combination, known as the Green Line, includes in its organization twenty-one different roads, with an aggregate of 3,330 miles. (Evidence, p. 779.)

Mr. Thomas E. Walker, general claim-agent of the line, says, "The Green Line is not a corporation, *but a combination of roads.*" The principle on which the combination is formed he states as follows: "These roads meet in convention, and agree to furnish a quota of cars, which is based on the amount of revenue derived from the business over each road. The calculation is based upon that, and each road furnishes a quota of cars. They agree to pay so much mileage per mile or per car for these cars." (Evidence, p. 780.)

There is but slight probability that these twenty-one roads, covering so large a portion of the South, bound together by this common interest, and meeting in council to arrange the details of their organization, will enter very earnestly into competition with each other in their respective localities.

It is true the line itself has some competition with other lines at the South, and somewhat effective competitors with the Chesapeake and Ohio, and the Baltimore and Ohio railroads to certain points on or near the Atlantic coast.

The rates to Charleston, Savannah, and other places easily reached by

* See testimony of Mr. Hayes, general manager of Blue Line. (Evidence, pp. 1 to 72.)

water, are fixed at Cincinnati, Saint Louis, &c., in competition with the two last-named roads, and are much lower than the rates from Nashville, where no such competition exists. There is at present a contest between the Chesapeake and Ohio, the Baltimore and Ohio, and the "Green Line" organization for the possession of a strip of country lying along the Atlantic coast in North Carolina, South Carolina, and Georgia, which may be reached by the sea from the termini of the two former roads at Richmond and Baltimore. It seems destined, however, to become a very narrow strip, for the roads of the Green Line, running into the interior from the sea-board, will, by a system of discrimination, make it to the interest of the interior to receive their freights over their long lines from the West, rather than over the shorter distances from the sea westward.

A very large proportion of the entire railway mileage of the country is divided between these different but by no means numerous systems of freight lines, each system having its various sub-divisions. Between the subdivisions there is entire unity of interest and action, but between the systems themselves there is yet some actual competition. The same motives which at first induced competition on the main trunk-lines, and subsequently in their outlying districts, and finally destroyed it in both, are operating with full force upon the *systems* of freight-lines, and may be reasonably expected to produce similar results. So long as the great systems are contending for dominion, competition will be found, but eventually, one of two things will take place, viz: a well-defined understanding of the territorial limits of each, or a general agreement as to rates. When either of these events, toward which we are rapidly tending, shall transpire, competition in the United States will have become a thing of the past. To the public it may sometimes come back as a pleasant memory, but to the railway companies it will never return to disturb their dreams of wealth and power.

Additional railway lines have been suggested as the means of increasing competition and reducing the cost of transportation. Is it probable that relief will be found in that direction if such lines are to be under corporate control? What reason have we to suppose that the same principles of combination which govern existing lines will not control the new ones? If, as already shown, competition with the water-routes, and "the highest charge the commodity will bear" now rule the rates, have we any guarantee that they will not do so on the additional lines? In fact every new line from the Mississippi to the Atlantic Ocean will add from seventy-five to one hundred millions of dollars to the capital on which the transportation business of the country must pay at least $5,000,000 to $7,000,000 annual interest, in addition to the cost of maintaining the new organization. Will not this afford an irresistible inducement to combine with existing companies, in order to make the largest possible profits out of the business to be performed? Is there anything in experience, or in the known principles of railway management, which teach us to hope that the new competing line would not at once participate in the councils of its rivals and be governed by their policy?

The case mentioned by Mr. Isaac Hinckley, president of the Philadelphia, Wilmington and Baltimore Railway, (Appendix, p. 219) is by no means exceptional. It is but an illustration of the general rule that competition among railways ends in combination and in enhanced rates. Such illustrations might readily be multiplied to any extent.

Having reluctantly reached the conclusion that the reduced cost of transportation demanded by the public is not to be anticipated from unregulated competition between existing railway companies, nor in competition to be induced by the construction of additional lines under private management and control, the committee will next consider the practicability of direct congressional regulation and the results probably attainable thereby.

2.—DIRECT REGULATION BY CONGRESS.

The reasons on which we base the opinion that Congress has the power to regulate inter-State commerce, when carried on by rail, are stated at some length in another part of this report. In this connection we have to do only with the *practicability* and *expediency* of its exercise *under existing circumstances*, and *with our present limited information on the subject.* In the discussion of this branch of the subject we wish it distinctly understood that the considerations presented apply to Federal regulation of the vast system of railways in the United States, and not to the smaller number of roads and less diverse conditions existing in a single State. The regulation of rates and fares by law is probably one of the most difficult problems ever presented even to the legislature of a State, but when extended to a great nation, composed of many States, having within their limits one-half the railway-mileage of the globe, and embracing every conceivable variety of conditions and circumstances, the problem becomes one of vastly greater difficulty.

Before considering the specific modes of proposed regulation, it may be of service to refer briefly to the conditions which affect the cost of transport by rail, all of which must be taken into account in establishing any general rule in regard to charges.

1st. The cost of the road on which interests and dividends are to be paid.

2d. The grades and curves. These conditions determine the net load that can be drawn by a locomotive of given power. The tractive power of an engine being about one-sixth of its weight on the driving-wheels, the load which a 33-ton engine can haul over various grades is about as stated in the following table:

Grades.	Hauling power.	No. of loaded cars.
	Tons.	
On a level	1,400	70
20 feet to the mile	655	32
40 feet to the mile	415	21
60 feet to the mile	300	15
80 feet to the mile	230	11
100 feet to the mile	180	9

It will be observed from the above table that the cost of transport depends largely, also, upon the fact as to whether the heaviest grades are encountered in the direction of the principal movement of tonnage or the reverse.

The number of freight-cars which may be safely drawn in a single train is also determined by the radius of the curves. On some roads of slight curves forty cars may be used, while on others of sharp curvatures it is unsafe to use more than fifteen or twenty.

3d. The character of the goods transported constitutes a material element in the cost. Goods in bulk may generally be transported cheaper than in small packages. Those which occupy a large space in proportion to weight increase the expense. Goods which require care in handling, or which are perishable, involve a responsibility for damages which must be borne by the carrier, and hence his charges must be higher. The greater cost of perishable goods is also due to the fact that trains carrying such goods in large quantities are obliged to be run at a higher rate of speed. In this country there are four general classes of goods in which the highest rate is generally   per cent higher than the lowest.

4th. The amount of business.* There is a class of expenditures on every road known as "constant expenditures," which are entirely independent of the number of trains that pass over it, such as interest on the cost of road and equipment, repair of road-bed, bridges, and ditches, and the replacement of ties and other wood-work. When distributed over a large number of train-miles, the average cost per train-mile, and consequently the average cost of transporting one ton per mile, is thereby reduced.

Under a second class of expenditures may be comprised all that are in some measure reduced with the increase of the number of train-miles, but not in the same proportion. To this class belong the general expenses, superintendence, the cost of adjustment of track, the compensation of engineers, &c.

The third class of expenditures increases in direct proportion as the number of trains over a road are increased.

To this class belong engines, wages, engine-repairs, fuel, &c.

* The data under this division are taken from a very valuable work recently prepared by Albert Fink, civil engineer, of Louisville, Ky., entitled "Cost of Transportation on American Railroads."

On page 32 of the evidence, Mr. Joseph D. Potts, president of the Empire Transportation Company, says:

"I had occasion to investigate two roads some three years ago and compare them. The one did a business, I think, of some 400,000,000 of tons one mile in a year; the other about 15,000,000, if I recollect right. The difference was very great.

"The cost per ton per mile on the road that did the large business was about one cent; on the route that did the small business it was about $5\frac{8}{10}$ cents."

"By Mr. DAVIS:

"Q. What caused that difference, if you examined?

"A. The large amount of fixed expenses and the small amount of tonnage moved. Out of every hundred tons of engines, cars, and freight moved over the smaller road, only 19 per cent. paid any money. I judge, though I do not know, that the kind of lading was light and bulky, and perhaps in very small quantities, while their fixed station expenses were probably large. It was a road that ran into New York. The road that did the large business—the Philadelphia and Reading—charged the public, I think, about a cent and three-quarters per ton per mile for doing the work. On the other it was 7.6 cents, and I think the Reading made much the most money on its capital."

5th. Freights can be transported at less expense on a road where the business is uniform than where it is fluctuating. The company must provide itself with sufficient rolling-stock and trained labor to meet the maximum demand. If that demand continues through only a small portion of the year, the charges must be higher to compensate for the losses during the period that the employés and the stock are compelled to remain comparatively idle.

Hon. Leland Sandford, president of the Central Pacific Railroad, says:

"Our car-equipment in 1872 comprised 3,198 cars, flat and box. Of this number, 182 made no mileage, leaving 3,016 cars that made all the movement of the year. The actual car-mileage made was 31,351,667 miles, equivalent to 313,516,670 ton mileage, while the *actual* ton-mileage was but 190,516,507, or 60 per cent. of the mileage which the cars were compelled to make, on account of the distance of empty mileage and irregular distribution of tonnage.

"It must not be lost sight of that this percentage represents but the *average* performance of our freight rolling-stock, and that in order to meet the excessive amount of work demanded of us during wheat seasons, it has been necessary to keep the entire 3,016 cars in commission.

"The actual freight-mileage capacity of these cars, if steadily worked, and allowing proper time for loading and unloading, is about 136,000,000, car-mileage, or 1,360,000,000 ton-mileage, while the actual ton-mileage performed, based upon the actual car-mileage, being but 310,000,000, we have the rather startling result of our actual work in car-mileage, being but 23 per cent. of the easily possible car-mileage of the equipment which the excessive fluctuations of business in this State forces us to keep on hand.

"As this 23 per cent. is still further reduced by the fact that, of the *actual* car-mileage made, but 60 per cent. was (on account of long distance hauled empty or imperfectly loaded) of *paying* ton-mileage, we have, as a final result, that the total tonnage of our California system of roads, including "throughs," is but 13.8 per cent. of the capacity of the stock which we are forced to keep and keep moving at different times of the year; in other words, out of 3,016 cars, but 416 would represent the actual earning ones, did they have full loads moving with regularity."

7th. Climatic influences must also be considered. This of course is a variable condition. On some of our northern roads the obstructions from ice and snow are very small some winters and very great in others. The losses sustained at times are enormous. Mr. William Bliss, general manager of the Boston and Albany Railroad, states that the total cost of moving the snow from the track on that road in the winter of 1871–'72, was $29,400, and that this was but a small part of the damages sustained; the principal loss being by the detention of trains, sometimes for two or three days. He expresses the opinion that the cost of maintaining a road is 12½ per cent. greater in the winter than in the summer; repairs of machinery 10 per cent. greater, and the power of the locomotive 10 per cent. less.

Mr. Strickland Kneass, assistant to the president of the Pennsylvania Railroad Company, estimates the cost of transportation on that road in winter fully 12 per cent. greater than in summer. He states that during the winter of 1872 and 1873 the cost of removing snow alone amounted to $35,298.

Mr. L. Millis, general superintendent of traffic on the Vermont Central Railroad, estimates that the cost of transportation in the winter on their road is from 70 to 75 per cent. more than in the summer. He states also that in some cases the cost of clearing the track after a single snow-storm, is greater than the receipts from transportation of freight for a month.

Mr. Thomas R. Sharp, master of transportation on the Baltimore and Ohio Railroad, says:

"The estimated increased cost of transportation during the winter months above that of the three summer months, on the Baltimore and Ohio Railroad is from 5 to 20 per cent.; varying according to the character of power employed, the direction of the traffic, the relative altitude above tide-water of the portion of the road carried over, and the severity of the winter."

8th. The cost of transport is diminished in proportion to the equality of transport each way. One of the most serious difficulties encountered in railway transportation is the proportion of dead weight to paying freights actually transported. An ordinary freight-car weighs about ten tons and carries ten tons. The average weight of a locomotive is about thirty tons. A train of thirty cars fully loaded carries one and one-tenth tons dead weight for every ton of paying freights. If the cars return empty, every net ton carried requires the movement of two and one-fifth tons of dead weight. The cost of moving a ton of dead weight (cars and locomotive) being the same as the cost of moving a ton of merchandise, it is evident that the cost of transport must differ very widely, according to the relative volume of its freights in each direction. Assuming the extreme case of a road which transports all its tonnage in one direction, the cost would be nearly twice as great as upon another transporting an equal quantity both ways.

9th. The cost of transportation per ton per mile diminishes as the distance increases, because the "constant expenses" are distributed over a greater number of train-miles, and hence the cost per ton per mile is less.

10th. There are various other incidental circumstances which materially affect the cost, among which may be mentioned the supply and quality of the equipment, the substantial character of the road, the price of labor, fuel, supplies, &c.

All of these conditions and circumstances vary in every State and on every road, but must be fully understood and carefully considered in order to frame a general law regulating charges, that shall operate fairly and justly upon all.

Railway regulation, though untried by Congress, is by no means a novel experiment in the States or in other countries. In England, to whose railway system ours corresponds more closely than to that of any other nation, the subject of regulation has been discussed for more than a third of a century, and experimented upon by Parliament in almost every conceivable form. Commenting on these experiments the Massachusetts railway commissioners say: "Nowhere has the system of special legislation been more persistently followed, and nothing, it may be added, could have been more complete than its failure. As the result of forty years' experience, reviewed in the recent elaborate report of the joint committee on amalgamation of railways, it may be said that the English legislation has neither accomplished anything it sought to bring about, nor prevented anything which it sought to hinder." We have already seen how complete was the failure to create and maintain competition or to prevent combinations and consolidations. The table of comparative charges on English and other railways hereafter submitted, shows what practical results have attended the effort to reduce charges by direct governmental regulation.

The recent report of the parliamentary committee on railway amalgamation reviews with great thoroughness the various modes of regulation which have been proposed and tried in England. As many of the modes therein mentioned are identical with those on which reliance seems to be placed in this country, and as the opinions expressed by that committee are the results of forty years' experience, and of the investigations of numerous able committees, we take the liberty of quoting the forms of "suggested regulations" discussed by them, with a brief statement of their conclusions as to each, to which we add our own conclusions regarding their practicability in the United States.

"Suggested regulations."

1. "Equal mileage-rates."
2. "Rates to be fixed by relation to cost and profit on capital."

3. "Immediate reduction of rates and fares."

4. "Periodical revision of rates and fares."

5. "Absolute limitation of dividends."

6. "Division of profits beyond a certain limit between companies and the public."

7. "Interchange of traffic; through rates and running powers."

8. "Publication of rates."

9. "Combinations and consolidations with competing lines to be prohibited."

10. "Railway companies to be required to receipt for quantity, and to account for the same at destination."

1. EQUAL MILEAGE RATES

they pronounce "impracticable," because—

a. "It would prevent railways from lowering their fares and rates so as to compete with traffic by sea or canal, or by a shorter or otherwise cheaper railway, and would thus deprive the public of the benefit of competition and the company of a legitimate source of profit."

b. "It would prevent railways from making perfectly fair arrangements for conveying, at lower rates than usual, goods brought in large and constant quantities, or for conveying for long distances at a lower rate than for short distances."

c. "It would compel a company to carry for the same rate, over a line which has been very expensive in construction, or which from gradients, or otherwise, is very expensive in working, at the same rates for which it carries over less expensive lines."

The difficulties here enumerated apply with far greater force in this country than in England. Our roads are much longer. Their circumstances and conditions are less uniform. The difference in cost of construction and expense of working different sections of the same road is greater. There is less uniformity in the amount of business on different roads and on different sections of the same road. A rate that would ruin one road, costing $100,000 per mile, would be excessive on another that cost only $25,000 per mile, if the amount of business on each be the same. On the other hand the more expensive road could, with a sufficiently large amount of business, make a profit at rates which would be ruinous on the cheaper one with a small amount of business. And e en on the same road, a rate that would be excessive on one section would not pay the running expenses on another section. It would be manifestly unjust to require local freights passing over a given number of miles, costing one million of dollars, to pay the same rate per mile that other local freights pay for carriage over a like distance on the same road, which cost five millions. Distance, also, is an important element in the economy of railway transportation, but it is not the only one, nor is it in fact always the most important element. Extortionate charges for short distances, and unjust discriminations against certain points, afford good ground for complaint, and doubtless demand a remedy; but that remedy to be effective, must be based upon sound principles. It is a fact susceptible of the clearest demonstration, that it actually costs more per mile to transport a short distance than a long one, and this principle has received universal recognition by railway managers. In Belgium, where, through state management, the cheapest and in many respects the best railroad system in existence has been developed, the charges on fourth-class goods are graded according to distance, as follows:

Distance.	Charge per ton per mile in 1868, including terminals.
	Cents.
15 miles	2.54
31 miles	1.86
46 miles	1.66
62 miles	1.38
77 miles	1 18
93 miles	1.02
108 miles	.92
124 miles	.86
139 miles	.80
155 miles	.74

A similar decrease in rates in proportion to increase of distance prevails in every country in Europe, and we may add on every road in the United States. The reasons for this universal rule are well stated in a recent paper prepared by W. M. Grosvenor, of Saint Louis, as follows:

"The regularity of decrease in rate charged corresponds with a general law governing all railway service, namely, cost of loading and unloading, and fixed expenses being the same, whether the trip is long or short; cost of transportation per ton per mile regularly decreases as distance increases, being cost of haulage plus fixed cost, divided by the number of miles. Thus, if cost of loading and unloading be 33 cents, and other items of fixed cost 27 cents per ton, the actual cost of haulage, (maintenance of track, repairs, &c., included,) being eighty-three hundredths of one cent per ton per mile, the cost for different distances will be 83+60 cents divided by distance, thus:

Miles.	Haulage.	Fixed.	Total.
10	83	6.00	6.83
20	83	3.00	3.83
30	83	2.00	2 83
40	83	1.50	2 33
50	83	1.20	2.03
60	83	1.00	1.83
80	83	.75	1.58
100	83	.60	1.43
150	83	.40	1.23
200	83	.30	1.13
300	83	.20	1.03
400	83	.15	.98
500	83	.12	.95
1,000	83	.06	.89

Now if it actually costs six and eighty-three one-hundredth cents per ton per mile to transport freight ten miles, and only eighty-nine one-hundredth cents to carry it a thousand miles, it is evident that a law establishing equal mileage-rates, without regard to distance, would prove a failure, because of its manifest injustice both to the public and to the company. The enforcement of such a rule of charges, instead of bringing relief to the producers in the distant interior of the continent, would add very largely to their present burthens. The average rates for transporting all freights on the leading trunk-lines between Chicago and New York in 1872 was about 1½ cents per ton per mile, which, on a bushel of wheat, would amount to about 44 cents. The actual average charge by rail per bushel that year was 33.5 cents. Hence, an equal mileage rate on those lines, if adjusted upon the basis of their average charges, would have reduced the value of the 213,000,000 bushels of wheat and corn moved that year about 10 cents per bushel, amounting to an aggregate loss to producers of $21,300,000, with no compensating gain to consumers. And as the price of wheat and corn at the West, as well that part which remains at home as that which is sent abroad, is fixed by the market-price in Liverpool, less the cost of transportation, the loss to the Northwestern States on the entire crop of that year, (estimated at over 1,000,000,000 bushels,) would have amounted to the enormous sum of $100,000,000. A permanent reduction of 10 cents per bushel on the value of the cereal crop of the Northwest, would reduce the value of the farms, in that section, by an amount which would build and equip all the trunk-lines of railroad from the interior to the seaboard.

Not only would an equal mileage-rate, if applied to the whole country, impose additional burthens on those sections most in need of relief, but it would tend to destroy whatever of competition now exists. This fact is demonstrated by the operation of the *pro-rata* law of the State of Illinois. At many points in that State the people have contributed largely to aid the construction of a second road for the purpose of securing competition. The two roads are not the same length. But the law says that both shall charge the same rate per mile. The longer one being compelled to charge more to the common point of destination is, of course, driven out of competition, and the shorter one takes a monopoly of the business. Hence it will be observed that one of the most valuable and salutary rules which obtain in railway transportation, viz, that the shortest line between two common points, all other things being equal, makes the rates for all other lines, is reversed by the principle of equal mileage rates. The people who have contributed to build competing roads thus find themselves taxed to pay the cost of transportation for others who have been less enterprising. A general *pro-rata* law applied to the whole country would indefinitely multiply such evil results at competing points, without any compensating benefits at other places. The non-competing points, would not be benefited, for if by reason of low rates, at the point of competition, a largely increased traffic can be created, from which the company can make a small profit, it will be enabled, to the extent of such profit, to reduce the rates at the intermediate point.

The committee are therefore of the opinion that no good results can be anticipated from an equal mileage-rate, but that a law establishing such a rule of charges for the United States would be impracticable and unjust both to the railroads and the public.

2. RATES TO BE FIXED BY RELATION TO COST, AND PROFIT ON CAPITAL.

This the parliamentary committee dismiss because attended with difficulties which are "practically insuperable." "The original cost of the particular line, the cost of carriage of the particular goods on that portion of the line, as compared with the cost of carriage of other goods on the same line, and the proportion of all these to the whole charges and expenses of the company," are items which (they say) "it might be difficult for the companies themselves to give, and impossible for a committee or Government department to ascertain. Still more difficult is the determination of profit." If the difficulties of this mode of regulation are found to be "practically insuperable" in Great Britain with 15,000 miles of railway, what shall be said of the United States with their 70,000 miles? In order to establish intelligently a rule of charges based upon cost and profit we must investigate thoroughly the circumstances and conditions of every one of the 1,300 roads. We must know all about each individual road, its original cost, how much of its capital is real and how much fictitious; how much was actually paid on its stock, and what proportion of the profits charged to capital account should have been charged to expenses. Having completed this detailed investigation, which would necessarily involve an examination and re-adjustment of the accounts of the company from its organization, we next turn our attention to its profits. In order to adjust charges to profits by a general rule of law, we must know what the actual profits are now, and what they will be in the future. This requires a knowledge of its grades and curvatures; the cost of fuel, supplies, and other items of working expenses; the amount of business it now does, and what it will continue to do; the economy or extravagance with which it will be managed; the condition and character of its construction and equipment; how long its iron, ties, and rolling-stock will last, and what it will cost to replace them; the storms of winter and the floods of summer it will probably encounter; and finally, the losses which will result from accidents of all kinds. This completed, we must study carefully the nature of its traffic so as to know what relation the various classes of goods bear to each other in cost of transportation; what charge each class will bear without injury to the business interests of the country, and how much the expense of carrying a ton of silk goods twenty-five miles per hour exceeds that of carrying a ton of corn ten miles per hour.

When we have thus informed ourselves with reasonable accuracy in regard to all these details, and many more that might be named, we will be prepared to commence the investigation of the next road on the list, and so on through the 1,300. By the time we have completed the investigation, the changed conditions and circumstances of the roads, and the rapid changes in the business of the country, will render a re-examination imperatively necessary.

The committee are therefore unable to find a practical solution of the transportation question in this mode of regulation.

3. Immediate reduction of rates and fares

Involves all the difficulties mentioned under the last proposition, for if the reduced rates are to stand the test of practical experiment, they must be just and reasonable, and hence they must be determined with reference to the cost and profitableness of the road. The committee on railway amalgamation say of this proposition: "It would be merely a temporary remedy, for the reason that a change which will give the company ample profit to-day may, through increased economy or other cause, be excessive to-morrow." The utmost that could be done would be the establishment of maxima rates for each road, which must be placed high enough to cover all contingencies, and hence it would probably effect no perceptible reduction in the present cost of transportation. In practice the maximum fares in England, France, and Prussia are rarely changed. The following comparison of parliamentary rates with the rates actually charged, taken from the "blue-book," and handed to the committee by Mr. J. M. Walker, president of the Chicago, Burlington and Quincy Railroad, illustrates the effect of maximum rates in England.

ENGLAND.

Commodities.	Rates allowed by Parliament.	Rates actually charged.
Lumber	6	4
Corn and other grain	7	4
Coal	$3\frac{5}{10}$	2
Flour	7	4
Stock	8	8
General merchandise	8	$2\frac{1}{2}$ to 5
Manufactured goods	8	$2\frac{1}{2}$ to $4\frac{1}{2}$

Maxima rates.

It is doubtless entirely practicable for State legislatures to establish *maxima* rates which will afford a remedy for local extortions and discriminations; and it is possible that in certain cases such rates may be established by act of Congress with beneficial results. But it is difficult to see how a general law of Congress, establishing *maxima* rates, can be framed that will materially *cheapen* the cost of transport on existing lines of railway between the interior of the continent and the seaboard.

A commission with authority to establish *maxima* rates subject to revision by the courts, has been suggested. But Congress acts only under delegated powers, and a serious constitutional question arises whether it can delegate its powers to another tribunal. I believe it is a well-settled principle of law that an agent cannot, without the authority of his principal, delegate his power to another agent; else such sub-agent may again delegate them, and so on without limit. Assuming, however, that no constitutional difficulties exist, the expediency of clothing the President with power to appoint commissioners authorized to establish rates that will increase or diminish the dividends on over $3,000,000,000 of railway capital is seriously questioned. If there is any truth in the oft-repeated assertions that railway companies already exercise a corruptive influence over legislative bodies, what may we expect when the powers which now belong to Congress shall be transferred to a commission whose duties will require them to decide what profits shall be made upon this immense capital?

Maxima rates, whether established by Congress or by a commission, must be high enough to pay the actual cost of transportation and leave a margin large enough to provide a fair return for capital honestly invested and to cover all contingencies. The actual average charge on all cereals moved by the trunk-lines of railway between Chicago and New York in 1872 was less than 12 mills per ton per mile. The evidence taken by the Committee on Transportation shows that the average cost of movement, exclusive of interest and dividends, was from 8 to 9 mills per ton per mile. Assuming the cost to be 8½ mills, there would be left for the payment of interest and dividends 3½ mills. The number of tons carried one mile on the Pennsylvania Railroad in 1872 was 1,190,052,975, which, at 3½ mills, gives $4,115,185. The actual cost of the road, with its equipment, was something over $42,000,000; hence, if the same rates had been charged on all the tonnage moved, the margin between the actual cost of movement and the actual average charges that year, would have paid a little less than 10 per cent. on the cost of the road. Is it probable that either Congress or a commission could have established a maximum rate with less margin above actual cost than the rates which were in fact imposed? The parliamentary committee of 1872 say:

"Legal *maxima* rates afford little protection to the public, since they are always fixed so high that it is, or becomes sooner or later, the interest of the companies to carry at lower rates. The same thing is true of terminal charges. The circumstances are so various and so constantly changing that any legal *maxima* which might now be fixed would probably be above the charges now actually made, certainly far above those which will hereafter be made. Indeed, attempts made in 1861 and 1866 to fix a maximum for terminals broke down, because the only maximum that could be agreed upon was so much beyond the charge then actually made to coal-owners that the coal-owners feared it would lead to a rise in that charge."

Captain H. W. Tyler, in his report to the secretary of the railway department, Board of Trade, says:

"The attempt to limit rates and fares by the principle of fixing a maximum has almost always failed in practice, and is almost always likely to fail, for the simple reason that the parliamentary committees and authorities by whom such limits are decided cannot do otherwise than allow some margin between the actual probable rate, so far as they can forecast it, and the maximum rate; and cannot foresee the contingencies of competition, of increase in quantities, of facilities, or economy in working, or of alteration in commercial conditions which may occur in the course of years after such limits have been arranged by them."

4. Periodical reduction of rates and fares

The parliamentary committee pronounce "inexpedient and impracticable," and suggest the following among other reasons, viz: "How is it to be performed, and by whom? If it is to be purely arbitrary, if no rule is to be laid down to guide the revisors, the power of revision will amount to a power to confiscate the property of the companies. It is not likely that Parliament would attempt the exercise of any such power itself, still less that it would confer such a power on any subordinate authority."

Assuming for the present that Congress would attempt the exercise of a power from which the Parliament of England shrinks, let us inquire how such revision of rates would be made in this country. Shall it be done by Congress itself, or by some tribunal acting under its authority? Surely not the latter, for the power of Congress over the subject is only a delegated power, which it cannot delegate to another. Nor is it probable that any one has ever dreamed of conferring on any tribunal the authority to decide arbitrarily and in advance what compensation one person shall receive for services to be performed for another. The revisions must, therefore, be made by Congress itself, if at all. It is said in the English reports that "the rates in the case of all the great companies are numbered by millions." In this country each of the 1,300 roads has its through rates, its rates to every station on its own line, and to every station on the lines with which it connects, its scores of special rates, and its numerous classifications of goods. A bill which should enumerate them all, if such a bill could be framed, could hardly be read through during the session, and if read, not one member in a dozen would be the wiser. If Congress should undertake the periodical revision of rates on the 70,000 miles of railroad in the United States, it must remain in constant session, and devote its attention exclusively to this work.

5. Absolute limitation of dividends.

This form of proposed regulation assumes that the passenger and shipper will receive, in the shape of reduced fares and charges, whatever excess of profits may remain after paying to the shareholder the limit allowed by law. It involves the power of revision, and the necessity for accurate and detailed information, referred to under the forms of regulation already discussed, and hence, in its practical application, would encounter many, if not all, of the difficulties therein mentioned. In England this form of regulation is pronounced "impossible and undesirable."* Impossible, because it involves the necessity of judging "what rates will enable the company to make the given dividend on a given capital," and of determining "what are the proper expenses of the companies and what economies they can practice." These are declared to be "matters which require the knowledge, skill, and experience of the managers themselves, and any attempt on the part of any government department to do it for them is impossible, unless the agents of the Government were to undertake an amount of interference with the internal concerns of the companies which is neither desirable nor practicable."

The assumption that what is withheld from the shareholders would be available for reduction of rates is declared to be a "fallacy, because the company, having no interest in making more than the fixed rate of profit, will have every inducement to use up the surplus in needless expenditure. * * * The result, therefore, of limiting the dividends of companies would be to deprive them, monopolists as they are, or will be, of the ordinary motives for efficiency or economy, and to impose upon government or Parliament an impracticable task, the result of which must be either to delude the public by giving a formal and groundless sanction to the schemes of the companies, or to take out of their hands the management of their own affairs."

The reasons thus forcibly presented against an absolute limitation of dividend are quite as applicable to the railroad system of America as to that of England. It is surely undesirable to increase the present extravagance and waste in railway management. The probable results of such a limitation are pretty clearly stated in the evidence of Mr. E. D. Worcester, secretary of the New York Central Road, (page 125 of the evidence,) in which facts are presented showing the effects of economical management in the increase of dividends, and the means by which profits could be readily reduced below the limit. If the dividend could not extend beyond a certain fixed amount, it would be to the interest of the company to do only enough business to produce that sum, and hence if the movement of one million tons at 2 cents per ton per mile, or of two million tons at 1 cent per ton per mile, would produce the profit limited to the company, the lesser amount of work would be preferred. The direct inducement, therefore, would be to increase the price and diminish the traffic, thereby giving to the public an inferior service, at an enhanced cost. It is apparent, also, that another result would be to stimulate the stock-watering process, which has already become so offen-

* Report of joint committee on railways amalgamation.

sive to the public, and which has so largely increased the cost of transportation, for, if the shareholder can receive only a certain fixed dividend on the amount of his capital, he will not be slow in finding some plausible excuse for increasing his stock.

One of the chief motives for the practice of stock-inflations which prevails on some of our leading roads, is the fear of offending public sentiment by an exhibit of actual profits. When public sentiment shall have crystallized into a law of absolute limitation, may we not expect to see this evil aggravated to an extent even more alarming than at present?

Such a limitation of dividends would also tend to discourage the construction of new and competing roads in localities where they are needed, for capital will not readily seek investment if the profits are limited, unless it be accompanied with a guarantee which no one proposes to give. This is illustrated by the fact that a bond of the New York Central Railroad, which guarantees 6 per cent., is worth as much in the market as its stock on the expectation of 8 per cent.

Your committee are therefore of the opinion that a law of Congress establishing this form of regulation would, even if practicable, afford no relief, but on the other hand it would result in a withdrawal of every inducement to economy; in increased expenditures and waste; in enhanced prices for inferior service; in an additional stimulus to the reprehensible practice of stock-watering, and in special contracts, jobbery, and favoritism. Unable to overcome the difficulties encountered by this mode of regulation, the advocates of limitation have in England proposed as a modification the following:

6. DIVISION OF PROFITS BEYOND A CERTAIN LIMIT, BETWEEN COMPANIES AND THE PUBLIC.

The theory upon which this proposition is based is, that a certain limit being fixed, the excess shall be divided between the public and the company, one portion being added to the dividend and the remainder being applied to the reduction of charges.

This modification would to a certain extent avoid the objection urged against an absolute limitation, viz,. that it would destroy all motive for economy of management; but, says the report from which we have just quoted, "There are other difficulties which it would not meet," viz, "What is, or ought to be, the sum available for dividend?" "In what specific fares or rates is the reduction to be made, and to what extent?" "No government department could undertake to say what the expenditure of a railway company ought to be, and what consequently is the amount properly divisible as profit; nor could a government department well undertake the difficult and obnoxious task of selecting special traffic or special rates for reduction. If a railway were a homogeneous concern, supplying a given article at a fixed price to all its customers, it would not be difficult to provide that when its dividends reached 10 per cent.

the price of the article should be reduced so much for every additional 1 per cent. added to the dividend. But when a railway company is a concern like the London and Northwestern Company, having 1,500 miles of railway in different parts of the country, carrying all sorts of traffic on the different parts of its line, and charging "millions" of special rates for special services, it would be a task beyond the capacity of any department to decide, as against the company, and among the innumerable claimants, what should be the amount or description of any particular reductions, and to whom and in what manner they should be given." This modification was once adopted in England, but it never went into effect.*

It has been tried in France, and on account of the difficulty of selecting rates and classifications of goods on which to apply it, the reduction has been abandoned, and one-half the surplus profit is paid into the national treasury. There is, therefore, but little encouragement to try the experiment in this country, where, by reason of the greater number of our roads, and the great diversity of the conditions and traffic, as well as the instinctive aversion of our people to meddlesome governmental interference in private affairs, vastly greater difficulties would be encountered than in France or England.

7. Interchange of traffic; through rates and running powers.

It is proposed by this mode of regulation, first, to give every company the power to make through rates to any point on the line of any other company and to require the companies over whose lines the goods are sent to forward them without delay or hinderance; and, second, to give every company the power to run its cars over the road of every other company, the compensation therefor to be fixed by agreement between the companies, or, in the event of their disagreement, by a tribunal to be especially appointed, by the proper judicial authority, for that purpose.

The parliamentary committee recommend under certain restrictions the adoption of the first proposition relating to through rates, and the rejection of the second as to "running powers." We are unable to see how any practical benefit would arise from either under existing system of management. If the through rates are fixed arbitrarily by Congress, or by a commission, it would involve all the difficulties heretofore mentioned under that form of regulation. If the charges upon the through line are to be the same on the line of the owning company as its own local rates, it would result in an increase rather than diminution of cost. If, as is proposed in England, every railway company is "to make through rates and fares from or to any station, on any other line, the rates to be divided as a general rule, according to mileage after allowing terminals," we can discover no reason why such an arrangement would result in decrease of rates.

---

* Report of joint committee on railway amalgamation, pages 36 and 37.

The second proposition is objectionable on several grounds, but chiefly because instead of stimulating competition, its direct tendency would be, if such power were enforced, to induce the railway companies of the whole country to combine in self-defense. It would also enable the strong companies to first bankrupt and then absorb the weaker ones, thereby stimulating and aiding consolidations. If, for instance, one of the great trunk-lines should desire to own a line which threatens competition, but which has a small amount of business, and a heavy interest account to meet, nothing would be easier than for the strong company to send its cars on the line of the weak one, and by carrying for a time at losing rates compel it to default in payment of its interest, and then buy it in, on its own terms.

We shall have occasion to refer to "running powers" in another connection, in which the objections above enumerated do not apply.

8. PUBLICATION OF RATES

is proposed as a remedy for the evils of unjust discrimination against one locality in favor of another, or in favor of one description of trade at the expense of another; as a preventive of higher rates for a short distance than for a longer one; and of uncertainty and favoritism by means of special contracts, rebates, drawbacks, and the thousand and one other means by which a rich and powerful company may, by the secret adjustment of rates, impose upon the public, and render fluctuating and precarious the business transactions of those who are compelled to use its line.

This proposed regulation proceeds upon the not unreasonable theory that the moral restraints of public opinion will have a salutary effect upon the companies, and that such publicity will tend to insure stability and certainty to the business of transportation, and to remove the discontent and suspicion of the public. And further it is argued that a company dealing honestly and fairly should court publicity, and challenge criticism by giving to the public every possible facility for obtaining information regarding its charges and its reasons for making them.

Hence in England the royal commission of 1867 and the committee of 1872 agree in urging that the companies should be compelled to exhibit, when required, at every station, a true list of the fares and rates charged from that station, and to give true information as to special contracts, drawbacks, and other deductions and advantages.

On this point a singular unanimity prevails in nearly all the countries of Europe; France, Prussia, Austria, Sweden, and Belgium all regard it as important and insist upon its enforcement. In all of these countries hand-books are published giving all the particulars regarding distance, classification, rates, special tariffs, &c. There is no doubt that a valuable reform in railway management may be attained by requiring such publication in this country, especially if it be accompanied, as in several European countries, with a provision prohibiting an increase of rates without reasonable public notice.

As many of the causes of complaint arise from fluctuations, discriminations, and favoritism, at and between points entirely within a State, the remedy for such abuses must be applied by the State legislature, if at all.

But there is a large class of cases in which inter-State traffic is alone concerned, for which the remedy is in the hands of Congress.

Your committee recommend that in all such cases within the jurisdiction of Congress, a publication of rates and fares be required, and that common carriers be prohibited from increasing such rates without reasonable notice to the public, to be prescribed by law.

9. COMBINATIONS AND CONSOLIDATIONS WITH COMPETING LINES TO BE PROHIBITED.

The consolidation of separate links, into through lines, is believed by the committee to be in the interest of the public as well as of the companies. In 1852 seventeen distinct companies operated the line between New York and Chicago. Ten of these companies constituted the line from Albany to Buffalo. By the various consolidations since made there are now but two companies—the New York Central and Lake-Shore line—between those cities. The practical effect of these consolidations has been to reduce rates and to greatly increase the efficiency of the line. Each separate company formerly had its own local interest to subserve, its own profits to make, and its own peculiar policy to enforce. Seventeen different organizations had to be maintained, at a heavy cost to the patrons of the line. No one company was under obligations to co-operate with another, except so far as its own individual interest was thereby subserved. Through lines of cars could be run only by complicated and embarrassing arrangements. In some cases through tickets could not be obtained from Albany to Buffalo. Freights could not be sent through but by agreement between the numerous companies, and, except so far as they agreed, a change of freight was required at each terminus. The consolidation of separate companies into through lines has introduced the system of pro-rating, and all the conveniences resulting from through business. Formerly goods sent from Chicago to New York had to be consigned to the care of several different agents along the line, thereby largely increasing the cost for commissions to middle-men, causing great delays in transmission and intolerable vexations in regard to losses. (Evidence, p. 157.) The only serious objection to consolidations of this kind is the centralization of power thereby effected, but we regard this as a far less evil than those to which we have referred.

There is, however, another class of consolidations, the design of which is not to cheapen and facilitate commerce, but solely to enlarge the powers of monopoly by destroying competition. This species of consolidation is as an unmixed evil, and wholly indefensible. It not only opens an almost boundless field for the centralization of a power already of threatening proportions, but its tendency and direct effect is the utter destruction of just and fair competition.

The State of Pennsylvania has incorporated a very wise provision in her new constitution, recently adopted, which prohibits all forms of consolidation between competing lines. A like provision, either in the constitution or laws of other States, would doubtless have a very beneficent effect. Your committee are of the opinion that Congress should co-operate with the several States in this matter by the enactment of laws regulating commerce among the States, which shall provide, with proper penalties for disobedience, that no railway corporation in the United States whose road forms a part of a continuous line between two or more States shall consolidate the stock, property, or franchise of such corporation with, or lease or purchase the works or franchises of, or in any way control, any other railroad corporation owning or having under its control a parallel or competing line; and that no officer of such railroad corporation shall act as an officer of any other railroad owning or having the control of a parallel or competing line.

10. Railway companies to be required to receipt for quantity, and to account for the same at its destination.

The enforcement of a regulation of this character would remedy an evil of no small magnitude, and one which falls peculiarly within the scope of national regulation. Hon. Benjamin Eggleston, of Cincinnati, testified that "a car-load of grain sent from Cincinnati to New York is always a little short. The cars are all sealed or lined, but the companies claimed that it shook out between the cracks, may be three or four bushels to each car. That is a toll that they are getting at almost every place where they have an elevator." (Evidence, p. 539.) Mr. Carlos Cobb, of the New York produce exchange, testifies that the "shortage" on a car-load of grain from Chicago to that city "varies from ½ to 10 per cent.; 1 to 3 per cent. not uncommon." * * Thefts along the line, and from railroad lighters, have not been of unfrequent occurrence. As bills of lading are usually given "quantity unknown," there is less responsibility, and doubtless less care, on the part of the men in charge than if the road had become liable for "quantity." In answer to a question from Senator Sherman, the witness replied, "I mean to say this, that a shortage of 10 per cent. has occurred without any ability to trace it, in several instances; but 1 to 3 per cent. is not uncommon." (Evidence, p. 302.) Mr. Hickok and other members of the New York produce exchange, corroborated this statement. Assuming the average shortage to be 2 per cent., it amounts to a loss of 3 cents per bushel on wheat when the market-price in New York is $1.50, a loss that falls wholly on the shipper from the western point. And as the western buyer knows by experience that the usual loss is from 1 to 3 per cent., and sometimes as high as 10 per cent., he will buy on a margin large enough to cover the greatest probable deficit. Hence the producer has to bear a loss even larger than the actual shortage. It may be said that a law compelling the carrier to receipt and account for quantity would render necessary an increased charge for transportation. This is doubted for two reasons: First, because the water-lines now account for quantity, and as the railways fix their prices in competition with the water-routes, they cannot, during the season of navigation, increase their prices. Second, the evidence taken by the committee shows that the rule of railway charges is "how much will the article bear," and as they usually put on *all it will bear*, when not in competition with water, it is likely that the effect of such a law would be to compel them to exercise greater care, instead of increasing the rate. But even if it should cause an increase of charges, the producer would then lose only the actual increased rate, instead of the undefined margin between 1 and 10 per cent. A congressional regulation of this kind would be peculiarly applicable to freight-lines, which are organized for the express purpose of carrying on inter-State traffic.

Having carefully considered the subject of direct congressional regulation of commerce among the several States when conducted upon railways, the committee are of the opinion that the assertion of such power by the national Government is of the utmost importance; that a remedy for some of the evils and defects of our railway system may be found through its present exercise; and that in the future complex relations likely to exist between railways and the public it may, and probably will, become indispensable. They are, however, forced to the conclusion that as a practical solution of the question of *cheap* transportation it is inadequate to meet the just demands of commerce, and that any attempt to work out the desired results through its agency would be to delude and disappoint the public. While they are of the opinion that under proper management many of the railways of the country could render a cheaper and more efficient service, and yet pay a liberal dividend upon an honest capital, the committee do not believe that, as they are now constructed, and under the present system of operating fast and slow trains on the same road, it is in their power, under any form of regulation that can be devised, to carry at rates low enough to answer the reasonable requirements for cheap commodities, produced at long distances from market. They therefore proceed to the consideration of the third general remedy suggested, namely:

3.—INDIRECT REGULATION AND REDUCTION OF CHARGES, THROUGH THE AGENCY OF ONE OR MORE RAILWAY LINES TO BE OWNED, OR CONTROLLED, BY THE GOVERNMENT.

It is proposed that the general Government shall own or control one or more railways, to be operated for freight-traffic exclusively, and at the lowest rate that will pay a reasonable return for the capital actually invested. This proposition proceeds upon the theory, that by reason of stock-inflations, extravagance and dishonesty in construction and management, and combinations among existing companies, the present railway-service of the country imposes unnecessary burdens upon its commerce; and that one or more railroads economically constructed, and operated, or controlled, by the Government in the interest of the public, would regulate all the others on fair business principles, remedy the abuses that now exist, check combinations, and thereby reduce the cost of transportation to reasonable rates. Its advocates recognize the fact, we have attempted to show, that competition among railways is unreliable, and daily becoming less effective. They insist that the only means of obtaining efficient and permanent competition, is through Government ownership, or control, of certain lines, with which combination will be impossible. The intelligence, numbers, and respectability of the advocates of this system of regulation entitle it to the most careful consideration. The committee regret that the data on which to base a conclusion as to its merits are not entirely satisfactory. They have earnestly addressed themselves to the inquiry in regard to the cost, capacity, and probable economical results to be anticipated from a road of this character, but, as no such railway exists in this country or elsewhere, they are unable to present answers to such inquiries, founded on practical results. The statistics furnished by actual railway operations in this country and in Europe, which will be presently presented, may, however, enable us to form a conclusion that will be of some value.

A MIXED BUSINESS INCREASES COST OF TRANSPORT.

It is urged that the present system of operating fast and slow trains on the same road, greatly increases the cost of transport, because of its interference with the movement of freight-trains, thereby causing great loss of time while waiting on side-tracks the passage of express trains. And that this cost is further increased by the high rate of speed which heavy freight-trains are compelled to make, between stations, in order to keep out of the way of express trains. The prevailing opinion among practical railroad operators is, that from eight to ten miles per hour is the most economical speed for freight-movement, but on account of the delays above mentioned, and the necessity of keeping out of the way of trains of a higher class, heavy freight-trains are often compelled to make twenty-five miles per hour. It is not easy to determine the enhanced expense caused by this interference, though it is doubtless considerable. The detention of freights resulting therefrom depends very much upon the amount of traffic on the particular road, and the regularity with which trains are run.

Mr. Isaac Hinckley, president of the Philadelphia, Wilmington and Baltimore Railroad, says that passenger-roads like the New York and

New Haven, and the Philadelphia, Wilmington and Baltimore Railroad, work at a great disadvantage in carrying freight, while a road like the Philadelphia and Erie works at great disadvantage comparatively, in carrying passengers, the latter being eminently a freight-road and the former passenger-roads. While it costs the Philadelphia and Erie per passenger 2.76 cents per mile, and for freights 1.86 cents per ton per mile, the cost per passenger per mile on the Philadelphia, Wilmington and Baltimore road is 1.92 cents, and the cost of freight 3.20 cents per ton per mile. (Evidence in postal-car investigation, page 71.)

Mr. H. D. Whitcomb, chief engineer of the Chesapeake and Ohio Railroad Company, expresses the opinion "that none of the leading railways are prepared to carry freight in large quantities or at a minimum cost. They are constructed for a mixed business, for slow and for fast trains, or rather they are constructed for fast trains, and, in some respects, such as in the inclination of the rails on curves, are not suited to slow trains. On a road, whether double or single track, doing a fair amount of business, freight-trains must be run at high rates of speed at intervals to clear the track for fast trains. This involves increased wear of machinery of the road and liability to accidents; the lighter loading of cars, or its equivalent heavier cars, thus increasing the dead weight. A large proportion of the expense of moving freight is due to the velocity with which it it is carried. Some expenses are in the proportion of the square of the velocity." A carefully-prepared statement, already quoted, from Mr. Albert Fink, vice-president of the Louisville, Nashville, and Great Southern Railroad, shows that "the cost of moving one gross ton per mile on a passenger-train is about twice as great as on a freight-train."

The schedule running-time for freights from Chicago to New York on the Pennsylvania line is ninety hours. (Evidence of Mr. Cassatt, p. 49.) On the New York Central line "freight-trains from New York to Chicago, if they make their proper connections, go through in eighty-four hours, allowing ample time for inspection of cars, and the transfers and taking the car-numbers at the different terminal points." (Evidence of Mr. Hayes, p. 13.)

This being the schedule-time on these leading lines, some idea of the delays incident to the present system of operation may be drawn from the following facts stated in a letter from Mr. Franklin Edson, president of the New York Produce Exchange, addressed to the chairman of the committee, under date of December 6, 1873. (Appendix, p. 176.)

"The time that goods are in transit from Chicago to New York by railway is from eight to ten days, and from that to fifteen and thirty days. If 30,000 bushels of grain are shipped from Chicago on any one day, destined to this city, a considerable portion, say a third, will be delivered in New York in eight and ten days, and the remaining portion may be anywhere from twelve to thirty days."

"Time-contracts for the transportation of property by rail are exceptional, and are, as a general rule, declined by the railway companies. The losses of property in transit by rail are frequent, a d especially so during the fall and winter months, when there is a pressure of business consequent upon the close of the water-lines by frost, and portions of shipments are not unfrequently a month or more in time of transit for long distances from interior points to this city. The time of the transit of property by rail from Buffalo to New York ranges from four to twenty days when tranported on the company's cars. Shipments of grain from Buffalo, to the extent of fifty cars or less by one shipper at one time, will, most of it, go through in four to five days, and the remaining portion will be probably eight, ten, twelve, fifteen, and twenty days. Shipments without this irregularity in time are the exception. The general rule is irregularity in transit, ranging, when transported on the cars of the railroad companies, from four to twenty, and even thirty days from Buffalo to New York. The larger portion of any one shipment from Buffalo is usually delivered in New York on the minimum time of four and five days, and the remaining portion of any one shipment of from twenty-five to fifty cars, irregularly in from eight to thirty days. The average time is, approximately, six to seven days, taking the whole of any one shipment of from twenty-five to fifty cars of freight."

If freights which should be carried in less than four days, on schedule time, are from eight to thirty days on the way, it is evident that the cost of such carriage is very largely increased by the present tardy and uncertain system.

CAPACITY OF A DOUBLE-TRACK FREIGHT-RAILWAY.

Opinions upon this point vary widely. Several authorities are submitted; Mr. Worcester (secretary of the New York Central Railway, evidence, pages 164, 165,) says "the practical capacity of a double-track road exclusively for freight is not yet fully ascertained. The theoretical capacity of such a line could be very easily stated, but the practical capacity depends on things that do not pertain entirely to the road itself. The theoretical capacity of a road might, in a general way, be said to be trains following each other at certain intervals uniformly during the twenty-four hours. That capacity could be very easily computed.

"Mr. CONKLING. What is your understanding of that?

"Mr. WORCESTER. The capacity of a road of that kind would be, I should say, enough to move 10,000,000 tons a year. I mean move and deliver or discharge that tonnage, taking the probable chances of blocks and accumulations. In other words, a road of that kind could be worked efficiently and effectively to that extent, when provided with the proper amount of equipment.

"Mr. CONKLING. That would be trains running how often each way?

"Mr. WORCESTER. About one hundred trains a day of twenty-five cars to a train.

"Mr. CONKLING. How many cars a day?

"Mr. WORCESTER. Two thousand five hundred cars. This estimate of tonnage is founded on what would be the actual freight in both directions. In round numbers we could send 2,500 cars from New York to Buffalo, and 2,500 cars from Buffalo to New York, but the cars going west could not run full loaded, and so the tonnage would, under any circumstances, fall below what the simple ability to move cars would indicate."

Mr. Hayes, general manager of the Blue Line, (evidence, pages 13, 14,) expresses the opinion that trains running at twelve miles per hour should not be permitted to run more frequently than once every fifteen minutes, and that "there would be no such necessity as that, because at the destination you could not handle the property." He thinks that including handling at terminals the practical capacity would not exceed a train for every thirty minutes. On the other hand, Mr. A. J. Cassatt, (general manager of the transportation department of the Pennsylvania Central Railroad, evidence, page 48,) in answer to the question, "How frequently could trains run in your judgment upon an exclusively freight road?" says, "I do not think you could run them closer than every fifteen minutes, on an average, throughout the twenty-four hours. We run our freight-trains in sections, with five minutes between each train; that is to say, we run from six to twelve trains, or sections, as we call them, on one schedule; but I do not think you could run trains closer, on an average, for twenty-four hours, than fifteen minutes apart, in each direction, on a double-track road, because if you did the slightest detention here or there would block everything back; you must make allowances for necessary delays and detentions.

"The CHAIRMAN. Would you not have to make an allowance for time to repair your track?

"Mr. CASSATT. That would be included in the fifteen minutes. I think you could run about one hundred trains a day, in each direction."

Mr. H. D. Whitcomb, chief engineer of the Chesapeake and Ohio Railroad Company, in a letter to the chairman of this committee, says:

"Suppose the repairs occupied one-half the time, and that the trains were kept five minutes apart, and that a road constructed between the Ohio and the Atlantic, as is entirely practicable, with a maximum grade going eastward of 20 feet per mile, the load of an ordinary locomotive would be three hundred and twelve tons net, or say thirty-one cars; at eight miles per hour there would be six and a half minutes between one locomotive and the next—nine trains an hour, or in one-half of twenty-four hours one hundred and eight trains, or in three hundred and twelve days 10,782,720 tons in one direction. On such a road, doing a maximum business, I believe freight could be carried at one-half the cost per ton that the maximum business is now carried on for on existing roads, that is, where the slow trains are necessarily interfered with by fast trains."

The committee therefore deem it safe to assume that the capacity of such a road is from eight to ten millions of tons each way, which may be very considerably increased by the adoption of the English block-system.

Economical results to be anticipated.

The cost of transportation by a railroad of this character involves so many unknown conditions, that any estimate of its probable economical results must be, to a considerable extent theoretical, and yet we think the data exists from which a reasonably correct conclusion may be drawn. A paper submitted to the committee by Mr. W. C. Kibbe, of the Continental Railway Co., (Appendix, page 153,) contains some valuable statistics, and an elaborate estimate on this point. Its computations are based upon a first class, steel-rail, double-track railroad, from Council Bluffs, Iowa, to New York City, 1,224 miles in length, estimated to cost when fully equipped $225,000,000, with grades not exceeding 30 feet to the mile going eastward, and 40 feet to the mile going west. The maximum curves are estimated to be 4°, or upon a radius of 1,433 feet, and the maximum speed of trains ten miles per hour, or, including stoppages, two hundred miles per day. Assuming that one hundred trains of thirty cars each, fully loaded, start daily each way from a given point on the first eight hundred miles from the sea-board, and fifty trains each way upon the western division of the road, there would be one thousand trains moving in both directions upon the road at all times, and the annual capacity would be 9,090,000 tons each way. Estimating the rate at six mills per ton per mile, on a tonnage of the same relative proportions in both directions, as actually existed in 1872 on the Erie, Pennsylvania, and Philadelphia and Reading Railroads respectively, and the various items of expenditure as reported by those companies, the financial results to be anticipated from a double track freight-railway, performing the amount of business above named, are stated as follows:

Expenses and earnings compared.

Interest account.—Estimated cost of road, including all stations and grounds, machine-shops, water-tanks, and all property and appliances appurtenant to the realty, $175,000,000, as follows:

Five per cent. interest on $87,500,000, first mortgage bonds.	$4, 375, 000
Eight per cent. dividend on $87,500,000, capital stock	7, 000, 000
Seven per cent. interest on $50,000,000, equipment bonds..	3, 500, 000
To annual sinking fund	1, 000, 000
Total annual interest account, including dividend and sinking-fund	15, 875, 000

which would be a daily expense of $43,496, and divided among one thousand trains, would amount, per train per day, to $43.49 .*

* The above calculation is on the basis of starting, on the average, one hundred trains each way on first eight hundred miles from the seaboard, and fifty trains each way upon the western division of the road daily, which would give, on whole road, one thousand trains moving in both directions at all times. The number of trains per day will vary with the demands of business. This estimate gives the daily average for the entire year.

P. S.—The equipment will consist of 1,500 engines and 52,700 cars.

Labor account.—We compute labor of all classes, officers, agents, skilled and unskilled labor, required in all departments for operating, replacement, maintenance of way, rolling-stock, &c., at ten and two-sevenths men per mile of single track, making a total aggregate on this road of 36,000 men, which, at the average wages of $2.50 per day, would amount to $90,000 per day, and, on the foregoing basis, to $90 per train per day.*

Material account, other than labor—Rolling-stock.—The Philadelphia and Reading Railroad Company gives the cost of repairs of engines and tenders per mile run at 2½ cents, which, upon the basis of operation given for this road, would be as follows, viz:

Cost of repairs of engines and tenders per mile per day, (two hundred miles, at 2½ cents per mile)	$5 00
The same company gives the cost of repairs and replacements of coal and freight cars at 19.7 cents each per day, which would be, per train of 30 cars	5 91
Total cost per train per day	10 91

The Pennsylvania Central Railway Company gives the cost of repairs of engines and tenders for 1871 at 6.8 cents per mile run, which, at above comparison—2.9 cents for materials and 3.9 cents for labor—would give for a run of two hundred miles, as follows:

Cost of materials used for repairs of engines and tenders, per train per day	5 80
The same company gives, as cost of repairs of freight cars, 18.3 cents per day, which, for 30 cars, would give, per train per day	5 49
Total cost per train per day	11 29

We have estimated cost of materials used for repairs of rolling-stock, adapted to the business, and the manner of operating, at $6.50 per train per day; but, to be sure of covering fully this item of cost, we give it in this estimate, as per train per day, $13.

The design of the company is, by the construction of its special freight cars, while preserving the requisite strength, capacity, and durability, to greatly reduce the weight of its grain and other cars, thereby saving largely in dead weight to be hauled, over those now in use for similar purposes by other roads.

Material account other than labor—Roadway.—The Baltimore and Ohio Railway Company gives as the cost of materials for maintenance of way on that road, at $914,174.53 per annum, equal to $666.30 per mile which on Continental Railway would give per train per day $6.39.

The Pennsylvania Central Railroad Company gives as the total cost

* The number of men employed in all capacities on the New York Central Railroad and the Philadelphia and Reading Railroad is ten men per mile, and the average wages paid is about $2 per day upon all the trunk roads in the country.

of maintenance of way $2,330 per mile per annum, which, after deducting the cost of labor on above basis, would give as the cost of materials used on roadway account, applied to the Continental, as follows: Cost of materials per train per day, $9.77. We give this estimate per train per day $12.20.*

We estimate the cost of materials for maintenance of way, with steel rails, 107 tons per mile, at $120 per ton, to last fifteen years; which would give per train per day	$8 21
Ties, 2,600 per mile, to last six years, and to cost 60 cents each, would give per train per day	2 49
Total	10 70

Experience has demonstrated the fact that steel rails are much the cheapest that can be laid down.

The chief engineer of the Philadelphia and Reading Railroad in his report of January, 1873, says that of 3,350 tons of solid steel rails laid down on his road since 1867, less than 15 tons have been moved from the track; and those have been taken from places where the life of iron rails had been found not to exceed four months.

Train supplies.

Coal, ten tons per day, at $3.50	$35 00
Oil and waste per day	5 00
Water	1 00
Total	41 00

Recapitulation.

Interest account, per train per day	$43 49
Labor account, per train per day	90 00
Material, rolling-stock, per train per day	13 00
Material, roadway, per train per day	12 20
Train supplies, per train per day	41 00
	199 69

Total expenses per train per day of moving 300 tons 200 miles, $199.69.

The Philadelphia and Reading Railroad Company gives as cost of running a train carrying 520 tons a round trip of 190 miles at $157.55, not including maintenance of way and rolling-stock, at which rate 300 tons could be moved 200 miles for $95.64. Add interest, $43.49, maintenance of way, $12.20, and it makes $151.33, leaving a margin of $48.36 per day in our favor for taxes, damages, &c.†

* Both of the above roads are substituting steel rails for iron as rapidly as possible, and when this substitution is completed it will result in a large reduction of the cost of materials for maintenance of roadway.

† All the items for operating and replacements, given above, are believed to be largely in excess of what will be the actual cost on this road.

Earnings.—The earnings of a train of 30 cars carrying 300 tons two hundred miles per day, at 6 mills per ton per mile, is $360.

Cost of running a train, including all expenses of the road, is, according to above estimate, per day $199.69.

The bulk of the freight, however, upon an east and west trunk-road, being from west to east, it will be necessary to compute earnings and costs in both directions, taking two trains, one moving east, the other west.

The Erie Railway Company for 1872 gives their eastward tonnage at 675,285 tons; westward tonnage, 274,846 tons. This ratio on Continental Road, the train-earnings would be as follows, viz:

For eastward train	$360 00
For westward train	146 52
Total for two trains per day	506 52
Cost of two trains per day	399 38
	107 14
Surplus profits, after paying interest and dividends, per train.	53 57

The Pennsylvania Central Railroad Company gives their rate of tonnage 1,000 tons east to 286 west, which would give on Continental Road a surplus per train per day of $31.79."

This computation, it will be observed, is based upon the several items of expenditure of the leading railways to which it refers, and upon an assumed charge of 6 mills per ton per mile. The lowest "surplus per train per day," resulting from a proportion of east and west tonnage corresponding to that of the Pennsylvania Railroad, gives for a year an excess of receipts over all expenditures, including interest and dividends, of $9,950,000 (31.79 × 1,000 × 313 = $9,950,000.) Estimated upon the proportionate tonnage in both directions on the Erie Railway, the excess of annual receipts over all expenditures is $16,767,410. This would seem to be a large enough margin for ordinary contingencies. In order to test the accuracy of the above estimate of expenditures, the committee have adopted a basis of comparison entirely different from that therein assumed. The above being based upon the various items of cost for labor, material, supplies, maintenance, replacement of road, buildings, &c., ours upon comparison of the cost per train-mile, which in railway reports usually includes every kind of expenditure except interest and dividends. Deducting the daily interest account for each train ($43.49) from the total estimated daily expenditures, as stated above, we have the cost per train, $156.20 for two hundred miles, or 78 cents per train-mile. Is this an underestimate? The average expense per train-mile in Great Britain, in 1870, was about 60 cents; on the India railways, 111 cents; on the Grand Trunk Railway of Canada, 92 cents. On the Massachusetts railroads it ranged from 99 cents to $1.78, averaging $1.31. On the following roads the train-mileage and total expenditures are reported for 1872, in Poor's Manual, from which we deduce the cost per train-mile as expressed in the third column as follows:

Name of railroad.	Total train-miles.	Total expenditures, exclusive of interest and dividends.	Cost per train-mile.
New York Central and Hudson River	13,380,957	$13,764,673	$1 03
Erie	12,318,504	12,727,422	1 04
Lake Shore and Michigan Southern	13,477,534	11,473,031	85
Illinois Central	5,888,226	4,846,854	82

The expenses per train-mile given on all the above-mentioned roads are computed by dividing the entire expenditures (except interest and dividends) by the whole number of miles run by fast as well as slow trains. Now, if it be borne in mind that on account of the more expensive character of equipment, greater damage done to the road, more costly service required, &c., the cost per train-mile for a passenger-train is from 25 to 50 per cent. higher than for a slow freight-train, it will be seen that a very considerable reduction should be made in favor of the proposed freight-road.

And again, the average cost per train-mile reported in England, India, and elsewhere, includes the small as well as the great lines; and as the "constant expenditures" are the same whether one train or one hundred trains per day move over a given road, it is obvious that the expense per train-mile must be very much less where the train-mileage is large than where it is small. For instance, assuming that on a given railroad the "constant expenses" are $4,000,000 per annum, and all other expenditures, which depend upon the number of miles run, are 40 cents per train-mile, the decrease of expense per mile in proportion to the increase of train-mileage will be expressed as follows:

Expenses per train, dependent upon train-mileage. Per mile run.	Constant expenses per annum.	Train-mileage per annum. No. of miles run.	Expenses per train-mile.
40 cents	$4,000,000	1,000,000	$4 40
40 cents	4,000,000	2,000,000	2 40
40 cents	4,000,000	5,000,000	1 20
40 cents	4,000,000	10,000,000	80
40 cents	4,000,000	20,000,000	60

Another practical illustration will be found in the fact that while the cost per train-mile on the Lake Shore and Michigan Southern line was only 85 cents, the cost on Minnesota roads, where the traffic is comparatively small, averages $1.41. That low rates would create an immensely increased traffic, and that the increased train-mileage would in turn greatly decrease the expenses per train is apparent, because a large proportion of the expenses, such as interest, dividends, maintenance of road-bed, bridges, and ditches, and replacement of ties and other wood-work, are, as before stated, entirely independent of the amount of business performed. And the expenses affected by the additional train-mileage do not increase in the same proportion, but in a much lower ratio. This is well illustrated by Mr. Joseph D. Potts, president of the Empire Transportation Company, in a paper entitled "The Science of Transportation," read before the American Social Science Association at New York, October 28, 1869, in which he says:

"Expenses are reduced when the volume of tonnage movement increases. This is, indeed, the fundamental condition of cheap transportation. The forwarding of one letter by special messenger across the continent would cost hundreds of dollars; but if sent by the Government mails only three pennies. The cheap service by the latter is possible, because it simultaneously performs a like service for multitudes. Property movement is governed by the same law.

"To exemplify, contrast certain operations in 1868 of two roads: The New York and Harlem is one hundred and thirty-one miles long. The Philadelphia and Reading, including its Harrisburgh branch, is one hundred and forty-seven miles long, and is mostly double-tracked. The Harlem moved in the whole year 287,000 tons; the Reading, 3,600,000 tons of coal and 1,200,000 tons of merchandise. The Harlem moved 15,000,000 tons one mile; the Reading, 366,000,000 tons of coal and 45,000,000 tons of merchandise one mile. Note the financial results: On the Harlem the expense per ton per mile was 5.78 cents, and on the Reading for coal 1.08 cents. The Harlem charged the public an average price per ton per mile of 7.62 cents, but the Reading on coal only 1.74 cents." The latter probably made the most money.

General Herman Haupt, an engineer of large experience, states that in 1856 it was found by the department of transportation on the Reading Railway "that the expenses that would be increased by an increased tonnage constitute but 24 per cent. of the whole expense of the department, and the whole increased expense amounted to only .53 of a mill per ton per mile. In the department of maintenance of way, the only item seriously affected by an increase of tonnage was the wear of the rail." * * "The renewals of rails both on the Pennsylvania and the Reading Railway was found to be covered by one-third of a mill per ton per mile. Only 9 per cent. of the maintenance of way expenses was increased by increased tonnage, the other items remaining stationary."

Your committee are therefore of the opinion that a charge of 78 cents per train-mile is nearly, if not quite, sufficient to meet all the necessary expenditures, including interest and dividends, on an exclusively freight-road, operated at a low and uniform speed, and performing a business equal to that above assumed.

Estimating the probable financial results to be secured by such a road upon the basis of a charge of 7½ mills per ton per mile, instead of 6 mills, we may add to all the above-mentioned items of expenditure nearly 50 per cent., and still have an annual surplus of from six to sixteen millions of dollars. The same rate of charges would allow an expenditure of $1.15 per train-mile, without diminishing the annual surplus of receipts; or, the expenditures and traffic remaining as above estimated, a charge of 7½ mills per ton per mile would give an annual surplus of $33,000,000.

Advantages and disadvantages both political and economic.

The fallacy, if there be any, in the financial results just submitted, will probably be found in the assumption that a regular and uniform traffic as large as that supposed will be obtained throughout the year. The wheat-crop of the Mississippi Valley is usually harvested in July and August, the corn-crop in October and November, and the great movement to eastern markets is mainly in September, October, and November; but with reliable transportation facilities, at the rates named, during the winter months, we are inclined to believe that this movement would be much more evenly distributed throughout the year than at present. And again, the local development of mineral and agricultural products and manufacturing industries that would be created by a road carrying at 6 mills per ton per mile would also go far toward supplying it with a uniform and steady traffic. In a country so rich in resources of every kind, and containing a population so enterprising as our own, it is difficult to conceive the results that would be produced by a constant and reliable means of transportation at this low rate. Not only would the local traffic be developed to an extent not now dreamed of, but the products of the West would, in a short time, be more than quadrupled. Six mills per ton per mile would carry a bushel of wheat or corn from the Mississippi to New York for about 20 cents. The average cost for the last five years has been by rail about 50 cents per bushel, and by water and rail (rail to Chicago and water to New York) 40 cents. Decrease the distance from market one-half, as would be the effect of such a road, and the valley of the Mississippi will feed the world. The future products of her incomparably fertile fields, and her unnumbered millions of animals will supply an ample tonnage for all the channels of commerce that can be made. The capacity and wonderful growth of that country are well illustrated by the State of Minnesota. Thirteen years ago she imported her breadstuffs; to-day she is first among the wheat-growing States of the Union, and yet less than five per cent. of her land is improved. One-half of her rich prairies under cultivation would produce more wheat than was raised in the entire country in 1870. Minnesota is but one of many in the bright galaxy of States which stand ready to pour their inexhaustible treasures upon any channel of commerce that will afford the necessary facilities.

The effects of a reduction of charges upon the increase of railway traffic and profits are well illustrated in the history of the Belgian railways. A reference to table (Appendix, page 227) will show that from 1837 to 1851, inclusive, the state railways of Belgium were worked at a heavy annual loss ranging from $62,766 in 1851 to $1,264,175 in 1841, the average annual loss for the 14 years being $444,982, and the aggregate loss for that period $6,229,747. In 1855, with four hundred and four miles of railway operated by the state, the net profits reached $601,594; but in 1856 they had fallen off again to $325,663.

"The minister then commenced a system of special scales of low charges, and finding these successful in particular places and for particular commodities, the system was generally extended until the entire charges for goods traffic had been modified and considerably reduced, the chief characteristic of the charges being the introduction of the principle that the charge per league should decrease as the distance the goods were carried increased." (Irish commission, second report, p. 8.)

The table of charges, (Appendix, page 227,) shows the nature and extent of those charges on fourth-class goods. The effect of such reductions is shown in the steady increase of net profits to the state, rising from $62,766 in 1856 to $1,819,997 in 1864. During the 22 years from 1835 to 1856, inclusive, the total excess of expenditures over receipts on all the state railways amounted to $3,803,997, while during the eleven years, from 1857 to 1867, inclusive, (the period of reduced charges,) the aggregate net profits from the working of the state railways amounted to $13,661,365.

The total cost of the state railways in Belgium to the end of the year 1867 was £10,426,619, and the amount actually redeemed from the profits of their business up to the same date £1,970,889. Hence it appears that while the debt had increased during the first twenty-two years by the amount above stated, it was reduced during the following eleven years (while the railways were worked at reduced rates) 19 per cent.

The effects of reduced rates on the increase of traffic are stated, in 1865, by M. Vandersteckelin, minister of public works, as follows:

"These reductions were commenced in 1856, when the weight carried was 2,545,000 tons, and the receipts were £466,244, giving on the average about 3*s.* 8*d.* per ton. In 1864 the weight carried was 5,251,000 tons, and the receipts were £695,232, or nearly 2*s.* 8*d.* per ton.

"The increase of tonnage at the end of the eight years was therefore 2,706,000 tons, or 106 per cent. The increase of gross receipts was £228,988, or 49 per cent.

"It was necessary to expend capital during this period for the supply of additional rolling-stock, and in providing station and other accommodation for the increased traffic. This expenditure amounted to £1,243,120, the interest on which at the rate of 5 per cent. per annum is £62,160."

The minister sums up by saying that "in eight years the charges on goods have been lowered on an average 28 per cent.; that the public have dispatched 2,706,000 additional tons of goods; that they have economized upwards of £800,000 on the cost of carriage; and yet the public treasury has realized £231,240 profit after having paid the cost of working and the interest of additional capital." (Irish commission, second report, page 12.)

A further reduction made in 1864 was followed by still more remarkable results. In 1863 the tonnage carried on state railways was 4,479,000 tons; in 1866 it had risen to 6,533,000 tons.

A reduction of fares on the London and Brighton, England, in 1869 produced like results.

"In June, 1868, when the fares were raised, they carried 8,000,000 passengers; in 1869 they carried only 7,782,000, but that year the fares were reduced and they carried 8,891,000, the next year 9,970,000, and in 1872 they still progressed and carried another million passengers.

"When the fares were reduced in 1868 and 1869, the traffic receipts for the twelve months were £1,274,000, but in 1869 and 1870 they were only £1,283,000, showing during the twelve months during which the increased fares were in force an increase only of £9,000; in fact, practically, they had been stationary. Then they began to reduce the fares, and although it took some little time before that alteration produced an effect upon the traffic, still in the next twelve months, 1870 and 1871, the traffic increased by £37,000, bringing it up to £1,320,000 for the half year. Then the operations of the reduced scale got into full work and the result was that in the next two years the receipts increased from £1,320,000 to £1,520,000. In other words, when they increased the fares they did not increase the traffic; but when they reduced them they increased the receipts £100,000 a year for two years successively."

These experiences ought to suggest to railway managers the policy of relying upon a large business at low rates, rather than upon high rates on a small traffic. In no country in the world are the possibilities in this direction so great as in the United States, and we may add, nowhere is this policy so imperatively demanded. Their variety of soil, climate, and productions, their infinite diversity of labor and enterprise, the long distances which intervene between producers and consumers, all point to the necessity of cheap communication, and promise the richest rewards for its accomplishment.

It will be seen by reference to Appendix, page 228, that in Belgium fourth-class goods, corresponding substantially to the same classification in this country, are carried a distance of one hundred and fifty-five miles for .37 of a penny, which is the equivalent of 7.4 mills per ton per mile, *including terminals*. Estimating the terminal expenses at only 15 cents per ton, the actual transportation charge would be 6.4 mills per ton per mile.

It cannot be said that the cheap construction of the Belgian railways enables the state to work them at rates lower than can be afforded in the United States, for including equipment, the state railways cost nearly £24,000, or $116,000 per mile. (Statement of M. Fassiaux, appended to report of the commission of 1866.)

A first-class double-track railroad of the best steel rails between the Atlantic Ocean and the Mississippi River should not cost, with ample equipment, over $100,000 per mile. The difference in the necessary cost would nearly counterbalance the difference in the value of money in the two countries. The heavy cost of the Belgian railways is accounted for by the fact that interest was charged to capital account while the lines were under construction, and the investment was necessarily unproductive, and also by the fact that for the sixteen years in which the expenditures exceeded the receipts, the deficiency was paid by the treasury and charged against the railways. But, notwithstanding their heavy cost and the low rate of charges, they paid 5½ per cent. in 1858, 6½ per cent. in 1860, and 7 per cent. in 1870; 7 per cent. in that country being equal to 10 or 12 per cent. in the United States. Nor is the tonnage moved on the Belgian railways so exceptionally large as to enable them to carry at lower rates than can be afforded on a great trunk-line in the United States. In the year 1866, when the low rates were maintained and the net profits to the state were $1,009,396, the four hundred and ninety miles of railway operated by the state carried 6,533,000 tons of goods of all classes. In 1873 the Pennsylvania Railroad moved 7,844,778 tons, (exclusive of fuel and other materials for the company's use,) being 21,912 tons for each mile of the Pennsylvania road, against 13,332 tons for each mile worked by the government of Belgium. A first-class railroad from the Mississippi Valley to the Atlantic, devoted exclusively to freight and carrying at low rates, would undoubtedly have a tonnage very much greater than that of the Belgian railways, and as it would have the advantage of long distances, less cost of construction, and no interference from fast trains, we can see no reason why it should not carry very nearly as cheaply.

Whether, therefore, the probable economical results be estimated from the various items of expenditure on existing roads, or from a comparison of the cost of per train-mile on leading railways in this and other countries, or upon the basis of actual charges on the state roads of Belgium, your committee are forced to the conclusion that the reduction of freight-charges to 6 mills per ton per mile, on fourth-class goods, such as western cereals, is not beyond what may reasonably be anticipated from an exclusively freight-railroad economically constructed and managed. But, in order to cover all contingencies, the committee add 25 per cent., making the charge 7½ mills per ton per mile. This estimate is sustained by Mr. Hayes, a railway operator of large experience, who says: "By running a train every half hour on grades where you could run, say thirty or thirty-five cars, you might possibly reduce the charge to three-quarters of a cent per ton per mile; that is, by taking that amount of business. The increased business diminishes the cost per ton upon your expenditure for roadway very rapidly." (Evidence, p. 12.) The evidence is very conclusive that trains may be run as often as once every fifteen minutes or less, which would reduce the cost very considerably below Mr. Hayes's estimate.

In an address delivered in 1873, before the American Association of Engineers at Louisville, Ky., Mr. W. P. Shinn, formerly general freight-agent of the Pittsburgh, Fort Wayne and Chicago Railway, stated that freights have been taken from Chicago to New York at 7 mills per ton per mile, and he insisted that even at this rate the traffic was profitable.

The average charge for the transportation of wheat from the Mississippi River to New York, by rail, for the last five years, is $16.50 per ton, equal to 15.2 mills per ton per mile, or 50 cents per bushel. At 7½ mills per ton per mile the cost of transport would be $8.83 per ton, or 26 cents per bushel.

The successful operation of such a railway would compel existing lines to adopt substantially the same system and the same rates. Heretofore railway operators have generally studied how to make the largest profits out of a given amount of traffic. By this means they would be compelled to study the cheapest modes of transport and the largest possible increase of business. Instead of stock-inflations, for speculative purposes, and profits squandered on favorites, or in useless expenditures, they would be compelled to seek the extension and improvement of their facilities. Railway transportation is yet in its infancy. We have learned how to transport by rail, but not how to do it cheaply. Under the stimulus of a competition that neither bribery nor combination could remove, the business talent and inventive genius of the country would be taxed to their utmost to devise the cheapest possible modes of transportation. The possibilities in this direction are as difficult to estimate as our existing achievements would have been fifty years ago. Take, for instance, the one matter of "dead weight." A loaded car carries only the equivalent of its own weight, (ten tons of paying freight.) It is said by practical railway operators of the largest experience that an improvement in construction which shall make a car of nine tons carry eleven tons of freight will enable such car, if run two hundred miles per day, to make a greater annual profit from the one additional ton, at the rate of 1 cent per ton per mile, than the entire car now makes under the present system. This is cited merely as an illustration of what may be accomplished in one direction. There are many other ways, such as improvements in motive-power and roadway, in which the cost may be very greatly reduced, and we have no doubt will be, when the proper stimulus to the study of economy is applied. Believing that the great benefits above-mentioned, and many others, may be secured through the agency of a Government freight-railway, the committee proceed to inquire how it may be obtained. The answer to this question necessarily implies:

1. That the Government shall construct one or more new lines; or,

2. That it shall purchase, by agreement with the owners, one or more existing roads; or,

3. That one or more existing roads shall be taken for public use, paying just compensation therefor; or,

4. That a new line, or lines, shall be subsidized with conditions as to charges and management, and a reservation of the right to take pos-

session and operate it upon fair and equitable terms, in the event of failure to comply with such conditions.

Various methods of operating the proposed Government railway have been suggested, among which may be named:

1. Actual management by Government officers or trustees of both the roadway and traffic.

2. The Government to furnish the roadway, and corporations or individuals to operate it with their own locomotives, cars, &c.

3. The entire ownership and operation of the line to be in the hands of a corporation, but subject by its charter to the supervision and control of the Government both as to charges and management.

The construction, purchase, or condemnation for public use of the proposed line of railway involves an expenditure of from $75,000 to $100,000 per mile, depending upon the character of the country through which it passes, making an aggregate expenditure for a line from the Mississippi River to the seaboard, of from one hundred millions, to one hundred and twenty-five millions of dollars. The subsidy plan would require a guarantee of interest on a portion of that sum, the balance to be raised by the stockholders. The former requires much the larger immediate expenditure, though neither method necessarily involves the loss of a dollar by the Government or the least increase of taxation. If properly guarded in the charter, both methods may, we believe, be made to re-imburse the Government to the last penny, without danger of failure. Either would imply an increase of the nominal obligations of the Government, but, unlike an indebtedness created by war, this obligation would be coupled with the amplest means of repayment. The property for which the money would be expended would itself provide the revenue to meet the interest on the increased debt. So far from increasing taxation it would, as before stated, vastly reduce the transportation taxes now paid by the public, and, by the increase of value which it would give to the productive property of the nation, it would actually diminish the burthen of our present indebtedness. The public debt of a nation is large or small according to the proportion it bears to the public wealth. There are two methods of diminishing this further. One is by taxation for its payment, thereby crippling the industries of the people and retarding the growth of the country; the other is by developing its commerce and stimulating its products, thereby increasing its wealth and diminishing the percentage which the debt bears to the taxable property out of which it must be paid. Hence we conceive that a judicious expenditure for works calculated to cheapen and facilitate the internal trade of a great country like ours does not add to the taxation of the people, but actually diminishes their burdens.

The various proposed methods of management all range themselves under one or the other of the following divisions:

1. By the Government directly, through its own agents or trustees.

2. By a kind of copartnership between the Government and private

corporations, by which the former shall furnish a portion of the capital, and the latter conduct the business.

Both of these propositions have been objected to on account of the increase of Federal power and patronage they would give, and the temptations to corruption they would introduce. Let us examine briefly these objections. The copartnership plan would doubtless confer less power and patronage than the other; but, in the judgment of the committee, it would be less efficient, and more productive of corruption. The experience of our Government in copartnerships with private corporations has not been such as to commend them to public favor. Nor is there anything in the experience of other countries which gives assurance of reduced charges under this plan. The corrupting tendency of this system would be found in the swarms of adventurers who would seek the aid of Government for speculative enterprises and personal gain; and in the fact that it would separate the ownership from the control of the property. The thing regulated would inevitably seek to control the regulator, and in a contest between private interest and the good-natured but somewhat slow-moving giant, known as the public, (where both are associated in the same enterprise,) seldom results in favor of the latter.

The next inquiry suggested is, are the real dangers to be apprehended from Government ownership greater than the evils existing and to be anticipated from the centralization of corporate power through railway combinations? If we take the only parallel illustration that can be drawn from experience in this country—the transmission and distribution of the mails by the Post-Office Department—we find nothing to excite our apprehensions. Though the employés of that Department are numbered by tens of thousands, and scattered throughout every part of the country; though they not only handle the money of the people by millions, but are also charged with the transmission of their business and political secrets, yet it is safe to say that since the origin of the Government no branch of the public service has given more satisfaction or been less tainted by corruption. Its intimate relations with the public cause it to be guarded with the utmost vigilance, and the people are less tolerant of malfeasance there than in any other department of the Government. So, too, the people's railway, if one should be constructed, would be so directly and intimately connected with the interests of the public that every dereliction of duty, or evidence of corruption, would be followed by the most speedy and condign punishment. No administration would venture to abuse a trust so sacred, whatever it might be guilty of in other matters.

But if it be true that consolidation is the natural and inevitable law of railway development, which no efforts thus far have been able to countervail, we may be compelled to choose between unlimited centralization of power in the hands of private corporations, and a limitation of that power through governmental interference. If power is to be measured by the wealth and patronage it controls, some conception may be formed of the vast influence wielded by the railway corporations of the country, from the fact that in 1872 their aggregate capital amounted to $3,159,423,057, and their gross revenues to $473,241,055. The wealth of these corporations is about equal to the entire wealth of the nation in 1840, and their revenues exceed the total revenues of the General Government by $151,063,382. In the matter of taxation, there are to-day four men representing the four great trunk-lines between Chicago and New York who possess, and who not unfrequently exercise, powers which the Congress of the United States would not venture to exert. They may, at any time, and for any reason satisfactory to themselves, by a single stroke of the pen reduce the value of property in this country by hundreds of millions of dollars. An additional charge of five cents per bushel on the transportation of cereals would have been equivalent to a tax of $45,000,000 on the crop of 1873. No Congress would dare to exercise so vast a power, except upon a necessity of the most imperative nature; and yet these gentlemen exercise it whenever it suits their supreme will and pleasure, without explanation or apology. With the rapid and inevitable progress of consolidation and combination, those colossal organizations are daily becoming stronger and more imperious. The day is not distant, if it has not already arrived, when it will be the duty of the statesman to inquire whether there is less danger in leaving the property and industrial interests of the people thus wholly at the mercy of a few men, who recognize no responsibility but to their stockholders, and no principle of action but personal and corporate aggrandizement, than in adding somewhat to the power and patronage of a government directly responsible to the people and entirely under their control.

The advocates of governmental ownership, recognizing the fact that there is a strong feeling in this country against intrusting Federal officials with any more power and responsibility than is absolutely necessary, have suggested the following among other means of obviating this difficulty:

1st. That the States through which the road shall be located shall appoint directors who shall have entire control over its operations, under general regulations of rates and charges to be prescribed by the Government. It is supposed that as these States will be most directly benefited, they will be most careful to see that the best men are selected And as the board thus chosen would have the appointment of officers and employés, no additional power would be conferred on the Federal Government.

2d. The contract system. This would be carried out by the Government owning the roadway, and permitting private persons or corporations to operate it upon terms prescribed by the Government, both as to superintendence and tariffs. By this method not only the tolls, but the tariff-sheets for the transportation of goods, could be prescribed.

The companies or individuals operating it would derive their compensation either from a certain percentage on the gross receipts, or from a certain fixed sum per ton per mile, as might be agreed upon. Under this system the Government will be absolute owner of the property for which the money is paid, and thus many of the evils incident to joint ownership, or copartnership, will be avoided. In this way there would be but a slight increase of Federal patronage, and the traffic might still be managed by independent companies. But as it would be exceedingly difficult, if not impossible, to prevent combinations among the operating companies, it may be doubted whether this system would be any more effectual than the present one in securing and maintaining the desired competition among carriers.

But it is argued by the opponents of the Government railway scheme, that it must fail for want of feeders from which to draw its traffic; that the existing roads would combine against it, and so adjust their tariffs as to prevent its receiving business, except from the country in immediate proximity to its line. Should this be attempted we think the remedy would be readily found. Congress might by law provide for "running powers," whereby the Government line should be open, upon fair and proper terms, to the cars of all other lines connecting with it, and the cars of the Government road should have similar rights on such connecting lines, upon terms to be settled by agreement, or in case of a failure to agree, upon payment of just compensation to be ascertained by a commission appointed for the purpose by the proper court. In cases to which the power of Congress to regulate does not extend, the legislature of the State can be relied upon to make the necessary provisions for such "running powers." This could hardly be called a very great stretch of constitutional power, for as these roads have themselves taken the property of private citizens for a public use, they cannot complain if the partial use of their property be in turn taken for the same purpose. The objection we have before mentioned to "running powers" under our existing system, viz, that such a regulation would tend to a more general combination among railways, does not apply to this case, because combination with the Government line would be impossible. Nor would such power be used for the purpose of injuring weaker lines.

Its opponents also urge the two not very consistent objections, viz:

First. That such a road could not be made to pay the interest on its cost, and hence the Government would suffer loss; and,

Second. That it would be unfair for the Government to enter into competition because it would injure honest stockholders in private corporations. In the same breath it is said that the Government could not manage it, without greater cost to the public, than roads are now operated by private corporations, and yet that it would introduce a competition that would prove ruinous to the latter.

We submit that neither of these objections is well founded, nor are they supported by the experience of other countries. The cheapest transportation in the world, as we have already shown, is afforded under government management. The only country that has fairly tested the principle of state competition disproves the assertion that state roads are more expensively and less efficiently managed than those under the control of private corporations.*

This brings us to the consideration of the practical results, in the matter of transportation charges, attained under the several systems we have discussed. Great Britain may represent the system of direct governmental regulation, without financial aid or copartnership; France, the system of financial aid and copartnership, with the most rigid surveillance and regulation; Belgium, the system of indirect regulation of the whole, through state ownership and management of a part, and entire non-interference with the private corporations, except in matters of safety and police. The following statement shows the charges per ton per mile on fourth-class goods on the leading roads in each of said countries for the distances named:

GREAT BRITAIN.

	Cent.
On the London and Southwestern and London and Northwestern Railways, for 192 miles, per ton per mile	3.16
On the Great Northern Railway, for 155 miles, per ton per mile	4.4
On the Great Northern, London, Chatham and Dover Railways, for 198 miles, per ton per mile	4.5
On the Great Northern, North Eastern, North British, and Highland Railways, for 594 miles, per ton per mile	1.98

FRANCE.

On the line between Paris and Orleans, for all distances over 186 miles, per ton per mile	1.74

BELGIUM.

On the Belgium State Railways, for all distances over 155 miles, per ton per mile	.74

* The experience obtained in Belgium of the working by the state of at least a portion of the railways existing in that country, is entirely in favor of that system. The lines worked by the state have been most successful financially, and are also those kept in the best order, and the working of which gives the greatest satisfaction to the commercial world and the public in general, as regards regularity of conveyance, cheapness of transit, and the comfort of travelers.

The state not being solely guided by the prospect of financial gain, but having constantly in view the interest of the public which it represents, is in a better position than private companies to introduce all desirable improvements, not only as regards the efficient performance of the service, but also as respects the cost of conveyance, without, however, altogether disregarding the increase of revenue which its operations may bring into the public treasury.

The state railways thus find themselves placed in constant comparison with the railways worked by private companies, on the one hand, stimulating them to general improvements; and on the other, acting as a sort of check against any attempt to realize extravagant profits at the cost of the public."—(Memorandum of C. A. Fasesiaux, Director-General of Belgian Posts, Railways, and Telegraphs. Royal Commission on Railways, Appendix M.

The remarkably low rates in Belgium furnish a powerful argument in favor of State ownership, and also in confirmation of the principle that *cheap* transportation is to be obtained only through *competition* under governmental control.

IV.—THE IMPROVEMENT OF NATURAL AND CONSTRUCTION OF ARTIFICIAL WATER-WAYS.

Under this fourth and last of the general remedies proposed the committee will consider the improvement and construction of water-routes between the interior and the sea-board, and the relative importance of each.

The investigations of the committee having led to the conclusion that the practical and substantial relief demanded by the public is to be found only in a Government freight-railway, or in the improvement and construction of water-channels, they have given to both of these subjects most earnest and careful consideration. Their conclusions with reference to the former are already stated. The investigation of the latter subject having been especially indicated by the Senate resolution under which they were appointed, the committee have devoted to it much more time and labor than to any other branch of their inquiries. They have personally inspected portions of nearly all the principal existing and proposed water-routes, and taken full and detailed testimony in regard to them, which will be found in the Appendix and the volume of evidence herewith submitted. As the evidence is somewhat voluminous, the committee have carefully grouped the facts relative to each route under their appropriate titles.

The investigations of the committee in regard to the various existing and proposed water-lines between the interior and sea-board embrace the cost of construction and improvement of such routes; their known or supposed commercial advantages; the cost of transport upon them; and such other facts as appear to have an important bearing upon the question of their relative importance as highways of commerce.

The deductions of the committee in regard to these lines are based upon the information embraced in the evidence and other papers accompanying this report, and upon official documents and other reliable sources of information. The several routes will be described in geographcal order, beginning with the most northerly one, as follows:

1st. The northern lake and canal route, embracing the lakes and New York and Canadian canals.

2d. The James River and Kanawha Canal.

3d. The Atlantic and Great Western Canal.

4th. The Mississippi River.

The committee have also instituted inquiries in regard to the following works:

The Niagara Ship-Canal; the Wisconsin and Fox River Canal; the

Illinois Canal; the Hennepin and Rock Island Canal; the improvement of the rivers between Lakes Huron and Erie; the improvement of the Ohio and other navigable tributaries of the Mississippi River; the Chesapeake and Ohio Canal, the Florida Ship Canal, and the canals of Pennsylvania.

These routes and parts of routes are delineated on the map, which may be found at the end of the appendix.

THE NORTHERN ROUTE, EMBRACING THE LAKES AND THE NEW YORK AND CANADIAN CANALS.

The merits of the various existing and proposed canals between the lakes and the seaboard at Montreal and at New York will be clearly appreciated by presenting them under a comparative statement, and by treating of the characteristics and advantages of each line separately.

The inauguration of the canal-systems of the State of New York and of Canada antedates the history of railroads.

The construction of the canals of Canada began in the year 1821, and was continued, for some years, with no other purpose than that of opening avenues for internal communication between the different sections of that colony. But the development of the resources of our Northwestern States consequent upon the opening of the Erie Canal, in the year 1826, soon led to the adoption of an extended system of improvements designed to compete for the rapidly-increasing commerce of that section of our country. That competition is more active to-day than ever before, and it constitutes an important feature in the question as to the best mode of transporting the surplus products of the West to the seaboard and to foreign countries. The spirit of enterprise which has characterized the province of Canada in the inauguration and construction of her canal-system has not been surpassed in boldness and persistent energy by those efforts which carried to successful completion the canal-system of New York, and which have made that State the first in the American Union in population and in wealth, and her chief sea-port, New York, the commercial and financial metropolis of the western world.

Immediately after the union of the provinces of Upper and Lower Canada, in 1840, when the total population was a very little more than one million, and the total revenues of the united provinces amounted to only $1,488,000, the legislature of Canada appropriated no less a sum than $2,000,000 for the construction of the Welland and Saint Lawrence Canals, and thus formally inaugurated the policy of opening the trade of our Western States to her chief sea-port, Montreal. At the present time there are fifteen canals in Canada, whose aggregate length is two hundred and seventeen and a half miles. These works, excepting the Rideau Canal, and the improvements of the Ottawa River have been constructed by the Canadian government, at a cost of $22,000,000. This sum includes the cost of improving the harbor of Montreal, also the cost of improving the Saint Lawrence between Montreal and Quebec, at a cost of $1,347,018, by means of which the draught of vessels navigating this part of the river has been increased from 11 to 20 feet.

The Rideau and Ottawa Canals were constructed at an early date by the British government, as a means of military defense, at a cost of $4,280,000.

The estimated cost of the works now projected, or in course of construction, amounts to $13,550,000. These works embrace the enlargement of the Welland and Saint Lawrence Canals for the passage of vessels of 1,000 tons from the ports on the upper lakes to Montreal without breaking bulk, and the deepening of the channel of the river below Montreal from 20 to 24 feet in depth, so as to admit the passage of steamers of 3,500 tons.

In this connection it may be mentioned that there have been constructed in Canada by private capital three thousand four hundred and fifty miles of railroad, at an estimated cost of $137,000,000.

The Canadian canals were opened for western trade in 1848, and their commercial results have fully met the expectations of their projectors. Not only have they enabled Canada to secure a share of the commerce of our Northwestern States, but the agricultural and commercial progress of the provinces of Ontario has not been surpassed by that of those States. The population of Ontario increased from 952,000 in 1851 to 1,620,851 in 1871. In 1851 Ontario raised 12,000,000 bushels of wheat; in 1861 the production had increased to 25,000,000 bushels.

The population of Montreal has increased as follows: In 1851, 57,715; in 1861, 91,159; and in 1871, 107,245. Statistics showing the growth of the commerce of that port may be found on page 79 of the appendix.

The following is a description of the works which have been constructed and which are projected in order to form continuous water-lines of transport between the eastern extremity of Lake Erie and the seaboard at Montreal and New York:

THE WELLAND CANAL AND SAINT LAWRENCE ROUTE.

The Canadian canals embrace the Welland Canal from Port Colborne, on Lake Erie, to Port Dalhousie, on Lake Ontario, forming a navigable route around the Falls of Niagara, and the six canals around rapids in the Saint Lawrence River, viz: the Gallops Canal, the Rapide Plat Canal, the Ferrans Point Canal, the Cornwall Canal, the Beauharnoris Canal, and the Lachine Canal. These latter are generally known as "the Saint Lawrence canals." A tabular statement showing the length and dimensions of these canals may be found on page 231 of the Appendix. The locks of the Welland Canal determine the size of vessels which can pass from Lake Erie to Lake Ontario. They are 150 feet long, 26½ wide, and 10¼ deep, and admit the passage of vessels of 500 tons burden, or of a capacity of 18,000 bushels of wheat. The Saint Lawrence canals have locks 200 feet long, 55 feet wide, and 9 feet deep, admitting the passage of vessels of 700 tons. The width of the Welland Canal at the surface varies from 58 to 110 feet, and the width of the Saint Lawrence canals at the surface vary from 90 to 150 feet. All these canals were devised by the best engineering skill, and they are constructed in the most thorough manner.

It is found that on the Welland it requires about 20 minutes, on the average, to pass a boat through each lock. There being only a single line of locks, the greatest number of vessels which can be passed eastward in a day is 36. The maximum capacity of vessels admitted being 500 tons, it appears that the ultimate annual capacity of the Welland Canal during the average season of 246 days amounts to 8,856 vessels, of an aggregate tonnage of 4,428,000 tons, both eastward and westward. During the year 1870 the total tonnage movement eastward amounted to 1,315,967 tons, or 30 per cent. of the capacity of the canal, upon the basis of the above computation.

The business of the Welland Canal has remained nearly stationary for several years, as appears from the following table of tonnage passing in both directions for a number of years:

	Tons.		*Tons.*
1860	2,182,593	1866	2,057,532
1861	2,348,155	1867	1,927,198
1862	2,495,774	1868	2,402,187
1863	2,637,479	1869	2,462,201
1864	2,479,559	1870	2,631,935
1865	2,003,883		

That the business of the Welland Canal has not very materially increased is undoubtedly due to the fact that a large proportion of the vessels built on the upper lakes during the last ten years are too large to pass through the locks of the present canal. The Welland Canal is now being enlarged so as to admit the passage of vessels of 1,000 tons, carrying about 50,000 bushels, or three times the capacity of vessels which can now pass through its locks. By the present mode of transport from lake-ports to Montreal, lake-vessels go no further than Kingston, at the head of the Saint Lawrence River. At that port grain is transshipped into barges, which are towed down the Saint Lawrence, and through the Saint Lawrence canals to Montreal, and there again transferred into ocean-vessels.

A difference of opinion exists as to the policy of enlarging the Saint Lawrence canals to the same size as the enlarged Welland Canal. Persons of large practical experience believe that the present barge system on the Saint Lawrence is more economical than would be the direct shipment of grain from Chicago and Milwaukee to Montreal in lake-vessels. The time required in the passage of barges through the canal is about the same as would be required for the passage of lake-vessels. The speed on this part of the route being very much less than on the lakes, it is believed that if lake-vessels were to continue their voyages to Montreal, the loss occasioned by a reduced number of round voyages during the season of navigation would greatly exceed the extra cost of transshipment at Kingston, amounting to only half a cent per bushel.

THE PROPOSED CAUGHNAWAGA AND CHAMPLAIN SHIP-CANAL ROUTE.

This route, from Lake Erie to New York, embraces the present Welland Canal, Lake Ontario, the Saint Lawrence River and canals to the village of Caughnawaga, eight miles above Montreal; a canal from Caughnawaga to Saint John's, on the Richelieu River; the Richelieu River and Lake Champlain to White Hall, New York; a ship-canal from White Hall to Fort Edward, on the Hudson River; slack-water navigation on the Hudson River from Fort Edward to Troy, and thence by the Hudson River to New York City.

It is proposed that the canal sections of this route shall have a breadth of 150 feet at the surface, 100 feet at the bottom, and a depth of 13 feet, the locks to be of the same dimensions as those on the enlarged Welland and Saint Lawrence Canals, viz: 270 feet long, 45 feet wide, and 12 feet deep, admitting the passage of lake-vessels of 1,000 tons, or 35,000 bushels capacity, from ports on the upper lakes to New York City.

The works to be constructed on this line are the Caughnawaga Canal from the Saint Lawrence to the Richelieu River, the enlargement of the present Champlain Canal from White Hall to Fort Edward, and the work involved by the slack-water navigation on the Hudson River from Fort Edward to Troy.

The length of the Caughnawaga Canal will be twenty-nine miles, and it will have but three locks, the total lockage being 29 feet. It is estimated that this work will cost about $3,000,000.

The artificial water-way from Lake Champlain to Troy will be sixty-five miles in length, of which twenty-five will be canal and forty miles slack-water navigation.

No computations have yet been made to determine the cost of a work of this size; but from the results of a former survey for a canal of smaller dimensions, it is roughly estimated that the entire work from Lake Champlain to the Hudson River at Troy will cost about $8,000,000. No estimate has been made of the probable cost of deepening the channel below Troy.

There is no doubt as to the abundance of the water-supply upon this line. The total length of the route from Chicago to New York will be one thousand six hundred and forty-four miles, of which one hundred and twenty-one miles will be canal, forty miles slack-water, and one thousand four hundred and eighty-three miles lake and river navigation. There will be on the line seventy-one locks, and the total lockage will be $736\frac{8}{10}$ feet.

The Caughnawaga Canal lies wholly within the territory of Canada. The Canadian parliament has heretofore refused to make this a government work, believing that its construction would not be conducive to the growth of Canadian commerce via Montreal. A charter for the construction of the canal has, however, been granted to a private corporation, of which Hon. John Young, of Montreal, is president. The term for which the charter was granted has not yet expired.

It is the opinion of this committee that government ownership and control of a canal is the only sure guarantee of free competition and cheap transportation upon it, and that such ownership and control can best secure the least possible charges for tolls, and the greatest possible exemption from delays and inconveniences affecting the value of a great navigable highway of commerce. This opinion appears to be fully sustained by practical results on the Erie Canal and on other canals in this country. The commercial and financial success of the policy pursued by the State of New York, in not only constructing but in retaining the ownership and control of her canals, has fully demonstrated the wisdom of that policy.

The spirit of liberality which has always been manifested by the Canadian government in according to American vessels like privileges with Canadian vessels upon her canals; the low rates of toll which have always prevailed, and the manner in which her canals have been constructed and managed, also sustain the committee in the view here expressed in regard to government ownership and control of canals, and increase their regrets that the Dominion government has not regarded the construction of the Caughnawaga canal with more favor. Whatever may be the value of this route as compared with others hereinafter named, there can be no doubt that it would form the cheapest possible line of transport between the Western States and the ports of New England on Lake Champlain. Upon the opening of the Caughnawaga Canal, a depot of supplies for nearly all of New England would probably be established at Burlington, or at some other point on Lake Champlain. These supplies could be brought from the West to Lake Champlain during the season of open navigation and stored for fall and winter distribution. From this point the New England markets could be supplied by means of direct and cheap railway transport.

The committee believe that upon the completion of the enlargement of the Welland and Saint Lawrence canals, and the construction of the Caughnawaga Canal, wheat and corn can be transported from ports on Lakes Superior and Michigan to Burlington, Vt., for 12 cents per bushel, and that the average cost of distribution by rail from the latter point to the consumers of New England need not exceed 10 cents per bushel, making the entire cost of transportation 22 cents per bushel. The average freight-charge during the last five years by rail from Chicago to Boston has been about 39 cents per bushel.

During the year 1872 the New England States received from the Western States 41,132,225 bushels of grain. Almost all of this immense supply was transported by rail. Assuming the average rail charge to be 37 cents, the saving in the cost of transport by the northern water-line would be 15 cents per bushel, and the total saving upon the quantity of grain above mentioned would have amounted to $6,169,834 in the year 1872.

The opening of the Caughnawaga route would not only afford cheap water-transport, but also the reduction on rates of rail-transport which such competition would induce. Reciprocal trade relations with the Dominion of Canada would introduce a strong element of competition, which, with the other causes named, would probably reduce transportation charges to the lowest practicable limits. It may be said that the remission of duties on wheat and corn imported from Canada would operate injuriously to the western producer. Without entering upon a discussion of the tariff question, the committee are of the opinion that such result need not be apprehended. As already shown, the effect of existing duties is to diminish Canadian competition on the lakes, and thereby to increase the cost of transport. That these duties are no protection to the western farmer is shown by the fact that Canada produces but little more of breadstuffs than she consumes, and only competes in our markets with wheat of a grade superior to the great bulk of American grain. The effect of the existing duties, so far as New England is concerned, is to shut her off from cheap water-transport, and to compel her to rely almost wholly upon the railways.

The proposed Caughnawaga Canal being entirely within the Dominion of Canada, of course the committee can make no further recommendations in regard to it, but they would express the hope that the future trade relations between the United States and the Dominion government may be so adjusted that the construction of this work may be found to be in the interest of both countries. The committee also express the hope that the State of New York will recognize the expediency of continuing this line by way of the Champlain Canal and the Hudson River to the city of New York, or, in the event of the State declining to enter upon the work, that the United States Government shall give the subject that attention to which its manifest merits entitle it. A detailed statement of the advantages of this route and the probable reduction in transportation charges to be effected by its construction, has been presented in a paper prepared by Hon. John Young, of Montreal. (See Appendix, page 136.)

THE ONEIDA LAKE ROUTE FROM OSWEGO TO TROY.

It is proposed to construct a canal from Oswego to Troy, N. Y., via Oneida Lake, for steam-barges carrying 25,000 bushels and barges in tow of such steamers carrying 28,000 bushels. The distance by this route from Oswego to Troy is one hundred and ninety-one and one-half miles, of which one hundred and sixty-eight and one-half miles is canal, the remaining twenty-three miles being through Oneida Lake.

Hon. William J. McAlpine, civil engineer, estimates that the work will cost $25,000,000, this estimate being for a canal 140 feet wide at the surface, and 120 feet at the bottom, and 10 feet deep, the locks being 185 feet long, 29 feet wide, and 9 feet deep. There will be sixty-eight locks on the line, with a total lockage of 609 feet.

It is estimated by Mr. McAlpine that the time of transporting grain from Oswego to New York will be reduced from six days, by the present Oswego and Erie Canal, to 2.63 days by the proposed Oneida Lake Canal, and that the cost of transport from Oswego to New York by the proposed route will be only 2.7 cents per bushel.

The report of Mr. McAlpine to the Oswego Board of Trade, containing a very full and elaborate statement of the advantages of this route, will be found in the appendix, page 101. Mr. McAlpine's long experience and high reputation as an engineer, and his thorough knowledge of the canal system of New York, entitle his statements to great consideration. He expresses the opinion that of all the existing or proposed water-routes through the State of New York, this one offers, all things considered, the greatest advantages, and promises the best results. Full information as to the reasons for this opinion may be found in the report of Mr. McAlpine.

Prior to the year 1858 the depth of water upon the Saint Clair flats compelled the use of vessels of such limited size upon the upper lakes that all the vessels composing the lake-marine were able to pass through the Welland Canal. At that time about one-half the total quantity of grain shipped from the West to eastern markets was received at Oswego. The deepening of the water on the Saint Clair flats, however, led to the construction of vessels of much greater depth and length than had formerly been employed, such vessels being too large to pass through the locks of the Welland Canal. The cheaper transport of grain on the lakes in vessels of larger size of course diverted the trade from the Oswego route to the Buffalo route, and the result has been that the commerce of Buffalo has increased very much, while the commerce of Oswego has fallen off.

About five-sixths of the grain shipped from Chicago and Milwaukee and other lake ports is now transferred to canal-boats at Buffalo, or is shipped east by the New York Central or the Erie Railway. Of the total eastward movement of freight by canal in 1872, 1,845,598 tons were shipped from Buffalo, and 610,424 tons from Oswego; and of the total westward-bound tonnage delivered by canal at these points 146,413 tons were delivered at Buffalo, and 10,182 tons at Oswego.

The enlargement of the Welland Canal now in progress will admit the passage of vessels of 1,000 tons, or of twice the capacity of the largest vessels which can now reach Oswego. There appears to be no doubt that this enlargement will lead to a very considerable increase in the transport of grain from the West to the East via Oswego. The construction of the Oneida Lake Canal upon the enlarged dimensions stated would undoubtedly reduce the present cost of transport from Oswego to Albany and to New York, and largely increase the business of that line.

The geographical position of Oswego [near the eastern extremity of lake-navigation,] and the extensive water-power which is there employed in the manufacture of flour, are both important commercial features of the Oswego route, especially in view of the fact, hereafter shown, that the time required for the transport of grain from Chicago and Milwaukee to New York via the Caughnawaga route, the Oswego route, and the Buffalo and Erie Canal route, is so nearly equal.

THE ERIE CANAL ROUTE.

The Erie canal-route from Lake Erie to New York embraces the lakes from Chicago to Buffalo, the Erie Canal from Buffalo to Troy, and the Hudson River from Troy to New York. The Erie Canal has performed so important a part in the development of the resources of the country that a specific statement is deemed proper as to the commercial and financial success of the work.

The Erie Canal.

At the close of our war for independence the spirit of enterprise and of adventure in the original thirteen States looked toward the settlement of that vast and fertile domain extending from the Alleghanies to the Mississippi.

The canal was at that time the only artificial highway of commerce, other than common roads, known to the world. Four canals were projected, viz, The Erie Canal, the Pennsylvania Canal, the Chesapeake and Ohio Canal, and the James River and Kanawha Canal. The Erie Canal is the only one ever completed. The route of this canal was found to be particularly favorable, both in its topographical and geographical features. The Appalachian range, encountered by all the other lines, is pierced at West Point by the Hudson River, and the completion of the canal to Buffalo and Oswego formed a connecting-link between tidewater at Albany and the chain of inland seas which extend to the center of the continent.

The construction of the Erie Canal was begun in the year 1817, and it was opened to Buffalo in 1825 and to Oswego in 1828.

A survey of the line having been made, application for aid in its construction was made to Congress in the year 1811 through a commission consisting of Clinton, Morris, Fulton, and others.

The sum asked for was $8,000,000.

In consequence of the threatened war with Great Britain, Congress declined to make the desired appropriation at that time. The State of New York, unwilling to postpone the construction of a work of such vast importance, not only to herself, but to the country, embarked at once in the enterprise. Since that time the State has neither sought nor received any assistance in the construction of her canals either from the National Government or from any State.

The Erie Canal was at first constructed for boats of 76 tons, but the developments of its commerce having surpassed even the anticipations of its projectors, both greater capacity and cheaper transportation were soon demanded. These objects were attained by the enlargement authorized in 1835, and completed in 1862, by which boats of 240 tons were admitted, and the cost of transport was reduced one-half.

The theoretical capacity of the canal was at the same time increased from five million to sixteen million tons.

The financial results of the Erie Canal.

The auditor of the canal department of the State of New York reported to the constitutional convention of 1867, in relation to the financial condition of the Erie Canal, at the close of the fiscal year 1866, as follows:

Receipts from tolls, with interest	$181, 828, 604
Total expenditures for construction, maintenance, and repairs, with interest	140, 430, 953
Net profit from Erie Canal	41, 397, 651

It appeared, therefore, at the end of the fiscal year 1866, that this great artificial highway of commerce had refunded every dollar expended upon it, and yielded to the State treasury a surplus of $41,397,651. This amount had, however, been absorbed in the construction of the Champlain and the lateral canals, the cost of the construction and maintenance of which had exceeded the receipts from tolls by the sum of $48,871,643. The State, therefore, had not been re-imbursed for the total amount of money expended for canal purposes by the sum of $7,473,992.

From a statement made by the auditor to the legislature, dated March 20, 1873, it appears that, during the twenty-six years ending with the fiscal year 1872, the total receipts from the Erie and Champlain Canals amounted to $81,952,010; and that the total expenditures for superintendence, repairs, maintenance, damages, and collection amounted to $22,075,570; showing a net income of $59,876,440, or 73 per cent. of the gross income during the period mentioned.

The net annual profits realized in operating the Erie and Champlain Canals amounted to the sum of $2,302,940.

Tolls have generally been so graded as to provide for the maintenance and operation of the State canals, with provision for gradually refunding to the State the sums raised by taxation in aid of their construction.

It appears from the auditor's report for the year 1872 that 39 per cent of the total tolls on eastward-bound tonnage received during the thirty-six years ending with the year 1872 was paid on commodities the growth or product of the State of New York, and that during the same period only 24 per cent. of the tonnage arriving at tide-water consisted of commodities the growth or production of the State of New York.

Statement.

Tolls received from merchandise transported on the Erie Canal, 1837 to 1872, inclusive:

From the State of New York	$33, 914, 923
From other States	52, 805, 831

Statement.

Total tonnage arriving at tide-water:

	Tons.
From the State of New York	13, 365, 142
From other States	43, 444, 137

Commercial results.

The financial results of the Erie Canal are, however, of small moment in comparison with its commercial results, the grandest of any material enterprise of modern times. Connecting the ocean with the great lakes, which interlace the heart of the continent, it developed the possibilities of the most productive area on the face of the globe, the value of the merchandise transported on the canals to the end of the year 1872 having amounted to the enormous sum of $6,065,060,698.

Soon after the completion of the Erie Canal, the State of New York assumed the first rank among the States of the Union, in population and wealth, and her chief seaport, New York City, became within a few years the commercial and financial metropolis of the Western World.

The development of the Western and Northwestern States is also largely due to the construction of this great work, it having been the only avenue for the transport of freights to the Atlantic States until about the year 1850.

Since that period the business of the canal has gradually increased, but the commerce between the interior and the seaboard has increased far beyond its capabilities, and now a very large proportion of that commerce seeks the more rapid transit afforded by railways. The canal, however, serves a purpose quite as important as that performed by the railroads, it being the principal avenue of transport for the heavier classes of merchandise. The Erie Canal is, also, by virtue of the cheapness of transport upon it, a most valuable regulator of freight-charges on competing railways. The further reduction of the cost of transport on the canal, by means of an enlargement, becomes, therefore, a matter of national importance, bearing as it does upon the cost of transport between the interior and seaboard, both by water and by rail.

Although the State of New York has not yet adopted the policy of entering upon the enlargement of the Erie Canal to meet the growing demands for transportation from the West to the sea-board, the necessity for such enlargement in view of the increased facilities which the Canadian government is now providing by the Saint Lawrence route, and the fact that a very large part of the surplus products of the West are being deflected from the canal to other lines of transport in this country, is having the effect of awaking public opinion in that State to the importance of the work. Statements in regard to this subject may be found in the evidence taken before the committee at Buffalo. (See page 193 of the evidence.) The comptroller of the State of New York, in his recent report to the legislature, says: "It is believed that this improvement, (enlargement of the Erie Canal for boats of 690 tons,) with steam as a motor, giving ten to eleven days time for the passage from Chicago and Milwaukee to New York, will secure and hold the trade of the Western and Northwestern States in perpetuity."

A valuable statement in regard to the importance of enlarging the Erie Canal, and its cost and practicability, may be found in a letter addressed to the chairman of this committee by Hon. F. A. Alberger, member of the New York State assembly, and late canal commissioner of that State. (See appendix, page 205.)

At this time, when the construction of artificial water-lines commands so much interest, not only as a means of providing cheap transportation, but of serving as a regulator of charges by rail, the practical results achieved in the State of New York by a former enlargement of the Erie Canal, and the deductions from such results as to the probable effect of a further enlargement, are deemed to be of especial value. The Erie Canal was originally constructed for boats of 78.62 tons. Subsequently it was enlarged for boats of 210 tons, and the results of such enlargement were found to correspond exactly with the predictions of the engineer, namely, a reduction in the cost of transport of 50 per cent. (See report of State engineer for the year 1863, pages 123 to 125, inclusive.)

In the year 1863 (act April 22, 1862) the legislature of the State of New York passed an act providing that when the Government of the United States should furnish the means for enlarging a single tier of locks, or building an additional tier, in whole or in part, with such other improvements of the canal as might be necessary to admit the passage of steamboats from the Hudson River to the lakes, the canal-board should in such case, without delay, put such work under contract. That act has never been repealed. Subsequently, in compliance with a request of the governor of the State, the President of the United States appointed an engineer to consult with the State engineers in regard to the subject. The engineer of the State of New York made the necessary surveys and estimates, and reported, in 1863, that the expense of constructing an enlarged tier of locks, for steamboats, and deepening the Erie Canal one foot, would amount to $10,380,170; that such enlargement would admit of the passage of boats engaged in commerce of 690 tons of burden, (present capacity 210 tons,) and that the results of such enlarged capacity would be a reduction of 50 per cent. in the cost of transport on the canals. In the language of his report, "At an expense of $10,380,170 the same results are obtained in cheapening the cost of transportation as by the original enlargement, at an expense of $32,008,850." (See report of State engineer for 1863, page 134.)

The result of a long series of experiments has demonstrated the fact that freights may be transported upon the Erie Canal in boats propelled by steam-power at less cost than in boats moved by animal-power.

Upon this subject attention is called to a letter addressed to Hon. F. A. Alberger, by Mr. D. M. Greene, engineer of the commission in charge of the late experiments in relation to this matter. (Appendix, p. 152.) There seems to be no doubt that upon a canal of larger dimensions the successful application of steam-power would be much more marked than in the case of the experiments already made.

The successful application of steam on canals must be regarded as an important advance in the economy of transportation.

COMPARATIVE ADVANTAGES OF THE THREE ROUTES BETWEEN THE PORTS OF THE UPPER LAKES AND NEW YORK, VIZ, THE CAUGHNAWAGA ROUTE, THE ONEIDA LAKE ROUTE, AND THE ERIE CANAL ROUTE.

The distance on each of the three routes from Chicago to New York is as follows:

	Miles.
Caughnawaga route	1,644
Oneida Lake route	1,411
Erie Canal route	1,395

The number of locks and feet of lockage and mileage of canals on the three routes are as follows:

Route.	Number of locks.	Feet of lockage.	Miles of canal.
Caughnawaga route	71	737	161
Oneida Lake route	95	955	194
Erie Canal route	71	655	350

Assuming in each case that the time consumed in passing through each lock is equal to the time required in a movement of half a mile on the canal, we obtain the equated length of canal navigation on each line as follows:

Equated canal distance, by assuming each lockage to be equal to one mile.

	Miles.
Caughnawaga route	197
Oneida Lake route	242
Erie Canal route	386

The total equated distances by the three lines appear to be as follows:

Route.	Equated canal navigation.	Lake and river navigation.	Total equated distances.
	Miles.	*Miles.*	*Miles.*
Caughnawaga route	197	1,483	1,680
Oneida Lake route	242	1,217	1,459
Erie Canal route	386	1,045	1,431

In this computation the slack-water navigation of forty miles on the Hudson River, from Fort Edward to Troy, is added to the canal distance.

The cost of transport, however, depends not upon the relative length of each of these routes, but upon the time required to make a single voyage, or, in other words, upon the number of voyages which can be made by a vessel during a season of navigation.

Assuming the speed of boats on canals, of the dimensions proposed, to be four miles per hour when propelled by steam, and the speed of propellers on the lakes and rivers to be eight miles per hour, and adding ten hours to the time by the Oswego and Buffalo route for the transshipment from lake-vessels into canal-boats, we find the time required to move grain from Chicago to New York, by the three routes, to be as follows:

By Caughnawaga route, 234 hours, or 9¾ days.

By Oswego route, 222 hours, or 9¼ days.

By Buffalo route, 237 hours, or 9⅞ days.

In practical business operations the time by each route may be considered to be ten days.

The committee do not, of course, present this as a precise statement of the actual comparative merits of the three routes, but simply as *an estimate*, based upon data which appear to be approximately correct.

It is stated by Hon. John Young, of Montreal, that on the eastward trip by the Caughnawaga route vessels can avoid 22 locks, of 162 feet lockage, by passing down the rapids. In that case the time of the eastward voyage by the Caughnawaga route will be reduced to about 9½ days. This would not, however, affect the general statement just made. Vessels, in making the westward passage on the Caughnawaga route, would of course be obliged to pass through all the St. Lawrence canals, and the time, as before stated, would be 9¾ days.

The relative economy of passing vessels of 1,500 tons burden through canals or of transferring cargoes from lake-vessels into canal-boats, is a question very materially affecting the cost of transport from the lakes to New York City by these three routes.

The time required to pass a large vessel through a canal-lock is much greater than the time required for the passage of an ordinary boat.

The average time required for a single lockage on the Erie Canal, for boats of 210 tons, is about ten minutes, whereas the time required for a single lockage of a lake-vessel of 500 tons on the Welland Canal is about twenty minutes. Vessels of about 1,500 tons will, of course, require more time. Again, the rate of movement on the enlarged canals here referred to is but half that upon the lakes. In this connection, therefore, the following facts must be taken into consideration: First, that lake-steamers of 1,500 tons cost about $105,000, and that the canal-barges, carrying an equal amount of freight, cost only about half as much—interest and cost of maintenance amounting to much more in the former than in the latter case. This fact is based upon the statement of Mr. McAlpine, page 106 of Appendix. Second, the greater cost for wages of crews upon lake-steamers, and the damages incident to passing large vessels through canal-locks.

These facts and the opinion of practical men clearly indicate that freights can be transported on canals much cheaper in barges than in vessels constructed in the expensive manner in which it is necessary to build vessels which navigate the lakes, and the profitable employment of which depends upon the largest possible number of trips which can be made during a season of navigation.

It is unnecessary for the committee to enter upon any detailed computation as to the precise difference of cost in the two cases. A practical illustration of the point may, however, be cited. Formerly, lake vessels were sent from Chicago to Montreal, through the Saint Lawrence canals, without breaking bulk. But it was afterward found to be cheaper to transfer grain at Kingston, and to send it down the Saint Lawrence in barges, the cost of such transfer being only *one half a cent per bushel.* It is stated by the secretary of the board of trade at Montreal that of the total quantity of grain received at that city during the year 1872, 9,055,000 bushels were transshipped at Kingston, and only 3,266,000 bushels were carried through to Montreal in lake vessels. Almost all the grain transported on the lakes in sailing-vessels was transferred to barges at Kingston.

In consequence of this change in the mode of transport, the quantity of grain shipped to Montreal has been largely increased within the last three years.

Since it has been proved, by practical experience, that the cheapest transport on the lakes is in vessels of the largest size yet constructed, the economy of transferring from lake vessels into canal-boats or barges is much more decided than in the case of the vessels of 500 tons burden which now pass through the Welland Canal.

But there is another circumstance which must have a very important bearing in determining the question as to the quantity of grain which can be transported by each of these routes from Chicago to New York, viz, the available supply of lake-tonnage, this being governed chiefly by the magnitude of the return cargoes from the eastern termini of the three routes. It is evident that, all things else being equal, the grain trade will be mainly controlled by that route on which the total expenses and profits of transportation are borne in part by westward-bound cargoes. This fact has already been alluded to in respect to the transport of grain upon the ocean.

The freight-charges from the upper lakes to a large commercial port at the eastern extremity of the lakes, or on the sea-board, will not only be lower in the aggregate than to a port the commerce of which is chiefly or exclusively confined to the grain trade, but will be less subject to violent fluctuations. In the former case the freight-charges will not be dependent upon the eastward movement of *grain only*, but upon the total movement eastward and westward of all the tonnage constituting the commerce of the port. Circumstances of this nature constitute the permanency of great commercial lines, and lead to the growth of great commercial centers, which, in their turn, by the force of imperious laws of trade, exercise a strong influence in determining commercial movements.

In this view, the route via Buffalo has very marked advantages over the other routes, both in respect to the economy of transport upon the lakes and upon the Erie Canal and its competing railroads. Buffalo is the western terminus of the Erie Canal and of the New York Central and Erie Railways, both of which roads transport freights during the season of navigation in connection with steamer lines on the lakes. There are also several other railways completed or in course of construction, having their western termini at Buffalo, and making that city a very important commercial center.

Large quantities of anthracite and bituminous coal are brought from the coal-fields of Western Pennsylvania to Buffalo for shipment to ports on the upper lakes, affording a large amount of return lake-freights and by this means reducing the cost of transport on eastward freight.

It is evident, that each of the other routes must command a share of the transport of grain to competing points in the State of New York and the New England States and to foreign countries, the magnitude of such shipments, as already remarked, being greatly dependent upon the amount of return freights which can be secured at the eastern lake termini of each route. In case one or all of the other routes shall be opened with the enlarged dimensions and improved facilities already mentioned, and no means are adopted for the cheapening of transport on the Erie Canal, it is probable that a very large proportion of the shipments of grain from the West to the East would be deflected from the route via Buffalo.

The Caughnawaga route presents, in one respect, commercial advantages which are not common to either of the other two, in the fact that it opens a line of water transport for grain from the West to New England.

As the rates of ocean freights depend largely upon the relation of the amount of merchandise seeking shipment to the amount of tonnage offering for such freights, it is manifestly in the interest of the western producer that for foreign shipments he shall have the full benefit of the option offered by the available amount of ocean tonnage at Montreal and at New York, especially at times when an unusually large amount of freights is seeking shipment to Europe.

The treaty of Washington secures to us the free navigation of the Saint Lawrence River, but not of the Welland and Saint Lawrence canals, which are owned and controlled by the Dominion government. Without the privilege of the free navigation of the Canadian canals, the right to the free navigation of the Saint Lawrence River would be of no practical value whatever.

A large part of the cereal products of the United States passes through the territory of Canada over the Grand Trunk Railway to the New England States, and merchandise is also sent by the same line from the Eastern to the Western States. The Canadian government has united with the Government of the United States in securing the greatest possible freedom of transit in such case. The Canadian government also allows importations to be made through Montreal from other countries to United States ports on the lakes, with the least possible detention and expense. It appears desirable, in the interests of both countries, that purchasers of American grain in Canada should have the option of re-exporting it to the United States without the payment of duties.

THE JAMES RIVER AND KANAWHA CANAL.

The James River and Kanawha Canal or Central Water-line is a project for connecting the James River at Richmond with the Ohio River at the mouth of the Kanawha by means of canal and slack-water and open river navigation. The project was originated in the latter part of the last century, and the route has since been carefully surveyed at various times. It is proposed that the canal portions of the line shall have a breadth of 70 feet at the surface, and a depth of 7 feet. The locks are to be 120 feet long and 20 feet wide, admitting the passage of boats of 280 tons burden.

The following is a description of the line:

First. The canal now constructed from Richmond to Buchanan, Va., a distance of 197½ miles, embracing the ship-lock and other works belonging to the James River and Kanawha Company at Richmond, composed of 160.75 miles of canal and 36.75 miles of slackwater. The present canal has a width, at surface, of 50 feet and a depth of 5 feet, with locks 100 feet long and 15 feet wide, admitting the passage of boats of 150 tons. The cost of the work already completed has been $10,436,869. It is proposed to enlarge this canal to the dimensions fixed for the entire line, viz, 70 feet wide at the surface and 7 feet deep.

Second. A canal from Buchanan to the Greenbrier River. This division of the route is 76½ miles in length, and is composed of 67.25 miles of canal and 9.95 miles of slackwater navigation. It embraces certain unfinished work between Buchanan and Covington, and includes the construction of a tunnel of $7\frac{8}{10}$ miles in length on the summit level through the Alleghany Ridge.

Third. The Greenbrier, New, and Kanawha Rivers, from the mouth of Howard's Creek to the Ohio River, a distance of 197.44 miles. This portion of the line will consist entirely of slack-water navigation, or of a canal and slack-water navigation, as the result of future surveys may prove to be most practicable.

LOCKAGE.

The lockage between the James River at Richmond and the Kanawha River at Lyken's Shoals is as follows:

Ascending from Richmond to summit-level	1,700 feet.
Descending from the summit-level to the Kanawha River	1,114 feet.
Total lockage	2,814 feet.

There will be 160 locks in ascending from Richmond to the summit, and 77 locks in descending from the summit to the Kanawha River, the total number of locks being 237.

LENGTH OF THE ENTIRE LINE.

The length of the entire line from Richmond to the Ohio River is as follows:

First division, Richmond to Buchanan	197.50 miles.
Second division, Buchanan to the mouth of Howard's Creek	76.50 miles.
Third division, mouth of Howard's Creek to Ohio River	197.44 miles.
Total	471.44 miles.

The entire line will be composed of—

Canal	231.00 miles.
Slack-water navigation	161.39 miles.
Open river	79.05 miles.
Total length	471.44 miles.

The effect of lockage on the various canals referred to in this report is arrived at by assuming each lock to be equivalent to half a mile in distance. The equated length of the line upon this basis will therefore be—

Actual length	471.44 miles.
237 locks, equivalent to	118.50 miles.
Total equated length	589.94 miles.

ESTIMATED COST.

The cost of enlarging the present James River Canal, and of constructing the additional works required, is estimated to be as follows:

First division, Richmond to Buchanan	$8,538,271 51
Second division, Buchanan to the mouth of Howard's Creek	21,880,156 56
Third division, mouth of Howard's Creek to the Ohio River	14,217,441 00
Ten per cent. added for contingencies on first and second divisions	2,986,420 00
Total	47,622,289 07

It should be stated here that the improvement of the Kanawha River from the Great Falls to its mouth was estimated by the late Mr. Lorraine to cost $3,000,000, including the Meadow River reservoir, and that this expenditure constitutes a part of the cost of the improvements of the Western rivers recommended in this report, and does not constitute a part of the cost of constructing the James River and Kanawha Canal. This amount, therefore, should be deducted from the above estimate.

It is also to be remarked that the distance from the Great Falls to the mouth of the Kanawha is 94.20 miles, and that this distance should be deducted from the length of the central water-line, as above stated, leaving the actual length of the line 377.24 miles, and its equated length 493.74 miles.

THE LORRAINE TUNNEL.

The Lorraine tunnel, through the Alleghany Ridge, is the most expensive and difficult work on the line in an engineering point of view. Experts have ascertained that the rock through which the tunnel is to be excavated is of a very favorable character. It is found that by means of six shafts of moderate depth fourteen working faces (including the two ends) can be secured.

The time required to construct the entire tunnel will, therefore, be limited by the time required in excavating the part of the tunnel between two shafts.

The supply of water for the portions of the line east and west of the tunnel is found to be abundant.

THE SUPPLY OF WATER FOR THE SUMMIT-LEVEL.

The summit-level is to be supplied with water from a reservoir on Anthony's Creek, a branch of the Greenbrier River.

All the engineers who have inquired into this subject agree in the statement that the supply of water will be abundant. If the supply from the reservoir mentioned should be deficient, other reservoirs can be constructed of equal capacity.

COMMERCIAL CONNECTIONS.

The James River and Kanawha Canal will form a navigable connection between the Atlantic sea-board at the capes of Virginia and the Mississippi River and its tributaries at the mouth of the Kanawha.

The value of such connection will be very greatly increased by the radical improvements of the Ohio River referred to in this report, and estimated to cost about $22,000,000. The vast deposits of iron and other minerals in the State of Virginia, and of coal, salt and lumber in West Virginia, on the line of this route, would supply an immense tonnage. The trade in these minerals which are found in the western part of the State of Pennsylvania, and in West Virginia and Ohio, now supply an immense commerce on the Ohio River.

TIME REQUIRED TO CONSTRUCT THE WORK.

It is the opinion of engineers who have carefully studied the subject that the entire line can be completed in from four to six years.

The foregoing facts are based upon careful surveys made by the late Mr. Edward Lorraine, civil engineer, by Mr. William R. Hutton, civil engineer, by W. G. Turpin, civil engineer, and by Col. W. T. Craighill, and other officers connected with the Engineer Corps of the War Department.

These surveys were very carefully made and are sufficient for the purposes of the estimates of cost already presented, but they are not of that nature in detail which is required for the satisfactory determination of the character and cost of all the structures which will be involved in the work. It will therefore be necessary to have new surveys made at important points between the east end of the tunnel and the Great Falls of the Kanawha.

ACTION BY THE STATES OF VIRGINIA AND WEST VIRGINIA.

In the year 1870 the States of Virginia and West Virginia, through their several memorials to Congress, proposed to relinquish their respective interests in this route, and partially constructed water-way, to the United States, and to turn over the work to the Government, to be constructed and managed as Congress might decide would best promote the prosperity and welfare of the whole country.

REPORT OF THE RECENT BOARD OF ENGINEERS.

Under an order of the War Department dated January 27, 1874, a board of engineers was convened, who were directed to report upon "all questions of practicability, plan, and probable cost for a water communication to the Ohio River by the way of the James and Kanawha Rivers, together with the probable time required for its completion, and the cost of maintenance when built." This board was constituted as follows:

J. G. Barnard, Colonel of Engineers and Brevet Maj. Gen., U. S. A.

Benj. H. Latrobe, civil engineer, of Baltimore, Md.

Q. A. Gillmore, Lieut. Col. Engineers, Brevet Maj. Gen., U. S. A.

Wm. P. Craighill, Major of Engineers, Brevet Lieut. Col., U. S. A.

G. Weitzel, Major of Engineers, Brevet Maj. Gen., U. S. A.

Thomas Turtle, First Lieutenant Engineers, U. S. A., recorder.

The report of the board is dated March 18, 1874. The following resolution was adopted:

"*Resolved*, That, in the opinion of this board, it is entirely practicable to connect the waters of the James and Ohio Rivers by a water navigation of 7 feet in depth."

In regard to the proposed tunnel, the board report that the rock through which it is to be excavated is of a material very easily excavated, and that shafts may be driven at distances apart seldom exceeding one mile.

The construction of reservoirs for the supply of the summit or tunnel level and their dependencies is deemed to be entirely practicable, and the supply of water is found to be abundant.

The board are unanimously of the opinion that a tunnel of the dimensions proposed, 52 feet wide by 34 feet high, "*should not be attempted*," and they "unite in the recommendation of a single tunnel with occasional turnouts, with which hereafter, if found necessary, a second tunnel may be combined."

The board unite in recommending a tunnel 34 feet wide, and 34 feet high, with turnouts every quarter of a mile for passing boats, and recesses at such points 52 feet wide. The estimated cost of such a tunnel, as stated by Mr. Benjamin H. Latrobe, is $16,192,487, and the cost of the whole line, according to the computation of the same engineer, is $49,626,845.

Several changes in the location of the tunnel are suggested, as follows:

First. That the level be raised 20 feet, in order to avoid the deep cutting in the narrow valley of Howard Creek.

Second. A change in the location of the east end of the tunnel from Fork Run to Bush Creek, so as to save two miles of canalling.

Third. A change in the location of the line of the tunnel, a line being proposed from Bush Creek to the Greenbrier River, making the total length of the tunnel a fraction over nine miles, and saving expensive canalling in the valley of Howard's Creek.

These modifications are not mentioned as matters of positive recommendation, but as subjects of further survey, with a view of obtaining the best possible location.

In regard to the plan proposed, "there are minor differences of opinion" among the members of the board, "applying to all that portion of the work east of the summit, which, however, will involve considerable differences of cost." These questions are confined to the expediency of adopting single or double locks, the enlargement of the present locks, or the construction of new ones, and revetting the sides of the canal.

The board recommend that the canal locks be increased from 20 to 23 feet in width, with a corresponding increase in the width of the slack-water locks west of the summit. It is stated that such an increased width will give an increased capacity of about one-fourth, and admit the passing of boats of 345 tons.

In regard to the part of the work west of the tunnel, the board expresses the following opinion: "With regard to the extension of the water-line from the mouth of Howard's Creek to the Great Falls, while the board is unanimous as to the question of practicability of a water connection, they are not so as to the proposed method of locks and dams or slack-water, and the differences involve very material differences in the probable cost of the work." The board agree, by formal resolution, "that it may be expedient to adopt canal navigation for this part of the work, with occasional exceptions."

The opinion is also expressed "that further surveys are necessary to the final adjustment of these plans."

In regard to the cost of maintaining the canal the board passed the following resolution:

Resolved, That, in the opinion of the board, the cost of maintenance (repairs and administration included) of the water-line, should not exceed one million dollars per annum.

In regard to cost and time required for the construction of the canal, the opinion is expressed that the entire work can be completed in six years, at a cost of not more than $60,000,000. It is added: "The cost may reasonably be expected to be within $55,000,000, and possibly it may not exceed $50,000,000."

DEDUCTIONS FROM THE STATEMENTS MADE BY THE BOARD OF ENGINEERS.

From the opinions expressed by the board of engineers it appears—

First. That the exact location of the tunnel is undetermined as yet. It is decided by the board that the size of the tunnel shall be changed to the dimensions above mentioned.

Second. That additional surveys are necessary in order to determine the questions as to whether it is better to construct a canal from the summit to the Kanawha River, or to adopt the present plan of slack-water navigation, and that additional surveys are necessary for determining the particular points referred in the report of the board.

These surveys should be made at the earliest day practicable, especially as to the exact location of the tunnel, and the character of the navigation west of the Alleghany Mountains. Construction can, however, be begun at once on the part of the line east of the summit.

The committee refer to a very complete statement in regard to this work, its history, topographical features, commercial bearings, &c., which has been prepared by Hon. Henry G. Davis, a member of this committee. This statement may be found on page 1 of the Appendix.

The committee are of the opinion that the construction of this canal would develop vast resources of coal and iron, now almost worthless for lack of the means of transportation. It would form a connection between tidewater at Richmond and 16,000 miles of inland navigation by the Kanawha and Ohio Rivers, and open a cheap and valuable channel of transport to the Atlantic coast for the cereal products of the West.

ATLANTIC AND GREAT WESTERN CANAL ROUTE.

It is proposed by this work to connect the Tennessee River, at Guntersville, Tenn., with the Atlantic Ocean at Savannah, Ga.

In the year 1870 the legislature of Georgia granted a charter to certain citizens of that State and of other States to construct this work. In 1871 Congress ordered a survey of the line, which survey was made in the years 1871 and 1872 by Major Walter McFarland, of the Corps of Engineers, United States Army.*

The right of way has been secured by the company on that portion of the line which lies within the State of Georgia, but it has not been secured through the State of Alabama. The greater part of that section of the line in the latter State passes through lands belonging to the United States.†

The company now ask aid from the United States Government in such manner as Congress may prescribe. The results of the surveys already made are stated by Major McFarland on page 756 of the evidence, and in his official report of May 25, 1872. These surveys are preliminary, but are sufficiently accurate to determine all questions of an engineering character, as to the practicability of the route.

The following is a general description of the line: Beginning at Guntersville, a point on the Tennessee River, 40 miles above the Muscle Shoals, the line follows Short Creek, by slack-water navigation, 17 miles; thence, by canal, 34 miles, to Will's Creek, and thence down, Will's Creek to its junction with the Coosa River, at a point two and a half miles below Gadsden, Ala. The Coosa River forms a part of the line from the latter point to Rome, Ga., a distance of 153 miles. Between these points the Coosa is now navigable at lowest stages for boats drawing two and a half feet. From Rome the line follows the Etowah River by slack-water navigation, 53 miles to the mouth of Owl Creek, from which point a canal is proposed to Macon, on the Ocmulgee River, a distance of 158¼ miles. Macon is situated at the head of flat-boat navigation on the Ocmulgee River.

LOCKAGE.

From the Tennessee there is an ascending lockage of 400 feet, and a descending lockage of 464 feet; total 864 feet. (Evidence, page 582.)

---

* See report Chief of Engineers, 1872, page 684.

† Report Chief of Engineers ,1872, page 697.

The slack-water navigation and canal on the part of the line from Rome to Macon have an ascending lockage of 266 feet and a descending lockage of 705 feet, or a total lockage of 971 feet. The lockage from the Tennessee River to Macon, therefore, amounts to 1,835 feet. To this is to be added the lockage at the Muscle Shoals, 134 feet, making the total lockage on the entire line of 1,969 feet.*

DISTANCES.

The following is a statement of the length of the several parts of the line:

	Miles.
Guntersville to Gadsden, canal and slack-water	51½
Gadsden to Rome, river navigation	153
Rome to mouth of Owl Creek, slack-water	53
Mouth of Owl Creek to Macon, canal	158¼
Total from Tennessee River to Macon	415¾

This portion of the line, 415¾ miles in length, embraces 70½ miles of slack-water, and 192¼ miles of canal; the remainder being river navigation.

The additional parts of the route between Saint Louis and the Atlantic Ocean are as follows:

Mississippi, Ohio, and Tennessee Rivers, from Saint Louis to Guntersville, 563 miles.

Ocmulgee River, Altamaha River, and coast navigation from Macon to Savannah, 500 miles.

A canal is to be constructed around the Muscle Shoals, on the Tennessee, a distance of 38½ miles,† with six locks, and a total lockage of 134 feet. The total lockage between the Tennessee River at Guntersville and the Ocmulgee River at Macon, amounts to 1,835 feet. Assuming one lock for each 10 feet of lockage, there will be 184 locks on the entire line. Assuming, also, that each lockage will be equivalent to half a mile of canal, the lockage on the entire line will add 92 miles to the distance from Guntersville to Macon. The canal around the Muscle Shoals will have six locks—equivalent to three miles. Adding the equivalent distance in lockage to the canal portions of the line, we obtain the following statement of the total distance from St. Louis to Savannah, Georgia:

		Miles.
St. Louis to Cairo: Open river		200.00
Cairo to Guntersville:		
Muscle-Shoals Canal	41.50	
Open river	325.00	
		366.50

*Evidence of Major McFarland, page 760 of the evidence.
† See McBrides's evidence, p. 773–4.

	Miles.	Miles.
Guntersville to Macon:		
Canal	284.25	
Slack-water	70.50	
Open river	153.00	
		507.75
Macon to Savannah: Open river		500.00
Total distance		1,574.25

SUMMARY OF DISTANCE FROM SAINT LOUIS TO SAVANNAH, GA.

Open river	1,178.00
Canal	325.75
Slack-water	70.50
Total distance	1,574.25

DIMENSIONS OF CANAL.

The canal is to be 70 feet wide at the surface and 5 feet deep, wtih locks 135 feet long by 27 wide, admitting the passage of boats 120 feet long by 26½ feet beam, and carrying 300 tons of freight.* Larger boats cannot be employed on account of the short turns on the Sand Mountain division.

It has been decided that the depth of five feet in the canal will be sufficient, in view of the average depth of the water which can be secured at a reasonable expense in the Tennessee, Coosa, and Ocmulgee Rivers during the entire year.

SUPPLY OF WATER.

The supply of water both on the canal from the Tennessee to the Coosa, and on the canal from the Coosa to the Ocmulgee is stated by Major McFarland to be sufficient for all the prospective demands of commerce, and even for a much larger canal than the one proposed.

COST.

The estimated cost of the entire work, providing for a double tow-path and a single line of locks, is as follows: †

Muscle Shoals Canal	$3,676,000
Canal from the Tennessee to the Coosa	11,570,607
Canal from the Coosa to the Ocmulgee	20,435,684
Improvements of the Tennessee, Coosa, and Ocmulgee Rivers, estimated ‡	4,000,000
Total cost of the works from Saint Louis to Savannah	39,682,291

Upon further examinations and estimates, † Major McFarland states that the above sum can be reduced $4,000,000, making the total cost of the route about $35,700,000.

* Evidence, page 758.
† See evidence, page 767.
‡ The cost of improving the Coosa, Ocmulgee, Altamaha, and inland coast navigation is not based upon survey, but upon a reconnaissance.

EXPENSIVE WORKS.

The only engineering works on the line of importance are, first, the aqueduct on the Chattahoochee, 117 feet high and375 feet long,* and a tunnel of 3,200 feet, or three-fifths of a mile.

TIME REQUIRED TO CONSTRUCT THE WORK.

No estimate has yet been made by the engineer as to the time required to construct the entire work. It is supposed by well-informed persons that it can be constructed in two years.

LENGTH OF SEASON OF NAVIGATION.

The results of several years of observation indicate that this line would be unobstructed by ice during the entire year.

CAPACITY.

The maximum capacity of this canal is ascertained in the mode adopted in computing the capacity of all other canals mentioned in this report, viz, by assuming that ten minutes are required for a single lockage. This will give three lockages in *each* direction in an hour, or 72 in a day.

Although this canal is designed for boats of three hundred tons, it appears that during the dry season, which embraced the months of July, August, September, and October, the stage of navigation on the Tennessee River will limit the tonnage of boats navigating the canal to 190 tons. (See testimony of Major McFarland, on page 583 of the evidence.) The total annual capacity of the canal to carry freights eastward may, therefore, be stated as follows:

	Tons.
190 tons × 72 lockages × 120 days, equal	1,641,600
300 tons × 72 lockages × 245 days, equal	5,292,000
Total annual capacity to carry freights eastward	6,923,600

Or, stated in bushels at 60 pounds, 231,120,000 bushels.

The capacity to carry westward being equal to the capacity to carry eastward, the annual capacity of this canal, for the transport of merchandise in both directions, will be 13,867,200 tons.

The above estimate of capacity is, of course, theoretical, being based upon the supposition that boats will present themselves regularly at the locks throughout the year. The practical capacity will be about 67 per cent. of this theoretical capacity, viz, 9,291,024 tons in both directions, or 4,645,512 eastward, equal to 154,850,400 bushels of wheat.

---

* Report of chief engineer, 1872, page 723.

Estimated time required to transport grain from Saint Louis to Savannah.

This estimate is made by assuming a speed of 8 miles an hour upon rivers and of 4 miles upon the canal and slack-water.

	Miles.	Speed per hour.	Hours.
River	1,178	8 miles.	147
Canal and slack-water	396¼	4 miles.	99
Total			246

This equals 10 days and 6 hours.

SPECIAL ADVANTAGES CLAIMED.

The special advantages claimed for this line by its advocates are as follows:

First. That it will never be obstructed by ice.

Second. That it does not descend so far into the heated region as to cause grain-cargoes to be injured by heat and moisture.

Third. That in addition to furnishing a highway of commerce from the West to the sea-board, it will also be the means of opening lines of transport by water from the Tennessee to the Coosa and Chattahoochee Rivers, which it crosses. These rivers empty into the Gulf of Mexico, and it is believed that, by means of a system of river and coast-line improvements, connections can be made with all the navigable rivers flowing into the Gulf between Louisiana and the peninsula of Florida.

It is also believed that a line of inland navigation can be formed along the coast of South Carolina, Georgia, and Florida, connecting with the rivers in these States which flow into the Atlantic Ocean. It is believed that by such means several thousand miles of river navigation can be connected with this work, extending into a very large part of these States, where it is desirable to increase the culture of cotton and to purchase large amounts of breadstuffs from other States.

No surveys have been made for the purpose of determining the cost or practicability of such navigable connections.

Upon this subject see testimony of Col. B. W. Frobel, on pages 115 to 172 of the evidence.

Fourth. It is stated that the line will open up a large home-market for the grain of the West which now seeks a market in foreign countries, thus reducing the cost of transport between the producer and the consumer, and leading to a very large increase in the production and exportation of cotton.

THE MISSISSIPPI AND TRIBUTARY RIVERS.

Prior to the opening of the New York and Canadian canals, and the construction of lines of railways from the West to the East, the Mississippi River, with its navigable tributaries, formed the only avenues of commerce between the territories embracing the present Western

States and other States of the Union, and also between the Western States and foreign countries. The construction of the canals and railroads mentioned, together with the closing of the Mississippi River by the war, the general paralysis of business at the South, and the increase in the size of ocean-vessels, have turned the greater part of that commerce eastward, to the markets of the Atlantic States, and to foreign countries, by the way of Montreal and New York, and other cities on the Atlantic seaboard. This deflection of the commerce of the West to the northern routes of transport, has not, however, in any sense diminished the value of the Mississippi River as a great commercial highway. In view of the facts we have stated in regard to the relative economy of water and rail transport for the surplus products of the West, and of the failure of railways to supply sufficiently cheap transportation to meet the demands of the rapidly-increasing commerce between the great central basin of the continent and the markets of the world, it is far more important now than ever before. Finding that no real and substantial relief is to be anticipated from additional railways under private control without regulation and that but little actual competition exists anywhere, except upon water-lines, public attention has of late been directed to the natural channels which seem to be so plainly indicated by the hand of the Great Architect of the continent. In searching earnestly for some practical method of reducing the burdens which now bear so heavily upon the producing interests of a large section of our country, the committee have been impressed with the conviction that no plan yet suggested promises more speedy and valuable results for the same expenditure of money than the improvement of the Mississippi River and its navigable tributaries.

The vast extent and wonderful fertility of the country which these rivers drain, the nature, variety, and location of the products seeking transportation, the almost incalculable commerce which demands the facilities they seem designed by nature to supply, all point to the expediency of availing ourselves at the earliest practicable moment of the advantages which they present.

That the commerce of New Orleans and of the entire Mississippi Valley is now greatly depressed and embarrassed by obstacles, not by any means insurmountable, is very obvious, and that the industrial interests of the country are unnecessarily taxed for the want of adequate improvements of the Mississippi River is demonstrable beyond a doubt.

Notwithstanding the present exceedingly adverse circumstances affecting this great river as a great commercial highway, which are hereinafter fully set forth, a glance at its existing commerce and advantages may serve to illustrate to some extent its future possibilities, and to suggest the necessity for governmental action. A statement of the advantages of any given route for the movement of grain necessarily involves a consideration of the areas which produce a surplus of cereal products. In illustration of this subject, we have appended to this report crop-maps, prepared by the Superintendent of the Census for 1870, from which it will be observed that the areas of greatest production are so located as to be peculiarly benefited by the improvements under consideration.

A valuable table prepared by Mr. J. R. Dodge, statistician of the Agricultural Department, showing the estimated yield of wheat, corn, rye, oats, and barley, for the year 1872, may also be found on page 199 of the appendix. It exhibits the yield of cereals in each State, and in several divisons of States.

It appears from the data in regard to the eastward and southward movements of grain from the Western and Northwestern States presented in the section of this report relating to the course of trade that 178,021,426 bushels, or 83 per cent. was shipped east by the lakes, the New York and Canadian canals and railroads during the year 1872, and that 35,000,000 bushels, or 17 per cent. was shipped south by the Mississippi River, and by railroads extending from the Western States into the Gulf States. The total quantity of grain received at New Orleans during the year 1872–'73 amounted to 13,249,576 bushels, or 38 per cent. of the total southern movement.

The statistics of production by counties given in the Census for 1870, and in the annual reports of the Agricultural Department in connection with the maps here republished, furnish an almost illimitable fund for theoretical computations as to the areas for which particular routes may be supposed to furnish the cheapest means of transport to home and foreign markets, and for conjectures as to what will be the results of improving or constructing particular routes. It is, however, proper in this report to treat only of facts as to the actual course of trade, and to mention only probable results of the construction or improvement of important commercial highways.

In addition to what has already been stated, a few words as to the course of trade eastward and southward may serve to show the actual and relative value of the Mississippi River as a highway of commerce between the interior and the seaboard.

The markets for the surplus grain-products of our western and northwestern States may, for the purpose of illustration, be stated as follows:

1st. Interior markets of the Atlantic States.

2d. The cities on the Atlantic seaboard.

3d. The Gulf States.

4th. Foreign countries.

No elaborate computations are necessary in order to show that the cost of transporting the surplus products of the West to markets of the North Atlantic States by the Erie Canal and railroads from the West to the East must be much less than would be the cost of transporting such products to ports on the Mississippi River, thence to New Orleans, thence to Atlantic seaports, and thence by rail or water to interior points. The quantity of grain consumed in these States, however, not including the large seaboard cities, amounted in the year 1872 to about 37,000,000 bushels, or about 18 per cent. of the total surplus grain of the West during that year.

It is also evident that the cheapest means of transporting grain from the State of Michigan, and from the portions of the States of Ohio, Indiana, Wisconsin, and Minnesota, bordering upon the lakes, is by the lakes and the New York and Saint Lawrence Canals and by railroads extending from the lake ports to ports on the Atlantic seaboard. The history of the actual course of trade between the West and the East during the last thirty years is a commentary upon this statement, which appears to place it beyond all question. A difference of opinion exists, however, in regard to the cost of transporting grain and other products of a very large part of the Western States, not embraced within the territory bordering on the lakes, both to Atlantic sea-ports and to the markets of Europe.

The most reliable data as to the cost of transportation over any two competing routes may be deduced from the actual freight-charges, where such charges are regulated under fair competition by the laws of supply and demand.

Two comparative statements will be given, based upon data for the year 1872, as follows:

FIRST STATEMENT.

		Rate per bushel. Cts. M.
Average freight-charges from Chicago to New York by lake and canal		26. 6
Average freight-charges from Saint Louis to New York:		
Saint Louis to New Orleans (average for the year)	13. 9	
Saint Louis to New York (average for the year)	13. 7	
		27. 6
Less by lake and canal route		1. 0

Adding transfer charges and marine insurance and we obtain the total cost of transportation in each case as follows:

	Cts. M.
Total cost of transportation from Chicago to New York	31. 4
Total cost of transportation from Saint Louis to New York	34. 0
Less by lake and canal route	2. 6

SECOND STATEMENT.

This statement relates to the transportation of grain from Chicago to Liverpool and from Saint Louis to Liverpool.

	Rate per bushel. Cts. M.
Average freight-charges from Chicago to Liverpool	45. 8
Average freight-charges from Saint Louis to Liverpool	40. 9
Less from Saint Louis to Liverpool	4. 9

Adding the transfer-charges and marine insurance and we obtain the total cost of transportation as follows:

	Cts. M.
Total cost of transportation from Chicago to Liverpool..........	53.7
Total cost of transportation from Saint Louis to Liverpool.......	47.3
Less from Saint Louis to Liverpool............................	6.4

The average high-water rate from Saint Louis to New Orleans during the year 1872 was only 11 cents per bushel (60 pounds,) whereas the average rate for the year was 13.9 cents, as stated above. Taking the high-water rate instead of the average for the year as above and we find the total freight-charge from Saint Louis to New York to be 1.9 cents less than the total freight charge from Chicago to New York, and the total cost of transport from Saint Louis to New York (including transfer and marine insurance) to be 3 mills less than the total cost of transportation from Chicago to New York. Taking the high-water rate from Saint Louis to New Orleans in the second statement we shall find the actual freight-charge from Saint Louis to Liverpool to be 7.8 cents less than the actual freight-charge from Chicago to Liverpool, and the total cost of transportation (including transfers and marine insurance) to be 9.3 cents less from Saint Louis to Liverpool than from Chicago to Liverpool.*

The comparisons with the high-water rates on the Mississippi River afford, perhaps, the best illustration of the possibilities of that line, because with the proposed improvements the navigation would be quite as good during the entire season as during high water at present. Mr. Henry C. Haarstick, vice-president and general superintendent of the Mississippi Valley Transportation Company, (barge line,) expresses the opinion that with the improved river wheat can be carried from Saint Louis to New Orleans, at a fair compensation, for 7½ cents per bushel, and that the possibilities of this route from Saint Louis to Liverpool are about 28½ cents per bushel. (Evidence, p. 623.) It is also shown by the exhibit of *actual expenses* of the tow-boat Future City, with five barges, (each barge 1,500 tons capacity,) and the whole costing $135,000, that the total cost from Saint Louis to New Orleans was seven-tenths of one mill per ton per mile—*equal to 5¼ mills on a bushel of wheat for the entire distance.* (Evidence, p. 851.) With a large and constant business, it is evident that the charges could be reduced below 7½ cents, and yet afford a liberal return for the capital invested.

On the other hand, it is probable that by the improvements already discussed the charges on the northern water-line could be considerably reduced. The estimate of the State engineer of New York is that the

* The freight-rates from Saint Louis to New Orleans are taken from the annual report of the Union Merchants' Exchange of Saint Louis and the freight-rates from New Orleans to New York and from New Orleans to Liverpool by Messrs. L. J. Higby, A. K. Miller, and J. F. Bordeau, merchants of New Orleans. The freight-rates from New York to Liverpool were furnished by the New York Produce Exchange.

proposed enlargement of the Erie Canal would reduce the cost of transportation one-half; and the estimates of Mr. McAlpine and others show that very large reductions can also be made by the construction of the Oswego and Oneida Lake route, and by the opening of the Caughnawaga and Lake Champlain route.

The foregoing comparative statements are submitted merely as indices of a general fact in regard to the economy of grain transportation from the interior to the sea-board and foreign countries. It is necessary also to consider other circumstances affecting the course of trade.

These circumstances will be discussed hereafter in connection with reasons why so small an amount of Western cereals now find their way to foreign markets via New Orleans.

The markets to which grain is now exported from New Orleans and the development of commerce with the tropical countries on this continent.

The receipts and exports of grain at New Orleans for five years, 1868–'69 to 1872–'73, inclusive, may be found on pages 842 and 843 of the evidence. The total receipts of corn during the period of five years amounted to 22,394,937 bushels, and the shipments to 9,259,310 bushels. The quantity of corn shipped to the various markets appears to be as follows:

	Bushels.
To New York	507, 323
To Boston	12, 925
To other ports of the United States	5, 124, 077
Total to ports of the United States	5, 644, 325
To Cuba	707, 589
To Great Britain	1, 837, 867
To other foreign ports	1, 069, 529
Total to foreign ports	3, 614, 985

The total receipts of wheat during the same period of five years amounted to 764,005 bushels. The shipments of wheat were as follows:

	Bushels.
To New York	135, 332
To Baltimore	2, 155
To other United States ports	400, 862
Total to United States ports	538, 349
	Bushels.
To Great Britain	137, 615
To other foreign ports	64, 685
Total to foreign ports	202, 300

Total exports of wheat, 740,649 bushels.

The receipts and shipments of wheat-flour are given on pages 847 and 848 of the evidence. The receipts during the year ending August 31, 1873, amounted to 1,046,124 barrels, and the shipments were as follows:

	Barrels.
To New York	9,965
To Boston	None.
To Philadelphia	None.
To other United States ports	363,961
Total to United States ports	373,926
To Great Britain	10,746
To Cuba	36,986
To other foreign ports	15,304
Total to foreign ports	63,036

Total shipments of wheat-flour, 436,962 barrels.

The shipments of corn, wheat, and wheat-flour from New Orleans to other United States ports are believed to have been almost exclusively to Gulf ports, and embrace the greater part of the shipments to home markets. About one-half the corn shipped to foreign countries was exported to Great Britain, and the other half is believed to have been exported to Cuba, Mexico, and Central America. The shipments of wheat from New Orleans are very small. The shipments of wheat-flour to United States ports embrace about 86 per cent. of the total shipments, and are chiefly to Gulf ports.

New Orleans is the only port for the shipment of grain by water from the Western States to the southern portions of the Gulf States, and by virtue of its geographical position, it enjoys superior advantages over every other American port for commerce between the Western and Northwestern States, and Mexico, Central America, and the West Indies. New Orleans also has marked geographical advantages in commerce between the United States and South America.

The following views expressed by Hon. W. M. Burwell, of New Orleans, on pages 853 and 855, inclusive, of the evidence, are worthy of very careful attention.

Mr. Burwell says:

"The subject upon which I am specially requested to report is in regard to the state of commerce between the Valley of the Mississippi and the Spanish American States. There are many of us who believe that the trade lines of latitude cross above us, and that a very large proportion of the western productions will move directly to Atlantic ports for exportation, as they will and have received the foreign importations through the same ports. I would say that in the estimation of many in this city, merchants and others, the most important object of improving the Mississippi River will be to establish a direct line of communication between the immense productive interior of the West and the consuming markets of and beyond the tropics. There is a physical impediment in the way which we ask Congress to remove; but there are diplomatic impediments also, which are even greater, as far as that line of trade is concerned, than the physical impediments to which I referred. The diplcmatic impediments consist in the want of reciprocal trade-treaties between the United States and the Spanish American States that are adjacent to or lie south of us. Gentlemen know, and especially members of the Senate of the United States, better than we do, the precise state of the treaties between the United States and the Spanish-American powers; and they will remember that, with the exception of a few special conventions, there has been scarcely any changes made in the treaty relations of those two great interests since almost the origin of the Government. Almost all our trade-treaties, as I understand, are based on the phrase of "the most favored nations;" and while such are the terms of our commercial treaties with Spain, and while it is true that we can carry American provisions or American manufactures into Spanish possessions on the same terms with any other power, yet, when the fact is that we are the only people producing corn and grain and hog products, that we do send to the Spanish-American possessions, it is perfectly plain that that which is a tax on the trade of the most favored nations is practically an oppressive tax upon the trade of the United States. The Spanish tax in Cuba is 40 cents on the bushel on corn, which is, altogether, equivalent to the entire cost of transportation from Iowa to New York. The tax there is $55 on an American horse, $19 on a mule, $8 on a barrel of flour, and 3½ cents on lard. And it is plain that a tax of 80 per cent., which is the average upon the products almost exclusively marketed by Americans, is an excessive tax when contrasted with the American tax upon the products of Cuba. We, as I understand, only tax two of the principal products of Cuba. We admit her coffee duty free, and we impose a tax of something upward of two cents on sugar, and a tax of some 75 per cent. on tobacco manufactured and not manufactured.

"Our schedule of duties, then, would not average 25 per cent. on her products, while hers averages on ours certainly 80 per cent. It seems to me as if the Government of the United States, the Senate, the diplomatic power, would or could, by any means, establish the same principle of reciprocity in regard to Cuba which has been so zealously sought to be re-established with Canada, there would be a draught of trade from the great interior West into the markets of gold and silver, of sugar and coffee, and that there would be a great gain to the people of the West in sending their trade in this direction, instead of being compelled to market it in Europe, and to import commodities received in exchange across the Atlantic Ocean. I confine myself, however, to say that the rate of Spanish duties in Cuba is not reciprocal with respect to our own.

"When we get to Mexico we find that the rate of duties there is still more excessive. As a matter of course we cannot control the legislation of Mexico, but there should be an immense demand for American western products there. Yet if an American commodity is landed at Vera Cruz, and pays all the charges, interest, Federal and State, municipal and railroad duties up to Mexico, your own consul has shown that the aggregate of this tax is 96 per cent. As one result, the people of the United States send to ten millions of people within three and one-half days of this place but about 10 per cent. of the commerce which they receive. That commerce is supplied to a very great extent, so far as it exists at all, from other countries."

The enormous taxes imposed on American products in Cuba, Mexico, and other tropical countries and colonies on this continent, appear fully to sustain Mr. Burwell in the views he has expressed in regard to the importance of measures having in view the establishment of reciprocal relations of trade tending to remove the present burdens upon commerce, and thus to increase very largely our exports to Mexico, Central America, the West Indies, and South America.

Some idea of the possible development of trade with these countries and islands may be formed by referring to the statistics of their population, our commerce with them, and their total commerce with all foreign countries.

Population.

Mexico	9,175,000
Central America	2,665,000
South America	26,259,000
West Indies	4,000,000
Total	42,099,000

Value of our imports from and of our exports to Mexico, Central America, the West Indies, and South America, 1873.

Countries.	Value of imports.	Value of exports.
Mexico	$18,566,154	$6,430,163
Central America	2,238,896	1,347,549
West Indies *	103,006,062	35,059,372
South America †	75,988,999	29,641,967
Total	199,800,111	72,479,051

It appears that the balance of trade with these countries during the year ending June 30, 1873, was against us by the sum of $127,321,060, the value of our exports having amounted to only $36\frac{3}{10}$ per cent. of the value of imports.

But the possibilities of commerce with those countries are indicated by comparing the value of our trade with them with the value of their total commerce with all foreign countries.

* Including also Dutch Guiana, French Guiana, and British Honduras.

† The only South American States named in our reports of commerce and navigation are the Argentine Republic, Brazil, Chili, Peru, Uruguay, Venezuela, British Guiana, and the United States of Colombia.

N. B.—The value of imports and exports are both expressed in United States currency.

TABLE A.—*Statement showing the value of the total commerce (exports and imports) of Mexico, Central America, the West Indies, and South America with the United States and with all foreign countries.*

Countries.	Value of total commerce.	Value of commerce with the United States.
Mexico	$25,000,000	$24,996,317
Central America	11,500,000	3,586,445
West Indies	250,000,000	138,065,434
South America	450,000,000	105,630,966
Total	736,500,000	272,279,162

TABLE B.—*Statement showing the value of the commerce of Great Britain with Mexico, Central America, the West Indies, and South America during the year* 1872.

Countries.	Value of imports into Great Britain.	Value of exports from Great Britain.
	Gold.	*Gold.*
Mexico	$2,158,409	$4,377,601
Central America	6,335,866	2,436,067
West Indies	52,239,930	33,250,137
South America	128,878,139	123,710,792
Total	189,612,344	163,774,597

The total value of the commerce of these countries and colonies and the value of their commerce with Great Britain and the United States may be stated as follows:

Countries.	Value.	Per cent.
Commerce with Great Britain	$397,560,308	54
Commerce with the United States	272,279,162	37
Commerce with all other countries	66,660,530	9
Total commerce	736,500,000	100

N. B.—Value of commerce with Great Britain is here reduced to United States currency.

The lesson which these statistics convey needs no further elaboration here.

With such facts before them, the committee do not hesitate to recommend that our Government shall at once adopt measures to establish more advantageous commercial relations with the countries above-mentioned, and especially such measures as will tend to increase the amount of our exports of grain and other farm products to them. The improvement of the Mississippi River, and the consequent development of a large commerce at New Orleans, will tend to bring us into closer relations with them, and thereby to give us that share of their trade to which our geographical position entitles us.

Trade between New Orleans and Great Britain.—Why cereals are not exported in larger quantities via New Orleans.

If all these things be true, if western products can be exported as cheaply, or nearly so, via New Orleans to New York, and apparently cheaper via New Orleans to Liverpool than by any other route; if its geographical position is so favorable for a large tropical trade, the question very naturally presents itself, why is not a very much larger quantity of grain shipped by that route? Why is it that, with all these advantages, so large a proportion of the heavy products of the West cross the Mississippi River and climb over high mountains, on expensive railways, rather than float down the river-current to the ocean? There are various circumstances which determine the course of trade besides the current rates of transportation. The magnitude of the grain business of a port depends upon the amount of available tonnage seeking freights, and this depends largely upon the general business of the port. This is true not only with respect to grain but of all commodities which will not bear the cost of a round trip. It is not true, however, in regard to more valuable commodities, such as cotton, tea, sugar, and other articles of commerce, which can bear freight-charges high enough to meet the necessary profits for both the inward and outward voyage.

This is illustrated by the statistics of imports and exports at New Orleans and New York, and of other commercial seaports of the United States. There are no available statistics indicating the weight and volume of the commodities exported from and imported into the several ports of the United States—only the values, and the amount of tonnage entered can be stated.

Value of imports and exports of ports of the United States during the year ending June 30, 1872.

Cities.	Value of imports.	Value of exports.	Tonnage entered from foreign ports.
	Dollars.	*Dollars.*	*Tons.*
Boston	70,398,185	21,443,154	881,486
New York	418,515,829	270,413,674	3,969,339
Philadelphia	20,383,853	20,982,876	417,911
Baltimore	28,836,305	18,325,321	368,136
Charleston	740,976	10,933,430	43,576
Savannah	627,410	28,246,607	139,523
Mobile	1,761,402	13,938,605	55,895
New Orleans	18,542,188	89,501,149	501,965
San Francisco	33,330,501	26,243,061	423,572

NOTE.—The value of imports is expressed in gold, and the value of exports in currency.

From this table it would seem that Boston, New York, Baltimore, and San Francisco are able, other things being equal, to offer the greatest inducements for the exportation of cheap commodities, because at each of those places the imports are greatly in excess of the exports, and consequently there is always a large amount of tonnage offering for outgoing shipments. Charleston, Savannah, Mobile, and New Orleans, on the other hand, have a very large excess of exports over imports, and consequently no very large additional exportation of cheap commodities is likely to take place at any of these ports until the conditions of trade are changed. At New Orleans the total value of exports for the year ending June 30, 1872, amounted to $89,501,149, of which cotton constituted $82,121,910, and the value of grain and flour amounted to only $1,212,133, over 93 per cent. of the value of the entire exports being cotton, and only about 1.3 per cent. consisting of flour and grain. The imports consisted largely of heavy commodities, such as pig-iron, salt, and railroad iron, and were carried at very low rates of freight. The above figures do not, however, represent the actual relative tonnage capacity entered and cleared. On this point Capt. Silas Weeks, of the Mississippi and Dominion Steamship Company, says that the tonnage of cargoes from Liverpool to New Orleans is about half that of outward cargoes, and that in consequence of the light return-cargoes the freight rates obtained by that company from Liverpool to New Orleans are not quite so much as from Liverpool to New York. The tendency of the laws of trade is always toward an equilibrium between the volume of imports and exports. Vessels which take a full paying cargo one way always seek return-cargoes, even at very low rates, rather than sail in ballast. Hence, although the distance from Liverpool to New Orleans is much greater than from Liverpool to New York, the rates are somewhat lower by the former route. The natural tendency of this fact is to stimulate the importation of merchandise at New Orleans destined to the Southern States and, also to the Western States. The question then arises, Why do not these States now receive their imported goods by the way of New Orleans? The answer, in our judgment, is found in the fact that the controlling influence of capital is directed almost exclusively in other channels. Money is a magnet of wonderful power. Both ships and merchandise obey its imperious mandates.

But why has not capital sought this route, if it be cheap and practcable? For several reasons. First. Because the rebellion crippled and paralyzed the South, while the war electrified and strengthened the commercial interests of the North. The commerce of the Mississsppi River which sought an outlet at New Orleans was larger before 1860 than at present. Capital, unable to find safe employment at New Orleans, sought the ports of the North, and by the construction of railroads and ships, new channels of commerce were created and old channels enlarged and improved.

The change in ocean-shipping from sailing to steam vessels, and the great increase in the size and draught of vessels has also tended to arrest the commerce of New Orleans. Merchandise is transported upon the ocean much more economically in large than in small vessels. But vessels of the largest size cannot pass the bar at the mouth of the Mississippi River, and hence for this reason, also, capital has sought other ports which offered the necessary facilities for economical ocean-transport, and the West, North, and East have poured out their wealth by hundreds of millions in the construction of artificial highways to such favored ports. The practical effect of the obstacles at the mouth of the river upon the tonnage of vessels entering, is shown by the average tonnage of steamers which entered the port of New Orleans during the last three years. (See page 845 of the evidence.) It is found by experience that from 3,000 to 5,000 tons is the most profitable size for ocean steamers, and yet during the last three years the average tonnage of steamers which entered the port of New Orleans has been under 1,050 tons. A reference to the same statistics will show the effect of the obstructions upon the smaller class of steamers also. In 1870–'71 the total number of steamers entered was 916, in 1871–'72 616, and 1872–'73 only 385. The practical effect, therefore, of the bar at the mouth of the river, and of other obstructions to be mentioned hereafter, has been to exclude from that port all vessels of the largest size, which carry freights most cheaply and advantageously, and to deter vessels of the smaller class from entering except for cotton, a cargo which commands higher rates of freight and fills the vessel without a corresponding increase of depth. Capt. A. K. Miller, of New Orleans, agent of the State Line Steamship Company, says that the vessels of his line could be loaded to 21 and 22 feet, but that on an average they are unable, on account of the bar, to load to more than 18 feet, and sometimes they are limited to 16½ or 17 feet, depending upon the condition of the Pass. He estimates that with a sufficient depth of water the saving in freight-charges would be fully 25 or 30 per cent.* It costs very little more to sail a fully loaded steamer than one carrying only three-fourths of her capacity, and the difference between the cost of navigating vessels 2,600 tons and of 2,000 tons is hardly appreciable. Captain Miller further testifies: "One of our ships is 600 tons larger than the others. We sail her with the same number of men. That makes the same amount for wages and provisions. There is no difference in the sailing of that vessel except some four or five tons of coal." (Evidence, p. 871.) He also mentions another fact which explains to some extent why the importations are not larger, namely, the cargoes from the other side being generally heavy articles, they are able to load only to a certain draught in order to get over the bar. The tonnage thus excluded in both directions would be clear profit, and would enable vessels to carry at much lower rates. If the mouths

* See also the evidence of Capt. Silas Weeks, agent of the Mississippi and Dominion Steamship Company, who says the loss in operating the largest vessels of his line, on account of shallow water on the bars, amounts to 30 per cent. (Evidence, p. 879.)

of the Mississippi were so improved that vessels of the largest size could reach New Orleans, the additional amount of cargo carried would increase the profits of the freighting business, and at the same time largely increase the commerce of the port. It is not surprising that under such circumstances capital does not eagerly seek investment in ocean-vessels for this port while other ports are free from such obstructions.

The heavy tax imposed upon commerce by the organization known as the Tow-boat Association also contributes very largely to the embarrassments of Mississippi River trade. Mr. William G. Coyle, president of the association, testified that the charge for towing a vessel in and out is from $1.40 to $1.50 per ton, amounting on a 2,000 ton vessel to $2,800, or $3,000 per trip, (Evidence, p. 889,) as will be seen by reference to the evidence of Major Howell, page 953, and Captain Follett, page 906. This association holds a practical control of the towing business at the mouth of the river, and the condition of the bar enables them to maintain this control. The committee refer to the evidence on this point for an illustration of the most indefensible monopoly ever known in the United States. It is proved to the satisfaction of the committee that the Tow-Boat Association have at times, for purposes designed to subserve their own interests, purposely obstructed and blockaded the passage formed through the bar by the United States dredge-boats, thus undoing work which had been done at great expense by the Government for the benefit of commerce.

In the opinion of the committee no individual or company should be allowed to exercise any exclusive right upon a natural navigable highway of commerce within the jurisdiction of the United States. It is the duty of the Government to maintain unrestricted freedom of commerce upon such waters. Any act on the part of an individual or corporation tending to obstruct or blockade such highways is an act of hostility to the commerce of the country, and demands such action on the part of the Government as will effectually prevent its continuance.

The committee recommend such legislation by Congress at the present session as may be necessary to place the channel through the bar at the mouth of the Mississippi under the control of the officer of the War Department in charge of that work, in so far as to confer upon him the power to regulate the passage of merchant-vessels through it; and the committee also recommend such legislation as may be proper to prevent any improper restraint upon free competition in the towing of vessels at New Orleans.

Another and perhaps the most potent cause why capital is not more readily invested in commercial enterprises by the New Orleans route will be found in the element of uncertainty, caused by the obstructions named. Capital in commercial enterprises seeks chiefly the more reliable channels of trade.

Exhibit E, page 843 of the evidence, shows the depth of the channel at the mouth of the river from July 1, 1871, to July 1, 1873; and also contains a statement, giving the number of vessels grounded, draught, time of detention, and cause; from which it appears that the detentions ranged from four hours to five and a half months. Five vessels were detained on the bar over four months in a single year. The loss suffered by the steamer Memphis by reason of such detention amounted to $31,609, not including loss of time and expenses of crew. To the Tow-boat Association alone she was compelled to pay $8,400. (Evidence, p. 849.)

These uncertainties sufficiently account for the fact that western products shun so dangerous and difficult a passage and that capital seeks other and more reliable channels. Let us suppose, for the purpose of illustration, a case of frequent occurrence. A merchant at Liverpool wishes to order a cargo of wheat or corn. Delay in the arrival of the vessel in which it is shipped will destroy his chance for speculation and disappoints his customers. He knows that from the northern ports he may rely upon receiving it at a certain time, while from New Orleans it may be three weeks or three months on the way. Can there be any doubt as to which port he will order? Again, a New Orleans trader purchases and ships to England a cargo of corn or wheat, and draws on his Liverpool consignee, relying upon the arrival of the cargo to meet his draft. The vessel is detained several weeks on the bar; his draft is protested and his credit suffers. He will not be likely to repeat the experiment. Nearly all the great ocean-steamer lines carry the mails, touching at various points on their voyage. The mails require certainty and celerity, and hence the port of New Orleans must be omitted from direct ocean mail-service.

These reasons appear fully to explain why there is lack of ocean-tonnage at New Orleans, and why the products of the West climb over mountains to reach the East rather than float down the river-current to the sea.

And yet, notwithstanding all these disadvantages and embarrassments, New Orleans is, in the value of her imports and exports, the second commercial seaport in the United States, her commerce being surpassed only by that of New York. In shipping she is the third port; her tonnage being exceeded only by that of New York and Boston. Her present commercial rank attained under all these adverse circumstances indicates the bright future that awaits her, and is a sure prophecy of the mighty volume of commerce which is destined at no distant day to find its way to the sea on the grandest internal water-way of the world.

Climatic difficulties.

It has been alleged that the Mississippi River can never become of great practical value for the transportation of cereals to foreign markets, because of the climatic influences at New Orleans and on the Gulf, which injure the products of the Northwestern States. On this point the committee have taken the testimony of a large number of gentlemen well informed on the subject, some of whose statements are as follows:

Capt. A. R. Miller, agent of the State Line Steamship Company, says: "During my experience in business we have shipped here on our ships about 220,000 bushels of corn, and have never, in any instance, heard complaint of any damage whatever; but, on the contrary, it has landed in as fine condition as when it was shipped." (Evidence, page 869.)

Mr. Lewis J. Higby, of New Orleans, testified:

"Mr. Chairman, as much has been said about this climatic influence, I will remark that my experience at the North in handling grain, from 1844 to 1868, was the largest of any one handler in Milwaukee, I having charge of the Milwaukee and Saint Paul elevator, and all the grain that the company brought in, and my experience here since 1868 to the present time, during five years, has been that we can keep grain here longer in the elevator than I could in Milwaukee—that is, in the summer time, I mean to say." * * * When grain comes here from Saint Louis, it is generally six or seven days on the way. It is put on barges which are about 15 feet between the joints, and between the joints there are 5 feet of grain, usually on deck, and then the windows are open forward and aft, and there is a continual draught through. Now, when that corn leaves Saint Louis, unless it is in the winter time, when there is no danger, in the summer time, when the warm weather continues, that draught passes through, and that grain is undergoing a drying process. When it gets here, it is in better order when it goes into the elevator or on board of a ship than it is in the spring of the year in Milwaukee or on the lake. We have stored grain here for four months during the summer time, and then the grain came out in very good order.

"Question. You say you find no more difficulty from damage to grain here than you did in Milwaukee?

"Answer. I do not have so much difficulty. At the same time I wish to be understood that grain will spoil anywhere, no matter where it is, if it is put in large quantities in the winter time and held until the germinating season. No grain will stand that in any place under some circumstances.

"Question. Why do you consider it safer here than North?

"Answer. It is for just these reasons that I speak of, that there are more of these humid hours. It is not all day that these hours occur at the North, nor is it so here. I have not known but two hours here within the past six months of that kind of what we call humid atmosphere. We have it up North more in the month of February. I recollect there once of losing twelve thousand bushels of corn in four days in the month of February. It was sold for 58 cents to a man, and he had taken part of it away, and backed out because it had changed grade. Those hours you have all experienced in the North or somewhere else, when there is seemingly no air, and the perspiration comes outside and stays on your skin."

Mr. Higby also submitted to the committee an account of the sale in Liverpool of a cargo of corn, of which he says:

"This cargo of mixed corn was shipped from here June 24, on the steamer Saint Louis. The thermometer stood at 94 the day it went on board, and it had as hot a passage through the Gulf as any cargo ever will have; yet when it arrived, which was in twenty-four days from the time of sailing, it sold at 2*s.* 6*d.* over the same grade from New York, as it was in better order." The consignees, John Stewart Oxley & Co., of Liverpool, say "the corn could not have been in better condition." (Evidence, p. 842.)

A committee of the Union Merchants' Exchange, of Saint Louis, confirmed the above statement, and also presented to the committee a list of eighteen cargoes of corn shipped from New Orleans to Europe, from February 11 to August 26, 1873, all of which arrived in good condition. One of these cargoes started on the steamer Memphis, April 23, and was detained on the bar forty-three days, but was not injured.*

Some of the witnesses have expressed a doubt as to whether corn sent by the Mississippi route always arrived in as good condition as by the railroads of the North and by the Saint Lawrence River, but after the most careful investigation of the subject, your committee are of the opinion that but little if any greater difficulty need be apprehended by this route than by any other.

The obstructions at the mouth of the Mississippi River and the proposed improvements.

At New Orleans the Mississippi River is about half a mile in width and nearly one hundred feet deep, but about one hundred and ten miles below that city it separates into several mouths, or passes. As these passes approach the sea they increase in width and become very shallow. Where the muddy waters of the Mississippi meet the waters of the Gulf, their motion is suddenly arrested, and the immense quantities of sediment, borne by the river from the many thousands of miles of alluvial shores above, are suddenly precipitated, and thus in the absence of littoral currents, bars and shallows are formed which encircle the entire delta. These bars are steadily advancing into the Gulf at the rate of about 340 feet in a year. The maximum depth of water at the mouths of the two largest passes varies from 12 to 16 feet in consequence of changes in the stage of water in the river, and of storms upon the Gulf. This has been the condition of the passes for many years, and it seems to be the regimen of the river under the action of natural forces.

Thirty or forty years ago this depth of water was sufficient for all the requirements of commerce, but for the large ocean-steamers now in use it is wholly inadequate.

Various modes of deepening the channel through the passes have been tried, among which may be mentioned the following, namely:

1. *Dredging.*—Under instructions of the War Department, Captain Talcott attempted, in 1839, to open the Southwest Pass with the ordinary bucket-drag. The gulf-waves, in a single storm, swept in "twice as much mud," as he had taken out.

2d. *By rake and harrow.*—This method was once tried under the direction and at the expense of the Government, by a tow-boat association, but their efforts were equally fruitless. The channel was temporarily opened to a depth of 18 feet, but again suddenly closed by a Gulf storm.

*See evidence of Captain Silas Weeks, agent of the Mississippi and Dominion Steamship Company, page 879.

3d. In 1868, '69, and '70, the Government caused to be constructed a steam-propeller dredge, at a cost of $350,000, which was placed under the command of an officer of the Navy. This experiment was faithfully made, but "it failed to maintain a much greater depth of water than that which nature has prescribed as the regimen depth of the pass." The results of this mode are at best only temporary, and to be of any service, the work must be continued from year to year, while the labors of an entire season are liable to be destroyed at any time by a single storm.

4th. *By concentration of the current.*—The Government entered into a contract with Messrs. Craig & Righter in 1836, to open a channel 1,000 feet wide and 18 feet deep, which was to be executed by closing all the passes except those designed for navigation. The contract was, however, never performed.

5th. *By the use of gunpowder.*—Blasting with gunpowder has also been tried without permanent success.

The difficulty with all these modes has been, that the work of months was liable to be destroyed at any time in a single night, by one of the severe storms which sweep over the Gulf. It is said that the money expended by the Government in these various experiments amounts to an aggregate of over $2,000,000. The present method of harrowing and scraping is probably the most effective yet adopted. This consists in constantly passing steam-vessels over the bar, which are provided with machines for stirring up the mud, the sediment thus loosened being carried by the current out into the deep water of the Gulf. This mode, like the others named, does not afford any permanent benefit. It is effectual only so long as the means employed are kept in motion. If the boats so employed are withdrawn, for even one month, the bar assumes its natural condition. By the means applied, channels have been opened, ranging from fifty to two hundred feet in breadth, and from 15 to 20½ feet in depth. When severe and long-continued storms occur, the work of deeping is often completely undone, and much time is again required to secure the maximum depth attainable.

The practical results of the means applied are stated in the report of the Board of Engineers dated January 13, 1874. (See page 78, Ex. Doc. No. 113, 43d Cong., 1st session.) The period of time referred to in the report was from July 1, 1872, to April 1, 1873.

Results.—Width of channel 50 to 150 feet; depth of channel 13 to 20 feet.

The depth of water ranged as follows: 19 to 20 feet, 39½ days; 17½ to 19 feet, 120 days; 17 feet, 90 days; 13 to 16½ feet, 22 days. The difficulties encountered and the practical results attained are summarized in the following statement of the board taken from the daily records:

"From July 1, 1872, to April 1, 1873, 53 vessels grounded at Southwest Pass, and were the cause of there being less than 18 feet in the channel. After November 1, to April 1, 1873, the dredge worked 58 days. Suspension of work on account of slack current, 62 days; fogs, 21 days; waves, 16 days; repairing, 36 days. The remainder of the time is accounted for in coaling, pulling grounded vessels out of the way, and suspension of work on Sundays. Operations at Pass àLoutre from April 1 to June 30, 1873, starting at 11½ feet depth on the bar, worked 78 days. From May 27 to July 1, the depth was 17½ feet at extreme low water of the Gulf."

Major Howell says of this mode of improvements:

"With the success attending the work of dredging the bar at Southwest Pass during the past two years, the commerce seeking the port of New Orleans has grown rapidly.

"Lines of steamships before in the trade have built new vessels for it; other old lines have been attracted to it; new lines have their vessels in course of construction; and sailing-vessels, in greater number than before, have engaged in it, all taking fuller cargoes, making quicker trips, with greater profit to owners and reduced expense to shippers. The cotton-trade of the upper cotton-region, for a time partially diverted from this route, is returning, and a grain-trade has been inaugurated, which promises to attain large proportions.

"While the great benefit already derived from dredging is acknowledged, there remains, in the minds of commercial men, doubt as to its continuance to meet the growing demand for deeper-draught vessels.

"There is yet more serious doubt regarding the continuance of suitable action on the part of Congress in making appropriations seasonably and in amount to prevent interruption of the work.

"Distrust in the continued effectiveness of dredging can only be overcome by long-continued success, and simply retards commercial progress. Distrust in the continued good will of Congress is of more serious import.

"The work in progress is dependent for its continuance on an annual appropriation; it is of a character requiring continued work; suspension for a few weeks or months will permit the natural agencies always at work to obliterate all evidences of previous improvement and return the channel across the bars at the river outlets to their normal and obstructed condition. Such occurrence would be disastrous in the extreme. It would ruin the commerce now promising such good results, ruin the merchants engaged in it, and destroy confidence in plans for its revival at any future time. Yet such occurrence is not improbable, as evidenced by the past record of the work.

"Legislative economy enters too largely into the spirit of American politics to permit of men engaged in legitimate business staking their wealth where it will depend on the turn legislation may take.

"What is required to inspire confidence in the future of the commerce of the Mississippi River is a permanent outlet, not one of uncertain tenure.

"Dredging, from its dependence on legislative action, does not offer such, nor do I believe it capable of offering more than a depth of 20 feet the year round, a depth not considered adequate." (See Ex. Doc. H. R. No. 113, 1st sess. 43d Cong.)

Fort Saint Philip canal.

In view of the inadequacy, uncertainty, continued expense, and substantial failure of all the experiments yet made, the question arises, *What method can be adopted which will afford a permanent deep-water passage from the Mississippi River to the Gulf?*

The method which is strongly recommended by a majority of the board of engineers appointed by the War Department for the purpose of passing upon the whole subject of the improvement of the mouth of the Mississippi River, and also by engineers not connected with the Government service, is to cut a canal from a point on the Mississippi River, a short distance below Fort Saint Philip, to the deep waters of Breton Sound, an arm of the Gulf of Mexico. The proposed work is, therefore, generally known as the Fort Saint Philip Canal. This canal was first proposed in the year 1832, since which time two or three surveys and reconnaissances have been made as to its proper location. The latest survey was made under direction of the Government by Capt. C. W. Howell, of the United States Engineer Corps, in the years 1871 and 1872, and his report was rendered in February, 1873. (For details in regard to the proposed canal see Ex. Doc. H. R. No. 113, 1st sess. 43d Cong.)

The line of canal by Captain Howell's survey extends from a point about seven miles below Fort Saint Philip, in an easterly direction, to a point a short distance south of Sable Point; the outer end being protected from the action of storms by jettees projecting some distance beyond the end of the canal. The plan provides for a canal which shall be about six miles in length, the prism being 200 feet wide at bottom, with slope sufficient to insure permanency, and the depth of 27 feet; a lift-lock 400 feet long and 80 feet wide, with 27 feet water on the miter-sill, a guard-lock at the east or Gulf end of the canal. Captain Howell estimates that this work will cost $7,400,000, and that the time required for its construction will be about three years, provided that appropriations are made as follows: $3,000,000 the first and second years, and the remainder during the third year. On the 30th of June, 1873, a board of engineers was constituted to consider and report upon the plan submitted by Captain Howell. That board consisted of J. G. Barnard, colonel of engineers, brevet major-general United States Army; John Newton, lieutenant-colonel of engineers, and brevet major-general United States Army; William P. Craighill, major of engineers, and brevet lieutenant-colonel United States Army: G. Weitzel, major of engineers, and brevet major-general United States Army; and C. W. Howell, captain of engineers, and brevet major United States Army. All the members of the board agreed as to the entire practicability of constructing the proposed work. The board, excepting General Barnard, presented a report approving the plan submitted by Captain Howell, as to its general engineering features; one member besides General Barnard being, however, of the opinion that the Gulf end of the canal should be located north of Sable Point, and that the river end should be located nearer to Fort Saint Philip. The board recommended the following changes in the details of the plan: Length of lock 500 feet, instead of 400 feet; width of lock 60 to 65 feet, instead of 80 feet; depth of water on sill of lock 25 feet, instead of 27 feet; sides of slope of canal, about from 1 to 4 feet. They also make the following statement:

"But it is suggested, in order to avoid beds and pockets of quicksand, known to exist at some points in this locality, that the precise line of the canal should not be decided upon until a more thorough examination of the substrata has been made by borings. It is not improbable that such an examination may indicate the expediency, and, perhaps, the necessity, not only of adopting a curve, or a series of curves, in preference to a straight line for the axis of the canal, but also of selecting other points of *termini* than those recommended by Captain Howell."

They also state:

"It is evident from the foregoing that the necessary and unavoidable absence of sufficient data to determine the best location for the line of the canal across the peninsula, including its *termini*, and particularly its *débouché* by jettees into Isle au Breton, renders it impossible to make a close estimate of its cost.

"A new estimate, resulting in part from a revision of that made by Captain Howell, has been rendered specially necessary in view of the modifications of plan recommended by the board. It is believed to be ample to cover the cost of constructing a canal of the dimensions given above, located within the limits designated. The estimate amounts to $10,273,000."

The dissenting opinion of General Barnard is based upon the following considerations:

1st. That the surveys made are insufficient, even to base an approximate estimate of cost upon.

2d. That the canal, if constructed, should be located farther north, and nearer to Fort Saint Philip.

3d. That the plan of locks and the method of constructing them involve objections of an engineering nature, which are mentioned.*

4th. That he believes the method by jettees at the mouth of one of the passses has not yet received proper attention.

In presenting these reports to the Secretary of War, Brig. Gen. A. A. Humphreys, Chief of Engineers says:

"Respecting the practicability of constructing a ship-canal from the river near Fort Saint Philip to the deep water of Isle au Breton Pass, all the members of the board agree that there is no doubt as to its entire practicability. To determine, however, the best line for the location of the canal across the peninsula, and the best point for its entering the river, and also the position and manner of its entering Isle au Breton Pass, requires further surveys, borings, and other examinations and measurements, and the preparation of plans based upon their results.'

The board of engineers were also ordered to report upon the practicability of improving the existing passes of the river, so as to afford the required depth of 25 feet.

The method by jettees projecting across the bar into the Gulf was considered, and pronounced impracticable on account of the cost, (about $9,500,000,) the improbability of maintaining such works intact, and the annual cost of extending them into the Gulf. The special difficulties in the application of the jettee system are considered to be:

* Ex. Doc. H. R., No. 113, 1st sess. 43d Congress, pp. 65–71.

1st. The absence of a littoral current, to carry off the sediment which is precipitated into the Gulf.

2d. The yielding nature of the banks and shoals.

3d. The abundance of deposits.

General Barnard also presented a dissenting opinion to this report, in which he favors the jettee plan. He does not recommend that the plan be at once adopted, but advises that further surveys and estimates be made, in order to determine the cost and practicability of applying this system of improvement to the South Pass, the smallest of the three great passes. In regard to the subject, he says:

"The question submitted, however, is not so much to recommend its trial (the jettee system) as to recommend its *consideration*, and that scrutiny and survey on which alone estimates can be based."

He adds the following as to the special advantages of the plan of improving one of the natural mouths of the Mississippi:

"If successful at all, (and I have endeavored to show that success is promised,) the cost will be a small fraction of that of the canal. On the other hand, the advantages of an open river mouth are inestimable. The needs of a navigation so great as that which now exists, and which in the future of the great Mississippi Valley must be fifty-fold increased, demand it.

"It is said that 'the time has come' when the needs of commerce demand the canal; but I answer *the time will come* when there will be the same cry for a navigation unimpeded by locks—*an open river mouth*—which we now hear for a canal. But in whatever aspect the question be regarded, the use of the river mouth for the next ten years is simply inevitable."

In regard to the jettee system, General Humphreys makes the following statement:

"After a careful investigation of the question of applying this method of improvement to the mouth of the Mississippi River, I am of the opinion that it does not present, either in its construction or cost, superior advantages to the canal plan. One of the chief objections to the jettee system is the unavoidable necessity of constantly extending the piers into the open sea, exposed to the full force of storms."*

The committee are unanimously of the opinion that prompt and vigorous measures should be adopted for a radical improvement of the mouth of the Mississippi River, adequate to the wants of commerce, but in view of all the facts presented to them, they reserve for the present any expression of opinion in regard to the best method to be adopted.

The improvement of the Mississippi River above the falls of Saint Anthony.

The Mississippi River has for several years been successfully navigated by steamboats from the falls of Saint Anthony to Sauk Rapids, a distance of seventy-eight miles. During navigable seasons small steamboats are also run on the various reaches of the river from Minneapolis

* The arguments for and against the proposed canal and jettee plan will be found in Ex. Doc. No. 113, first session Forty-third Congress.

to Leech Lake, the entire distance being about six hundred and seventy-five miles.

In consequence of obstructions caused by bowlders and bars, and the construction of the railroad from Saint Paul to Saint Cloud, there has been but very limited navigation on the river above Saint Anthony's Falls for several years.

The city of Minneapolis, at the falls of Saint Anthony, is one of the largest lumbering and milling points in the United States. The value of products manufactured in that city in 1873 amounted to $13,859,689, and her commercial business to $12,321,200, making a total of $26,180,889. Of lumber alone over 167,000,000 feet were manufactured. The maximum capacity of her flouring mills now in operation and in process of construction, as stated by those best informed, will equal 6,000 barrels per day, or over 1,800,000 barrels per year, affording a home market for over 8,000,000 bushels per annum of the surplus wheat of Minnesota.

It is believed that, by means of improvements in the river, involving a very moderate cost, a continuous line of navigation can be secured to the lakes near the head-waters of the Mississippi, forming a cheap line of transport, and securing incidentally all the advantages of competition with the railroads.

A reconnaissance of the river from the falls of Saint Anthony to Leech Lake was made in the year 1869, by Frank Cook, civil engineer, under the direction of General G. K. Warren, of the United States Engineer Corps. In his report to General Warren dated January 22, 1870, (Ex. Doc. 285, 41st Cong. 2d session,) Mr. Cook presents some valuable information in regard to the improvement of the Upper Mississippi, and the plan of reservoirs for supplying the river both above and below the falls of Saint Anthony during dry seasons. At Sauk Rapids a lockage of 18 feet will form a connection with a reach of the river requiring but little improvement in order to extend navigation to Little Falls. At this point a lockage of 14 feet will form a connection with another navigable reach extending to the mouth of Pine River, thence by improvements, such as the removal of bowlders and the opening of cut-offs, navigation can be extended to the Pokegama Falls. At that point a lockage of 30 feet will form a connection with navigable waters on the river above, and with Leech Lake and Winnebagoshish Lake.

It appears, from the report of Mr. Cook, that by means of the lockages at the three points mentioned, continuous navigation can be opened a distance of six hundred and seventy-five miles above the Falls of Saint Anthony. A United States Government supply-boat, connected with the Chippewa agency, has been employed for several years on the Mississippi and its tributaries above Pokegama Rapids, navigating the river on a reach of two hundred and sixty-two miles. In view of well-established facts as to the cheapness of transport on constant navigable rivers, and the possibility of opening a line of navigation of six hundred and seventy-five miles by means of locks at only three points, the total lockage amounting to but 62 feet, the river passing through a fertile area of the most productive wheat-growing State in the Union, there can be no question as to the importance of a survey for the purpose of determining the practicability and cost of such works. The accomplishment of this very desirable object, however, depends entirely upon the permanent maintenance of the Falls of Saint Anthony, a result which may be secured at a very trifling cost in comparison with its great importance.

But the most important recommendation made by Mr. Cook relates to the subject of *natural reservoirs* for the supply of the Mississippi River, both above and below the Falls of Saint Anthony during the seasons of low water. It is stated that by means of a dam at Pokegama Falls a supply of 37,057,638,400 cubic feet of water can be secured by raising the water in Winnebagoshish and Leech Lakes 2 feet, and it is also stated that by means of a dam, raising Lake Mille Lacs half a foot, a supply of water can be secured amounting to 10,036,224,000 cubic feet.

The total area of country furnishing drainage for this supply is six hundred and sixty square miles.

In regard to the benefits which would be secured to the navigation of the Mississippi River at Saint Paul, General Warren makes the following statement:

"It would supply at Saint Paul the difference between a 2-foot and 3-foot navigable stage for three hundred and ninety-five days; the difference between a 2 and 4 foot stage for one hundred and fifty-six days; the difference between a 2 and 5 foot stage, eighty-three days; the difference between a 3 and 4 foot stage, two hundred and sixty days; the difference between a 3 and 5 foot stage, one hundred and five days; and the difference between a 4 and 5 foot stage, for one hundred and seventy-nine days. It would do as much above the Falls of Saint Anthony."

The estimated cost of the reservoir-plan is $114,000. As the season of low water in the Upper Mississippi does not usually last over ninety days, it is believed that, by a comparatively trifling expenditure, the present uncertain and difficult navigation may be increased to a permanent depth of from 4½ to 5 feet during the entire season. The portion of the river which would thus be converted into permanently good navigation is over fifteen hundred miles in length, and located in the very heart of the most productive wheat-region on the continent. There are very few improvements which promise such valuable results at a cost comparatively so insignificant.

One of the most favorable features of the proposed plan is that the dams being low and the areas of supply very large, there will be little danger of the dams being carried away by freshets. In case of such accident no serious damage would be incurred, as the discharge of water would not be sufficiently rapid to overflow the valley below. In a report to the War Department, dated December 22, 1873, (Ex. Doc. 145, 43d Cong., 1st sess.,) Maj. F. U. Farquhar, of the United States Engineer Corps, recommends that a complete survey be made of the navigable portions of the Mississippi River above the Falls of Saint Anthony, and he also states that the improvement of the river between Saint Anthony and Saint Cloud requires at this time an appropriation of $43,034.75.

In view of the foregoing facts, the committee recommend—

That an appropriation be made for a survey of the Mississippi River from Saint Anthony's Falls to such point above as it may be found practicable to secure a sufficient depth of water for steamboat-navigation, and for the purpose of such surveys as may be necessary, in order to determine the practicability of forming reservoirs at the head-waters of the Mississippi for the supply of that river during dry seasons; and that an appropriation be made at the present session of Congress, for the improvement of the Mississippi River between Saint Anthony's Falls and Saint Cloud.

The improvement of the Mississippi River between Saint Paul and Saint Louis.

The following information in regard to the improvement of the Mississippi River between Saint Louis and Saint Paul has been furnished to the committee in reply to a letter of inquiry, addressed to General A. A. Humphreys, Chief of the Engineer Corps, United States Army:

Two dredge-boats have been employed between Rock Island Rapids and Saint Paul since the year 1867 in deepening sand-bars and in removing snags and overhanging trees. By this means from 3 to 3½ feet of water have been secured during the greater portion of the season of navigation. A new boat is now required which will cost about $30,000. It is thought that it will be necessary to construct wing-dams or jettees at certain points, and at places where the river divides into several channels it may be necessary to close all but one channel, in order to secure the requisite depth of water at some of the worst sand-bars during the lowest stages in the river. No estimate can be made at this time as to the cost of completing the improvements on this part of the Mississippi.

The Rock Island Rapids are being improved by means of excavating the natural channel so as to give a width of 200 feet and a navigable depth of 4 feet at extreme low water. This excavation is all in rock. The remaining work to be done will require an appropriation of $112,000.

No improvements are contemplated on that part of the river between Rock Island Rapids and the upper end of the Keokuk Rapids, the ruling depth at low water being now 4 feet. The plan adopted several years ago, and now being carried out for the improvement of the Keokuk Rapids, is the construction of a canal extending along the Iowa shore a distance of 7.6 miles. This canal varies in width from 250 to 300 feet, and it will have a minimum depth of 5 feet, with two lift-locks and one guard lock, each lift-lock being 350 feet long and 80 feet wide. Certain rock excavations are also required at Montrose by means of a thorough cut 200 feet wide and 5 feet deep along the natural channel of the river. The estimated cost of completing these works is $800,000. No improvements are now contemplated in that part of the river between the lower end of the Keokuk Rapids and Saint Louis, the ruling depth at low water being at present about 4 feet. A dam is being constructed across the slough behind Ellis Island for the purpose of improving the harbor of Alton, Illinois. Works are also in progress between the mouth of the Missouri and the mouth of the Meramec for the preservation and improvement of the harbor of Saint Louis.

The improvement of the Mississippi River between Saint Louis and Cairo, and at points between Cairo and Memphis.

In regard to the permanent improvement of the Mississippi River in such manner as to secure *a depth of* 10 *feet between Cairo and Saint Louis at the lowest stages of the river*, the committee refer to a letter addressed to Hon. E. O. Stanard, by Col. J. H. Simpson, of the United States Engineer Corps, which may be found on page 600 of the evidence. The method proposed is that of contracting the water-way at points where the great width of the river causes shoals and bars to be formed, together with the protection of the banks and the removal of sunken wrecks and snags.

Colonel Simpson states that his predecessor estimated the cost of these improvements at $2,996,000, but he believes that a more accurate estimate of cost can be made from the results of very thorough surveys now in progress.

The Chief of Engineers, in his late annual report, recommends that an appropriation of $50,000 be made for the purpose of completing this survey; also that an appropriation of $600,000 be made for the prosecution of the present work of improvements on the Mississippi River, between the mouth of the Missouri and the mouth of the Ohio.

The commerce of the Mississippi River.

No adequate estimate can be formed of the value of the commerce on the Mississippi River, nor of the value of the total commerce of the towns situated upon it. An idea of the magnitude of this commerce may, however, be formed when it is considered that the value of the commerce of the cities and towns on the Ohio River amounts to the enormous sum of $1,623,000,000. The National Government has provided no means of arriving at a knowledge of such important facts as this in regard to the internal commerce of the country. The collection of the necessary data from private sources, and from data prepared by boards of trade, State and city governments, would alone require the constant labor of one person for a year.

Not only is the commerce of the Mississippi River crippled by the existence of the bar at its mouth, a difficulty which can be entirely overcome by an expenditure of a sum probably not exceeding $10,000,000, but the value of the river above is greatly depreciated by obstructions which may be overcome very readily by engineering skill, and at an expense quite insignificant in comparison either with the present value of its commerce, or with the increase of trade which may be expected as the natural result of such improvements. Hitherto the improvement of the Mississippi has been carried on merely by sporadic efforts. Appropriations have from time to time been made and money expended, without any general plan as to the ultimate results which were to be attained. The committee recommend that the necessary surveys and estimates be made at the earliest practicable moment, in order to mature a plan for the radical improvement of the river, and of all its navigable tributaries.

Such a plan should comprehend the establishment of a given depth of water on the Mississippi River in some such manner as the following:

1st. Improvements designed to secure a depth of from 8 to 10 feet from Saint Louis to New Orleans, at the lowest stages of the river.

2d. Improvements designed to secure a depth of 5 feet at the lowest stages between Saint Louis and Saint Paul.

3d. Improvements designed to secure a depth of 4½ feet in the river above Saint Anthony's Falls.

Having adopted a plan of this kind for the radical improvement of the river, all works should be carried out with this general object in view.

It is much more practicable to establish such a plan now than it was a few years ago, for the reason that the successes and failures of past efforts have enabled engineers to discover the nature of the difficulties which will be met, and to adopt the best methods of improvement. Diverse opinions still exist among some of our ablest engineers as to the best means to be adopted in specific cases, but it is believed that sufficient practical knowledge has already been gained to determine a general plan of future operations, both in regard to the Mississippi River and its principal navigable tributaries. The time has arrived for thorough measures, and the necessary plans and estimates upon which such measures must be based should be prepared at once.

It is impossible to overestimate the commercial results likely to follow such improvements. With the well-established facts before us in regard to the much greater cheapness of transport by navigable rivers than by railways, it cannot be doubted that such improvements would increase the commerce of the Mississippi very greatly, and, at the same time, afford relief to a large area in the Western States now fettered in its growth and prosperity, by the cost of transporting agricultural products to both home and foreign markets.

Men of large practical experience state that if 8 feet of water can be obtained between Saint Louis and New Orleans at all stages of the river, the average cost of transporting grain between these cities would not exceed 7½ cents per bushel. The present freight charge from New Orleans to Liverpool averages only 27 cents, and with improvements at the mouth of the river may be reduced to 18 or 20 cents. Hence, by these improvements a saving of from 18 to 20 cents per bushel may be effected. The highest rate of freight on corn from Saint Louis to New Orleans, during the year 1872, was $36\frac{2}{5}$ cents per bushel, and the lowest rate $9\frac{4}{5}$ cents. The highest rate prevailed when there was less than 5 feet of water on the worst bars, and the lowest rate when there was over 8 feet on those bars. The average low-water rate in 1872 was $21\frac{2}{5}$ cents and the average high-water rate 11 cents, or only about half the low-water rate. When the river falls to its lowest stages the largest boats are laid up, and smaller ones are employed, the cost of transport in such boats being much greater than in the larger size. Besides, this mode of business entails upon the owners of steamboat property a very serious loss in consequence of the capital invested in the larger boats lying idle during the low stages of the river. The average lifetime of these large and expensive boats is only about eight years; the loss from depreciation is therefore very large. This expense, together with the cost of maintenance and interest on capital, constitutes a heavy burden upon transporter and shipper alike.

The precise nature of the difficulties of navigation below Saint Louis will perhaps be more clearly appreciated from the following statement showing the condition of river-navigation below that city during the last nine years.

Average stage of water each year for nine years.

Number of days less than 4 feet	$3\frac{4}{9}$
Number of days over 4 feet and less than 6	$52\frac{2}{9}$
Number of days over 6 feet and less than 8	$103\frac{5}{9}$
Number of days over 8 feet and less than 10	$69\frac{1}{9}$
Number of days over 10 feet	$136\frac{6}{9}$

It appears that during nearly one half the year the commerce of Saint Louis was more or less affected by low water. Capable engineers have clearly proved that all these embarrassments to commerce in consequence of low water can be overcome at a cost which, in comparison with the benefits to be secured, is quite insignificant.

The fact that oftentimes the river is not closed by ice below Saint Louis during the entire winter season constitutes that city a valuable winter port for the shipment of western produce. The average suspension of navigation on account of ice does not exceed ten or twelve days.

The importance of the improvement of the Mississippi River, above Saint Louis, may be demonstrated from present high and low water rates; the cost of transporting grain from points above Keokuk during high water being about one half the low-water rates.

Persons best informed on this subject believe that upon the completion of the entire river improvements, and with the largely increased business which is expected to result therefrom, grain can be transported in barges from Saint Paul to New Orleans at a fair profit for from 12 to 15 cents per bushel. Capt. W. F. Davidson, a gentleman of large experience in river navigation, has expressed the opinion that, with the improved river, the cost per bushel from Saint Paul to New Orleans need not exceed 12 cents; estimating the probable cost at 15 cents per bushel to New Orleans, and at 27 cents from there to Liverpool, (the present average,) and the two transfers at Saint Louis and New Orleans at 1 cent each, the entire cost from Saint Paul to Liverpool would be 44 cents. The present cost by the cheapest routes, including elevator and terminal charges at western lake ports, and at Buffalo and New York, averages about 71 cents per bushel. A saving of 27 cents per bushel could therefore be effected, which, on the corn and wheat crops of Iowa and Minnesota alone would amount to over $36,000,000 per annum, more than enough to pay every year double the cost of the entire improvements.*

Estimates of the cost of the various improvements of the Mississippi River and its tributaries have been prepared by the Union Merchants' Exchange of Saint Louis. These estimates amount to the sum of $16,010,000, and are supposed to cover the entire cost of the radical improvements of these rivers, except the Ohio.

In view of the great advantages to be derived from these works, the amount of the above estimates is certainly very small. It is also small in comparison with the cost of the Erie Canal and the Saint Lawrence Canals, the former constructed by the State of New York, and the latter by the Canadian government, for the purpose of opening up the northern water-lines from the West to the Atlantic seaboard.

Cost of the proposed improvement of the Mississippi River and its tributaries	$16, 010, 000
Cost of the Erie Canal	43, 639, 000
Cost of the Canadian canals when works now in progress are completed	35, 550, 000

Such benefits as are anticipated from the improvements of the Mississippi have been more than realized from the improvement of the principal harbors on Lake Michigan, where the depth has been increased from 7 to 14 feet; and also by the improvements in the passages between Lakes Huron and Erie.

THE OHIO RIVER.

The improvement of the Ohio River in such manner as to secure from Pittsburgh to Cairo a depth of 6 feet of water at all seasons is believed by the committee to be one of the most important works for which the National Government can appropriate money. Even in its present condition of high and low water†—sometimes a depth sufficient to

* This estimate is based upon the fact that the price of wheat and corn are fixed by the price at Liverpool, less the cost of transportation, and hence any reduction of transportation-charges increases the value of the entire crop to the extent of such reduction.

† The rise and fall of the Ohio at Cincinnati is 62½ feet.

float the largest ocean-vessel, and at other times unnavigable in its upper portions for the smallest flat-boat—it is one of the most important highways of commerce on this continent. In the interests which it touches not only in the States bordering upon it, but also in all the States of the Mississippi Valley, few other highways present commercial considerations more truly national in their bearing and extent. Its improvement would doubtless develop resources of wealth vastly exceeding in value the expenditures required.

The Ohio River, from Pittsburgh to its mouth, at Cairo, is nine hundred and sixty-seven miles in length. Six States border upon it, viz, Pennsylvania, West Virginia, Ohio, Kentucky, Indiana, and Illinois, and the territory drained by it embraces 214,000 square miles. An elaborate statement of the commerce of the cities and towns on the Ohio River was prepared in the year 1868, by W. Milnor Roberts, United States engineer, which statement is here presented with certain corrections in relation to the cities of Pittsburgh, Cincinnati, and Louisville, which are based upon statistics of the trade of these cities during the year 1872.

Pittsburgh, Pa	$300,000,000
Wheeling, W. Va	30,000,000
Pomeroy, Ohio	8,000,000
Ironton, Ohio	5,000,000
Steubenville, Ohio	8,000,000
Portsmouth, Ohio	12,000,000
Maysville, Ohio	8,000,000
Ripley, Ohio	5,000,000
Cincinnati, Ohio	518,000,000
Madison, Ind	12,000,000
Jeffersonville, Ind	5,000,000
Louisville, Ky	424,000,000
New Albany, Ind	15,000,000
Evansville, Ind	12,000,000
Wabash River, Ind	15,000,000
Smithland, Ky	30,000,000
Paducah, Ky	40,000,000
Cairo, Ill	20,000,000
354 other points	156,000,000
	1,623,000,000

These estimates are the best that could be obtained. It is probable, however, that the total value here stated is less than the actual value of the commerce of the towns mentioned, as the increase of the population and commerce of the Ohio has been very rapid since 1868, when Mr. Roberts's report was made. Only an official census could enable the committee to arrive at an accurate statement in relation to this subject.

Coal and other mineral interests are among the most important depending at the present time upon the Ohio River for transport. The coal bordering on the Upper Ohio and its tributaries covers an extent of territory estimated at 122,000 square miles, and embraces all the varieties of coal required in the arts, and for fuel. These coal-fields extend throughout the western slope of the Allegheny range in Pennsylvania, West Virginia, and Kentucky, and are also found extensively in the State of Ohio. The city of Pittsburgh is now the center of the coal-trade. The shipments of coal by river during the year 1873 amounted to about 60,000,000 bushels, or 2,300,000 tons, and yet nearly as much coal is consumed in the immense manufacturing establishments of that city as is shipped to points below.

The value of the steamers, barges, and boats owned at Pittsburgh and employed in the coal business is estimated at $5,000,000. Almost all the coal consumed in the cities and towns and country bordering on the Mississippi River and its navigable tributaries below Saint Louis, consumed by steamers on the Mississippi River, and, to a great extent, by ocean-steamers from New Orleans, is shipped on the Ohio River from Pittsburgh and vicinity, and from the Kanawha River in West Virginia. During a single rise in the river 46 fleets, composed of 369 barges and carrying 4,156,000 bushels of coal, have been shipped from Pittsburgh within the space of three days. A statement in regard to the resources of West Virginia in coal and iron, by Professor David T. Anstead, of England, may be found on page 452 of the evidence. But those vast resources largely await improvements in the navigation of the Kanawha and Ohio Rivers, the cost of which would be quite insignificant in proportion to the amount of wealth which would be developed.

As pertinent to this subject the following statement from the letter of the chairman of the commission for the improvement of the Ohio is given:

"The bituminous-coal area of the United States is given at 133,132 square miles, in the geological surveys so far published, while Great Britain, France, and Belgium contain but 14,096 square miles, or a little over one-tenth. Of this 133,132 square miles of bituminous-coal deposit, the Ohio States contain 100,000. The relation of fuel to manufactures is too well understood to need comment to show where the manufacturing population of the United States will be. The value of minerals and manufactures to the wealth of a nation has been too clearly demonstrated in the national life of Great Britain to require argument to show what one hundred thousand square miles of coal will be to the seven Ohio States, if only eleven thousand has been of such incalculable value to Great Britain. What food, what transportation, then, will not this nation's workshop need for its workers?"

The tide of emigration in this country has passed over and around resources of mineral wealth here, the development of which may even surpass the riches of the fertile prairies of the West, and yet this immense commerce and the development of these vast mineral resources are dependent upon the rising and falling waters of an uncertain stream.

By examining the crop-maps at the end of the Appendix it will be seen, that the Ohio River passes through one of the largest and most productive corn-producing areas of the country, embracing the southern part of Ohio and the northern part of Kentucky; and that the Ohio River is almost contiguous to one of the largest and richest wheat-producing areas of the country, embracing a large part of the States of Ohio and Indiana, of which Cincinnati and Louisville are the principal receiving and shipping points. Besides, those portions of the States of Ohio, Kentucky, and Indiana, bordering on the upper and middle sections of the Ohio River, produce immense surplus quantities of beef, pork, and other provisions, together with all other kinds of agricultural products raised in this latitude, which require cheap transport, and which go to make up the immense commerce of the Ohio River towns, amounting in value to over $1,623,000,000, as already stated. These surplus products find large and valuable markets in the Gulf States, and are exported to a considerable extent to tropical countries on this continent, and to other foreign countries, via New Orleans.

Railroads have been constructed within a few years from the States of Ohio, Indiana, and Illinois direct to the Gulf States, but the Ohio and Mississippi Rivers form not only the cheapest line of transport, but the competition of the river-route regulates the rail-routes to a very great extent, and thereby reduces very much the cost of transportation by rail.

Upon this subject the committee refer to the testimony taken before them at Cincinnati and at Louisville, and particularly to the statements made by Mr. Thomas Sherlock, of Cincinnati, (page 523 to 528 of the evidence.)

Mr. Sherlock states that the railroads always raise their rates when the water in the river is so low that the larger boats cannot be run, and when navigation is entirely suspended on account of ice or low water.

The railroad lines from Cincinnati to New Orleans raise their rates from 50 cents per 100 pounds during high water to 82 cents per 100 pounds during low water.

The improvement of the Ohio River.

The question as to the best mode of improving the Ohio River is one of great difficulty, the decision of which must depend upon the result of practical experiments.

A board of commissioners for the improvement of the Ohio River was created in the year 1872 by the joint action of the States of Pennsylvania, Ohio, West Virginia, Kentucky, Tennessee, Indiana, and Illinois. This commission presented a memorial to Congress, dated December 16, 1872, in which they make the following judicious reference to the subject of improvement:

"How or in what detail this improvement is to be made we make at this time no presentation. When the Government shall have provided the means, the skill of the Engineer Corps of the United States will find a satisfactory plan beyond a doubt. The question is not one of engineering, but of finance."

In a series of resolutions adopted by the commission at Washington, February 12, 1874, they do not attempt to pass upon the merits of any one of the various plans proposed. The question, therefore, turns upon the results arrived at by the United States engineers, who have given to this subject years of study and personal examination.

The nature of the difficulties involved may be briefly stated as follows: The Ohio River descends 426 feet between Pittsburgh and Cairo, the distance being nine hundred and sixty-three miles. In consequence of this great descent the velocity of the current varies from one and one-half to three and one-half miles per hour. The coal-tows of Pittsburgh consisting of a number of boats or barges, and the steamers which propel them, require 6 feet of water in the river in order to pass down with safety. These tows and fleets of tows also require a wide channel in order to be navigated safely and economically. In view of these necessities of commerce, there are two essential conditions imposed upon any plan which may be adopted, viz:

1st. That whatever structures may be placed in the river they shall be so low that at a fair rise in the river the coal-fleets can pass over them without impediment.

2d. That the improvements adopted shall secure a depth of at least 6 feet of water at the lowest stages of the river.

In the year 1870 W. Milnor Roberts, United States engineer, a gentleman of eminence in his profession, presented a report, after a thorough survey and examination of the river, and of the various plans suggested for its improvement. He recommended the adoption of the plan of locks and dams with chutes, estimated to cost $23,777,662.

It is believed by Mr. Roberts that by this means the flow of water at low stages will be greatly retarded, that the number of days each year in which coal can be transported will be increased, and that a depth of three feet to Cairo will be secured at the lowest stages of the river. He recommended, however, that before applying the system to the entire river, as an experiment, six dams with locks and chutes should be constructed between Pittsburgh and Beaver Shoals, a distance of twenty-seven miles, at an estimated cost of $2,000,000. Another plan has since been proposed by a board of engineers, composed of G. Weitzel, major of engineers, brevet major-general United States Army, and W. E. Merrill, major of engineers and brevet colonel, appointed by order of the War Department, dated April 16, 1872. The report of this board is dated January 31, 1874, (Ex. Doc. No. 127, Forty-third Congress, first session.) It embraces a valuable sketch of the practical results of various plans adopted for river improvements in this and other countries, together with descriptions of several plans not yet tried. Fifteen plans and combinations of plans are mentioned. The plan recommended for trial is the invention of Mr. F. R. Brunot, with modifications suggested by the board.

It consists of 66 locks and dams, with chutes 200 feet wide, opened and shut by means of hydraulic gates, which can be lowered and raised at will. The estimated cost of each one of these structures is $300,000, and the estimated cost of applying the system to the entire river, omitting the hydraulic gate below Louisville, where there is a greater depth of water and less velocity of current, is about $20,000,000. The board, however, recommend that the merits of the plan be first tested by means of a practical experiment at dam No. 1, on the Monongahela River, opposite the city of Pittsburgh. The estimated cost of the experimental structure is $80,000; the chute to be only 100 feet wide. The Monongahela Navigation Company, through their president, Hon. J. K. Moorhead, offer the use of this dam for the purpose of the experiment mentioned, and agree to pay one-half of the expense incurred, without any charge for the use of the dam, or for such tools and working machinery as they may have on hand, the chutes and gate to become the property of the company, and the United States to be at no expense for its removal, or for the restoration of the dam to its original condition, in case the experiment does not succeed. The board recommend that Congress shall appropriate the sum of $40,000 for the purpose of making the experiment. This whole matter has been referred to Gen. A. A. Humphreys, Chief of Engineers United States Army, who recommends that the measure suggested by the board be adopted.

In view of these recommendations and the opinions of the Chief of Engineers of the War Department, the committee recommend an appropriation for the purpose of making the experiment referred to.*

THE LOUISVILLE CANAL.

The most formidable natural obstacle to the navigation of the Ohio River is the "falls," between Louisville and Portland. These falls or rapids have a descent of 25.7 feet in a distance of four and one-half miles. Steamers and tows pass over them during the highest stages of the river, but at all ordinary stages and during low water they are impassable either by steamers or barges.

In the year 1825 a charter was granted by the State of Kentucky for the construction of a canal around the falls. This canal was opened in the year 1831. In the year 1857 the ownership of it was transferred to the United States, and the work has since been held in trust by the directors of the original Louisville and Portland Canal Company, the

* A valuable statement in regard to the navigation of the Ohio River below Cincinnati, by the local board of United States inspectors of steam-vessels at that city, may be found on page 228 of the appendix. The committee also present a letter from George H. Thurston, esq., chairman of the executive committee of the board of commissioners for the improvement of the Ohio River, embracing valuable statistics and other information, which may be found on page 87 of the appendix.

United States Government having since greatly enlarged the canal, so that it will now admit the passage of the largest vessels employed on the Ohio River.

A bill has already passed the Senate at the present session of Congress, providing for the payment of certain outstanding bonds of the Louisville and Portland Canal Company, and the assumption of the entire control of the work by the United States Government, the rate of tolls to be so graded that the receipts shall simply be sufficient to pay for the current expenses of maintaining and operating the work.

THE IMPROVEMENT OF THE KANAWHA RIVER BELOW THE GREAT FALLS.

The radical improvement of the Kanawha River from its mouth to Great Falls, a distance of 94.20 miles, requires the adoption of a plan which will insure the same depth at low water as is proposed to be secured on the Ohio, viz, 6 feet at the lowest stages. Such an improvement would afford a constant channel for the transport of coal, with the exception of about a month each year, when navigation is closed on account of ice.

It is stated by W. Milnor Roberts, United States engineer, in his report rendered in the year 1870, that "among the items of export for 1869, passing Point Pleasant into the Ohio from the Kanawha River, was 1,873,528 bushels of salt and 2,763,000 bushels of coal."

The treasurer of the Kanawha Improvement Company states that this trade has probably increased 100 per cent. since Mr. Roberts's report was made.

Mr. Lorraine, late chief engineer of the James River and Kanawha Canal, presents two estimates, each providing for boats drawing six feet.

The first, amounting in round numbers to $2,000,000, contemplates an open-dam improvement as far up as Paint Creek Shoal, with waterways 120 feet in width, and with 6½ feet depth; and from this point to the Great Falls a lock and dam improvement, with locks 240 feet long, 40 feet wide, and 7 feet depth of water. This estimate includes the cost of a reservoir at Meadow River.

The second estimate, amounting in round numbers to $3,000,000, contemplates a lock and dam improvement throughout.

By a plan of improvement, consisting of dams with open chutes below Paint Creek Shoals, and of dams with locks between that point and Lyken's Shoals, it was estimated that the cost would be $2,000,000.

The cost of improving the Kanawha by the method of locks and dams, with chutes and movable gates, would be about $3,300,000, viz, eleven dams, locks, and chutes, at $300,000 each.

In view of the importance of developing the vast mineral resources of West Virginia herein referred to, the committee recommends that, as soon as the Engineer of the War Department can determine upon the best plan for the radical improvement of the Kanawha River, the necessary appropriations shall be made by Congress for that work.

THE WISCONSIN AND FOX RIVERS IMPROVEMENT.

The Wisconsin and Fox Rivers have formed an important highway of commerce for nearly two hundred years. It was by this route that, in 1673, Marquette and his companions discovered the Upper Mississippi, and along which were made, by the French missionaries and traders, the earliest settlements in the West.

It was the wish of the founders of the republic to preserve this great natural water-route unobstructed, and to make it a permanent means of communication between the lakes and the Mississippi. In the ordinance for the government of the territory of the United States northwest of the river Ohio, adopted July 14, 1787, it is provided that the navigable waters leading into the Mississippi and the Saint Lawrence, and the carrying-places between the same, shall be common highways, and forever free.

The same provision, in substance, is embodied in an act of Congress relating to said territory, passed August 7, 1789, after the adoption of the Constitution of the United States; in an act of Congress establishing the territorial government of Wisconsin, approved April 20, 1836; in an act of Congress relating to the admission of Wisconsin as a State into the Union, approved August 6, 1846; and in the constitution of the State of Wisconsin.

In 1839, under the direction of the War Department of the Government, a preliminary survey of the rivers and an estimate of the cost of their improvement were made by Captain Cram, of the United States Topographical Engineers.

In 1846, by an act of Congress approved August 8, 1846, a grant of lands was made to the State of Wisconsin, on the admission of such State into the Union, for the purpose of improving the navigation of the Fox and Wisconsin Rivers in the Territory of Wisconsin, and of constructing a canal to unite the said rivers at or near the portage, in which the declaration was re-asserted that this should be free for the commerce of the United States.

The State of Wisconsin, at first by its board of public works and afterward by corporations duly created therefor, undertook to improve the navigation of these rivers. Over two millions of dollars, including the proceeds of the lands granted by Congress, were expended. The Fox River was improved so as to pass, in low water, boats of four feet draught from Green Bay to Lake Winnebago, and of two and a half feet from Lake Winnebago to the Wisconsin River. Little or no work was done upon the Wisconsin, owing to the uncertainty attending the navigation of the Wisconsin, and the inadequate depth of the channel in the Fox River. The improvement failed to meet in any great degree the requirements of commerce. It did not admit of the passage of boats up the

Wisconsin from the Mississippi, and was of little benefit, excepting on the line of the Fox River. There its benefits are apparent in the extraordinary development of that portion of the State—a development which is traceable not only to the utilization of water-power, but probably in a greater degree to the competition, although necessarily small, existing between water and rail.

In 1870 Congress directed the Secretary of War to adopt such a plan for the improvement of the Wisconsin as should be approved by the Chief of Engineers, and authorized him to appoint arbitrators to ascertain the sum which ought to be paid for the transfer of all rights in the works of improvement then held by a corporation created under the laws of Wisconsin. In ascertaining this sum the arbitrators credited the United States with the proceeds of all lands granted by Congress in aid of the work, the proceeds, with the costs of sale, amounting to about $1.25 per acre, and fixed the sum to be paid to said corporation at $145,000. In 1871 Congress made an appropriation therefor, and a deed of transfer was made and delivered to the United States. Additional appropriations for the work, according to the plan approved by the Chief of Engineers, to the extent of $400,000, have been made by Congress.

In reference to this work, Colonel Houston, the engineer in charge, says: "The work now is in the hands of the Government, different from any other work of this character, and the appropriation that was made last year is too small an appropriation to carry on the work to advantage."

Nature and condition of the work of improvement.

The Wisconsin River, having its rise in the northern part of the State of Wisconsin, runs southerly until it approaches the Fox River, turns abruptly southwesterly, and, running in that course one hundred and eighteen miles, empties into the Mississippi at Prairie du Chien.

The Fox River, having its rise in the southern part of Wisconsin, runs northwesterly until it approaches the Wisconsin River, turns abruptly northeasterly, and running in that course one hundred and sixty miles, (to be reduced to one hundred and fifty-three miles,) empties into Lake Michigan at Green Bay.

The course of the two rivers below the portage, the point of nearest approach, is surprisingly straight, and nearly upon a due line passing through Prairie du Chien and the Straits of Mackinaw.

The divide, or portage, separating the Wisconsin River waters, leading into the Gulf of Mexico, from the Fox River waters, leading into the Saint Lawrence, is a level sand prairie, without rock, and in width one and one-half miles. The Wisconsin at the portage is at the summit-level. It is about 7 feet higher than the Fox at the portage, about 200 feet higher than Lake Michigan at the mouth of the Fox, and 169 feet higher than the Mississippi at the mouth of the Wisconsin.

Already a canal at the portage connects the Wisconsin and the Fox, and a slack-water communication extending from the portage to Green Bay, a distance of one hundred and sixty miles, overcomes, by locks and dams, the fall of 200 feet, and connects the Wisconsin River with Lake Michigan.

The Fox River from its mouth to Oshkosh, on Lake Winnebago, has a low-water channel of about 4 feet, and from Lake Winnebago to the portage of about 3 feet. At stages of high water, boats of 3, 4, and even 5 feet draught have passed from Lake Michigan up the Fox River, and down the Wisconsin into the Mississippi River. As late in the season as June boats of three hundred tons burden have made the passage. In stages of low water the Wisconsin cannot be navigated on account of the drifting sand.

Compared with the Erie Canal.

The Erie Canal is three hundred and fifty miles long, nominally 7 feet deep; has seventy-one locks 110 feet by 18 feet; a total lockage of 654 feet, and admits the passage of boats of about two hundred tons.

The Wisconsin and Fox Rivers improvement to have five feet draught, to be 271 miles in length, of which 118 are to be unobstructed river and 153 slack-water navigation; with 27 locks, 160 feet by 35 feet, and a total lockage of 195 feet; water at the summit-level greatly in excess of the quantity required, and not to exceed six miles of canal in all, including the short canals around the dams,* and will pass boats of over 500 tons.

The present motive-power on the Erie Canal is horse-power. On the improvement steam is proposed. The rate of movement on the canal, including lockages, does not exceed one and a half miles per hour; while on the improvement it will be five to seven miles per hour.

An impediment, and possibly the greatest, in the way of the improvement of rivers, is the sudden and great rise of water at certain seasons of the year. In the Ohio River the floods rise above low-water mark as high as sixty feet, and in the Illinois, Rock, and Chippewa Rivers as high as thirty feet. But not so in the Wisconsin. The difference between high and low water mark is, at the mouth ten feet, and at the portage six feet. Two mountains of rock, twenty miles above the portage, situated at each side and close against the river, by reducing the channel, hold back the floods.

Maj. Charles R. Suter, in his report of the survey of this river, made January 2, 1867, says:

"Twenty-three miles above Portage City the river passes through the Dalles, and is there very much reduced in width. The Dalles act as a dam to prevent any very great rise in the Lower Wisconsin. The average yearly rise is about six feet. In the spring of 1866 it rose nine feet, which is the greatest height it has attained for many years. The rise in the river just above the Dalles on this occasion was more than fifty feet."

---

* See Colonel Houston's Report, 1873, and evidence, p. 232.

The proposed improvement will permit the passage of vessels more than double the size of those on the Erie Canal, and at a speed at least three times as great. The annual capacity of this line for the movement of tonnage will be more than twice that of the Erie Canal. Assuming the capacity of the vessels to be 500 tons, the time for passage of a lock 10 minutes, and the number of days of navigation 220, the ultimate capacity for the movement of freights eastward will be 7,920,000 tons per annum—equal to 264,000,000 bushels of 60 pounds.

The construction of this work will afford water competition with all the railways which now connect the Mississippi River with the lakes, between Burlington, Iowa, and Saint Paul, Minn. It is difficult to state precisely all the benefits that may be anticipated from such competition, but an approximate estimate may be made by comparing the present railroad charges, between the river and the lakes, with actual results obtained on similar water-courses and applied to this route. The following tables present such an estimate:

Table showing the distances from the river ports named to Chicago and to Green Bay.

From—	To Chicago by rail.	To Green Bay via the Fox and Wisconsin Rivers.
	Miles.	*Miles.*
Saint Paul	406	484
Winona	306	366
La Crosse	275	331
Prairie du Chien	245	271
Dubuque	188	328
Savannah	156	384
Fulton	136	402
Rock Island	182	438
Burlington	207	529

NOTE.—The above distances "by rail" are as given by the several railroads connecting Chicago with said river ports. The distances by river are furnished by the War Department.

Table showing the actual cost of transport by rail to Chicago and the estimated cost by the Fox and Wisconsin improvement from the river ports named to Green Bay.

From—	Cost per bushel of sixty pounds to Chicago by rail.	Cost per bushel of sixty pounds to Green Bay via Fox and Wisconsin Rivers.	Saving by the improvement.
Saint Paul	$0 19.3	$0 06.4	$0 12.9
Winona	18.4	4.8	13.6
La Crosse	18.4	4.4	14
Prairie du Chien	18.4	3.6	14.8
Dubuque	17	4.2	12.8
Savannah	18	5.1	12.9
Fulton	17.5	5.3	12.2
Rock Island	15	5.8	9.2
Burlington	12	7	5
Average	17.1	05.2	11.9

The actual average rail-rates in above table are taken from the freight-tariffs of the several railroads during the season of navigation in 1872. The water-rates to Green Bay are computed upon the basis of the actual average charges which prevailed on the Mississippi River, between Saint Paul and Saint Louis, during the season of high-water navigation in 1872, and also upon the actual average charges on the Mississippi from Saint Louis to New Orleans the same year, namely, $4\frac{4}{10}$ mills per ton per mile. As the Fox and Wisconsin improvement will have 5 feet depth of water, and pass vessels of at least 500 tons burden at the rate of 5 or 6 miles per hour, with only six miles of canal on the entire route, it is believed that the rate named will afford a liberal compensation to the carrier. The carrier's charges on the Erie Canal, which passes boats of only 210 tons, at the rate of $1\frac{1}{2}$ miles per hour, have ranged from 5 to 7 mills per ton, and including tolls, a little less than 10 mills. It is believed that an enlargement of the Erie Canal that will pass boats of 600 tons will reduce the cost of transport one-half. This route being substantially open river and slack-water for the entire distance, with steam motive-power, will be able to afford as cheap transportation as the Erie Canal with the proposed enlargement. A much more just comparison, however, is the one above made with *actual* river-charges.

In case the above estimate be considered too low for the water-route, the following is also submitted, it being based upon an assumed charge of 6 mills per ton per mile *down* the Mississippi River and through the Fox and Wisconsin improvement, and 8 mills per ton per mile *up* the Mississippi. The following are the results of such comparison:

From—	Actual cost per bushel of sixty pounds to Chicago by rail.	Estimated cost per bushel of sixty pounds to Green Bay via the Fox and Wisconsin improvement and the Mississippi River.	Saving by the improvement.
Saint Paul	$0 19.3	$0 8.7	$0 10.6
Winona	18.4	6.5	11.9
La Crosse	18.4	5.9	12.5
Prairie du Chien	18.4	4.8	13.6
Dubuque	17	5.1	11.9
Savannah	18	7.5	10.5
Fulton	17.5	7.9	9.6
Rock Island	15	8.8	6.2
Burlington	12	11.5	5
Average	17.1	7.4	9.7

Computing the cost at the rates last named, which are higher than the usual river charges, and about equal to the average carriers' charges on the Erie Canal, we find the average cost for all the ports named by the proposed water-route to be only 7.4 cents per bushel, against 17.1 cents by rail, showing a saving of 9.7 cents per bushel. The surplus of wheat and corn in Iowa and Minnesota in 1873 being over 60,000,000 bushels, the annual saving to be effected by the proposed improvement will amount to $6,000,000, or twice as much for a single year as the entire cost of the work. To this must be added a similar saving per bushel on the wheat and corn of Nebraska, and of a large part of Illinois and Wisconsin. By referring to the crop-map in the appendix, showing the localities in which a surplus of wheat is produced, it will be observed that this improvement connects the lakes by direct water communication with the largest and most productive wheat region on the continent, and seems especially designed to afford for it the cheapest possible outlet to market. It is the shortest and cheapest connection with the most prolific wheat areas of Minnesota, Northern Wisconsin, and Iowa; and it passes through the richest wheat-producing region of Central Wisconsin. The four counties of Dane, Dodge, Columbia, and Fond du Lac, situated directly upon the proposed route, produced in 1869 an aggregate surplus of over 7,000,000 bushels of wheat. The other counties of Wisconsin which are closely contiguous to the Mississippi River produced an aggregate surplus of over 3,500,000 bushels, making a total surplus of over 10,500,000 bushels in Wisconsin, which would be benefited to the extent of the reduction above estimated.

Minnesota, with only 5 per cent. of her lands under cultivation, produced a surplus last year of over 22,000,000 bushels; a reduction of 9.7 cents* per bushel in the cost of transportation would make a present saving to that State of $2,131,000 per annum, or more than two-thirds of the entire cost of the improvement. When one-half of her lands shall be brought under cultivation, as they will be within a very few years, the saving will be over $21,000,000 per annum.

To all these vast benefits must be added a like reduction on the cost of transportation for the lumber of Michigan and Eastern Wisconsin, for the coal and salt from districts east of the lakes, for the iron of Lake Superior, and for general merchandise.

It is stated that in the ten years, from 1855 to 1864, inclusive, the total number of tons moved one mile by the New York Central Railroad was 2,132,073,612, and by the Erie Railroad 2,587,274,914 tons; by the New York canals 8,175,803,065 tons; and the average charges of the Central Railway were 2.6 cents, Erie Railway, 2.22 cents, and the canals, .91 cents per ton per mile. Had the freights which were carried by canal for the ten years been carried by rail, the additional freight-charges would have amounted to $122,637,045.97.

The special advantages presented by this route are these:

1. It runs on a direct line to the center of the great surplus wheat area of the country, which supplies the bulk of the grain shipments east, and to or near the centers of the surplus areas of other grains.

* The average saving from all Minnesota ports, including La Crosse and Prairie du Chien, Wis., is 12 cents per bushel, as will be seen by reference to the last table. This would make a saving on last year's surplus of $2,640,000.

2. It has less canal, less lockage, and costs less than any other proposed route.

3. Its point of connection with the lake at Green Bay is nearly two hundred miles nearer to the eastern markets than the southern end of Lake Michigan. By the opening of the Sturgeon Bay Canal, one mile in length, to be completed in 1874, Green Bay becomes a port at which nearly all of the shipping of the lakes will touch.

4. Congress has already directed the Secretary of War to improve the Wisconsin, and has prescribed the plan of improvement; no further action of Congress being necessary excepting to make additional appropriations.

The proposed Fox and Wisconsin improvement is only an extension of the Erie Canal to the Mississippi River—the completion of the great work inaugurated by De Witt Clinton in 1817. From it like results may reasonably be expected to flow. The population and products of the country west of the Mississippi River are vastly greater to-day, than they were west of the lakes when the Erie Canal was commenced. In 1826, after its completion to Buffalo, Mr. Clinton delivered a speech in honor of the event, in which, giving loose reins to his enthusiasm, he ventured to predict that in fifty years from that date Buffalo, then an Indian trading-station, and Chicago, a frontier post, would contain a population each of 100,000 souls. The 400,000 people at Chicago and the teeming millions in the Mississippi Valley prove how inadequate was even the prophetic vision and ardent enthusiasm of a Clinton to anticipate the wonderful progress of the imperial West. The same wise statemanship which rendered this progress possible, points to a connection of the lakes and Erie Canal with the Mississippi River, as one of the means of relieving the overburdened West, of cheapening the price of bread at the East, and of contributing to the prosperity of both sections of the country The great benefits it will confer, for the comparatively insignificant exditure required, confirms the wisdom of the founders of the republic when, by the ordinance of the 14th of July, 1787, they provided that "the navigable waters leading into the Mississippi and the Saint Lawrence, and the carrying places between the same, shall be common highways, and forever free."

Colonel Houston, United States engineer in charge of this work, estimates its entire cost at $3,000,000, a sum totally insignificant in comparison with the results to be obtained. Owing to the inadequacy of the sums heretofore appropriated, the improvement has progressed very slowly, and at much greater expense than was necessary. In view of the great benefits to be obtained, the committee are of the opinion that liberal appropriations should be made to complete the improvement at the earliest practicable moment.

ROCK ISLAND AND HENNEPIN CANAL.

It is proposed to connect the Illinois River, at Hennepin, a point 19 miles below the southern terminus of the Illinois and Michigan Canal, with the Mississippi River, at Watertown, a point about 8 miles above Rock Island.

At the instance of certain public meetings, held at various points in the State of Illinois during the year 1866, a preliminary survey of the Hennepin Canal route was made by Col. J. O. Hudnutt, civil engineer. The dimensions of the canal and its locks upon which Col. Hudnutt based his calculations were as follows: Prism, 60 feet at surface, 36 feet at bottom, and 6 feet deep. Locks, 160 feet long, 21 feet wide, and 11 feet lift. Capacity of boats, 250 tons.

Length of canal, main line	64 miles.
Navigable feeder from Rock River	38 miles.
Total length	102 miles.

Estimated cost a little over $4,500,000. Colonel Hudnutt declared that this would be the cheapest canal ever constructed in the United States.

A very careful survey and series of estimates was made for a canal upon nearly the same route by Mr. Gorham P. Low, civil engineer, under the direction of the War Department, in the year 1870. The estimates were for a ship-canal of the following dimensions: Prism, 160 feet at surface, 132 feet at bottom, and 7 feet deep. Locks, 350 feet long and 75 feet wide. The dimensions of the feeder estimated upon were 140 feet width at surface, 112 feet at the bottom, and 7 feet deep.

Length of canal, main line	65. 31 miles.
Feeder	38. 12 miles.
Total length	103. 43 miles.
Estimated cost, main line	$10, 208, 840
Navigable feeder from Dixon, on the Rock River, to the summit	2, 270, 850
Total cost	$12, 479, 693

The lockage was found to be as follows: From the Illinois River at Hennepin to the summit-level, 19 locks, with an ascent of 207 feet, and thence by a descent of 92 feet by 9 locks to the Mississippi River. There will be no lift-locks upon the feeder, and only one guard-lock. Mr. Low states that the locks contemplated in his estimate would admit a steamer and tow of barges capable of carrying 2,000 tons or 66,666 bushels of wheat. He states that the supply of water on the summit-level will be sufficient for 67 passages eastward daily of such tows, carrying 134,000 tons of freight or 4,466,666 bushels of wheat. This would afford an annual capacity for the transport of grain eastward of 1,071,999,840 bushels for each season of 240 days, or eleven times the largest amount of grain ever received at Chicago during one year.

The foregoing estimates being based upon the requirements of a gunboat canal, Mr. Low also proposed estimates for a commercial canal of the same dimensions as those assumed by Colonel Hudnutt in 1866, viz, prism 60 feet surface, 36 feet bottom, and 6 feet deep, with locks 150 feet long and 21 feet wide, admitting the passage of boats of 280 tons.

Assuming the canal to have a single line of locks, and the time of the passage of a lock to be 10 minutes, the ultimate capacity of the canal to pass freights eastward would be 4,838,400 tons per annum—equal to 161,280,000 bushels of grain during a season of navigation of 240 days, or 1⅗ times the largest amount of grain received at Chicago during any one year.

The estimated cost of the work was as follows:

Main line	$2, 896, 911
Feeder	1, 002, 812
Total cost	3, 899, 723

The present locks of the Illinois and Michigan Canal will not admit of the passage of boats of 280 tons. In order that the navigation may be uniform, the locks will have to be enlarged. No estimate has been made of the cost of such enlargement.

The improvements on that portion of the Illinois River which has already been completed under appropriations made by the State of Illinois and the United States, together with the Illinois and Michigan Canal, would form with the Hennepin Canal a continuous line of canal and slack-water navigation from Chicago to the Mississippi River, the distances being as follows:

	Miles.
Illinois and Michigan Canal, Chicago to La Salle	96
Slack-water, Illinois River, La Salle to Hennepin	19
Hennepin Canal, Illinois River to Mississippi River	65
Total distance	180

The improvements of the Mississippi River, now in progress, will afford 761 miles of continuous navigation between Saint Louis and Saint Paul (except during the winter months) for barges which can be passed through the Hennepin and the Illinois and Michigan Canals to the city of Chicago, thus affording water competition with all the railway lines which cross the Mississippi River between Saint Louis and Saint Paul. All the advantages which would be realized from such competition cannot of course be precisely stated. An approximate estimate may be made of the advantages to be expected from the construction of this work, in connection with the improvements of the Mississippi River between Saint Louis and Saint Paul, which will probably be completed within two years. Such an estimate is presented in the following table. The rates and distances between Chicago, Saint Paul, Winona, La Crosse, Prairie du Chien, Du Luth, Savannah, and Fulton are given by "rail" and "rail and river" during the season of navigation by the Northwestern Railway and its river connections. The rail distances to Rock Island and Burlington, Iowa, are given by the lines of railway from Chicago to the several points respectively. The distance from Chicago to all of these points by the Illinois and Michigan Canal, the Hennepin Canal, and Missisippi River are also stated.

The actual average rail-rates are taken from the freight tariffs of the several roads for the season of navigation of the year 1872, and the water-rates are computed upon the following basis: the cost of transport on the canals and slack-water between Chicago and the Mississippi River is assumed to be the same as the average cost of transport eastward on the Erie Canal during the year 1872, viz., 10$\frac{6}{10}$ mills per ton per mile; and the cost of transport on the Mississippi River is assumed to be the same when improved as the average charges on that river between Saint Louis and New Orleans during the year 1872.

	Distances.				Rates per 100 pounds.			
	Distance by rail and river.	Canal and Mississippi River.			Rail rates per 100 pounds.	Water rates per 100 pounds.		
		Canal.*	River.†	Tot'l canal and river.		Canal.	River.	Total water rates.
	Miles.	*Miles.*	*Miles.*	*Miles.*	*Cents.*	*Cents.*	*Cents.*	*Cents.*
Saint Paul to Chicago	458, water and rail.	180	389	569	33.8	9.5	8.6	18.1
Winona to Chicago	340, all rail	180	271	451	30.7	9.5	6.0	15.5
La Crosse to Chicago	305, all rail	180	236	416	30.7	9.5	5.2	14.7
Prairie du Chien to Chicago	245, all rail	180	176	356	30.7	9.5	3.9	13.4
Dubuque to Chicago	188, all rail	180	119	299	28.4	9.5	2.6	12.1
Savannah to Chicago	156, water and rail.	180	65	245	30.0	9.5	1.4	10.9
Fulton to Chicago	136, all rail	180	45	225	29.2	9.5	1.0	10.5
Rock Island to Chicago	182, all rail	180	9	189	25.0	9.5	0.2	9.7
Burlington, Iowa, to Chicago	207, all rail	180	82	262	20.0	9.5	2.0	11.5

* The canal-distance includes the Illinois and Michigan Canal from Chicago to La Salle, 96 miles. The slack-water navigation from La Salle to Hennepin, 19 miles; and the Hennepin Canal, from Hennepin to the Mississippi River, 65 miles.
† The above river-distances were furnished by the War Department.

The following table gives the cost of transport per bushel by the two lines between Chicago and the several river-towns mentioned:

	Actual average rail rates per bushel.	Assumed water rates per bushel.	Water rates less than rail rates.
Saint Paul to Chicago	20.3	10.9	9.4
Winona to Chicago	18.4	9.3	9.1
La Crosse to Chicago	18.4	8.8	9.6
Prairie du Chien to Chicago	18.4	8.0	10.4
Dubuque to Chicago	17.0	7.3	9.7
Savannah to Chicago	18.0	6.5	11.5
Fulton to Chicago	17.5	6.3	11.2
Rock Island to Chicago	15.0	5.8	9.2
Burlington, Iowa, to Chicago	12.0	6.9	5.1
Average	17.1	7.8	9.4

Assuming a charge of six miles per ton per mile *down* the river, and eight miles per ton per mile *up* the river, as in the estimate made for the Fox and Wisconsin improvement, the results would be as stated in the following table:

	Actual average rail rates per bushel.	Assumed water rates per bushel.	Water rates less than rail rates.
	Cents.	*Cents.*	*Cents.*
Saint Paul to Chicago	20.3	12.7	7.6
Winona to Chicago	18.4	10.5	7.9
La Crosse to Chicago	18.4	9.9	8.5
Prairie du Chien to Chicago	18.4	8.8	9.6
Dubuque to Chicago	17.0	7.8	9.2
Savannah to Chicago	18.0	6.8	11.2
Fulton to Chicago	17.5	6.5	11.0
Rock Island to Chicago	15.0	5.9	9.1
Burlington to Chicago	12.0	7.6	4.4
Average	17.1	8.5	8.6

The average water-rates appear to be but 50 per cent. of the present average rail-rates. The average saving in the transport of grain from the river towns mentioned to Chicago, upon the basis of the results here obtained, appears to be 8.6 per bushel. The total surplus quantity of wheat and corn in the States of Iowa and Minnesota during the year 1872 is estimated at 60,000,000 bushels.

If we assume that this saving of 8.6 cents per bushel would be effected on the transport of this quantity, either by water-carriage or by the effect of water-carriage in causing a reduction of rail-rates, we find that the reduced cost of transporting the surplus wheat and corn of Minnesota and Iowa to Chicago will amount, on the crop of a single year, to the sum of $5,160,000, or $1,261,000 more than will be required to construct the Hennepin Canal.

The general effect of the construction of the Hennepin Canal in reducing the cost of transportation from the Mississippi River, and the territory west of that river, may also be inferred from the actual results of transport on that part of this water-line which has already been constructed from Chicago to La Salle. The Illinois and Michigan Canal competes with the Rock Island and Pacific Railroad for the transport of grain from La Salle to Chicago—100 miles.

The following statement gives the average rail-freight charges from this point to Chicago, and also from points on the railroads equally distant from Chicago to that city. This statement is computed from data furnished by Hon. Joseph Utley, president of the Illinois and Michigan Canal, which may be found on page 193 of the appendix.

Comparative charges for the transport of grain to Chicago by rail from points 100 miles distant on five different railroads:

	Average charge per 100 pounds.
Chicago, Rock Island and Pacific	8 cents.
Chicago, Burlington and Quincy	14 cents.
Chicago and Northwestern	18 cents.
Chicago and Alton	12 cents.
Illinois Central	16 cents.

The rate on the Chicago, Rock Island and Pacific Railroad, which competes with the Illinois and Michigan Canal, appears to be only 53 per cent. of the average charge for the same distances on the other roads.

A more marked exhibition of the effect of water competition in reducing rail freight charges is also given by Mr. Utley. The freight-charges on the Chicago, Rock Island and Pacific Railroad is only 8 cents per hundred pounds from Henry to Chicago, between which points there is water competition, while the rate from Tiskilwa, only 12 miles farther west than Henry, and beyond the effect of canal competition, is 15 cents per hundred pounds, or nearly as much for 12 miles as for 100 miles. Discriminations such as this are, however, characteristic of rail transport in all parts of the country.

This route presents two special advantages:

1st. It passes through the center of the richest corn-producing area, and it forms a connection with the Mississippi River, which passes through the richest wheat-producing area on this continent. This may be seen by referring to the crop-maps in the appendix.

2d. Its eastern terminus is at Chicago, the largest grain-market in the West, where there is always a large supply of lake-tonnage.

The following extract from a letter addressed to the chairman of this committee by Charles Randolph, esq., secretary of the board of trade of Chicago, is worthy of careful attention:

"If this water-way were completed it would, in effect, give an unbroken line of transportation by water from the head-waters of the Mississippi to the ocean, either via the Saint Lawrence or the Hudson Rivers. Freights, say on grain, could be reduced nearly, or quite, one-half of the general average between all points on the Mississippi River and Lake Michigan. * * * * * What the Erie Canal is to the regulation of freight-rates across the State of New York, this would be across the State of Illinois, and, indeed, of Wisconsin too, for all railroads running eastward from the Mississippi River would be brought within the influence of its competition."

It is also proposed that the western terminus of the canal shall be at a point on the Mississippi about 20 miles above Rock Island. Such a change in the location of the line would present these advantages: 1st, it would reduce the distance from Chicago to all points on the river above the western terminus of the canal; 2d, it would reduce the amount of lockage, and 3d, the obstacle to navigation presented by the Rock Island rapids would be avoided.

It has also been proposed to substitute a line running from Chicago almost directly west and striking the great eastern bend of the Mississippi River at or near Fulton, Ill. The practicability of neither of these two lines has yet been determined by means of a survey.

OTHER WATER-LINES REPORTED UPON BY THE COMMITTEE.

In addition to the foregoing routes, the following water-lines are reported upon by the committee:

THE IMPROVEMENT OF THE ILLINOIS RIVER

By means of the improvements of the Illinois River, now in progress, it is proposed to secure a depth of 7 feet of water at its lowest stages. The method adopted is that of dams and locks, or slack-water navigation. The locks are to be 350 feet long and 75 feet wide, or large enough to accommodate Mississippi River steamers. The fall of the river from La Salle to its mouth, a distance of 228 miles, is only 29 feet and 4 inches. Only four locks will, therefore, be required. One of these locks has already been constructed at Henry, at a cost of $400,000. This lock affords a depth of 7 feet in the river from that point to La Salle, the southern terminus of the Illinois and Michigan Canal, a distance of thirty miles. The entire success of this lock in securing the required depth of water may be considered to have determined the proper method for the radical improvement of the entire river.

The legislature of Illinois at its last session appropriated the sum of $400,000 from the revenues of the Illinois and Michigan Canal and the river improvement, for the construction of another lock at the mouth of Copperas Creek, a point sixty miles below Henry. It is estimated that the entire cost of the improvements of the Illinois River, including locks, dams, and dredging, will amount to about $1,400,000.

The Illinois River passes through the principal corn area of the West, as may be seen by referring to the crop-map in the appendix.

The route composed of the Illinois and Michigan Canal, the Illinois River, and the Mississippi River will form a very direct and valuable commercial line between Chicago and Saint Louis and the large districts of country tributary to those cities.

THE CANALS OF PENNSYLVANIA.

The committee desire to call attention to a paper prepared by Col. James Worrall, of Harrisburgh, Pa., in regard to the existing and projected canals of that State, which may be found on page 96 of the appendix.

Three water-routes are proposed—one from Montezuma, a point on the Erie Canal, one hundred and fifty miles east of Buffalo, to the mouth of the Susquehanna River, and two routes for a canal to connect Pittsburgh with Chesapeake Bay, at the mouth of the Susquehanna River.

The statements thus presented by Colonel Worrall, which are indorsed by Senator Cameron, are sufficient to warrant the committee in recommending that, before any general system of water improvements is adopted, proper inquiries and surveys shall be made, in order to determine the practicability of said routes and their respective merits as compared with other proposed canals.

THE CHESAPEAKE AND OHIO CANAL.

The Chesapeake and Ohio Canal was one of the first lines proposed between the West and the seaboard.

Its construction was begun in the year 1828, and it was completed to Cumberland, Md., on the eastern slope of the Alleghany Range, in the year 1851, at a cost of $11,071,000.

This route, in its topographical features and in the commercial results which it is expected to subserve, is quite similar to the James River and Kanawha route. The total distance from Washington to Pittsburgh is 314 miles. From Pittsburgh a canal may be constructed to Lake Erie, the distance being 119 miles.

The division of the canal already constructed from Washington to Cumberland is 184½ miles in length.

It is proposed that the western portion of the line shall consist of slack-water navigation on the Youghiogheny and Monongahela Rivers. The Monongahela River has already been improved by means of slack-water navigation to the mouth of the Youghiogheny, and a company has been formed for improving the Youghiogheny by locks and dams to Connelsville, at the mouth of Castleman's River, leaving but 90 miles of canal to be constructed from Cumberland to the point just mentioned.

During the year 1873 a survey of the route was made by Colonel Sedgwick, of the United States Engineer Corps, who reported that the canal will attain an elevation of 2,100 feet above tide-water, and involve a tunnel at the summit-level of five miles in length.

Colonel Sedgwick estimates the cost of completing the canal at $19,900,000.

He reports that the water supply is abundant, as did the United States engineers who made surveys of the line in the years 1824 and 1825.

The line from Cumberland to Pittsburgh passes through one of the most valuable coal and iron deposits in the United States.

A very interesting statement in regard to this line may be found on page 195 of the Appendix. This statement was prepared by Mr. A. P. Gorman, president of the Chesapeake and Ohio Canal.

THE FLORIDA SHIP-CANAL ROUTE.

Two routes have been proposed for artificial waterways across the peninsula of Florida, connecting the Gulf of Mexico with the Atlantic Ocean.

First. A coast-line from New Orleans through Lake Pontchartrain, Mississippi Sound, by means of short canals and land-locked bodies of water along the gulf to the peninsula of Florida; and thence by canal and slack-water navigation to Fernandina on the Atlantic coast. This line will involve very little lockage.

Another water-line, consisting of canals, slack-water navigation, and rivers already navigable, has been proposed from the mouth of the Saint John's River to the Gulf. The western terminus of this line has not yet been decided upon, three points having been proposed, viz, the mouth of the Suwanee River, the mouth of the Withlockooche River, and Tampa Bay.

The object of this route is to enable sea-going vessels to avoid the dangerous passage around the Florida Keys.

The committee recommend that the necessary surveys or reconnaissances be made, in order to determine the practicability and probable cost of these lines.

NIAGARA SHIP-CANAL.

The project of constructing a canal on the American side of the Niagara River, to connect Lake Erie with Lake Ontario, has been agitated at various times during the last fifty years. The completion of the Erie Canal from Albany to Buffalo, in the year 1826, formed a direct route from the Hudson River to Lake Erie, and thus avoided the immediate necessity for the construction of a canal from Lake Erie to Lake Ontario, a work which would have been required, in order to open a commercial line from the East to the West, if the canal from Albany to Oswego only had been constructed. At an early date, however, the necessity for such a connection between the lakes forced itself upon the attention of the Canadian government, in order to open up the commerce of the Northwestern States to Montreal, and to foreign countries beyond the sea, by the Saint Lawrence route. This purpose was accomplished by the construction of the Welland Canal from Port Colborne, on Lake Erie, to Port Dalhousie, on Lake Ontario, in connection with the Saint Lawrence River Canals. For several years after the construction of the Welland Canal about half of the commerce between the West and New York passed through the Welland Canal to Oswego, and thence by canal to the Hudson River. That commerce, however, fell off very much in consequence of the building of lake vessels which were too large to pass through the locks of the Welland Canal. This fact caused a renewed demand for the construction of a ship-canal on the American side of the Niagara River, the principal reasons urged being, 1st, That the United States should not be dependent upon Canada for so important a military and commercial connection; 2d, That a canal could be constructed on the American side only eight miles long, whereas the Welland Canal is twenty-eight miles long; and, 3d, as already stated, that the locks of the Welland Canal were not large enough for the merchant-vessels of the upper lakes.

Again, however, the enterprise of Canada, by the enlargement of the Welland Canal, a work now in progress, has preceded action in this country. By means of this enlargement a large proportion of the vessels of the upper lakes will be able to pass from Lake Erie into Lake Ontario. While there does not appear to be an immediate necessity for the construction of an additional canal on the American side of the Niagara River, in view of the fact that American vessels are accorded by the Dominion government the same privileges as Canadian vessels in passing through the Welland Canal, yet the committee are of the opinion that the shorter distance between the navigable waters of Lakes

Erie and Ontario, and the more favorable topographical features of the country on the American side, point to the necessity for the construction of an American Niagara ship-canal at no distant period, in order to meet the demands of the rapidly-increasing commerce between the East and the West.

The following general description of the lines surveyed by Col. C. E. Blunt, of the Corps of Topographical Engineers, U. S. A., in the year 1868, will afford an idea of the nature of the proposed work:

No. 1. From steamboat landing at Lewiston to Schlosser, 7.5 miles; estimated cost, $12,095,438.

No. 2. From Five-mile Meadow, below Lewiston, to Schlosser; length 9.38 miles; estimated cost, $11,128,438.

No. 3. From a point 1,500 feet south of steamboat landing at Lewiston to Schlosser, 7.8 miles; estimated cost, $11,031,916.

No. 4. From the mouth of Four-mile Creek, on Lake Ontario, to Schlosser, 14.43 miles; estimated cost, $12,673,520.

No. 5. From Wilson, at the mouth of Twelve-mile Creek, on Lake Ontario, to the Niagara River, between Cayuga and Tonawanda Creeks; length, 18.35 miles; estimated cost, $13,993,638.

No. 6. From the head of Olcott Harbor, Eighteen-mile Creek, on Lake Ontario, to the north end of Tonawanda Island, 25.28 miles; estimated cost, $12,893,170.

In addition, a line was surveyed from Tonawanda Creek to Buffalo Harbor, fifteen miles, the estimated cost being $11,000,000; this line being intended for the purpose of avoiding the current in the Niagara River between Lake Erie and the entrance to the proposed canal.

The difference of elevation between Lake Erie and Lake Ontario to be overcome by lockage amounts to about 316 feet by each line.

In view of the enlargement of the Welland Canal, now in progress by the Dominion government, and of the more urgent necessity for improvements elsewhere, the committee refrain from recommending immediate action by this Government in relation to the proposed Niagara ship-canal. It may be doubted, however, whether the depth and size of the locks proposed by the Dominion government will long afford the necessary facilities for the rapidly-increasing size of our lake vessels, and hence the necessity for a Niagara ship-canal of adequate dimensions may not be long delayed.

THE PACIFIC COAST.

The investigations of the committee have, under the terms of the resolution by which it was created, been confined chiefly to questions relating to the transportation of the surplus products of the Western and Northwestern States of the interior to the seaboard. The committee have, however, felt that, in treating of a subject so truly national in all its bearings, the interests of the States of the Pacific coast should not be neglected. Senators Mitchell, of Oregon, and Casserly, of California, were, in June, 1873, appointed a sub-committee to investigate and report upon the commercial interests of that section of the country. Mr. Casserly having resigned his seat in the Senate in November, 1873, the duty has devolved chiefly upon Mr. Mitchell.

The rapid development of the States of California and Oregon in population, in commerce, and in mineral and agricultural wealth is a matter of history, the truthful recital of which bears almost the impress of fiction. The resources of all that vast territory lying west of the Rocky Mountain range present possibilities, the full development of which waits upon the means of transport to the sea-ports of the Pacific coast.

The value of the exports of gold and silver, breadstuffs, provisions, and other articles from California, Oregon, and Washington Territory during the year 1873 was as follows:

Breadstuffs	$20, 113, 574
Gold and silver coin and bullion	14, 490, 977
All other articles	5, 826, 080
Total	40, 430, 631

The above statement does not, however, embrace the value of the commodities shipped from the Pacific States to the other States of the Union.

According to our annual statistics of foreign commerce for the year 1873, it appears that San Francisco was the third city of the Union in the value of domestic exports, New York being first and New Orleans second. And it also appears that San Francisco was the third city in the value of imports, New York being first and Boston second.

Wheat appears to be the chief exportable product of the Pacific coast. During the year 1873 the exports of wheat amounted to 18,235,708 bushels; this amount comprising 35 per cent. of the entire exports of wheat from the United States to foreign countries. It is estimated that the exports of wheat from Oregon during the year 1874 will amount to nearly 5,000,000 bushels, an increase of about 4,000,000 bushels since the year 1872. Oregon and Washington Territory also produce immense quantities of lumber and timber, and wool is becoming an important article of commerce in all the Pacific States.

The committee desire especially to call attention to the importance of improving that great natural highway of the Pacific coast, the Columbia River, with its principal tributary, the Willamette.

Portland is situated at the head of ship-navigation. Improvements are required in the channel of the river below that city for sea-going vessels; also in the Columbia above the mouth of the Willamette, and in the Willamette above Portland for steamboat and barge navigation. The western part of the Territory of Idaho and the eastern part of the State of Oregon and of the Territory of Washington form one of the richest agricultural sections on the continent. The Columbia River is, at the present time, the only avenue of commerce from this region to the seaboard.

On the Columbia River there are two obstructions to navigation, consisting of rapids and falls; these are, 1st, the Dalles, fourteen miles in length, and, 2d, the Cascades, four miles in length.

Several years ago the Oregon Steam Navigation Company obtained a charter from Congress for the construction of portage-railroads around these rapids, by which means that company now holds an absolute monopoly of the commerce of the Columbia between the seaboard and the territory east of the Cascade Mountains. No other persons or companies can engage in the business of transporting merchandise on the Columbia River. The freight-charges imposed by this company are so burdensome as to stifle enterprise, and prevent the legitimate development of commerce and agriculture. Wheat worth $1.25 at Portland is worth but 40 cents at Wallula, only 230 miles distant by river.

For transporting a ton of merchandise from Portland to Umatilla, a distance of 200 miles, a freight-charge of $25 is imposed. This is at the rate of 12½ cents (gold) per ton per mile.. The freight charges on wheat from Wallula to Portland are $6 per ton on regular boats, twice a week, and $8 per ton on special boats.

The average rate of transport from Chicago to New York by the water-line is only 9.6 mills per ton per mile, and the rate by all rail 12.1 mills. In comparison with these rates, the extortionate nature of the charges imposed on the Columbia River may be clearly appreciated.

The people of Oregon desire that the National Government, which has exclusive jurisdiction of all natural navigable streams, shall improve the rapids of the Columbia River by means of canals and locks so as to admit the passage of river-steamers and barges. It is believed, also, that portage-railroads can be constructed by the Government at a cost not exceeding $300,000; and in view of the pressing demand for the opening of free commerce on the Columbia River, this plan is thought to be the one which should be first adopted.

The required improvements of the Willamette and of the Columbia, below the mouth of the Willamette, consist in the removal of sand-bars by dredging, and the construction of such works as may be necessary to maintain the required depth of water in the channel.

But aside from these improvements of such obvious necessity, the development of the State of Oregon and of the Territories of Idaho and Washington depends largely upon the completion of at least two main-trunk-railway lines connecting the State of Oregon and Washington Territory with the States east of the Rocky Mountain range.

To such main-trunk lines numerous lateral lines would soon be constructed, reaching to all points and leading to that general development of the country which has followed the extension of the railway-system throughout the interior and the Atlantic States.

The committee recommend that appropriations be made at the present session of Congress for surveys of the Cascades and Dalles of the Columbia River, and of the Willamette River, with a view to the improvements above indicated.

SUMMARY OF CONCLUSIONS AND RECOMMENDATIONS.

The following general summary of the conclusions and recommendations of the committee are respectfully submitted:

Firstly. One of the most important problems demanding solution at the hands of the American statesman, is by what means shall cheap and ample facilities be provided for the interchange of commodities between the different sections of our widely extended country.

Secondly. In the selection of means for the accomplishment of this object, Congress may, in its discretion and under its responsibility to the people, prescribe the rules and regulations by which the instruments, vehicles, and agencies employed in transporting persons or commodities from one State into or through another shall be governed, whether such transportion be by land or by water.

Thirdly. The power "to regulate commerce" includes the power to *aid* and *facilitate* it by the employment of such means as may be appropriate and plainly adapted to that end; and hence Congress may, in its discretion improve, or create, channels of commerce on land, or by water.

Fourthly. A remedy for some of the defects and abuses which prevail under existing systems of transportation, may be provided by direct congressional regulation, but for reasons, stated at length in this report, it is seriously doubted if facilities, sufficiently *cheap* and *ample* to meet the just and reasonable requirements of commerce, can ever be obtained by this method

Fifthly. Whatever may be the limit of the power of Congress over interstate commerce, it is believed that the attempt to regulate the business of transportation by general congressional enactments establishing rates and fares on 1,300 railways, aggregating nearly one-half the railway mileage of the world, and embracing an almost infinite variety of circumstances and conditions, requires more definite and detailed information than is now in the possession of Congress or of your committee. Believing that any ill-advised measures, in this direction, would tend to postpone indefinitely the attainment of the desired object—*cheap* transportation—the committee deem it expedient to confine their recommendations, in this regard, to such measures only as may be enacted with entire safely, reserving other matters of legislation for further inquiry and consideration. They therefore recommend for present action the following:

1. That all railway companies, freight-lines, and other persons, or organizations of common carriers, engaged in transporting passengers or freights from one State into or through another, be required, under

proper penalties, to make publication at every point of shipment from one State to another, of their rates and fares, embracing all the particulars regarding distance, classifications, rates, special tariffs, drawbacks, &c., and that they be prohibited from increasing such rates above the limit named in the publication, without reasonable notice to the public, to be prescribed by law.

2. That combinations and consolidations with parallel or competing lines are evils of such magnitude as to demand prompt and vigorous measures for their prevention.

3. That all railway companies, freight-lines, and other organizations of common carriers, employed in transporting grain from one State into or through another, should be required, under proper regulations and penalties to be provided by law, to receipt for *quantity* and to deliver the same at its destination.

4. That all railway companies and freight organizations, receiving freights in one State to be delivered in another, and whose lines touch at any river or lake port, be prohibited from charging more to or from such port than for any greater distance on the same line.*

5. Stock-inflations, generally known as "stock-waterings," are wholly indefensible; but the remedy for this evil seems to fall peculiarly within the province of the States who have created the corporations from which such practices proceed. The evil is believed to be of such magnitude as to require prompt and efficient State action for its prevention, and to justify any measures that may be proper and within the range of national authority.

6. It is believed by the committee that great good would result from the passage of State laws prohibiting officers of railway companies from owning or holding, directly or indirectly, any interest in any "*non-co-operative* freight-line" or car company, operated upon the railroad with which they are connected in such official capacity.

7. For the purpose of procuring and laying before Congress and the country such complete and reliable information concerning the business of transportation and the wants of commerce, as will enable Congress to legislate intelligently upon the subject, it is recommended that a Bureau of Commerce, in one of the Executive Departments of the Government, be charged with the duty of collecting and reporting to Congress information concerning our internal trade and commerce; and be clothed with authority of law, under regulations to be prescribed by the head of such Department, to require each and every railway and other transportation company engaged in inter-State transportation to make a report, under oath of the proper officer of such company, at least once each year, which report should embrace, among other facts,

* This provision, it is believed, will prevent the discriminations now practiced against such ports, and will enable States which are separated from water-lines by intervening States to reach such lines at reasonable cost. Congress has no power to regulate commerce wholly within a State, and hence States bordering upon such water-lines will regulate the rates to ports within their own territory.

the following, namely: 1st. The rates and fares charged from all points of shipment on its line in one State to all points of destination in another State, including classifications and distances, and all drawbacks, deductions, and discriminations; 2d. A full and detailed statement of receipts and expenditures, including the compensation paid to officers, agents, and employés of the company; 3d. The amount of stock and bonds issued, the price at which they were sold, and the disposition made of the funds received from such sale; 4th. The amount and value of commodities transported during the year, as nearly as the same can be ascertained, together with such other facts as may be required by the head of such Bureau, under the authority of law.

Sixth. Though the existence of the Federal power to regulate commerce to the extent maintained in this report is believed to be essential to the maintenance of perfect equality among the States as to commercial rights; to the prevention of unjust and invidious distinctions which local jealousies or interests might be disposed to introduce; to the proper restraints of consolidated corporate power, and to the correction of many of its existing evils, yet your committee are unanimously of the opinion that the problem of *cheap* transportation is to be solved through *competition*, as hereinafter stated, rather than by direct congressional regulation of existing lines.

Seventh. Competition, which is to secure and maintain *cheap* transportation, must embrace two essential conditions: 1st, it must be controlled by a power with which combination will be impossible; 2d, it must operate through cheaper and more ample channels of commerce than are now provided.

Eighth. Railway competition, when regulated by its own laws, will not effect the object; because it exists only to a very limited extent in certain localities; it is alway unreliable and inefficient; and it invariably ends in combination. Hence, additional railway-lines, under the control of private corporations, will afford no substantial relief, because self-interest will inevitably lead them into combination with existing lines.

Ninth. The only means of securing and maintaining reliable and effective competition between railways is through national or State ownership, or control, of one or more lines, which, being unable to enter into combinations, will serve as regulators of other lines.

Tenth. One or more double-track freight-railways, honestly and thoroughly constructed, owned or controlled by the Government, and operated at a low rate of speed, would doubtless be able to carry at much less cost than can be done under the present system of operating fast and slow trains on the same road; and, being incapable of entering into combinations, would no doubt serve as a very valuable regulator of all existing railroads within the range of their influence.

Eleventh. The uniform testimony deduced from practical results in this country, and throughout the commercial world is, that water-routes, when properly located, not only afford the cheapest and best-known means of transport for all heavy, bulky, and cheap commodities, but that they are also the natural competitors, and most effective regulators of railway-transportation.

Twelfth. The above facts and conclusions, together with the remarkable physical adaptation of our country for cheap and ample water-communications, point unerringly to the improvement of our great natural water-ways, and their connection by canals, or by short freight-railway portages under control of the Government, as the obvious and certain solution of the problem of *cheap* transportation.

Thirteenth. After a most careful consideration of the merits of various proposed improvements, taking into account the cost, practicability, and probable advantages of each, the committee have come to the unanimous conclusion that the following are the most feasible and advantageous channels of commerce to be created or improved by the National Government in case Congress shall act upon this subject, viz:

1st. The Mississippi River.

2d. A continuous water-line of adequate capacity from the Mississippi River to the city of New York, via the northern lakes.

3d. A route adequate to the wants of commerce, through the central tier of States, from the Mississippi River, via the Ohio and Kanawha Rivers, to a point in West Virginia, and thence by canal and slack-water, or by a freight-railway, to tide-water, in Virginia.

4th. A route from the Mississippi River, via the Ohio and Tennessee Rivers, to a point in Alabama or Tennessee, and thence by canal and slack-water, or by a freight-railway, to the ocean.

In the discussion of these four existing and proposed channels of commerce, we shall, for the sake of brevity, designate them respectively, the "Mississippi route," "Northern route," "Central route," and "Southern route."

THE MISSISSIPPI ROUTE.

The improvements necessary on the Mississippi route are; 1. The opening of the mouth of the river, so as to permit the free passage of vessels drawing 28 feet—estimated cost, $10,000,000. 2. The construction of reservoirs at the sources of the river—(if upon a careful survey they shall be deemed practicable)—estimated cost, $114,000. 3. Improvements upon a system to be provided by the War Department, at all intermediate points, so as to give from 3 to 5 feet navigation above the Falls of Saint Anthony; from 4½ to 6 feet from that point to Saint Louis; and from 8 to 10 feet from Saint Louis to New Orleans, at the lowest stages of water; estimated cost, $5,000,000.

The total cost of the Misssissippi improvements may, we think, be safely estimated at $16,000,000.

THE NORTHERN ROUTE.

The improvements suggested on this route are:

1st. The Fox and Wisconsin Rivers improvement, by which 5 feet of navigation will be secured, during the entire season, from the Mississippi River to Green Bay, thereby affording the shortest and cheapest connection between the centers of wheat production and the eastern markets, and a continuous water-channel from all points on the Mississippi River and its tributaries to the Atlantic Ocean. Estimated cost, $3,000,000.

2d. The construction of the Hennepin Canal (65 miles long) from a point on the Mississippi River, near Rock Island, to the Illinois River at Hennepin, thereby affording the shortest and cheapest route from the largest areas of greatest corn production to the east, and a connection by water between the river system of the West, the northern lakes, and the Atlantic Ocean. Estimated cost, $4,000,000.

3d. The enlargement and improvement, with the concurrence of the State of New York, of one or more of the three water-routes from the lakes to New York City, namely: The Erie Canal from Buffalo to Albany; the Oneida Lake Canal from Oswego to Albany; or the Champlain Canal from Lake Champlain to deep water on the Hudson River, including such connection as may be effected between Lake Champlain and the Saint Lawrence River with the co-operation of the British Provinces. Estimated cost, $12,000,000.

Total cost of northern route from the Mississippi River to New York City, $19,000,000.

The enlargement of the Welland Canal, now in progress, with the construction of the Caughnawaga Canal, and the proposed enlargement of the Champlain Canal, will enable vessels of a 1,000 tons to pass from western lake ports to ports in Vermont and to New York City. The Erie Canal, enlarged as proposed, will pass vessels of about 700 tons.

THE CENTRAL ROUTE.

The plan of improvement for this route contemplates—

1st. The radical improvement of the Ohio River from Cairo to Pittsburgh, so as to give six to seven feet of navigation at low water. Estimated cost, $22,000,000.

2d. The improvement of the Kanawha River from its mouth to Great Falls, so as to give six feet of navigation at all season. Estimated cost, including reservoirs, $3,000,000.

3d. A connection by canal or by a freight-railway from the Ohio River or Kanawha River, near Charleston, by the shortest and most practicable route, through West Virginia, to tide-water in Virginia; the question as between the canal and freight-railway to be decided after the completion of careful surveys and estimates. If by canal and slack-water, the estimated cost is $55,000,000; if by a freight-railway, the cost would probably not exceed $25,000,000.

The total expenditure necessary for the improvement of the Ohio and Kanawha Rivers is estimated at $25,000,000. The amount necessary to complete the connection with tide-water depends upon the nature of the improvement, as above stated.

THE SOUTHERN ROUTE.

The plan suggested by the committee for the southern route contemplates; 1. The improvement of the Tennessee River from its mouth to Knoxville, so as to give 3 feet of navigation at lowest stages of water. Estimated cost, $5,000,000. 2. A communication by canal, or freight-railway, from some convenient point on the Tennessee River in Alabama or Tennessee, by the shortest and most practicable route to the Atlantic Ocean. The railway, if constructed, will be about 430 miles long; the question as between the canal and railway to be decided after a careful survey and estimate of both shall have been completed. If by canal, the cost will be about $35,000,000. If by railway, probably about $30,000,000. Large portions of all of the above routes have been surveyed, and careful estimates prepared by the War Department. It is recommended that appropriations be made at the present session of Congress, for completing the surveys of the entire system of improvements proposed, in order to determine accurately the cost of each route, and to enable the Government to enter at once upon the work, if the same shall be deemed practicable and expedient, after such surveys shall have been completed.

In presenting this general plan of improvements, the committee wish to be distinctly understood that the ordinary annual appropriations for other important works, in aid of commerce should not be omitted.

The cost of the entire improvement, will depend upon the decision to be hereafter made between the canals and the freight-railway portages, on the central and southern routes. If the canals be constructed, the total cost will be about $155,000,000. If the railways be chosen, the total cost will be about $120,000,000.

An actual expenditure of $20,000,000 to $25,000,000 per annum will be required for five years, (in addition to the loan of Government credit as above stated,) when the whole work can be completed. The resulting benefits, will, for all time, annually repay more than double the entire cost.

In view of the fact that private companies invariably combine with each other against the public, it is recommended that no aid be given to any route to be owned or controlled by private corporations, but that the four great channels of commerce suggested, shall be improved, created, and owned by the Government, and stand as permanent and effective competitors with each other, and with all the railways which may be within the range of their influence.

The committee believe that the water-routes suggested should constitute free highways of commerce, subject only to such tolls as may be necessary for maintenance and repairs. If, however, Congress shall deem it expedient to require them to provide interest on the cost of construction, and the means for ultimate redemption of the principal, the whole improvements will involve only a loan of Government credit.

NATIONAL CHARACTER OF THE PROPOSED IMPROVEMENTS.

By reference to the map of the United States it will be seen that the completion of the system of improvements proposed will provide four great competing commercial lines from the center of the continent to the Atlantic seaboard and the Gulf of Mexico. It will also be observed, by reference to the crop-maps republished with this report, that these routes lead directly from, or through, the greatest areas of production, to those sections which constitute the greatest areas of consumption; thus dividing their benefits equitably between producers and consumers, and contributing to the development and prosperity of the whole country. The Great Architect of the continent seems to have located its rivers and lakes with express reference to the commercial necessities of the industrious millions who now and shall hereafter occupy it. The plan of improvements suggested by the committee merely follows the lines so clearly indicated by His hand.

The proposed improvements are so located as to distribute their benefits with great equality among all the States east of the Rocky Mountains. Twenty-one of those States are situated directly on one or more of said routes; two States—Kansas and Nebraska—are so situated as to enjoy the full benefits of reduced cost of transportation from the Mississippi River by all of the proposed lines. Eleven States, viz, Maine, New Hampshire, Massachusetts, Connecticut, Rhode Island, Delaware, Maryland, New Jersey, North Carolina, Florida, and Texas, nearly all of which consume largely the food of the West, and most of which are to a great extent dependent upon the West for a market for their manufactures and other products, are directly connected by the waters of the ocean with their several termini. The proposed improvements will, therefore, connect by the cheapest known means of transport every one of the thirty-four States, east of the Rocky Mountains, with all the others, and but one State in the Union will be without water-connection with the whole world. The accomplishment of so great a result, by an expenditure of money comparatively so small, illustrates the wonderful provisions of nature for cheap commercial facilities on this continent.

These four great channels of commerce under public control, and hence unable to combine with each other or with existing lines of transport, will, by the power of competition, hold in check all the railways radiating from the interior to the seaboard, and, by affording cheap and ample means of communication, will solve the problem of cheap transportation. If local railways discriminate against them, it will be in the power of the States whose boundaries they touch to prescribe regulations for the correction of such discriminations. A law of Congress prohibiting discriminations against river or lake ports, will enable the other States not directly upon any of said lines to reach them at reasonable rates. The committee submit that no scheme of public improvement could be more eminently national in its character, nor diffuse its benefits more generally and equitably, than the one proposed, and they believe that the entire system of improvements indicated should be considered and acted upon as a whole.

Let us now consider more specifically the benefits and advantages to be anticipated from each route and from the entire system, when completed.

1.—BENEFITS ANTICIPATED FROM THE NORTHERN ROUTE.

From all points on the Mississippi River between Minneapolis, Minn., and Quincy, Ill., the average railway rate to lake ports in 1872 was 17 cents per bushel of 60 pounds. From Chicago to New York, by rail, the average charge during that year was 33½ cents per bushel, and the average rate by water was $26\frac{6}{10}$ cents per bushel, making the all-rail charges through from the Mississippi to New York 50½ cents, and the rail and water charges, exclusive of terminals, $43\frac{6}{10}$ cents per bushel. In the section of this report devoted to the Fox and Wisconsin River Improvement, and the Hennepin Canal, we have shown that an average saving can be effected through their agency, of at least 10 cents per bushel on all the cereals transported from points west of the Mississippi River and north of the southern line of Iowa. It is believed by those who have studied the subject, that the enlargement of the New York canals so as to pass boats of 600 to 1,000 tons, will reduce the cost of transportation on that part of the line 50 per cent. The establishment of reciprocal trade relations with the Dominion of Canada, which shall induce the construction of the Caughnawaga Canal, (if such an arrangement can be made,) and which will encourage Canadian shipmasters to compete for the carrying trade on the lakes, will also materially cheapen the cost of transport to New England. The evidence taken by your committee fully justifies the opinion that by the enlargement of the New York canals, the construction of the Caughnawaga Canal, and the use of the enlarged Canadian canals, the cost of transport from Chicago to Burlington, Vt., and to New York City will not exceed from 12 to 15 cents per bushel, making the entire cost from the Mississippi River to Burlington, Vt., or to New York, not more than 22 cents per bushel, against the present cost of $43\frac{6}{10}$ cents by water, and 50½ cents by rail. We may, therefore, reasonably estimate that by the proposed improvements upon this route a saving can be effected of 20 cents per bushel, or $6.70 per ton, on all the East tonnage moved between that river and the East.

BENEFITS ANTICIPATED FROM THE CENTRAL ROUTE.

Assuming a charge of 4 mills per ton per mile on the Mississippi River, and on the improved Ohio and Kanawha Rivers,* a charge of 8 mills per ton per mile on the James River and Kanawha Canal, and 6 mills per ton per mile on the slack-water improvement, the following statement will represent the cost of transport from Cairo, Ill., to Richmond, Va., by the central water line:

Cairo to Great Falls of the Kanawha, 790 miles, 4 mills per ton per mile	$3.16
From Great Falls to Richmond the distance (equating each lock at one-half mile of canal) is 509 miles, of which 348 is canal (equated) and 161 is slack-water.	
348 miles canal, at 8 mills per ton per mile	2.78
161 miles of slack-water, at 6 mills per ton per mile	96
Total per ton for entire distance	†6.90

Equal to 20.4 cents per bushel of 60 pounds.

If the freight railway from the Kanawha to tide-water be adopted, instead of the canal and slack-water improvement, the cost of transport from the Ohio River to the ocean will, it is believed, be substantially the same as above stated.

The central route would be closed by ice only about 30 days each year, and hence it would be an active competitor with all the railways from the Mississippi River to the Atlantic, at times when competition is now suspended by reason of frost on the northern water-route. The effect of such a regulator of railway charges would be to greatly reduce the present winter rates, and, by the constant competition it would maintain, to compel uniformly low charges on all rail and water lines from the interior to the eastern and southern seaboard. Its advantages would be greatest, however, to the central tier of States. Four of the largest interior cities of the continent—St. Louis, Cincinnati, Louisville, and Pittsburgh—are situated directly upon it. The trade of these cities, together with the other towns and cities on the Ohio River, is now far in excess of our entire foreign commerce. A vast area of the richest agricultural and mineral country in the world is directly tributary to it, and only awaits reasonable facilities for transportation, to develop a commerce the magnitude of which it is difficult now to conceive.

---

* The evidence taken by the committee, and already stated in this report, shows that average charges by the Ohio and Mississippi Rivers is now only from 3½ to 4½ mills per ton per mile, and in many cases only 2 mills.

† It is due to this route to say that the above estimates of cost are fully 50 per cent. higher than those relied upon by its advocates. The committee have adopted them from superabundant caution, preferring to understate the benefits to be anticipated from all the routes, rather than to exaggerate them. The successful application of steam as a motor on canals will doubtless reduce the cost of transport by this line very much below the figures named.

BENEFITS ANTICIPATED FROM THE SOUTHERN ROUTE.

Assuming the same rate of charges as in the estimate just made for the central route, viz, 4 mills per ton per mile on open river, 6 mills per ton per mile on slack-water navigation, and 8 mills per ton per mile by canal, the following will represent the cost of transport by this route from Cairo to the ocean:

Open river, 980 miles, 4 mills per ton	$3 92
Slack-water, 70 miles, 6 mills per ton	42
Canal, 325 miles, 8 mills per ton	2 60
Total per ton for entire distance	*6 94

Equal to 20.8 cents per bushel of 60 pounds.

It is believed that a freight railway from the vicinity of Guntersville, Ala., or Chattanooga, Tenn., would enable this route to accomplish very nearly the same results. This route will never be obstructed by ice, and hence will afford unfailing competition throughout the year. Its greatest advantages, however, will be found, not so much in furnishing a highway of commerce to the sea-board, as in opening up a valuable connection between the grain-growing States of the West and the cotton-plantations of the South, whereby each section will have the full benefit of those crops for which its soil and climate are best adapted. It will connect with various southern rivers, penetrating a very large portion of the cotton districts of the South. It is believed that eventually inland navigation will be obtained at small expense along the coast of South Carolina, Georgia, and Florida, connecting with the rivers in those States which flow into the ocean. By this route the center of the cotton-producing region can be reached from the center of the corn area at a cost not exceeding 15 to 18 cents per bushel; and hence, in addition to the creation of a new competing avenue to the sea, the home market for food that will be developed, and the increased production of cotton that will be induced, will much more than compensate for the entire cost.

BENEFITS ANTICIPATED FROM THE MISSISSIPPI ROUTE.

The evidence submitted with this report justifies the conclusion, that upon the completion of the entire improvement of the Mississippi River, wheat and corn can be transported from Minnesota, Iowa, Wisconsin, Illinois, Indiana, Missouri, and other States above Cairo, to New Orleans for an average of 12 cents per bushel, and that the cost from Saint Paul will not exceed 17 cents. The average rate from New Orleans to Liverpool in 1872 was about 27 cents, (currency,) which can be reduced, as hereinbefore shown, to 18 or 20 cents by the improvement at the mouth of the river. Estimating the cost from Saint Paul to New Orleans at

* The same remark should be made with reference to this route just made with regard to the "central," viz, that the estimates of the committee are much higher than those of its special advocates.

17 cents, the two transfers at Saint Louis and New Orleans at 1 cent each, and the charge from New Orleans to Liverpool at 20 cents, the total from Saint Paul to Liverpool will be 39 cents per bushel. The charge in 1872 from Saint Paul to Liverpool, including transfers and terminals at Chicago, Buffalo, and New York, by the cheapest route, averaged 67.5 cents per bushel. The saving to be effected by the improvements of this route may therefore be estimated at 28 cents per bushel from Saint Paul to Liverpool, with a proportionate reduction from all other points on the river.

In view of the benefits and advantages to be derived from each of the four proposed routes, and from their combined influence when in constant competition with each other, and with the railroad-system of the country, it is, in the judgment of your committee, entirely safe to say that the completion of the system of improvements suggested will effect a permanent reduction of 50 per cent. in the cost of transporting fourth-class freights from the valley of the Mississippi to the seaboard, and that the cost of carrying a bushel of wheat or corn to the markets of the East, and of the world, will be reduced at least 20 to 25 cents per bushel below the present railway-charges, and that a similar reduction will be effected on return-freights.

The actual movement of grain to the eastern and southern markets in 1872, as shown by the carefully prepared statistics submitted with this report, amounted to about 213,000,000 bushels. An average saving of 20 cents per bushel on the surplus moved that year would have amounted to over $42,000,000, or more than two-thirds of the entire expenditure necessary to complete the proposed routes, in addition to the loan of Government credit as before stated. But for the fact that large quantities of corn were unable to find a market, on account of the high transportation-charges, the amount moved would have been very much greater. Hence, in addition to the saving in transportation above named, a benefit perhaps equally great would have been conferred upon the producer in affording him a market for his surplus products.

To this must be added the enhanced value which such reduction would give to the improved lands of the West, amounting, in the eight Northwestern States of Indiana, Illinois, Iowa, Minnesota, Wisconsin, Missouri, Kansas, and Nebraska, in 1870, to 55,841,000 acres. Estimating the productive capacity of these lands at an average of only twenty bushels per acre, (the average of corn, oats, &c., being, in fact, very much greater,) an addition of only ten cents per bushel (one-half the estimated saving) to the value of the cereals those States are capable of producing, would give a net profit of $2 per acre, which is is the equivalent of ten per cent. interest on a capital of $20, and hence equal to an increase in the value of lands to that extent. Twenty dollars per acre, added to the value of improved lands in those States, would exceed an aggregate of $1,100,000,000. This calculation assumes that one-half of the reduction will inure to the benefit of the consumer and the other half to the producer.

Add to all this the increased value of farms in other States, the increased value of unimproved lands, the enhanced value of cotton-plantations, the benefits to accrue from reduced cost of movement of the products of the mine, the foundry, the factory, the workshop, and of the thousands of other commodities demanding cheaper transportation, and some conception may be formed of the vast additions to be made to our national wealth and prosperity by the system of improvements under consideration. In comparison with the great benefits reasonably to be anticipated, their cost is utterly insignificant.

The probable effect of such reduction in the cost of internal transportation upon our exports and foreign balances of trade is also worthy of the most careful consideration. America and Russia are the great food-producing nations of the world. Great Britain is the principal market. For many years America and Russia have been active competitors for the supply of that market. Until recently, the farmers of the West have had the advantage of the wheat-producers on the Don and the Volga; but, a few years ago, Russia, inaugurated a system of internal improvements by which the cost of transporting her products from the interior to the seaboard is greatly reduced. The result is shown by the importations of wheat into the United Kingdom during two periods of five years each.

Imports of wheat from Russia and America into the United Kingdom from 1860 *to* 1864, *compared with the imports from* 1868 *to* 1872.

1860 to 1864, inclusive.		1868 to 1872, inclusive.	
From—	Wheat.	From—	Wheat.
	Bushels.		*Bushels.*
Russia	47,376,809	Russia	117,967,022
United States	127,047,126	United States	116,462,380

An *increase* during the latter period as compared with the former of 70,590,213 bushels from Russia, and a *decrease* of 10,584,746 from the United States.

The cheaper mode of handling grain by elevators has not yet been adopted by Russia, but doubtless will be very soon. When this shall be done, and her wise system of internal improvements, which have already turned the wavering balances in her favor, shall be completed, she will be able to drive us from the markets of the world, unless wiser counsels shall guide our statesmanship than have hitherto prevailed. In fact, as the increased size of ocean-vessels is constantly decreasing the cost of ocean-transport, and our wheat-fields are yearly receding farther westward from the lakes, it is not impossible that when she shall have driven us from the markets of Europe, she will become our active competitor in Boston and Portland, if cheaper means of internal transport be not provided.

A condition of things equally unsatisfactory exists with regard to our chief article of export, cotton. High transportation-charges from the grain-fields of the Northwest to the cotton-fields of the South have compelled the planter to devote his cotton-lands to the production of wheat and corn, for which they are by nature unsuited, thereby reducing the product of cotton and diminishing the market for grain. The effect upon our cotton exportations is shown by the following statement:

Receipts of cotton in Great Britain in 1860 compared with 1872.

1860.		1872.	
From—	Cotton.	From—	Cotton.
	Pounds.		*Pounds.*
United States	1, 115, 890, 608	United States	625, 600, 080
All other countries	275, 048, 144	All other countries	783, 237, 392

Our cotton exports have fallen off nearly 50 per cent., while other countries have gained nearly 300 per cent. This is doubtless largely due to the war, which stimulated the production of cotton in India; but it is also attributable to a great extent to the causes above mentioned, and to the system of internal improvements inaugurated by Great Britain in India, for the express purpose of rendering herself independent of us for the supply of cotton. Every cent unnecessarily added to the cost of transportation is to that extent a protection to the cotton-planters of India and the food-producers of Russia, against the farmers of the West and the cotton-planters of the South.

The cry of despair which comes from the over-burdened West, the demand for cheaper food heard from the laboring classes at the East and from the plantations of the South, and the rapid falling off of our principal articles of export, all indicate the imperative necessity for cheaper means of internal communication. If we would assure our imperiled position in the markets of the world, re-instate our credit abroad, restore confidence and prosperity at home, and provide for a return to specie payment, let us develop our unequaled resources and stimulate our industries by a judicious system of internal improvements.

A reference to the expenditures of our Government* since the adoption of the Constitution will show that in some matters we have been sufficiently liberal, but in appropriations for the benefit of commerce and for the development of our vast resources, most parsimonious. For public buildings, including those in the District of Columbia, and custom-houses, post-offices, and court-houses in other parts of the country,

*See Appendix, pages 184 to 186, inclusive, showing the expenditures for various purposes from the adoption of the Constitution to June 30, 1873.

we have expended over $62,000,000; while for the improvement of the 20,000 miles of western rivers, through which should flow the life-currents of the nation, we have appropriated only $11,438,300. For the improvement of these great avenues of trade, which were designed by nature to afford the cheapest and most ample commercial facilities for the teeming millions who inhabit the richest country on the earth, we have expended an average of $133,100 per annum; while for public buildings we have appropriated an average of over $750,000 a year. Is it not high time that all expenditures not absolutely necessary be suspended, and that the imperative necessities of the country receive attention?

England, in order to encourage and stimulate the culture of cotton in India for the supply of her factories at home, guaranteed interest on an expenditure for internal improvements in that distant country amounting to over $400,000,000. The most advanced nations of ancient and modern times have regarded their highways of commerce of the first importance, and, in exact proportion to the excellence of those highways, have been the development of national resources and power, and the augmentation of national wealth.

It may be said that in the present financial condition of the country, and with our heavy burden of indebtedness, we cannot afford to enter upon the system of improvements indicated It is true our debt is large, and our industrial enterprises are temporarily deranged, but our resources are immeasurable, and need only a liberal and wise statesmanship to insure their full development.

As we have already stated, the public debt of a nation is great or small according to the proportion it bears to the public wealth and to the commercial prosperity of the people who have it to pay. A debt that would have crushed the United States in 1800 would scarcely be felt to-day. In the exact proportion that our wealth increases, the burden of our debt diminishes. For instance, in 1840 the entire national wealth was estimated at $3,764,000,000. At the close of the rebellion our national indebtedness had reached $3,300,000,000. Hence to have paid the debt of 1865 in the year 1840 would have required 90 per cent. of all the property in the country. On the 1st of March, 1874, our debt was $2,154,880,066. Our national wealth is estimated at over $30,000,000,000. While, therefore, the debt of 1865 would have consumed almost the entire property, public and private, owned in the United States in 1840, the payment of our present debt would require only about 7 per cent. of our present wealth. It is therefore apparent that the burden of the debt of 1874 is less than one-twelfth as great on our present property as the debt of 1865 would have been in 1840. If by the development of our resources we can maintain the same ratio of increase during the next twenty-five years that we have since 1850, the debt of the nation (if no further payments be made) will amount to only about 1 per cent. on the national wealth in 1900. In other words, with the full development of our resources, which it is in the power of wise statesmanship to induce, the entire debt can be paid in the year 1900 by the assessment of a tax but little greater than is now required to meet the current expenditures of the Government. If it be true, then, that the burden of a nation's debt diminishes in exactly the same ratio as its wealth increases, is it not the dictate of wisdom and sound policy to pay only so much of our debt as may be necessary to keep our faith and maintain our credit, and to devote whatever surplus revenues may remain to such improvements as are required for the full development of our unequaled resources?

I concur in the main in the foregoing report, prepared by the chairman; it contains, however, certain statements and assertions of law and of fact, and recommendations relative to the power of Congress and its exercise, from which I dissent.

ROSCOE CONKLING.

The undersigned, members of the committee, do not agree that Congress can exercise the power "to regulate commerce among the several States," to the extent asserted in this report.

T. M. NORWOOD.
N. G. DAVIS.
JOHN W. JOHNSTON.

MAPS AND CHARTS ACCOMPANYING THIS REPORT.

1. Crop-map in relation to the production of corn.
2. Crop-map in relation to the production of wheat.
3. Crop-map in relation to the production of cotton.
4. Map of the United States, showing the system of improvements recommended by the committee.
5. Statistical chart showing the average rate of freight on grain from Chicago to New York each month during the years 1869 to 1873, inclusive, by lake and canal, by lake and rail, and by all-rail lines.
6. Statistical chart showing the quantity of wheat shipped from Chicago by lake and by rail each month during the five years from 1869 to 1873, inclusive.
7. Statistical chart showing the quantity of corn shipped from Chicago by lake and by rail during each month of the five years from 1869 to 1873, inclusive.

CONTENTS OF APPENDIX.

LETTERS AND REPORTS.

TABLES.

CONTENTS OF APPENDIX.

LETTERS AND REPORTS.

TABLES.

○

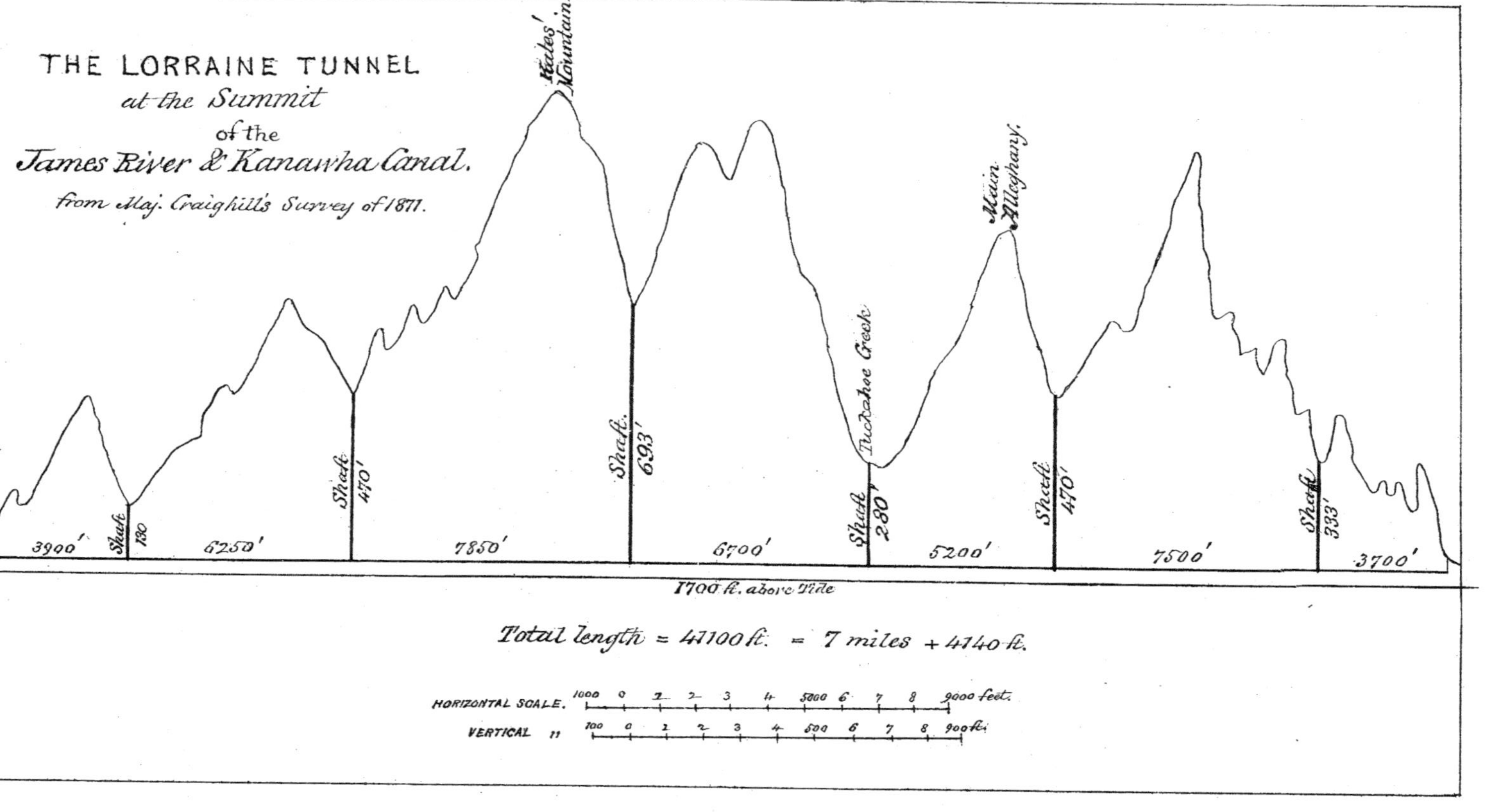

The heights and distances given on the above, have been taken from the scales on the original map.

APPENDIX.

The subject of the James River and Kanawha Canal having been especially referred to Hon. Henry G. Davis, of the committee, the following report has been presented by him and accepted:

REPORT BY HON. HENRY G. DAVIS, AS A COMMITTEE OF ONE IN REGARD TO THE JAMES RIVER AND KANAWHA CANAL, OR CENTRAL WATER-LINE.

This route is a project contemplating the completion of a continuous line of water-communication from the waters of the Ohio River, at the mouth of the Kanawha River, in the State of West Virginia, to the waters of the Chesapeake Bay and the Atlantic Ocean, at the mouth of the James River, in the State of Virginia.

ITS HISTORY.

1. *Its origin.*—The idea of a water communication between the valley of the Ohio River and the valley of the James River has for its author no less a distinguished person than George Washington himself, though it is popularly supposed to have originated with General Spotswood, when on the 20th of August, 1716, he set out from Williamsburgh on his expedition over the Blue Ridge. Upon the conclusion of the Revolutionary War, General Washington was so impressed with the importance of a water-line across the Alleghanies that during the year 1784 he made a personal exploration of the country, traveling for that purpose many hundreds of miles. The result of his observations was communicated to Benjamin Harrison, the then governor of Virginia, who communicated the subject to the legislature in a special message, dated October 18, 1784. It was largely owing to the influence and instrumentality of General Washington that the legislature of Virginia, on the 5th of January, 1785, passed "An act for clearing and improving the navigation of the James River." By this act the first or old James River Company was incorporated. This company was organized August 25, 1785, and on the next day General Washington was elected its first president, which position he held for some years. This organization continued until the 17th day of February, 1820, on which day the legislature passed "An act to amend the act for clearing and improving the navigation of the James River, and for uniting the eastern and western waters by the James and Kanawha Rivers." By this act the rights and interests of the James River Company were transferred to the Commonwealth, and by an act passed February 24, 1823, all the rights, powers, duties, and privileges of the president and directors were conferred on the board of public works, whose transactions were to be still in the name of the James River Company. This organization continued until the year 1835. The James River and Kanawha Company, under which organization the constructed canal is now being worked, was incorporated March 16, 1832, and organized May 25, 1835. By the charter the whole interest of the Commonwealth in the works and property of the then existing James River Company was transferred to the James River and Kanawha Company.

II. *Its progress to the present time.*—The first James River Company was required to make the James River navigable for vessels drawing one foot of water, at least, from the highest practicable place to the Great Falls, beginning at Westham, and from said falls to make such canal or canals, with sufficient locks, as would open navigation to tide-water; and the said company constructed a canal around the falls of James River, extending from the city of Richmond to Westham, a distance of about seven miles, and improved the bed of the river by sluices as high up as Buchanan. The second James River Company, on State account, enlarged and reconstructed the former canal from Richmond to Westham, and extended the same to Maiden's Adventure, in Goochland County, a distance of twenty-seven miles; constructed a turnpike road from Covington to the mouth of Big Sandy River, two hundred and eighty miles long, and improved the Kanawha River by wing-dams and sluices from Charleston to its mouth, a distance of fifty-eight miles. The James River and Kanawha Company commenced the construction of the new canal from Richmond to Lynchburgh in 1836, and the work was completed about the 1st of December, 1840. The part known as the second division of the canal, extending from Lynchburgh to Buchanan, was commenced in the mean time and prosecuted up to the year 1842, when, for want of funds, it was abandoned. On the 1st of March, 1847, an appropriation was made by the Virginia legislature, and the work on this division was again commenced in July, 1847, and completed in November, 1851. In August, 1853, some fifteen miles of the part known as the third division of the canal was contracted for, but, owing to a lack of funds, the work was suspended in the fall of 1856. The company at this time labored under severe embarrassment on account of its heavy indebtedness to the State of Virginia, which indebtedness, with accrued interest, amounted in the year 1860 to about $7,200,000. To relieve this embarrassment the legislature, on the 23d of March, 1860, passed an act increasing the capital stock of the company to $12,400,000, (the original capital stock having been $5,000,000,) in shares of $100 each, and the board of public works, on behalf of the Commonwealth, subscribed for 74,000 shares thereof, and issued State bonds for the remaining 2,000 shares, to be applied to the extinguishment of the floating debt of the company. The company was also authorized to borrow not exceeding $2,500,000 at a rate of interest not exceeding 7 per cent. It was then hoped that the company would be able to complete the work on the third division. About this time a French gentleman, representing a company of European capitalists, proposed to enter into an engagement to complete the canal to the Ohio River on an enlarged scale. His propositions were acceded to, and the requisite legislation obtained from the State, but the civil war intervening, the project was abandoned. During and since the war the company has done nothing toward the contemplated enlargement and completion of the canal, owing to a lack of funds, but has worked and kept in order the constructed portion of the canal, which extends to the town of Buchanan.—(Ex. Doc. 110, 41st Cong., 3d sess., pp. 51-53.)

III. *Contemplated enlargement of the canal and extension of the route.*—The contemplated extension of the route includes the enlargement of the constructed canal so as to conform to the dimensions now fixed for the canal-portion of the entire line. Then the finishing of the canal, which followed the valley of the James and Jackson Rivers from Buchanan to Covington, a distance of forty-seven miles. From Covington the line, as projected, to the Greenbrier River, crossed Jackson River by an aqueduct, and followed the valley of Dunlap's Creek to Crow's tavern, at the base of the Alleghany Mountains. There the line left the valley of Dunlap's Creek, and followed the bed of Fork Run to the summit-level, where it pierced the mountains by a tunnel 2.6 miles long, at an elevation of 1,916 feet above tide. It descended thence the valley of Tuckahoe and Howard Creeks by canal to the Greenbrier and New Rivers, down which, as well as down the Kanawha River, slack-water navigation was projected to the Ohio River, a distance of two hundred miles, making a total distance, from Richmond to the mouth of the Kanawha River, of 486.13 miles. This plan was the result of a survey made by Captain McNeil, of the United States Corps of Engineers, hereinafter referred to, and was adopted by the company. In 1868 Mr. E. Lorraine, the then engineer of the company, *advised the adoption of a new location*, which was the same as Captain McNeil's, except that it pierced the mountains by a tunnel about (estimated) nine miles in length, and reduced the elevation of the summit-level to 1,700 feet, thereby saving three and a half miles, in actual length, of canal, and twenty and a half miles of equated length—considering the saving of time in lockages, and cost of working and repairs. *The plan as now proposed* by W. P. Craighill, major United States Engineers, in a survey made, under his direction, in 1870, adopts the general line as surveyed and reported by Messrs. McNeil and Lorraine. He proposes to pierce the mountains at the same elevation as Mr. Lorraine, *but reduces the length of it to* 7.8 *miles*. He also changes Captain McNeil's plan from Lyken's Shoals to the mouth of the Kanawha River, by substituting open-river navigation instead of slack-water navigation, equalizing the fall throughout the length by low dams at regular intervals, having sluices to permit the passage of vessels. The constructed canal has a width at water-line of 50 feet, and a depth originally of 5 feet. The dimensions proposed for its extension west of Buchanan, as well as for the enlargement of the constructed portion, are 70 feet width at water-line, with a depth of 7 feet. The locks are to be 120 by 20 feet, of cut stone throughout, and in all respects of first-class masonry. The towing-path is to be 12 feet wide; berme-bank, 8 feet wide; the exterior slopes to be 1½ base to 1 perpendicular, and interior slopes 2 base to 1 perpendicular. After striking the Greenbrier River the route is to follow the Greenbrier, New, and Kanawha Rivers to the Ohio River, at Point Pleasant. For the Greenbrier and New Rivers, and the Kanawha River to Lyken's Shoals, Mr. Hutton, who surveyed this portion of the line, under direction of Major Craighill, recommends a continuous slack-water improvement, broken at two points only by short sections of canal—one at Anderson's, the other a short distance below the falls of Greenbrier.

IV. *Surveys.*—The first surveys were of the Jackson, Greenbrier, New, and Kanawha Rivers, made under the direction of Virginia, by Messrs. Moore and Briggs, in 1817-'19, contemplating a slack-water navigation for batteaux of 1½ to 2 feet draught, and a portage over the mountain.

The next were made by Captain McNeil, of the United States Topographical Engineers, in 1826-'28, for a canal and slack-water navigation. From Dunlap's Creek to the Greenbrier River full examinations and surveys were made, resulting in a location by way of Fork Run and Howard's Creek, passing the mountains by a tunnel 2.6 miles long, at an elevation of 1,916 feet above tide. This location was adopted by the company, but afterward abandoned.

In 1838 Ed. H. Gill, an experienced civil engineer, made a minute and careful survey and report on the improvement of the Kanawha River, under the direction of Charles Ellet, jr., then chief engineer, and in 1841 made an examination of the Greenbrier and

New Rivers. He recommended a system of locks from pool to pool, combined with wing-dams for the Kanawha River; a mixed system of canal and slack-water for the Greenbrier River and of locks and dams suitable for steamboat navigation for New River. His report is approved in general terms by Benjamin Wright and Charles Ellet, and, with some reservations, by Charles B. Fisk, all eminent civil engineers.

On the 5th day of November, 1851, Professor Fourney, a geologist, reported his minute examination of the site of Anthony's Creek reservoir, and of other reservoirs.

On the 20th day of January, 1852, Mr. E. Lorraine, a civil engineer, reported on the water-supply for the summit-level, having spent an entire year, 1851–'52, gauging the streams and surveying the country in the vicinity of the summit-level. He located and calculated the capacity of the reservoir on Anthony's Creek.

These reports of Mr. Lorraine and Professor Fourney were approved by Walter Gwin, a distinguished civil engineer.

Another survey and estimate for improving the Kanawha were made under the direction of Mr. Charles B. Fisk, in 1855, by John A. Byers, on the plan of sluice-dams at short intervals on the ripples, with a view to obtain 5 feet depth of water.

A project was also submitted to the directors of the Kanawha improvement in 1860, by Charles Ellet, jr., their engineer at that time, who proposed, after clearing out the sluices and confining the water to the channels, to supply from reservoirs the quantity needed for purposes of navigation beyond the natural flow of the stream.

In 1868 Mr. E. Lorraine, the then engineer of the company, advised the adoption of a new location, which, by the use of a tunnel about nine miles in length, reduced the elevation of the summit-level 216 feet, thus making it 1,700 feet above tide.

In 1872 a survey of the Great Kanawha River, from the Great Falls to its mouth, was made by Mr. Lorraine, under the direction of W. P. Craighill, major of United States Engineers, by virtue of an act of Congress passed June 10, 1872. Mr. Lorraine presented two estimates, each providing for a continuous and uninterrupted navigation throughout the year for boats drawing 6 feet of water. The first, which method is recommended by Major Craighill, contemplates an open dam improvement as far up as Paint Creek Shoals, with water-ways 120 feet wide and 6½ feet deep, and, from this point to the Great Falls, a lock and dam improvement, with locks 240 by 40 feet and 7 feet depth of water, and a reservoir at Meadow River. The second contemplates a lock and dam improvement throughout. Mr. Lorraine based his remarks and calculations on surveys of the river made by Mr. E. H. Gill in 1838, the elaborate survey made under his direction in 1856 by Mr. John A. Byers, and the subsequent measurements and reports on the improvement of the river by reservoirs by Charles Ellet, jr.

By a law of Congress passed in July, 1870, a survey of the James River and Kanawha Canal route was authorized, for the purpose of throwing additional light upon the question, first, of the practicability, and, second, of the cost, if practicable, of opening a continuous line of navigable waters between Richmond and the Ohio River. This survey was given by Gen. A. A. Humphreys, Chief of Engineers United States Army, into the charge of W. P. Craighill, major of United States Engineers. Major Craighill divided the work into two parts, and placed Mr. Walter Gwynn Turpin, an eminent civil engineer, "in charge of the examination of the line of the canal from Richmond to Buchanan, with a view to a determination of the cost of its enlargement to a size which would adapt it to the extended use it would receive when it became a link in the great central water-line between the Atlantic slope and the Valley of the Mississippi." He assigned Mr. William R. Hutton, an engineer of eminent ability, "the duty of ascertaining the best manner, if any existed, of continuing the communication by water from the end of the old canal—meaning the completed works to Buchanan, and the route as definitely located from Buchanan to the mouth of Fork Run, in Alleghany County—to the waters of the Ohio River." The results of the conclusions arrived at by these gentlemen will be spoken of more specifically hereafter. It is sufficient now to say that they, in common with all who have preceded them, agree in reporting the work a necessary one, and of practicable construction beyond controversy.

In 1872 Congress made an additional appropriation for a further examination of the line of the James River and Kanawha Canal from the mouth of Howard's Creek to the Ohio River. This examination was made by Mr. E. Lorraine, under the direction of Major Craighill. The detailed survey and report of Mr. Lorraine have been made to Congress the present session. Mr. Lorraine recommends that the slack-water shall be continued from Lykens's Shoals, as heretofore reported, to Paint-Creek Shoals, on the Kanawha.

V. *The capital stock of the canal, and how it is held.*—The capital stock of the James River and Kanawha Company is $12,400,000, which is held as follows:

By the State of Virginia	$10,400,000
By the city of Richmond	576,800
By the city of Lynchburgh	67,300
By the Washington and Lee University	10,000
By private stockholders	1,345,900
Total	12,400,000

Of this State stock $7,400,000 is preferred stock. Probably more than one-third of the private stock is now owned by the original subscribers, at a cost per share of $100 principal money. Probably one-third is held by private citizens, at a cost of from $15 to $20 per share, bought in 1860 or 1861. The remaining one-third, or perhaps less than one-third, has probably changed hands since the war at from $3 to $6 per share. During the last session of Congress it was proposed to fill the blank in the bill in reference to this subject, as the price to be paid private parties per share for their stock, with the sum of $25; but it is thought some of it would be surrendered for less. The advantages accruing to the cities of Richmond and Lynchburgh would be so great that their stock, if necessary, would likely be surrendered without charge. (Ev. of C. S. Carrington, pp. 234–6.)

VI. *Debt of the canal.*—The debt on the canal is $1,250,000, secured by two mortgages, one for $750,000 and the other for $500,000. There is a contingent liability for an alleged debt of $100,000 or more, which is the subject of litigation now pending in the court of appeals of Virginia. All of this debt, except that necessary to repair the canal after the unprecedented flood of September, 1870, was created before and during the war. The mortgages were both executed since the war, and the interest has been paid on all the bonds which have been issued under the mortgages. It was proposed to fill the blank in the bill introduced in Congress last session with the sum of $1,500,000, which would cover the mortgages, the contingent liability above mentioned, and the contingency of possible indebtedness of that portion of the line running through the State of West Virginia. (Ev. of C. S. Carrington, pp. 236–8.)

VII. *Length of canal now completed and cost of the same.*—The completed canal extends from Richmond to Buchanan, along the James River, a distance of one hundred and ninety-seven and a half miles, which includes the Richmond dock and tide-water connection, a mile in length. A portion of the line between Buchanan and Covington has also been constructed, but the canal is not in working condition beyond Buchanan.

There are three connections completed. There are two on that portion of the line extending from Richmond to Lynchburgh, one connecting the canal with the south side of the James River, and known as the Southside Connection, and the other connecting on the north side, with the improvement on the Rivanna River. The other connection is on that portion of the line between Lynchburgh and Buchanan, and extends from the mouth of North River to Lexington, a distance of nineteen and three-fourths miles.

The cost of the completed canal, including the three connections, was $10,436,869, and was expended as follows:

The Richmond dock and tide-water connection	$851,312
From Richmond to Lynchburgh	5,837,628
From Lynchburgh to Buchanan	2,422,556
The completed portion from Buchanan to Covington	511,094
The Southside connection	162,685
The Rivanna River connection	115,043
The North River Improvement connection	536,551
Total cost	10,436,869

VIII. *The outlet from Richmond to the sea and the harbor of Norfolk.*—The outlet to the Atlantic Ocean from Richmond, the eastern terminus of the canal, is by way of the James River to Newport News, a distance of one hundred and four miles, and from Newport News to the Capes of Virginia, by Hampton Roads and the Chesapeake Bay, a distance of twenty-two miles, making a total distance of one hundred and twenty-six miles. The James River is a large body of water, capable of accommodating vessels of from 12 to 15 feet draught, and it is estimated that with additional improvements that are now in progress under the direction of the United States Government, and will cost some $250,000, there will be at least 18 feet of water at high tide.

The harbor of Norfolk, or Hampton Roads, occupies one of the most important and commanding positions on the Atlantic coast of the United States. It is a well-sheltered harbor, and opens right upon the sea, with beautiful offings. It surpasses all others, with the single exception, perhaps, of New York and Sandy Hook, and is its peer in all the requirements of navigation, both as to facility of ingress and egress, certainty of land-fall, depth of water, and holding-ground. Says M. F. Maury, LL.D., &c., in his book entitled "Physical Survey of Virginia:" "The Chesapeake Bay is a 'king's chamber' in the bosom of Virginia, which no belligerent may enter with other than good intent. * * * This noble sheet of water, with its spacious harbors, is large enough to accommodate shipping sufficient to afford transportation for all the products and merchandise of the West were they a thousand-fold more abundant than they are. * * * * Then there is the Gulf-Stream, that mighty river in the ocean, upon the verge of which Norfolk stands. It flows up with a current which, without the help of sweeps, sails, or steam, will carry the European-bound vessel out of Norfolk at the rate of one hundred miles a day, directly on her course. Then at the sides of this and counter to it are eddies which favor the same vessel on her return to Norfolk. These hawse her along, and shorten her voyage by many a mile."

DESCRIPTION OF THE ROUTE.

The James River and Kanawha Canal, or "central water-line," extends from the city of Richmond, Va., to Point Pleasant, or the mouth of the Kanawha River, in West Virginia, a distance of 471.44 miles. As already constructed, the canal proper has a width at water-line of 50 feet, at bottom of 30 feet, and a depth of 5 feet. The locks are 100 by 15 feet in the clear. The dimensions of the prism of the enlarged canal are proposed to be 70 feet at water-line, 56 feet at bottom, and 7 feet deep—the same as the prism of the Erie Canal. The locks, as proposed, will be larger than those of the Erie Canal, being 120 by 20 feet, while those of the latter are but 110 by 18 feet.

Mr. Lorraine, in his description of this line, divided it into six divisions, and it is so spoken of in the surveys and papers in reference to it. The divisions were as follows: 1. From Richmond to Lynchburgh. 2. From Lynchburgh to Buchanan. 3. From Buchanan to Covington. 4. From Covington to the Greenbrier River. 5. The Greenbrier and New Rivers to Lykens's Shoals, on the Kanawha River. 6. From Lykens's Shoals, on the Kanawha River, to the mouth of the Kanawha River.

We, however, in speaking of this work, shall treat it as composed of but three divisions, viz: 1. The canal as now constructed from Richmond to Buchanan, but which is to be enlarged in order that it may be made to conform to the dimensions fixed for the entire line. 2. The canal from Buchanan to the Greenbrier River. This division includes the incomplete but partially constructed works between Buchanan and Covington, the Summit-level and the Lorraine Tunnel. 3. The Greenbrier, New, and Kanawha Rivers, from the mouth of Howard's Creek, on the Greenbrier, the western end of the canal portion, to the Ohio River at the mouth of the Kanawha.

(For an outline of the route, see map at the end of the Appendix.)

I. *The canal as now constructed from Richmond to Buchanan, and its proposed enlargement.*—This division of the canal is 197.50 miles in length, including the Richmond dock and tide-water connection, a mile in length. It is composed of 159.75 miles of canal and 36.75 miles of slack-water navigation. The dock at Richmond is 4,100 feet long, has an average width of 100 feet, and is from 11 to 15 feet in depth. It has a granite wall for its whole length on the north side, and for about 1,000 feet on the south side. Above the large dock is a continuation called the "Upper lock," surrounded by a granite wall. This upper portion is 800 feet long and 200 feet wide. The docks are connected by means of five locks with a commodious basin, also surrounded by a granite wall. The ship-lock, by means of which vessels enter the dock, is 180 feet long, between the gates 35 feet wide, has a lift of 15 feet, and will pass vessels of 500 tons.

The width of the canal on this division is, as before stated, 50 feet at water-line, 30 feet at bottom, and the depth 5 feet. The locks are 100 by 15 feet. The proposed enlargement will make the canal as follows: 70 feet wide, 5 at water-line, 6 feet at bottom, and 7 feet deep. The enlarged locks will be 120 by 20 feet. On this division, exclusive of the dock and ship-lock, there are 90 locks, of a total lift of 812 feet.

The structures embrace three connections, the necessary guard and accommodation locks, 33 dams, 15 aqueducts, 199 culverts, 158 road-bridges, and 48 drains. Of the 90 locks, some 30 are built of rubble masonry, faced with timber and plank, and some 60 of cut-stone.

The total cost of the work on this division, including the lock and tide-water connection and the feeders, has been $9,025,775.

II. *The canal from Buchanan to the Greenbrier River.*—This division of the canal is 76.50 miles in length. It is composed of 67.25 miles of canal, and 9.25 miles of slack-water navigation. It embraces (A) a certain unfinished work from Buchanan to Covington, and the construction of the canal to a point on Fork Run, at the eastern end of the Lorraine tunnel; (B) the Lorraine tunnel of 7.8 miles in length, through the Allegheny summit; and (C) the construction of the part on the western slope of the Alleghany ridge, from the west end of the Lorraine tunnel to the Greenbrier River, at the mouth of Howard Creek. (See map at the end of the Appendix.

(A.) The partially-completed work on this division is between Buchanan and Covington, and consists of the following structures: The completion of the Mason tunnel, 198 feet in length; the excavation of 800 feet of the Marshall tunnel, which is to be 1,900 feet in length; the completion of the foundations of two of the dams up to the surface of low-water mark, and the partial construction of 10 lift-locks, and the abutments and piers of three of the aqueducts across James River. The prism of the canal, and the size of the locks, will be the same as the proposed enlargement, mentioned in the first division.

The structures on this portion of this division will embrace two tunnels, viz: the

Marshall tunnel, of 1,900 feet length, (partially excavated,) and the Mason tunnel, of 198 feet length, (completed;) the nesessary dams, aqueducts, and road-bridges, one culvert, two waste-weirs, and one waste. (NOTE.—By means of these two tunnels five and five-eighth miles of distance are saved.)

The cost of the work done on this division was $511,094.

(B.) *The Lorraine tunnel and the water-supply for the summit-level.*

1. *The Lorraine tunnel.*—This tunnel forms the summit-level of the canal, from which it descends on one side to the Atlantic Ocean, and on the other side to the Ohio River, and is one of the most interesting features of the great work. A few years ago men would have been appalled at the apparent magnitude of the work, but it is no longer deemed an extraordinary undertaking. Eminent engineers of great professional ability and experience, after due examinations and surveys, have, in their official reports, and not less carefully prepared papers, expressed clear and decided opinions, without dissent or qualifications, favorable to the practicability of the construction of the proposed tunnel.

Captain McNeil's line ascended the valley of Fork Run to an elevation of 1,916 feet above tide, and there pierced the ridge with a tunnel of 2.6 miles in length, whence it descended the valley of Howard's Creek to the Greenbrier River.

Mr. Lorraine, by his survey made in 1868, proposed to establish the summit at a level of 1,700 feet above tide, or 20 feet above the level of Greenbrier River, at the mouth of Howard's Creek, and pass through the Alleghany Mountains by a tunnel about nine miles in length.

The line now recommended by Maj. W. P. Craighill, of United States Engineers, by a survey made under his direction in 1870, commences at the mouth of Fork Run, ascends that stream by a canal 70 feet wide at water-line, with a depth of 7 feet; locks to be 120 by 20 feet, and six in number, of 12 feet lift each, to the summit-level, at 1,700 feet above tide. It then pierces the main range of the Alleghany Mountains, passing under Tuckahoe and Katis Mountains, by a tunnel 7.8 miles long, with a section of 52 by 34½ feet, being 46 feet wide at water-line, and 7 feet deep. It emerges into the valley of Howard's Creek, which it descends to the Greenbrier River, by three locks of 10 feet lift each. The extreme length of the tunnel is 40,380 feet, and, for the purpose of diminishing the depth of shafts, has been located upon a curve of nearly thirty miles radius, although in construction the tunnel would be made straight from shaft to shaft. The shafts vary in depth from 333 to 693 feet, and the greatest distance between any two of them is 7,500 feet. The length of the Mount Cenis tunnel is seven and a half miles, and of the Hoosac tunnel four and three-fourths miles. Mr. William R. Hutton, chief engineer in charge of this portion of the survey made in 1870, says: "The distinguishing feature of the low level is the long tunnel, longer even than that of Mount Cenis, just now reaching completion; differing from that work, however, in one important particular, that while the Mount Cenis tunnel was excavated exclusively from the two ends, the one now in consideration can be worked from six shafts, as well as from the ends, forming fourteen faces upon which simultaneous progress can be made." (Ex. Doc. 110, Forty-first Congress, 3d session, p. 18.) The rock through which the excavation will be made is slate and sandstone of variable quality, from a sandstone shale to the most solid character of rocks. Lying below the summits, crossed at a depth of 1,000 to 1,300 feet, it is reasonable to suppose that a large portion of the rock will be sufficiently firm and solid to stand without a lining arch. Mr. Hutton, however, in his estimate has provided for arching one-half of the whole length of the tunnel. The cost of the tunnel is estimated by Mr. Hutton at $13,253,310. (Same, p. 26.) In regard to the tunnel, Mr. Benjamin H. Latrobe, of Baltimore, who has had long experience in tunneling, and especiallyas consulting engineer of the Hoosac tunnel, and who visited the Mount Cenis tunnel in Europe, and made observation of its operations, in a letter to Mr. Lorraine, dated May 1, 1868, says: "That he (Mr. Latrobe) has driven more than one tunnel in slates and sandstones, such as will be met with in the Alleghany tunnel. That he was well acquainted with the character of those rocks, and knows that very rapid progress could be made in them, and that the strike and dip of the strata at that locality were as favorable as possible to safe and speedy working." (Same, pp. 61, 62.) He further says that he cannot hesitate to pronounce the proposed tunnel entirely practicable. General Charles P. Stone, in a letter to Charles S. Carrington, esq., president of the James River and Kanawha Company, dated October 13, 1868, says: "As regards the feasibility of the succession of tunnels, (referring to the long tunnel and its shafts,) I think there can be no question." (Same, p. 74.) Maj. W. P. Craighill, in his report heretofore referred to, says: "The question of practicability is settled by the data furnished by the reports hereto attached." (Same, p. 61.) The reports attached are those of Mr. Hutton and Mr. Turpin, and the letters of Messrs. Lorraine, Latrobe, and Stone, heretofore referred to. In short, all the engineers who have surveyed or spoken of the tunnel are agreed as to its practicability.

2. *The water-supply for the summit-level.*—The supply of water for the summit-level will

come mainly from the Greenbrier River, which is a stream of an average width of 100 feet; but as this river may not at all times furnish a sufficient quantity, recourse must be had to reservoirs to meet the deficiency, if any exists. Mr. Hutton says: "These (reservoirs) may be constructed on the river (Greenbrier) itself, but the very complete surveys made by Mr. Lorraine for a reservoir on Anthony's Creek, one of its tributaries, show that site to be a desirable one, both as to cost and sufficiency." (Same, p. 18.) On the question of the site proposed, Mr. Lorraine says: "As doubts have been suggested as to the adaptation of this valley (Anthony's Creek) for the purpose of a reservoir, and vague surmises expressed as to fissures and caverns in the sides of the mountain through which the water would leak out, an eminent practical geologist was employed to make an examination of the geological structure of the site of this reservoir, who reported that if the engineers had the choice of the rocks of this region it would be difficult to show how they could make a better disposition of them." (Same, p. 57.)

Anthony's Creek reservoir.—Where Anthony's Creek passes through the Greenbrier Mountain there is a narrow defile, which has been selected as a site for a dam or mound, which, when erected, will arrest the water that flows down the creek, and convert the valley above into a reservoir or lake. This reservoir will be nine miles long, will have an average width of half a mile, a superficial area of 2,753 acres, and a mean depth of 60 feet. The mound will be 126 feet high and 395 feet long. The reservoir will contain 178,000,000 cubic yards of water, which was ascertained by an accurate survey of its superficial area. The annual quantity of water discharged by Anthony's Creek has been ascertained by daily gauges of the creek for a whole year, and the total amount per annum found to be 210,526,955 cubic yards, an average discharge per diem of 576,786 cubic yards. These gauges of the creek were taken during the last half of the year 1851 and the first half of the year 1852, during which time the quantity of rain, as ascertained by the rain-gauges which were kept in that vicinity, was 34¼ inches, which has been ascertained to be considerably below the average; so it is safe to assume that the average daily supply of 576,786 cubic yards is within the mark. Now, let us see how much water the canal at this point will demand, assuming that the canal will enjoy a full trade, and that the boats will pass through the locks at the summit as fast as possible. Mr. Hutton, in his report on this subject, says: "On the Erie Canal 198 boats have actually been passed through a single lock in one day. We may then safely assume a capacity for 180 boats. The tonnage of the boats which will be used will be about 280 tons, but as the freight going West will not be more than one-fourth of that from the West, we will average them at 180 tons." (Same, p. 18.) He further says: "We have assumed a trade of 180 boats per day, but it will be prudent to provide a supply of water for 200. Allowing them one and one-half locksful of water to each boat passing the summit-level, we will require 300 locksful of water per day for a maximum trade. The greatest lift between Greenbrier and Covington, the portion of the line to be supplied from the summit-level, is 14 feet, and the locks being 120 by 20 feet, we have:

300 locks, 120 by 20 by 14, equal to cubic feet per day	10,080,000
Evaporation on 21.9 miles, (the tunnel being excluded,*) ⅛ inch per mile per day	225,264
Filtration, cubic feet	5,240,400
Waste at structures, cubic feet	43,200
Leakage at lock-gates	1,728,000
Total cubic feet	17,316,864
The minimum flow of the Greenbrier River, as gauged by Captain McNeil, was 97 feet per second, or per day	8,380,800
Leaving to be supplied from other sources	8,936,064
The reservoir surveyed by Mr. Lorraine will contain 4,806,000,000 cubic feet, and the observed discharge of the stream, (where it has been gauged,) for a year of much less than the average rain-fall is	5,484,229,000
Diminish this by the evaporation of ¼ of an inch per day, for one year, from the surface of the reservoir	899,405,100
And we have available for the canal	4,584,823,900
Suppose the flow of the Greenbrier to continue at its minimum for an average period of 120 days, the total quantity to be furnished would be, cubic feet	1,072,327,680
Or a surplus of	3,512,496,220

* "That portion of the canal occupied by the tunnel, being through solid rock, will be subject to no more loss by leakage and evaporation than will be supplied by percolation through the roof and sides of the tunnel, and this is therefore excluded from the calculation."—(*See* Ex. Doc. No. 110, 41st Cong., 3d sess., p. 57.)

Some persons not familiar with the subject have expressed fears that a reservoir supplied chiefly from rain-fall might fail to furnish the anticipated supply. On this point Mr. Hutton says: "It is well to observe that the valley of the Greenbrier River is extremely favorable for the construction of reservoirs, with which it might be filled throughout its length of 60 miles, in which any desired amount of water from the spring and winter floods might be stored up for use in time of drought." (Same, p. 19.)

Mr. James M. Harris, present engineer of the James River and Kanawha Company, testifies that "there cannot be the least reason to doubt that there will be any deficiency in water to supply the largest canal the Government may deem proper to construct." (Evidence before committee, p. 232.) The proposed means, as above stated, of supplying any possible deficiency in the supply of water for the summit-level are proven to be amply sufficient by competent and skilled witnesses, and there seems to be no doubt on the matter whatever.

(C.) *The construction of the part of the canal from the west end of the Lorraine tunnel to the Greenbrier River.*—The canal from the west end of the Lorraine tunnel emerges into the valley of Howard's Creek, which it descends, by three locks of ten feet lift each, to the Greenbrier River. The distance from the mouth of Fork Run to the mouth of Howard's Creek, at the Greenbrier River, is 12.6 miles, and the cost of construction, exclusive of the tunnel, is estimated to be $2,383,474.

The estimated cost of this division from the town of Buchanan to the mouth of Fork Run, is $6,128,585.62.

Lockage on the second division.—There are 70 ascending locks from Buchanan to the Lorraine tunnel, with a total lockage of 888 feet, and 3 descending locks from the western end of said tunnel to the Greenbrier River, at the mouth of Howard's Creek, with a total lockage of 30 feet, making 73 locks in all, with a total lockage of 918 feet.

III. *The Greenbrier, New, and Kanawha Rivers, from the mouth af Howard's Creek, on the Greenbrier, to the Ohio River, at the mouth of the Kanawha.*—The length of this division is 197.44 miles. The canal ceases from the time the line strikes the Greenbrier River at the mouth of Howard's Creek, (except in two cases, at Anderson's and again a short distance below the falls of Greenbrier, short canals of large dimensions are introduced to avoid very expensive locations for dams, which would otherwise be required,) and a continuous slack-water navigation is projected down the Greenbrier River to the New River, and down the New River to Lykens's Shoals, on the Kanawha River, a distance of 113.44 miles. From Lykens's Shoals to the mouth of the Kanawha River open navigation is proposed, the fall throughout the length being equalized by dams at regular intervals, having sluices to permit the passage of vessels. On this division there are 74 locks and —— dams, and the fall to Lykens's Shoals on the Kanawha, is 1,084 feet. The locks are to be 240 by 40 feet.

The cost of the proposed improvements on these rivers, so as to secure 6 feet of water all the year round, is estimated by Mr. Hutton as follows:

Down the Greenbrier and New Rivers to Lykens's Shoals, on the Kanawha River	$13,243,541
From Lykens's Shoals to mouth of the Kanawha	973,900
Total cost of this division	14,217,441

Greenbrier and New Rivers.—Of New River Mr. Hutton says: "New River is, particularly in its lower portions, of a different character (from the Greenbrier,) the banks being composed almost entirely of bowlders, among or over which the construction of a canal presents formidable difficulties. These, however, are not in the way of a slack-water improvement as is now recommended." (Ex. Doc. 110, 41st Cong., 3d sess., p. 20.) The length of the Greenbrier River, from the mouth of Howard's Creek to the New River, is 49.086 miles. The length of New River, from the mouth of the Greenbrier to the mouth of the Gauley River, where it is merged into the Kanawha, is 67.433 miles. Eminent engineers, such as Wright, Gill, Fisk, Ellet, Lorraine, Hutton, Harris, &c., have examined and surveyed the proposed route through these streams, and, with singular and entire unanimity, concur in the practicability and feasibility of the proposed improvements. As regards the supply of water for any deficiency that may exist in these rivers, Mr. Hutton says:

"The large locks on the slack-water will transmit the daily tonnage estimated for the canal in 120 lockages, requiring for a maximum lift of 15.5 feet, (on the Greenbrier,) with 25 per cent. added for waste; 120 by 200 by 40 by 155 by 1.25, 18,600,000 cubic feet.

	Cubic feet.
Which being supposed necessary for one hundred and twenty days, the required supply will be	2,232,000,000
But Anthony's Creek reservoir will furnish beyond the quantity needed for the canal	3,512,496,220
Showing a surplus to meet contingencies of	1,280,496,220

(Same, p. 20.)

The Kanawha River.—The Great Kanawha River is formed by the united waters of the New River, the Greenbrier River, and the Gauley.

The upper portion of the Kanawha, from the mouth of Gauley to the foot of Lykens's Shoals, requires the same kind of improvement as the Greenbrier and New Rivers, the fall being too great for any open navigation. From Lykens's Shoals to the mouth of the Kanawha open-river navigation is proposed.

The present improvement on the Kanawha.—The present improvement consists of channels or "chutes," excavated through the shoals, and occasionally of slight wing-dams of stone or gravel, extending from either bank of the river to the chutes, for the purpose of concentrating the water in the chute. This improvement extends up as far as the foot of Loup Creek Shoal. These chutes are from one hundred to one hundred and twenty feet wide.

The proposed plans of improvement on the Kanawha.—Mr. Lorraine, in his report to Major Craighill, dated December 9, 1872, recommends that the improvement be by open dams and a reservoir on Meadow River, a combination and improvement of the plans proposed by Mr. Fisk in 1854, and by Mr. Ellet in 1858. This recommendation is indorsed by Major Craighill. (Rep. Chief Eng., 43d Cong., 1st sess., p. 839.)

1. *The improvement by open dams.*—This plan of improvement consists of the construction of low dams extending from either bank of the river to the channel, leaving a water-way in the dam of sufficient width and depth for the passage of steamboats and barges. These dams will be placed at intervals along the stream so as to give it a grade of two feet to the mile on the shoals, the fall from one pool to another being so slight as to offer but little resistance to ascending boats. The water-ways in the dams are to be 94 feet at the bottom and 120 feet wide at the top, with 6½ feet depth of water.

2. *The reservoir on Meadow River.*—Mr. Lorraine, in said report, estimates the probable deficiency in the supply of water in the Kanawha to be supplied by the Meadow Lake at 130,291,200 cubic feet per day. The annual drainage into Meadow Lake, as computed by Mr. Ellet, is 10,722,000,000 cubic feet, the capacity of the lake being 13,587,815,000 cubic feet. Then divide 10,722,000,000 by 130,291,200, and the result (82) will be the number of days during which Meadow Lake will be able to supply the deficiency. But if the water from this reservoir proves insufficient, there is the surplus that will remain in the Anthony's Creek reservoir, after supplying the summit-level, to fall back upon. As hereinbefore shown, it is estimated that Anthony's Creek reservoir will have a surplus of 3,512,496,220 cubic feet of water, to be devoted to the service of the Greenbrier River. This will of course pass into the Kanawha, and after allowing one-twentieth for evaporation during its passage, will supply the Kanawha with 37,076,348 cubic feet per day, for 90 days, or nearly one-third the quantity needed to keep the water-ways full. It must, therefore, be conceded, says Mr. Lorraine, that there will be an abundant supply of water for full navigation during the ordinary dry season.

RECAPITULATION.

Length of the whole line and the character of each division.

	Miles.
Richmond dock and tide-water connection	1.00
I. The first division, extending from Richmond to Buchanan, 159.75 miles of canal, and 36.75 miles of slack-water	196.50
II. The second division, extending from Buchanan to the Greenbrier River, 67.25 miles of canal, and 9.25 miles of slack-water	76.50
III. The third division, extending from the mouth of Howard's Creek, on the Greenbrier, to the mouth of the Kanawha, 115.39 miles of slack-water, and 79.05 miles of open-river navigation, and 3 miles of canal	197.44
Total	471.44

Total equated length of the line.

Assuming each lock to be equivalent to half a mile in distance, the equated length of the entire line appears to be as follows:

	Miles.
Actual length	471.44
237 locks, equivalent to	118.50
Total equated length of the line	589.94

The entire line will be composed of—

	Miles.
Canal	231.00
Slack-water navigation	161.39
Open-river	79.05
Total equated length	471.44

Probable cost of enlarging and completing the James River and Kanawha Canal and the Kanawha River improvements.—The following are the estimates reported by Major Craighill, as the result of the survey made under his directions in 1870, contemplating the probable cost of enlarging and completing the James River and Kanawha Canal, and the improvements on the Kanawha River, "in a substantial manner, proportionate to the importance of the work and the gravity of the results which would attend any stoppage of its use, caused by failures in its mechanical structures." (Ex. Doc. 110, 41st Cong., 3d sess.)

Cost of enlarging first division, extending from Richmond to Buchanan, including Richmond dock and ship-lock and tide-water connection. (Ex. Doc. 110, 41st Cong., 3d sess.):

Dock and ship-lock	$1,300,000 00	
Tide-water connection	334,937 00	
Richmond to Lynchburgh	4,811,326 00	
Lynchburgh to Buchanan	2,092,008 51	
		$8,538,271 51
Cost of second division, extending from Buchanan to mouth of Howard's Creek, and the Greenbrier River, including Lorraine tunnel:		
Buchanan to Covington	$4,036,577 11	
Covington to mouth of Fork Run	2,206,795 45	
Mouth of Fork Run to Greenbrier River, exclusive of tunnel	2,383,474 00	
Lorraine tunnel	13,253,310 00	
		21,880,156 56
Cost of third division, extending from mouth of Howard's Creek, on the Greenbrier, to mouth of Kanawha:		
Greenbrier and New Rivers to Lykens's Shoals on the Kanawha	$13,243,541 00	
Lykens's Shoals to mouth of Kanawha	973,900 00	
		14,217,441 00
Add ten per cent. to amounts on first and second divisions for contingencies		2,986,430 00
Total estimated cost		47,622,289 07

It may be proper to add that while Mr. Hutton has included in his estimate of cost for improving the Kanawha River the Meadow River reservoir, yet he thinks it need not be near so large as contemplated by Mr. Ellet, and consequently has reduced the cost of the reservoir to $250,000.

It will be noted that this estimate of cost ($47,622,289.07) far exceeds the estimates made by any previous survey, the highest being that made by Mr. Lorraine, and including the tunnel, then estimated to be about nine miles in length, amounting to but $37,363,911.

H. D. Whitcomb, esq., chief engineer of the Chesapeake and Ohio Railroad, in his evidence before the committee, says he considers the estimates given by Major Craighill amply sufficient, even if the tunnel were shale throughout, and had to be arched from end to end. Mr. Whitcomb built nineteen tunnels on the Chesapeake and Ohio Road, under his own observation, one of which was through the Alleghany Mountains, at an elevation of some 2,060 feet above tide, and not over a mile distant from the proposed Lorraine tunnel. (pp. 212, 213.)

Gen. Herman Haupt, who was connected with the Hoosac tunnel as engineer and contractor, and has had considerable experience otherwise in relation to tunnels, also indorses the estimate of the cost of the tunnel. (p. 20.)

Mr. James M. Harris, present engineer of the James River and Kanawha Company, says he thinks the estimates of costs are very full. To use his own words: "The work can be done for the estimate. It is from 50 to 75 per cent. higher than I have had the same sort of work estimated and done." He further says: "I have never had it done in that locality, but I think it can be done much cheaper there than where I had it done, if the price of labor be the same." (p. 233.)

Probable time required to complete the enlargement and improvement.—On this point Mr. William R. Hutton, assistant under Major Craighill, says: "Provided funds are supplied to keep pace with their economical expenditure, the opening of the line will be governed by the time necessary to complete the long or Lorraine tunnel. If we suppose a progress of 30 feet per month to be made in each shaft, and 100 feet per month in each heading, (and double this has been made in the Mount Cenis tunnel,) then the longest time will be consumed in the west heading of shaft No. 4, and the east heading of shaft No. 5, (see profile of tunnel.) which will require five years and two months from the date of commencement. Ten months may be consumed in preparation and in trimming up after the opening is made through. We may, therefore, safely say that the work can be completed in six years from the time it is put into the hands of a competent contractor." (Ex. Doc. 110, 41st Cong., 3d sess.)

Mr. Lorraine estimates the time that would probably be consumed in excavating the tunnel at four years, "which is about as quickly as the New River or Greenbrier sections could be completed under the most favorable circumstances." (Same, p. 60.)

Mr. Benjamin H. Latrobe, of Baltimore, Md., a civil engineer of large experience, who was consulting engineer of the Hoosac tunnel, and visited and made personal inspections of the Mont Cenis tunnel in Europe, in a letter to Mr. Lorraine, dated May 1, 1868, sums up his deductions of the time necessary to excavate the long tunnel, and says that the work could be finished and in operation at the end of four years. He closes his letter in the following words: "In conclusion, I will add that I never felt, in giving a professional opinion, more perfect confidence in its soundness, and the certainty with which the results predicted can be realized." (Same, p. 62.)

General Charles P. Stone, civil engineer, in a letter to Col. C. S. Carrington, president of the James River and Kanawha Company, dated October 12, 1868, says, referring to Mr. Lorraine's report as to time and cost: "He has certainly overestimated the necessary cost of the shafts, and that very considerably, and his estimate of time is perfectly safe. I speak positively on this matter, because speaking from experience in shaft-sinking through very much the same kind of rock as he will probably have to contend with." (Same, pp. 74, 75.)

Mr. H. D. Whitcomb, chief engineer of the Chesapeake and Ohio Railroad, says that he thinks the estimate of time made by Mr. Lorraine sufficient, and puts the maximum of time, taking into consideration all contingencies, at five years.

It may be noted at this point that Mr. Lorraine's estimate of the time is based upon the construction of a tunnel about nine miles in length, whereas the actual length now determined on is but 7.8 miles. (Evidence before committee, p. 213.)

General Herman Haupt, who was a contractor and engineer on the Hoosac tunnel, says: "The Lorraine tunnel is only a collection of smaller tunnels, and, in this particular, presents much less difficulty and uncertainty than the tunnels of the Alps or Hoosac." He further says: "I should think, from the time when the shafts were sunk to the grade of the tunnel, it ought not to require more than four and a half or five years at the outside, even taking into consideration all the difficulties that we may reasonably expect to encounter in the progress of such a work." (Same, p. 220.)

Length of season of navigation by this route.—It is the official duty of the superintendent of the James River and Kanawha Canal to report, annually, the time during the year of suspension of navigation by ice. Colonel Carrington, president of the company, says: "The estimate of the time of suspension of navigation by ice is fifteen days for the eastern and western portion of the line, and thirty days for the middle or mountainous," per annum.

Mr. Lorraine says on this point: "By examining the reports of the James River and Kanawha Company it will be seen that, from 1840 to 1848, there was no suspension of navigation by ice reported, except twelve days in 1845. If there were any others they must have been so slight as not to have attracted attention, or to have been deemed unworthy of comment. From 1848 to 1868, a period of twenty years, during which time all suspensions of navigation by ice have been reported by the superintendents, the total number of days in which the navigation was so suspended amounts to 302, an average of fifteen days for each year. As these reports apply to the canal as high up as Buchanan, west of the Blue Ridge, it will be reasonable to infer that, when the canal reaches its highest elevation in the Alleghanies, it will not be closed by ice, on an average, more than thirty days in the year." (Ex. Doc. 110, 41st Cong., 3d sess., p. 70.)

Colonel Carrington says: "From my observation during my connection with the canal since 1867, and from information derived from intelligent parties with long experience in navigation on the canal, I believe that these suspensions would have been greatly reduced in time and number by the use of ice-boats. Indeed, it is not improbable that ice-boats and a full traffic would have kept open the navigation during the whole year." (Evidence before committee, p. 251.)

H. D. Whitcomb, chief engineer of the Chesapeake and Ohio Road, says: "That the time of obstruction by ice would not be more than a month or six weeks at the outside, perhaps from about Christmas to the middle of February, and many winters not half that time." (Same, p. 217.)

Dr. A. E. Summers, a member of West Virginia senate, and a resident of Charleston the capital of that State, says that he does not think the freezes on the Kanawha River will average more than a week to ten days, and it has been frequently the case that the whole winter has passed without any freezing of the river. (Same, p. 308.)

W. F. Goshorn, president of the Kanawha River board, testifies that the Kanawha River is sometimes open for navigation during the whole year. (Same, p. 314.)

Territory for the trade of which this line will form a competing point. Its area, population, and most important cereal productions.—The portion of the Mississippi Valley and lake country interested in the opening of a direct line of transportation, extending the navigation of the Ohio and Mississippi Rivers to the sea-board, and for which this line will form a competing point, is composed of some nineteen States and Territories, aggregating in area 1,212,164 square miles, in population 18,946,733 people, and in important cereal productions a grand total of 1,023,352,583 bushels. From these totals there should be deducted at least one-fourth for that portion of the territory lying contiguous to the lake-lines, and for which the "central water-line" could not fairly claim to be a competing point, leaving an area of 909,123 square miles, a population of 14,210,050 people, and a total of 767,514,438 bushels of cereals. It may be noted at this point that the opening of this line to the Ohio River would place some 17,000 miles of inland steamboat navigation in connection with tide-water.

The area, population, and important cereal productions of the States and Territories above mentioned will be found in the annexed tables, compiled from the census of 1870:

TABLE No. 1.—*Area and population.*

State or Territory.	Square miles.	Population.
The United States, including the Territories—total	3, 603, 884	38, 558, 371
Virginia	38, 348	1, 225, 163
West Virginia	23, 000	442, 014
Western Pennsylvania, estimated at one-third of whole	15, 333	1, 173, 984
Tennessee	45, 600	1, 258, 520
Kentucky	37, 680	1, 321, 011
Arkansas	52, 198	484, 471
Ohio	39, 964	2, 665, 260
Indiana	33, 809	1, 680, 637
Illinois	55, 410	2, 589, 891
Michigan	56, 451	1, 184, 059
Wisconsin	53, 924	1, 054, 670
Minnesota	83, 531	439, 706
Iowa	55, 045	1, 194, 020
Missouri	65, 350	1, 721, 295
Kansas	81, 318	364, 399
Nebraska	75, 995	122, 993
Dakota	150, 932	14, 181
Montana	143, 776	20, 595
Colorado	104, 500	39, 864
Total	1, 212, 164	18, 946, 733

TABLE No. 2.—*Principal cereals.*

State or Territory.	Bushels wheat.	Bushels rye.	Bushels corn.	Bushels oats.	Bushels barley.	Bushels buckwh't.
The United States, including Territories—total	287, 745, 626	16, 918, 795	760, 944, 549	282, 107, 157	29, 761, 305	9, 821, 721
Virginia	7, 398, 787	582, 264	17, 649, 304	6, 857, 555	7, 259	45, 075
West Virginia	2, 483, 543	277, 746	8, 197, 865	2, 413, 749	50, 363	82, 916
Tennessee	6, 188, 916	223, 335	41, 343, 614	4, 513, 315	75, 068	77, 437
Kentucky	5, 728, 704	1, 108, 933	50, 091, 006	6, 620, 103	238, 486	3, 443
Arkansas	841, 736	27, 645	13, 382, 145	528, 777	1, 921	226
Ohio	27, 882, 159	846, 890	67, 501, 144	25, 347, 549	1, 715, 221	180, 341
Indiana	27, 747, 222	457, 468	51, 094, 538	8, 590, 409	356, 262	80, 231
Western Pennsylvania, estimated at one-third	6, 524, 332	1, 192, 547	11, 567, 335	12, 159, 528	176, 520	844, 057
Illinois	30, 128, 405	2, 456, 578	129, 921, 395	42, 780, 851	2, 480, 400	168, 862
Michigan	16, 265, 773	144, 508	14, 086, 238	8, 954, 466	834, 558	436, 755
Wisconsin	25, 606, 344	1, 325, 294	15, 033, 998	20, 180, 016	1, 645, 019	408, 897
Minnesota	18, 866, 073	78, 088	4, 743, 117	10, 678, 261	1, 032, 024	52, 438
Iowa	29, 435, 692	505, 807	68, 935, 065	21, 005, 142	1, 960, 779	109, 432
Missouri	14, 315, 926	559, 532	66, 034, 075	16, 578, 313	269, 240	36, 252
Kansas	2, 391, 198	85, 207	17, 025, 525	4, 097, 925	98, 405	27, 826
Nebraska	2, 125, 086	13, 532	4, 736, 710	1, 477, 562	216, 481	3, 471
Dakota	170, 662	....	133, 140	114, 327	4, 118	179
Montana	181, 184	1, 141	320	149, 367	85, 756	988
Colorado	258, 474	5, 235	231, 903	322, 940	35, 141	178
Total	224, 540, 216	9, 891, 750	581, 708, 437	193, 370, 155	11, 283, 021	2, 559, 004

What Virginia and West Virginia propose to do.—The States of Virginia and West Virginia propose to relinquish to the Government of the United States their interests in the work, which amount to some $10,400,000, of which $7,400,000 is perferred stock, representing money actually expended in prosecuting the work to Buchanan, and in the incomplete works between Buchanan and Covington; and will turn the whole line over to the Government, to be completed in such manner as Congress may prescribe. If Congress shall see fit to complete the work by direct appropriation, without a return of principal and interest, the two States further agree that the line, as soon as completed, shall be thrown open to the public free of toll, except so far as necessary to keep the work in repair. They further agree "That the work shall be prosecuted either under the management of the company, subject to such regulations and restrictions as Congress may impose, or by commissioners appointed by the States of Virginia and West Virginia, who will hold the property as a sacred trust for the benefit of the whole country, under like regulations; or that the prosecution of the work and the management of the property, when it shall have been completed, shall be committed to a board of eleven trustees, one of whom shall be appointed by the President of the United States, and one each by the States of Iowa, Missouri, Arkansas, Illinois, Indiana, Kentucky, Ohio, Virginia, West Virginia, and Maryland, as recommended by the National Board of Trade at its annual session in December, 1869, or in any other way in which its construction and management will best promote the prosperity and welfare of the whole country." Any pledge, however, given by the two States, looking to the relinquishment of the interests of the company, or the exemption of tolls must, of course, be subordinate to the rights of creditors and private stockholders of the company, which, in view of the small amount involved, admit of easy adjustment.

The legislature of the State of West Virginia, by a joint resolution adopted December 21, 1872, provided for the appointment by the board of public works of nine commissioners on the part of the State, to confer and negotiate with any commissioners or persons who may be authorized by law, on behalf of the United States, in regard to a transfer to the United States of the rights, privileges, and franchises of this line, so far as the said State has any interest in them. The resolution also provides that the action of the commissioners shall be submitted to the legislature for their action. In pursuance of said resolution the board of public works has appointed the following gentlemen as commissioners: Messrs. A. J. Pannell, James Morrow, jr., William H. Travers, Charles F. Scott, James D. Armstrong, Jonathan M. Bennett, William A. Quarrier, A. T. Caperton, and John Douglass. The commissioners met on the 16th of December, 1873, and effected a permanent organization by the election of Allen T. Caperton president and Charles F. Scott secretary.

General remarks.—As to the importance and necessity of a line of water-communication, such as this, to connect the grain-growing section of our country and the seaboard, there can be no question. In the message of President Grant to the Forty-second Congress we find these words: "The attention of Congress will be called at its present session to enterprises for the more certain and cheaper transportation of the constantly-increasing surplus of the western and southern products to the Atlantic sea-board. The subject is one that will force itself upon the legislative branch of the Government sooner or later, and I suggest that immediate steps be taken to gain all available information to inevitable and just legislation regarding a route to connect the Mississippi Valley with the Atlantic."

Practicability of the route.—The highest professional skill in this country, civil and military, has testified that the work is practicable, at a cost inconsiderable in comparison with the large benefits to inure. When civil and hydraulic engineers of the celebrity and professional eminence of Wright, Gwin, Fisk, Gill, Ellet, Lorraine, Craighill, Turpin, Harris, Hutton, Latrobe, and others that might be mentioned, unite in pronouncing an improvement of practicable accomplishment, as has been done in this instance, the question is concluded from further discussion by unprofessionals.

Action of conventions and boards of trade in regard to this line.—Several of the States, through their legislatures, have adopted memorials in favor of the completion of this line, as the most feasible and practicable plan. The Louisville Board of Trade, on the 7th of October, 1868, indorsed this line, and reiterated it "with increased confidence" in 1873. The National Board of Trade, in December, 1868, at its meeting in Cincinnati, appointed a committee, consisting of delegates from the States of Kentucky, Missouri, Louisiana, Tennessee, Maine, Massachusetts, New York, Iowa, Illinois, Minnesota, Ohio, Pennsylvania, Maryland, and Virginia, to consider the resolutions of indorsement of this line adopted by the Louisville Board of Trade. This committee assembled at the White Sulphur Springs, West Virginia, in August, 1869, and, after a session of some two weeks, agreed to a report which sets forth the necessity of a water-line, and recommends this route as certainly the most central, and, as they believed, the most practicable route for such a water-line.

Important mineral productions on this line.—Professor David I. Ansted, who has practiced engineering, as connected with geology, for 28 years, and has visited most of the important coal and iron fields in the world, says: "I find on the line of this proposed communication (referring to this line) one of the most remarkable iron-fields that exist in any part of the world as at present known. It contains every variety of the most valuable ores, and these ores are distributed in such a manner as to be more accessible than, I think, in any other districts. * * * * They include the most valuable of all the known iron-ores, magnetic oxide."—(Ev. before com., pp. 277, 278.) He also says that there are about twenty distinctly workable seams of coal in the middle of the district, all of them above the water-line. "They lie almost horizontally, and are capable of being worked at a cheaper rate than any coals which exist on a large scale in any part of Europe. They include beds of coal of various thickness, * * * * all thick enough to be worked in the most effective manner without any waste."—(*Id.*, p. 278.) A late authentic work on the subject of the Kanawha coals says: "They (the Kanawha coal-fields) are regarded by eminent geologists as the finest deposit of coal in the world. * * * * The veins lie horizontally, and vary from 3 feet to 15 feet in thickness, and the aggregate thickness of the various veins, in some localities, amounts to 40 and even 50 feet of solid coal." The varieties of coal are mainly bituminous, cannel, and splint. Then there are the Kanawha salines, which have a present capacity of 3,250,000 bushels, which would be much enlarged if there was cheaper and more reliable transportation.

Distances.	To New York, via lakes.	To capes of Virginia, via James River and Kanawha Canal.	Difference in favor of capes.
From Cairo, mouth of Ohio River, 704 miles of river-navigation, to mouth of Kanawha, 471.44 miles, which is composed of 197 miles of open river and slack-water navigation, and 274 miles (which includes 46 miles of slack-water navigation) of, say, canal-navigation, 126 miles of navigation by James River below tide-water and by Hampton Roads and Chesapeake Bay, or, altogether, 1,027 miles of river and 274 miles of, say, canal-navigation		1, 301	
From Cairo, via Miami and Erie Canal, (618 miles canal, 652 river, and 252 lake)	1, 522		221
From Cairo, via Portsmouth, Ohio and Erie Canal, (661 miles canal, 754 river, and 190 lake)	1, 605		304
From Cairo, via Illinois and Michigan Canal, (454 miles canal, 650 river, and 1,042 lake)	2, 146		845
From Cairo, via Gulf route, (1,202 miles river and 1,850 ocean)	3, 052		1, 751
From Louisville, (658 miles river and 274 canal,) as above		932	
From Louisville, via Miami Canal, (618 miles canal, 283 river, and 252 lake)	1, 153		221
From Louisville, via Portsmouth, Ohio and Erie Canal, (661 miles canal, 385 river, and 190 miles lake)	1, 236		304
From Louisville, via Gulf, (1,571 river and 1,850 ocean)	3, 421		2, 489
From Louisville, via rail	887		
From Cincinnati, (526 miles river and 274 canal,) as above		800	
From Cincinnati, via Miami Canal, (618 canal, 151 river, and 252 lake)	1, 021		221
From Cincinnati, via Portsmouth, Ohio and Erie Canal, (661 canal, 253 river, and 190 lake)	1, 104		304
From Cincinnati, via Gulf, (1, 703 miles river and 1,830 ocean)	3, 553		2, 753
From Cincinnati, via rail	777		
From Point Pleasant, (323. 44 miles river and 274 miles canal)		597. 44	
From Point Pleasant, via Gulf, (1,906 miles river and 1,850 ocean)	3, 756		3, 159
From Wheeling, (496 miles river and 274 canal)		770	
From Wheeling, via Gulf, (2,079 miles river and 1,850 ocean)	3, 929		3, 151
From Pittsburgh, (586 miles river and 234 canal)		860	
From Pittsburgh, via Gulf, (2,169 miles river and 1,850 ocean)	4, 019		3, 159
From Pittsburgh, via rail	444		
From Memphis, (1,260 miles river and 274 canal)		1, 540	
From Memphis, via Gulf, (963 miles river and 1,850 ocean)	2, 813		1, 273
From Memphis, via rail	1, 123		
From Memphis, (rail to Norfolk, 921 miles, and ocean to New York, 293 miles)	1, 214		
From Saint Louis, (1,205 miles river and 274 canal)		1, 479	
From Saint Louis, via Gulf, (1,380 miles river and 1,850 ocean)	3, 230		1, 751
From Saint Louis, via Illinois and Michigan Canal, (454 miles canal, 466 river, and 1,042 lake)	1, 962		483
From Saint Louis, via rail	1, 110		
From mouth of Illinois River, (1,252 miles river and 274 canal)		1, 526	
From mouth of Illinois River, (454 miles canal, 425 river, and 1,042 lake)	1, 921		395
From Kansas City, (1,476 miles river and 274 canal)		1, 750	
From Kansas City, via Gulf, (1,651 miles river and 1,850 ocean)	3, 501		1, 751
From Kansas City, via rail	1, 385		
From Omaha, (1,784 miles river and 274 canal)		2, 058	
From Omaha, via Gulf, (1,959 miles river and 1,850 ocean)	3, 809		1, 751
From Omaha by rail to Chicago, thence lake and Erie Canal, (493 rail, 1,042 lake, 352 canal, and 151 river)	2, 038		
From Omaha, all rail	1, 450		
From Keokuk, (1,417 miles river and 274 canal)		1, 691	
From Keokuk, (259 miles rail, 1,042 lake, 352 canal, and 151 river)	1, 795		104
From Davenport, (1,559 miles river and 274 canal)		1, 833	
From Davenport, (say as above, from Keokuk)	1, 795		*38
From Dubuque, (river 1,650 miles and 274 miles canal)		1, 924	
From Dubuque, (225 miles rail, 1,042 lake, 352 canal, and 151 river)	1, 770		154
From Dubuque, all rail	1, 182		742
From La Crosse, (1,835 miles river and 274 canal)		2, 109	
From La Crosse, (260 miles rail, 1,042 lake, 352 canal, and 151 river)	1, 805		304
From Saint Paul, (2,005 miles river and 274 canal)		2, 279	
From Saint Paul, (260 miles rail, 321 river, 1,042 lake, and 352 canal)	1, 975		304
From Saint Paul, all rail	1, 366		927

* Against capes.

Distances.	To Liverpool, via Gulf.	To Liverpool, via capes of Virginia.	Difference in favor of capes of Virginia.
Cairo, (1,027 miles river, 274 canal, and 3 270 ocean)		4, 571	
Cairo, (1,202 miles river and 4,750 ocean)	5, 952		1, 381
Cincinnati, (526 miles river, 274 canal, and 3,270 ocean)		4, 070	
Cincinnati, (1,703 miles river, 4,750 ocean)	6, 453		2, 383
Mouth of Illinois River, (1,252 miles river, 274 canal, and 3,270 ocean)		4, 796	
Mouth of Illinois River, (1,427 miles river and 4,750 ocean)	6, 177		1, 381
Omaha, (1,784 miles river, 274 canal, and 3,270 ocean)		5, 328	
Omaha, (1,959 miles river and 4,750 ocean)	6, 709		1, 381
Saint Louis, (1,205 miles river, 274 canal, and 3,270 ocean)		4, 749	
Saint Louis, (1,380 miles river and 4,750 ocean)	6, 130		1, 381
Saint Paul, (2,005 miles river, 274 canal, and 3,270 ocean)		5, 549	
Saint Paul, (2,180 miles river and 4,750 ocean)	6, 930		1, 381

	Miles.
Hampton Roads to New York, via ocean	293
Hampton Roads to New York, via inland route, viz: by Chesapeake Bay, Chesapeake and Delaware Canal, and Delaware and Raritan Canal	343
Hampton Roads to Philadelphia, by ocean and Delaware Bay	300
Hampton Roads to Philadelphia, by inland route, viz: by Chesapeake Bay and Chesapeake and Delaware Canal	223
Hampton Roads to Baltimore, by Chesapeake Bay	200
Hampton Roads to Washington City, by Chesapeake Bay and Potomac River	182

JAMES RIVER AND KANAWHA CANAL PROJECT.

REPORT OF BOARD OF ENGINEERS.

ARMY BUILDING, NEW YORK, *March* 18, 1874.

GENERAL: The board of engineers convened by Special Orders 17, War Department, Adjutant-General's Office, January 27, 1874, to examine and report upon the James River and Kanawha Canal project, respectfully report that they met and organized at the office of the engineer in charge, at Richmond, Va., on the 5th of February.

(The part of the report here omitted relates to the journey made by the board in the examination of the route.)

Before the re-convening of the board on call of the president, March 9, two of the members, Mr. Latrobe and Colonel Craighill, who had been appointed a committee to examine the estimates, devoted much of the time to this duty, in which they were assisted by Mr. Harris, Mr. Hutton, and Mr. Turpin. They also visited the Hoosic tunnel for the purpose of obtaining information bearing upon tunnel-construction; and the president visited Syracuse to obtain from the actual experience of the Erie Canal important facts concerning water-consumption and lock arrangements.

The board having re-convened in New York on the 9th, were favored with the attendance of Mr. Harris, chief engineer of the James River and Kanawha Canal, and of Mr. Hutton, and their several reports and estimates were gone over again by the full board.

The foregoing account of the proceedings of the board will show that for so vast a subject these examinations could be but of a very general character. In such a case the obvious mode of proceeding was, first, to satisfy themselves that the projects presented had been conscientiously made up by competent engineers, and that their data, their *facts*, their surveys, &c., (to the extent at least purported,) were *reliable*. The board, at the outset, unhesitatingly affirms this to be the case in the projects submitted. The project differs by a world-wide difference from a mere reconnaissance of a new route. A large part of it lies over a work actually constructed; another portion over an extension of that same work, actually commenced, but as yet incomplete. Another portion, connecting with the last-named, and extending over the summit to the Greenbrier, was as early as 1825–'26 the subject of very accurate surveys and estimates by the subsequently eminent engineer, the late Major McNeill, United States Topographical Engineers. With his accurate topography before them, the surveys have been repeated, and again-repeated since, and projects revised and plans made, with all this accumulated information. A great modification, indeed, of the first plans has been made, first, by the late lamented Mr. E. Lorraine, (approved by all subsequent engineers,) in the introduction of the long tunnel. But to modern engineers such tunnels are no novelty, and its existence in the present plan throws no element of uncertainty, either as to practicability or cost. So, too, with regard to water-supply, there can be no reason to call in question the results of the surveys and the protracted observations, extending through a whole year, of the late Mr. Lorraine.

With regard to a very important part of the line—the Greenbrier and New Rivers slack-water improvement from Howard's Creek to the Great Falls of the Kanawha—the engineer in charge has officially stated that he has not had adequate means of surveying, and, therefore, that the plans have not been founded on such perfect knowledge of the bed of the river and of its regimen as would be desirable; nevertheless, the board bear witness that the efforts of the late Mr. Lorraine, and of his successor, (at the time assistant in this work,) Mr. Harris, have been most strenuous to supply the deficient information, and that their plans for locks and dams have been most carefully and conscientiously made up, while lacking in some elements for satisfactory location or for precision of estimate. Having convinced themselves of the reliability of the data, by proper evidence, the board must necessarily make these data the basis of their own opinions; and if these diverge from those upon which the plans have been based, it must, in general, be in consequence of modification of those plans being judged necessary.

With these preliminary remarks, a brief description of the project, as presented to our consideration, will now be given.

The James River and Kanawha Canal is a project for connecting the James River at Richmond with the Ohio River at Point Pleasant, by means of a canal and slack-water navigation. The canal to be constructed will have a width of 70 feet at the water-line, with a depth of seven feet, its locks to be 120 feet between the gates and to have a width of chamber of 20 feet. The tonnage of the boats to be used on it will be about 280 tons.

The slack-water navigation is to begin at the Greenbrier River, at the end of the canal, and to continue down this, the New, and the Kanawha, to the Ohio River. The locks for this navigation are designed to be 240 feet by 40 feet, with 7 feet depth of water, and to accommodate a barge of 700 tons, or four boats for the enlarged canal.

From Paint Creek Shoals, on the Kanawha, to the Ohio River, it is proposed to improve the navigation by means of open sluice-dams.

To furnish the supply of water for this improvement, it is proposed to construct two reservoirs; the first in the valley of Anthony's Creek, a tributary of the Greenbrier River, and the second in the valley of Meadow River, a tributary of the Gauley River.

The execution of the project involves work which may be subdivided as follows:

1st. The enlargement of the existing canal from Richmond to Buchanan.

2d. The construction of the projected and definitely located portion of the canal from Buchanan to the mouth of Fork Run.

3d. The construction of the canal up Fork Run to the summit-level, 1,700 feet above tide, under the Tuckahoe and Katis Mountains, by a tunnel of 7⅓ miles long, and thence down the valley of Howard's Creek to the Greenbrier River.

4th. The slack-water improvement of the Greenbrier, New, and Kanawha Rivers to Paint Creek Shoals, (with occasional short canal, to avoid expensive location of dams.)

5th. The open sluice-dam improvement of the Kanawha River from Paint Creek Shoals to its junction with the Ohio River.

Concerning this project, the board is required to report upon "*all questions of practicability, plan, and probable cost, for a water-communication to the Ohio by the way of the James and Kanawha Rivers, together with the probable time required for its completion, and the cost of maintenance when built.*"

On the first point—practicability of a water-communication—a resolution adopted unanimously shows the sense of the board:

"*Resolved*, That in the opinion of this board it is entirely practicable to connect the waters of the James and Ohio Rivers by a water-navigation of 7 feet in depth."

In this connection we remark that the route from Richmond as far as Covington (243.77 miles) is, from the first-named place to Buchanan, 196½ miles, an established work, to be merely *enlarged;* and between Buchanan and Covington (47.27 miles) a partially executed work. There could be no doubt of the practicability of *enlargement*, unless some unusual obstacle interposed; on the contrary, we are assured by the engineers in whose charge the existing work now is, and to whom it is thoroughly well known, that not only is enlargement practicable, but that it has been carefully estimated for.

The remaining portion of *open-canal* route between Covington and the Greenbrier has been, almost throughout its whole length, examined by the board, and it is their opinion that it is as practicable to make the open-canal part as in parts where the work has been already executed.

With regard to the tunnel, as presented to us, it is of about the same length as the Mont Cenis tunnel; and it has a very great advantage over this, that, whereas that was wholly driven from the ends, the proposed tunnel will be driven from shafts of moderate height and at distances seldom exceeding one mile. The rock, too, is of a material very easily excavated.

With regard to the proposed reservoirs on Anthony's Creek and Meadow River, the question of practicability depends solely upon that of building dams of the required height, about which no question has been raised. The drawing of water in large volumes and the controlling of its draught, under a head of sixty or more feet, may, indeed, require unusual arrangements and extraordinary precautions; all, however, perfectly practicable.

With regard to the extension of the water-line *from the mouth of Howard's Creek, on the Greenbrier, to the Great Falls,* while the board is unanimous as to the question of practicability of a "water-communication," they are not so as to the proposed method of locks and dams (or slack-water) navigation; *and the difference involves very material differences in the probable cost of the work.* All concur, however, in the opinion, as expressed by formal resolution, "that *it may be expedient to adopt canal-navigation for this part* of the line, with occasional exceptions, where it may be desirable, in consequence of peculiarly favorable reaches or the necessity of water-supply."

Concerning the further extension of the water-communication of 7 feet at low water, from the Great Falls to the mouth of the Kanawha, no question of practicability has been raised, *i. e.*, that by dams and sluices, *or else* by locks and dams, it may be accomplished.

In the question of practicability, that of water-supply at the summit is necessarily involved. Accepting as reliable the surveys and observations of Anthony's Creek and its water-shed, the question of quantity of water available from that source is accepted with them. Taking actual experience *on the Jordan summit of the Erie Canal* for estimating water-consumption, the demand would be somewhat greater than in the estimates presented to us; nevertheless a large surplus still remains, while, on the other hand, the whole Greenbrier Valley, from near Howard's Creek to its sources, lies above the proposed summit-level, and a large portion of its water-shed (five times that of Anthony's Creek) may be by reservoirs converted into gathering-ground for the canal. The board therefore are unanimous in the opinion that an ample water-supply can be commanded.

On the second point submitted, viz. the plan, there are minor differences of opinion applying to all that portion east of the summit, (or, more generally speaking, to all everywhere which shall be *open canal;*) which, however, will involve *very considerable differences, as to cost.* These differences refer to whether the proposed plans with single locks shall be accepted as they are, or whether the locks, remaining single, shall be enlarged; or, finally, whether double locks shall be everywhere constructed and the sides of the prism be revetted.

So far as regards the tunnel, the board is unanimously of opinion that a tunnel of the dimensions proposed, (52 broad by 34 high,) *i. e.*, wide enough for *passing* everywhere, should not be attempted, and, on the suggestion of one of our members, unite on the recommendation of a single tunnel with *turn-outs of dimensions* which will be fully set forth in his individual report, with which hereafter, *if found necessary, a second tunnel may be combined.* It is also suggested that the tunnel and canal construction may be facilitated by raising the level 20 feet, so as to avoid the deep cutting in the narrow valley of Howard's Creek, *or improved by a radical change of location,* taking a point near the railroad-crossing in the ravine of *Brush Creek* (or Jerry's Run) for the eastern terminus, and the same point on Howard's Creek for the western. By this it is supposed two miles of canalling would be saved and the location laid in a more *open valley* (Bush Creek) *than Fork Run;* or, finally and possibly, by starting from the last-named point and tunneling a distance scarcely exceeding that originally designed by Mr. Lorraine, (nine miles and a fraction,) the valley of the Greenbrier may be reached, by which the expensive canalling in Howard's Creek ravine and the feeder would be wholly dispensed with. These modifications *of location* are not mentioned as matters of positive recommendations, but as subjects *for further survey,* with a view to having the best possible location.

The board here remark, too, that in so long a tunnel the question of *traction* assumes a very predominant importance. Diminution of the great cost of such works impels the fixing of the very narrowest dimensions admissible. On the other hand, resistance to traction increases so rapidly, as the dimension of the tunnel is made to approximate to the dimension of the boat, that it becomes a very important question how those dimensions should be fixed; whether the dimension of width (by which the cost of excavating and arching is much diminished) may not be compensated by an increase of depth, and finally, that the *mode* of traction be positively fixed before the tunnel section and interior arrangements are finally determined. The long experimental difficulties encountered on the St. Quentin tunnel, $3\frac{1}{4}$ miles long, (Belgium,) and the Pouilly tunnel, $2\frac{1}{10}$ miles long, (France,) in applying horse-power and steam, show that the tunnel cannot be economically and successfully planned till the matter is entirely settled. Were the question still in the form originally presented to us, *i. e.*, of a single tunnel wide enough for passing, this matter of traction would play a less important part, for there would be a wide water-way, (in which, nevertheless, there is still an increase of 25 per cent. in the traction, according to Mr. Hutton's calculations;) but with a narrow tunnel, the question becomes of very great importance.

Concerning the plans for lock and dam navigation on the Greenbrier, New, and Kanawha Rivers, there is difference of opinion as to the applicability of the system, while it is admitted that further surveys are necessary to the final adjustment of these plans The engineer in charge states officially to the board, "I would not build dams on bowlders, but I have no doubt of our ability to carry the work through the New River section successfully by the use of the ultimate resort of a canal at points where others fail."

As four of the New River dams (beside several others) are in the projects before us founded where, as yet, the bed-rock has not been discovered, the above statement is conclusive that the plans need revision. As there is not complete unanimity (as before observed) concerning the success of the slack-water method of navigation in this locality, the objection to it must be left for discussion in the individual reports.

On the third point submitted to the board, viz., the probable cost, the resolution of the board, "That, in the opinion of the board, the water-line by the James River and Kanawha route, with seven feet depth, may be completed in six years at a cost of not more than $60,000,000, allowing an unusually broad margin for contingencies, which cannot be accurately measured. The cost may reasonably be expected to be within $55,000,000, and possibly not exceed $50,000,000," expresses the sense of the majority of the board both as to probable cost and time of completion.

It has already been stated that the estimates submitted by the engineer have been revised, and, in general, deemed adequate to the work proposed; indeed, the only increase in the scale of prices has been a moderate one, applied to the summit tunnel, at the recommendation of one of our members whose experience has made him particularly authoritative on this subject. One of the members of the board does not concur in the above specified probable cost, his dissent being founded on non-concurrence in the portion of the plans which involve slack-water navigation, and on the necessity of doubling the locks, or increasing with their dimensions those of the canal prism, in order to accommodate the expected traffic.

Concerning the fourth and last point submitted, viz., "The benefits to commerce to be derived from the construction of such a work," the board can only speak in general terms. Indeed, it cannot be expected of its members, most of whom are little conversant with the statistics of commerce and with those intricate details which are involved in questions merely of profit on capital invested, to speak otherwise than in general terms. In such terms the following resolution expresses the unanimous opinion of the members: "In the opinion of the board this route presents extraordinary claims as the measure of relief to the population of the Western States, in furnishing them for their bulky productions cheap transportation to a market, and for fostering the commerce of the United States, by developing immense mineral resources now neglected."

A glance at the map of the United States east of the Rocky Mountains shows that the northern frontier is skirted by the great lakes and the St. Lawrence River, furnishing, with the adjunct of the Erie Canal, water-transportation to the sea-board to the entire northern border, the Mexican Gulf forms the southern boundary, and by aid of the rivers which it receives, and especially by the Mississippi, furnishes water-transportation to the regions through which these rivers ramify; on the other hand, there is a great central region for which these routes to the sea-board and a market are too long. If we regard the Mississippi River as a great north and south or meridian line of transportation bisecting the country, as distinguished from the lakes and the Gulf, which skirt the northern and southern boundaries, we shall find that while this great central axis sends out to the westward its numerous great and parallel arms to the foot of the Rocky Mountains, by which it draws to itself the freight-commerce of this vast region, it directs one single central arm—the Ohio—to the eastward and toward the Atlantic sea-board; and that the natural and shortest prolongation of this arm to the Atlantic sea-board is the Kanawha, and by implication the "central water-line" upon which we are called to report. With these general remarks, we believe, we may in this report dismiss the subject, referring for statistics especially relating to it to the numerous printed documents and to appended statements of several of the individual members.

It could hardly be expected that on all points connected with so vast a project there should be perfect unanimity. Hence, while unanimous in the foregoing, the several members deem that the full exhibition of their several views requires individual expressions of opinion which will be appended to this.

Respectfully submitted.

J. G. BARNARD,
Colonel of Engineers and Brevet Major-General, U. S. A.
BENJ. H. LATROBE,
Civil Engineer.
Q. A. GILLMORE,
Lieutenant-Colonel of Engineers, Brevet Major-General.
WM. P. CRAIGHILL,
Major of Engineers, Brevet Lieutenant-Colonel.
G. WEITZEL,
Major of Engineers, Brevet Major-General, U. S. A.
THOMAS TURTLE,
First Lieutenant of Engineers, Recorder.

Average freight charges from Saint Louis to New Orleans, by the Barge Line, for seven years.

Articles.	1866.		1867.		1868.		1869.		1870.		1871.		1872.	
	High water.	Low water.	High water.	Low water.	High water.	Low water.	High water.	Low water.	High water.	Low water.	High water.	Low water.	High water.	Low water.
Flour ....per barrel..	$0 45	$0 55	$0 54	$0 73	$0 31	$0 49	$0 30	$0 40	$0 38	$0 56	$0 26 1-2	$0 65	$0 43	$0 77
Corn ....per bushel..	12 2-3	15 2-5	15 1-3	20 1-2	8 7-10	13 3-4	8 2-5	11 1-5	10 3-5	15 7-10	7 1-2	18 1-5	11	21 2-5
Rye ....do....	12 2-3	15 2-5	15 1-3	20 1-2	8 7-10	13 3-4	8 2-5	11 1-5	10 3-5	15 7-10	7 1-2	18 1-5	11	21 2-5
Oats ....do....	7 1-5	8 4-5	8 3-5	11 7-10	5	7 4-5	4 4-5	6 2-5	6 1-10	9	4 3-10	10 2-5	6 9-10	12 3-10
Bacon...per 100 pounds..	22 1-2	27 1-2	27	36 1-2	15 1-2	24 1-2	15	20	19	28	13 2-5	32 1-2	21 1-2	38 1-2
Ham...............do....	22 1-2	27 1-2	27	36 1-2	15 1-2	24 1-2	15	20	19	28	13 2-5	32 1-2	21 1-2	38 1-2
Pork.........per barrel..	67 1-2	82 1-2	81	1 09 1-2	46 1-2	83 1-2	45	60	57	84	40	97 1-2	64	1 15 1-2
Beef............... do....	67 1-2	82 1-2	81	1 09 1-2	46 1-2	83 1-2	45	60	57	84	40	97 1-2	64	1 15 1-2
Lard ....per 100 pounds..	22 1-2	27 1-2	27	36 1-2	15 1-8	24 3-8	15	20	19	28	13 2-5	32 1-2	21 1-2	38 1-2
Hay ....do....	32 1-2	37 1-2	37	46 1-2	25 1-2	34 1-2	25	30	29	38	23 2-5	42 1-2	31 1-2	48 1-2

High-water rates include the months of April, May, June, July, and August. Low-water rates the balance of the year. The year 1873, for the months of January, February, and March, the rate for flour averaged 82 cents per barrel; for April, May, June, and July, 28¾ cents per barrel.

Statement showing the average freight-charges by steamboat from Saint Louis to New Orleans during the seven years, 1866 to 1872 inclusive.

	Year.						
	1866.	1867.	1868.	1869.	1870.	1871.	1872.
	Cents.	*Cents.*	*Cents.*	*Cents.*	*Cents.*	*Cents.*	*Cents.*
Wheat per bushel	24¾	31	17	17 1-10	22 1-5	*	*
Flour per barrel	75	92 1-5	51	46¼	64	68	71½
Corn per bushel	23 7-10	28¾	16	16	20¾	20	20
Rye do	23 7-10	28¾	16	16	20¾	20	20
Oats do	13 1-5	16⅓	9	9 1-10	11¾	11½	11½
Bacon per 100 lbs	41 1-5	51½	28 1-5	28½	37	36	36⅔
Hams do	41 1-5	51½	28 1-5	28½	37	36	36⅔
Pork per barrel	114	141	86	71	104	106	108
Beef do	114	141	86	71	104	106	108
Lard per 100 lbs	41 1-5	51½	28 1-5	28½	37	36	36⅔
Hay do	41 1-5	51½	28 1-5	28½	37	45½	46

NOTE.—This table was prepared by George H. Wagner, secretary of the Union Merchants' Exchange of Saint Louis.

* None shipped.

The following table was prepared for the committee by Messrs. J. H. Ashbridge & Co., merchants of New Orleans:

*Statement showing rates of freights for corn from New Orleans to Liverpool during the past five years.**

Month.	Description.	1869.		1870.		1871.
		Steam.	Sail.	Steam.	Sail.	Steam.
January	Bulk	No quotation	No quotation	No quotation	9¾*d*	No quotation.
	Sacks	do	12*d*	do	No quotation	Do.
February	Bulk	do	No quotation	do	10	Do.
	Sacks	12	10½	do	No quotation	Do.
March	Bulk	No quotation	No quotation	do	do	Do.
	Sacks	11	10	do	do	Do.
April	Bulk	No quotation	No quotation	do	do	Do.
	Sacks	9	8	do	do	Do.
May	Bulk	No quotation	No quotation	do	10½	10.
	Sacks	do	8¼	do	No quotation	No quotation.
June	Bulk	10	No quotation	do	10½	Do.
	Sacks	No quotation	8½	do	No quotation	Do.
July	Bulk	do	9½	do	do	Do.
	Sacks	do	No quotation	do	do	Do.
August	Bulk	do	do	do	do	Do.
	Sacks	do	do	do	do	Do.
September	Bulk	do	do	do	do	Do.
	Sacks	do	do	do	do	Do.
October	Bulk	do	do	do	do	Do.
	Sacks	do	do	do	do	Do.
November	Bulk	do	do	do	do	Do.
	Sacks	do	12	do	do	Do.
December	Bulk	do	10¼	do	10½	Do.
	Sacks	do	No quotation	do	No quotation	Do.

* The quotations of rates in this table are expressed in English sterling money.

tatement showing rates of freights for corn from New Orleans to Liverpool, &c.—Continued.

Month.	Description.	1871.	1872.		1873.	
		Sail.	Steam.	Sail.	Steam.	Sail.
January	Bulk	10¼	12	10⅜*d*	No quotation	No quotation.
	Sacks	No quotation	No quotation	No quotation	....do	Do.
February	Bulk	10¼	12	10	....do	Do.
	Sacks	No quotation	No quotation	No quotation	....do	Do.
March	Bulk	....do	11½	9¾	....do	Do.
	Sacks	....do	No quotation	No quotation	....do	Do.
April	Bulk	10 and 15	10	9	16	15.
	Sacks	No quotation	No quotation	No quotation	No quotation	No quotation.
May	Bulk	9¾	8¾	8½	....do	15.
	Sacks	No quotation	No quotation	No quotation	....do	No quotation.
June	Bulk	9¾	....do	10	15	Do.
	Sacks	No quotation	....do	No quotation	11	Do.
July	Bulk	9½	....do	10½	14	12.
	Sacks	No quotation	....do	No quotation	11	No quotation.
August	Bulk	....do	....do	11¼	13	12.
	Sacks	....do	....do	No quotation	No quotation	No quotation.
September	Bulk	....do	13¾*d*	11½*d*	14	Do.
	Sacks	....do	No quotation	No quotation	No quotation	Do.
October	Bulk	....do	....do	13¼	14	Do.
	Sacks	....do	....do	No quotation	No quotation	Do.
November	Bulk	....do	....do	13¼	14	Do.
	Sacks	....do	....do	No quotation	No quotation	Do.
December	Bulk	10½	....do	....do	13¾	Do.
	Sacks	No quotation	....do	....do	No quotation	Do.

Number of bushels of corn exported from New Orleans to Europe each month during the year 1872

[Prepared for the United States Senate Committee on Transportation, by the Collector of Customs at New Orleans.]

Month.	Bushels.	Month.	Bushels.
January	4, 353	August	46, 326
February	33, 669	September	68, 590
March	21, 448	October	103, 899
April	80, 600	November	74, 017
May	323, 772	December	....
June	141, 818		
July	113, 590	Total	1, 012, 082

Monthly receipts, exports, and prices of grain at Saint Louis for two years.

WHEAT.

Month.	Receipts. 1872.	Receipts. 1871.	Month.	Exports. 1872.	Exports. 1871.
	Bushels.	*Bushels.*		*Bushels.*	*Bushels.*
January	224, 396	278, 017	January	79, 362	26, 365
February	216, 143	287, 011	February	58, 669	34, 390
March	388, 195	464, 167	March	71, 607	6, 741
April	476, 547	388, 946	April	51, 667	5, 344
May	324, 777	513, 419	May	79, 491	5, 580
June	166, 591	386, 663	June	41, 376	56, 536
July	271, 459	1, 222, 727	July	65, 274	383, 347
August	821, 517	1, 084, 617	August	137, 422	113, 760
September	1, 091, 375	929, 869	September	113, 506	165, 702
October	997, 493	681, 135	October	91, 068	94, 839
November	465, 107	405, 300	November	67, 607	93, 725
December	254, 312	329, 018	December	61, 428	62, 203
By wagons	310, 075	341, 021			
			Total	918, 477	1, 048, 532
Total	6, 007, 987	7, 311, 910	On hand December 31	637, 388	525, 977
In store January 1	525, 977	329, 746	Ground in city mills	4, 978, 099	6, 067, 147
Total	6, 533, 964	7, 641, 656	Total	6, 533, 964	7, 641, 656

Receipts of wheat for twenty-three years.

Year.	Bushels.	Year.	Bushels.	Year.	Bushels.
1850	1, 794, 721	1858	3, 835, 759	1866	4, 410, 305
1851	1, 712, 776	1859	3, 508, 732	1867	3, 571, 593
1852	1, 645, 387	1860	3, 555, 871	1868	4, 353, 591
1853	2, 075, 872	1861	2, 654, 787	1869	6, 736, 454
1854	2, 126, 272	1862	3, 559, 336	1870	6, 638, 253
1855	3, 312, 854	1863	2, 621, 020	1871	7, 311, 910
1856	3, 747, 224	1864	3, 315, 828	1872	6, 007, 987
1857	3, 218, 410	1865	3, 452, 722		

Exports of wheat for eight years.

Year.	Bushels.	Year.	Bushels.	Year.	Bushels.
1865	67, 710	1868	542, 234	1871	1, 048, 532
1866	635, 818	1869	1, 715, 005	1872	918, 477
1867	321, 888	1870	634, 562		

Prices of wheat on the first day of each month.

1872.	White.			Red.				Spring.		
	No. 1.	No. 2.	No. 3.	No. 1.	No. 2.	No. 3.	No. 4.	No. 1.	No. 2.	No. 3.
January	......	....	......	$1 63	$1 54	$1 44 *a* 1 46	$1 40	......	$1 26 *a* 1 28	$1 23
February	$1 75	$1 65	$1 58	......	1 63 *a* 1 69	1 60	1 55	......	1 30	1 27
March	1 75	1 72	1 65	1 80	1 75 *a* 1 76	1 70	1 66	......	1 39	1 36
April	1 97	1 85	1 82	......	1 90	1 82	1 75	......	1 39 *a* 1 40	......
May	......	2 20	2 00	2 20	2 10	1 96	1 83	......	1 38 *a* 1 40	......
June	......	2 15	2 00	2 05	2 00	1 80	1 75	$1 50	1 40	......
July	1 43	....	1 55	......	1 50	....	......	......	....	......
August	......	1 60 *a* 1 70	1 53	......	1 60 *a* 1 65	....	......	......	....	......
September	1 75	1 65	1 55	1 75	1 65	1 50 *a* 1 55	1 40	......	1 25 *a* 1 26	......
October	1 90	1 85	1 75	......	1 82 *a* 1 85	1 70	1 50	......	1 24 *a* 1 25	1 15
November	1 95	1 75	1 65	1 90	1 80	1 60 *a* 1 63	1 35	......	1 11	1 02
December	2 00	1 90	1 75	2 00	1 90	1 71 *a* 1 73	1 50	......	1 16	1 07

CORN.

Monthly receipts and exports at Saint Louis for two years.

Months.	Receipts.		Months.	Exports.	
	1872.	1871.		1872.	1871.
	Bushels.	*Bushels.*		*Bushels.*	*Bushels.*
January	780, 772	207, 055	January	529, 675	132, 815
February	681, 625	287, 695	February	473, 753	259, 399
March	1, 071, 742	675, 830	March	1, 028, 036	478, 975
April	1, 269, 339	694, 302	April	1, 123, 538	538, 505
May	1, 387, 046	715, 770	May	1, 365, 430	572, 015
June	1, 504, 662	802, 105	June	1, 089, 266	715, 046
July	778, 405	714, 902	July	753, 043	544, 023
August	598, 898	322, 417	August	496, 645	271, 140
September	243, 009	210, 548	September	349, 745	195, 070
October	412, 153	335, 355	October	324, 028	200, 790
November	478, 690	222, 447	November	337, 347	196, 982
December	231, 970	562, 735	December	159, 233	365, 089
By wagons	41, 075	139, 573			
Total	9, 479, 387	6, 030, 734	Total	8, 029, 739	4, 469, 819
			On hand December 31	181, 115	124, 921
On hand January 1	124, 921	19, 765	Ground into meal	1, 111, 324	853, 672
			City consumption	282, 130	602, 057
Total	9, 604, 308	6, 050, 499	Total	9, 604, 308	6, 050, 499

Receipts of corn for seventeen years.

Year.	Bushels.	Year.	Bushels.	Year.	Bushels.
1872	9, 479, 387	1866	7, 233, 671	1860	4, 249, 729
1871	6, 030, 734	1865	3, 162, 310	1859	1, 639, 857
1870	4, 708, 838	1864	2, 369, 590	1858	892, 104
1869	2, 395, 713	1863	1, 361, 310	1857	2, 485, 786
1868	2, 800, 277	1862	1, 734, 219	1856	938, 546
1867	5, 155, 480	1861	4, 515, 040		

Exports for eight years.

Year.	Bushels.	Year.	Bushels.	Year.	Bushels.
1872	8, 079, 739	1869	1, 298, 863	1866	6, 757, 199
1871	4, 469, 849	1868	1, 611, 618	1865	2, 591, 158
1870	3, 630, 060	1867	4, 318, 937		

Prices of corn, in bulk, on the first day of each month.

Months.	No. 2 mixed.	No. 2 yellow.	No. 2 yellow mixed.	No. 2 white mixed.
January	$0 42	$0 43	$0 42	$0 46
February	$0 40 *a* 41	41½	41½	44
March	40 *a* 40½	41	40½	44
April	40½ *a* 41	41	41	46
May	46 *a* 47	47	47	47½
June	46½ *a* 47	47	47	53½
July	38 *a* 39	40	41	47
August	39	40	39	48
September	35	36	35½	38
October	38	40	38½	40
November	33	33	33	41
December	32 *a* 32½	33	33	34

OATS.

Monthly receipts and exports at Saint Louis for two years.

RECEIPTS.			EXPORTS.		
Months.	1872.	1871.	Months.	1872.	1871.
	Bushels.	*Bushels.*		*Bushels.*	*Bushels.*
January	300, 178	137, 154	January	117, 439	92, 963
February	286, 983	292, 969	February	95, 172	186, 652
March	361, 556	337, 686	March	294, 828	230, 833
April	311, 204	346, 915	April	290, 481	245, 997
May	732, 710	435, 319	May	511, 345	288, 610
June	835, 159	369, 209	June	634, 089	272, 902
July	360, 715	697, 102	July	361, 266	266, 942
August	617, 540	433, 663	August	325, 387	264, 118
September	424, 796	539, 629	September	237, 490	230, 648
October	623, 885	342, 580	October	282, 470	202, 806
November	361, 450	228, 776	November	215, 226	145, 306
December	201, 624	188, 097	December	99, 401	56, 803
By wagons	50, 000	9, 000			
			Total	3, 464, 594	2, 484, 582
Total	5, 467, 800	4, 358, 099	City consumption	2, 062, 756	1, 725, 132
Stock January 1	238, 087	89, 702	Stock December 31	178, 537	238, 087
Total	5, 705, 887	4, 447, 801	Total	5, 705, 887	4, 447, 801

Receipts of oats for seventeen years.

Year.	Bushels.	Year.	Bushels.
1872	5, 467, 800	1863	3, 845, 877
1871	4, 358, 099	1862	3, 135, 043
1870	4, 519, 510	1861	1, 735, 157
1869	3, 461, 814	1860	1, 832, 634
1868	3, 259, 132	1859	1, 267, 624
1867	3, 445, 388	1858	1, 690, 010
1866	3, 568, 253	1857	1, 624, 158
1865	4, 173, 227	1856	1, 029, 908
1864	4, 105, 040		

Exports for eight years.

Year.	Bushels.	Year.	Bushels.
1872	3, 467, 594	1868	1, 925, 579
1871	2, 484, 582	1867	2, 244, 756
1870	3, 144, 744	1866	2, 624, 044
1869	2, 903, 002	1865	3, 083, 864

Prices of oats on the first day of each month.

Months.	No. 2 mixed.	No. 2 white.	Months.	No. 2 mixed.	No. 2 white.
	Per bushel.	*Per bushel.*		*Per bushel.*	*Per bushel.*
January	\$0 37 to \$0 37½	\$0 37 to \$0 37½	July	\$0 29 to \$0 29½	— to \$0 31
February	— to 37½	— to 38½	August	— to 32	— to 34
March	— to 37	— to 37	September	24 to 25	— to 28
April	36 to 36½	— to 37	October	27½ to 28	— to 29
May	— to 43	— to 45	November	— to 25½	— to 26½
June	— to 42½	— to 43	December	24¾ to 25	— to 26

RYE.

Monthly receipts and exports at Saint Louis for two years.

RECEIPTS.			EXPORTS.		
Months.	1872.	1871.	Months.	1872.	1871.
	Bushels.	*Bushels.*		*Bushels.*	*Bushels*
January	48, 691	7, 213	January	8, 073	1, 542
February	30, 078	13, 382	February	8, 824	4, 286
March	44, 022	20, 248	March	20, 990	9, 013
April	37, 060	33, 822	April	18, 211	20, 873
May	19, 831	19, 960	May	14, 830	11, 973
June	15, 466	16, 347	June	7, 782	12, 894
July	8, 526	44, 166	July	5, 201	19, 710
August	29, 704	37, 625	August	9, 418	16, 500
September	50, 617	33, 047	September	15, 474	13, 347
October	57, 835	69, 631	October	16, 503	14, 203
November	18, 965	36, 347	November	12, 969	10, 865
December	9, 776	36, 048	December	11, 933	3, 550
By wagons	1, 016	6, 500			
Total	377, 587	374, 336	Total	150, 208	138, 756
Stock January 1	48, 601	3, 243	Stock December 31	134, 645	48, 601
			City consumption	141, 335	190, 222
Total	426, 188	377, 579	Total	426, 188	377, 579

Receipts of rye for sixteen years.

Year.	Bushels.	Year.	Bushels.
1872	377, 587	1864	140, 533
1871	374, 336	1863	205, 918
1870	210, 542	1862	253, 552
1869	266, 056	1861	117, 080
1868	367, 961	1860	159, 974
1867	250, 704	1859	123, 058
1866	375, 417	1858	45, 900
1865	217, 568	1857	30, 442

Exports for eight years.

Year.	Bushels.	Year.	Bushels.
1872	150, 208	1868	192, 555
1871	138, 756	1867	56, 076
1870	100, 254	1866	225, 460
1869	110, 947	1865	32, 445

Prices of rye on the first of each month.

Months.	No. 2.	Months.	No. 2.
January	73 cts.	July	60 cts.
February	77½ cts.	August	60 cts.
March	82 cts.	September	54 cts.
April	77 cts.	October	63 cts.
May	83 cts.	November	55 cts.
June	80 cts.	December	62 cts.

BARLEY.

Monthly receipts and exports at Saint Louis for two years.

RECEIPTS.			EXPORTS.		
Months.	1872.	1871.	Months.	1872.	1871.
	Bushels.	*Bushels.*		*Bushels.*	*Bushels.*
January	63, 412	21, 569	January	3, 425	1, 773
February	64, 980	29, 762	February	7, 398	5, 990
March	95, 972	54, 679	March	3, 412	8, 219
April	132, 167	73, 504	April	4, 978	6, 667
May	46, 286	29, 056	May	4, 773	4, 459
June	6, 034	10, 113	June	4, 044	1, 134
July	1, 465	14, 292	July	3, 528	2, 102
August	30, 552	70, 534	August	3, 451	4, 552
September	123, 778	209, 205	September	4, 564	10, 108
October	393, 699	217, 462	October	16, 304	7, 932
November	219, 974	110, 319	November	22, 375	7, 141
December	75, 167	30, 722	December	9, 314	2, 766
By wagon	10, 000	5, 000			
			Total	87, 566	62, 843
Total	1, 263, 486	876, 217	City consumption	1, 111, 557	810, 028
Stock, January 1	66, 262	62, 916	Stock December 31	130, 625	66, 262
Total	1, 329, 748	939, 133	Total	1, 329, 748	939, 133

Receipts of barley for twelve years.

Year.	Bushels.	Year.	Bushels.	Year.	Bushels.
1872	1, 263, 486	1868	634, 591	1864	326, 060
1871	876, 217	1867	705, 215	1863	182, 270
1870	778, 518	1866	548, 797	1862	290, 925
1869	757, 600	1865	846, 230	1861	201, 434

Exports for eight years.

Year.	Bushels.	Year.	Bushels.	Year.	Bushels.
1872	87,566	1869	57,134	1866	89,751
1871	62,843	1868	64,426	1865	50,000
1870	70,451	1867	55,720		

Prices of barley on the first of each month.

Months.	Prime to choice spring.	Prime to choice winter.	Months.	Prime to choice spring.	Prime to choice winter.
January	\$0 67½ to \$0 68	\$0 65 to \$0 75	July	....	....
February	....	75 to 85	August	....	....
March	62½ to —	75 to —	September	\$0 45 to \$0 60	....
April	61 to —	75 to 80	October	75 to 90	....
May	— to 75	80 to 82½	November	65 to 85	\$0 72
June	55 to 70	— to 75	December	45 to 75	....

Average monthly prices of wheat per bushel, at Winona, Minnesota, from A. D. 1859 to A. D. 1872, inclusive.

[Prepared for the use of the United States Senate Committee on Transportation, by D. Sinclair, esq., of Winona, Minnesota.]

Year.	January.	February.	March.	April.	May.	June.	July.	August.	September.	October.	November.	December.
1859	\$0 60	\$0 60	\$0 60	\$0 63.7	\$0 75	\$0 75	\$0 75	\$0 52	\$0 53	\$0 58.2	\$0 60.6	\$0 73.2
1860	84.2	88	92	82.5	1 02.4	1 02.5	1 05	74	79.7	73.6	64.5	53.5
1861	60.2	60	62	62.7	71.8	70	*61.8	†56.2	†60	63.8	57.5	56.7
1862	55.8	61.2	65.5	62.4	61.8	65.5	....	82	74.5	77.8	69	75.6
1863	89.2	99.2	95.2	95.4	1 05	1 06.2	94	79.7	78.4	85.5	84.2	84.8
1864	94.5	89	89.6	95	98	1 19.8	1 81.5	1 64.2	1 53	1 19.2	1 32.4	1 27
1865	1 22	1 09	89.2	82.5	88.4	90.7	81.7	96.8	1 08	1 18.2	1 12.4	98
1866	94.4	94	1 02.7	1 10.8	1 40	1 76.2	1 65	1 57	1 58.7	1 54.2	1 57.5	1 68
1867	1 83	1 77.5	1 95	2 34.2	2 55	1 77	1 72	1 61.2	1 53	1 72.8	1 64.7	1 65.7
1868	1 88.5	1 81.2	1 70	1 80	1 97.7	1 78.7	1 59	1 50	1 33	1 13	95	97
1869	96.8	1 00	86.2	86.2	1 03.4	1 04.2	1 18	1 19.5	1 03.5	81.8	71	66
1870	65.5	68.5	68.7	65	84.2	1 00	1 05	94	86	87.2	83.6	87.5
1871	1 08	1 09	1 10	1 13	1 14	1 18	1 03	89.8	1 00	1 04.2	1 12	1 11.4
1872	1 13	1 13.7	1 15	1 17.7	1 46	1 28	1 10	1 11	1 04.7	1 11	1 05	1 05

Average monthly prices of No. 2 spring-wheat at Milwaukee.

[Prepared for the United States Senate Committee on Transportation, by William J. Langston, esq., secretary of the Board of Trade of Milwaukee.]

Month.	1872.	1871.	1870.	1869.	1868.
January	\$122 25	\$119 44	\$78 84	\$113 40	\$201 09
February	124 25	123 30	80 47	118 47	196 41
March	123 50	125 33	81 72	108 81	189 65
April	126 37	127 36	80 11	105 84	196 42
May	146 37	127 11	96 53	113 00	202 38
June	138 50	128 04	116 15	116 57	188 96
July	123 25	115 83	117 32	131 96	176 03
August	130 87	109 15	109 03	138 44	175 26
September	120 62	116 36	101 72	121 15	152 11
October	113 00	120 34	104 24	95 54	132 44
November	118 75	120 00	101 56	87 68	113 50
December	114 37	119 56	105 88	83 34	113 26

*Currency. †Gold.

Shipments of wheat from Milwaukee, by rail and by water, each month for ten years, 1863 to 1872, inclusive.

Year.	How shipped.	Bushels.											
		January.	February.	March.	April.	May.	June.	July.	August.	September.	October.	November.	December.
1863	By rail		224							1,207	325		
	By water				1,443,485	1,544,110	1,843,866	1,178,609	672,296	2,440,168	2,600,669	1,102,879	6,762
1864	By rail	397	562		2,367	3,956		1,662	410			1,200	1,325
	By water				927,566	2,726,046	2,230,236	819,773	550,003	486,532	675,904	564,540	
1865	By rail			423	1,759	56,926	25,254	15,279	45,916	90,343	31,741	25,798	19,342
	By water				210,367	676,445	930,539	1,264,940	1,176,238	1,542,723	2,543,839	1,799,902	22,000
1866	By rail	19,966	42,280	69,760	175,757	111,827	93,931	24,757	41,319	52,170	55,114	26,830	44,647
	By water				574,818	1,806,571	1,536,382	907,961	590,358	1,111,828	2,673,593	1,704,880	10,000
1867	By rail	31,189	79,530	18,689	112,185	38,169	7,458	7,491	3,000	6,469	11,688	7,187	9,051
	By water				337,805	337,932	405,134	357,412	187,463	2,481,986	3,402,939	1,793,685	2,066
1868	By rail	18,998	22,490	56,013	102,216	68,493	16,991	30,787	7,193	59,839	46,213	8,522	28,456
	By water			7,600	782,220	1,118,168	702,838	524,135	408,218	2,144,808	2,613,000	1,086,864	24,574
1869	By rail	32,319	82,412	65,491	86,906	16,035	10,024	4,359	2,023	2,603	16,549	4,647	9,058
	By water				757,414	1,934,313	2,890,355	1,568,358	417,961	1,373,264	2,488,425	2,511,273	
1870	By rail	26,999	32,924	11,193	124,300	20,116	26,675	18,121	15,919	13,958	10,475	19,474	41,874
	By water				1,138,966	2,506,071	2,009,068	1,822,122	1,646,880	1,685,909	2,558,091	2,391,863	16,850
1871	By rail	3,083	5,974	38,495	20,441	9,031	6,351	11,497	19,218	124,782	82,160	1,320	4,365
	By water			16,200	1,750,323	2,182,741	1,643,869	1,205,111	979,528	2,115,324	2,154,478	1,022,886	12,500
1872	By rail	3,423	11,490	20,463	94,399	136,885	58,309	26,582	49,619	176,622	99,474	84,224	92,090
	By water				81,643	702,373	1,466,778	1,137,201	825,362	2,239,833	2,587,823	1,674,952	

Shipments of wheat, wheat-flour, corn, rye, oats, and barley, from Milwaukee, by rail and by lake, for fifteen years, 1858 to 1872, inclusive.

[Prepared for the United States Senate Committee on Transportation, by William J. Langston, esq., secretary of the Chamber of Commerce.]

Year.	Wheat.		Wheat-flour.		Corn.		Rye.		Oats.		Barley.	
	By water.	By rail.	By water.	By rail.	By water.	By rail.	By water.	By rail.	By water.	By rail.	By water.	By rail.
	Bushels.	*Bushels.*	*Barrels.*	*Barrels.**	*Bushels.*	*Bushels.*	*Bushels.*	*Bushels.*	*Bushels.*	*Bushels.*	*Bushels.*	*Bushels.*
1858	3, 994, 213	....	298, 688	....	43, 958	....	5, 378	....	562, 067	....	63, 178	....
1859	4, 712, 657	20, 300	282, 087	869	41, 234	4, 838	10, 397	....	299, 733	10, 663	53, 986	8, 650
1860	7, 532, 554	36, 054	446, 089	11, 454	34, 947	2, 257	9, 735	....	48, 379	16, 303	26, 104	2, 501
1861	13, 201, 715	98, 780	373, 471	301, 471	1, 485	....	29, 810	....	1, 200	....	5, 220	....
1862	14, 908, 907	6, 773	440, 275	271, 130	9, 489	....	125, 612	689	75, 921	3, 173	10, 045	34, 855
1863	12, 835, 864	1, 756	472, 619	130, 907	88, 989	....	82, 520	1, 527	817, 502	14, 098	66, 151	67, 296
1864	8, 980, 609	11, 879	357, 317	57, 516	132, 940	31, 846	12, 108	6, 108	720, 184	81, 310	....	23, 479
1865	10, 166, 993	312, 784	450, 961	116, 615	34, 351	36, 852	51, 444	....	304, 066	22, 406	6, 875	22, 722
1866	10, 876, 391	758, 358	393, 872	326, 493	460, 747	29, 661	254, 652	677	1, 616, 391	20, 304	8, 988	10, 000
1867	9, 246, 448	352, 004	486, 680	435, 583	196, 320	69, 929	103, 356	3, 439	557, 567	64, 902	21, 656	9, 166
1868	9, 411, 879	466, 211	552, 996	464, 603	76, 247	266, 470	47, 630	47, 406	486, 871	49, 668	36, 088	55, 355
1869	13, 940, 701	332, 051	691, 701	529, 357	49, 121	44, 685	22, 732	97, 930	311, 928	39, 840	3, 760	74, 275
1870	15, 766, 025	361, 813	783, 200	442, 741	47, 278	55, 895	34, 158	28, 336	122, 459	87, 728	308, 706	160, 519
1871	13, 082, 990	326, 477	721, 099	490, 328	391, 098	28, 035	176, 182	32, 714	714, 937	57, 982	491, 492	84, 971
1872	10, 616, 975	953, 600	507, 168	727, 833	1, 532, 255	35, 698	89, 885	119, 866	1, 149, 143	173, 691	615, 384	322, 341

* Five bushels to the barrel.

Shipments of wheat from Chicago, 1863 to 1872.

[Furnished to the Senate Committee on Transportation, by Charles Randolph, esq., secretary Board of Trade of Chicago.]

How shipped.	Jan.	Feb.	Mar.	Apr.	May.	June.	July.	Aug.	Sept.	Oct.	Nov.	Dec.	Total.
1863.	*Bushels.*	*Bushels.*	*Bushels.*	*Bushels.*	*Bushels.*	*Bushels.*	*Bushels.*	*Bushels.*	*Bushels.*	*Bushels.*	*Bushels.*	*Bushels.*	*Bushels.*
By lake			500	684, 777	1, 070, 550	1, 212, 650	1, 068, 250	615, 050	2, 325, 325	1, 986, 300	1, 679, 250	3, 900	10, 646, 552
By canal				15, 446	3, 000	9, 557	3, 676		6, 353	6, 484	12, 366		56, 882
By railroad	14, 463	21, 789	14, 393	3, 363	4, 854	353	13, 073	706	6, 090	5, 506	2, 763	2, 508	89, 861
Total	14, 463	21, 789	14, 893	703, 586	1, 078, 404	1, 222, 560	1, 084, 999	615, 756	2, 337, 768	1, 998, 290	1, 694, 379	6, 408	10, 793, 295
1864.													
By lake				1, 070, 275	1, 227, 575	1, 738, 767	1, 168, 800	1, 291, 150	1, 283, 525	1, 278, 900	907, 575	17, 000	9, 983, 567
By canal				17, 446	14, 287	743	6, 892		927	25, 843	26, 929		93, 067
By railroad	9, 927	5, 734	1, 341	9, 728	28, 337	8, 239	29, 686	4, 369	34, 838	22, 505	10, 548	8, 140	173, 392
Total	9, 927	5, 734	1, 341	1, 097, 449	1, 270, 199	1, 747, 749	1, 205, 378	1, 295, 519	1, 319, 290	1, 327, 248	945, 052	25, 140	10, 250, 026
1865.													
By lake				388, 150	1, 267, 275	880, 625	980, 300	632, 000	592, 350	1, 006, 175	737, 700	18, 000	6, 502, 575
By canal				9, 291	4, 816	4, 343	15, 224	22, 716	22, 461	76, 616	90, 817		246, 284
By railroad	4, 334	2, 409	9, 563	4, 597	10, 165	33, 665	68, 292	244, 395	131, 815	135, 528	130, 487	90, 778	866, 028
Total	4, 334	2, 409	9, 563	402, 038	1, 282, 256	918, 633	1, 063, 816	899, 111	746, 626	1, 218, 319	959, 004	108, 778	7, 614, 887
1866.													
By lake				32, 925	197, 950	341, 263	200, 521	452, 412	1, 509, 435	1, 954, 500	1, 138, 900		5, 827, 846
By canal				28, 356	42, 688	45, 556	17, 179	20, 201	7, 224	74, 554			235, 758
By railroad	106, 439	136, 117	241, 525	424, 572	415, 700	559, 967	203, 009	257, 845	434, 366	581, 500	452, 988	241, 275	4, 055, 303
Total	106, 439	136, 117	241, 525	485, 853	656, 338	946, 726	420, 709	730, 458	1, 951, 025	2, 610, 554	1, 591, 888	241, 275	10, 118, 907
1867.													
By lake				30, 984	51, 028	197, 390	71, 823	1, 303, 421	2, 597, 231	2, 449, 161	1, 791, 149		8, 492, 187
By canal				51, 004	24, 604	12, 266	7, 502	16, 351	17, 322	27, 743	8, 867		165, 659
By railroad	241, 058	211, 188	254, 477	303, 225	143, 938	62, 496	185, 225	35, 481	48, 792	193, 285	134, 599	85, 513	1, 899, 277
Total	241, 058	211, 188	254, 477	385, 213	219, 570	272, 152	264, 550	1, 355, 253	2, 663, 345	2, 670, 189	1, 934, 615	85, 513	10, 557, 123
1868.													
By lake				281, 508	659, 696	559, 805	216, 634	1, 291, 641	2, 050, 153	2, 697, 986	1, 127, 016	12, 208	8, 896, 647
By canal				12, 785	14, 056	6, 729	6, 019	11, 378	13, 365	10, 888			75, 220
By railroad	52, 969	42, 234	104, 848	298, 221	174, 001	84, 859	36, 768	63, 851	76, 584	108, 587	159, 109	200, 785	1, 402, 816
Total	52, 969	42, 234	104, 848	592, 514	847, 753	651, 393	259, 421	1, 366, 870	2, 140, 102	2, 817, 461	1, 286, 125	212, 993	10, 374, 683

Shipments of wheat from Chicago, 1863 *to* 1872—Continued.

[Furnished to the Senate Committee on Transportation, by Charles Randolph, esq., secretary Board of Trade of Chicago.]

How shipped.	Jan.	Feb.	Mar.	Apr.	May.	June.	July.	Aug.	Sept.	Oct.	Nov.	Dec.	Total.
1869.													
By lake				610, 948	1, 888, 330	2, 171, 416	1, 410, 838	1, 126, 026	1, 355, 568	1, 918, 689	797, 699		11, 279, 514
By canal				15, 852	13, 087	8, 544	240	13, 500	5, 704	11, 635	350		68, 912
By railroad	236, 213	489, 758	420, 019	251, 992	127, 189	73, 748	26, 379	16, 576	26, 083	80, 056	63, 602	84, 208	1, 895, 823
Total	236, 213	489, 758	420, 019	878, 792	2, 028, 606	2, 253, 708	1, 437, 457	1, 156, 102	1, 387, 355	2, 010, 380	861, 651	84, 208	13, 244, 249
1870.													
By lake				1, 095, 234	1, 129, 382	1, 484, 044	1, 883, 052	1, 619, 204	1, 660, 697	2, 519, 035	2, 038, 431		13, 429, 069
By canal				21, 252	11, 376	20, 430	21, 343	15, 409	8, 347	2, 406			100, 563
By railroad	329, 373	271, 852	445, 637	817, 676	113, 027	107, 928	141, 192	346, 681	87, 691	69, 366	128, 629	43, 901	2, 902, 953
Total	329, 373	271, 852	445, 637	1, 934, 162	1, 253, 785	1, 612, 402	2, 045, 587	1, 981, 294	1, 756, 735	2, 590, 807	2, 167, 050	43, 901	16, 432, 585
1871.													
By lake			42, 440	2, 252, 654	1, 515, 666	1, 239, 220	873, 892	1, 491, 839	2, 040, 393	1, 714, 947	949, 872		12, 120, 923
By canal				1, 000	8, 393	10, 467	3, 533	15, 570	5, 932	32, 560	20, 495		97, 950
By railroad	35, 245	59, 759	150, 010	88, 591	103, 108	42, 847	35, 075	55, 569	45, 394	25, 205	19, 304	26, 469	686, 576
Total	35, 245	59, 759	192, 450	2, 342, 245	1, 627, 167	1, 292, 534	912, 500	1, 562, 978	2, 091, 719	1, 772, 712	989, 671	26, 469	12, 905, 449
1872.													
By lake				49, 532	272, 591	519, 564	492, 722	2, 487, 016	1, 280, 590	2, 465, 626	1, 264, 229		8, 831, 870
By canal			5, 090	36, 848	22, 060	14, 808	15, 261	34, 647	16, 254	33, 110	27, 932		206, 010
By railroad	39, 971	63, 918	146, 715	368, 171	340, 584	111, 829	81, 144	369, 597	398, 025	355, 780	433, 036	413, 396	3, 122, 166
Total	39, 971	63, 918	151, 805	454, 551	635, 235	646, 201	589, 127	2, 891, 260	1, 694, 869	2, 854, 516	1, 725, 197	413, 396	12, 160, 046

Shipments of flour from Chicago, 1863 to 1872, inclusive.

[Furnished to the Senate Committee on Transportation, by Charles Randolph, esq., secretary of the Board of Trade of Chicago.]

How shipped.	Jan.	Feb.	Mar.	April.	May.	June.	July.	Aug.	Sept.	Oct.	Nov.	Dec.	Total.
1863.	*Barrels.*	*Barrels.*	*Barrels.*	*Barrels.*	*Barrels.*	*Barrels.*	*Barrels.*	*Barrels.*	*Barrels.*	*Barrels.*	*Barrels.*	*Barrels.*	*Barrels.*
By lake	....	....	2	73, 993	238, 701	180, 716	101, 546	86, 165	183, 484	204, 706	130, 944	7, 088	1, 207, 345
By canal	....	....	11	250	1, 654	88	91	52	336	159	215	....	2, 856
By railroad	18, 630	19, 381	12, 047	25, 156	43, 029	33, 430	22, 470	12, 850	32, 033	25, 172	30, 112	38, 574	311, 884
Total	18, 630	19, 381	12, 060	99, 399	282, 384	214, 234	124, 107	99, 067	215, 853	230, 037	161, 271	45, 662	1, 522, 085
1864.													
By lake	....	....	....	67, 270	230, 195	197, 842	119, 490	97, 237	126, 387	105, 590	86, 404	4, 378	1, 034, 793
By canal	....	....	....	45	116	175	391	93	35	15	263	....	1, 133
By railroad	8, 749	14, 524	12, 529	70, 188	23, 751	28, 968	12, 644	7, 216	6, 725	15, 650	21, 974	26, 499	249, 417
Total	8, 749	14, 524	12, 529	137, 503	254, 062	226, 985	132, 525	104, 546	133, 147	121, 255	108, 641	30, 877	1, 285, 343
1865.													
By lake	....	....	....	17, 404	111, 812	110, 474	86, 452	49, 057	108, 961	107, 269	53, 226	1, 701	646, 356
By canal	....	....	....	29	43	42	75	126	85	290	10	....	700
By railroad	9, 708	8, 916	19, 380	29, 541	37, 089	66, 293	67, 202	70, 083	84, 042	90, 615	68, 732	94, 771	646, 372
Total	9, 708	8, 916	19, 380	46, 974	148, 944	176, 809	153, 729	119, 266	193, 088	198, 174	121, 968	96, 472	1, 293, 428
1866.													
By lake	....	....	....	4, 619	77, 628	63, 508	67, 923	53, 491	80, 567	78, 139	54, 513	1, 103	481, 491
By canal	....	....	....	11	57	67	9	30	7	37	....	....	218
By railroad	68, 930	94, 462	105, 060	113, 247	121, 766	111, 414	56, 175	80, 737	147, 371	244, 496	197, 835	158, 323	1, 499, 816
Total	68, 930	94, 462	105, 060	117, 877	199, 451	174, 989	124, 107	134, 258	227, 945	322, 672	252, 348	159, 426	1, 981, 525
1867.													
By lake	....	....	....	6, 405	46, 297	51, 959	35, 985	74, 393	153, 261	165, 231	114, 998	1, 838	650, 367
By canal	....	....	....	43	103	168	101	30	15	27	25	....	512
By railroad	188, 407	150, 324	145, 983	100, 666	67, 395	45, 087	77, 153	67, 549	125, 961	161, 651	113, 030	121, 370	1, 364, 576
Total	188, 407	150, 324	145, 983	107, 114	113, 795	97, 214	113, 239	141, 972	279, 237	326, 909	228, 053	123, 208	2, 015, 455
1868.													
By lake	....	....	....	59, 624	109, 780	83, 330	70, 354	74, 639	121, 327	137, 158	112, 877	5, 476	774, 565
By canal	....	....	....	38	15	2	10	96	17	376	....	....	554
By railroad	113, 867	106, 011	167, 306	201, 132	79, 766	71, 350	39, 099	120, 153	174, 670	119, 007	136, 019	296, 120	1, 624, 500
Total	113, 867	106, 011	167, 306	260, 794	189, 561	154, 682	109, 463	194, 888	296, 014	256, 541	248, 896	301, 596	2, 399, 619

Shipments of flour from Chicago, 1863 to 1872, inclusive—Continued.

How shipped.	Jan.	Feb.	Mar.	April.	May.	June.	July.	Aug.	Sept.	Oct.	Nov.	Dec.	Total.
	Barrels.	*Barrels.*	*Barrels.*	*Barrels.*	*Barrels.*	*Barrels.*	*Barrels.*	*Barrels.*	*Barrels.*	*Barrels.*	*Barrels.*	*Barrels.*	*Barrels.*
1869.													
By lake		62	50	11, 983	128, 695	141, 310	95, 300	96, 398	89, 795	152, 639	112, 925	115	829, 272
By canal				112	28	101		75		415	205		936
By railroad	262, 640	210, 446	241, 936	241, 726	108, 396	67, 496	32, 829	23, 424	38, 620	59, 172	90, 815	131, 355	1, 508, 855
Total	262, 640	210, 508	241, 986	253, 821	237, 119	208, 907	128, 129	119, 897	128, 415	212, 226	203, 945	131, 470	2, 339, 063
1870.													
By lake				14, 642	89, 135	76, 579	46, 367	57, 903	87, 874	115, 928	85, 404	561	574, 393
By canal				64	68	891	274	295	789	129			2, 510
By railroad	138, 819	143, 263	136, 254	154, 915	67, 119	48, 769	53, 258	63, 743	46, 809	80, 561	97, 595	97, 969	1, 129, 074
Total	138, 819	143, 263	136, 254	169, 621	156, 322	126, 239	99, 899	121, 941	135, 472	196, 618	182, 999	98, 530	1, 705, 977
1871.													
By lake			117	64, 576	82, 471	91, 338	53, 729	54, 108	62, 367	46, 089	32, 767	1, 143	488, 705
By canal				276	512	546	82	93	122	117	36		1, 784
By railroad	103, 978	88, 304	93, 943	80, 667	38, 642	40, 042	30, 023	41, 000	60, 047	65, 394	69, 824	85, 221	797, 085
Total	103, 978	88, 304	94, 060	145, 519	121, 625	131, 926	83, 834	95, 201	122, 536	111, 600	102, 627	86, 364	1, 287, 574
1872.													
By lake				1, 137	47, 998	32, 725	26, 918	23, 965	38, 850	31, 490	20, 246	188	223, 457
By canal				25	387	216	309	155	6	73	30		1, 201
By railroad	83, 271	79, 433	89, 918	105, 808	98, 499	91, 111	50, 602	49, 040	60, 835	115, 450	142, 527	170, 176	1, 136, 670
Total	83, 271	79, 433	89, 918	106, 970	146, 884	124, 052	77, 829	73, 100	99, 691	147, 013	162, 803	170, 364	1, 361, 328

Shipments of corn from Chicago, 1863 to 1872, inclusive.

[Furnished to the Senate Committee on Transportation, by Charles Randolph, esq., secretary of the Board of Trade of Chicago.]

How shipped.	Jan.	Feb.	Mar.	April.	May.	June.	July.	Aug.	Sept.	Oct.	Nov.	Dec.	Total.
	Bushels.	*Bushels.*	*Bushels.*	*Bushels.*	*Bushels.*	*Bushels.*	*Bushels.*	*Bushels.*	*Bushels.*	*Bushels.*	*Bushels.*	*Bushels.*	*Bushels.*
1863.													
By lake				3, 133, 950	3, 910, 550	5, 914, 975	4, 727, 850	3, 165, 000	2, 188, 425	856, 925	849, 250	2, 475	24, 749, 400
By canal													
By railroad	13, 620	63, 446	95. 609	17, 485	23, 905	8, 848	15, 799	5, 883	23, 148	6, 457	9, 817	18, 033	302, 050
Total	13, 620	63, 446	95, 609	3, 151, 435	3, 934, 455	5, 923, 823	4, 743, 649	3, 170, 883	2, 211, 573	863, 382	859, 067	20, 508	25, 051, 450
1864.													
By lake				743, 060	1, 559, 375	3, 085, 575	2, 171, 800	1, 673, 925	1, 563, 600	523, 950	586, 400	85, 850	11, 993, 475
By canal				5, 581	8, 673	16, 377	2, 634	2, 013	10, 369	1, 880	1, 233		48, 760
By railroad	4, 255	9, 476	14, 428	22, 280	19, 322	5, 121	12, 020	2, 462	3, 402	4, 217	21, 070	75, 164	193, 217
Total	4, 255	9, 476	14, 428	770, 861	1, 587, 370	3, 107, 073	2, 186, 454	1, 678, 400	1, 577, 371	530, 047	608, 703	161, 014	12, 235, 452
1865.													
By lake				1, 018, 550	1, 540, 575	3, 016, 150	3, 849, 150	4, 233, 725	5, 534, 825	3, 632, 425	1, 553, 900	42, 300	24, 421, 600
By canal				7, 842	3, 612	15, 151	37, 320	13, 105	13, 669	16, 850	5, 723		113, 272
By railroad	210, 500	182, 769	139, 981	130, 036	109, 320	34, 148	37, 705	9, 463	10, 751	12, 890	11, 935	12, 871	902, 369
Total	210, 500	182, 769	139, 981	1, 156, 428	1, 653, 507	3, 065, 449	3, 924, 175	4, 256, 293	5, 559, 245	3, 662, 165	1, 571, 558	55, 171	25, 437, 241
1866.													
By lake				1, 399, 702	5, 154, 897	5, 387, 050	5, 748, 161	5, 217, 750	3, 540, 355	3, 161, 640	1, 644, 300	4, 000	31, 257, 855
By canal				8, 455	20, 460	18, 879	10, 144	31, 050	18, 600	17, 967			125, 555
By railroad	147, 937	76, 894	99, 704	280, 962	167, 094	332, 892	168, 059	21, 756	17, 267	10, 553	2, 087	44, 566	1, 369, 771
Total	147, 937	76, 894	99, 704	1, 689, 119	5, 342, 451	5, 738, 821	5, 926, 364	5, 270, 556	3, 576, 222	3, 190, 160	1, 646, 387	48, 566	32, 753, 181
1867.													
By lake				934, 152	2, 184, 754	2, 848, 805	4, 376, 665	3, 287, 973	2, 808, 692	1, 824, 483	1, 623, 529	51, 119	19, 940, 172
By canal				200	5, 500	29, 645				6, 260			41, 605
By railroad	77, 478	180, 828	266, 588	195, 267	124, 161	28, 258	9, 215	2, 230	15, 469	10, 623	87, 952	287, 359	1, 285, 428
Total	77, 478	180, 828	266, 588	1, 129, 619	2, 314, 415	2, 906, 708	4, 385, 880	3, 290, 203	2, 824, 161	1, 841, 366	1, 711, 481	338, 478	21, 267, 205
1868.													
By lake				2, 251, 347	3, 161, 072	3, 147, 674	3, 284, 475	4, 328, 257	2, 844, 540	1, 541, 006	1, 070, 649	42, 051	21, 671, 071
By canal				5, 000	12, 985	27, 958	11, 500	21, 724	29, 200	12, 800			121, 167
By railroad	276, 273	464, 437	397, 661	587, 349	332, 497	33, 325	23, 450	7, 522	14, 205	28, 230	124, 927	683, 512	2, 978, 388
Total	276, 273	464, 437	397, 661	2, 843, 696	3, 506, 554	3, 208, 957	3, 319, 425	4, 357, 503	2, 887, 945	1, 582, 036	1, 195, 576	730, 563	24, 770, 626

Shipments of corn from Chicago, 1863 to 1872, inclusive—Continued.

How shipped.	Jan.	Feb.	Mar.	April.	May.	June.	July.	Aug.	Sept.	Oct.	Nov.	Dec.	Total.
1869.	*Bushels.*	*Bushels.*	*Bushels.*	*Bushels.*	*Bushels.*	*Bushels.*	*Bushels.*	*Bushels.*	*Bushels.*	*Bushels.*	*Bushels.*	*Bushels.*	*Bushels.*
By lake	....	2, 350	4, 270	1, 426, 242	1, 893, 774	2, 454, 010	, 856, 692	2, 977, 790	3, 594, 059	1, 899, 874	901, 974	8, 905	17, 019, 940
By canal	....	....	....	....	159	....	25, 198	....	24, 230	15, 800	....	....	65, 387
By railroad	505, 262	333, 016	881, 373	839, 151	464, 170	237, 914	62, 812	153, 559	319, 510	428, 961	125, 946	149, 807	4, 501, 481
Total	505, 262	335, 366	885, 643	2, 265, 393	2, 358, 103	2, 691, 924	1, 944, 702	3, 131, 349	3, 937, 799	2, 344, 635	1, 027, 920	158, 712	21, 586, 808
1870.													
By lake	....	....	....	307, 510	1, 822, 585	1, 597, 500	2, 574, 096	2, 858, 762	1, 901, 319	1, 370, 415	1, 162, 100	4, 100	13, 598, 387
By canal	....	....	....	....	27, 393	14, 980	....	22, 317	5, 358	....	....	....	70, 048
By railroad	223, 782	369, 318	488, 429	577, 747	383, 572	438, 837	274, 623	230, 012	165, 695	175, 956	297, 995	482, 976	4, 108, 942
Total	223, 782	369, 318	488, 429	885, 257	2, 233, 550	2, 051, 317	2, 848, 719	3, 111, 091	2, 072, 372	1, 546, 371	1, 460, 095	487, 076	17, 777, 377
1871.													
By lake	....	....	83, 218	2, 988, 280	3, 523, 330	5, 905, 169	6, 830, 102	5, 400, 303	3, 739, 237	2, 211, 547	3, 391, 990	127, 700	34, 200, 876
By canal	....	....	....	....	....	....	....	....	....	....	....	....	....
By railroad	199, 325	166, 955	603, 752	288, 167	193, 256	101, 267	131, 038	114, 602	154, 616	160, 090	125, 063	277, 023	2, 515, 154
Total	199, 325	166, 955	686, 970	3, 276, 447	3, 716, 586	6, 006, 436	6, 961, 140	5, 514, 905	3, 893, 853	2, 371, 637	3, 517, 053	404, 723	36, 716, 030
1872.													
By lake	22	....	1, 000	1, 445, 606	2, 568, 080	6, 850, 326	7, 574, 131	7, 829, 558	6, 264, 918	6, 819, 201	2, 214, 145	22, 521	41, 589, 508
By canal	....	....	....	....	....	....	....	....	....	....	....	....	....
By railroad	725, 856	534, 097	442, 952	1, 018, 271	694, 000	369, 036	265, 458	323, 947	444, 015	329, 991	184, 107	92, 314	5, 424, 044
Total	725, 878	534, 097	443, 952	2, 463, 877	3, 262, 080	7, 219, 362	7, 839, 589	8, 153, 505	6, 708, 933	7, 149, 192	2, 398, 252	114, 835	47, 013, 525

Rates of freight on shipments of grain from Chicago to New York by water (lake and canal) from 1868 to 1872, inclusive.

[Compiled from auditor's tables.]

Months.	Rate in cents per bushel.				
	1868.	1869.	1870.	1871.	1872.
April	......	......	......	......	......
May	20	19	16	16	18
June	19	21	16	16	21
July	18	18	15	16	23
August	22	19	15	18	22
September	25	22	15	23	27
October	27	29	21	27	31
November	28	32	20	25	28

Rates of freight on shipments of grain from Chicago to New York, by lake and rail, from 1868 to 1872, inclusive.

[From report of Chicago Board of Trade.]

Months.	Rate in cents per bushel.				
	1868.	1869.	1870.	1871.	1872.
April	28	26	22	22	......
May	26	25	20	21	25
June	25	25	21	21	23
July	25	23	20	22	23
August	26	20	20	24	23
September	33	22	23	28	32
October	34	27	25	32	37
November	35	36	29	32	38

Rates of freight on grain and other fourth-class freights from Chicago to New York by the all-rail lines, 1860 to 1872, inclusive.

[Prepared for the Senate Committee on Transportation, by Mr. C. M. Gray, general freight agent Lake Shore and Michigan Southern Railway Company.]

	Rate in cents per 100 pounds.												
	1860.	1861.	1862.	1863.	1864.	1865.	1866.	1867.	1868.	1869.	1870.	1871.	1872.
January	60	60	95	105	110	160	80	90	85	70	70	65	65
February	55	65	100	105	110	160	70	80	85	65	70	65	65
March	50	57½	85	85	100	160	70	70	80	50	60	50	60
April	45	60	65	80	75	100	70	50	70	50	50	45	50
May	42½	55	55	70	75	70	55	50	60	50	45	45	45
June	40	50	50	67	75	70	60	75	50	47	45	40	45
July	45	45	50	60	87	70	65	70	55	45	45	45	45
August	45	45	55	60	80	70	65	70	60	50	45	50	45
September	55	55	70	55	95	70	85	75	65	65	50	55	55
October	60	90	85	75	95	95	100	85	70	65	60	65	65
November	65	95	95	95	115	130	105	85	75	70	65	65	65
December	65	95	105	110	160	130	90	85	75	70	65	65	65

Monthly average price of No. 2 spring-wheat at Chicago, 1868 *to* 1872, *inclusive.*

[Compiled from Chicago Board of Trade Report.]

Months.	1868.	1869.	1870.	1871.	1872.
January	$2 03. 7	$1 14. 5	$0 78. 9	$1 16. 7	$1 23. 1
February	2 01. 4	1 15. 8	81	1 23. 7	1 24. 7
March	1 95	1 12	77. 4	1 25. 6	1 21. 7
April	1 95. 9	1 11. 5	80. 3	1 27. 5	1 24. 7
May	2 02. 3	1 07. 2	95. 4	1 27. 2	1 47. 9
June	1 91. 5	1 16. 2	1 09. 5	1 28	1 42. 5
July	1 84	1 31. 4	1 12	1 18. 1	1 25
August	1 72. 2	1 38. 2	1 08. 9	1 10. 1	1 36
September	1 54	1 23. 3	99. 2	1 17. 3	1 21. 2
October	1 29. 2	1 01. 8	1 05. 9	1 18. 1	1 12. 5
November	1 12	88. 8	1. 01. 4	1 20. 3	1 07
December	1 14. 2	84. 3	1. 05. 5	1 19	1 14

Monthly average price of western mixed corn at Chicago, 1868 *to* 1872, *inclusive.*

[Compiled from Chicago Board of Trade Reports.]

Month.	1868.	1869.	1870.	1871.	1872.
January	$0 85. 6	$0 56. 1	$0 71. 9	$0 47. 3	$0 40. 8
February	80	59	70. 2	51. 9	40. 4
March	83. 1	....	71. 5	53. 9	37. 6
April	81. 8	53. 8	82. 1	54. 2	40. 2
May	88. 4	57. 7	87	53. 8	46
June	85. 4	61. 9	83. 1	53. 3	44. 2
July	88. 5	80. 5	82. 7	51	41
August	97. 4	90. 4	73. 8	45. 3	41. 4
September	94	83. 9	63. 9	46. 6	36. 2
October	86. 4	67	59. 7	47. 1	32. 3
November	76. 1	73. 4	60. 9	46. 1	31. 7
December	63. 5	76	50. 3	41	30. 8

Statement of through-charges per ton per mile on grain and fourth-class freight from Chicago to New York, all rail, 963 *miles, via Michigan Central and connecting roads.*

[Prepared for Senate Committee on Transportation, by H. E. Sargent, general superintendent Michigan Central Railroad.]

Date.	Through rate per 100 pounds.	Rate per ton per mile.
	Cents.	*Cents.*
1871. January 1 to March 5	65	1. 35
March 6 to March 8	60	1. 25
March 9 to March 18	55	1. 14
March 19 to June 13	45	. 935
June 14 to July 22	40	. 831
July 23 to August 11	45	. 935
August 11 to September 28	50	1. 04
September 29 to October 6	55	1. 14
October 7 to October 28	60	1. 25
October 29 to December 31	65	1. 35
1872. January 1 to March 26	65	1. 35
March 27 to April 4	60	1. 25
April 5 to May 1	55	1. 14
May 2 to May 18	50	1. 04
May 19 to September 3	45	. 935
September 4 to September 11	50	1. 04
September 12 to September 17	55	1. 14
September 18 to October 17	60	1. 25
October 18 to December 31	65	1. 35
1873. January 1 to April 15	65	1. 35
April 16 to April 22	60	1. 25
April 23 to April 28	55	1. 14
April 29 to May 20	50	1. 04
May 21 to September 5	45	. 935
September 6 to September 15	50	1. 04
September 16 to November 12	55	1. 14

Shipments of corn from Buffalo by rail and by canal each month for ten years, 1863 *to* 1872, *inclusive.*

[Prepared for the United States Senate Committee on Transportation, by William Thurstone, Secretary of the Board of Trade of Buffalo, N. Y.]

Year.	How shipped.	January.	February.	March.	April.	May.	June.	July.	August.	September.	October.	November.	December.
		BUSHELS.											
1863	By canal					3, 772, 915	4, 574, 224	3, 984, 686	3, 076, 860	2, 863, 104	786, 900	388, 406	
1864	do					817, 189	2, 100, 436	2, 034, 725	1, 716, 121	1, 566, 670	909, 619	404, 513	
1865	do					1, 168, 898	1, 684, 946	2, 766, 062	3, 394, 718	3, 506, 346	4, 002, 128	2, 610, 290	
1866	do					2, 324, 472	5, 314, 294	4, 456, 006	4, 820, 399	5, 004, 876	2, 206, 350	2, 454, 148	
1867	do					862, 455	1, 817, 970	3, 291, 570	3, 065, 640	2, 201, 710	2, 600, 640	1, 259, 086	
1868	do					2, 662, 671	2, 093, 754	2, 349, 096	2, 021, 288	3, 179, 553	970, 259	967, 587	9, 000
1869	do					959, 631	1, 171, 434	839, 017	1, 191, 183	2, 048, 935	1, 816, 497	630, 553	
1870	do					197, 008	664, 407	1, 232, 637	1, 506, 062	1, 114, 400	783, 996	557, 396	
1871	By rail	17, 400	3, 750	25, 500	257, 336	757, 301	348, 009	695, 679	638, 822	563, 398	278, 951	183, 144	550, 761
	By canal				505, 293	1, 574, 434	2, 878, 193	4, 720, 040	3, 669, 227	3, 037, 055	1, 347, 213	2, 552, 768	
1872	By rail	105, 536	15, 200	18, 200	53, 900	746, 405	395, 682	413, 166	667, 460	196, 705	100, 993	68, 913	170, 000
	By canal					2, 463, 992	6, 045, 416	6, 569, 777	5, 775, 687	5, 280, 791	3, 633, 265	3, 551, 754	

Shipments of wheat from Buffalo by rail and by canal each month for ten years, 1863 *to* 1872, *inclusive.*

Year.	How shipped.	January.	February.	March.	April.	May.	June.	July.	August.	September.	October.	November.	December.
1863	By canal					2, 700, 597	2, 683, 015	1, 369, 080	1, 605, 570	2, 593, 101	4, 285, 718	3, 036, 746	
1864	do					2, 815, 589	3, 785, 890	2, 208, 848	1, 444, 437	1, 704, 980	1, 595, 690	2, 212, 918	
1865	do					754, 202	1, 795, 940	1, 026, 619	1, 428, 344	907, 428	2, 337, 861	2, 235, 197	
1866	do					576, 577	920, 484	357, 259	292, 369	916, 901	2, 309, 962	2, 239, 894	
1867	do					71, 660	114, 392	112, 960	489, 810	2, 608, 280	3, 862, 248	2, 706, 599	
1868	do					793, 339	489, 157	296, 430	571, 709	2, 486, 591	3, 196, 327	2, 248, 964	72, 680
1869	do					1, 720, 737	3, 392, 589	1, 740, 231	2, 392, 169	2, 254, 005	4, 675, 128	2, 407, 912	
1870	do					1, 878, 477	2, 719, 878	1, 753, 132	1, 644, 888	1, 962, 914	3, 448, 093	2, 994, 960	
1871	By rail	121, 487	118, 683	33, 287	468, 458	665, 076	390, 719	325, 645	315, 593	118, 092		41, 686	37, 444
	By canal				618, 245	1, 749, 487	2, 035, 627	1, 104, 590	2, 558, 640	4, 029, 997	3, 836, 041	2, 982, 813	
1872	By rail	36, 350	69, 865	53, 422	79, 911	59, 251	90, 542	612, 243	216, 808	358, 981	146, 713	366, 465	350, 000
	By canal					182, 283	926, 217	1, 402, 185	705, 814	2, 205, 323	3, 374, 226	2, 257, 494	

NOTE.—No returns of rail-shipments during the years 1863 to 1870, inclusive. Canal closed during January, February, March, and April.

Average price of Milwaukee No. 2 spring wheat, at the port of Buffalo, each month during the last five years, 1868 to 1872, inclusive.

[Prepared for the United States Senate Committee on Transportation, by Mr. William Thurstone, Secretary Board of Trade of Buffalo, N. Y.]

Year.	PRICE PER BUSHEL EACH MONTH.											
	January.	February.	March.	April.	May.	June.	July.	August.	September.	October.	November.	December.
1868	$2 20	$2 19	$2 18	$2 20	$2 18	$2 02½	$1 86	$1 93	$1 71	$1 45½	$1 35	$1 40
1869	1 56	1 40	1 35	1 25	1 26	1 28	1 38½	1 42½	1 33	1 15	1 09	1 10
1870	1 05	1 04	1 02½	97	1 05	1 21½	1 22½	1 15	1 05	1 15½	1 16	1 22
1871	1 33½	1 38	1 41½	1 39	1 36	1 39	1 30	1 21	1 31	1 41	1 38½	1 35
1872	1 39	1 42½	1 45	1 47½	1 61	1 50	1 36	1 43	1 42	1 40	1 34	1 38

Average price of No. 2 Western mixed corn, at the port of Buffalo, each month during the last five years, 1868 to 1872, inclusive.

Year.	PRICE PER BUSHEL EACH YEAR.											
	January.	February.	March.	April.	May.	June.	July.	August.	September.	October.	November.	December.
1868	$1 11	$1 05	$1 08	$1 03	$1 00	$0 95	$0 97	$1 10	$1 08	$1 00	$0 96	$1 00
1869	97	90	88	80	67	71½	86	1 00	92	80	88	98
1870	95	94½	94	1 00	99	92	90½	83	73	71½	73½	64
1871	68½	71	72	62	60½	63	59½	56	60	65½	63	59
1872	59	59	58	60	59	52	51	52	53	52	49	50

Receipts of wheat at Buffalo each month during the last five years, 1868 *to* 1872, *inclusive.*

[Prepared for the United States Senate Committee on Transportation, by Mr. William Thurstone, secretary Board of Trade, Buffalo, N. Y.]

Year.	BUSHELS.											
	January.	February.	March.	April.	May.	June.	July.	August.	September.	October.	November.	December.
1868	12, 708	14, 718	16, 809	196, 720	902, 814	624, 352	405, 640	1, 077, 779	3, 229, 295	3, 470, 210	2, 625, 588	433, 528
1869	10, 966	700	363	1, 108	1, 758, 048	3, 885, 043	2, 891 186	2, 299, 540	2, 651, 916	3, 021, 065	3, 609, 379	378, 989
1870	417	710		154, 758	3, 171, 237	2, 902, 569	2, 369, 048	2, 161, 117	1, 996, 656	3, 903, 877	2, 684. 592	286, 954
1871	1 133			2, 094, 039	1, 938, 315	2, 481, 109	1, 637, 915	2, 870, 031	3, 875, 192	4, 961, 695	2, 544, [illegible]77	121, 200
1872		350			333, 377	1, 279, 166	1, 645, 055	1, 064, 721	2, 866, 724	4, 012, 750	2, 922, 225	180, 574

Receipts of corn at Buffalo each month during the last five years, 1868 *to* 1872, *inclusive.*

Year.	BUSHELS.											
	January.	February.	March.	April.	May.	June.	July.	August.	September.	October.	November.	December.
1868		1, 750		921, 578	2, 304, 953	2, 663, 249	2, 830, 679	3, 277, 790	3, 219, 489	1, 007, 027	2, 675, 755	222, 471
1869					1, 703, 681	2, 148, 021	1, 485, 216	1, 977, 256	2, 488, 217	1, 209, 738	620, 952	52, 087
1870				83, 834	935, 754	1, 035, 779	2, 014, 390	2, 204, 177	1, 073, 853	1, 164, 552	564, 826	246, 837
1871			1, 800	2, 191, 805	2, 013, 886	3, 800, 186	5, 407, 220	4, 258, 650	3, 160, 180	2, 126, 714	725, 329	465, 473
1872					5, 169, 356	5, 349, 243	5, 351, 423	6, 341, 932	4, 709, 980	4, 885, 375	2, 773, 278	62, 600

NOTE.—During the months of January, February, March, and about three-fourths of April, receipts are by steamer International by Grand Trunk Railroad only, navigation by lake opening about end of April.

Shipments of wheat, wheat-flour, corn, rye, oats, and barley from Buffalo, by rail and by canal, for fifteen years, from 1858 to 1872, inclusive.

[Prepared for the United States Senate Committee on Transportation, by Mr. William Thurstone, secretary Board of Trade, Buffalo, N. Y.]

Year.	Wheat, bushels.		Wheat-flour, barrels.		Corn, bushels.		Rye, bushels.		Oats, bushels.		Barley, bushels.	
	Rail.	Canal.	Rail.	Canal.	Rail.	Canal.	Rail.	Canal.	Rail.	Canal.	Rail.	Canal.
1858	....	8, 294, 690	....	771, 602	....	5, 478, 343	....	64, 528	....	1, 916, 214	....	204, 293
1859	....	6, 168, 068	....	220, 486	....	2, 157, 538	....	36, 587	....	953, 169	....	308, 506
1860	....	13, 951, 458	....	180, 853	....	10, 306, 048	....	50, 804	....	1, 285, 646	....	130, 189
1861	....	23, 713, 713	....	306, 236	....	19, 112, 112	....	282, 726	....	1, 705, 935	....	134, 341
1862	....	27, 751, 766	....	451, 814	....	22, 487, 185	....	658, 480	....	2, 164, 778	....	201, 744
1863	....	19, 404, 308	....	469, 792	....	18, 980, 442	....	361, 718	....	6, 527, 598	....	419, 157
1864	....	16, 148, 386	....	126, 820	....	9, 757, 022	....	517, 131	....	11, 178, 564	....	235, 133
1865	....	10, 202, 154	....	142, 018	....	18, 476, 331	....	629, 758	....	7, 900, 451	....	514, 951
1866	....	7, 772, 217	....	52, 325	....	25, 548, 596	....	972, 647	....	8, 922, 433	....	1, 301, 715
1867	....	10, 109, 718	....	15, 468	....	14, 931, 812	....	736, 578	....	9, 409, 686	....	1, 206, 733
1868	....	10, 369, 030	....	5, 774	....	15, 099, 136	....	633, 899	....	10, 423, 504	....	209, 128
1869	998, 496	16, 363, 480	....	51, 928	2, 320, 378	7, 816, 960	11, 606	76, 792	967, 791	3, 983, 046	128, 975	82, 429
1870*	....	16, 738, 613	....	76, 471	....	5, 911, 668	....	378, 322	....	5, 572, 254	....	831, 024
1871	2, 636, 170	19, 028, 316	....	47, 731	4, 320, 591	20, 695, 305	18, 750	986, 517	1, 658, 718	6, 649, 439	416, 001	825, 420
1872	2, 440, 551	11, 001, 069	....	5, 172	3, 032, 160	30, 934, 606	4, 825	210, 705	1, 227, 247	4, 598, 237	396, 082	1, 729, 772

* Figures during the year 1870 were not made public by the owners of the elevators. The estimated aggregate was 6,250,000 bushels.

NOTE.—No record kept of rail-shipments previous to 1869, and since then only of the grain that is shipped by the Erie and Central Railroads from elevators at this port having connection therewith by tracks laid down to said elevators.

Receipts of wheat, wheat-flour, corn, rye, oats, and barley at Buffalo, by rail and by lake, for fifteen years, from 1858 *to* 1872, *inclusive.*

[Prepared for the United States Senate Committee on Transportation, by Mr. William Thurstone, secretary Board of Trade, Buffalo, N. Y.]

Year.	Wheat, bushels.		Wheat-flour, barrels.		Corn, bushels.		Rye, bushels.		Oats, bushels.		Barley, bushels.	
	Rail.	Water.	Rail.	Water.	Rail.	Water.	Rail.	Water.	Rail.	Water.	Rail.	Water.
1858	....	10, 761, 550	....	1, 536, 109	....	6, 621, 668	....	125, 214	....	2, 275, 241	....	308, 371
1859	....	9, 234, 652	....	1, 420, 333	....	3, 113, 653	....	124, 693	....	394, 502	....	361, 560
1860	....	18, 502, 649	....	1, 122, 335	....	11, 386, 217	....	80, 822	....	1, 209, 594	....	262, 158
1861	....	27, 105, 219	....	2, 159, 591	....	21, 024, 657	....	337, 764	....	1, 797, 905	....	313, 757
1862	....	30, 435, 831	....	2, 846, 022	....	24, 388, 627	....	791, 564	....	2, 624, 932	....	423, 124
1863	....	21, 240, 348	....	2, 978, 089	....	20, 086, 952	....	422, 309	....	7, 322, 187	....	641, 449
1864	....	17, 677, 549	....	2, 028, 520	....	10, 478, 681	....	633, 727	....	11, 682, 637	....	465, 057
1865	....	13, 437, 883	....	1, 788, 393	....	19, 840, 901	....	877, 676	....	8, 494, 799	....	820, 563
1866	....	10, 479, 694	....	1, 313, 543	....	27, 894, 798	....	1, 245, 485	....	10, 227, 472	....	1, 606, 384
1867	....	11, 879, 685	....	1, 440, 056	....	17, 873, 638	....	1, 010, 693	....	10, 933, 166	....	1, 802, 598
1868	....	12, 555, 215	....	1, 502, 731	....	16, 804, 067	....	947, 323	....	11, 492, 472	....	637, 124
1869	....	19, 228, 546	....	1, 598, 487	....	11, 549, 403	....	126, 093	....	5, 459, 347	....	651, 339
1870	....	20, 556, 722	....	1, 470, 391	....	9, 410, 128	....	626, 154	....	6, 846, 983	....	1, 821, 154
1871	....	22, 606, 217	....	1, 278, 077	....	26, 110, 769	....	1, 095, 039	....	9, 006, 409	....	1, 946, 923
1872	....	14, 304, 942	....	762, 502	....	34, 643, 187	....	301, 809	....	6, 050, 045	....	3, 088, 925

NOTE.—No record kept of rail-receipts. Included in the water (by lake) receipts are the receipts per steamer International, bringing the produce carried by Grand Trunk Railway of Canada.

NOTE.—See Thurstone's report for 1872, page 19.

Average price of No. 1 Milwaukee Club wheat at Oswego, for each month during the last five years, 1868 to 1872, inclusive.

Prepared for the United States Senate Committee on Transportation, by Mr. J. L. McWhorter, secretary of the Board of Trade of Oswego, N. Y.]

Year.	Price per bushel each month.											
	Jan.	Feb.	Mar.	Apr.	May.	June.	July.	Aug.	Sept.	Oct.	Nov.	Dec.
1868	$2 47	$2 48	$2 44	$2 45	$2 32	$2 15	$2 03	$2 12	$1 90	$1 65	$1 56	$1 68
1869	1 71	1 69	1 54	1 45	1 37	1 34	1 47	1 55	1 46	1 29	1 25	1 28
1870	1 26	1 20	1 18	1 13	1 16	1 28	1 32	1 35	1 22	1 25	1 27	1 40
1871	1 44	1 51	1 56	1 50	1 46	1 43	1 34	1 33	1 42	1 51	1 48	1 50
1872	1 51	1 56	1 59	1 64	1 74	1 67	1 48	1 57	1 61	1 55	1 55	1 61

Average price of western mixed corn at Oswego for each month during the last five years, 1868 to 1872, inclusive.

Year.	Price per bushel each month.											
	Jan.	Feb.	Mar.	Apr.	May.	June.	July.	Aug.	Sept.	Oct.	Nov.	Dec.
1868	$1 24	$1 25	$1 25	$1 15	$1 03	$0 95	$1 00	$1 10	$1 13	$1 05	$1 05	$1 04
1869	1 02	1 00	99	90	75	80	86	1 04	1 01	86	96	1 08
1870	1 07	1 03	1 01	1 03	1 08	99	92	89	82	78	79	79
1871	78	84	87	75	68	66	64	59	66	71	69	67
1872	67	71	71	71	66	60	56	57	59	60	59	59

Receipts of wheat, wheat-flour, corn, rye, oats, and barley at Oswego for fifteen years, from 1858 to 1872, inclusive.

[Prepared for the United States Senate Committee on Transportation, by Mr. J. L. McWhorter, secretary of the Board of Trade of Oswego, N. Y.]

Year.	Wheat, bushels.		Wheat-flour, barrels.		Corn, bushels.		Rye, bushels.		Oats, bushels.		Barley, bushels.	
	American.	Canadian.	American.	Canadian.	American.	Canadian.*	American.	Canadian.	American.	Canadian.	American.	Canadian.
1858	5, 984, 397	611, 039	62, 036	34, 627	2, 913, 618	....	14, 077	83, 981	447, 216	190, 117	190, 425	359, 542
1859	4, 019, 908	854, 685	28, 921	36, 030	804, 646	....	10, 060	172, 377	123, 275	128, 259	225, 999	552, 420
1860	8, 550, 399	1, 101, 165	29, 734	91, 665	5, 016, 041	....	34, 786	209, 525	110, 680	277, 736	103, 598	1, 223, 317
1861	8, 851, 131	1, 270, 315	24, 723	94, 333	5, 642, 262	....	102, 608	279, 079	48, 786	67, 598	11, 194	1, 162, 357
1862	10, 213, 810	767, 322	159, 876	75, 506	4, 528, 962	....	74, 709	57, 960	181, 514	5, 770	74, 709	975, 652
1863	8, 104, 169	681, 256	53, 674	61, 618	2, 676, 387	....	60, 144	56, 211	130, 012	303, 135	179, 703	1, 644, 964
1864	4, 670, 856	1, 004, 917	11, 651	39, 999	1, 279, 137	....	40, 151	52, 792	652, 530	139, 400	7, 516	1, 760, 787
1865	5, 191, 043	1, 084, 876	12, 948	19, 402	2, 480, 006	....	45, 831	380, 038	357, 321	28, 415	114, 849	2, 992, 932
1866	4, 745, 411	771, 918	1, 929	6, 180	3, 492, 207	....	143, 917	428, 477	226, 116	130, 422	174, 299	4, 130, 504
1867	4, 339, 345	939, 941	1, 549	2, 028	3, 420, 784	....	49, 876	188, 301	205, 691	69, 793	191, 887	2, 528, 447
1868	6, 079, 583	890, 751	758	412	3, 679, 346	....	25, 902	142, 878	683, 154	....	102, 925	2, 031, 385
1869	7, 348, 415	441, 284	3, 218	304	1, 818, 170	....	27, 240	306, 762	62, 331	....	32, 724	3, 167, 023
1870	6, 084, 345	766, 067	5, 696	56	940, 484	....	25, 769	284, 338	366, 724	60, 960	277, 422	3, 268, 149
1871	5, 912, 703	856, 149	1, 552	....	3, 416, 765	....	122, 076	182, 186	124, 800	....	252, 804	3, 219, 484
1872	3, 360, 966	792, 543	10	100	1, 921, 901	....	17, 072	164, 661	89, 801	....	95, 107	2, 695, 931

* No receipts from Canada.

Receipts of wheat at Oswego for each month during the last five years—1868 *to* 1872, *inclusive.*

[Prepared for the United States Senate Committee on Transportation, by Mr. J. L. McWhorter, secretary of the Board of Trade of Oswego, N. Y.]

Year.	Bushels received in—											
	January.	February.	March.	April.	May.	June.	July.	August.	September.	October.	November.	December.
1868	...	...	...	241, 449	979, 139	811, 661	336, 215	328, 470	1, 263, 662	1, 336, 377	1, 510, 369	162, 992
1869	...	...	...	184, 364	713, 081	1, 098, 031	863, 441	844, 644	1, 333, 688	1, 301, 549	972, 572	478, 317
1870	...	...	...	263. 927	755, 814	761, 669	960, 604	1, 013, 288	654, 384	1, 201, 946	1, 062, 800	185, 980
1871	...	...	...	450, 434	923, 332	878, 404	596, 051	768, 355	962, 076	977, 210	1, 085, 390	127, 600
1872	...	...	...	381, 999	397, 330	361, 346	319, 108	450, 670	601, 411	709, 854	847, 101	84, 670

Receipts of corn at Oswego for each month during the last five years—1868 *to* 1872, *inclusive.*

Year.	Bushels received in—											
	January.	February.	March.	April.	May.	June.	July.	August.	September.	October.	November.	December.
1868	...	...	...	109, 109	626, 264	547, 126	842, 058	415, 771	614, 756	370, 144	154, 118	...
1869	...	...	...	5, 055	271, 766	222, 623	232, 106	231, 061	479, 473	162, 981	130, 855	82, 251
1870	...	...	...	15, 930	127, 411	158, 118	93, 885	216, 162	71, 711	72, 110	146, 129	39, 028
1871	...	...	...	150, 578	491, 750	820, 030	797, 144	461, 312	152, 889	42, 328	424, 935	75, 799
1872	...	...	...	17, 480	512, 557	236, 240	348, 854	296, 228	85, 132	60, 260	295, 741	19, 400

Shipments of wheat, wheat-flour, corn, rye, oats, and barley from Oswego, by rail and by canal, for fifteen years—1858 to 1872, inclusive.

[Prepared for the United States Senate Committee on Transportation, by Mr. J. L. McWhorter, secretary Board of Trade of Oswego, New York.]

Year.	Wheat.		Wheat-flour.		Corn.		Rye.		Oats.		Barley.	
	By rail.	By canal.	By rail.	By canal.	By rail.	By canal.	By rail.	By canal.	By rail.	By canal.	By rail.	By canal.
	Bushels.	*Bushels.*	*Barrels.*	*Barrels.*	*Bushels.*	*Bushels.*	*Bushels.*	*Bushels.*	*Bushels.*	*Bushels.*	*Bushels.*	*Bushels.*
1858	....	4, 071, 391	....	467, 886	....	2, 397, 805	....	97, 459	....	614, 414	....	540, 574
1859	....	2, 198, 882	....	253, 510	....	474, 215	....	205, 866	....	233, 304	....	767, 206
1860	....	6, 786, 606	....	421, 032	....	4, 538, 841	....	165, 687	....	401, 514	....	1, 201, 101
1861	....	7, 695, 262	....	433, 546	....	5, 160, 682	....	367, 870	....	96, 645	....	1, 089, 466
1862	....	7, 408, 513	....	499, 835	....	3, 729, 206	....	113, 969	....	156, 653	....	948, 845
1863	....	6, 061, 611	....	374, 593	....	2, 538, 755	....	99, 733	....	444, 352	....	1, 803, 365
1864	177, 577	3, 129, 648	283, 794	263, 672	22, 413	914, 639	1, 450	98, 384	32, 987	777, 968	3, 669	1, 867, 800
1865	60, 346	2, 678, 667	253, 865	277, 814	31, 135	1, 928, 315	....	404, 740	8, 783	322, 968	28, 363	2, 848, 766
1866	171, 816	2, 190, 335	476, 582	156, 791	119, 476	2, 871, 747	....	560, 648	9, 237	316, 716	19, 827	4, 184, 632
1867	173, 737	2, 511, 331	487, 435	74, 761	231, 466	2, 740, 227	9, 676	241, 692	22, 718	270, 689	8, 246	2, 608, 752
1868	283, 667	2, 358, 231	519, 009	46, 741	246, 596	2, 912, 235	32	146, 963	16, 096	628, 042	13, 973	1, 948, 892
1869	173, 856	4, 711, 984	492, 996	68, 161	292, 386	1, 020, 893	1, 826	306, 019	7, 428	69, 541	84, 948	2, 783, 064
1870	137, 251	3, 857, 727	482, 694	105, 925	196, 797	361, 911	3, 248	264, 346	61, 118	247, 053	164, 648	3, 246, 104
1871	231, 527	4, 105, 784	437, 939	93, 997	392, 098	2, 507, 799	1, 260	223, 235	54, 734	112, 913	190, 628	3, 028, 164
1872	261, 147	1, 928, 850	591, 407	44, 202	357, 581	969, 587	5, 820	241, 125	28, 283	42, 750	180, 625	2, 590, 500

N. B.—No record of shipments by rail previous to 1864.

Wheat received at Cincinnati by railroads, by Ohio River, and by canals—1863 to 1872, inclusive.

[Prepared for the United States Senate Committee on Transportation, by William T. Tibbetts, esq., secretary of Cincinnati Chamber of Commerce.]

Year.	By railroad.	By river.	By canal.
	Bushels.		
1863	1, 740, 491	Included in figures in the first column.	Included in figures in the first column.
1864	1, 650, 759		
1865	1, 678, 395		
1866	1, 545, 892		
1867	1, 474, 987		
1868	780, 933		
1869	1, 075, 348		
1870	1, 195, 341		
1871	866, 459		
1872	762, 144		

Wheat shipped from Cincinnati by rail, by river, and by canal—1863 to 1872, inclusive.

Year.	By railroad.	By river.	By canal.
	Bushels.		
1863	1, 177, 108	Included in figures in the first column.	Included in figures in the first column.
1864	943, 737		
1865	686, 893		
1866	873, 775		
1867	972, 982		
1868	406, 349		
1869	702, 622		
1870	806, 775		
1871	469, 893		
1872	323, 405		

NOTE.—The figures given are for the commercial year, ending August 31 each year.

Wheat-flour received at Cincinnati by railroads, by Ohio River, and by canals—1863 to 1872, inclusive.

[Prepared for the United States Senate Committee on Transportation, by William T. Tibbetts, esq., secretary Cincinnati Chamber of Commerce.]

Year.	By railroad.	By river.	By canal.
	Barrels.		
1863	619, 710	Included in figures in the first column.	Included in figures in the first column.
1864	546, 983		
1865	671, 900		
1866	659, 046		
1867	577, 296		
1868	522, 297		
1869	571, 280		
1870	774, 344		
1871	705, 579		
1872	582, 930		

Wheat-flour shipped from Cincinnati by rail, by river, and by canal, 1863 to 1872, inclusive.

Year.	By railroad.	By river.	By canal.
	Barrels.		
1863	404, 570	Included in figures in the first column.	Included in figures in the first column.
1864	393, 268		
1865	436, 186		
1866	514, 450		
1867	412, 008		
1868	352, 896		
1869	387, 083		
1870	576, 677		
1871	538, 498		
1872	410, 501		

NOTE.—Figures for commercial years, ending August 31.

Corn received at Cincinnati by railroad, by Ohio River, and by canals—1863 *to* 1872, *inclusive.*

[Prepared for the United States Senate Committee on Transportation, by William T. Tibbetts, esq. secretary Cincinnati Chamber of Commerce.]

Year.	By railroad.	By river.	By canal.
	Bushels.		
1863	1, 504, 430	Included in figures in the first column.	Included in figures in the first column.
1864	1, 817, 046		
1865	1, 262, 198		
1866	1, 427, 766		
1867	1, 820, 955		
1868	1, 405, 366		
1869	1, 508, 509		
1870	1, 979, 645		
1871	2, 068, 900		
1872	1, 829, 866		

Corn shipped from Cincinnati by rail, by river, and by canal—1863 *to* 1872, *inclusive.*

Year.	By railroad.	By river.	By canal.
	Bushels.		
1863	265, 934	Included in figures in the first column.	Included in figures in the first column.
1864	445, 260		
1865	342, 753		
1866	305, 873		
1867	549, 942		
1868	278, 586		
1869	94, 392		
1870	192, 250		
1871	336, 314		
1872	123, 316		

NOTE.—Figures all for commercial years ending August 31.

Monthly average price of No. 2 *spring-wheat at Montreal*—1868 *to* 1872, *inclusive.*

[Compiled from reports of Board of Trade of Montreal. Prepared for the United States Senate Committee on Transportation, by William Patterson, esq., secretary of Board of Trade of Montreal, Canada.]

(GOLD VALUES.)

Months.	1868.	1869.	1870.	1871.	1872.
January	....	....	....	....	....
February	....	....	....	....	....
March	....	....	....	....	....
April	....	....	....	....	....
May	$1. 567	$0. 982	$0. 973	$1. 31	$1. 375
June	1. 491	1. 021	1. 133	1. 305	....
July	1. 432	1. 117	1. 185	1. 21	1. 305
August	1. 404	1. 165	1. 115	1. 177	1. 368
September	1. 275	1. 118	1. 05	1. 287	1. 425
October	1. 165	1. 002	1. 131	1. 334	1. 345
November	1. 143	. 985	1. 14	1. 30	1. 325
December	....	....	....	....	....

Monthly average price of western mixed corn at Montreal—1868 *to* 1872, *inclusive.*

[Compiled from the board of trade reports, Montreal. Prepared for the United States Senate Committee on Transportation, by William Patterson, esq., secretary of Board of Trade, Montreal, Canada.]

(GOLD VALUES.)

Months.	1868.	1869.	1870.	1871.	1872.
January	....	....	....	....	....
February	....	....	....	....	....
March	....	....	....	....	....
April	....	....	....	....	....
May	.795	.61	....	.665	.613
June	.74	....	.95	.625	.57
July	.77	.725	.95	.62	.53
August	.82	.89	.79	.597	.56
September	.84	.90	.725	.625	.58
October	.84	....	.74	.655	.56
November	.85	....	.737	.64	.53
December	.887	....	.81	.632	.565

Annual receipts of western wheat and corn at Kingston—1850 *to* 1872.

Prepared for the United States Senate Committee on Transportation, by William Patterson, esq., secretary of Board of Trade, Montreal, Canada.]

Year.	Wheat.	Corn.	Year.	Wheat.	Corn.
1850	145, 472	....	1862	5, 079, 417	1, 913, 010
1851	148, 364	31, 622	1863	3, 135, 055	653, 855
1852	28, 936	109, 906	1864	1, 813, 152	121, 978
1853	....	117, 537	1865	1, 686, 718	640, 041
1854	33, 301	253, 912	1866	274, 252	1, 442, 912
1855	372, 258	472, 924	1867	2, 064, 509	700, 692
1856	651, 882	679, 905	1868	1, 461, 272	999, 515
1857	1, 443, 919	380, 844	1869	5, 092, 071	171, 220
1858	1, 228, 468	169, 781	1870	4, 839, 591	165, 283
1859	347, 376	90, 688	1871	5, 546, 193	2, 766, 449
1860	1, 184, 062	218, 929	1872	2, 754, 148	6, 300, 959
1861	2, 850, 677	1, 013, 554			

Receipts of wheat-flour at Montreal, via Grand Trunk Railroad and via Lachine Canal, each month for ten years, 1863 *to* 1872, *inclusive.*

[Prepared for the United States Senate Committee on Transportation, by William Patterson, esq., secretary of the Board of Trade, Montreal, Canada.]

Year.	How received.	BARRELS.											
		January.	February.	March.	April.	May.	June.	July.	August.	September.	October.	November.	December.
1863	Via Grand Trunk Railroad	32, 191	29, 156	34, 453	27, 923	86, 924	41, 807	18, 043	29, 525	10, 332	37, 771	37, 525	49, 647
	Via Lachine Canal	....	....	....	....	224, 433	168, 186	67, 352	67, 619	36, 870	76, 681	78, 656	15, 385
1864	Via Grand Trunk Railroad	23, 259	40, 018	55, 833	23, 199	40, 593	22, 094	9, 271	24, 966	12, 520	52, 872	40, 741	25, 762
	Via Lachine Canal	....	....	....	....	115, 564	97, 227	39, 147	64, 885	38, 772	59, 566	41, 039	12, 668
1865	Via Grand Trunk Railroad	20, 960	21, 151	44, 594	37, 104	29, 353	26, 617	18, 040	10, 655	13, 656	52, 619	41, 923	40, 406
	Via Lachine Canal	....	....	....	....	88, 753	67, 964	65, 901	51, 883	26, 303	54, 100	72, 803	13, 633
1866	Via Grand Trunk Railroad	20, 114	19, 804	12, 408	36, 236	51, 157	18, 598	24, 233	13, 723	11, 726	52, 619	38, 249	49, 712
	Via Lachine Canal	....	....	....	....	77, 710	40, 970	42, 795	34, 431	23, 864	80, 340	73, 169	8, 849
1867	Via Grand Trunk Railroad	28, 394	38, 886	31, 528	40, 120	23, 568	26, 505	26, 359	17, 961	14, 688	46, 241	44, 789	39, 192
	Via Lachine Canal	....	....	....	....	56, 073	25, 518	37, 003	42, 181	28, 829	67, 787	52, 329	3, 216
1868	Via Grand Trunk Railroad	27, 691	22, 778	21, 937	63, 554	33, 952	29, 849	38, 145	21, 049	34, 472	37, 424	65, 776	55, 341
	Via Lachine Canal	....	....	....	700	70, 688	30, 697	27, 603	18, 816	51, 041	66, 084	65, 777	7, 688
1869	Via Grand Trunk Railroad	36, 134	29, 024	27, 392	27, 100	41, 923	52, 930	57, 821	43, 230	43, 232	49, 440	57, 696	81, 402
	Via Lachine Canal	....	....	....	....	68, 794	59, 497	56, 198	44, 119	53, 479	76, 882	71, 046	6, 790
1870	Via Grand Trunk Railroad	22, 366	28, 100	24, 828	38, 667	49, 867	54, 326	48, 578	62, 497	24, 022	34, 392	48, 778	38, 555
	Via Lachine Canal	....	....	....	....	99, 102	63, 284	59, 095	77, 129	59, 061	92, 267	94, 335	9, 815
1871	Via Grand Trunk Railroad	20, 863	27, 949	28, 534	45, 598	60, 444	37, 942	36, 096	40, 604	56, 234	72, 186	92, 151	39, 100
	Via Lachine Canal	....	....	....	....	109, 541	58, 272	40, 298	39, 060	36, 449	43, 464	61, 086	5, 842
1872	Via Grand Trunk Railroad	48, 489	30, 500	20, 200	25, 500	91, 290	58, 875	51, 367	31, 641	28, 515	98, 113	68, 401	48, 345
	Via Lachine Canal	....	....	....	....	67, 946	41, 545	30, 870	25, 755	30, 159	62, 932	50, 561	4, 881

Receipts of wheat at Montreal, via Grand Trunk Railroad and via Lachine Canal, each month for ten years—1863 to 1872, inclusive.

[Prepared for the United States Senate Committee on Transportation, by William Patterson, esq., secretary of the Board of Trade, Montreal, Canada.]

Year.	How received.	BUSHELS.											
		January.	February.	March.	April.	May.	June.	July.	August.	September.	October.	November.	December.
1863	Via Grand Trunk Railroad..	30, 422	66, 880	27, 004	1, 700	21, 360	32, 923	30, 615	20, 308	21, 800	98, 938	62, 193	58, 599
	Via Lachine Canal	....	....	....	....	1, 210, 470	1, 252, 308	634, 501	810, 096	190, 077	414, 783	439, 627	18, 237
1864	Via Grand Trunk Railroad..	30, 800	22, 311	39, 752	4, 900	26, 601	32, 375	20, 152	24, 130	16, 850	89, 808	47, 650	35, 700
	Via Lachine Canal	....	....	....	....	491, 105	1, 021, 663	670, 893	957, 820	413, 296	155, 919	58, 943	....
1865	Via Grand Trunk Railroad..	46, 315	16, 400	32, 860	36, 950	20, 107	8, 050	9, 420	21, 700	32, 200	50, 900	107, 644	64, 483
	Via Lachine Canal	....	....	....	....	277, 250	523, 939	461, 339	248, 285	79, 852	210, 563	354, 011	46, 406
1866	Via Grand Trunk Railroad..	25, 600	25, 200	3, 850	9, 450	18, 550	16, 950	21, 750	17, 900	14, 150	88, 870	52, 540	85, 240
	Via Lachine Canal	....	....	....	....	75, 998	92, 338	56, 582	81, 058	14, 491	132, 761	98, 643	18, 576
1867	Via Grand Trunk Railroad..	22, 470	20, 408	25, 200	21, 894	51, 250	21, 700	29, 400	12, 960	5, 950	94, 100	44, 300	40, 750
	Via Lachine Canal	....	....	....	....	67, 512	86, 100	65, 029	140, 270	409, 401	1, 015, 128	608, 474	49, 359
1868	Via Grand Trunk Railroad..	9, 450	2, 809	3, 898	11, 705	39, 200	44, 450	26, 590	29, 209	52, 985	56, 700	67, 960	28, 000
	Via Lachine Canal	....	....	....	....	144, 774	333, 014	143, 260	73, 073	315, 356	458, 821	389, 690	195, 925
1869	Via Grand Trunk Railroad..	11, 200	10, 500	12, 930	4, 049	42, 100	98, 567	29, 353	29, 433	25, 900	36, 084	44, 744	54, 246
	Via Lachine Canal	....	....	....	....	403, 870	1, 376, 485	642, 706	821, 488	1, 411, 292	1, 230, 375	961, 044	89, 980
1870	Via Grand Trunk Railroad..	9, 450	7, 700	2, 800	33, 250	74, 250	64, 050	28, 204	6, 590	350	2, 100	350	....
	Via Lachine Canal	....	....	....	....	1, 057, 060	1, 050, 526	625, 829	1, 295, 574	557, 546	665, 426	1, 001, 655	5, 794
1871	Via Grand Trunk Railroad..	....	2, 100	350	1, 750	700	20, 650	17, 910	31, 596	150, 250	257, 375	208, 810	30, 349
	Via Lachine Canal	....	....	....	....	1, 559, 937	1, 054, 412	409, 180	1, 015, 016	1, 146, 001	1, 204, 747	1, 113, 660	....
1872	Via Grand Trunk Railroad..	27, 300	21, 525	7, 000	3, 530	15, 650	32, 225	63, 014	2, 894	56, 976	238, 050	46, 900	13, 700
	Via Lachine Canal	....	....	....	....	312, 848	229, 089	410, 817	282, 372	784, 657	1, 413, 435	703, 332	....

Shipments of wheat from Montreal to Great Britain each month during the last five years—1868 *to* 1872, *inclusive—in sailing-ships.*

[Prepared for the United States Senate Committee on Transportation, by William Patterson, esq., secretary of the Board of Trade, Montreal, Canada.]

Year.	NUMBER OF BUSHELS.											
	January.	February.	March.	April.	May.	June.	July.	August.	September.	October.	November.	December.
1868	....	6, 631	....	....	65, 109	212, 503	138, 773	596	104, 906	239, 076	259, 624	17, 126
1869	29, 030	....	....	....	199, 244	940, 381	811, 119	449, 124	1, 128, 226	953, 968	976, 235	8, 782
1870	16, 809	25, 100	36, 779	....	531, 770	767, 505	909, 422	1, 154, 226	384, 554	454, 010	1, 204, 472	38, 088
1871	34, 397	41, 348	1, 947	30, 144	1, 114, 278	915, 145	682, 035	1, 032, 587	877, 427	1, 274, 573	1, 361, 362	126, 682
1872	42, 958	68, 744	18, 925	1, 600	80, 800	256, 514	379, 469	196, 579	520, 232	852, 293	999, 109	70, 875

Shipments of corn from Montreal to Great Britain each month during the last five years—1868 *to* 1872, *inclusive—in steamships.*

[Prepared for the United States Senate Committee on Transportation, by William Patterson, esq., secretary of the Board of Trade, Montreal, Canada.]

Year.	NUMBER OF BUSHELS.											
	January.	February.	March.	April.	May.	June.	July.	August.	September.	October.	November.	December.
1868	....	....	....	....	89, 515	205, 328	136, 829	169, 410	86, 201	25, 378	17, 761	....
1869	....	....	....	....	28, 183	23, 036	21, 971	....	....	5, 104	....	....
1870	....	....	....	....	308	....	....	....	....	....	....	....
1871	....	....	....	6, 033	297, 821	414, 250	257, 639	492, 971	409, 176	376, 085	545, 399	....
1872	....	....	....	....	616, 493	1, 459, 679	1, 644, 179	1, 236, 215	1, 083, 697	817, 836	587, 407	57, 378

No. 1.—*Average rates of freight on wheat and corn, by sail, from Montreal to Liverpool each month during the last five years,* 1868 *to* 1872, *inclusive.*

[Prepared for the United States Senate Committee on Transportation by William Patterson, esq., secretary of the Board of Trade of Montreal, Canada.]

Year.	Freight per 480 pounds.						
	May.	June.	July.	August.	September.	October.	November.
	s. d. *s. d.*	*s. d.* *s. d.*	*s. d.* *s. d.*	*s. d.* *s. d.*	*s. d.* *s. d.*	*s. d.* *s. d.*	*s. d.* *s. d.*
1868 ..	4 0 to 4 6	4 0 to 4 6	– — to – —	– — to – —	4 9 to – —	5 4½ to 5 9	5 3 to – —
1869 ..	3 4 to 3 9	5 6 to 6 6	– — to – —	6 0 to 6 6	7 2 to 8 0	7 0 to – —	7 0 to – —
1870 ..	5 6 to 5 10½	4 3 to 5 0	4 0 to 4 6	6 0 to – —	4 10½ to – —	4 6 to 5 3	4 6 to 5 3
1871 ..	4 9 to 5 9	5 8¼ to 6 7	5 8½ to 6 1	6 4 to 6 7½	7 0 to 7 6	6 9 to 7 3	7 0 to 7 6
1872 ..	4 2 to 4 6	4 11 to 5 9	6 0 to 6 4½	5 9 to 6 4½	6 7½ to 7 3	8 1½ to 9 0	7 0 to 8 0

No. 2.—*Average rates of freight on wheat and corn, by steam, from Montreal to Liverpool each month during the last five years,* 1868 *to* 1872, *inclusive.*

Year.	Freight per 480 pounds.						
	May.	June.	July.	August.	September.	October.	November.
	s. d. *s. d.*	*s. d.* *s. d.*	*s. d.* *s. d.*	*s. d.* *s. d.*	*s. d.* *s. d.*	*s. d.* *s. d.*	*s. d.* *s. d.*
1868 ..	6 10½ to – —	5 6 to 6 0	4 2½ to – —	4 0 to – —	– — to – —	6 5¼ to 6 9	6 6 to 7 6
1869 ..	4 4¼ to 5 0	5 1¼ to 5 5¼	5 7½ to 5 10	5 4½ to 6 3	7 4½ to – —	8 10 to – —	8 4 to – —
1870 ..	5 6 to 5 9	5 11 to 6 9	4 0 to 4 6	6 0 to – —	5 3 to 5 9	4 10½ to 6 0	6 3 to 6 9
1871 ..	5 6 to 6 3	6 9½ to 7 3	5 9 to 6 3	6 6 to 7 6	7 4½ to 7 9	8 4 to 8 9	8 4 to 8 9
1872 ..	4 6 to 4 9	5 0 to 5 6	5 10½ to 6 5	5 9 to 6 4½	6 7½ to 7 3	8 9 to 9 2	7 3 to 8 9

MEMORANDUM.—In explanation of the figures in these two tables, it is to be noted that ocean-rates of freight from Montreal are at so much in sterling shillings and pence (free of primage) per 480 pounds of wheat, or Indian corn, or pease. The averages inserted in No. 1 are those for these grains to Liverpool by sailing-ships, and those filled into No. 2 are averages to that port by steamships.

WM. J. PATTERSON.

MONTREAL, *September* 12, 1873.

Statement showing the rate of insurance on grain (wheat and corn) in first-class sailing-vessels and first-class iron steamers on the voyage from Montreal to Liverpool.

[Prepared for the United States Senate Committee on Transportation by Hon. Hugh McLennan, president Board of Trade of Montreal, Canada.]

Date.	Sailing-vessels.	Steam-vessels.
	Per cent.	*Per cent.*
April to May 10	2	1
May 11 to June	1½	⅞
June	1½	⅞
July	1½	⅞
August	1½	⅞
September 1 to 15	2	1
September 16 to 30	2½	1¼
October 1 to 15	3	1½
October 16 to 30	4	2
November 1 to 5	4½	2½
November 6 to 10	5½	2¾
November 11 to 15	6½	3
November 11 to 16	....	3
November 17 to 24	....	3½

The above rates are for the iron clippers and mail-steamers. Other vessels pay somewhat higher rates, according to description and class. All rates less 15 per cent. discount.

Monthly average prices of No. 2 Milwaukee spring-wheat in Liverpool and New York for the undermentioned years.

[Prepared for the United States Senate Committee on Transportation by Mr. E. H. Walker, statistician of the New York Produce Exchange.]

Month.	New York, per bushel, 60 pounds.			Liverpool, per cental, 100 pounds.		
	1870.	1871.	1872.	1870.	1871.	1872.
				s. d.	s. d.	s. d.
January	120	146	156 2-3	8 3	11 0	11 7
February	118	152½	158 3-4	7 8	11 4	11 7
March	114¾	159⅛	155 3-5	8 4	11 5	11 1
April	115½	156½	158 5-8	8 3	11 10	10 9
May	121	151⅝	172 2-3	8 7	11 8	11 7
June	129	151	168	9 1	11 1	12 0
July	127	143	151	9 10	10 11	11 4
August	136	135	159 1-4	9 3	10 10	11 3
September	120	150	158 1-4	8 4	11 0	12 6
October	119	153	157 1-4	8 9	11 7	11 11
November	132⅓	152	156 2-3	10 3	11 5	11 8
December	138	153	158	10 8	11 4	11 4
Average, year	124	150¼	159 1-4	8 11	11 3	11 7

Monthly average price of No. 1 Milwaukee spring-wheat in New York from 1862 to 1872, inclusive.

[Prepared for the United States Senate Committee on Transportation, by Mr. E. H. Walker, statistician of the New York Produce Exchange.]

Month.	1862.	1863.	1864.	1865.	1866.	1867.	1868.	1869.	1870.	1871.	1872.
January	$1 32	$1 45	$1 53½	$2 20	$1 76	$2 46	$2 49	$1 65	$1 22	$1 46½	$1 56½
February	1 34½	1 61½	1 59	2 16	1 71	2 35	2 50	1 68	1 22¾	1 53⅞	1 60¼
March	1 32½	1 52¼	1 64	1 87½	1 70	2 56	2 50	1 53⅞	1 20	1 59	1 58¾
April	1 26¾	1 52½	1 71	1 61	1 77	2 64	2 57	1 47½	1 17	1 58¾	1 62½
May	1 00	1 37½	1 61¼	1 38½	2 04	2 80	2 41	1 49⅞	1 25¾	1 53⅜	1 77½
June	99½	1 38½	1 87	1 39	2 25	2 41	2 22¾	1 49	1 36	1 52	1 74½
July	1 13	1 22½	2 42½	1 36½	2 19	2 41	1 99¾	1 56	1 41½	1 47	1 52¼
August	1 18	1 05	2 66½	1 42½	2 17	2 15	2 09⅜	1 68½	1 41¼	1 38	1 59¾
September	1 15	1 11	2 22½	1 60½	2 24	2 27	2 00	1 57¾	1 22¾	1 54	1 65½
October	1 24	1 34	1 90	1 76½	2 39	2 31	1 74	1 40¼	1 32	1 53	1 63
November	1 25	1 41	2 20	1 77	2 40	2 27	1 59	1 33½	1 32⅞	1 56	1 59½
December	1 30	1 42	2 29	1 73¼	2 30	2 34	1 66⅛	1 34	1 29½	1 56	1 64½

Monthly average price of Western mixed corn in New York from 1862 to 1872, inclusive.

[Prepared for the United States Senate Committee on Transportation, by Mr. E. H. Walker, statisticia of the New York Produce Exchange.]

Month.	1862.	1863.	1864.	1865.	1866.	1867.	1868.	1869.	1870.	1871.	1872.
January	$0 64¼	$0 85	$1 26¼	$1 88	$0 79	$1 10¾	$1 36	$1 02⅝	$1 05¼	$0 85½	$0 75
February	64	94½	1 27¼	1 87	76	1 16¼	1 25	95	1 03¾	86	73
March	59¼	91½	1 32½	1 81	82½	1 30¼	1 19	85	1 11⅜	78⅜	69
April	59¼	90	1 33	1 39	83½	1 35	1 14	86⅜	1 11¾	77⅔	73
May	51½	76¼	1 43¼	1 08½	88	1 15	1 07	80¾	1 07½	74	74
June	49½	75½	1 54	86	85¾	1 04	1 09	97¼	1 10	70½	65½
July	54	68	1 60¾	81½	82	1 10	1 20	1 14½	1 05	66⅔	62
August	58½	69	1 55½	89	84½	1 23	1 21	1 16¾	91¼	66⅜	62⅜
September	59¾	78	1 60¾	91½	1 01½	1 39	1 15	1 07	92½	71 1-6	64¼
October	59¼	98	1 54	90½	1 27½	1 35	1 15	1 09⅝	91	77¼	64 1-7
November	69	1 12	1 78	94	1 13	1 38	1 13½	1 12	76⅞	77¼	64⅛
December	76½	1 26	1 91¼	93	1 18	1 40	1 08¼	98	81⅞	78	65⅓

Monthly average price of Western mixed oats in New York from 1862 to 1872, inclusive.

[Prepared for the United States Senate Committee on Transportation, by Mr. E. H. Walker, statistician of the New York Produce Exchange.]

Month.	1862.	1863.	1864.	1865.	1866.	1867.	1868.	1869.	1870.	1871.	1872.
January	......	$0 71	$0 91¼	$1 06	$0 58¼	$0 64	$0 87½	$0 77½	$0 59⅞	$0 61⅞	$0 55
February	......	75¼	90	1 10½	56¾	60	84¾	76¼	56⅜	65⅞	53
March	......	83	89¼	1 02	53¼	63	84	70¾	56	69	53½
April	......	87	88	84½	57½	72	86	77⅓	60⅞	68	52⅓
May	$0 40	74¼	87¾	57¾	59	85	86½	81½	65¾	67 1-5	52⅓
June	43	78½	93	70	56	77½	84⅓	78⅜	64½	65⅜	50¼
July	46	76	99	64½	50	80½	84¼	81	62¾	63¾	43¼
August	53¼	57	96¾	62	44	84¾	82½	71¼	53	50	43
September	57¾	68	90	56¼	46	70½	82	65⅜	50⅞	59¾	42½
October	58¾	80	85¼	60	59	80	73½	63¼	53¼	52	43¾
November	64	85	96	60½	67	79	72¾	65	58⅝	52¾	46½
December	69	90	1 04	60½	63	85	78	64	60⅞	55⅛	49⅜

Monthly average rates of ocean-freights from New York to Liverpool, on flour, wheat, and corn for the year 1872.

[Prepared for the United States Senate Committee on Transportation, by Mr. E. H. Walker, statistician of the New York Produce Exchange.]

Month.	Flour, per barrel, 216 pounds.		Wheat, per bushel, 60 pounds.		Corn, per bushel, 56 pounds.	
	Steam.	Sail.	Steam.	Sail.	Steam.	Sail.
	s. d.	s. d.	s. d.	s. d.	s. d.	s. d.
January	1 7½	1 3	0 6½	0 6	0 6¼	0 5¾
February	1 7	1 4	0 6 7-18	0 5⅞	0 6	0 5½
March	1 6	1 3	0 5⅝	0 5½	0 5 2-7	0 5 1-5
April	1 9	1 6	0 4	0 5½	0 4 1-6	0 5
May	2 0	1 9	0 5 3-5	0 5	0 5 1-9	0 5 1-5
June	2 6	2 0	0 7¾	0 6¼	0 7½	0 7½
July	2 4	2 1½	0 9⅓	0 9	0 8 3-5	0 8⅛
August	3 0	2 8¾	0 9¼	0 9⅜	0 8⅓	0 8¼
September	3 6	3 1½	0 10¾	0 10¼	0 10	0 9½
October	3 9	3 6	0 10⅞	0 10⅜	0 9⅛	0 8⅝
November	3 0	3 6	0 9 1-5	0 9	0 8¼	0 7¾
December	3 0½	3 5¼	0 9⅓	0 9⅜	0 8⅛	0 7⅝
Average, year	2 8	2 6½	0 7 5-9	0 7½	0 7 1-6	0 6 11-12

Monthly average rates of ocean-freights from New York to Liverpool, on flour, wheat, and corn for the year 1871.

[Prepared for the United States Senate Committee on Transportation, by Mr. E. H. Walker, statistician, of the New York Produce Exchange.]

Months.	Flour, per barrel, 216 pounds.		Wheat, per bushel, 60 pounds.		Corn, per bushel, 56 pounds.	
	Steam.	Sail.	Steam.	Sail.	Steam.	Sail.
	s. d.	s. d.	s. d.	s. d-	s. d.	s. d.
January	3 0	2 6¾	0 7	0 5 1-8	0 7	0 5½
February	2 8	2 5 13-16	0 7½	0 6 ⅝	0 7 1-5	0 5½
March	2 2¾	2 1	0 6 1-7	0 6	0 6	0 6
April	2 0	2 3½	0 7⅝	0 7	0 8	0 7 1-6
May	2 5¾	2 7	0 7 1-5	0 7¾	0 7½	0 7
June	1 9	1 11	0 8¼	0 7 1-10	0 8	0 7 3-5
July	1 10½	1 8¼	0 8½	0 7¾	0 8 1-5	0 7⅓
August	2 9¾	2 7	0 10	0 9	0 9 1-7	0 8 3-5
September	3 4⅓	3 0	0 11½	0 11	0 10 10-13	0 8 4-5
October	2 4⅓	2 3	0 11	0 10 1-6	0 11	0 9
November	3 0 1-7	2 9 4-5	0 8 7-24	0 7⅞	0 7 4-5	0 6⅓
December	3 0¾	2 9	0 7⅓	0 6½	0 6½	0 6 7-12
Average, year	2 6 9-14	2 5	0 8 3-8	0 7 3-5	0 8 1-11	0 7 1-11

Grain received at Montreal and at Buffalo—1845 *to* 1872.

Year.	Received at Montreal.	Received at Buffalo.	Year.	Received at Montreal.	Received at Buffalo.
	Bushels.	*Bushels.*		*Bushels.*	*Bushels.*
1845	2, 577, 639	5, 581, 790	1859	3, 389, 017	21, 530, 722
1846	3, 063, 130	13, 366, 167	1860	5, 423, 354	37, 053, 115
1847	3, 388, 791	19, 153, 187	1861	14, 487, 734	61, 460, 601
1848	3, 004, 401	14, 641, 012	1862	16, 824, 864	72, 872, 454
1849	2, 616, 122	14, 665, 188	1863	12, 452, 897	64, 735, 510
1850	2, 577, 639	12, 059, 559	1864	8, 822, 029	51, 177, 146
1851	2, 870, 289	17, 740, 781	1865	7, 584, 449	51, 415, 188
1852	3, 389, 088	20, 390, 504	1866	8, 819, 364	58, 388, 087
1853	3, 667, 360	15, 956, 526	1867	7, 876, 819	50, 700, 060
1854	3, 396, 666	22, 252, 235	1868	7, 551, 911	49, 949, 856
1855	3, 272, 740	24, 472, 278	1869	12, 143, 166	45, 007, 163
1856	4, 499, 067	25, 753, 967	1870	11, 580, 613	46, 613, 096
1857	4, 612, 727	19, 578, 695	1871	15, 884, 687	67, 155, 742
1858	5, 027, 786	26, 812, 980	1872	16, 811, 382	62, 260, 332

Statement showing the exports of wheat, wheat-flour, and corn from Montreal and from New York—1860 to 1872, inclusive.

Years.	WHEAT.		WHEAT-FLOUR.		CORN.		TOTAL.		Total.
	Exported from New York.	Exported from Montreal.	From New York.	From Montreal.	From New York.	From Montreal.	Wheat, wheat-flour, and corn exported from New York and from Montreal.		
							New York.	Montreal.	
	Bushels.	*Bushels.*	*Bushels.*	*Bushels.*	*Bushels.*	*Bushels.*	*Bushels.*	*Bushels.*	*Bushels.*
1860	1, 880, 908	1, 645, 209	5, 342, 400	1, 249, 051	1, 580, 019	24, 387	8, 803, 327	2, 918, 647	11, 721, 974
1861	21, 320, 775	5, 584, 727	11, 994, 736	2, 726, 739	6, 874, 372	1, 447, 114	40, 189, 883	9, 758, 580	49, 948, 463
1862	28, 164, 879	6, 500, 796	14, 663, 101	2, 688, 646	14, 115, 962	1, 774, 546	56, 943, 942	10, 963, 988	67, 907, 930
1863	25, 956, 155	3, 741, 146	12, 721, 405	2, 772, 094	10, 889, 962	638, 281	49, 567, 522	7, 151, 521	56, 719, 043
1864	17, 294, 391	2, 406, 531	10, 081, 179	3, 861, 319	2, 642, 588	21, 974	30, 018, 158	6, 289, 824	36, 307, 982
1865	5, 518, 937	787, 938	7, 292, 803	2, 866, 504	1, 052, 407	734, 849	13, 864, 147	4, 389, 291	18, 253, 438
1866	....	83, 278	....	2, 588, 391	....	1, 870, 223	....	4, 541, 892	4, 541, 892
1867	424, 425	1, 576, 528	2, 799, 994	2, 560, 594	11, 015, 828	681, 708	14, 240, 247	4, 818, 830	19, 059, 077
1868	7, 208, 373	1, 081, 958	5, 001, 516	3, 076, 254	7, 369, 647	782, 497	19, 579, 536	4, 940, 709	24, 520, 245
1869	8, 379, 924	5, 595, 332	5, 150, 142	4, 347, 301	3, 694, 386	108, 018	17, 224, 452	10, 050, 651	27, 275, 103
1870	20, 077, 434	5, 973, 048	8, 532, 018	4, 389, 808	401, 939	6, 043	29, 011, 391	10, 368, 899	39, 380, 290
1871	18, 090, 794	7, 680, 834	9, 188, 514	4, 089, 798	4, 662, 238	2, 870, 998	31, 941, 546	14, 641, 630	46, 583, 176
1872	17, 889, 037	3, 818, 450	5, 121, 157	3, 748, 189	18, 331, 147	7, 546, 390	41, 341, 341	15, 113, 029	56, 454, 370

Statement showing the quantities of wheat and corn received at New York and Montreal each year, from 1862 to 1872, inclusive, the total for this period, and the total for the first four and for the last four years of this period.

Year.	Wheat.		Wheat-flour.		Corn.		Total.	
	Received at New York.	Received at Montreal.	Received at New York.	Received at Montreal.	Received at New York.	Received at Montreal.	Received at New York.	Received at Montreal.
	Bushels.	*Bushels.*	*Bushels.*	*Bushels.*	*Bushels.*	*Bushels.*	*Bushels.*	*Bushels.*
1862	27, 069, 259	8, 534, 172	23, 656, 536	5, 285, 709	17, 290, 114	2, 661, 261	68, 015, 909	16, 481, 142
1863	17, 901, 208	5, 599, 143	20, 328, 102	5, 369, 787	13, 993, 075	862, 534	52, 222, 385	11, 741, 464
1864	13, 281, 068	4, 194, 217	17, 802, 279	3, 864, 577	7, 281, 880	158, 564	38, 365, 227	8, 217, 358
1865	8, 674, 829	2, 648, 674	16, 139, 470	3, 519, 972	14, 701, 967	934, 421	39, 516, 266	7, 103, 067
Four years' total	66, 926, 364	20, 866, 206	77, 926, 387	18, 040, 045	53, 267, 036	4, 616, 780	198, 119, 787	43, 543, 031
1866	5, 766, 664	773, 208	12, 247, 456	3, 169, 692	22, 218, 519	2, 117, 208		
1867	9, 706, 894	2, 939, 295	12, 726, 320	3, 323, 331	15, 024, 221	891, 605		
1868	12, 950, 068	2, 426, 869	12, 851, 937	3, 556, 399	18, 995, 072	1, 086, 152		
1869	23, 952, 250	7, 462, 033	15, 918, 925	4, 388, 827	10, 691, 749	141, 982	50, 562, 924	11, 992, 842
1870	23, 913, 748	6, 508, 315	18, 544, 234	4, 775, 728	9, 230, 340	83, 656	51, 688, 322	11, 367, 799
1871	26, 763, 967	8, 224, 805	16, 092, 306	4, 282, 920	26, 849, 916	3, 171, 757	69, 706, 189	15, 679, 482
1872	16, 221, 907	4, 665, 314	13, 672, 638	4, 148, 878	40, 757, 115	7, 656, 440	70, 651, 660	16, 470, 632
Four years' total	90, 851, 872	26, 860, 467	64, 228, 103	17, 596, 353	87, 529, 120	11, 053, 835	242, 609, 095	55, 510, 755
Total	186, 201, 772	53, 886, 045	179, 980, 203	45, 685, 820	197, 033, 968	19, 765, 580	682, 553, 388	

Wheat (including wheat-flour) exported from the United States in the years 1830, 1840, 1850, *and* 1860 *to* 1873, *inclusive.*

Year.	COUNTRIES TO WHICH EXPORTED.									
	Great Britain and Ireland.	Canada and other British possessions in North America.	West Indies and Central American States.	Brazil.	China.	France.	Belgium.	Portugal.	All other countries.	Total.
	Bushels.	*Bushels.*	*Bushels.*	*Bushels.*	*Bushels.*	*Bushels.*	*Bushels.*	*Bushels.*	*Bushels.*	*Bushels.*
1830	1, 499, 856	686, 452	754, 880	885, 312	567	254, 655			1, 487, 030	5, 568, 752
1840	3, 410, 104	3, 012, 206	2, 019, 840	890, 991	4, 500	332, 762	225		588, 982	10, 259, 610
1850	1, 980, 892	1, 375, 253	1, 549, 866	1, 316, 088	14, 202		9		606, 867	6, 843, 177
1860	3, 765, 017	4, 899, 810	2, 209, 640	2, 259, 558	177, 941	28, 599	17, 943	74, 194	2, 534, 633	15, 907, 335
1861	35, 441, 987	7, 106, 293	2, 142, 197	1, 640, 754	196, 136	1, 789, 196	235, 364	25, 764	2, 117, 268	50, 694, 959
1862	32, 983, 012	7, 812, 330	2, 425, 628	1, 679, 859	109, 920	10, 180, 160	1, 336, 101	343, 405	2, 388, 355	59, 258, 770
1863	35, 400, 971	10, 924, 143	2, 828, 429	1, 839, 690	469, 981	500, 060	680, 712	839, 547	2, 432, 128	55, 915, 661
1864	22, 487, 892	8, 013, 480	3, 191, 936	1, 835, 883	526, 315	363, 114	150, 256	153, 586	2, 967, 311	39, 689, 773
1865	7, 623, 579	6, 628, 949	3, 107, 501	1, 650, 780	160, 452	42, 340	140, 659	159, 447	2, 143, 884	21, 657, 591
1866	2, 582, 806	5, 484, 029	2, 174, 472	1, 332, 648	798, 669	360	247	83, 906	2, 945, 691	15, 402, 828
1867	5, 208, 960	2, 097, 790	1, 588, 872	751, 285	656, 230	41, 436	4, 518	4, 800	1, 642, 997	11, 996, 888
1868	14, 549, 623	4, 711, 906	2, 408, 703	1, 114, 402	336, 668	314, 799	70, 239	216, 120	1, 562, 342	25, 284, 802
1869	15, 198, 420	5, 645, 332	2, 931, 741	1, 738, 814	621, 907	37, 544	20, 334	150, 265	2, 156, 897	28, 501, 264
1870	33, 137, 888	8, 654, 303	3, 435, 344	1, 692, 976	826, 764	1, 166, 856	264, 112	763, 376	2, 217, 494	52, 159, 113
1871	28, 012, 329	12, 340, 967	3, 754, 029	2, 050, 528	372, 670	769, 107	1, 214, 347	514, 146	1, 718, 976	50, 747, 090
1872	20, 495, 859	6, 096, 938	3, 773, 858	1, 719, 972	688, 309	1, 430, 799	1, 294, 635	447, 800	1, 790, 317	37, 738, 487
1873										
Total										

NOTE.—Canada—exports less imports.
This table includes flour, which is reduced to wheat, upon the basis of $4\frac{1}{2}$ bushels to the barrel.

Statement showing the number of bushels of corn (including corn-meal) exported from the United States, 1850 to 1873.

Year.	COUNTRIES TO WHICH EXPORTED.						
	Great Britain and Ireland.	Canada and other British possessions in North America.	West Indies and Central America.	Germany.	France.	All other countries.	Total.
1850	23, 831, 504	270, 727	1, 656, 508	....	....	1, 659, 397	27, 418, 136
1860	1, 945, 129	1, 247, 701	795, 557	115, 774	20	378, 519	4, 482, 700
1861	8, 138, 866	2, 178, 576	878, 699	28, 730	21, 060	245, 565	11, 491, 496
1862	14, 485, 515	3, 648, 163	1, 100, 205	43, 784	277, 745	363, 777	19, 919, 189
1863	10, 793, 027	4, 719, 689	955, 937	45, 761	73	636, 781	17, 151, 268
1864	2, 253, 125	1, 500, 563	946, 967	4, 729	30	440, 708	5, 146, 122
1865	765, 205	1, 668, 462	886, 128	12, 318	....	178, 289	3, 610, 402
1866	9, 910, 880	3, 181, 684	1, 034, 877	39, 761	....	98, 549	14, 365, 751
1867	12, 205, 784	2, 726, 138	827, 046	22, 720	....	245, 259	16, 026, 947
1868	8, 712, 236	2, 654, 442	874, 287	44, 201	35, 426	172, 930	12, 493, 522
1869	4, 274, 807	2, 673, 016	915, 460	120, 451	54, 889	21, 564	8, 060, 187
1870	66, 352	888, 626	968, 611	42, 570	237	174, 091	2, 140, 487
1871	5, 910, 325	3, 247, 881	1, 110, 493	113, 728	77, 771	213, 355	10, 673, 553
1872	25, 786, 359	7, 913, 582	834, 094	737, 014	161, 520	294, 421	35, 726, 990
1873	....	....	....	....	....	....	....

Statement showing the number of bushels of wheat, wheat-flour, (reduced to bushels,) and corn exported to foreign countries from Portland, Boston, New York, Philadelphia, Baltimore, and New Orleans, 1856 to 1873, inclusive.

Year.	PORTS.					
	Portland, Me.	Boston.	New York.	Philadelphia.	Baltimore.	New Orleans.
1856	38, 782	840, 972	16, 492, 538	2, 441, 178	3, 530, 783	5, 170, 238
1857	16, 612	956, 197	21, 011, 750	2, 845, 474	3, 987, 607	4, 315, 844
1858	29, 630	734, 150	10, 706, 395	1, 810, 558	3, 218, 459	3, 867, 666
1859	16, 667	684, 941	6, 263, 722	999, 027	1, 791, 848	862, 847
1860	28, 939	794, 800	8, 803, 327	1, 202, 651	1, 874, 815	589, 005
1861	939, 624	1, 247, 355	40, 189, 883	4, 207, 207	4, 111, 310	167, 630
1862	388, 506	2, 257, 460	56, 943, 942	5, 334, 523	2, 736, 347	....
1863	52, 788	1, 666, 514	49, 567, 522	3, 631, 859	2, 566 964	169, 521
1864	44, 815	1, 380, 663	30, 018, 158	1, 863, 970	1, 663, 219	184, 598
1865	427, 410	1, 122, 132	13, 864, 147	1, 306, 435	1, 302, 750	138, 751
1866	....	....	....	....	....	....
1867	20, 314	506, 051	14, 240, 247	1, 222, 829	1, 407, 678	150, 666
1868	70, 002	844, 472	19, 579, 536	1, 104, 736	1, 741, 369	807, 559
1869	37, 473	838, 163	17, 224, 452	552, 222	1, 735, 791	1, 391, 194
1870	72, 096	802, 945	29, 011, 391	1, 710, 202	2, 517, 794	1, 717, 183
1871	141, 696	1, 232, 515	31. 941, 546	1, 571, 478	3, 477, 532	1, 255, 612
1872	94, 149	2, 282, 955	41, 341, 341	4, 435, 885	6, 572, 375	1, 195, 558
1873	39, 594	1, 896, 217	41, 432, 766	3, 893, 167	7, 520, 930	1, 189, 484

Total value of certain articles imported into Great Britain, and value of the same imported from the United States, for the year 1871.

[Compiled from the British reports of trade and navigation.]

Articles.	Total value imported.		Value imported from the United States.		Per cent. from U. S.
	Pounds.	Dollars.	Pounds.	Dollars.	
Cereals:					
Wheat	26, 816, 891	129, 793, 752	9, 514, 207	46, 048, 762	35. 4
Corn	6, 482, 807	31, 376, 786	2, 837, 992	13, 735, 881	43. 7
Oats	4, 170, 518	20, 185, 307	....	....	....
Rye	68, 333	330, 732	3, 040	14, 714	4. 4
Barley	3, 400, 048	16, 456, 232	30, 413	147, 198	. 8
Total cereals	40, 938, 597	198, 142, 809	12, 385, 652	59, 946, 555	33. 6
Provisions:					
Beef	635, 353	3, 075, 108	515, 986	2, 497, 372	81. 2
Pork	693, 096	3, 354, 585	361, 297	1, 748, 677	52. 1
Hams	196, 185	949, 535	99, 346	480, 835	50. 0
Bacon	2, 529, 724	12, 243, 864	1, 820, 512	8, 811, 278	71. 9
Butter	6, 939, 040	33, 584, 954	394, 359	1, 908, 698	5. 6
Cheese	3, 341, 496	16, 172, 841	2, 014, 805	9, 751, 656	60. 3
Lard	1, 310, 012	6, 340, 458	1, 203, 866	5, 826, 711	92. 0
Total of these provisions	15, 644, 906	75, 721, 345	6, 410, 171	31, 025, 227	40. 9
Cotton	55, 907, 070	270, 590, 219	33, 090, 939	160, 160, 145	59. 1
Tallow	3, 134, 531	15, 171, 130	551, 827	2, 670, 843	17. 6
Wool	17, 470, 471	84, 557, 080	....	....	....
Tobacco	2, 462, 670	11, 919, 323	1, 624, 665	7, 863, 378	65. 9
Seeds of all kinds	8, 742, 962	42, 315, 936	553, 738	2, 680, 092	63. 3
Petroleum	614, 017	2, 971, 841	597, 438	2, 891, 560	97. 2
Total	88, 331, 721	427, 525, 529	36, 418, 607	176, 266, 058	51. 3

Exports of wheat, flour, corn, rye, oats, and barley from various ports of the United States to foreign ports—1856 *to* 1872, *inclusive.*

Ports.	WHEAT, BUSHELS.										
	1856.	1857.	1858.	1859.	1860.	1861.	1862.	1863.	1864.	1865.	1867.
New York	5, 057, 569	9, 588, 506	4, 960, 152	1, 390, 828	1, 880, 908	21, 320, 775	28, 164, 879	25, 956, 155	17, 294, 391	5, 518, 937	424, 425
Boston	17, 994	3, 652	2, 336	....	2, 760	16, 970	5, 989	1, 483	....	897	860
Philadelphia	359, 473	597, 942	167, 164	29, 904	127, 740	1, 627, 845	2, 210, 776	1, 501, 632	447, 003	202, 404	30, 954
Baltimore	274, 937	989, 087	249, 031	62, 649	15, 045	1, 097, 416	531, 137	411, 856	66, 583	2, 766	....
New Orleans	1, 066, 773	1, 353, 480	596, 442	107, 031	2, 189	3	....	....	1, 050	....	....
San Francisco	33, 088	35, 932	6, 564	9	948, 220	2, 379, 617	1, 539, 835	1, 777, 213	1, 793, 196	46, 141	4, 883, 232
All others	1, 315, 043	2, 001, 732	2, 944, 507	1, 411, 595	1, 178, 291	4, 795, 431	4, 826, 956	7, 512, 075	4, 079, 489	4, 166, 007	806, 940
Total	8, 154, 877	14, 570, 331	8, 926, 196	3, 002, 016	4, 155, 153	31, 238, 057	37, 289, 572	36, 160, 414	23, 681, 712	9, 937, 152	6, 146, 411

Ports.	WHEAT, BUSHELS.					FLOUR, BARRELS.					
	1868.	1869.	1870.	1871.	1872.	1856.	1857.	1858.	1859.	1860.	1861.
New York	7, 208, 373	8, 379, 924	20, 077, 434	18, 090, 794	17, 889, 037	1, 649, 471	1, 735, 981	1, 314, 869	965, 623	1, 187, 200	2, 665, 497
Boston	1, 397	....	....	81, 914	134, 581	175, 503	204, 807	154, 901	150, 531	174, 450	268, 518
Philadelphia	79, 764	43, 099	988, 390	383, 686	1, 168, 102	314, 846	296, 674	233, 651	191, 879	178, 688	404, 813
Baltimore	10, 769	8, 348	820, 931	263, 743	906, 353	587, 993	541, 427	551, 088	345, 891	363, 493	444, 026
New Orleans	31, 830	168, 833	398, 862	12, 510	....	251, 501	428, 436	474, 906	133, 193	80, 541	21, 767
San Francisco	....	5, 530, 624	7, 939, 030	5, 993, 427	2, 263, 085	114, 572	43, 122	6, 683	22, 580	57, 820	186, 455
All others	8, 608, 766	3, 427, 008	9, 359, 468	9, 568, 832	4, 061, 922	1, 416, 740	461, 606	776, 071	622, 127	569, 404	332, 680
Total	15, 940, 899	17, 557, 836	36, 584, 115	34, 304, 906	26, 423, 080	3, 510, 626	3, 712, 053	3, 512, 169	2, 431, 824	2, 611, 596	4, 323, 756

Exports of wheat, flour, corn, rye, oats, and barley from various ports of the United States to foreign ports, &c.—Continued.

Ports.	FLOUR, BARRELS.										CORN, BUSHELS.
	1862.	1863.	1864.	1865.	1867.	1868.	1869.	1870.	1871.	1872.	1856.
New York	3, 258, 467	2, 826, 979	2, 240, 262	1, 620, 623	622, 221	1, 111, 448	1, 144, 476	1, 806, 004	2, 041, 892	1, 138, 035	4, 012, 350
Boston	486, 841	361, 704	300, 436	247, 423	108, 605	181, 718	182, 117	176, 964	220, 027	155, 604	33, 215
Philadelphia	521, 466	380, 005	296, 489	225, 582	58, 872	72, 530	82, 409	146, 929	140, 156	125, 642	664, 898
Baltimore	337, 291	371, 690	338, 667	260, 525	141, 781	247, 166	246, 662	350, 540	489, 216	356, 251	609, 878
New Orleans	....	....	27, 649	19, 302	29, 542	67, 695	167, 363	264, 337	163, 146	89, 911	2, 941, 711
San Francisco	93, 762	149, 989	168, 710	42, 149	283, 873	277, 642	390, 519	340, 736	198, 223	267, 083	....
All others	184, 206	1, 299, 688	185, 134	188, 938	55, 212	118, 224	218, 327	287, 823	301, 181	382, 009	2, 030, 828
Total	4, 882, 033	4, 390, 055	3, 557, 347	2, 604, 542	1, 300, 106	2, 076, 423	2, 431, 873	3, 463, 333	3, 653, 841	2, 514. 535	10, 292, 880

Ports.	CORN, BUSHELS.										
	1857.	1858.	1859.	1860.	1861.	1862.	1863.	1864.	1865.	1867.	1868.
New York	3, 611, 330	1, 829, 333	527, 591	1, 580, 019	6, 874, 372	14, 115, 962	10, 889, 962	2, 642, 588	1, 052, 407	11, 015, 828	7, 369, 647
Boston	30, 914	34, 760	7, 552	7, 015	22, 054	60, 687	37, 363	28, 701	7, 832	16, 469	25, 344
Philadelphia	912, 499	591, 965	105, 668	270, 815	757, 704	777, 150	420, 205	82, 767	88, 912	926, 951	698, 587
Baltimore	562, 099	489, 532	167, 690	224. 052	1, 015, 777	687, 401	482, 533	72, 635	127, 622	769, 664	618, 353
New Orleans	1, 034, 402	1, 134, 147	111, 522	224, 382	69, 679	....	73, 604	59, 128	51, 892	17, 727	471, 102
San Francisco	....	....	60	85	50	100	150	40	....	1, 774	333
All others	1, 354, 074	686, 408	799, 915	1, 027, 787	1, 938, 608	3, 263, 598	4, 215, 659	1, 210, 835	1, 484, 061	2, 141, 410	1, 964, 124
Total	7, 505, 318	4, 766, 145	1, 719, 998	3, 314, 155	10, 678, 244	18, 904, 898	16, 119, 476	4, 096, 694	2, 812, 726	14, 889, 823	11, 147, 490

Exports of wheat, flour, corn, rye, oats, and barley from various ports of the United States to foreign ports, &c.—Continued.

Ports.	CORN, BUSHELS.				RYE, BUSHELS.								OATS, BUSHELS.
	1869.	1870.	1871.	1872.	1864.	1865.	1867.	1868.	1869.	1870.	1871.	1872.	1864.
New York	3, 694, 386	401, 939	4, 662, 238	18, 331, 147	120, 176	2, 145	99, 075	481, 713	47, 028	157, 000	37, 400	763, 397	63, 269
Boston	18, 637	6, 607	160, 480	1, 448, 156			38		40	40	45		2, 897
Philadelphia	138, 283	60, 632	557, 090	2, 702, 394	24			16, 198	530				1, 046
Baltimore	617, 464	119, 433	1, 012, 320	4, 062, 893		255		30					2, 942
New Orleans	469, 228	128, 805	508, 945	790, 959									5, 980
San Francisco	271	550	900	1, 168		70		167	86	36			124, 343
All others	2, 108, 928	674, 149	2, 924, 336	7, 154, 933	34, 760	129, 989	48, 240	3, 241	1, 817	530	12, 229	31, 570	105, 278
Total	7, 047, 197	1, 392, 115	9, 826, 309	34, 491, 650	154, 960	132, 459	147, 353	501, 349	49, 501	157, 606	49, 674	794, 967	305, 755

Ports.	OATS, BUSHELS.							BARLEY, BUSHELS.						
	1865.	1867.	1868.	1869.	1870.	1871.	1872.	1864.	1865.	1868.	1869.	1870.	1871.	1872.
New York	75, 955	505, 806	47, 355	94, 214	29, 005	40, 728	45, 782	4, 645	65			100	52, 160	39, 352
Boston	2, 331	4, 373	3, 396	4, 776	1, 325	3, 039	2, 117					30		
Philadelphia	449	20, 992	12, 293	7, 302	3, 985	4, 119	17, 212	469						6
Baltimore	13, 467	5, 553	16, 266	6, 194	2, 687	2, 059	6, 798	6	5		3, 280		2	
New Orleans	2, 070	15, 342	21, 512	22, 610	27, 364	34, 300	33, 875	9	44				33	
San Francisco	8, 777	266, 323	10, 891	51, 523	37, 023	42, 296	36, 437	56, 063	29, 062	8, 631	54, 472	253, 882	287, 619	33, 010
All others	215, 068	7, 506	10, 841	295, 252	20, 128	21, 031	120, 754	5, 290	15, 062	1, 179	1, 325	1, 378	279	14, 523
Total	318, 117	325, 895	122, 554	481, 871	121, 517	147, 572	262, 975	66, 482	44, 248	9, 810	59, 077	255, 490	340, 093	86, 891

Average price of mixed corn at the port of London each month during the last five years, from 1867 to 1871, inclusive.

[Furnished to the United States Senate Committee on Transportation by Hon. Adam Badeau, United States consul at London.]

Year.	Price per four hundred and eighty pounds each month.											
	January.	February.	March.	April.	May.	June.	July.	August.	September.	October.	November.	December.
	s. d.	*s. d.*	*s. d.*	*s. d.*	*s. d.*	*s. d.*	*s. d.*	*s. d.*	*s. d.*	*s. d.*	*s. d.*	*s. d.*
1867	38 3	37 10½	37 11	40 10½	41 7½	39 6	36 10½	36 6	37 6	43 4½	45 8	46 7
1868	(*)	(*)	(*)	(*)	......	......	......	......	......	......	......	......
1869	(*)	(*)	(*)	(*)	......	......	......	......	......	......	......	......
1870	(*)	(*)	(*)	(*)	......	......	......	......	......	......	......	......
1871	(†)	(†)	......	......	......	......	......	......	......	......	......	......

* Not recorded this year. † No arrivals.

Average price of American spring-wheat at the port of London each month during the last five years, from 1867 to 1872, inclusive.

[Furnished to the United States Senate Committee on Transportation by Hon. Adam Badeau, United States consul at London.]

Year.	Price per four hundred and ninety-six pounds each month.											
	January.	February.	March.	April.	May.	June.	July.	August.	September.	October.	November.	December.
	s. d.	*s. d.*	*s. d.*	*s. d.*	*s. d.*	*s. d.*	*s. d.*	*s. d.*	*s. d.*	*s. d.*	*s. d.*	*s. d.*
Spring, 1867	63 6	62 7½	61 6	62 3	62 7½	62 6	62 6	62 9½	63 0	69 9	70 1	69 9
Spring, 1868	71 3	71 3½	71 3	71 4½	69 0	63 3	58 6	52 3½	53 4	51 2	48 5	48 4½
No. 1 spring, 1869	50 0	50 0	48 4½	45 6	44 6	46 10	47 10	49 7½	48 7½	46 9½	43 9	42 1
No. 2 spring, 1870	42 0½	39 8	40 4½	40 8	42 6	46 3	49 3	48 10½	45 4½	45 4	49 3	50 3
No. 2 spring, 1871	51 11	52 6	55 0	56 1½	57 0	57 7	54 2	52 8	54 3	56 0	56 10½	56 11
No. 2 spring, 1872	57 0	58 4	57 6	57 0	58 6	58 6	57 10	58 0	58 6	59 2½	59 0	58 10

Liverpool imports of breadstuffs for the past ten years.

[Prepared for the United States Senate Committee on Transportation Routes, by John Bingham & Co., merchants, Liverpool.]

Year.	Wheat.	Barley.	Oats.	Beans.	Pease.	Indian corn.	Flour.	
	Quarters, (of 480 pounds.)	Quarters, (of 400 pounds.)	Quarters, (of 320 pounds.)	Quarters, (of 480 pounds.)	Quarters, (of 504 pounds.)	Quarters, (of 480 pounds.)	Sacks, (of 280 pounds.)	Barrels, (of 196 pounds.)
1863	1, 473, 869	48, 405	192, 487	176, 787	46, 049	808, 718	253, 483	835, 869
1864	1, 483, 495	38, 743	217, 268	57, 198	36, 747	421, 500	385, 937	576, 161
1865	626, 437	64, 900	230, 561	59, 592	50, 097	500, 906	552, 443	113, 389
1866	542, 040	127, 648	276, 743	125, 107	64, 207	1, 086, 101	536, 293	85, 517
1867	1, 831, 985	82, 027	171, 767	207, 267	139, 966	928, 527	392, 665	124, 262
1868	1, 920, 147	81, 821	174, 957	337, 781	53, 039	1, 012, 153	137, 307	213, 941
1869	2, 599, 851	63, 067	180, 392	178, 011	19, 266	988, 428	356, 286	533, 678
1870	2, 209, 155	21, 223	115, 847	188, 803	70, 085	924, 922	252, 663	378, 613
1871	2, 567, 233	64, 428	197, 231	338, 584	54, 086	1, 227, 423	265, 540	351, 235
1872	2, 496, 390	32, 778	165, 774	193, 093	84, 063	1, 598, 477	432, 011	182, 789

Board of trade return of foreign grain and flour imported into the United Kingdom from January 1, 1863, *to December* 31, 1872.

[Prepared for the United States Senate Committee on Transportation Routes.]

Year.	Wheat.	Flour of wheat.	Total wheat and flour of wheat.	Barley.	Oats.	Beans.	Pease.	Maize.
	Cwts.	*Cwts.*	*Cwts.*	*Quarters.*	*Quarters.*	*Quarters.*	*Quarters.*	*Quarters.*
1863	24, 364, 171	5, 218, 977	29, 583, 148	2, 078, 717	2, 376, 473	488, 436	299, 154	2, 964, 765
1864	23, 196, 714	4, 512, 391	27, 709, 105	1, 388, 119	2, 039, 708	212, 665	249, 731	1, 473, 118
1865	20, 962, 963	3, 904, 471	24, 867, 434	2, 195, 738	2, 766, 672	223, 150	170, 534	1, 644, 577
1866	23, 156, 329	4, 972, 280	28, 128, 602	2, 361, 481	3, 216, 213	308, 973	269, 296	3, 342, 001
1867	34, 645, 569	3, 592, 969	38, 238, 538	1, 591, 442	3, 420, 778	462, 611	352, 473	1, 992, 767
1868	32, 639, 768	3, 093, 022	35, 732, 790	2, 124, 007	3, 001, 907	628, 576	259, 663	2, 657, 698
1869	37, 695, 828	5, 401, 555	43, 097, 383	1, 789, 702	1, 759, 304	421, 604	234, 308	3, 925, 358
1870	31, 026, 142	4, 815, 488	35, 841, 630	2, 106, 889	4, 170, 894	379, 688	437, 548	4, 134, 144
1871	39, 407, 646	3, 984, 638	43, 392, 284	2, 383, 895	3, 947, 391	694, 173	228, 813	3, 878, 521
1872	41, 990, 228	4, 396, 059	46, 386, 287	4, 221, 879	4, 048, 470	685, 420	286, 683	5, 964, 778

Prices of American wheat, flour, and Indian

[Prepared for the United States Senate Committee on Trans

	January.		February.		March.		April.		May.	
1863.	*s. d.*	*s. d.*	*s. d.*	*s. d.*	*s. d.*	*s. d.*	*s. d.*	*s. d.*	*s. d.*	*s. d.*
Wheat, spring.....per 100 lbs.	9 0 to	9 3	8 6 to	9 3	8 9 to	9 0	9 0 to	9 3	8 10 to	9 0
Californian.....do....	11 4	12 0	10 10	12 0	10 10	11 6	10 6	11 6	10 3	11 0
Indian corn.......per 480 lbs.	29 9	30 0	29 0	29 6	28 6	28 9	29 6	30 0	29 9	30 0
Flour.................per bbl.	23 0	24 6	23 0	24 6	20 0	22 0	21 6	22 6	21 6	22 6
1864.										
Wheat, spring.....per 100 lbs.	8 0	8 3	8 0	8 4	7 10	8 1	7 6	7 9	7 6	7 8
Californian.....do....	9 9	10 3	10 0	10 6	9 9	10 2	9 0	9 6	8 9	9 6
Indian corn.......per 480 lbs.	30 0	30 3	29 0	29 3	28 0	—	27 6	28 0	27 9	28 0
Flour.................per bbl.	21 0	22 0	21 0	22 0	20 6	21 0	19 0	19 9	18 9	19 6
1865.										
Wheat, spring.....per 100 lbs.	7 10	8 0	7 7	7 10	8 0	8 3	8 2	8 5	8 5	8 6
Californian.....do....	9 0	9 6	8 10	9 4	8 9	9 3	9 0	9 6	9 3	9 8
Indian corn.......per 480 lbs.	27 6	28 0	27 0	27 6	28 0	28 3	30 0	30 3	29 0	29 3
Flour.................per bbl.	20 6	21 6	20 6	22 0	20 6	21 0	20 6	21 9	21 0	22 0
1866.										
Wheat, spring.....per 100 lbs.	9 3	10 0	9 3	9 10	9 0	9 8	9 2	9 9	9 6	10 0
Californian.....do....	11 0	11 4	11 0	11 4	11 0	11 4	11 0	11 4	11 0	11 4
Indian corn.......per 480 lbs.	29 0	—	28 6	28 9	29 0	29 3	28 9	29 0	30 0	30 3
Flour.................per bbl.	25 6	26 6	25 0	26 0	22 0	24 0	21 0	24 0	22 0	25 6
1867.										
Wheat, spring.....per 100 lbs.	11 3	13 0	11 0	12 6	11 0	12 6	12 0	13 0	—	—
Californian.....do....	13 4	14 0	13 0	13 9	13 0	13 6	13 9	14 3	13 6	14 0
Indian corn.......per 480 lbs	41 6	—	37 0	—	44 0	—	40 0	44 3	39 9	—
Flour.................per bbl.	—	—	—	—	—	—	—	—	—	—
1868.										
Wheat, spring.....per 100 lbs.	14 9	15 0	14 10	15 5	14 9	15 0	14 10	15 6	13 6	13 9
Californian.....do...	15 10	16 6	15 10	16 8	15 10	16 6	15 9	16 4	14 3	15 4
Indian corn.......per 480 lbs	45 3	45 6	42 6	—	42 3	—	38 3	38 6	38 6	39 0
Flour.................per bbl	32 0	37 0	32 0	38 0	32 0	38 0	32 0	37 0	31 0	34 6
1869.										
Wheat, spring.....per 100 lbs.	10 3	10 6	9 10	10 2	9 4	9 6	8 8	8 9	9 0	9 2
Californian.....do....	11 6	12 3	10 6	11 0	9 10	10 6	9 0	9 6	9 6	10 3
Indian corn.......per 480 lbs	34 3	34 6	31 0	—	30 6	30 9	26 6	27 0	27 6	—
Flour.................per bbl.	25 6	27 6	24 0	26 0	22 6	24 6	21 0	22 6	21 0	22 6
1870.										
Wheat, spring.....per 100 lbs.	8 4	8 6	7 11	8 4	8 5	8 9	8 2	8 8	8 10	9 0
Californian.....do....	9 0	9 9	8 11	9 6	9 2	10 0	9 0	9 10	9 6	11 0
Indian corn.......per 480 lbs	27 9	—	26 9	27 0	28 3	28 6	39 3	—	29 9	30 0
Flour.................per bbl	20 0	21 0	19 6	26 0	19 0	20 6	18 6	20 0	20 0	22 0
1871.										
Wheat, spring.....per 100 lbs.	11 2	11 4	11 0	11 3	11 2	11 3	11 3	11 5	11 1	11 2
Californian.....do....	12 0	12 7	11 9	12 6	11 10	12 6	12 2	12 9	12 2	12 8
Indian corn.......per 480 lbs.	—	—	36 0	36 3	34 3	34 6	33 0	—	33 0	33 3
Flour.................per bbl.	27 0	28 0	26 0	27 6	26 6	28 0	26 6	28 0	26 6	28 0
1872.										
Wheat, spring.....per 100 lbs.	11 4	11 10	11 6	11 8	11 0	11 2	11 4	11 6	12 0	12 3
Californian.....do....	12 6	13 6	12 3	13 3	11 9	12 8	12 0	12 10	12 10	13 9
Indian corn.......per 480 lbs.	30 0	30 3	28 0	28 6	28 6	—	29 0	—	28 6	28 9
Flour.................per bbl.	26 6	29 0	26 0	28 6	26 0	28 6	27 6	30 0	29 0	31 6

corn in Liverpool for the past ten years.

portation Routes by John Bingham & Co., merchants, Liverpool.]

June.		July.		August.		September.		October.		November.		December.	
s. d.	s. d.	s. d.	s. d.	s. d.	s. d.	s. d.	s. d.	s. d.	s. d.	s. d.	s. d.	s. d.	s. d.
8 6 to	8 9	8 3 to	8 6	7 6 to	7 9	6 9 to	7 3	7 0 to	7 6	7 6 to	7 9	8 0 to	8 3
10 3	11 0	10 0	11 0	10 0	10 6	9 6	10 0	9 6	10 0	9 9	10 3	9 9	10 3
27 0	—	27 0	27 3	26 6	26 9	26 9	27 0	28 3	28 6	29 0	29 3	30 0	—
20 6	21 6	20 6	21 0	20 0	21 0	18 0	20 0	18 0	20 0	18 0	20 6	20 0	21 0
8 0	8 3	8 0	8 3	7 9	8 0	7 2	7 4	7 0	7 4	7 4	7 7	7 8	8 0
9 3	9 9	9 6	10 6	9 6	10 0	8 9	9 6	8 6	9 0	9 0	9 6	9 0	9 6
29 0	29 3	29 9	30 0	30 0	30 3	27 6	27 9	27 3	27 6	28 0	28 6	28 3	28 6
20 6	21 0	21 0	21 6	20 6	21 0	19 0	20 6	19 6	20 0	19 6	21 0	20 0	21 6
8 3	8 6	8 0	8 2	9 2	9 4	9 0	9 3	9 8	9 10	9 11	10 3	9 0	10 0
9 3	9 8	9 3	9 6	10 0	11 0	10 0	10 9	10 9	11 3	11 0	11 6	11 0	11 6
28 0	28 6	31 0	31 6	30 3	30 6	29 3	29 6	28 9	29 0	29 6	29 9	29 6	29 9
21 0	22 0	21 0	22 6	23 0	24 0	22 6	23 6	—	—	—	—	27 0	28 0
10 9	11 3	10 0	10 6	9 0	10 3	11 2	11 8	11 0	12 3	11 3	12 6	11 0	12 3
11 9	12 0	11 6	12 0	10 9	11 6	12 3	12 6	13 3	14 6	13 6	15 0	13 6	14 6
29 3	29 6	26 6	26 9	26 0	26 3	28 9	29 0	33 6	33 9	39 9	40 0	38 0	-
—	—	—	—	—	—	26 6	29 0	28 0	30 0	—	—	—	—
—	—	—	—	10 9	11 3	—	—	13 9	14 1	13 2	13 10	14 0	14 2
12 9	13 9	13 0	13 6	12 9	13 0	13 6	14 2	16 0	16 6	15 0	16 0	15 3	16 0
38 9	39 0	35 0	35 3	35 6	35 9	42 0	—	50 0	—	49 0	—	47 0	—
—	—	—	—	—	—	—	—	—	—	33 0	35 0	32 6	36 0
12 9	13 0	11 4	11 8	11 3	11 9	11 8	11 9	10 6	11 4	10 1	10 6	10 4	10 8
13 0	13 9	11 10	12 9	12 9	13 6	12 6	13 6	12 3	13 0	11 9	12 6	11 6	12 0
35 0	—	35 3	35 6	34 9	35 0	36 3	36 6	38 0	—	39 3	39 6	38 3	38 6
31 0	33 0	28 6	30 6	27 6	29 6	27 6	29 6	26 6	28 6	25 0	27 0	25 0	27 0
9 2	9 6	9 5	9 9	9 8	9 10	9 8	9 9	9 4	9 6	8 9	9 0	9 0	—
10 0	10 9	10 6	11 0	10 6	11 6	10 6	11 3	10 4	10 10	9 4	10 0	9 8	10 3
—	—	—	—	—	—	—	—	—	—	—	—	—	—
22 0	24 0	22 6	24 6	24 0	26 0	23 0	25 0	23 6	24 6	21 6	22 6	21 0	22 0
9 3	9 5	10 4	10 6	9 3	9 6	9 2	9 4	10 0	10 4	10 2	10 4	10 4	10 6
10 0	10 10	11 0	12 0	10 0	10 9	9 8	10 6	10 9	11 6	11 0	11 9	11 6	12 0
31 6	31 9	35 0	—	29 9	—	29 3	29 6	30 0	30 3	31 0	31 3	32 0	32 3
22 6	24 0	26 0	27 0	24 6	26 0	22 0	23 6	23 0	25 0	23 6	25 6	25 6	26 6
10 9	10 11	10 3	10 5	10 6	10 8	11 2	11 5	11 5	11 8	11 3	11 7	11 3	11 6
11 9	12 4	11 5	11 11	12 2	12 3	12 10	13 8	13 2	14 0	12 10	13 9	12 9	13 6
31 0	31 6	31 3	—	29 9	30 0	32 6	—	33 6	33 9	32 6	33 0	31 6	31 9
26 0	28 0	—	—	26 0	27 0	26 0	28 0	26 6	29 0	26 0	29 0	26 0	28 6
12 0	12 6	11 1	11 4	11 11	12 1	12 6	13 0	11 10	12 4	11 8	12 3	12 0	12 4
12 6	13 3	11 9	12 7	12 0	13 0	13 3	14 3	12 8	13 10	12 6	13 6	12 6	13 6
27 0	—	27 9	—	28 0	28 3	29 9	30 0	28 6	—	29 3	—	29 0	29 3
29 0	31 0	26 6	28 6	28 0	30 6	29 0	32 6	30 0	34 0	30 0	34 0	30 0	34 0

The following tables were prepared by Messrs. Richardson, Spence & Co., merchants, of Liverpool, having been obtained for the use of the Senate Committee on Transportation by Hon. Lucius Fairchild, United States consul at Liverpool:

Receipts of American wheat at the port of Liverpool each month for five years, 1868 to 1872, inclusive.

Year.	QUARTERS.											
	January.	February.	March.	April.	May.	June.	July.	August.	September.	October.	November.	December.
1868	12, 102	13, 964	25, 882	23, 704	58, 889	54, 376	31, 228	11, 653	11, 060	69, 850	48, 641	47, 514
1869	31, 091	45, 278	67, 095	39, 005	37, 327	64, 768	149, 442	114, 863	161, 272	200, 419	167, 981	135, 122
1870	69, 780	38, 067	40, 799	79, 635	98, 259	67, 173	100, 664	72, 376	124, 260	110, 365	75, 640	137, 349
1871	97, 127	73, 842	34, 097	57, 071	75, 492	106, 051	144, 098	69, 117	176, 329	196, 127	124, 385	122, 761
1872	42, 726	50, 375	91, 147	34, 488	76, 173	40, 040	85, 821	91, 287	88, 688	113, 147	152, 044	89, 840

Receipts of corn from United States (Atlantic ports) at the port of Liverpool each month for five years, 1868 to 1872, inclusive.

Year.	QUARTERS.											
	January.	February.	March.	April.	May.	June.	July.	August.	September.	October.	November.	December.
1868	59, 309	58, 509	45, 176	51, 484	53, 751	54, 503	44, 634	54, 678	34, 217	19, 866	9, 428	14, 316
1869	37, 835	66, 490	16, 704	33, 645	20, 494	10, 476	14, 070	618	203	341		6
1870					4	1			145	2	244	2, 686
1871	12, 812	10, 208	46, 338	48, 218	51, 672	118, 012	78, 541	49, 765	83, 376	85, 626	63, 374	89, 074
1872	72, 881	48, 616	102, 047	51, 999	111, 268	123, 482	110, 559	159, 980	97, 767	84, 322	90, 574	72, 520

Average price of American No. 2 spring-wheat at the port of Liverpool each month during the last five years, 1868 to 1872, inclusive.

Year.	Price, per cental of 100 pounds, each month.											
	January.	February.	March.	April.	May.	June.	July.	August.	September.	October.	November.	December.
	s. d.	s. d.	s. d.	s. d.	s. d.	s. d.	s. d.	s. d.	s. d.	s. d.	s. d.	s. d.
1868	14 4	14 3	14 2	14 5	13 9	12 4	11 0	10 9	10 11	10 2	9 9	9 9
1869	9 11	9 9	9 0	8 7	8 8	8 9	9 3	9 10	9 9	9 2	8 7	8 0
1870	7 10	7 6	8 0	7 11	8 2	8 11	9 2	9 2	8 5	8 10	9 7	9 10
1871	10 2	10 7	10 10	10 10	10 10	10 8	10 1	10 0	10 9	11 3	11 0	10 11
1872	11 0	....	....	10 10	11 5	11 10	10 11	11 3	12 3	11 8	11 4	11 3

Average price of American mixed corn at the port of Liverpool each month during the last five years, 1868 to 1872, inclusive.

Year.	Price, per quarter of 480 pounds, each month.											
	January.	February.	March.	April.	May.	June.	July.	August.	September.	October.	November.	December.
	s. d.	s. d.	s. d.	s. d.	s. d.	s. d.	s. d.	s. d.	s. d.	s. d.	s. d.	s. d.
1868	45 9	42 9	41 2	39 10	38 3	34 6	34 4	35 0	36 1	37 7½	38 9	38 7
1869	34 11	31 3	29 7	28 1	27 1	27 1½	30 0	....	....	....	....	....
1870	....	....	....	....	....	....	....	....	....	....	....	....
1871	32 6	36 0	35 1	33 2	34 0	31 4	30 10	30 4	32 0	33 5	33 3	32 1
1872	31 0	29 7	28 1	27 11	28 6	27 3	26 7	27 5	29 2	29 6	28 9	28 7

Average freight and charges for the transportation of wheat from the countries here mentioned to Liverpool during the years 1863 *to* 1872, *inclusive.*

[Furnished to the United States Senate Committee on Transportation by Hon. Lucius Fairchild, United States consul at Liverpool.]

Countries.	Freight per quarter of 480 pounds.	Freight per quarter of 480 pounds.	Freight per quarter of 480 pounds.	Freight per quarter of 480 pounds.	Freight per quarter of 480 pounds.	Freight per quarter of 480 pounds.	Freight per quarter of 480 pounds.	Freight per quarter of 480 pounds.	Freight per quarter of 480 pounds.	Freight per quarter of 480 pounds.
	1863.	1864.	1865.	1866.	1867.	1868.	1869.	1870.	1871.	1872.
RUSSIA.	*s. d.* *s. d.*	*s. d.* *s. d.*	*s. d.* *s. d.*	*s. d.* *s. d.*	*s. d.* *s. d.*	*s. d.* *s. d.*	*s. d.* *s. d.*	*s. d.* *s. d.*	*s. d.* *s. d.*	*s. d.* *s. d.*
Baltic ports	3 0 to 3 6	3 0 to 3 6	3 0 to 3 6	3 0 to 3 6	3 0 to 3 6	3 0 to 3 6	3 0 to 3 6	3 0 to 3 6	3 0 to 3 6	3 0 to 3 6
Black Sea, Sea of Azof, and other ports	6 6 to 7 3	6 6 to 7 3	6 6 to 7 3	6 6 to 7 3	6 6 to 7 3	6 6 to 7 3	6 6 to 7 3	6 6 to 7 3	6 6 to 7 3	6 6 to 7 3
UNITED STATES. (*a*)										
Atlantic ports	5 6 5 6	6 0 6 0	7 0 7 0	6 0 6 0	6 6 6 6	6 6 to 6 9 6 6 to 6 9	7 0 to 7 6 7 0 to 7 3	6 6 6 6 to 7 0	6 6 to 7 0 6 6	8 0 to 8 3 8 0
San Francisco	*55 0	*60 0	*62 6	*65 0	*60 0	*62 6	*65 0	*55 0	*60 0	*80 0 to 82 6
TURKEY AND THE ARCHIPELAGO	5 0 to 5 6	5 0 to 5 6	5 0 to 5 6	5 0 to 5 6	5 0 to 5 6	5 0 to 5 6	5 0 to 5 6	5 0 to 5 6	5 0 to 5 6	5 0 to 5 6
Coast to Syria and Cyprus	5 0 to 6 0	5 0 to 6 0	5 0 to 6 0	5 0 to 6 0	5 0 to 6 0	5 0 to 6 0	5 0 to 6 0	5 0 to 6 0	5 0 to 6 0	5 0 to 6 0
Molana and Wallachia	8 0	8 6	8 6 to 9 0	7 6 to 8 0	10 0	8 6	8 0	8 6	8 3 to 8 6	9 0
BRITISH NORTH AMERICA	6 6 to 7 0	7 0 to 7 6	7 3 to 7 6	7 0	6 9 to 7 6	7 0	7 3 to 8 0	8 3	7 6 to 8 0	8 0
EGYPT.										
Alexandria and Port Said	4 0 to 4 6	4 6 to 4 9	4 9 to 5 3	5 0 to 5 6	5 0 to 5 3	4 6 to 5 0	4 6	4 3 to 4 6	4 6 to 5 0	5 0
CHILI.										
All ports	*70 0	*65 0	*60 0	*70 0	*67 6	*80 0	*45 0	*40 0 to 42 6	*60 0	*62 6 to 65 0
AUSTRALIA	*50 0 to 52 6	*60 0	*62 6	*65 0 to 70 0	*67 6	*75 0 to 80 0	*45 0	*40 0	*57 6 to 60 0	*80 0 to 82 6
AUSTRIAN PORTS.										
Gulf of Venice and Adriatic Sea	5 6 to 5 9	5 6 to 5 9	5 6 to 5 9	5 6 to 5 9	5 6 to 5 3	5 6 to 5 9	5 6 to 5 9	5 6 to 5 9	5 6 to 5 9	5 6 to 5 9
Prussian ports	3 3 to 3 9	3 3 to 3 9	3 3 to 3 9	3 3 to 3 9	3 3 to 3 3	3 3 to 3 9	3 3 to 3 9	3 3 to 3 9	3 3 to 3 9	3 3 to 3 9
And Germany	1 6 to 2 3	1 6 to 2 3	1 6 to 2 3	1 6 to 2 3	1 6 to 2 3	1 6 to 2 3	1 6 to 2 3	1 6 to 2 3	1 6 to 2 3	1 6 to 2 3

(*a*) In 1872 and 1873 freights ranged very high, say £5 to £6 per ton.

* Per ton.

Average freight charges for the transportation of Indian corn from the countries here mentioned to Liverpool during the years 1863 to 1872, inclusive.

[Furnished to the United States Senate Committee on Transportation by Hon. Lucius Fairchild, United States consul at Liverpool.]

Countries.	Freight per quarter of 480 pounds.	Freight per quarter of 480 pounds.	Freight per quarter of 480 pounds.	Freight per quarter of 480 pounds.	Freight per quarter of 480 pounds.	Freight per quarter of 480 pounds.	Freight per quarter of 480 pounds.	Freight per quarter of 480 pounds.	Freight per quarter of 480 pounds.	Freight per quarter of 480 pounds.
	1863.	1864.	1865.	1866.	1867.	1868.	1869.	1870.	1871.	1872.
RUSSIA.										
Northern ports.	*s. d.* *s. d.*	*s. d.* *s, d.*	*s. d.* *s. d.*	*s. d.* *s. d.*	*s. d.* *s. d.*	*s. d.* *s. d.*	*s. d.* *s. d.*	*s. d.* *s. d.*	*s. d.* *s. d.*	*s. d.* *s. d.*
Baltic, Finland, Gulf of Bothnia, and White Sea	3 3 to 3 6	3 3 to 3 6	3 3 to 3 6	3 3 to 3 6	3 3 to 3 6	3 3 to 3 6	3 3 to 3 6	3 3 to 3 6	3 3 to 3 6	3 3 to 3 6
Southern ports.										
Black Sea, Sea of Azoff, and other ports	6 6 to 7 3	6 6 to 7 3	6 6 to 7 3	6 6 to 7 3	6 6 to 7 3	6 6 to 7 3	6 6 to 7 3	6 6 to 7 3	6 6 to 7 3	6 6 to 7 3
TURKEY.										
Moldavia and Wallachia	8 0	8 6	8 6 to 9 0	7 0 to 8 0	10 0	8 6	8 0	8 0	8 6	9 0
British North America	6 6 to 7 0	7 0 to 7 6	7 3 to 7 6	7 0	6 9 to 7 6	7 3 to 8 0	8 3	7 6 to 8 0	7 6 to 8 0	8 0
United States	5 6	6 0	7 0	6 0	6 6	6 9	7 0 to 7 6	6 6 to 7 0	6 6	8 0
Atlantic	5 6	6 0	7 0	6 0	6 6	6 9	7 0 to 7 6	6 6 to 7 0	6 6	8 0
Pacific*	....	....	....	....	....	....	....	....	....	....

*No Indian corn comes from the Pacific.

Statement showing the quantity and value of corn and corn-meal imported into the United Kingdom (England, Ireland, and Scotland) from 1853 to 1871, with the quantity and value of the same imported from the United States. (Values stated in gold.)

[Compiled from the British reports of trade and navigation.]

Year.	Corn imported.					Average price of corn imported.	
	Total.		From the United States.			Total.	From United States.
	Bushels.	*Dollars.*	*Bushels.*	*Dollars.*	*Pr. cent.*	*Dollars.*	*Dollars.*
1860	14, 828, 329	15, 340, 525	3, 456, 890	3, 482, 278	23. 4	1. 03	1. 07
1861	24, 740, 439	23, 639, 237	13, 801, 870	13, 069, 467	55. 8	. 94	. 94
1862	22, 001, 912	18, 512, 612	12, 274, 414	10, 221, 344	55. 8	. 84	. 83
1863	23, 780, 433	19, 587, 010	8, 496, 321	6, 911, 482	35. 8	. 82	. 81
1864	12, 235, 068	9, 581, 873	556, 296	481, 048	4. 5	. 81	. 86
1865	13, 259, 418	10, 827, 631	3, 310, 259	2, 765, 794	25. 0	. 81	. 83
1866	26, 758, 870	21, 952, 003	13, 001, 279	10, 613, 496	48. 6	. 82	. 81
1867	15, 956, 227	18, 581, 026	8, 951, 350	10, 483, 813	56. 1	1. 16	1. 17
1868	22, 959, 230	23, 436, 194	8, 0[illegible]1, 416	8, 432, 234	34. 9	1. 02	1. 04
1869	35, 340, 304	28, 742, 301	2, 721, 354	2, [illegible]6, 945	8. 0	. 80	. 80
1870	33, 525, 048	28, 039, 242	57, 462	52, 557	. 1	. 83	. 90
1871	33, 669, 440	31, 376, 785	14, 652, 730	13, 735, 881	43. 5	. 93	. 93
1872	49, 065, 340	42, 294, 323	33, 961, 366	29, 512, 427	69. 2	. 862	. 869

Statement showing the quantity and value of wheat and wheat-flour imported into Great Britain from 1860 to 1872, with the quantity and value of the same imported from the United States. (Values stated in gold.)

[Compiled from the British reports of trade and navigation.]

Year.	Wheat and wheat-flour imported.					Average price of wheat imported.	
	Total.		From the United States.			Total.	From United States.
	Bushels.	*Dollars.*	*Bushels.*	*Dollars.*	*Pr. cent.*	*Dollars.*	*Dollars.*
1860	58, 915, 534	98, 978, 097	17, 254, 953	30, 023, 618	29. 2	1. 68	1. 74
1861	69, 659, 375	115, 634, 562	28, 916, 637	48, 579, 950	41. 5	1. 66	1. 68
1862	92, 570, 775	137, 014, 747	40, 287, 083	61, 236, 366	43. 5	1. 48	1. 52
1863	57, 157, 618	73, 733, 327	21, 977, 249	28, 790, 196	38. 4	1. 29	1. 31
1864	53, 829, 443	59, 212, 387	18, 811, 204	22, 761, 556	34. 9	1. 10	1. 21
1865	48, 241, 295	57, 889, 554	2, 797, 347	3, 468, 710	5. 8	1. 20	1. 24
1866	54, 827, 133	79, 539, 342	1, 840, 960	2, 816, 668	3. 3	1. 45	1. 53
1867	73, 055, 321	136, 613, 450	9, 504, 567	19, 104, 179	13. 0	1. 87	2. 01
1868	68, 144, 617	119, 253, 079	12, 606, 326	23, 952, 019	18. 5	1. 75	1. 90
1869	82, 969, 172	111, 178, 690	28, 597, 813	40, 036, 938	34. 4	1. 34	1. 40
1870	68, 891, 418	93, 689, 128	28, 106, 889	38, 506, 369	40. 8	1. 36	1. 37
1871	82, 709, 501	126, 545, 536	29, 167, 285	45, 500, 964	35. 2	1. 53	1. 56
1872	88, 877, 406	140, 202, 816	17, 984, 117	30, 393, 157	22. 4	1. 619	1. 697

Average price per bushel, in gold, of corn imported into the United Kingdom from each country from 1860 to 1872, inclusive.

[Compiled from the reports of trade and navigation of Great Britain.]

Country whence imported.	1860.	1861.	1862.	1863.	1864.	1865.	1866.	1867.	1868.	1869.	1870.	1871.	1872.
United States	$1 07	$0 94	$0 83	$0 81	$0 86	$0 83	$0 81	$1 17	$1 04	$0 80	$0 90	$0 93	$0.869
Germany	......	......	......	......	......	......	......	......	1 02	71	......	......	......
Turkey	1 06	96	86	83	80	81	81	1 15	99	80	83	92	.859
Russia	1 04	99	86	83	81	79	80	1 23	99	80	83	92	.888
British North America	......	94	83	79	1 17	84	88	1 08	95	80	90	93	.826
Wallachia and Moldavia	1 03	96	86	82	82	82	81	1 07	97	80	85	91	.841
Austria	......	95	......	85	76	77	79	......	......	......	......	91	.847
Morocco	1 10	94	83	79	......	83	86	1 19	......	......	......	93	.878
France	1 06	97	......	83	84	80	83	1 15	1 19	80	80	99	......
Egypt	90	93	80	81	......	......	......	1 16	1 04	80	70	1 14	.87
Italy	1 02	......	......	......	......	......	......	......	1 04	80	80	......	......
Denmark	......	......	......	......	......	......	......	......	......	......	......	......	......
Holland	......	......	......	......	......	......	......	......	......	......	......	......	......
Australia	......	......	......	......	......	......	......	......	......	......	......	......	......
Chili	......	......	......	......	......	......	......	......	......	......	......	......	......
Portugal	......	1 06	......	......	......	......	......	1 28	1 24	......	......	......	......
Azores	......	1 10	......	......	......	......	......	1 20	......	......	......	......	......
All other countries.	1 04	......	81	83	85	81	90	1 11	1 13	80	80	1 03	.952
Total average.	1 03	94	84	82	81	81	82	1 16	1 02	80	83	93	.862

Average price per bushel, in gold, of wheat imported into the United Kingdom from each country from 1860 to 1872, inclusive.

[Compiled from the British annual reports of trade and navigation.]

Countries whence imported.	1860.	1861.	1862.	1863.	1864.	1865.	1866.	1867.	1868.	1869.	1870.	1871.	1872.
United States	$1 74	$1 68	$1 52	$1 31	$1 21	$1 24	$1 53	$2 01	$1 90	$1 40	$1 37	$1 56	$1.697
Russia	1 55	1 69	1 42	1 17	1 09	1 13	1 39	1 80	1 63	1 27	1 29	1 48	1.548
Germany	1 76	1 81	1 66	1 48	1 29	1 31	1 61	2 00	1 88	1 45	1 50	1 71	1.774
Turkey	1 58	1 66	1 27	1 17	1 09	1 10	1 33	1 68	1 70	1 23	1 21	1 35	1.423
British North America	1 69	1 47	1 45	1 24	1 11	1 16	......	2 02	1 70	1 32	1 40	1 56	1.725
Wallachia and Moldavia	1 33	1 39	1 67	1 12	1 10	98	1 34	1 74	1 59	1 22	1 16	1 38	1.415
Austria	......	1 68	1 53	1 38	......	1 16	1 32	......	......	......	1 72	......	1.617
France	1 76	1 79	1 52	1 34	1 21	1 21	1 33	1 78	1 62	1 36	1 43	1 33	1.696
Egypt	1 35	1 20	1 04	1 01	1 08	......	1 61	......	1 51	1 22	1 11	1 44	1.317
Italy	1 64	1 64	......	......	......	......	1 32	1 86	1 96	......	......	......	1.781
Denmark	1 56	1 70	1 29	1 29	1 12	1 13	1 41	1 79	1 63	1 30	1 30	1 52	1.763
Holland	1 61	1 72	......	......	......	......	......	......	......	......	......	......	......
Australia	......	......	1 34	......	......	......	......	2 12	2 10	1 58	1 70	1 70	1.774
Chili	......	1 78	1 64	......	1 23	1 20	1 77	1 90	1 97	1 52	1 56	1 67	1.702
Portugal	......	......	......	......	......	......	......	......	......	......	......	......	1.637
Spain	1 98	1 97	......	......	......	1 27	1 53	1 95	......	......	......	......	1.765
Sweden	1 52	1 70	......	......	......	......	......	......	......	1 28	1 31	......	......
Belgium	......	......	......	......	......	......	1 35	......	......	......	1 50	......	......
India	......	......	......	......	......	......	......	......	1 27	......	......	1 43	1.486
Syria and Palestine	......	......	......	......	......	......	......	......	......	......	1 05	......	......
Italy and Greece	......	......	......	......	......	......	......	......	......	......	1 16	......	......
All other countries,	1 65	1 64	......	1 39	1 12	1 19	1 40	1 84	1 61	1 32	1 23	1 62	1.692
Total average..	1 68	1 66	1 48	1 29	1 10	1 20	1 45	1 87	1 75	1 34	1 36	1 53	1.619

Wheat (including wheat-flour) imported into the United Kingdom from 1860 to 1872, inclusive.

[Compiled from the reports of trade and navigation of Great Britain.]

Countries whence imported.	1860.	1861.	1862.	1863.	1864.	1865.	1866.	1867.	1868.	1869.	1870.	1871.	1872.
	Bushels.	*Bushels.*	*Bushels.*	*Bushels.*	*Bushels.*	*Bushels.*	*Bushels.*	*Bushels.*	*Bushels.*	*Bushels.*	*Bushels.*	*Bushels.*	*Bushels.*
United States	17, 254, 953	28, 916, 637	40, 287, 083	21, 977, 249	18, 811, 204	2, 797, 347	1, 840, 960	9, 504, 567	12, 606, 326	28, 597, 813	28, 106, 839	29, 167, 285	17, 984, 117
Russia	10, 449, 623	8, 382, 993	10, 617, 264	8, 371, 024	9, 555, 903	15, 108, 574	17, 138, 674	26, 444, 683	18, 766, 752	17, 149, 507	19, 276, 776	29, 287, 898	33, 486, 089
British North America	2, 430, 243	6, 275, 315	9, 478, 328	5, 926, 995	3, 419, 521	986, 451	94, 850	1, 558, 677	1, 490, 542	6, 340, 153	6, 351, 685	7, 061, 181	4, 026, 716
Germany	12, 420, 946	11, 557, 842	14, 140, 393	10, 115, 521	12, 680, 854	13, 374, 847	12, 557, 936	14, 508, 529	13, 428, 698	14, 016, 968	8, 332, 879	7, 949, 815	9, 676, 055
Egypt	1, 578, 120	2, 718, 488	6, 072, 288	4, 282, 320	684, 820			2, 709, 978	6, 043, 108	1, 904, 539	195, 906	1, 674, 616	4, 368, 423
Turkey	532, 790	759, 208	2, 243, 672	521, 824	644, 409	720, 798	722, 870	4, 874, 676	5, 531, 861	5, 063, 135	1, 433, 877	1, 544, 228	1, 043, 482
Wallachia and Moldavia	779, 200	1, 091, 984	876, 872	244, 644	238, 762	351, 014	263, 538	1, 011, 776	2, 494, 063	1, 843, 164	247, 113	1, 109, 698	496, 837
Chili	32, 568	676, 254	642, 529		356, 311	317, 076	638, 397	3, 916, 225	2, 758, 067	1, 083, 319	1, 200, 913	1, 101, 240	3, 132, 095
Australia			347, 402	38, 880				1, 584, 602	361, 298	495, 367	172, 931	690, 156	1, 038, 203
Denmark	2, 183, 381	1, 872, 754	1, 162, 704	1, 095, 401	1, 448, 859	1, 283, 824	1, 050, 947	1, 054, 597	1, 525, 388	1, 455, 782	1, 083, 121	547, 939	1, 141, 661
France	8, 506, 606	2, 522, 365	3, 642, 107	3, 464, 127	5, 328, 255	11, 309, 949	14, 977, 256	3, 996, 221	1, 580, 810	4, 019, 588	1, 978, 889	340, 222	8, 500, 394
Austria		1, 580, 264	1, 658, 183	207, 454	68, 006	1, 149, 174	2, 596, 413					1, 560, 988	853, 003
India									301, 571			410, 709	292, 441
Spain	1, 019, 760	2, 406, 934	591, 495			230, 274	1, 611, 920	845, 001					1, 200, 429
Italy	585, 360	278, 219					215, 583	427, 972	600, 941				1, 002, 854
Sweden	263, 418	121, 048								117, 390	68, 790		
Holland	236, 304	89, 448							62, 322	257, 457	46, 411		
Syria and Palestine											98, 136		
Italy and Greece											70, 477		
Belgium							488, 764				37, 697		
Brazil			116, 496										
Portugal													101, 800
Argentine Confederation									46, 567				
All other countries	642, 262	409, 622	693, 959	912, 179	592, 539	611, 967	629, 025	617, 817	546, 303	624, 990	188, 978	263, 526	533, 407
Total	58, 915, 534	69, 659, 375	92, 570, 775	57, 157, 618	53, 829, 448	48, 241, 295	54, 827, 133	73, 055, 321	68, 144, 617	82, 969, 172	68, 891, 418	82, 709, 501	88, 877, 406

Corn, including meal, imported into the United Kingdom from 1860 to 1872, inclusive.

[Compiled from the reports of trade and navigation of Great Britain.]

Countries whence imported.	1860.	1861.	1862.	1863.	1864.	1865.	1866.	1867.	1868.	1869.	1870.	1871.	1872.
	Bushels.	*Bushels.*	*Bushels.*	*Bushels.*	*Bushels.*	*Bushels.*	*Bushels.*	*Bushels.*	*Bushels.*	*Bushels.*	*Bushels.*	*Bushels.*	*Bushels.*
United States	3, 456, 890	13, 801, 870	12, 274, 414	8, 496, 321	556, 296	3, 310, 259	13, 001, 279	8, 951, 350	8, 031, 416	2, 721, 354	57, 462	14, 652, 730	33, 961, 366
Germany	......	......	......	......	......	......	......	......	321, 198	475, 834	......	......	......
Turkey	2, 084, 952	4, 487, 784	3, 181, 896	8, 052, 280	6, 874, 158	5, 897, 914	8, 900, 957	2, 706, 508	7, 986, 344	23, 921, 674	21, 667, 440	8, 540, 440	3, 279, 230
Russia	2, 075, 688	987, 376	1, 745, 464	1, 842, 840	2, 615, 844	2, 205, 945	862, 269	461, 925	1, 329, 762	1, 209, 236	5, 023, 450	4, 172, 976	847, 702
British North America	......	947, 272	2, 710, 197	736, 689	470	564, 364	1, 604, 610	630, 993	682, 490	67, 694	24, 800	2, 692, 138	7, 115, 792
Wallachia and Moldavia	5, 248, 432	2, 483, 384	1, 001, 936	2, 736, 856	1, 174, 525	1, 004, 735	1, 128, 406	200, 323	2, 227, 046	3, 949, 652	4, 426, 948	2, 556, 102	1, 896, 826
Austria	......	363, 432	......	753, 456	153, 135	65, 551	85, 611	......	......	......	......	312, 098	311, 312
Morocco	......	430, 584	547, 352	128, 296	......	76, 026	231, 009	268, 044	......	......	......	246, 336	713, 214
France	1, 201, 272	139, 936	......	80, 264	311, 974	134, 279	866, 434	1, 870, 893	356, 922	332, 624	743, 364	193, 246	......
Egypt	257, 040	496, 624	439, 960	805, 456	......	......	......	410, 647	1, 075, 452	21, 732	22, 428	151, 810	744, 002
Italy	149, 872	......	......	......	......	......	......	......	572, 978	2, 474, 234	1, 388, 482	......	......
Denmark	103, 192	......	......	......	......	......	......	......	......	......	......	......	......
Portugal	......	78, 520	......	......	......	......	......	220, 924	182, 278	......	......	......	......
Azores	......	87, 920	......	......	......	......	......	79, 851	......	......	......	......	......
All other countries	250, 991	235, 737	100, 693	147, 975	548, 666	345	78, 295	154, 769	193, 344	166, 270	170, 674	151, 564	195, 896
Total	14, 828, 329	24, 540, 439	22, 001, 912	23, 780, 433	12, 235, 068	13, 259, 418	26, 758, 870	15, 956, 227	22, 959, 230	35, 340, 304	33, 525, 048	33, 669, 440	49, 065, 340

Value of the principal domestic exports of the United States during the year ending June 30, 1872. (Stated in the order of magnitude.)

[The values here given are in currency.]

	Articles.	Value.	Per cent. of total.
1	Cotton, unmanufactured	$180,684,595	33.4
2	Bread and breadstuffs	84,586,273	15.7
3	Gold and silver, and manufactures of	72,891,479	13.5
4	Provisions	59,696,670	11.2
5	Mineral oils	34,058,370	6.2
6	Tobacco	26,659,921	4.9
7	Wood, and manufactures of	15,240,872	2.8
8	Iron and steel, and manufactures of	8,747,106	1.6
9	Tallow	6,973,189	1.2
10	Oil-cake	3,966,368	.7
11	Seeds	3,839,108	.7
12	Leather, and manufactures of	3,684,029	.67
13	Naval stores	3,387,864	.63
14	Furs and fur-skins	3,343,005	.64
15	Spirits of turpentine	2,521,357	.45
16	Silver-bearing ore	2,473,238	.44
17	Sewing-machines	2,436,085	.43
18	Cotton, manufactured	2,304,431	.42
19	Coal	1,961,606	.35
20	Drugs, chemicals, and medicines	1,783,630	.32
21	Live animals	1,773,716	.31
22	Agricultural implements	1,547,413	.29
23	Hides and skins	1,445,178	.26
24	Animal and fish oils	1,421,567	.25
25	Sugar and molasses	1,189,233	.21
26	Ordnance stores	1,168,347	.2
27	Railroad cars	1,022,181	.19
28	Dyestuffs	975,571	.18
29	Fruit, dried and green	804,469	.14
30	Quicksilver	691,637	.11
31	Paper and stationery	633,048	.1
32	Soap	615,963	.1
33	Distilled spirits	591,499	.1
34	Vegetable oils	556,016	.1
35	Glass and glassware	547,112	.1
36	Books and other publications	465,153	.08
37	Manures	439,398	.08
38	Wearing apparel	427,799	.07
39	Hops	408,305	.07
40	Musical instruments	401,194	.07
41	Carriages and carts	397,818	.07
42	Perfumery	377,577	.06
43	Hair, and manufactures of	374,167	.06
44	Cordage, rope, and twine	362,343	.06
45	Ginseng	341,616	.06
46	Candles, tallow and other	341,210	.06
47	Marble and stone	322,287	.05
48	Hemp, and manufactures of	317,873	.05
49	Copper, and manufactures of	287,735	.05
	Total value	541,486,521	100.00

Tonnage entered from foreign countries at Boston, New York, Philadelphia, Baltimore, Charleston, Savannah, Mobile, New Orleans, San Francisco, and all other sea-ports, from 1830 *to* 1873.

Year.	Boston.	New York.	Philadelphia.	Baltimore.	Charleston.	Savannah.	Mobile.	New Orleans.	San Francisco.	All other sea-ports.	Total.
	Tons.	*Tons.*	*Tons.*	*Tons.*	*Tons.*	*Tons.*	*Tons.*	*Tons.*	*Tons.*	*Tons.*	*Tons.*
1830	108, 328	305, 181	77, 016	61, 121	72, 541	26, 378	15, 316	118, 636	....	314, 610	1, 099, 127
1840	245, 333	545, 931	87, 702	82, 140	60, 177	63, 651	66, 772	255, 477	....	346, 665	1, 753, 848
1850	478, 859	1, 145, 331	132, 370	99, 588	96, 619	57, 017	96, 020	349, 949	130, 864	424, 895	3, 011, 512
1855	707, 924	1, 735, 907	185, 975	165, 127	88, 833	47, 050	69, 832	435, 863	172, 947	568, 151	4, 177, 609
1860	718, 587	1, 973, 812	185, 162	186, 417	126, 411	92, 648	160, 909	632, 598	235, 001	688, 539	4, 999, 884
1861	771, 948	2, 320, 927	183, 408	225, 110	56, 371	10, 036	67, 646	68, 993	205, 602	649, 659	4, 559, 700
1862	619, 435	2, 509, 749	171, 882	123, 688	....	....	....	....	231, 698	535, 727	4, 192, 179
1863	639, 828	2, 554, 858	194, 443	128, 565	....	....	....	....	256, 584	430, 429	4, 204, 707
1864	681, 189	2, 382, 192	188, 938	102, 752	....	....	....	50, 588	299, 558	481, 474	4, 186, 691
1865	655, 035	2, 075, 477	159, 579	88, 466	....	....	....	50, 970	321, 253	476, 962	3, 827, 742
1866	725, 424	2, 697, 325	222, 552	132, 836	19, 113	35, 407	68, 710	228, 339	338, 130	538, 100	5, 005, 936
1867	731, 930	2, 754, 605	286, 735	203, 618	29, 077	39, 982	47, 577	253, 729	310, 896	607, 480	5, 265, 029
1868	642, 478	2, 865, 252	278, 440	216, 727	43, 790	84, 188	88, 544	326, 216	413, 673	610, 645	5, 569, 953
1869	779, 371	3, 101, 691	292, 595	225, 302	29, 691	81, 974	61, 210	381, 883	443, 735	634, 361	6, 031, 813
1870	793, 927	3, 093, 186	300, 006	272, 290	36, 332	86, 110	70, 249	458, 447	393, 983	753, 926	6, 258, 456
1871	836, 104	3, 413, 436	369, 616	315, 734	48, 104	142, 902	103, 822	566, 797	353, 493	840, 119	6, 990, 127
1872	881, 486	3, 969, 339	417, 911	368, 136	43, 576	139, 523	55, 895	501, 965	423, 572	966, 703	7, 768, 106
1873	819, 819	4, 211, 624	466, 817	397, 167	48, 040	135, 456	47, 139	522, 791	548, 477	1, 197, 059	8, 394, 389

Value of imports from foreign countries at Boston, New York, Philadelphia, Baltimore, Charleston, Savannah, Mobile, New Orleans, San Francisco, and all other sea-ports, from 1860 *to* 1873, *inclusive.*

[The values stated in gold.]

Year.	Boston.	New York.	Philadelphia.	Baltimore.	Charleston.	Savannah.	Mobile.	New Orleans.	San Francisco.	All other sea-ports.	Total.
1860	$39, 366, 560	$233, 692, 941	$14, 626, 801	$9, 784, 773	$1, 569, 570	$782, 061	$1, 050, 310	$22, 922, 773	$9, 577, 921	$28, 792, 544	$362, 166, 254
1861	44, 014, 151	222, 966, 274	12, 625, 448	9, 449, 105	806, 480	175, 328	368, 357	11, 960, 869	8, 506, 506	24, 777, 635	335, 650, 153
1862	23, 957, 621	142, 215, 636	9, 883, 586	5, 817, 190	....	....	....	....	8, 366, 238	15, 531, 458	205, 771, 729
1863	27, 083, 272	177, 254, 415	7, 392, 785	4, 484, 399	....	....	....	1, 425, 567	10, 682, 409	24, 597, 073	252, 919, 920
1864	30, 263, 853	229, 506, 499	9, 141, 672	5, 835, 503	....	....	....	1, 483, 692	15, 065, 478	38, 266, 598	329, 562, 895
1865	24, 540, 494	154, 139, 409	7, 319, 520	4, 816, 454	....	....	....	1, 475, 657	6, 173, 011	35, 969, 622	234, 434, 167
1866	....	....	....	....	....	....	....	....	....	....	....
1867	....	....	....	....	....	....	....	....	....	....	....
1868	37, 039, 736	242, 580, 659	14, 527, 765	12, 930, 733	497, 300	474, 078	523, 217	11, 386, 858	19, 503, 987	32, 160, 475	371, 624, 808
1869	44, 636, 967	295, 117, 682	15, 967, 556	15, 863, 032	401, 244	748, 977	413, 437	11, 414, 893	18, 088, 901	34, 661, 566	437, 314, 255
1870	47, 524, 845	293, 990, 006	14, 560, 797	19, 512, 468	505, 699	1, 001, 917	1, 349, 488	14, 993, 754	21, 834, 103	47, 464, 510	462, 377, 587
1871	53, 652, 225	357, 909, 770	17, 728, 006	24, 672, 871	621, 559	1, 090, 717	1, 579, 806	19, 427, 238	20, 384, 907	44, 426, 609	541, 493, 708
1872	70, 398, 185	418, 515, 829	20, 383, 853	28, 826, 305	749, 976	627, 410	1, 761, 402	18, 543, 188	33, 330, 501	47, 202, 117	640, 338, 766
1873	68, 083, 307	426, 321, 427	25, 393, 150	29, 287, 603	746, 139	820, 258	1, 097, 164	19, 933, 344	39, 422, 604	52, 512, 151	663, 617, 147

Value of exports of domestic produce at Boston, New York, Philadelphia, Baltimore, Charleston, Savannah, Mobile, New Orleans, San Francisco, and at all other sea-ports, from 1860 *to* 1873, *inclusive.*

[The values stated in currency.]

Year.	Boston.	New York.	Philadelphia.	Baltimore.	Charleston.	Savannah.	Mobile.	New Orleans.	San Francisco.	All other sea-ports.	Total.
1860	$13, 530, 770	$129, 630, 955	$5, 512, 755	$8, 804, 606	$21, 179, 350	$18, 351, 554	$38, 670, 183	$107, 812, 580	$7, 388, 394	$31, 308, 127	$373, 189, 274
1861	12, 947, 276	137, 379, 956	9, 865, 051	12, 949, 625	5, 455, 581	267, 096	8, 472, 001	6, 823, 357	10, 414, 468	24, 125, 075	228, 699, 486
1862	12, 183, 046	152, 377, 961	11, 054, 630	8, 375, 303	....	....	....	....	11, 765, 218	17, 373, 421	213, 069, 519
1863	19, 150, 215	221, 917, 978	12, 236, 197	11, 013, 871	....	....	....	....	9, 944, 114	31, 622, 623	305, 884, 998
1864	15, 240, 097	211, 237, 222	10, 166, 098	8, 741, 755	....	....	....	....	48, 198, 072	26, 451, 955	320, 035, 199
1865	19, 219, 499	219, 379, 873	10, 978, 603	11, 794, 546	....	....	....	3, 259, 882	12, 814, 694	28, 759, 661	306, 306, 758
1866	....	....	....	....	....	....	....	....	....	....	....
1867	17, 298, 307	207, 382, 457	16, 585, 132	10, 995, 348	11, 789, 918	16, 668, 684	22, 093, 154	82, 995, 294	23, 712, 255	29, 056, 763	438, 577, 312
1868	15, 690, 873	236, 031, 239	14, 384, 761	13, 857, 391	9, 913, 776	24, 646, 219	22, 610, 975	58, 538, 524	23, 790, 164	34, 837, 791	454, 301, 713
1869	13, 118, 827	185, 384, 264	14, 585, 173	13, 657, 530	7, 421, 188	21, 057, 728	20, 541, 510	75, 131, 704	27, 540, 018	35, 523, 173	413, 961, 115
1870	12, 251, 267	209, 972, 491	16, 903, 072	14, 330, 248	10, 772, 071	29, 749, 058	22, 422, 631	107, 658, 042	32, 186, 021	42, 847, 242	499, 092, 143
1871	12, 961, 291	285, 530, 775	17, 903, 027	15, 037, 855	12, 387, 524	32, 857, 902	21, 874, 703	93, 953, 081	20, 791, 414	49, 221, 079	562, 518, 651
1872	21, 443, 154	270, 413, 674	20, 982, 876	18, 325, 321	10, 933, 430	28, 246, 607	13, 938, 605	89, 501, 149	26, 243, 061	49, 191, 841	549, 219, 718
1873	27, 039, 225	313, 129, 963	24, 203, 125	19, 344, 177	14, 200, 041	32, 675, 500	12, 249, 866	104, 329, 965	38, 716, 497	63, 244, 204	649, 132, 563

Tonnage entered at the port of Quebec from foreign ports, from 1853 to 1872, inclusive.

Year.	Tons.			Year.	Tons.		
	Sail.	Steam.	Total.		Sail.	Steam.	Total.
1853	567, 857	2, 821	570, 678	1864	637, 209	61, 045	698, 254
1854	607, 598	11, 328	618, 926	1865	671, 145	75, 851	746, 996
1855	348, 430	....	348, 430	1866	590, 120	75, 611	665, 731
1856	460, 561	16, 599	477, 160	1867	549, 216	76, 167	625, 383
1857	588, 352	21, 092	609, 444	1868	558, 600	87, 911	646, 511
1858	481, 720	19, 933	501, 653	1869	573, 353	100, 861	674, 214
1859	462, 305	48, 679	510, 984	1870	619, 145	109, 301	728, 446
1860	616, 199	50, 759	666, 958	1871	515, 764	107, 710	623, 474
1861	703, 908	71, 894	775, 802	1872	650, 512	132, 804	783, 316
1862	549, 773	72, 025	621, 798				
1863	738, 025	59, 881	797, 906	Grand total	11, 489, 792	1, 202, 272	12, 692, 064

Statement showing the tonnage entered, and the imports and exports, at New York and at Montreal, each year, from 1860 to 1872, inclusive. (Values stated in gold.)

Year.	Tonnage entered.		Value of imports.		Value of exports.	
	At New York.	At Montreal.	At New York.	At Montreal.	At New York.	At Montreal.
					Currency.	
1860	1, 973, 812	118, 216	$233, 692, 941	$15, 479, 453	$120, 630, 955	$6, 020, 715
1861	2, 320, 927	248, 351	222, 966, 274	16, 814, 161	137, 379, 956	10, 415, 738
1862	2, 509, 749	259, 901	142, 215, 636	20, 529, 893	152, 377, 961	8, 765, 594
1863	2, 554, 858	195, 809	177, 254, 415	18, 841, 885	221, 917, 978	7, 557, 799
1864	2, 382, 192	142, 046	229, 506, 499	25, 651, 738	211, 237, 222	5, 654, 186
1865	2, 075, 477	134, 758	154, 139, 409	19, 842, 948	219, 379, 873	5, 361, 184
1866	2, 697, 325	189, 280	....	28, 792, 921	....	9, 674, 823
1867	2, 754, 005	185, 354	....	28, 378, 117	207, 382, 457	10, 287, 418
1868	2, 865, 252	186, 104	242, 580, 659	22, 919, 704	236, 031, 239	11, 758, 851
1869	3, 101, 691	251, 557	295, 117, 682	24, 097, 648	185, 384, 264	16, 748, 410
1870	3, 093, 186	306, 065	293, 990, 006	31, 524, 861	209, 972, 491	19, 027, 153
1871	3, 413, 436	344, 323	357, 909, 770	35, 504, 334	285, 530, 775	19, 133, 519
1872	3, 969, 339	391, 926	418, 515, 829	45, 675, 016	270, 413, 674	17, 081, 771

Total tonnage entered at the ports of Montreal, Boston, New York, Philadelphia, Baltimore, New Orleans, and San Francisco, for each year from 1853 to 1873, inclusive.

Year.	Montreal.	Boston.	New York.	Philadelphia.	Baltimore.	New Orleans.	San Francisco.
	Tons.	*Tons.*	*Tons.*	*Tons.*	*Tons.*	*Tons.*	*Tons.*
1853	59, 712	582, 490	1, 755, 521	183, 944	119, 089	511, 878	252, 820
1854	72, 305	653, 443	1, 840, 007	191, 673	156, 448	492, 434	208, 952
1855	48, 139	707, 924	1, 735, 907	185, 975	165, 127	435, 863	172, 947
1856	69, 962	682, 165	1, 681, 659	173, 178	153, 323	663, 067	168, 352
1857	65, 712	714, 821	2, 035, 649	189, 102	163, 381	612, 286	149, 242
1858	70, 183	665, 442	1, 694, 219	156, 671	156, 810	583, 776	147, 175
1859	85, 319	734, 167	1, 890, 144	180, 421	189, 982	659, 083	221, 439
1860	118, 216	718, 587	1, 973, 812	185, 162	186, 417	632, 398	235, 001
1861	248, 351	771, 948	2, 320, 927	183, 408	225, 110	68, 993	205, 602
1862	259, 901	619, 435	2, 509, 749	171, 882	123, 688	....	281, 698
1863	195, 809	639, 828	2, 554, 858	194, 443	128, 565	....	256, 584
1864	142, 046	681, 189	2, 382, 192	188, 938	102, 752	50, 588	299, 558
1865	134, 758	655, 035	2, 075, 477	159, 579	88, 466	50, 970	321, 253
1866	189, 280	725, 424	2, 697, 325	222, 552	132, 836	228, 339	338, 130
1867	185, 354	731, 930	2, 754, 005	286, 735	203, 618	253, 729	310, 896
1868	186, 104	642, 478	2, 865, 252	278, 440	216, 727	326, 216	413, 673
1869	251, 557	779, 371	3, 101, 691	292, 595	225, 302	381, 882	443, 737
1870	306, 065	793, 927	3, 093, 186	300, 006	272, 290	458, 447	393, 983
1871	344, 323	836, 104	3, 413, 436	369, 619	315, 734	566, 797	353, 493
1872	391, 926	881, 486	3, 969, 339	417, 911	368, 136	501, 965	423, 572
1873	....	819, 819	4, 211, 624	466, 817	397, 167	522, 791	548, 477

Number of tons transported on the New York canals, New York Central Railroad, and Erie Railway from 1853 to 1872, inclusive.

Year.	New York State canals.	New York Central Railroad.	Erie Railway.	Total number of tons transported by railway.
1853	4, 247, 853	360, 000	631, 069	991, 054
1854	4, 165, 862	549, 804	743, 250	1, 293, 054
1855	4, 022, 617	670, 073	842, 048	1, 512, 121
1856	4, 116, 082	776, 112	943, 215	1, 719, 327
1857	3, 344, 061	8[illegible]8, 791	978, 066	1, 816, 8[illegible]7
1858	3, 665, 192	765, 407	816, 954	1, 582, 361
1859	3, 781, 684	834, 319	868, 073	1, 702, 392
1860	4, 650, 214	1, 028, 183	1, 139, 554	2, 167, 737
1861	4, 507, 635	1, 167, 302	1, 253, 418	2, 420, 720
1862	5, 598, 785	1, 387, 433	1, 632, 955	3, 020, 388
1863	5, 557, 692	1, 449, 604	1, 815, 096	3, 264, 700
1864	4, 852, 941	1, 557, 148	2, 170, 798	3, 727, 946
1865	4, 729, 654	1, 275, 299	2, 234, 350	3, 509, 649
1866	5, 775, 220	1, 602, 197	3, 242, 792	4, 844, 989
1867	5, 688, 325	1, 667, 926	3, 484, 546	5, 152, 472
1868	6, 442, 225	1, 846, 599	3, 908, 243	5, 754, 842
1869	5, 859, 080	2, 281, 885	4, 312, 209	6, 594, 094
1870	6, 173, 769	4, 122, 000	4, 852, 505	8, 974, 505
1871	6, 467, 888	4, 532, 056	4, 844, 208	9, 376, 264
1872	6, 673, 370	4, 393, 965	5, 564, 274	9, 958, 239

Statement showing the railway-fares on English railways for first, second, and third class passengers from point to point herein mentioned, and the distances by rail between such points.

[Compiled for the United States Senate Committee on Transportation Routes to the Seaboard, by the Board of Trade of Great Britain.]

Journeys.		Distances.	Railway-fares.			Remarks.
From—	To—		First-class.	Second-class.	Third-class.	
		Miles.	£ *s.* *d.*	£ *s.* *d.*	£ *s.* *d.*	
London	Inverness	592	4 10 0	3 10 0	2 2 6	Return tickets usually $1\frac{2}{3}$ fares.
Do	Aberdeen	542	4 0 0	3 0 0	2 0 0	
Do	Glasgow	406	3 10 0	2 11 0	1 13 0	Via London and North-western.
Do	Edinburgh	398	3 10 0	2 11 0	1 13 0	Via Great Northern.
Do	Carlisle	299	2 14 9	2 0 0	1 4 2½	
Do	Liverpool	202	1 15 0	1 6 0	0 16 9	
Do	Fleetwood	231	2 0 0	1 10 0	0 19 1	
Do	Holyhead	264	2 6 10	1 15 4	1 1 10½	
Do	Leeds	225	1 13 0	1 4 0	0 15 5½	
Do	Manchester	189	1 12 6	1 4 0	0 15 6	Several competing lines.
Do	Milford	285	2 8 3	1 16 2	1 6 3	
Do	Bristol	118	1 0 10	0 15 8	0 9 10	
Do	Plymouth	247	2 6 6	1 12 10	0 18 8	
Do	Southampton	76	0 15 6	0 11 0	0 6 6	
Do	Brighton	50	0 10 0	0. 7 9	0 4 3	No competition. Extra fares by special express.
Do	Dover	78	0 18 6	0 13 6	0 6 6	Extra fares by continental express.
Do	Norwich	113½	1 3 9	0 19 0	0 12 3	Government rate by slow trains, third class, 9*s.* 5½*d.*
Do	Hull	174½	1 10 6	1 3 0	0 13 6	
Manchester	Bristol	191	1 10 6	1 1 6	0 13 7	
Do	Newcastle	158	1 4 9	0 18 7	0 11 9	
Do	Scarboro'	117	0 19 0	0 14 3	0 9 0	
Do	Hull	88	0 15 8	0 11 9	0 7 5	
Do	Edinburgh	221	1 17 0	1 6 6	0 18 5½	Via Midland and North British.
Do	Glasgow	225	1 17 0	1 6 6	0 18 6	Do.
Edinburgh	....do	47	0 5 6	0 4 0	0 2 6	Keen competition.
Bristol	Newcastle	301	2 15 0	2 0 6	1 5 6	
Do	Edinburgh	426	3 10 0	2 11 0	1 12 5	
Liverpool	Yarmouth	265	2 8 2	1 17 0	1 2 2	

B.—*Statement showing the rate per ton for the transmission of through-freights on English railways.*

Compiled for the United States Senate Committee on Transportation Routes to the Seaboard, by the Board of Trade of Great Britain.

Points between which the rates of freight are stated. From—	To—	Railways composing the route mentioned.	Double or single track.	Distances. Miles.	1st class. s. d.	2d class. s. d.	3d class. s. d.	4th class. s. d.	5th class. s. d.	Class S. s. d.	Class M. s. d.
London	Inverness	Great Northern, Northeastern, North British, and Highland.	About 100 miles of single track.	594	48 4	60 0	80 0	115 0	135 0	36 8	36 8
Do	Edinburgh	Great Northern, Northeastern and North British.	Double	398	41 8	51 8	70 0	100 0	120 0	31 8	31 8
Do	Glasgow	do	do	445	41 8	51 8	70 0	100 0	120 0	34 2	34 2
Do	Newcastle	Great Northern, Northeastern	do	274	31 8	35 0	50 0	80 0	100 0	20 0	20 0
Do	Grimsby	Great Northern	do	155	28 4	40 0	50 0	60 0	70 0	18 4	18 0
Do	Carlisle	London and Northwestern	do	298	36 8	41 8	55 0	80 0	100 0	30 0	Not quoted.
Do	Liverpool	do	do	201	27 6	32 6	37 6	50 0	70 0	29 0	15 10
Do	Milford	Great Western	do	285	42 6	47 6	57 6	72 6	107 6	25 0	16 8
Do	Bristol	do	do	118	22 6	27 6	35 0	40 0	50 0	12 6	10 0
Do	Plymouth	do	do	247	32 6	37 6	45 0	60 0	90 0	20 0	16 8
Birmingham	do	do	do	220	28 4	35 0	48 4	60 10	98 4	20 3	20 0
Do	Southampton	London and Southwestern, and London and Northwestern.	do	192	25 0	30 0	40 0	50 0	60 0	20 0	Not quoted.
London	Brighton	London, Brighton and South Coast	do	50	8 4	12 1	16 8	21 3	Not quoted.	6 1	4 10
Do	Dover	London, Chatham and Dover	do	78	10 0	11 3	17 11	26 8	36 8	8 4	Not quoted.
Do	Ramsgate	do	do	79	9 7	11 3	15 5	20 5	32 6	7 6	do
Wolverhampton	Yarmouth	Great Eastern, London and Northwestern	do	214	35 0	43 4	51 8	76 8	110 0	22 6	18 4
Dover	Birmingham	London, Chatham and Dover, Great Western	do	209	33 4	41 8	51 8	70 0	85 0	23 4	Not quoted.
Do	Bristol	do	do	198	36 8	47 6	60 0	72 6	80 0	22 6	do
Do	Sheffield	London, Chatham and Dover, Great North'n, and Manchester, Sheffield and Lincolnshire	do	242	43 4	48 4	62 6	85 0	105 0	25 0	do
Bristol	Newcastle	Midland, Northeastern	do	301	37 6	42 6	55 0	83 4	105 0	25 0	do
Do	Edinburgh	Midland, Northeastern, North British	do	424	41 8	51 8	70 0	100 0	120 0	31 8	do
Liverpool	Dundee	London and Northwestern, Caledonian	do	301	26 8	31 8	40 0	60 0	80 0	24 2	do
Do	Edinburgh	do	do	227	25 0	28 4	32 6	60 0	80 0	21 8	do
Do	Grimsby	Manchester, Sheffield and Lincolnshire	do	136	23 4	28 4	40 0	50 0	60 0	16 8	15 0
Do	Yarmouth	Manchester, Sheffield and Lincolnshire, Great Eastern.	do	265	33 4	41 8	50 0	70 0	90 0	23 4	Not quoted.
Manchester	Glasgow	London and Northwestern, Glasgow and Southwestern.	do	249	26 8	30 0	35 0	50 0	80 0	21 8	do
Do	Edinburgh	London and Northwestern, North British	do	222	31 8	35 0	40 0	55 0	85 0	25 0	do

NOTE.—Where Class M rates are not quoted, they are usually about the same as Class S. In addition, there are a large number of special rates quoted by the companies for special kinds of traffic, and to traders doing a large freight business with the companies.

C.—*Rates of wages paid by English railway companies.*

[Compiled for the United States Senate Committee on Transportation-Routes to the Seaboard by the Board of Trade of Great Britain.]

Rank.	Pay.	Remarks.
Conductors, (1st-class guards)	28*s*. to 30*s*. per week.	For long routes, however, and special service up to 40*s*. per week.
Engine-drivers	5*s*. 6*d*. to 8*s*. per day.	
Stokers or firemen	3*s*. 6*d*. to 5*s*. 6*d*. per day.	
Baggagemen, (2d-class guards)	25*s*. to 28*s*. per week.	
Brakemen, (occasional guards)	21*s*. to 22*s*. per week.	
Signalmen	20*s*. to 30*s*. per week.	Varying greatly with the responsibility of the post. In special cases, over 30*s*.

D.—*Statement showing the rates per ton for the transportation of through-freights on English canals.*

[Compiled for the United States Senate Committee on Transportation-Routes to the Seaboard by the Board of Trade of Great Britain.]

Points between which the rates of freight are stated.		Canals composing the routes here mentioned.	Distance.	Rates of freight per ton for the entire distance on commodities of these classes.*						Remarks.
From—	To—			S.	First class.	Second class.	Third class.	Fourth class.	Fifth class.	
			Miles.	*s. d.*	*s. d.*	*s. d.*	*£ s. d.*	*£ s. d.*	*£ s. d.*	
Manchester	Macclesfield	Ashton, Peak Forest and Macclesfield Canals.	$26\frac{1}{4}$	5 10	9 2	10 0	0 10 10	0 15 0	1 0 0	In cases where parties provide their own boats, towage, &c., *toll* only is charged. The tolls on the different canals vary as under—Lime, salt, &c., $\frac{1}{2}d.$ to $\frac{3}{4}d.$ per ton per mile; coal, coke, &c., $\frac{3}{4}d.$ to $1\frac{1}{2}d.$ per ton per mile; bricks, iron, stone, 1*d.* to $1\frac{1}{2}d.$ per ton per mile; grain, malt, &c., $\frac{3}{4}d.$ to $1\frac{1}{2}d.$ per ton per mile; timber, lead, and general goods, 1*d.* to 2*d.* per ton per mile. P. S.—These remarks apply only to the canals belonging to the Manchester, Sheffield, and Lincolnshire Railway Company—viz., the Ashton, Peak Forest, and Macclesfield Canals. Rates on canals vary according to the nature of country through which the canals pass, the period at which the parliamentary powers were obtained, and the amount of competition.
Manchester	Bollington	Ashton, Peak Forest and Macclesfield Canals.	$24\frac{1}{4}$	6 8	7 6	8 4	0 10 0	0 15 0	1 0 0	
Manchester	Marple	Ashton and Peak Forest Canals	15	4 2	5 0	6 8	0 7 6	0 10 0	0 15 0	
Manchester	New Mills	do	$18\frac{1}{2}$	4 2	5 10	6 8	0 7 6	0 8 4	0 12 6	
Manchester	Whaley Bridge	do	21	5 0	7 6	8 4	0 9 2	0 13 4	0 15 10	
Manchester	Chapel-le-Frith	do	$24\frac{1}{2}$	5 0	8 4	9 2	0 10 0	0 15 0	1 0 0	
Manchester	Hyde	do	9	3 4	5 0	5 10	0 6 8	0 10 0	0 12 6	
Manchester	Ashton	Ashton Canal	$6\frac{1}{2}$	3 0	5 0	5 10	0 6 8	0 7 6	0 10 0	
Manchester	Stockport	do	$7\frac{1}{2}$	2 6	5 0	5 0	0 5 10	0 8 4	0 10 0	
Liverpool	Macclesfield	River Mersey, Bridgewater Canal, Rochdale Canal, Ashton, Peak Forest, and Macclesfield Canals.	$74\frac{1}{2}$	10 10	14 2	15 10	0 18 4	1 2 6	1 10 0	
Liverpool	Bollington		$72\frac{1}{2}$	14 2	15 0	15 10	1 0 0	1 5 0	1 10 0	
Liverpool	Marple	River Mersey, Bridgewater Canal, Rochdale Canal, Ashton and Peak Forest Canals.	$63\frac{1}{4}$	10 10	12 6	14 2	0 15 10	0 19 2	1 2 6	
Liverpool	New Mills		$66\frac{3}{4}$							
Liverpool	Whaley Bridge		$69\frac{1}{4}$	12 6	14 2	15 10	0 17 6	1 0 0	1 5 0	
Liverpool	Chapel-le-Frith		$72\frac{3}{4}$	10 0	15 0	17 6	1 0 0	1 5 0	1 13 4	
Liverpool	Hyde		$57\frac{1}{4}$	9 2	10 10	12 6	0 14 2	0 16 8	1 1 8	
Liverpool	Ashton	River Mersey, Bridgewater Canal, Rochdale Canal, and Ashton Canal.	$54\frac{3}{4}$	8 4	10 0	11 8	0 13 4	0 15 10	1 0 0	
Liverpool	Stockport		$55\frac{3}{4}$	7 6	8 4	10 0	0 11 8	0 14 2	0 17 6	

* These rates are per ton of 2,240 pounds. See classification-book for articles included in each class

MEMORANDUM, WITH SEPARATE TABLES, A TO D.

Rates of freights from foreign ports to ports in Great Britain.

[Prepared for the United States Senate Committee on Transportation-Routes to the Seaboard, by R. Valpy, esq., of the statistical and commercial department of the Board of Trade of Great Britain.]

WHEAT—	1868.	1869.	1870.	1871.	1872.
Imported into England from ports on the Black Sea ....bushels..	15, 453, 736	13, 561, 249	15, 558, 118	21, 604, 857	29, 123, 969
Average price at Odessa....per bushel..	....	4*s.* $3\frac{1}{4}$*d.*	4*s.* 5*d.*	4*s.* $6\frac{3}{4}$*d.*	....
Average price in England.......do......	7*s.* $4\frac{1}{2}$*d.*	5*s.* $7\frac{3}{4}$*d.*	5*s.* 6*d.*	6*s.* 5*d.*	6*s.* $9\frac{1}{4}$*d.*
Imported into England from north of Europe ports..................bushels..	15, 606, 650	16, 026, 318	10, 299, 977	13, 226, 022	11, 998, 324
Average price at chief port of exportation......................per bushel..	6*s.* 0*d.*	5*s.* 1*d.*	5*s.* $10\frac{1}{2}$*d.*	5*s.* 11*d.*	....
Average price in England.......do......	8*s.* $7\frac{3}{4}$*d.*	6*s.* 8*d.*	6*s.* 6*d.*	7*s.* 5*d.*	7*s.* 9*d.*
Imported into England from American ports..........................bushels..	10, 907, 352	24, 335, 090	22, 840, 471	24, 712, 840	16, 098, 350
Average price in New York.. per bushel..	....	$1 39	....	....	....
Average price in England.......do......	7*s.* $10\frac{1}{2}$*d.*	5*s.* $11\frac{3}{4}$*d.*	5*s.* $10\frac{1}{2}$*d.*	6*s.* 2*d.*	6*s.* 8*d.*
Average price of native in England..........................do......	7*s.* 11*d.*	6*s.* 0*d.*	5*s.* 10*d.*	7*s.* 1*d.*	7*s.* 1*d.*
Average rate of freight from Odessa to England ....per bushel..	....	....	....	....	....
Average rate of freight from chief Baltic wheat-ports to England. ..per bushel..	....	....	....	....	....

R. VALPY.

STATISTICAL AND COMMERCIAL DEPARTMENT
BOARD OF TRADE, WHITEHALL,
October 22, 1873.

TABLE A.—*Rates charged by the Great Western Railway Company for the carriage of grain and flour, (wheat, barley, oats, beans, &c.,) between local stations, during the years* 1868, 1869, 1870, 1871, *and* 1872.

[Prepared for the United States Senate Committee on Transportation, by R. Valpy, esq., of the statistical and commercial department of the Board of Trade of Great Britain.]

Miles.	Per ton.	Remarks.	Miles.	Per ton.	Remarks.
	s. *d.*			*s.* *d.*	
10	2 6	2-ton lots.	35	5 10	2-ton lots.
15	2 9		40	5 10	
20	3 4		45	6 8	
25	4 2		50	6 8	
30	5 0				

TABLE B.—*Rates charged by the Great Western Railway Company for the carriage of grain and flour, (wheat, barley, oats, beans, &c.,) over long distances, in competition with grain sent by vessels to contiguous ports, during the years* 1868, 1869, 1870, 1871, *and* 1872.

[Prepared for the United States Senate Committee on Transportation, by R. Valpy, esq., of the statistical and commercial department of the Board of Trade of Great Britain.]

Miles.	Per ton.	Remarks.	Miles.	Per ton.	Remarks.
	s. *d.*			*s.* *d.*	
120	12 6	In lots of 4 tons and upward.	170	16 8	In lots of 4 tons and upward.
130	13 4		180	17 6	
140	14 2		190	18 4	
150	15 0		200	19 2	
160	15 10		210	20 0	

TABLE C.—*Scale of rates charged for the conveyance of live-stock over the Great Western Railway, from the year 1868 to 1872.*

[Prepared for the United States Senate Committee on Transportation, by R. Valpy, esq., of the statistical and commercial department of the board of trade of Great Britain.]

	Small wagon, not exceeding 13 feet 6 inches in length, capable of holding 7 fat or 10 lean beasts, 30 fat or 35 to 40 lean sheep.			Medium wagon, not exceeding 15 feet 6 inches in length, capable of holding 8 fat or 12 lean beasts, 35 fat or 40 lean sheep.			Large wagon, about 18 feet in length, capable of holding 10 fat, 14 to 16 lean beasts, 40 fat or 50 to 60 lean sheep.			Small wagon, 13 feet 6 inches, capable of holding 20 fat calves or pigs, 35 to 40 stone calves or pigs.			Medium, 15 feet 6 inches, capable of holding 25 to 30 fat calves or pigs, 40 to 50 stone calves or pigs.			Large, 18 feet, capable of holding 30 to 35 fat calves or pigs, 50 to 60 stone calves or pigs.		
	£	*s.*	*d.*	£	*s.*	*d.*	£	*s.*	*d.*	£	*s.*	*d.*	£	*s.*	*d.*	£	*s.*	*d.*
10 miles		6	0		7	0		7	9		6	6		7	3		8	3
20 miles		11	0		12	9		14	6		12	0		13	6		15	9
30 miles		16	0		18	6	1	1	0		17	3		19	9	1	3	0
40 miles	1	1	0	1	4	6	1	7	9	1	2	9	1	6	0	1	10	3
50 miles	1	6	0	1	10	3	1	14	6	1	8	3	1	12	3	1	17	6
70 miles	1	14	6	1	19	0	2	6	3	1	17	6	2	3	3	2	10	9
80 miles	1	19	6	2	4	6	2	12	9	2	2	9	2	9	6	2	17	9
100 miles	2	9	9	2	15	3	3	5	9	2	13	3	3	1	6	3	12	0
120 miles	2	16	0	3	3	6	3	13	6	3	1	0	3	11	0	4	3	6
150 miles	3	9	9	3	19	3	4	11	9	3	16	0	4	8	6	5	4	3
180 miles	4	3	6	4	14	9	5	9	9	4	11	0	5	6	0	6	4	9
200 miles	4	12	9	5	5	3	6	2	0	5	1	0	5	17	9	6	18	6

TABLE D—*Scale of rates charged by Great Western Railway Company for imported lean cattle going to grazing districts.*

	Beasts, per head.		Sheep, per head.		
	s.	*d.*	*s.*	*d.*	
123 miles 128 miles	4	6	1	6	Minimum charge 60*s.*
164 miles 170 miles	4	9	1	8	Mimimum charge 67*s.* 6*d*
185 miles 194 miles	5	0	1	9	Minimum charge 70*s.*

Statement of freight shipped on through bills of lading from Chicago to Europe, via Lake Shore and Michigan Southern Railway, during the year ending December 31, 1873.

Steamship lines.	Via—	Bacon.	Lard.	Beef, pork, Tallow, &c.	Flour.	Grain—wheat.	Wheat in pounds.
		Boxes.	*Tierces.*	*Packages.*	*Barrels.*	*Bushels.*	
Cunard	Boston	56, 673	12, 785	7, 182	300	117, 786	46, 647, 702
Other steamers	do	19, 543	9, 331				14, 024, 832
National	New York	7, 230	2, 080				5, 503, 506
White Star	do	2, 103	1, 217				2, 946, 520
Anchor	do	11, 528	10, 933	1, 813	7, 275	226, 272	24, 765, 921
Great Western	do	1, 183	374				245, 217
Sail	do	1, 718	200				954, 100
Allan Hooper's	Baltimore do	10, 307	3, 362				7, 345, 084
American Red Star	Philadelphia do	2, 250	1, 350			268, 733	18, 306, 929
Allan Do	Portland Montreal	16, 484	19, 748	8, 293	5, 900	14, 160	21, 011, 938
Total		129, 019	61, 380	17, 288	13, 475	626, 951	141, 751, 749

1873 .... 70, 846 tons.
1872 .... 52, 604 tons.

Increase .... 18, 242 tons.

G. MACDONALD,
General Western Agent Foreign Business.

C. M. GRAY,
Assistant General Freight Agent.

No. 12.—*Length of season of navigation for ten years.*

OPENING OF STRAITS OF MACKINAW.

Year.	Opened.	Year.	Opened.
1854	Apr. 25	1864	Apr. 23
1855	May 1	1865	Apr. 21
1856	May 2	1866	Apr. 29
1857	May 1	1867	Apr. 23
1858	Apr. 6	1868	Apr. 19
1859	Apr. 4	1869	Apr. 23
1860	Apr. 13	1870	Apr. 18
1861	Apr. 25	1871	Apr. 3
1862	Apr. 18	1872	Apr. 28
1863	Apr. 17	1873	....

OPENING AND CLOSING OF THE ERIE CANAL.

Year.	Opened.	Closed.	Number of days.
1863	May 1	Dec. 18	232
1864	Apr. 30	Dec. 8	223
1865	May 1	Dec. 12	226
1866	May 1	Dec. 12	226
1867	May 6	Dec. 10	218
1868	May 6	Dec. 7	215
1869	May 6	Dec. 18	226
1870	May 10	Dec. 8	212
1871	Apr. 24	Nov. 28	220
1872	May 13	Nov. 30	202
Average	....	....	220

Comparative length of the season of navigation on the Erie Canal, on the Welland Canal, and on the Saint Lawrence Canals.

Year.	Number of days of navigation each year.			Year.	Number of days of navigation each year.		
	Erie canal.	Welland canal.	Saint Lawrence canals.		Erie canal.	Welland canal.	Saint Lawrence canals.
1848	223	254	233	1858	226	245	215
1849	219	249	234	1859	212	252	220
1850	234	256	223	1860	232	250	229
1851	235	263	215	1861	224	249	224
1852	241	246	226	1862	224	245	215
1853	245	261	209	1863	223	245	217
1854	217	246	216	1864	223	243	224
1855	224	241	212	1865	226	243	227
1856	213	232	215	1866	226	239	223
1857	224	229	209	1867	224	239	....

Statement showing the production of cereals in the United States, the quantity consumed, and the quantity exported, 1840 to 1872, inclusive.

Year.	Production.	Consumed in the United States.	Consumed per capita.	Exported.	Per centage exported.
	Bushels.	*Bushels.*	*Per cent.*	*Bushels.*	*Per cent.*
1840	615, 525, 302	602, 326, 253	35. 21	13, 199, 049	2
1850	867, 453, 967	851, 502, 312	36. 8	15, 951, 655	1. 8
1860	1, 239, 039, 945	1, 216, 084, 810	38. 68	22, 955, 135	1. 8
1862	952, 702, 889	868, 358, 849	35. 23	84, 344, 040	8
1863	789, 580, 656	712, 121, 706	28. 18	77, 458, 950	9. 7
1864	916, 427, 263	868, 988, 145	33. 79	47, 439, 118	5
1865	1, 127, 459, 185	1, 100, 178, 958	31. 43	27, 280, 227	2. 4
1866	1, 342, 570, 666	1, 309, 233, 591	36. 67	33, 337, 075	2. 5
1867	1, 329, 729, 400	1, 298, 147, 835	35. 82	31, 581, 565	2. 5
1868	1, 450, 758, 900	1, 411, 070, 840	38. 13	39, 688, 060	2. 7
1869	1, 491, 412, 100	1, 458, 399, 134	38. 73	33, 012, 966	2
1870	1, 629, 027, 600	1, 571, 737, 079	41. 03	57, 290, 521	3. 5
1871	1, 528, 776, 100	1, 464, 070, 299	37. 44	64, 705, 801	4
1872	1, 656, 198, 100	....	....	....	....

POPULATION, CEREAL PRODUCTS, AND RAILROAD MILEAGE OF THE STATES OF OHIO, INDIANA, ILLINOIS, MISSOURI, KANSAS, NEBRASKA, IOWA, MINNESOTA, WISCONSIN, AND MICHIGAN.

Year.	Population.	Cereal products.					Railroad mileage.
		Wheat.	Barley.	Oats.	Rye.	Corn.	
		Bushels.	*Bushels.*	*Bushels.*	*Bushels.*	*Bushels.*	
1840	3, 351, 542	27, 517, 732	472, 199	30, 334, 613	1, 140, 624	105, 853, 405	196
1850	5, 403, 595	43, 842, 037	831, 517	42, 328, 731	839, 507	222, 208, 502	1, 276
1860	9, 091, 879	95, 004, 185	4, 908, 723	62, 950, 678	4, 101, 158	406, 146, 464	11, 055
1870	12, 966, 930	194, 763, 878	10, 608, 389	159, 600, 494	6, 472, 904	439, 111, 805	23, 769

LETTER ADDRESSED TO THE CHAIRMAN OF THIS COMMITTEE BY GEO. H. THURSTON, ESQ., OF PITTSBURGH, IN REGARD TO THE IMPROVEMENT OF THE OHIO RIVER.

PITTSBURGH, *October* 1, 1873.

SIR: As chairman of a committee, for whose report the people of the whole country look with much anxiety, permit me to occupy a brief portion of your time with some statistics bearing upon the importance of the improvement of the navigation of the Ohio River, and the necessity of the Government rendering that stream the great central water highway of the nation, which it can become.

The improvement of the navigation of this great water-course has been for years the subject of annual discussion in Congress; but to those only who do business upon its waters, and the people of the great cities along its course, does the importance to the future, as well as the present, of the whole nation seem to be understood.

The wonder arises that, in the grand march of the nation to its present magnitude, no statesman has seen, or, if so, failed to act, on the absolute certainty that the Ohio River, from its very geographical position, would, of unavoidable necessity, have to be made a capacious avenue of transportation, to meet the daily wants of the millions who would fill its valleys and develop the resources of the seven States that form its water-shed.

Congress after Congress virtually ignores the creation of one of the great transportation facilities of the nation, and year after year reluctantly votes a few thousands for surveys, and snag-boats for the Ohio, "a tub to the whale," but cheerfully gives millions after millions for improvements upon the coasts, to the neglect of a navigation one-fourth longer than the whole sea-coast line of the country. In that 16,000 miles of inland-river navigation there are, in the fifteen States along its banks, 20,268,000 people; and in those eighteen States, with greater or less shore along the sea-coast, but 15,931,000 including New York, with 4,400,000 inhabitants, who are more nearly interested in the lakes, or nearly thirty per cent. more inhabitants directly interested in the improvement of the Ohio than in the harbors of the ocast-line. The seven immediate States of the Ohio Valley, under whose appointment a body of commissioners are now striving to obtain enlarged governmental action for the improvement of the Ohio, have 13,400,000 population, or nearly ninety per cent. as many inhabitants as in the eighteen sea-coast States, and one hundred per cent. more than in the balance of the river States.

The importance not only now, but in the future, of the seven Ohio States, the following statistical statements will show so forcibly, I believe, that they will make their own argument as to the duty of the Government:

By the census of 1870 we find that the seven Ohio valley States had in that year 13,459,377 inhabitants, while the eighteen States having territory bordering on our sea-coast, had 15,931,152 of a population. In 1830, when the future necessity of the improvement of the Ohio began to be urged, the seven Ohio States had 4,156,033 inhabitants, the eighteen sea-coast States 8,288,651. In forty years the census of 1870 shows the growth of population in the sea-coast States has been but little over ninety per cent., while that of the Ohio States has been two hundred per cent. Under the same ratios, at the end of another forty years the sea-coast States will have 30,269,189 inhabitants, and the Ohio States 40,258,131. Should the progress of the nation be as great then in the next forty years as in the past, and the indications are that it may be greater rather than less, the seven Ohio States in population, and by analogy of reasoning in wealth, will be as powerful an empire in all respects as the whole United States now is. What then will be the wants of those States for transportation? What that of the other States of the Union? What should the Ohio River be made in view of this?

There were in the other eight States interested in the Ohio River in 1860 about 4,846,793 inhabitants; in 1870 there were 6,743,398, or an increase of thirty-three per cent. in the last ten years. At the same rates of increase there will be, in forty years from 1870, a population of 15,734,262 inhabitants—as many as there now are in all the sea-coast States, and half as many as there will be in those States forty years from now. It also appears that at the present time there are in the seven Ohio States within ten per cent. of the population of the coast States, and in the seven Ohio and eight Mississippi States interested in the navigation of the Ohio, there is twenty per cent. more population than in the sea-board States; and in the forty years there will be over fifty per cent. more, even if those States maintain the same ratios of increase as in the past forty years.

But let us look a little into the increase in the wealth of the territory of the Ohio valley during the past twenty years only.

In 1850 the valuation of property, real and personal, of the seven States of the Ohio was $2,089,002,652; in 1860 it was $5,171,001,897; in 1870 it is given in the census at $10,726,839,301—the valuation of that of the whole of the United States being only $30,068,518,507. In the eighteen sea-coast States, the valuation in 1850 was given at $4,324,577,745; in 1860 it was stated at $8,030,198,734; and in 1870, according to the census, it is $14,229,392,389. From this it would seem that the valuation of property in the seven Ohio States had increased, in the past *ten years* over *one hundred* per cent., and in twenty years over *five hundred* per cent.; while in the sea-coast States it had increased only seventy-five per cent. in the past ten years, and about three hundred and thirty per cent. in twenty years, including in that period of time California with her great mineral developments. Under the same ratios of increase, as in the past ten years, the census valuation of the Ohio States will be in 1890, or but a little over sixteen years from now, over thirty-two billions of dollars—more than ten times our national debt. This is allowing the increase to be from 1870 to 1880 the same per cent. as from 1860 to 1870, and from 1880 to 1890 only one-half that per cent. At the same period the sea-coast States would, under the same ratios, be given at only a little over thirty billions. It will easily be seen from these statistics how soon the seven Ohio States will as much exceed the eighteen coast States in wealth as they will in population.

It is assumed in all governments that statesmanship is the crowning talent of its rulers, and that the carrying out of measures which, while meeting the wants of the people in the present, prepares at the same time for the greater needs of the future, cannot fail to be that most conductive to the continued prosperity of a nation, and the expenditures, therefore, the least burdensome to the masses. The improvement of the Ohio is not merely a question of the transportation wants of the thirteen million people inhabiting now the seven Ohio States, with property valued at ten billions of dollars, important as the question is under such figures; but it is a question inside of sixteen years, of over twenty-five millions of sectional population and thirty billions of property.

What shall be said for the States of the Mississippi Valley, who feel to-day, as well as those of the Ohio, the imperative necessity of addition to the transportation facilities of the nation of such a grand water-highway as thirty millions of money will render the Ohio? In 1850 the value of the real and personal property of the eight Mississippi States was returned at only $705,803,959. In 1860 it was stated at $2,534,564,571; in 1870 it is given at $3,811,396,291, notwithstanding the great loss to four of the eight States in personal property by the consequences of the rebellion. For nearly all the purposes of national progress, the Ohio is as important to the eight Mississippi States as to those of the Ohio. In sixteen years from now, then, there will be not only the vast population of the latter States, and their vaster wealth, but that of the other river States, needing, in the same increased ratios over present necessities, such cheap transportation facilities as the Ohio can be made to furnish.

Considering that it is at all times assumed that from eight to ten years will be needed to complete any system of improvement of the Ohio, productive of navagation facilities demanded even now, it would seem, from the few statistics presented, that no time is to be lost in setting about the work if the necessities of the people are to be met. To-day fifty per cent. of the population of the United States, forty per cent. of all the States and Territories, and forty per cent. of the census-return of the real and personal property valuation of the nation, needs and asks that the Ohio be sufficiently improved to meet not only the wants of to-day, but those that the statistics of the nation show, will be of such immense magnitude in the years now so near at hand.

Let me further present the importance of these seven Ohio States from a mineralogical position, as bearing upon their future necessites for the greatest possible facilities for water transportation.

The bituminous-coal area of the United States is given at 133,132 square miles, in the geological surveys so far published, while Great Britain, France, and Belgium contain but 14,096 square miles, or a little over one-tenth. Of this 133,132 square miles of bituminous-coal deposit, the Ohio States contain one hundred thousand. The relation of fuel to manufactures is too well understood to need comment to show where the manufacturing population of the United States will be. The value of minerals and manufactures to the wealth of a nation has been too clearly demonstrated in the national life of Great Britain to require argument to show what one hundred thousand square miles of coal will be to the seven Ohio States, if only eleven thousand has been of such incalculable value to Great Britain. What food, what transportation, then, will not this nation's workshop need for its workers?

How fast this magnet of fuel is concentrating, in the Ohio States, the manufacturing interests of the nation, the comparative statistics of the number of the manufacturing establishments and their product, in the eighteen sea-coast States, and the seven Ohio States, in 1850 and in 1870 indicates. In 1850 there were, according to the census, in the eighteen sea-coast States, 65,273 manufacturing establishments, producing $639,771,163. In 1860 there were 66,959, producing $1,121,308,395. In the seven Ohio States in 1850, there were 36,277 factories, yielding $284,452,696 in products. In 1860 there were 49,099 factories, yielding $568,115,147. In 1870 the census gives 101,580 manufacturers in the sea-coast States, yielding $2,237,236,305 products, and in the seven Ohio States, 97,568 factories, yielding products to the value of $1,408,916,550. From these census statistics it appears that the increase in the eighteen sea-coast States has in twenty years been 36,307 factories, and $1,597,465,138 in product; while in the seven Ohio States the *increase* was 63,291 factories, and $1,124,483,854 in product. It is obvious that the factories of the Ohio States, being of more recent existence, were of less magnitude than the older ones of the eastern coast, including the mammoth manufacturing corporations of New England, and of course of less productive capacity. It will be observed that the ratio of increase in the Ohio States is about one hundred and seventy-five per cent., and only about fifty-six per cent. in the eighteen sea-coast States, or as *three to one;* while the increase in products is only twenty-five per cent. less than in the older manufacturing sections. Under the ratio of increase of the past ten years only, there will be in the seven Ohio States in twenty years from 1870 over two hundred and fifty thousand factories. Their production, taking only the average indicated by the census of 1870, will be three billions six hundred millions of dollars, or fifty per cent. more than the whole imports and exports of Great Britain to and from all countries.

It is for the transportation wants of this wonderful manufacturing empire, surpassing in extent that of Great Britain, Belgium, and France, the three great manufacturing fields of Europe as seven to one, that the improvement of the navigation of the Ohio River is of such national importance. Is it necessary in the knowledge of what the manufacturing industries of those three European nations have been, to ask what would be the action of their statesmen did similar opportunities for internal navigation exist within their governments?

The character of the seven Ohio States is, by reason of their mineral deposits, so settled, that it is obvious that a manufacturing population will largely predominate; and wheat as well as other subsistence articles have to be largely supplied to these States from others. The sixteen sea-coast States even now depend on the West for two-thirds of their food, and the question of their supply, under the increasing ratio of population in the future, assumes an overwhelming magnitude. Cheap transportation is, therefore, one of the provisions for the future comfort and prosperity of the people that wise rulers should lose no time in preparing. How distinctly the geographical position of producers and consumers of food in the United States suggests the central route of the Ohio Valley as the line of a cheap transportation facility; and how decidedly the advantages of water over rail transportation indicate the Ohio River as that facility.

But to bring the question yet nearer our own day: It is assumed that it will require from eight to ten years to complete any system of improvement that will render the Ohio the water highway it should be made. By the census ratios already quoted, there will be in *sixteen* years from now 27,000,000 people in the seven Ohio States. These under the consumption statistics already given, will require for food, of wheat alone, 162,000,000 bushels, and the sixteen sea-coast States, in the same period, 138,000,000 bushels, for their 23,000,000 inhabitants. Deducting the annual product of wheat in those twenty-three States, there remains about 140,000,000 bushels which must be obtained from States beyond the Mississippi. This 140,000,000 bushels of wheat represents 4,200,000 tons of transportation. Three million and seventy thousand tons of this must go to the sea-coast States to meet the absolute necessities for food; the other one million one hundred and twenty-nine thousand tons, to the Ohio States.

The saving to consumers, if the Ohio shall be rendered the great water highway it can and should be, in the transportation of this great bulk of *wheaten food only*, a few figures show, leaving to the natural suggestions arising from these statistics the enormous saving on the other great mass of life's necessities and luxuries, which must also result to the people of all sections of the nation.

Grain, it is claimed, can be carried on railroads for one and a half cents per ton per mile, and on the Ohio River for three mills per mile. Under these figures 3,070,000 tons of wheat carried from Saint Louis to Pittsburgh by rail, say 800 miles, would cost for transportation $36,840,000; by river say 1,100 miles, would cost $10,131,000—a saving to the consumer of over $26,700,000. The other 1,129,000 tons taken from Saint Louis to Portsmouth, Ohio, say 800 miles, as an average distance of the distribution, would cost by river $3,725,700; by rail, say 500 miles, would cost $8,467,500—a saving of nearly $5,000,000 to the consumers. It may be argued that this wheat being brought to Pittsburgh must be carried to the eastern cities, and the cost of that carriage as necessary to fully meet the consumer should be deducted from the apparent saving by water transportation *via* the Ohio. Assuming then the objective points to be New York, Philadelphia, and Baltimore, and the average distance 375 miles, the transportation would be, at one and a half cents per ton per mile, a little over seventeen and a quarter millions, making the entire transportation by river and rail about 27,500,000, while entirely by rail its cost would be over $54,000,000, leaving saving of $27,000,000 in one year, or about all of the supposed necessary expenditure to render the Ohio the great transportation facility desired. The further negative point might be asserted, that the same tonnage could be carried *via* the lakes and the New York Canal to New York for about the same cost as *via* the Ohio River, and the Allegheny Valley, Pennsylvania and Connellsville Railroads. It must not be forgotten that other points than New York will need the wheat, and that the capacity of the New York Canal is now taxed to its uttermost, so that giving it the advantage of the very cheap lake navigation, it would still have to be carried from Dunkirk to New York, four hundred and sixty miles, by rail. Making Dubuque the shipping point, thence by rail to Chicago, by lake to Dunkirk, and thence by rail to New York, the cost of transportation will be nearly $42,000,000, against $27,000,000 by the Ohio River route—a saving to the consumer, by reason of the improvement of the Ohio, of $15,000,000, or one-half in a year of the assumed cost of the improvement, great as the expense seems. Any contrast by lake and New York Canal is unnecessary, as the latter water transportation facility being now over-crowded, the same ratios of increased population, production and consumption, which justify the foregoing figures, will, even if its capacity should be enlarged, cause it to occupy the same neutral position in estimates of savings in transportation as now, by reason that local ratios of increase would consume the capacity and afford no relief for the increased wheat transportation under consideration.

When, therefore, the transportation of this one article alone, of which nearly definite statistics can be arrived at, is taken as the unit of computation for the whole increased tonnage seeking transportation seventeen years from now, it will be readily seen that $30,000,000 or $40,000,000 expended in the substantial improvement of the Ohio River is a national economy, not an extravagant scheme of internal improvements. That it is an absolute necessity staring the nation in the face; a wise precaution to prepare for the coming millions of population, the thunder of whose tread can even now be faintly heard reverberating down the aisles of time.

I have the honor to be, most respectfully, your obedient servant,

GEO. H. THURSTON,

Chairman Executive Committee Board of Commissioners for the Improvement of the Ohio River.

Hon. WILLIAM WINDOM,
Chairman of the Senate Committee on Transportation,
Washington, D. C.

LETTER ADDRESSED TO THE CHAIRMAN OF THIS COMMITTEE BY J. J. WISTAR, ESQ., PRESIDENT OF PENNSYLVANIA CANAL COMPANY.

OFFICE OF THE PENNSYLVANIA CANAL COMPANY,
Philadelphia, May 19, 1873.

DEAR SIR: In reply to your circular note of the 15th instant, requesting documents, facts, and statistics embraced within the Senate resolution in charge of your committee, I would respectfully state as follows, viz:

The canal lines under my superintendence are—

I. The Pennsylvania Canal.

II. The Delaware and Raritan Canal.

The first-named lies wholly upon the waters of the Susquehanna and its tributaries, embracing in all a length of 360 miles. It is consolidated from various short lines, originally constructed by the State, subsequently sold to and operated by sundry small corporations, and finally, by sundry measures of purchase, lease, merger, &c., consolidated into the present company. The dimensions, tonnage, &c., of the various lines differed very much, but recently the company has enlarged the dimensions of the main line extending from Wilkesbarre to Columbia, 151 miles, with the following results, which, for greater convenience, I give in tabular form—they apply to this enlarged portion only, viz:

	Dimension of locks.	Minimum depth of water.	Minimum width of prism on bottom.	Capacity of cargo.
	Feet.	*Feet.*	*Feet.*	*Gross tons.*
In 1867	17 × 90	4½	28	80
In 1873	17 × 180	6¼	34	300

Arrangements have also been carefully made—

1st. For the constant maintenance of the navigation during the season, by strengthening the structures and banks, and covering the latter with stone, either in the form of paving, riprapping, or macadamizing, so as to avoid all breeches, accidents, jams, and other interruptions, and utilize the whole time of the boats' crews and animals in constant movement.

2d. For the prompt loading and discharge of boats, for the same reasons.

In 1866 the tonnage was moved in 1,600 boats. In 1872 a larger tonnage was moved in 752 boats.

In 1866 the actual cost of movement, including boat-service, labor, motive-power, &c., but excluding the maintenance of the canal, averaged 10 mills per gross ton per mile.

In 1873 it averages about 5 mills per gross ton per mile, and, it is confidently believed, will be reduced to 4 mills in a short time, when the full result of the improvements shall have been realized.

It is difficult to reduce to an average the remaining element of cost, viz, *maintenance of the canal,* since it depends wholly upon the volume of tonnage, there being no appreciable wear and tear. Upon railroads each ton moved is the cause of an appreciable wear, or consumption of the line; but, upon canals, when the annual cost of keeping up and operating the work is once provided for by the revenue arising from a given tonnage, any additional quantity of tonnage may be moved without the addition of any appreciable expense for wear. Hence, the larger the tonnage the less per ton per mile is the expense of maintenance. Upon a well-built canal, with a large tonnage it is very small, being confined almost entirely to the decay of the perishable materials, and the operation of the locks, ferries, &c.

I should add that the Pennsylvania Canal is fed, or supplied with water, entirely from concurrent streams of ample dimensions, and its gradients, or lockage, is uniformly in the direction of the tonnage.

The Delaware and Raritan Canal extends from Bordentown to New Brunswick, and, with a navigable feeder, embraces 67 miles of canal, lying entirely in the State of New Jersey. Together with the adjacent bays and rivers it forms a coast-wise line of interior navigation between Philadelphia and New York of the first importance. Its annual tonnage exceeds 3,000,000 gross tons, with a constant increase, and the number of vessels engaged in its navigation is given in the following extract from a report made last year by the superintendent of the steam-towing department, F. B. Stevens, esq., viz:

In the year 1871, 15,862 vessels, carrying on the average 167 tons each, passed from the south to the north out of the canal into the Raritan. And in the same year the total number of vessels of all descriptions that passed out at Sandy Hook was 9,974, averaging 540 tons each.

The tonnage delivered into the Raritan through the Delaware and Raritan Canal in 1871 was 2,647,430 gross tons.

The tonnage delivered in that year by the Erie Canal into the Hudson was 2,365.-068 gross tons.

The tonnage delivered into the Raritan in 1871 was equal to the tonnage of the whole foreign trade, taken both in American and foreign vessels, that passed out at Sandy Hook during that year.

The tonnage delivered into the Raritan in 1871 was about three times as great, in one direction, as that of the Suez Canal in the same year in both directions. The tonnage that passed through the Suez Canal in both directions in 1871 was 761,367 tons. I have given all the above amounts of traffic for the year 1871, as that is the last year for which complete returns have been made.

The summit-level of this canal has a lockage-elevation of 56.26 feet above low tide.

The dimensions of the locks are 24 by 220 feet, and the width of the canal-prism on the bottom 40 feet; the depth of water from 8 to 10 feet, being equal to the depth of water which can be carried over the obstructions in the Raritan River, which have recently received the attention of Congress, and are now being surveyed and examined by its orders with a view to their removal. Any improvement which may be effected by Congress in the navigation of that river will be promptly followed by a corresponding deepening of the canal, for the size of the cargo has a very important result in the cost of transportation.

The expense of the chief elements of cost, viz, boat-service, labor, and motive-power does not increase in proportion with the increased number of tons carried in the cargo. Hence, when these expenses are averaged upon a cargo of 300 tons, they amount to not much over half as much *per ton* as when averaged upon a cargo of 150 tons.

The tonnage of this canal is of such miscellaneous character, and is transported in such various vessels, moved by wind, steam, and animals, and the work has come so recently under its present superintendence, that I am not prepared to give any average cost of transportation. Of course it is cheaper for staples than any other mode, or it would not command the business, since it controls no tonnage of its own, and competition, both by rail and outside vessels, is on this route extremely active.

The locks are all operated by steam, and the animal-towage, as well as the steam-towage, in the adjacent navigable waters of the United States, is conducted by the canal, such having been found necessary in order to secure prompt movement and the lowest cost for the service.

As no specific information is named in your circular, I am uncertain whether I have covered the ground desired. I abstain from advancing any theories, or general statements with regard to extended transportation by artificial navigation, since I do not understand that you desire anything more than facts.

In respect of the canals which now exist, I feel that I ought not to leave the subject without inviting your attention to two points, which are of vital importance to them, because it seems to me that justice to existing lines comes first in order before the creation of new ones.

I. Since canals now bear all the national and State taxation which is imposed on competing railroads, they should not bear any specific tax on boats unless the same is imposed on cars. The means or implements of transportation should be either free or taxed in both cases. At present the tonnage and enrollment tax is demanded from all boats which reach tide-water, (which includes all boats,) while there is no tax on cars. The district court of the United States, at Philadelphia, in *The boat Ohio, Boyle, claimant*, ads. *United States, libellants*, has decided that canal-boats are not "vessels" subject to the enrollment act, notwithstanding which they are now constantly seized, and taxes, penalties, and costs exacted from them, to the great loss and harassment of the laborious men who are chiefly their owners, and who vainly appeal to the companies for protection.

II. I respectfully submit that the authorities of the United States, viz, Congress should exert their constitutional authority to prevent the closing of the navigable and tide-water rivers of the United States, which constitute the connecting links and necessary outlets of all existing canals. Competing railroads find it very convenient, under State charters, to shut out cheaper lines of transportation by obstructing them with low bridges and narrow draws.

I could point out several such cases, where an annual tax, in the shape of increased cost of transportation, has been imposed on large communities, by small branch railroads of little importance, and that exclusively of a local character.

I am very far from opposing bridges or any other improvements, but I contend that when they cross great lines of water transportation on the navigable and tidal waters of the United States, such conditions should be imposed on their construction by the general laws of the United States, as would prevent the confiscation of prior rights, which is at this moment taking place in at least one locality.

These conditions should be, first, by requiring sufficient height for steam-tugs and their tows of barges to pass under without obstruction, and, secondly, by requiring the construction of draws of sufficient width for vessels other than barges to pass through without breaking up the tows, and putting them together again. In my opinion, in order to protect the existing water-lines and navigable rivers, a clear height of forty, (40) feet from high water to the bottom bridge-chords should be required in all cases by general laws. Should this be neglected but a few years longer, I believe that the existing navigable lines will be extinguished much faster than new ones are likely to be constructed, notwithstanding the great advantages to the whole country offered by both.

It will afford me pleasure to offer such further information to the committee as they may require, either verbally or otherwise.

Very respectfully, your obedient servant,

J. J. WISTAR,
President.

Hon. WILLIAM WINDOM,
Chairman of the Senate Committee on Transportation, Washington, D. C.

LETTER ADDRESSED TO THE CHAIRMAN OF THIS COMMITTEE BY HON. JOSEPH UTLEY, PRESIDENT OF THE BOARD OF CANAL COMMISSIONERS OF THE STATE OF ILLINOIS.

BOARD OF CANAL COMMISSIONERS, PRESIDENT'S OFFICE,
Dixon, Ill., March 7, 1874.

SIR: In reply to your interrogatories, under date of February 21, 1874, I have the honor to reply:

The length of the Illinois and Michigan Canal, from the Chicago River to the Illinois River, at La Salle, is ninety-six miles.

The canal is 60 feet wide at water-surface and 42 feet wide at bottom, with a uniform depth of 6 feet, with the exception of the summit, at the northern end, which is about 8 feet deep.

There are fifteen locks, with a total lockage of 145 feet, descending from Lake Michigan to the Illinois River at La Salle.

The size of the chamber of the locks is 109 feet long by 18 feet wide, admitting boats of one hundred and sixty tons burden.

The total cost of the canal was $6,557,681.50. The expense of maintenance, amount of tolls, and number of days of navigation for each year, for the last twenty-five years, are stated in the annexed table:

Exhibit from 1848 *to* 1873, *inclusive.*

Year.	Ordinary repairs.	Extraordinary repairs, renewals, and hyd. works.	Gross expenses.	Tolls.	Canal opened.	Canal closed.	No. of days open.
1848	$36, 452	$6, 744	$43, 197	$87, 890	April 19	Nov. 29	224
1849	43, 922	26, 999	70, 922	118, 375	April 20	Dec. 6	231
1850	38, 418	19, 996	58, 415	125, 504	Mar. 22	Dec. 6	259
1851	39, 447	19, 027	58, 475	173, 300	Mar. 15	Dec. 8	269
1852	42, 816	10, 692	53, 508	168, 577	Mar. 29	Dec. 8	255
1853	40, 383	4, 486	44, 870	173, 372	Mar. 14	Dec. 12	274
1854	36, 587	16, 654	53, 242	198, 326	Mar. 15	Dec. 2	263
1855	38, 216	32, 657	70, 873	180, 519	April 3	Dec. 12	253
1856	33, 101	58, 357	91, 458	184, 310	April 8	Dec. 4	241
1857	37, 256	65, 825	103, 082	197, 830	May 1	Nov. 20	204
1858	36, 115	21, 972	58, 088	197, 171	April 1	Dec. 1	244
1859	34, 026	40, 406	74, 432	132, 140	Mar. 16	Dec. 3	264
1860	34, 308	48, 275	82, 583	138, 554	Mar. 8	Nov. 26	264
1861	39, 238	15, 823	55, 061	218, 040	Mar. 4	Nov. 28	270
1862	40, 024	15, 337	55, 362	264, 657	April 1	Dec. 3	247
1863	49, 294	13, 021	62, 715	210, 386	Mar. 4	Dec. 1	271
1864	47, 535	18, 572	66, 107	156, 607	Mar. 10	Dec. 1	265
1865	39, 255	85, 614	124, 869	300, 810	April 10	Nov. 15	218
1866	43, 716	72, 647	116, 363	302, 958	April 11	Oct. 31	203
1867	46, 152	116, 504	162, 656	252, 231	April 10	Nov. 15	209
1868	52, 984	69, 067	122, 052	215, 720	April 4	Oct. 31	210
1869	49, 514	42, 251	91, 765	238, 759	April 7	Nov. 15	222
1870	43, 098	65, 597	108, 695	149, 635	April 7	Oct. 8	184
1871	54, 555	42, 667	97, 222	159, 050	April 6	Nov. 25	234
1872*	42, 785	46, 090	88, 876	165, 874	April 1	Dec. 1	144
1873	†53, 525	27, 573	81, 098	166, 641	April 10	Nov. 20	225

NOTE.—The figures in the above table from 1848 to May 1, 1871, are as given by the trustees of the Illinois and Michigan Canal.

* Tolls were reduced from 25 to 35 per cent. March, 1872.

† In this amount is $15,400 paid collectors, lock-tenders, and superintendent, which would leave the amount properly chargeable to ordinary repairs $38,125.

Average length of season of navigation $240\frac{7}{26}$ days.

No sufficient data can be obtained to determine the dates of the opening and closing of navigation in the Illinois River.

In answer to your second interrogatory, I would say that I know of no act of Congress giving the State authority to take control of the improvement of the Illinois River, but some time subsequent to 1861 Congress made an appropriation of $85,000 for the improvement of the said river, a small portion of which was expended in dredging, and the balance diverted by the United States Engineer Department to the improvement of the Mississippi River.

The legislature of the State of Illinois, in 1869, made an appropriation of $400,000 for the improvement of the Illinois River; and authorized the canal commissioners to construct a lock and dam in the river below its junction with the Illinois and Michigan Canal, so as to secure at least 7 feet of water in the channel at all seasons of the year.

In April, 1869, Congress passed a law appropriating $2,000,000, to be expended under the direction of the Secretary of War, for the repair, preservation, and completion of works for the improvement of rivers and harbors.

On the 25th of June, 1869, the honorable Secretary of War allotted $85,000 for the improvement of the Illinois River, the work to be done and expenditures to be made under the direction of Bvt. Maj. Gen. J. H. Wilson, United States Army.

On the 4th of August, 1869, the canal commissioners and D. C. Jeune, State engineer, met General Wilson at his office, where it was determined that the interests of commerce and the largest and most useful improvement of the river could be secured by expending the $85,000 in dredging out the bars and deepening the channel of the river between Henry and Copperas Creek, a distance of 60 miles, where the next lock in the series should be built.

At the session of Congress in 1870, an appropriation of $100,000 was made for the improvement of the Illinois River.

On the 31st of August, 1870, the canal commissioners, accompanied by Engineers D. C. Jeune and Wm. Gooding, met General Wilson at Peoria, and after examining the various plans for improving the Illinois River, it was mutually agreed that the amount ought to be expended in dredging the bars below the point where the former appropriation of $85,000 will be exhausted, and as shall apply to the different points on the river where other locks and dams should be built.

The last Congress of the United States having made an appropriation of $100,000 for the improvement of the Illinois River, and believing that the interest of the whole people would be promoted by expending at least a portion of that sum in putting in the foundation of the proposed lock at Copperas Creek, the governor of this State directed the commissioners to make an application to Colonel Macomb, United States engineer in charge, for that purpose.

The result of the application, and the governor's personal efforts at the Department in Washington, is fully explained by the accompanying correspondence:

"ROCK ISLAND, ILLINOIS, *April* 30, 1873.

"DEAR SIR: With a view of making the most advantageous application of the recent appropriation by Congress of $100,000 for the improvement of the Illinois River, I should like to be informed as to the provision made by the State of Illinois toward the same end. I should also be pleased to have any suggestions from you as to the particular work upon the river that would, in you opinion, best subserve the public interests, taking into consideration what has been done already toward this improvement.

"I remain, very respectfully, your obedient servant,

"J. N. MACOMB,
" *Colonel Engineers U. S. A.*

"To JOSEPH UTLEY, Esq., *Chairman of Board of Canal Commissioners, Illinois.*"

"DIXON, ILLINOIS, *May* 1, 1873.

"MY DEAR SIR: Your note of the 30th April is before me. In reply to your inquiries as to provisions made by the State of Illinois for the further improvement of the Illinois River, permit me to say that the legislature of the State has made an appropriation of the net revenue of the Illinois and Michigan Canal to the amount of $430,000 for the purpose of improving the Illinois River, and authorized the canal commissioners to commence the building of a lock and dam at Copperas Creek, as soon as there shall be accumulated the sum of $100,000; that sum will not be available until about the 15th of September next. Consequently the canal commissioners would most respectfully ask that a sum sufficient to put in the foundation for a lock at Copperas Creek be expended for that purpose by the United States the coming summer, out of the $100,000 appropriated by Congress, at its last session, for the improvement of the Illinois River. You are aware that the State has built a lock and dam at Henry, thirty miles below the junction of the Illinois and Michigan Canal and the Illinois River, at a cost of $400,000, and by an agreement made with General Wilson, your predecessor, the sum of $85,000 allotted by the Secretary of War for the improvement of the Illinois River was expended in dredging the bars between Henry and the proposed lock at Copperas Creek, a distance of sixty miles, thereby giving seven feet of water at all seasons of the year, when the lock and dam at Copperas Creek shall be completed. Thus you will see that perfect harmony has existed between the United States Engineer Department and the authorities of this State as to the improvement of the Illinois River. By complying with the request indicated above you will hasten the completion of this important work fully one year, and, in my judgment, it will best subserve the interest of commerce, and be the most economical expenditure that can be made of the appropriation by both the United States and the State governments.

"I remain, your most obedient servant,

"JOSEPH UTLEY,
"*Canal Commissioner.*

"Col. J. N. MACOMB, *Engineer Department, U. S. A., Rockford, Ill.*"

"DIXON, ILLINOIS, *July* 10, 1873.

"GOVERNOR: "You will see by the inclosed advertisement that the United States Engineer Department has decided to use so much of the appropriation of $100,000, made by the last Congress for the improvement of the Illinois River, as shall be necessary to build the foundation for the lock at Copperas Creek, thus saving to the State one year in time and about $80,000 in money in the construction of that important work. The well-known ability and large experience of Colonel Macomb, United States engineer in charge, is a sure guarantee that the work will be done in the most thorough and substantial manner.

"Your obedient servant,

"JOSEPH UTLEY,
"*Canal Commissioner.*

"His Excellency JOHN L. BEVERIDGE, *Springfield, Ill.*"

Thus you will see that perfect harmony has existed between the United States Engineer Department and the authorities of the State of Illinois in adopting plans for the improvement of the Illinois River.

The first lock and dam, located at Henry, was completed on the 11th of January, 1872, at a cost of $400,000, securing seven feet of water in the channel a distance of thirty miles—up to the junction of the Illinois and Michigan Canal with the Illinois River.

Two years' experience has satisfactorily demonstrated that the improvement will accomplish all that its most ardent supporters have predicted.

The legislature at its last session made an appropriation of $430,000 from the net revenues of the canal and river improvement for the construction of another lock and dam at the mouth of Copperas Creek, sixty miles below the one at Henry.

In answer to your third interrogatory, I would say: The locks in the Illinois River below the canal are not being built under the direction of Government engineers, but are being built of a size recommended by United States Government engineers, and of sufficient capacity for the passage of gun-boats, and much larger and more expensive than is required for the ordinary wants of the commerce of the State of Illinois.

To your fourth interrogatory, the fall of the Illinois River from La Salle to the mouth of the river, a distance of two hundred and twenty-eight miles, is but twenty-nine feet and four inches.

It will require but three more locks and dams, making five in all, to complete the improvement, so as to make slack-water navigation through the entire length of the river, giving seven feet of water in the channel at all seasons of the year.

In answer to your fifth, although very desirable, I do not feel authorized to say that the State of Illinois will at present enlarge the canal-locks to the size of the locks in the river, or increase the depth of the canal to the same depth that will be obtained in the river when the improvement is completed.

To your sixth, as to the effect of the Illinois and Michigan Canal and Illinois River in reducing freights on competing railways, by referring to the following table you will there see that the canal has a very marked and decided influence in reducing charges on competing railways:

	Miles.	First class, per 100 lbs.	Second class, per 100 lbs.	Wheat, per 100 lbs.	Corn, per 100 lbs.	Remarks.
CHICAGO AND ROCK ISLAND RAILROAD.						
		Cents.	*Cents.*	*Cents.*	*Cents.*	
La Salle to Chicago	100	....			......	Most of the grain is stored through the winter at La Salle.
Winter rates	......	45 to 50	30	9	9	
Summer rates	......	15 to 20	30	7	7	
Henry to Chicago	128	....	......	9	8	Henry, on Illinois River and Peoria branch of Chicago, Rock Island and Pacific Railroad.
Tiskilwa	122	50	40	......	15	Tiskilwa, on main line of the Chicago, Rock Island and Pacific Railroad, and 12 miles from Illinois River.
CHICAGO, BURLINGTON AND QUINCY RAILROAD.						
Princeton to Chicago	105	60	50	23	15	
Kewanee to Chicago	132	63	53	26	21	
Burlington to Chicago, (on Mississippi River)	207	65	50	30	20	
CHICAGO AND NORTHWESTERN RAILROAD.						
Dixon to Chicago	98	50	45	22	18	
Morrison to Chicago	126	62	56	24	21	
CHICAGO AND ALTON RAILROAD.						
Bloomington to Chicago	126	50	45	21	15	
ILLINOIS CENTRAL RAILROAD.						
Paxton to Chicago	103	62	53	20	17	
Champaign to Chicago	128	64	53	21	18	

NOTE.—I have found it quite difficult to get all the information which you desire under this head, but the figures given are believed to be correct.

The seventh interrogatory. The cost of constructing the three additional locks and dams to complete the whole system for the improvement of the Illinois River, cannot exceed the sum of one million four hundred thousand dollars. To which should be added the cost of the additional necessary dredging, say one hundred and fifty thousand dollars.

This comparatively small expenditure of money secures a channel of seven feet deep and at least 200 feet wide the whole length of the river, from La Salle to Saint Louis, a distance of 228 miles.

Eighth interrogatory. The size adopted for the locks for the improvement of the Illinois River is 350 feet long, between the gates, and 75 feet wide; built of cut-stone masonry in a thorough and substantial manner.

Ninth interrogatory. The State has made no further appropriation for the improvement of the Illinois River beyond what is required to complete the lock and dam at Copperas Creek.

In conclusion I will say that the navigation on the Illinois River is very unreliable below the lock and dam now constructed on account of the numerous bars which obstruct navigation during the season of low water; there is not over two feet of water on the Lancaster flats, and at the mouth of Copperas Creek.

Your obedient servant,

JOSEPH UTLEY.
Canal Commissioner.

To the Hon. WILLIAM WINDOM,
Chairman of Senate Committee on Transportation.

LETTER FROM COL. JAMES WORRALL, CIVIL ENGINEER, OF PENNSYLVANIA, TO HON. SIMON CAMERON, UNITED STATES SENATOR, IN ADVOCACY OF THE ROUTES THROUGH PENNSYLVANIA.

To Senator WINDOM: I indorse to you, for consideration of the Committee on Transportation over which you preside, the inclosed opinions of Colonel Worrall, civil engineer, of Pennsylvania. He has devoted years of study to the subject, and has brought to bear, in this examination, professional culture and practical experience.

Very respectfully, &c.,

SIMON CAMERON.

Washington, D. C., December 10, 1873.

HARRISBURGH, PA., *November* 25, 1873.

MY DEAR SIR: The subject of great water-communications seems as yet to have inspired no very active interest in Pennsylvania. Yet I question much whether there is a State in the Union which has better claims for notice in that particular at the hands of the General Government.

This you may remember I mentioned to you on one occasion last winter, when you agreed with me; fully informed as you were as a citizen of the interior of the State in this very important matter.

I took the liberty of addressing the Hon. William Windom, chairman of the Senate committee having this subject under consideration, who was kind enough to reply to me stating that my representations would receive attention at the hands of the committee.

I now, however, knowing the interest you take in all subjects of benefit to the great State you so well represent in the Senate, will endeavor to make to you a statement laying down the claims of Pennsylvania in such a manner as that I hope they can be easily understood.

One of the duties of the Committee on Transportation-Routes is to find where a great line or great lines of water communication should be located.

Thanks to the most favorable physical geography of our great State, a grand system of such lines might be constructed across her territory, and for cheapness and shortness I question whether any other lines could surpass them.

The Erie Canal will, no doubt, attract the attention of the committee as one of the most important water avenues that can be constructed, joining the East and the West.

The first of the great Pennsylvania lines that I shall mention to you will use a portion of that canal at its western end, and reach the sea equally soon in time and distance; that is to say, in a distance of about five hundred miles, in round numbers, from Buffalo.

It must be premised, however, that before the Pennsylvania system could be brought into play, the desire of Baltimore would have to be gratified by the construction of a ship-canal through the Delaware peninsula, using, probably, the Sassafras River, and creating a port on the estuary of the Delaware.

That canal constructed, its sea-port would become the sea-port of the Pennsylvania system, and that sea-port would, by the line I propose, be probably not one mile further from Buffalo than the port of New York is by way of the Erie Canal at this moment.

One hundred and fifty miles from Buffalo, on the line of the Erie Canal, at a place called Montezuma, the Seneca Lake invites the passing produce to turn aside and move along its waters, thus reaching the upper north branch of the Susquehanna at Elmira, and from thence following the north branch and the main stem of the Susquehanna, finally reach the Cheasapeake Bay, from whence it finds the sea at the Baltimore sea-port on the Delaware Bay.

The distance, as has been stated, is not a mile longer; indeed, it is most probably shorter than the distance by the way of Albany to New York. There is a delay caused by lockage operating against this proposed route. But apply the advanced science of engineering to its construction, and there will be found no other adverse discrepancy. The extra lockage would not exceed ten or twelve hours in delay, and those hours would be made up by the insurance of safety, considering the dangers of towing on the Hudson River, and the aid of later engineering experience. The elevation to be overcome will be about 350 feet above Lake Erie, or say 895 feet above the level of the sea. There is no want of water; and as for the country through which the canal is to pass, it is not surpassed on this continent—perhaps not in the world.

Canal communication on a small scale has existed for the whole distance, except for the twenty miles or so proposed to be made through the peninsula, and a five or six hundred ton canal is as easily made and supplied with water for the whole way as on the line of the Erie Canal to Albany.

The connection even from Oswego, on Lake Ontario, by this line to the ocean, though somewhat longer, (about thirty-three miles,) might well rival the old route.

At Oswego, at Rochester, at Syracuse the committee no doubt heard representations in favor of the Erie Canal made by prominent citizens.

Every word that recommends the New York system is equally applicable to this; and were this thoroughly examined by competent engineers of the present day; were its advantages ascertained; were the canal constructed under the science of engineering, with its improved experience up to the present time, I question much whether the line would not prove itself, as a national undertaking, superior in many respects to the Erie Canal.

Of course nothing *can* be done without a careful survey. The *prima facie* characteristics of this line call for such a survey at the hands of the General Government, certainly before choice be made of the Erie Canal, as the best possible work that can be created between the termini.

Thus Pennsylvania puts forth her claim in comparison with that of New York as regards a connection between Lake Erie and Lake Ontario and the sea-board.

Let us now look at what she has to present in regard to the Ohio Valley and the Atlantic.

A connection between the Ohio and New York City by water would be so much longer than such connection through any of the other competing States, that it can scarcely be entered in the way of competition.

It is questionable whether there is any such connection at all practicable except by way of the great lakes, and such a connection would be fifty per cent. at least longer than any other.

Pennsylvania, then, is left in competition with Maryland and Virginia alone; the connection with the sea through the more southern States being so far removed as to be independent of rivalry.

The sea-board may be reached from the Ohio by three different routes, commencing at Pittsburgh.

The first ascends the Alleghany River to the mouth of the Kiskiminetas, and thence by the Conemaugh reaches the Alleghany Mountains, through which a tunnel would connect the eastern and western waters, and the valley of the Juniata would be used to reach the Susquehanna, and thence the sea at our new sea-port on Delaware Bay, a distance of something over four hundred miles, say at the utmost four hundred and twenty-five miles. A canal has existed on this whole line except through the summit of the mountain, which was overcome by a portage railway.

The second ascends the Alleghany River still further, and by the Red Bank (already surveyed and pronounced practicable by competent engineering authority) or by the Clarion, (as yet not thoroughly examined) reaches the summit of the mountain, through which, by a tunnel, it would connect the upper waters of the west branch of the Susquehanna and thence reach the sea by this great water-course and terminate at the same port. This last, by the longest route chosen, would not exceed four hundred and fifty miles in length.

The third line ascends the Monongahela, and following its tributaries to the Alleghany Mountains, by a tunnel connects with the waters of the Potomac, and by the route of the Chesapeake and Ohio Canal debouches at Washington.

Its length to Washington City would be about three hundred and fifty miles; but it must be remembered that Washington is, by tide and bay navigation, about one hundred and sixty miles from Hampton Roads, and until a shipment reaches that point it has not attained the open ocean, which it may be said to have reached when it shall have arrived from the West at our port on the Delaware Bay. So the route to the sea by the Chesapeake and Ohio Canal may be called some sixty miles longer, at the least, than the longest of the other routes.

The topographical difficulties of the Chesapeake and Ohio route are no whit easier than those of the Kiskiminetas line. The summits are not more than fifty miles apart, and the elevation is essentially the same, say about 2,000 feet above the level of the sea. The tunnels would both be long—in the neighborhood of four miles—and water is not more difficult to procure at the one than at the other. In short, they have both been pronounced practicable by the highest engineering authority and opinion, which was invited by the United States Government.

The west branch route has an elevation less than twelve hundred feet above the level of the sea, and the tunneling on that route would not be so expensive as on the two others.

A survey of these routes I have not any doubt would decide in favor of either of the Pennsylvania lines as against the Maryland line, and all we ask is that a careful scientific examination of the whole ground be made a condition-precedent of any choice.

A route more nearly approaching successful rivalry with ours, is the route of the James River and Kanawha Canal. This, if I remember rightly, would not much exceed ours in distance to Norfolk, but I believe the physical, or, as I have called them, topographical difficulties, would far exceed those of Pennsylvania.

There is a long tunnel spoken of, and an uncertainty as to water, not met with in Pennsylvania.

I may mention incidentally that the James River and Kanawha Canal commences at or near the mouth of the Kanawha on the Ohio, ascends to the Alleghany Mountains, (in the vicinity of Greenbrier White Sulphur Springs,) which, crossing by a tunnel, it connects with the headwaters of the James River and debouches at Richmond, Va. It will have its warm advocates before the committee, so I need not say more about it.

If the Government entertains any idea of making or assisting to make a great water-transportation route to the sea-board, let Pennsylvania not be forgotten; that is all that is asked for her. The State is so fortunately situated that all the greatest railway lines, and I believe all the greatest canal lines, must cross her territory if the most favorable physical geography for their construction be taken into the account.

With regard to the more southern routes, I mean more southerly than the Virginia route, that they are of very great importance is not to be gainsaid. Routes to the sea from the great southern branches of the Ohio are of paramount importance. But they must, nevertheless, be considered local in comparison with the great northern and middle routes, routes, that is, having for their sea-port no point south of Norfolk.

In the first place, the coast navigation of the United States on the Atlantic side south of Hampton Roads and of the Virginia capes is unsafe.

It is so dangerous as to compel a charge at the hands of underwriters largely in excess of the percentage of insurance submitted to, I believe, anywhere else in the world. So that a first-class water communication would have an undesirable terminus, if striking the ocean anywhere below the entrance to Chesapeake Bay. As local works, however, there can be no doubt of the success of the great Georgia and Alabama canals. The prospective production of that country is simply incalculable. So soon as the political asperities subside in those States, and the people of our whole country can feel as thoroughly protected in person and property there as they do in the North and in the West, an access of industrial movement and prosperity will be inaugurated in that region, which even in the most active and stirring portions of the North and West will never have been exceeded.

It needs but the mere nervous excitement occasioned by the civil war to subside to be succeeded by an at present inconceivable activity.

Then the vast physical material and economical advantages of those States will be availed of, and canals and railways will build themselves. The Coosa will be joined to the Tennessee and "wild Altamaha" will cease to "murmur in its woe."

But still the southern sea-board will remain dangerous, and the time may come when goods from the interior bound for that coast will take a channel improved inside the sand-spits as they are called, and, protected by them from the dangers of Cape Lookout and Cape Fear, whose names alone suggest disaster, reach one of the most capacious harbors in the world, at Norfolk, and thence move out upon the open ocean.

The coast is admirably adapted for such a navigation, one of the safest and cheapest possible. A sloop navigation accommodating vessels of nine or ten feet draught extends now along the shore, for hundreds of miles, requiring very little improvement to make it continuous from Norfolk to Florida.

A canal across the Floridian peninsula would extend that navigation to the Gulf States when the outside navigation would be abandoned and its dangers be avoided.

These are things to be looked to in contemplating the prospective commerce of this great country, and when they shall be accomplished, what a commanding position will be that of Norfolk—undoubtedly the most important sea-port on this great continent.

I trust I have not been betrayed into writing too long a letter, but if I have, the importance of the subject must be my excuse.

Other States have stood up for the great work that might be constructed within their borders. The committee of the Senate has been heard of north, south, east, and west of us—and if their attention has not been attracted to Pennsylvania, it is no doubt because Pennsylvania has not pressed her claims.

Would it not then be surprising if Pennsylvania should at last be discovered to possess greater advantages for the location of these great works than any other State in the Union—seeing that her citizens have seen this national committee assemble and meet at various parts of the United States, listen to discussions of the propriety of building works elsewhere, and let the time pass over without a word in favor of their own territory?

I trust that the crude and hurried suggestions contained in this paper may have the effect to draw the attention of the committee to our unparalleled advantages.

I know that the paper cannot be placed in better hands than yours, so many years of whose life have been devoted to the practical service of your native State, and the nation at large.

I know that you will not neglect the claims of the old Keystone of the Federal Union.

I am, sir, very respectfully, your obedient servant,

JAMES WORRALL,
Civil Engineer.

Hon SIMON CAMERON,
United States Senate, Washington, D. C.

PROCEEDINGS OF THE OSWEGO BOARD OF TRADE AND ITS SPECIAL COMMITTEE, TOGETHER WITH THE REPORT OF THE HON. WM. J. McALPINE, TO THE COMMITTEE ON THE SUBJECT OF TRANSPORTATION-ROUTES FROM THE WEST TO THE SEABOARD.

BOARD OF TRADE ROOMS,
Oswego, N. Y., September 1, 1873.

Proceedings of the special committee of the Oswego Board of Trade, on the subjects of cheap transportation and water-routes from the West to the sea-board.

Immediately on its being brought to the attention of the Oswego Board of Trade that the Senate of the United States had raised a special committee to take into consideration the various routes of transportation from the Western States to tide-water, and to report upon the same to the Senate at its next annual session, the Oswego Board of Trade took cognizance of the matter, and appointed a special committee to take into consideration the whole subject as far as related to the great water-routes from the West to the sea-board.

Full powers were given to the committee, with instructions to consider the subject in all its bearings, to procure all the information possible, and to secure the best engineering talent for the service of the board.

The following-named gentlemen were appointed on the committee:

Messrs. G. B. Sloan, W. D. Smith, F. B. Lathrop, A. H. Failing, J. C. Churchill, J. L. McWhorter, B. Doolittle, I. L. Jenkins, G. Mollison, M. Merick, J. W. Pitkin, of Oswego, W. Foster of Cleveland, Oswego County, and W. S. Nelson, W. Johnson, D. W. Gardner, G. M. Case, and J. N. Pratt of Fulton.

The committee met and appointed Hon. John C. Churchill, chairman, and Mr. John L. McWhorter, secretary.

Hon W. J. McAlpine was appointed consulting engineer, with whom were associated Engineers Greene, of Troy, and Kimball, of Fulton.

Hon. William Windom, chairman of the Senate committee, visited Oswego, explained in full the objects of his committee, and requested certain detailed statistical information.

Upon his return to Washington, in a lengthy communication addressed to this committee, he asked for an engineer's report on the whole subject-matter, which would embody the views of this committee and its engineer in the fullest detail.

This communication was laid before Mr. McAlpine with instructions to make a full report based upon surveys and reports heretofore made on the line from Oswego to the Hudson and on new surveys to be made of the proposed lines from Fulton on the Oswego River to the Oneida Lake.

The report printed herewith contains his views and suggestions with regard to the whole subject-matter.

All the statistical information required by Mr. Windom, and which is contained in various elaborate tables of great length, covering the details of the grain and flour transportation and manufacturing business of Oswego for a long series of years, and which were compiled by Mr. H. C. Stillman, the statistical secretary of the board, were laid before Mr. Windom at Washington, for the use and information of his committee.

For further information reference is made to the report of Mr. McAlpine and the reports of the chairman and secretary of this committee.

The Hon. JOHN C. CHURCHILL,
Chairman Special Committee of Oswego Board of Trade on Cheap Transportation:

SIR: I have the honor to present the report of the Hon. Wm. J. McAlpine, civil engineer.

Mr. McAlpine has embodied his report in the form of replies to certain queries laid before this committee by the Hon. William Windom, United States Senator from Minnesota, and chairman of the Senate Special Committee on Transportation Routes to the Seaboard.

In addition to furnishing replies to Senator Windom's communication to this committee, Mr. McAlpine has expressed very clearly his own views relative to the several water-routes from the head of lake navigation to tide-water, the cost of construction of the Oswego route, and the relative cost of transportation by the said routes to the sea-board.

It is with much gratification I am enabled to state that, as will appear by reference to the report, Mr. McAlpine decides in favor of the Oswego water-route, and shows most conclusively that a ton of freight or bushel of grain can be transported from Chicago via the enlarged Welland Canal, or the projected Niagara ship-canal, Lake Ontario, the Oswego route via Oneida Lake, the improved Erie Canal from the Oneida Lake junction to Troy or Albany and the Hudson River to New York, much more cheaply and quickly than by the Erie Canal route via Buffalo, or the Saint Lawrence and Lake Champlain routes, were either of those routes improved to their best capacity.

Very respectfully,

JOHN L. McWHORTER,
Secretary.

J. L. McWhorter, Esq.,
Secretary Special Committee Oswego Board of Trade on Cheap Transportation:

Sir: I hereby respectfully submit answers to inquiries made by the Hon. Wm. Windom, chairman of the United States Senate Committee on Transportation Routes to the Seaboard, under dates of July 20 and 31, 1873, as follows:

1st. As to titles and dates of reports by Childs, Kirkwood, and McAlpine upon canal-routes from Lake Ontario to the seaboard.

These reports, together with other professional papers, and a large portion of my library, have been contributed to the library of the American Society of Engineers, and are, therefore, not accessible to me at this time, but may be examined at the society rooms, 63 William street, New York.

2d. In order to institute a comparison between the canal-route from Oswego to Troy via Oneida Lake and the route via proposed Caughnawaga Canal, I desire two statements of distances as follows:

OSWEGO ROUTE VIA ONEIDA LAKE.

	Miles.
Oswego Canal improvement	21
Canal thence to Oneida Lake	13½
Oneida Lake	23
Oneida Lake Canal	6
Erie Canal to Troy	128
Total	191½

LOCKAGE.

	No.	Feet lockage.
Oswego Canal	13	113
Canal to Oneida Lake	2	9
Oneida Lake Canal	7	60
Erie Canal to Troy	46	427
Total	68	609

CAUGHNAWAGA CANAL-ROUTE.

	Miles.
From point in Lake Ontario opposite Oswego to Saint Lawrence River at Kingston	22
Saint Lawrence River navigation	134
Saint Lawrence Canal navigation	35½
Caughnawaga	34½
Richelieu River	23
Lake Champlain	111
Champlain Ship-Canal	25
Hudson River to Troy	40
Total	425

LOCKAGE.

	No.	Feet of lockage.
Saint Lawrence River Canal	22	162
Caughnawaga Canal	3	29
Champlain	8	83.8
Hudson River improvement	11	116
Total	44	390.8

Showing a difference in distance in favor of the Oswego route of 233½ miles, and a difference in lockage in favor of the Champlain route of 218$\frac{2}{10}$ feet. Taking each lock as equivalent to a mile of canal, the difference is 209½ miles in favor of the Oswego route.

The eastward and westward lockage of the two routes are as follows:

OSWEGO ROUTE.

	Feet.
Ascending eastward	182
Descending eastward	427

CAUGHNAWAGA ROUTE.

	Feet.
Ascending eastward	79
Descending eastward	$311\frac{8}{10}$

It will be observed that there is an apparent error in the difference of level between Lake Ontario and the Hudson of $12\frac{2}{10}$ feet as shown above. This difference results from the fall in the Saint Lawrence and Richelieu Rivers, which is not included in the lockage.

The number of locks between Kingston and Caughnawaga is 22, a few of which may be avoided by light-draught vessels.

3d. Proposed dimensions in prism and locks of the Caughnawaga Canal.

In 1855 the government of Canada requested John B. Jervis, esq., to survey and estimate the cost of a canal from the Saint Lawrence to Lake Champlain.

The plan reported upon by Mr. Jervis was as follows:

PRISM.

	Feet.
Width at surface from 124 to 150, and in places even	250
Width at bottom, minimum	80
Depth of water	11

LOCKS.

	Feet.
Length	200 to 230
Width	36
Depth of water on miter-sill	10

In 1869, the late John B. Mills made a survey of the Caughnawaga Ship-Canal for vessels of 500 tons capacity; the plan now suggested would provide for the passage of boats of 1,000 to 1,200 tons, and the proposed dimensions of prism and locks are as follows:

PRISM.

	Feet.
Width at surface, minimum	150
Width at bottom, minimum	100
Depth of water	13

LOCKS.

	Feet.
Length of chamber	270
Width	45
Depth of water on miter-sill	12

4th. Proposed dimensions of prism and locks of Oneida Lake Ship-Canal.

These are as follows:

PRISM.

	Feet.
Width at surface	140
Width at bottom	120
Depth of water	10

LOCKS.

	Feet.
Length of chamber	185
Width of chamber	29
Depth of water on miter-sill	9

5th. Dimensions and capacity in tons of cargo (2,000 lbs.) or in bushels of wheat (60 lbs.) of the boats which it is proposed to employ on each of these routes.

The boats which it is proposed to employ on the Oswego route will be as follows:

	Feet.
Length	170
Beam	28
Draught of water	9
Capacity, tons	750
Capacity, bushels, wheat	25,000

The capacity of the boats proposed for the Caughnawaga route will be 1,000 to 1,200 tons, or from 33,000 to 40,000 bushels of wheat. These dimensions must of course conform to those of the Saint Lawrence River canals, and hence will be about as follows:

	Feet.
Length	185
Beam	34
Draught of water not to exceed	9

The proposed Champlain ship-canal prism is put at 110 feet wide, with a depth of 10 feet of water, and the locks will be 270 feet long by 45 feet wide, with a depth of 9 feet on the miter-sills.

The capacity of the boats will be about 1,000 tons, or 33,000 bushels of wheat.

6th. Speed assumed in lake and river navigation on each route.

In my opinion it will not be found economical to exceed the following speeds:

On lakes, eight miles per hour.

On rivers, six miles per hour.

7th. Speed of movement on canals on each route:

It is assumed that a speed of four miles per hour may be maintained on the canals of both routes, between locks, and that, including lockage, except possibly on the Welland, an average speed of three and a half miles per hour may be maintained; indeed, there is scarcely a doubt but that, on the Oneida Lake route, an average of three and a half miles per hour may be maintained between Oneida Lake and Troy and between Oswego and Phœnix. Upon this route it is proposed to tow a single barge; *i. e.*, machinery will be put in only half the barges.

I am of the opinion that this mode of transportation, under the circumstances, will be found most economical, although the duration of each trip will be somewhat greater than where each barge is provided with machinery for its propulsion.

While towing, a speed of three and a half miles per hour may be maintained between locks, or an average of three miles per hour, including lockage.

The models of boats designed for lake and river service, will, of course, admit of a higher rate of speed on canals of suitable size than can be obtained economically with ordinary canal-boats.

8th. Time consumed in each lockage in each route.

In ordinary practice, with boats of 750 to 1,000 tons capacity, the time consumed at each lock will be about fifteen minutes, except on the Welland Canal, where it varies at present from twenty to thirty minutes, but on the enlarged canal will not exceed fifteen minutes.

9th. Estimated time required to make the passage from a point on Lake Ontario opposite Oswego, to Troy, by the Caughnawaga canal route.

Allowing fifteen minutes for each lockage, and taking the speed as heretofore stated, the time will be as follows:

	Hours.
From point as stated to Kingston, lake	2.75
From Kingston to Caughnawaga, river	22.33
From Kingston to Caughnawaga, canal	14.
From Caughnawaga to Saint John's, canal	9.4
From Saint John's to Rouse's Point, river	3.83
From Rouse's Point to Whitehall, lake	13.87
From Whitehall to Fort Edward, canal	9.
From Fort Edward to Troy, river	9.41
Total	84.59

Or, $3\frac{52}{100}$ days.

10th. Estimated time required to make the passage from Oswego to Troy by the Oneida Lake route.

Estimating as before, the time will be—

	Hours.
From Oswego to Phœnix, canal	8.5
From Phœnix to Oneida Lake, canal	3.75
Through Oneida Lake, lake	3.83

	Hours.
From Oneida Lake, canal	3.25
Higginsville to Troy, canal	43.5
Total	62.83

Or, $2\frac{63}{100}$ days,

Showing a difference of 0.89 of a day in favor of the Oswego route, or 21 hours.

	Hours.
By the Caughnawaga route the steaming time is	73.59
Time in locks	11
Total	84.59
While by the Oswego route the steaming time is	45.88
Time in locks	16.95
Total	62.83

Showing a difference in steaming time of about twenty-eight hours in favor of the Oswego route.

Considering the difference in steaming time and the reduced rate of consumption of fuel while the barges are locking, the difference between the two routes may be put at one day, or $28\frac{4}{10}$ per cent. in favor of the Oswego route.

Considering time alone, the difference is $25\frac{7}{10}$ per cent. in favor of the Oswego route.

In this connection it may not be out of place to state that average time from Oswego to Troy by the Oswego and Erie Canals is about six days.

Collecting results for convenience of reference, we have:

	Days.
Time from Oswego to Troy, via Oswego and Erie Canals	6
Via Caughnawaga route	3.52
Via Oneida Lake route	2.63

11th. Estimated cost of transportation per ton of 2,000 pounds or bushel of wheat of 60 pounds from Chicago to New York, via the enlarged Welland Canal and Caughnawaga canal-route.

In making this estimate it will be assumed that the cost will depend upon the cost of the vessel, its capacity and life-time, and upon the daily cost of running it. It will also depend upon the condition as to whether full or only partial cargoes may be secured, and whether or not constant employment is allowed. In the present case we may assume that the vessels will secure cargoes of at least one-fourth for the return-trip, but as the rates paid are usually double those paid for eastward-bound freight, the result will be equivalent to half cargoes westward bound with uniform rates east and west.

The expense of the round trip will be charged to the single trip in this proportion, *i. e.*, $\frac{2}{3}$ to down trip and $\frac{1}{3}$ to up trip.

The several elements of cost will then be:

1. Interest on cost of vessel, say 7 per cent.
2. Maintenance, say 10 per cent.
3. Running expenses.

Vessels of 750 tons capacity will be considered in all cases, except between Chicago and Oswego, where 1,500 tons will be estimated for.

A propeller of 750 tons, fitted for service upon the lakes, will cost about $60,000.

The annual interest upon this sum	$4,200
Maintenance, 10 per cent	6,000
Total	10,200

This sum for the season of navigation, of say two hundred days, will amount to $51 per day, adding fuel, $60, and crew, $29. The total daily expense for interest, maintenance, and running, amounts to $140.

Detentions are estimated at two days at each end of the route, or four days for the round trip.

The average speed will be about the same both ways, considering the general current tending toward tide-water.

The time consumed in making a single trip will be:

	Hours.
Chicago to Port Huron, lake	75
Port Huron to Detroit, lake	3.12
Port Huron to Detroit, river	5.0
Detroit to Lake Erie, river	3.5

	Hours.
Through Lake Erie to Port Colbourn, lake	12.75
Port Colbourn to Dalhousie, Welland Canal	12
Dalhousie to point opposite Oswego, lake	17.25
Thence to Troy as before	84.59
Troy to New York, river	25.69
Total	240.88

Say 10 days.

The duration of a round trip with the assumed detentions, will therefore be 24 days, at a cost of—

20 days' steaming, at $140	$2,800
4 days in port, at $80	320
Total	3,120
⅔ for the down trip is	2,060

Which represents the cost of transportation of 750 tons, or 25,000 bushels of wheat 1,644 miles.

The cost per ton per bushel, and per ton per mile, will therefore be:

Cost per ton	$275
Cost per bushel	8¼ cts.
Cost per ton, mile	1¼ cts.

Tolls and insurance not included.

12th. Estimated cost of transportation per ton of 2,000 lbs., or bushel of 60 lbs., from Chicago to New York, via the enlarged Welland Canal and Oneida Lake Ship Canal route.

	Hours.
From our last estimate we have the time from Chicago to Oswego	130.62
From Oswego to Troy, as before	62.83
From Troy to New York, as before	25.67
Transshipment at Oswego	24
Total	243.12
	Days.
Or from Chicago to New York	10⅛

In this case it is proposed to employ vessels of 1,500 tons, or 50,000 bushels capacity, between Chicago and Oswego, and to transfer cargoes into 750-ton canal-vessels at the latter place.

The cost to be estimated will therefore be made up of these several items, as follows:

1. Cost from Chicago to Oswego.
2. Cost of transshipment at Oswego.
3. Cost from Oswego to New York.

Vessels of 1,500 tons, suited to lake service, will cost $105,000, and the daily expense will be made up thus, estimated as before:

Interest and maintenance	$89 25
Fuel, oil, and waste	120 00
Crew, say	40 75
Total	250 00
	Hours
The time to Oswego will be	130.62

Or 5.44 days; say 5½ days.

With 4 days' detention, the round trip will be made in 15 days, at a cost of—

11 days' steaming, at $250	$2,750 00
4 days in port, at $130	520 00
Total	3,270 00
⅔ for the down trip is	2,180 00

Which represents the cost of transporting 50,000 bushels of wheat from Chicago to Oswego.

The cost per bushel will therefore be $4\frac{36}{100}$ cents.

The cost of transfer from the lake propeller to the proposed steam-barge, with improved modern machinery and appliances, will not exceed ¼ cent per bushel.

The proposed steam-barges to ply between Oswego and New York are estimated to cost $35,000 each, and the daily expense of maintaining and running them together, with interest, will be:

Interest and maintenance	$29 75
Fuel, oil and waste	60
Crew	25 25
Total	115 00

The time from Oswego to New York will as previously estimated be:

	Hours.
Oswego to Troy	62.83
Troy to New York	25.67
Total	88.50

Or $3\frac{7}{10}$ days.

The round trip will therefore be made in $11\frac{4}{10}$ days, (detentions as before,) at an expense of—

Seven and four-tenths days steaming, at $110	$814
Four days in port, at $50	200
Total	1,014
Two-thirds for down trip is	676

Which represents the cost of transporting 25,000 bushels of wheat from Oswego to New York.

The cost per bushel will therefore be $2\frac{705}{1000}$ cents.

SUMMARY.

Cost from Chicago to Oswego	4.36	cents
Cost transshipment at Oswego	.5	cent.
Cost from Oswego to New York	2.705	cents.
Total	7.565	cents.
Cost per ton		$2 52
Cost per bushel	7.575	cents.
Cost per ton, mile	$1\frac{7}{10}$	mills.

If each steam-barge tow a single barge, carrying 28,000 bushels, (3,000 bushels being taken as equivalent to machinery,) the daily expense of the two boats will be about $140, and the time between Oswego and New York will be increased to $4\frac{1}{2}$ days, (allowing for reduced speed and time for locking towed barge;) with the assumed detentions, the duration of the round trip will be thirteen days, at a cost of—

Nine days steaming, at $140	$1,260 00
Four days in port, at $80	320 00
Total	1,580 00
Three-fourths for down trip is	1,053 33

Which represents the cost of transporting 53,000 bushels of wheat from Oswego to New York. The cost per bushel will therefore be $1\frac{987}{1000}$ cents.

SUMMARY.

Cost per bushel from Chicago to Oswego	4.36	cents.
Cost per bushel transshipment at Oswego	.5	cent.
Cost per bushel Oswego to Troy	1.987	cents.
Total	6.847	cents.
Cost per ton		$2.282
Cost per bushel say	$6\frac{7}{8}$	cents.
Cost per ton, mile	$1\frac{62}{100}$	mills.

In this connection it is thought best to add estimates of the cost of transportation from Chicago to New York via Buffalo and Erie Canal.

1st. Employing 1,500-ton vessels on the lakes in connection with the present mode of transportation on the Erie Canal.

Estimates made as in preceding cases, give the following results:

Cost per bushels, Chicago to Buffalo	4.13 cents.

Cost transshipment at Buffalo	.5	cent.
Cost from Buffalo to New York	8	cents.
Total	12.63	cents.
Cost per ton		$4 21
Cost per ton, mile, (1,395 miles)	$3\frac{2}{100}$	mills.
Time from Chicago to New York	18	days.

2d. Employing same class of vessels upon the lakes, and steam upon the present Erie Canal in boats carrying 200 tons, at an average speed of three miles on the canal, and five miles on the Hudson River. In this case we obtain the following results:

Cost per bushel, Chicago to Buffalo	4.13	cents.
Cost of transshipment at Buffalo	.5	cent.
From Buffalo to New York	3.984	cents.
Total	8.614	cents.
Cost per ton		$2.871
Cost per ton, mile, (1,395 miles)	$2\frac{6}{100}$	mills.
Time from Chicago to New York	12	days.

3d. Employing 1,500-ton vessels on the lake, and steam-barges of 750 tons on the Erie Canal and Hudson River, as proposed for the Oneida Lake route:

Cost per bushel, from Chicago to Buffalo	4.13	cents.
Cost transshipment at Buffalo	.5	cent.
Cost from Buffalo to New York	3.7	cents.
Total	8.33	cents.
Cost per ton		$2 78
Cost per ton, mile (1,395 miles)	2	mills.

4th. Employing same vessels on the lakes and canals, except that each steam-barge tows a single barge, carrying 28,000 bushels. Here fifteen minutes is allowed for each lockage of each barge, and a speed of 3½ miles per hour is assumed between locks, while the speed on the Hudson River is assumed at 5 miles per hour.

Estimating as before, we have the cost of transportation of 53,000 bushels from Buffalo to New York $1,501.33, or at the rate of 2.83 cents per bushel.

Taking the several elements of cost between Chicago and New York, we have:

	Cents per bushel.
Cost from Chicago to Buffalo	4.13
Cost of transshipment to Buffalo	.5
Cost from Buffalo to New York	2.83
Total	7.46

Cost per ton, $2.49.
Cost per ton, mile, (1,395 miles,) 1.79 mills.
Time from Chicago to New York, 13 days.

The foregoing results are arranged for convenient reference in the following

Table showing cost of transportation from Chicago to New York by various water-routes.

Routes.	Distance.	Time.	Cost of transportation. Per ton.	Per bushel of wheat.	Per ton, mile.	Per cent.
	Miles.	*Days.*		*Cents.*	*Mills.*	
Via Buffalo and Erie Canal, present	1,395	18.	$4 21	12.63	3.2	100
Via Buffalo and Erie, steam, on present canal	1,395	12.	2 87	8.61	2.06	68
Via Buffalo and Erie, 750-ton barges, on canal	1,395	11.4	2 78	8.33	2.00	66
Via Caughnawaga route	1,644	10.	2 75	8.25	1.25	65
Via Oneida Lake route	1,411½	10.2	2 52	7.565	1.70	59
Via Oneida Lake route, towing single barge	1,411½	11.	2 28	6.847	1.62	54

Tolls and insurance not included in any case.

Instituting a comparison between the results in the two particular cases mentioned by Senator Windom, we find that the times from Chicago to New York are practically the same, except in the case of towing a single barge, where it is a day longer by the Caughnawaga route.

Comparing the cost per ton and per bushel, we find a difference of 47 cents per ton, and of 1.4 cents per bushel, in favor of the Oneida Lake route, the cost in the latter case being 17 per cent. less than by the Caughnawaga route.

The proposed Oneida Lake route will have an ultimate capacity of at least 15,000,000 tons in 212 days or during the season of navigation. The annual saving in the cost of transportation, at 47 cents per ton, will, therefore, be over $7,000,000 upon the full capacity of the canal, or 2⅓ million of dollars upon a traffic of 5,000,000 tons, representing the annual interest at 7 per cent. upon one hundred and thirty-three and one-third million of dollars respectively.

13th. "Do you contemplate the employment of lake-sailing and steam-vessels from Chicago to New York by the Oneida Lake Canal route, or do you assume that there must be a transshipment from lake-vessels to canal-boats or barges? If the latter, what point do you think must be the port of transshipment?"

The employment of lake-sailing vessels and steamers from Chicago to New York by the Oneida Lake route is not contemplated, for the reason that the canal enlargement from Oswego to Troy, together with the improvements of the Hudson River, would have to be made of at least equal depth and dimensions with the enlarged Welland Canal, thus very largely increasing the cost of such enlargement and improvement.

Besides the large sailing-vessels and steamers (with their more costly appointments and greater number of officers and men,) are not adapted to the safe and economical navigation of the long reaches of canal and narrow river-navigation, such as exist between Oswego and New York.

This will be obvious when it is considered that a lake propeller of 1,500 tons costs about $105,000 if of wood, and $175,000 if of iron; while the proposed barges will not cost to exceed $35,000. Two of these barges, costing $70,000, will have the same capacity as the large lake-propeller, costing from $105,000 to $175,000.

Where half the barges are towed, the cost of two barges, one with and the other without machinery, will not exceed $50,000, while their aggregate carrying capacity will exceed that of the lake-propeller of 1,500 tons, costing $105,000. The saving will consist, of course, in reduced interest, maintenance, and insurance, and in reduced expenses of crews.

It is proposed to transship at Oswego. This can be done expeditiously and cheaply with modern machinery, and will in many cases save the grain from deterioration from heat to an extent far greater than the cost of transshipment.

14th. "What will be the dimensions of the Welland Canal, in prism and locks, when the present enlargements shall have been completed."

PRISM.

	Feet.
Width at surface	150
Width at bottom	105
Depth of water	13

LOCKS.

Length in chamber	270
Width in chamber	45
Depth on miter-sill	12

15th. "What will be the dimensions of the largest vessels, draught of water, and tonnage of same, (carrying capacity in tons of 2,000 pounds,) which can pass the enlarged Welland Canal?"

The enlarged Welland Canal will admit of the passage of vessels 250 feet long, drawing at least 12 feet of water.

The carrying capacity of vessels of fair model, will be about 1,500 tons, or 50,000 bushels of wheat with fuller models. Vessels of even larger capacity could pass these locks, but it is not likely that such vessels will be employed. The capacity for corn will be $\frac{1}{15}$ greater than for wheat, or 53,333 bushels.

16th. A statement is desired of the estimated cost of the Oneida Ship-Canal as follows:

Improvement of Oswego River;
Canal from Oswego River to Oneida Lake;
Canal from Oneida Lake to Mohawk River;
River improvement of Mohawk River.

Only approximate estimates can be made. These will be based upon profiles of recent surveys of the route from the Oswego Canal at Phœnix to Oneida Lake, and upon the estimate made in 1863–'64, by the then State engineer of New York, of the cost of removing bench-walls, deepening the canal, and constructing a single tier of enlarged locks, for the passage of gun-boats of 600 tons, to lakes Erie and Ontario. With these guides, and together with my own intimate knowledge of the route and of the cost of works generally, I submit the following:

Estimate of cost of the proposed Oswego Ship-Canal, from Oswego to Troy, via Oneid Lake

Oswego Canal improvement to Phœnix	$2,600,000
Canal from Phœnix to Oneida Lake	1,250,000
Oneida Lake Canal to Higginsville	1,300,000
Erie Canal, Higginsville to Troy	19,850,000
Total	25,000,000

17th. "What time do you estimate would be required to construct the Oneida Lake Ship-Canal and River improvements connected with it?"

The works could probably be done in from three to four years.

18th. "Please to state the following distances: Chicago to Port Colbourne; Welland Canal, (enlarged;) Port Dalhousie to Oswego."

	Miles.
Chicago to Port Colbourne	896
Welland Canal, (enlarged)	30
Port Dalhousie to Oswego	138

19th. "Is the general proposition true that increased size of canal in prism and locks causes a reduction in the cost of transportation? Such proposition has been stated; but I observe that a different opinion is held in the report to the New York legislature, dated February 25, 1873, entitled Steam on the Canals, (see pages 6, 7, and 13,) in relation to the Delaware and Raritan Canal."

Assuming that the dimensions of the prism and locks of a canal are exactly adapted to each other, and to the boats navigating the canal, and that proper proportions are observed in the design of the boats, the general proposition referred to is true.

The dimensions of the prism of a canal determine the size and capacity of the boats which can be most economically used upon it, it being assumed, of course, that the quantity of freight requiring movement is such as to keep the boats constantly employed during the season of navigation.

The locks of the Delaware and Raritan Canal were purposely constructed of sufficient length to admit of the passage of two boats, a steamer and barge, at a single lockage.

These locks, 220 feet long, of course admit the passage of boats of 600 tons carrying capacity; but such boats, or even those of 500 tons, have not been found economical, for the reason that they are not suited to the prism of the canal, and also because on account of their inordinate lengths, the crews required to manage such boats are out of proportion to the cargoes carried.

Experience has shown that boats 110 feet long by 23 feet 3 inches wide are best adapted to the prism of that particular canal. The fact that longer boats, having a larger carrying capacity, have been tried and found to be less economical on this canal, in no wise affects the truth of the general proposition referred to, when such proposition is correctly and fully stated.

20th. "Do you think that if the locks of the Erie Canal are made longer and wider, that the cost of transportation on that canal would be reduced, with its present size of prism?"

It is exceedingly doubtful whether the lengthening and widening of the locks of the Erie Canal would alone effect any reduction in the cost of transportation. Reduced speed or extra cost of towage and extra risks incurred would, in my judgment, fully compensate for any practicable gain in carrying capacity in the present prism of the Erie Canal.

In case steam should be successfully introduced upon the Erie Canal it may be found expedient to *double* the *length* of the locks, so that a steamer with a single boat in tow may pass at a single lockage. Such an arrangement would no doubt result in a somewhat diminished cost of transportation, and would be more economical than single steamers passing the present locks without tows.

21st. "Is it the opinion of Mr. McAlpine that the reduced cost of transportation on the enlarged Welland Canal, and on the proposed Oneida Lake Ship-Canal, would keep pace with the reduced cost of transportation on a double-track (steel) freight-railroad, such as that which the New York Central Company is now constructing?"

It is *decidedly* so. If the most extravagant claims of those who are or have been engaged in railroad transportation are ever realized, the cost of transporting wheat from Chicago to New York by rail will still be at least 20 cents per bushel, or nearly three times the estimated cost by the Oneida Lake Ship-Canal route.

22d. "What is the estimate of Mr. McAlpine as to the cost per mile from Oswego to New York by the proposed Oneida Lake Canal and by double-track freight-railroads just alluded to?"

I estimate the cost to be as follows:

Oswego to New York, single steam-barge, 750 tons	$2\frac{61}{100}$ mills.
Oswego to New York, towing a single barge	$1\frac{92}{100}$ mills.
Cost by double-track (steel) railway	*9 to 10 mills.

Taking the entire distance from Chicago to New York the cost per mile by water (Oneida Lake) is, as already stated, $1\frac{61}{100}$ mills, or about *one-sixth* of the minimum probable cost by rail. At 9 mills per ton mile the cost of transporting a bushel of wheat from Chicago to New York via Lake Shore and New York Central routes is, 982 miles, at 9 mills, $8.83 per ton, or 26½ cents per bushel.

It is to be understood that in all cases the estimated cost of transportation includes interest and cost of maintenance, except in the case of the canals where *tolls* are omitted.

23d. "What is the length of wharfage in the harbor of Oswego, what depth of water, and what the nature of the bottom of the harbor?"

The old harbor of Oswego has a wharfage of about *three* miles, and the depth at low water varies from nine to thirteen feet.

The bottom is rock, except in the basins, where it is mud and clay.

The new harbor covers an area of 100 acres. The shore line inclosed has an extent of $1\frac{1}{10}$ miles, and is capable of being developed by slips into a wharfage of four miles.

The curve-line of twelve feet depth at low water is about 600 feet from the breakwater, and between the two there is a depth at low water of from twelve to twenty-five feet.

The bottom is of rock, covered by from one to five feet of sand.

24th. "Has any estimate been made of the cost of deepening Oswego H bor?"

We have no information of any such estimate having been made.

Materials for the answers 23 and 24 have been kindly furnished by Maj. John M. Wilson, U. S. Engineer Corps, brevet colonel United States Army, in charge of harbor-works on Lake Ontario and river Saint Lawrence.

Answers to inquiries made by Senator Windom under date of July 31, 1872.

1st. "What is the capacity, in tons weight (2,000 lbs.) of cargo, and in bushels of wheat of 60 lbs., of vessels which can now pass through the Welland Canal?"

The average capacity is 540 tons, or 18,000 bushels. In the report of the canal commissioners respecting the inland navigation of the Dominion of Canada, dated 24th February, 1871, the capacity of the present locks of the Welland Canal is variously stated at 400 and 500 tons.

It is understood, of course, that the capacity for given dimensions, may vary between wide limits, depending upon the greater or less fullness of the models of vessels.

2d. "What are the present terminal charges, at Oswego—elevation, commission, storage, &c.?"

One cent per bushel covers all charges, elevation—storage, commission, &c., for the *first* five days, ¼ cent additional is charged for each additional ten days until December 15, of each year.

3d. "Please state the time now consumed in transportation by water, thus: Chicago to Port Colbourne; Welland Canal; Port Dalhousie to Oswego; Chicago to New York."

CHICAGO TO PORT COLBOURNE.

By steam	5 days.
By sail	8 days.

WELLAND CANAL.

By steam	1 day.
By sail	2 days.

PORT DALHOUSIE TO OSWEGO.

By steam	16 hours.
By sail	30 hours.
Oswego to Troy	6 days.
Troy to New York	2 days.

*Recent official estimates, based upon precise knowledge of all the facts, so far as developed upon the New York Central and Hudson River Railroad, show a remarkable coincidence with this estimate, and leave very little doubt of its entire reliability.

CHICAGO TO NEW YORK.

Including necessary detentions at Oswego and Troy, Oswego to transship, and Troy to make up tows, the time from Chicago to New York, via Oswego, is about 17 days with steam on the lakes, or about 21 days with sail on the lakes.

The present time, via Buffalo and the Erie Canal, is as follows:

Chicago to Buffalo, steam	5 days.
Transship at Buffalo	1 day.
Buffalo to Troy	10 days.
Troy to New York	2 days.
Total	18 days.

4th. "What proportion of the time required in passing through the Welland Canal is consumed in movement, and what proportion in lockage?"

In cases of steamers about *half* the time is consumed in lockage, and the balance in movement and detentions.

In case of sailing-vessels about *one-quarter* of the time is consumed in lockage and the remainder in movement and detentions.

It is stated that "by the proposed New American Niagara Ship-Canal, which will be eight miles long, a steamer carrying 50,000 bushels or more can pass from Lake Erie to Lake Ontario in ten hours, or in eight hours, if the canal be provided with double locks."

This canal will no doubt be built sooner or later; and especially will it be built in the event of a failure upon the part of the government of the Dominion of Canada to offer equal and the most ample facilities for the traffic of the United States.

Lest there should be any apprehension that the efficiency or value of the proposed Oneida Lake Ship-Canal may be impaired by hostile legislation upon the part of a foreign government, attention is called to the fact that more than *nine-tenths* of the business of the Welland Canal is derived from the United States territory, and therefore that the expenditure of money in the enlargement of this important channel of commerce will be rendered worthless if Canada shall at any time fail to place American bottoms upon the same footing with provincial ones, and compel the construction of the "American Niagara Ship-Canal."

By the canal referred to, the navigation of Lakes Erie and Ontario may be connected upon the American side upon a route better adapted to navigation, and more economical than that of the proposed enlarged Welland Canal.

Respectfully submitted.

WM. J. McALPINE.

To the honorable the Committee of the Senate of the United States on Routes of Transportation:

The committee of the Oswego Board of Trade, in submitting the views of Hon. William J. McAlpine, desire to add a few suggestions for your committee. The appointment of your committee, and the extraordinary powers given you in prosecuting your inquiries, are evidence of the great national necessity which has forced this subject of new and improved routes of transportation between the East and the West upon the attention of the executive and legislative departments of the Government.

Our six Northwestern States have already reached an annual cereal production of over 500,000,000 bushels, or 75 bushels to each individual of their population, while our six Northeastern States, (New England,) produce less than six bushels to each individual. To introduce these growing populations of the East to this wealth of production of the West, on terms that shall insure to the one cheap food and the other a fair and remunerative price for their crop, is a problem of the highest statesmanship and of the most enlarged philanthropy.

The improvement of our railways, as experience has abundantly shown, has failed to make transportation by rail as cheap as by water, while the ease with which these corporations can combine to put up freights, and the impossibility of such combination being long successful upon the water, where high freights start into activity every ship-yard upon the lakes and boat-yard upon the canals and rivers to remedy the difficulty, points unerringly to the water-routes of the country as *the great regulator of its freight tariffs.*

The enlargement of the Welland Canal, recently entered upon by the Canadian government, and to be completed within the next three years, will enable vessels carrying 1,500 tons or 50,000 bushels of wheat to enter Lake Ontario. It will make the great lakes a great Mediterranean Sea, extending with unbroken navigation from Du Luth to Ogdensburgh. It cannot fail largely to increase the amount of western produce coming into Lake Ontario, and which from that lake will find its way to market.

Prior to 1858, before which time the depth of water upon the Saint Clair Flats compelled the use of vessels of a size fitted to the navigation of the Welland Canal, as its locks were then and now constructed, the amount of wheat and flour received at Buffalo and Oswego were nearly equal. But with the increase of the size of vessels used on the upper lakes, which are excluded from Lake Ontario by the size of the locks of the Welland Canal, Buffalo has gained an advantage which has enabled her to monopolize substantially the grain seeking a market by the way of the canals of the State of New York.

A fact which will be important for the committee to consider in connection with the subject of enlarged canals, and especially with the use of barges involving transshipment of cargoes, has recently developed itself. The embarrassments attending the navigation of the canals and rapids of the Saint Lawrence with lake vessels, made the competition of that route, carried on by such vessels, comparatively unfelt by the routes through Buffalo and Oswego. The recent introduction of facilities for transshipment at Kingston, and the transfer of grain at that point to large barges destined to Montreal, there to be put on board ocean vessels, has changed all this. This route now draws more heavily, year by year, upon the business both of Buffalo and Oswego, and has proved, by the experience of the last two years, that grain destined to Liverpool can be carried cheaper by that than by any other route—and this, too, with the disadvantage of being obliged to use vessels carrying 18,000 bushels through the Welland Canal, against those carrying from 30,000 or 50,000 by the way of Buffalo. How greatly this advantage will be increased when the enlargement of the Welland Canal is completed, will be readily understood. Unless our Government, adopting the wise policy of our provincial neighbors, shall make corresponding improvement in our routes of transportation, we shall see our foreign grain export finding its way to market over foreign territory and in foreign bottoms, enriching our commercial rivals at our expense.

In presenting the Oneida route, we claim for it that it is the oldest and shortest, and, properly improved, will be the cheapest and best between the valleys of the lakes and Upper Mississippi and the Atlantic seaboard.

I.—THE ONEIDA LAKE ROUTE IS THE OLDEST ROUTE.

Nature insured this in providing the remarkable continuation of lake and river navigation in the direction most advantageous for commerce, and with but a single interruption. From 1727, when the English gained their first foothold upon Lake Ontario, at the mouth of the Oswego River, for nearly a century the Mohawk River, Wood Creek, the Oneida Lake, and Oneida and Oswego Rivers formed the regular line of communication between the Valley of the Hudson and that of the lakes. Very considerable sums were spent in its improvement. The break at Fort Schuyler (now Rome) was supplied by a canal one mile long, which made the water-way continuous from Albany to Oswego.

The supplies for the forts intended to guard this route from French and Indian attack; the goods of the fur-traders, and the traffic with the Indian tribes, all passed over this route. The attention of the ablest statesmen of this and other States was called to its advantages, and it was regarded as the permanent water-route between the East and West. But before the commencement of the construction of its present canals by the State of New York, interests had sprung up which had a controlling influence on the question of their location. The valleys of the lakes of Central New York and of the Genesee and Niagara Rivers had been occupied by an enterprising and rapidly-increasing population, whose necessities demanded an outlet to market. The same cry was heard from those localities that comes to us now from the West. Wheat upon the Genesee bore but one-third its price upon the Hudson, and brought little profit to its producer. The Erie Canal was primarily, and wisely, too, located where it is to meet this pressing necessity. But this necessity has long since passed, and when the General Government is called upon to aid works of internal improvement, it has a right to demand that the best and cheapest routes shall be selected.

II.—THE ONEIDA LAKE ROUTE IS THE SHORTEST BETWEEN THE LAKES AND THE HUDSON.

Three routes have been proposed: By the Saint Lawrence and Lake Champlain, by Buffalo and the Erie Canal, and by Oswego and the Oneida Lake.

The actual miles of these routes are as follows:

	Miles.
Chicago to Albany, by the Saint Lawrence and Lake Champlain	1,495
Chicago to Albany, by Buffalo and the Erie Canal	1,277
Chicago to Albany, by Oswego and Oneida Lake	1,262

These distances are each made up of lake, river, and canal navigation, and the difference between them will best be shown by reducing the distances to equivalents of one of these methods of navigation.

The cost of moving a ton a mile by each of these methods has been stated by very competent authority as follows: 1½ mills per mile on the lakes, 2 on the rivers, 4 on ship-canals, and 6 on the Erie Canal.

From them we derive the following distances of navigation by ship-canal, equivalent to each of the above routes.

Chicago to Albany, by Buffalo and Erie Canal:

	Miles.
925 miles lake-navigation = ship-canal navigation	346⅞
352 miles Erie-Canal navigation = ship-canal navigation	528
Chicago to Albany, by Erie Canal = ship-canal navigation	874⅞

Same route, with Erie Canal enlarged to ship-canal:

925 miles lake navigation = ship-canal navigation	346⅞
352 miles ship-canal navigation = ship-canal navigation	352
Chicago and Albany by Erie Canal enlarged = ship-canal navigation	698⅞

Chicago to Albany, by way of Oswego and Onieda Lake:

1,063½ miles lake-navigation = ship-canal navigation	398¾
198½ ship-canal = ship-canal navigation	198½
Chicago to Albany, by Oswego and Oneida Lake = ship-canal navigation.	597¼

Chicago to Albany, by way of Lake Champlain:

1,173 miles lake-navigation = ship-canal navigation	439⅞
165 miles ship-canal navigation = ship-canal navigation	165
157 miles river-navigation = ship-canal navigation	78½
Chicago to Albany, by Albany and Lake Champlain = ship-canal navigation	683⅜

That is, the Oneida Lake route has an advantage over either of the others, even supposing each of them to have been enlarged to ship-canals, equal to nearly one hundred miles of ship-canal navigation; as compared with the present Erie Canal route, the advantage would be equal to nearly three hundred miles of such navigation.

III.—THE ONEIDA LAKE ROUTE PROPERLY IMPROVED IS THE CHEAPEST.

This necessarily follows from the conclusions arrived at under our last proposition. But a more satisfactory proof of this will be found in the report of Mr. McAlpine, and particularly in his answer to the 11th and 12th questions submitted by your honorable chairman.

IV.—THIS ROUTE IS THE BEST FOR OTHER CONSIDERATIONS.

As compared with the Champlain route:

1. It has the advantage of being entirely within our own territory excepting the Welland Canal. The use of that canal is secured to us by the treaty of Washington, which also secures to the people of Canada very important privileges—including among others the navigation of Lake Michigan, and the use of the Saint Clair Flats Canal, and should the treaty be infringed, or interpreted or applied in a hostile manner by the Canadian authorities, we can withhold privileges equally important to them. But the true remedy, and one which should long since have been applied, we have in our hands, in the construction of the Niagara Ship-Canal.

The treaty of Washington also protects us in the use of the canals and the rapids of the Saint Lawrence, forming part of the Champlain route. But this protection does not extend to the proposed Caughnawaga Canal, and unfriendly legislation or action as to this canal, intended to advance the interests of Montreal at the expense of American ports, could not be claimed as an infringement of the letter or spirit of the treaty.

Besides, if our Government should adopt the Champlain route, what probability is there of the construction of the Caughnawaga Canal? Our own Government will not expend its money on foreign soil. The Canadian government have little interest in building a canal, the principal effect of which would be to divert the trade which they hope to concentrate at Montreal. If built by private capital, the tolls necessarily charged to re-imburse the outlay would largely increase the difference in favor of the American route heretofore shown.

2. It has the advantage of two weeks earlier navigation in the spring and two weeks later in the fall, and that at the time when the pressure of freights for movement is the greatest.

3. It escapes the fogs of the Saint Lawrence, which any one acquainted with the navigation of that river knows to be a serious inconvenience, especially in autumn.

As compared with the Erie Canal:

1st. This route has the advantage of avoiding most of the cities and large villages which are so numerous along the Erie Canal, and which, by their claims for land damages, would increase the cost of construction of an enlarged canal, and by their numerous street bridges would greatly embarrass and retard its navigation.

2d. The supply of water is ample for all purposes and for all time.

The point where difficulty for want of water would exist, if at all, is the summit-level at Rome. But upon this point, more water for purposes of artificial navigation could be turned than almost any other in the State of New York. The waters of the Mohawk, Black River, Fish Creek, and the Chenango Canal, now concentrated there, are ample, and if found insufficient, the rough and wild forest country around the heads of those streams furnishes unlimited opportunity for the construction of reservoirs at a minimum of expense.

The deficiency of water along the line of the Erie Canal west of Syracuse is well known, and it is believed to be impossible to furnish points of that route with the water required by the lockages of a canal with boats carrying 750 tons.

3d. It improves the communication between us and the dominion of Canada.

We have now a large, valuable, and growing trade with that country, and one susceptible of great increase by proper effort on our part. The merchants of Upper Canada formerly received most of their goods from or through New York, and their exports sought a market through the same port. Much of this trade has been diverted to Montreal by the improved navigation of the Saint Lawrence, but would be regained by us by the construction of the work we advocate.

It may be asked, if this route has so great advantages, why has it not been improved by the State of New York?

The answer is easy. For a long time the State of New York, with a large canal debt, sought to make the rate of tolls such as not only to suffice for the payment of the interest and gradual extinction of the principal of that debt, but also to pay in part the current expenses of the State government. While this policy prevailed the Oneida Lake route was an object of hostility, lest, by its fewer miles of canal paying tolls and comparative cheapness, it should divert trade from the Erie Canal, and thereby lessen the receipts of the State. So strong has this feeling been that the greatest draught of water permitted upon the Oneida River improvement, at one end of the Oneida Lake, is 3½ feet, against 7 feet in the Erie and Oswego Canals; and when, years ago, the Oneida Lake Canal, at the other end of that lake, became innavigable for want of repairs, it has been impossible to this day to procure its restoration to a navigable condition. But the State of New York has abandoned substantially the idea of profit from its canals, and with this abandonment the only objection the State could have to the improvement of this route has disappeared.

The fact that the canals of the State of New York have been mainly the channels of the commerce of other States is a sufficient reason why their improvement should be the work of the General Government. The last report of the canal auditor of this State shows that in 1837—twelve years after western production had felt the stimulus of the construction of our canals—nearly five-sixths of the tonnage arriving at tide-water from the Erie and Oswego Canals was the product of the State of New York, and only one-sixth the product of other States. In 1872, on the other hand, nearly eleven-twelfths of the tonnage arriving at tide-water by these canals was the product of other States and Territories, and only one-twelfth the product of this State.

The benefit to be derived from the enlargement of our canals is national, and not local, and for that reason the work should be done at the national expense, and when done should be under national control.

The capacity of the proposed canal is estimated by Mr. McAlpine at 15,000,000 tons per annum. This certainly would be sufficient to relieve the present pressure of western production. When found insufficient to meet the demands of the wonderful growth of our great Northwest, the enlargement of the Erie Canal can be properly entered upon. But it would be wise for the Government to make its first essay upon *that route which offers the largest and most certain returns.*

LETTER IN REGARD TO THE WISCONSIN AND FOX RIVERS IMPROVEMENT, ADDRESSED TO THE CHAIRMAN OF THIS COMMITTEE BY BREESE J. STEVENS, ESQ.

WASHINGTON, D. C., *March* 2, 1874.

SIR: In reply to your communication of the 17th ultimo, calling for information in designated particulars as to the Wisconsin and Fox Rivers and their present and proposed improvement, I have the honor to submit the following:

THE FOX AND WISCONSIN RIVERS IMPROVEMENT—HISTORICAL.

The Fox and Wisconsin Rivers have been an important highway for nearly two hundred years. They were the route by which, in 1673, Marquette and his companions discovered the Upper Mississippi, and along which were made, by the French missionaries and traders, the earliest settlements in the West.

It was the wish of the founders of the Republic to preserve this great natural water-route unobstructed, and to make it a permanent means of communication between the lakes and the Mississippi. In the ordinance for the government of the territory of the United States northwest of the river Ohio, adopted July 14, 1787, it is provided that the navigable waters leading into the Mississippi and the Saint Lawrence, and the carrying places between the same, shall be common highways and forever free.

The same provision, in substance, is embodied in an act of Congress relating to said territory, passed August 7, 1789, after the adoption of the Constitution of the United States; in an act of Congress establishing the territorial government of Wisconsin, approved April 20, 1836; in an act of Congress relating to the admission of Wisconsin as a State into the Union, approved August 6, 1846, and in the constitution of the State of Wisconsin.

In 1839, under the direction of the War Department of the Government, a preliminary survey of the rivers, and an estimate of the cost of their improvement, were made by Captain Cram, of the United States Topographical Engineers.

In 1846, by an act of Congress, approved August 8, 1846, a grant of lands was made to the State of Wisconsin, on the admission of such State into the Union, for the purpose of improving the navigation of the Fox and Wisconsin Rivers, in the Territory of Wisconsin, and of constructing a canal to unite the said rivers at or near the portage.

In 1854 and 1855 acts of Congress were passed by which the grant of lands to Wisconsin was defined and enlarged.

After the admission of Wisconsin into the Union, by an act of its legislature, approved August 8, 1848, a board of public works was created, through which the work of improving the said rivers, by the application thereto of the proceeds of the sale of the lands granted by Congress, was undertaken by the State.

It soon became apparent that the moneys realized from the sale of lands were insufficient to meet the obligations of the State, issued by its board of public works, as they became due; and in 1853 the work was turned over to the Fox and Wisconsin Improvement Company, a corporation created under an act of the legislature of Wisconsin, approved July 6, 1853. In 1856, by an act of the legislature of Wisconsin, approved October 3, 1856, the lands granted by Congress then unsold were granted by the State, through the said company, to trustees, with power to sell, and the proceeds to hold in trust, for the payment of State indebtedness, the completion of the work, thereafter for the payment of bonds issued by the said company, and the balance, if any, for the company itself.

In February, 1866, the trustees, in execution of the powers contained in the deed of trust made to them, and pursuant to a judgment of the circuit court of Fond du Lac County, sold at public sale at Appleton, Wisconsin, the works of improvement and the balance of lands granted by Congress then unsold, and applied the proceeds to the purposes expressed in the deed of trust.

The proceeds were sufficient to pay in full the expenses of the trust, the then outstanding State indebtedness, and to provide a fund sufficient to complete the work according to the plan specified in the act approved October 3, 1856.

Under an act of the legislature of Wisconsin, approved April 13, 1861, and the acts amendatory thereof, the purchasers at said sale, on the 15th day of August, 1866, filed their certificate in the office of the secretary of state, and thereby became incorporated as the Green Bay and Mississippi Canal Company, holding, as such company, the said works of improvement.

Under instructions from the Engineer Department of the United States, issued in July, 1866, Maj. Gen. G. K. Warren took charge of the surveys of the Fox and Wisconsin Rivers. These were continued by the United States under the supervision of General Warren, and his successor, Col. D. C. Houston, until completed and perfected.

The latest report, with estimates, was submitted to the present Congress.

By an act of Congress approved July 7, 1870, the Secretary of War was directed to adopt such a plan for the improvement of the Wisconsin River as should be approved by the Chief of Engineers, and also was authorized to appoint a board of arbitrators to ascertain how much, in justice, ought to be paid to the Green Bay and Mississippi Canal Company for the transfer of its property and rights, including locks, dams, canals, &c., in and to the line of water communication between Portage City and Green Bay—the arbitrators in making their award being required to take into consideration the amount of money realized from the sale of lands theretofore granted by Congress to the State of Wisconsin to aid in the construction of said water communication, and to deduct the amount thereof from the actual value of the works of improvement as found by said arbitrators.

The act also provided that all tolls to be received by the Government from the work should be deposited in the Treasury until the Government should be re-imbursed all moneys it should expend on the work.

The arbitration took place in 1871. It appeared that the moneys expended by the Green Bay and Mississippi Canal Company and its predecessors in interests considerably exceeded the sum of two million dollars, exclusive of interest. The arbitrators fixed the present value at $1,048,070, from which was deducted the full amount of money realized from the sale of lands granted by Congress, $723,070, leaving a balance of $325,000, all of which was to be paid to the company in case the Secretary of War should elect to take with the improvements the water-powers and the personal property; and in case he should elect not to take the latter or either, the value of the water-powers was fixed at $140,000, and of the personal property at $40,000, leaving as applicable to the improvement the balance of $145,000.

The Secretary of War elected to take the improvement only, and by act of Congress, approved June 10, 1872, an appropriation was made therefor. In October, 1872, the company delivered its deed of conveyance to the United States covering the works of improvement, &c., and received the sum of $145,000.

In his statement to your committee (p. 230, testimony) Colonel Houston is in error in the supposition that a portion of the lands granted by Congress were not sold, and were still held by the company. At the trustee's sale in 1866, pursuant to the judgment of the court, all of the lands were sold, and the full proceeds were applied to the payment and full satisfaction of the construction-indebtedness outstanding. The error doubtless arose from the fact that some of the parties who were afterward incorporated as the Green Bay and Mississippi Canal Company were purchasers at the public sale, and as individuals, not as a company, continued to hold, undisposed of, some of the lands purchased.

The moneys for which the Government received credit on the purchase from the company as the amount realized on the sale of the lands granted by Congress, with the expenses of sale, were about equal to $1.25 for every acre of land granted.

It is perhaps proper to say that the award was not satisfactory to the Green Bay and Mississippi Canal Company, especially as many of the corporators were heavy losers in both that and the preceding company.

Subsequent appropriations for this work, $100,000 in 1870, and $300,000 in 1873, were made by Congress, all of which have been expended under the direction of Colonel Houston. To your committee the colonel says, (p. 231 of testimony:) "*I wish to say that the work now is in the hands of the Government different from any other work of this character*, and the appropriation made last year is too small an appropriation to carry on the work to advantage."

NATURE AND CONDITION OF THE WORK OF IMPROVEMENT.

The Wisconsin River, having its rise in the northern part of the State of Wisconsin, runs southerly until it approaches the Fox River, turns abruptly southwesterly, and, running in that course one hundred and eighteen miles, empties into the Mississippi at Prairie du Chien. The Fox River, having its rise in the southern part of Wisconsin, runs northwesterly until it approaches the Wisconsin River, turns abruptly northeasterly, and, running in that course one hundred and sixty miles, (to be reduced by improvement to one hundred and fifty-three miles,) empties into Lake Michigan at Green Bay.

The course of the two rivers below the Portage, the point of nearest approach, is surprisingly straight, and nearly upon a due line passing through Prairie du Chien and the Straits of Mackinaw. The divide, or portage, separating the Wisconsin River waters, putting into the Gulf of Mexico, from the Fox River waters, putting into the Saint Lawrence, is a level sand prairie, without rock, and in width one and one-half miles. The Wisconsin at the portage is at the summit-level. It is about eight feet higher than the Fox at the portage, and about two hundred feet higher than Lake Michigan at the mouth of the Fox, and one hundred and sixty-nine feet higher than the Mississippi at the mouth of the Wisconsin.

Already a canal at the portage connects the Wisconsin and the Fox, and a slack-water communication extending from the portage to Green Bay, a distance of one hundred and sixty miles, overcomes by locks and dams the fall of two hundred feet, and connects the Wisconsin River with Lake Michigan. The Fox River, from its mouth to Oshkosh, on Lake Winnebago, has a low-water channel of about four feet, and from Lake Winnebago to the portage of about three feet. At stages of high water, boats of three, four, and even five feet draught have passed from Lake Michigan up the Fox River and down the Wisconsin into the Mississippi River. As late in the season as June boats of three hundred tons burden have made the passage. In stages of low water the Wisconsin cannot be navigated on account of the shifting sand.

The slack-water improvement now in operation chiefly extends from the portage to the mouth of the Fox, and consists of levels formed by dams, extending across the river, around one end of each of which there are short canals, and in the canals, locks. In all there are twenty-two locks; more locks than levels. The height overcome a

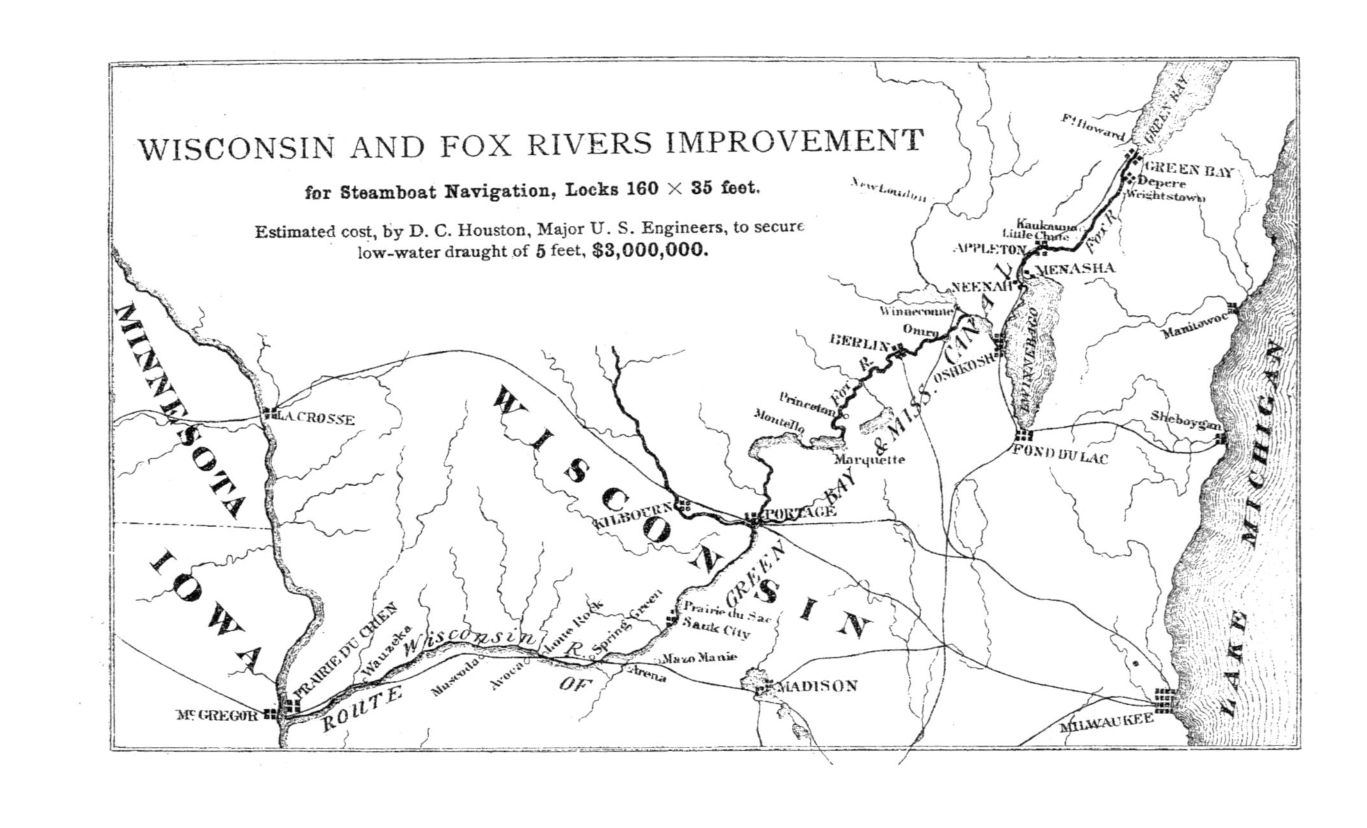
WISCONSIN AND FOX RIVERS IMPROVEMENT
for Steamboat Navigation, Locks 160 × 35 feet.
Estimated cost, by D. C. Houston, Major U. S. Engineers, to secure low-water draught of 5 feet, $3,000,000.
MINNESOTA
IOWA
WISCONSIN
LAKE MICHIGAN
GREEN BAY
Ft Howard
GREEN BAY
Depere
Wrightstown
Kaukauna
Little Chute
APPLETON
MENASHA
NEENAH
Fox R.
Winneconne
Omro
BERLIN
OSHKOSH
WINNEBAGO
CANAL
BAY & MISS.
Princeton
Montello
Marquette
Manitowoc
Sheboygan
FOND DU LAC
PORTAGE
KILBOURN
GREEN
Prairie du Sac
Sauk City
Mazo Manie
Arena
MADISON
MILWAUKEE
LACROSSE
Mc GREGOR
PRAIRIE DU CHIEN
Wauzeka
Wisconsin R.
Lone Rock
Spring Green
Muscoda
Avoca
ROUTE OF

little exceeds two hundred feet, while the lockage does not exceed one hundred and ninety-five feet. The canal at the portage is about two miles in length, while the canals at the dams are only long enough to furnish approaches to the locks.

Taking all together, there are about six miles of canal. That at the portage is seventy feet wide, and at trifling expense can be made of any required width and depth, while the approaches to the locks are in many cases wider than seventy feet and in all cases of sufficient width for the locks. The locks are 160 feet long by 35 feet wide, being nearly fifty per cent. longer and over one hundred per cent. wider than the enlarged locks on the Erie Canal, and wider than any in the country excepting on the Albemarle and Chesapeake Canal and the locks at Louisville, Ky.

To supply water to the Fox River, in case at any time it should be needed, the Wisconsin River is at the summit-level, with a volume at the portage at low water, according to Colonel Houston, of three thousand feet per second.

The plan of improvement which, pursuant to the act of July 7, 1870, has met the approval of the Chief of Engineers, and has been adopted by the Secretary of War, contemplates for the Fox River, from portage to Green Bay, the repair, and, in some cases, reconstruction, of the dams and locks now standing; the construction of five additional locks, and the dredging out of the channel; and for the Wisconsin River from portage to Prairie Du Chien, a "river improvement" proper. It is not proposed to throw any dam across the Wisconsin River, but to so contract the channel by means of wing-dams, &c., that for all practical purposes the river will be as free and open as before.

At the time of making his preliminary survey in 1867 and 1868 General Warren was in doubt whether a river improvement proper was practicable on the Wisconsin, and, therefore, recommended experimental work on the Wisconsin in order to test its practicability, and also made estimates for canal improvements, one consisting of short canals connecting navigable sections of the river, and the other of a canal the whole distance. The experimental work has proven the entire practicability of improving the Wisconsin by wing or side dams, so that the channel of the river the entire distance will be free, open, and unobstructed by dams. The dams already built have been sufficiently tested; some of them by the freshets and ice of two seasons. The result is, that for the sections of the river upon which the work has been done, about forty miles, there is a reliable low-water channel of about four feet draught, at the lowest places, and it is expected, with the work already done on these sections, that the operation of the river itself will, in another season, increase the depth so that the channel, in the lowest water, at the lowest places, will be five feet and over. To the inquiries submitted by you as chairman of the committee, and by Mr. Davis, Colonel Houston makes the following reply:

"The CHAIRMAN. I see your report states the fact as to the availability of the Wisconsin River for commercial purposes with these improvements. Have you any doubt as to its being made entirely available?

"Colonel HOUSTON. No, sir; it can be made navigable for vessels drawing five feet of water."

*   *   *   *   *   *   *

"Mr. DAVIS. I understand you that that three millions was for the improvement from the Mississippi River to Green Bay?

"Colonel HOUSTON. Yes, sir.

"The CHAIRMAN. And that would make five feet navigation from the river to the lake?

"Colonel HOUSTON. Yes, sir.

"The CHAIRMAN. Did you make a detailed estimate of the cost?

"Colonel HOUSTON. Yes, sir.

"The CHAIRMAN. Is that in print?

"Colonel HOUSTON. It will be next winter; it is in the report to the Secretary of War."*

It may be proper to add that steamboats drawing between three and four feet have in low water passed the length of the completed work on the Wisconsin under full head of steam without in any degree checking speed.

A navigable channel of five feet draught is greater than the low-water channel of the Upper Mississippi, stated by Colonel Houston (evidence, page 231) at three or four feet, and as great as the present like channel of the Lower Mississippi between Saint Louis and Cairo, stated by Governor Stannard and others at five feet. (See evidence, page 595.) If river-boats can reach the lakes it is not deemed important, for the present, at least, that lake-boats should reach the Mississippi. That time, however, is thought by some to be near at hand when the same barge will be towed over both river and lake.

The current in the Wisconsin is estimated by Major Suter, in his report of January, 1867, (p. 75,) at two miles per hour, *and is said to be remarkably uniform*, while the average current in the Mississippi and the Gulf-stream is estimated by the Saint Louis memorialists at *four miles*, and the current in the western end of the Erie Canal near Black Rock by D. M. Greene, the New York State engineer, at *three miles*. *So that when the* *improvement is completed the navigable channel of* five *feet draught at low water from Prairie Du Chien to Green Bay, connecting the Mississippi with the lakes,* 271 *miles, at its reduced length, will consist of* 6 *miles of ordinary canals, having twenty-seven locks and* 265 *miles of open river; of which latter* 147 *miles will be as level as the lakes and* 118 *miles with a current only one-half of the average current of the Mississippi, and not as great as in the western end of the Erie Canal,**

The accompanying map No. 1, prepared by the Government engineer, shows the line of this route.

ITS PRACTICABILITY IN COMPARISON WITH NEW YORK CANALS.

There are twelve canals in the State of New York, of an aggregate length of 886½ miles. The construction of these canals was commenced in 1817, and the Erie was completed in 1825. The enlargement was commenced in 1835, and the construction account closed in 1862, although practically completed in 1859.

The cost of the twelve canals, including enlargement and land-damages, was $65,644,848. To this add interest on loans and the cost of repairs and management up to 1865, inclusive, and the total cost to New York was $107,853,056. The amount of tolls received, inclusive of the year 1865, was $93,272,287, enough *even then,* into $14,580,769, to pay off in full the entire cost of the canals.

Of these canals the Erie is the only eastern and western through canal. The remaining eleven are lateral canals, feeders to the Erie, and outlets for from two to four counties each. Two or three of these lateral canals are self-sustaining. The remainder only become so by crediting to them the tolls on freights which they bring into the Erie. Without this credit, tolls on the lateral canals, with the exception of two or three, have not more than paid, and in most cases have not paid, the cost of repairs and management.

The receipts from tolls on the Erie Canal alone, up to 1865, inclusive, have paid:

1. Cost of the original Erie Canal.
2. The enlargement, including improvements and land damages.
3. Interest on loans.
4. The total cost of repairs and management up to 1865, inclusive.
5. A net profit amounting to $15,622,836. In all the extraordinary sum of $83,629,243.

As the account has been kept by the State of New York, the credit to the Erie is much greater than this. To raise a portion of the moneys expended upon the canals, the State sold its bonds on long time. To meet these bonds at maturity, the income from the canals was put at interest, and the amount so realized was greater than the accrued interest upon the bonds issued. According to statistics taken by Mr. Elmore Walker, of New York, from the reports of the auditor of New York, and submitted to a convention at Rochester in 1870, the credit to the Erie Canal (being net income over all expenditure) on the 30th of September, 1866, one year later than the above, was stated to be, not $15,622,836, as given, but the great sum of $41,436,490.64.

The length of the enlarged Erie Canal is 350 miles.

The length of the improvement, Green Bay to the Mississippi, will be 271 miles.

The summit-level of the Erie Canal is at Buffalo, 654 feet above the Hudson River at Troy.

The summit-level of the improvement is at the Portage, about 200 feet above Lake Michigan at Green Bay, and 169 feet above the Mississippi at the mouth of the Wisconsin.

The waters received into the Erie Canal at Buffalo are in great part wasted at Lockport. From that point eastward the canal is supplied by artificial feeders.

For all practical purposes, the summit-level of the canal is the long level from Syracuse to Utica, (55 miles,) a level fed by 10 artificial feeders, built at great cost, of which the largest and most expensive is the Black River Canal. The supply of water is still insufficient, and it is proposed to build other feeders for this level.

The full volume of the Wisconsin River, three-fifths as large as the Mississippi at Saint Paul, is at the summit-level of the improvement, having, according to General Warren, an average discharge at its mouth of 10,000 feet per second; and, according to Colonel Houston, a low-water discharge at Portage of 3,000 feet per second. (P. 232 of testimony.)

The bottom of the Erie Canal, throughout the long level, is an artificial bottom, from ten to thirty feet above the level of the country through which it passes. At Syracuse the New York Central Railway passes under the canal. At Utica the bottom is on a level with the second-story windows of many of the houses on the river side of the town. The city sewers, the street and highway drains, and the various streams and rivulets along this level, all pass under the canal. At Rochester the Genesee River passes under it, and at Schenectady the Mohawk.

*See page 231 of the evidence. See also Reports 1871, 1872, 1873, containing those of Captain Nader, who has had immediate supervision of the work under Colonel Houston. As far back as 1871 Captain Nader says: "The results of the experiments and investigations have clearly determined the feasibility of improving the river-bed by means of dams (wing-dams) at a comparatively moderate cost."

The bottom of the Wisconsin improvement, as built and projected, is a natural bottom, safe, and not liable to break away, and passes neither over nor under other bodies of water.

On the enlarged Erie Canal there are seventy-one locks, 110 feet long by 18 feet wide.

Upon the improvement, on the Fox River side, there are built and projected about twenty-seven locks, of which all but two are 160 feet long and 35 feet wide. Of the two referred to, both to be enlarged, one is 140 and the other 145 feet long.

The depth of the Erie Canal is nominally seven feet, but practically six feet or less.

The present depth of the eastern end of the improvement, from Lake Winnebago to Green Bay, is about four feet. The proposed depth for the entire improvement is five feet.

The bottom of the Erie Canal is narrow and the locks small, only permitting the passage of narrow boats, which, for the most part, are sharp at the bottom, to avoid friction.

The improvement, and the locks upon the improvement, will permit boats to pass which are flat-bottomed and 50 per cent. longer and 100 per cent. wider than the boats upon the canal.

It is estimated that the tonnage which will sink a river-boat four inches, will sink an Erie Canal boat one foot, so that for the purposes of commerce a depth of five feet in the improvement is more than equal to a depth of seven feet in the canal. As the improvement now is, boats of greater tonnage have been passed than can pass the canal. The motive-power on the canal is horse-power, and on the improvement steam. The rate of movement of freights on the canal is one and one-quarter miles per hour, and on the improvement, (when running,) from five to seven. In 1871, the arbitrators went over the improvement from Green Bay to Portage at an average of seven miles per hour, running movement.

Both are eastern and western through routes, the one a continuation of the other, and later an effort will be made to show that the commerce demanding the improvement to-day is little less in amount than the commerce seeking the Erie Canal. Six of the eleven side-canals of New York cost from two to six millions each, and the remainder less.

In length they vary from 38 to 124 miles. They are fed in part by artificial feeders. The Genesee Valley Canal has 112 locks, the Chemung Canal 116 locks, with 1,015 feet of lockage, and the Black River Canal 109 locks, with 1,082 feet of lockage. They are outlets for two, or at the most, four counties each.

The improvement of the Wisconsin and Fox Rivers, with a length less by nearly 100 miles than the Erie Canal, less than one-third of the lockage, abundant water on the summit-level rendering artificial feeders unnecessary, a natural and not an artificial bottom, no streams to cross, about one-third the number of locks, with only six miles of canal and the balance open river, giving a rate of movement four and perhaps five times that of the canal, with a corresponding saving in transportation charges, is estimated to cost the Government, not the great cost of the Erie, but about as much as the *average* cost of a side-canal of New York, and is the outlet for six States and a vast territory beyond.

ITS PRACTICABILITY IN COMPARISON WITH OTHER RIVER IMPROVEMENTS.

(Its comparison with other water-routes for transportation will be given later.)

Compared with the improvements proposed for other rivers putting into the Mississippi, the proposed improvement of the Wisconsin, is in length and feet of fall not greater than the rivers having the least number of miles in length and the least number of feet of fall, and not more than half as great as the rivers having the greatest number.

An impediment, and possibly the greatest, in the way of the improvement of rivers, is the sudden and great rise of water at certain seasons of the year. In the Ohio the floods rise above low-water mark as high as sixty feet, and in the Illinois, Rock, and Chippewa as high as thirty feet. But not so in the Wisconsin. The difference between high and low water mark is, at the mouth, ten feet and at the Portage six feet. Two mountains of rock, twenty miles above the Portage, situated at each side, and close against the river, by reducing the channel, hold back the floods.

Maj. Charles R. Suter, in his report of the survey of this river, made January 2, 1867, says:

"Twenty-three miles above Portage City the river passes through the Dalles, and is there very much reduced in width. The Dalles act as a dam to prevent any very great rise in the Lower Wisconsin. The average yearly rise is about six feet. In the spring of 1866 it rose nine feet, which is the greatest height it has attained for many years. The rise in the river just above the Dalles, on this occasion, was *more than fifty feet.*"

COST.

Finally, after careful surveys and a study of the river, extending over six years, and experiments in its improvement which have been tested by freshets and ice, many of them for two years or more, it is now reported by the engineers in charge *that the channel of the Wisconsin River, unobstructed by dams, can be improved, and that a channel of five feet draught in low water, from Prairie du Chien to Green Bay, through the Wisconsin and the Fox, can be had at a cost in the whole, in addition to the appropriations heretofore made, not to exceed $3,000,000.**

COMPARISON WITH CERTAIN OTHER WATER-ROUTES FOR TRANSPORTATION.

The greatest canal in the world is the Yun-ho or Imperial Canal of China, 650 miles long, 200 to 1,000 feet broad, and 10 feet deep. There are 400 canals in China with a length in the aggregate of 12,000 miles, whereby China is enabled to sustain one of the most crowded populations of the world, 333 to the square mile, or, if restricted to the cultivated portions, nearly 600. Holland sustains a population of 593 to the square mile, and has scarcely a village without its water-road. Introduced into England in 1755, later than into any other of the European countries, the canals connecting many of the towns, especially in the southern part of Great Britain, have now in the aggregate a length of over 2,000 miles.

These and similar facts teach the lesson that in order to enable this country to sustain a dense population by the development of its resources, it is necessary that all, at least, of the proposed water-routes, should ultimately be opened. It is believed that all will be necessary, practicable, and in the end profitable. A comparison of the northern route by way of the Wisconsin and Fox Rivers, with certain others, simply shows its relative importance. It is not deemed necessary to call attention to more than a few of the characteristics of each of the several routes, nor to enter into a thorough discussion of even those characteristics which are mentioned.

Distances from New York.

The following tables give the distances to New York by this and other routes. No attempt has been made to equate the distances by making allowance for delay and expense of lockages. An investigation into their characteristics will show that the doctrine of equation may be applied with advantage to this over most of the proposed routes, but it is thought that the decisive advantage is not likely to turn upon any mere margin of distance established by equation.

The following table is designed to represent the Wisconsin and Fox Rivers improvement in comparison with the Illinois River and Illinois and Michigan Canal improvement:

* Testimony, pp. 231, 232, Colonel Houston's letter, Appendix, p. —. Colonel Houston's report, 1873. Reports General Warren and Colonel Houston to War Department every year, 1867 to 1873, inclusive.

TABLE No. 1.—*Exhibiting the Wisconsin and Fox Rivers improvement route to New York, in comparison with the Illinois River and Illinois and Michigan Canal route.*

Distances from—		No. of miles, place to place.	No. of miles, total.	In favor of Illinois route.	In favor of Wisconsin route.
SAINT LOUIS TO NEW YORK.					
By Illinois and Michigan Canal route.	From Saint Louis to Grafton, (mouth Ill.)	41			
	From Grafton to Chicago	334			
	From Chicago to Buffalo	*1,100			
	From Buffalo to Albany	350			
	From Albany to New York	150			
			1,975		
By Wisconsin and Fox Rivers route.	From Saint Louis to Prairie du Chien	*500			
	From Prairie du Chien to Green Bay	278			
	From Green Bay to Buffalo	*875			
	From Buffalo to New York	500			
			2,153	178	
PRAIRIE DU CHIEN TO NEW YORK					
By Illinois and Michigan Canal route.	From Prairie du Chien to Grafton	460			
	From Crafton to Chicago	334			
	From Chicago to Buffalo	*1,100			
	From Buffalo to New York	500			
			2,394		
By Wisconsin and Fox Rivers route.	From Prairie du Chien to Green Bay	278			
	From Green Bay to Buffalo	*875			
	From Buffalo to New York	500			
			1,653	......	741
SAINT PAUL TO NEW YORK.					
By Illinois and Michigan Canal route.	From Saint Paul to Grafton	*710			
	From Grafton to Chicago	334			
	From Chicago to Buffalo	*1,100			
	From Buffalo to New York	500			
			2,644		
By Wisconsin and Fox Rivers route.	From Saint Paul to Prairie du Chien	*250			
	From Prairie du Chien to Green Bay	278			
	From Green Bay to Buffalo	*875			
	From Buffalo to New York	500			
			1,903	......	741

* Approximate.

From table No. 1 it appears that Saint Louis is nearer to New York by the Illinois improvement than by the Wisconsin improvement 178 miles; while Prairie du Chien, Saint Paul, and all other points north of Prairie du Chien, are nearer by the Wisconsin improvement 741 miles. The point equi-distant from New York by either route is 89 miles north of Grafton, at the mouth of the Illinois, and 370 miles south of Prairie du Chien, at the mouth of the Wisconsin. That point is 130 miles north of Saint Louis and 60 south of Keokuk, and near to the town of Louisiana. All points north of the town of Louisiana are, by the Wisconsin route, nearer to New York than by the Illinois route.

The following table is designed to represent the Wisconsin and Fox Rivers improvement in comparison with the Kanawha and James Rivers improvements:

TABLE No. 2.—*Statement showing the Wisconsin and Fox Rivers improvement-route to New York in comparison with the Kanawha and James Rivers improvement-route.*

Distances from—		Number of miles, place to place.	Number of miles, total.	In favor of Kanawha route.	In favor of Wisconsin route.
CAIRO TO NEW YORK.					
By Kanawha and James Rivers route.	From Cairo (mouth Ohio) to Point Pleasant (mouth Kanawha)	*735			
	From Point Pleasant to Richmond	485			
	From Richmond to Hampton Roads	125			
	From Hampton Roads to New York	*650			
			1,995		
By Wisconsin and Fox Rivers route.	From Cairo to Prairie du Chien	*675			
	From Prairie du Chien to Green Bay	278			
	From Green Bay to Buffalo	*875			
	From Buffalo to New York	500			
			2,328	333	
PRAIRIE DU CHIEN TO NEW YORK.					
By Kanawha and James Rivers route.	From Prairie du Chien to Cairo	*675			
	From Cairo to Point Pleasant	*735			
	From Point Pleasant to Richmond	485			
	From Richmond to Hampton Roads	125			
	From Hampton Roads to New York	*650			
			2,670		
By Wisconsin and Fox Rivers route.	From Prairie du Chien to Green Bay	278			
	From Green Bay to Buffalo	*875			
	From Buffalo to New York	500			
			1,653	......	1,017

* Approximate.

From table No. 2 it appears that Cairo, at the mouth of the Ohio, is nearer to New York by the Kanawha improvement than by the Wisconsin improvement 333 miles; while Prairie du Chien, at the mouth of the Wisconsin, and all points north of Prairie du Chien, are nearer by the Wisconsin improvement 1,017 miles. The point equi-distant from New York by either route is 166 miles north of Cairo, 508 miles south of Prairie du Chien, and south of the city of Saint Louis.

Comparing the Wisconsin route with the Gulf-route, via New Orleans, and taking New Orleans as the initial point, the distance from that city to New York by Gulf and ocean is about 2,200 miles, and by the Wisconsin route about 3,358 miles, making in favor of the former about 1,158 miles. The point equi-distant from New York is 580 miles above New Orleans and 674 miles below Saint Louis.

Cost.

The Wisconsin route, connecting the Mississippi and the Lakes, to have 5 feet draught, to be 271 miles in length, of which 118 are to be unobstructed river and 153 slack-water navigation, with 27 locks, 160 feet by 35 feet, a total lockage of 195 feet, water at the summit-level in quantity twenty times that required, and not to exceed 6 miles of canal, including the short canals around the dams, is *estimated to cost* $3,000,000.*

The rate of movement will be as great as the rate upon other rivers, and nearly equal to the rate upon the lakes, with an average, little, if any, less than six miles per hour. In 1871 the arbitrators passed over the route from Green Bay to Portage, through all the locks and canals, at an average running time of 7 miles per hour. There is less canal than on any other route, unless regarded in connection with the New York or Canadian canals as a part of the northern through route. Reasons will be given later for the belief that the rate of movement and the capacity of the New York canals will be doubled or trebled by the use of steam and the completion of certain improvements. With the canals as they now are, and the Wisconsin route opened, freights can be regularly moved to the city of New York from the Mississippi, at Prairie DuChien, in 18 days, exclusive of transhipments, and with the canals improved, in 13 days, and possibly in less time, and the return trip can be made in the same number of days; while by the Gulf-

*Colonel Houston's report, 1873. Testimony, p. 232.

route it is thought that the outgoing trip, exclusive of transhipment, will take at least 25 days, and the return trip considerably longer. The increased interest upon capital invested by both shipper and carrier, and the increased expense, are important items in favor of the northern route.

New York the terminal point or market.

In this comparison of routes the city of New York is taken as the terminal point to be reached, inasmuch as it is considered the market of the country at which products reach their highest home-value. The home-value of the products of a country is largely, if not wholly, dependent upon their value in the markets of the world. It is highest in that port from which they can be transported to those markets at least expense. The rates of transportation upon sea-going vessels from the port of New York are less than from any other port on this continent. Until New York shall cease to be the moneyed center of the country, and cease to have the best facilities of all ports for rapid and extended distribution, she will continue to be the chief market of the country. It is certain that she is the present moneyed center and the present market of the country. It is not certain that the glory of this possession will soon or ever pass from her. While it is hers she will control the exports of the country.

These views seem to be confirmed by the following table, designed to show the relations which, in 1872, the imports and exports of the country and of several of its cities bore to each other:

TABLE NO. 3.—*Statement designed to show the values of imports and exports, (exclusive of moneys,) and shipping-tonnage for* 1872, *of the United States and several of its cities; the values per ton, and the percentage which the value of imports of the respective cities bears to the value of imports of the United States.*

1872.	United States.	New York City.	New Orleans.	Boston.	Philadelphia.
Exports, (value,) exclusive of moneys	$549, 219, 718	$270, 413, 674	$89, 501, 149	$21, 443, 154	$20, 932, 876
Imports, (value,) exclusive of moneys	$640, 338, 766	$418, 515, 829	$18, 542, 188	$70, 398, 185	$20, 383, 853
Tonnage*	7, 768, 106	3, 969, 339	501, 965	881, 486	417, 911
Value, per ton	$82. 43	$105. 50	$36. 93	$79. 85	$48. 77
Per cent. of value of imports to value of imports of United States	....	. 65+	. 03–	. 11–	. 03+

* This is the tonnage capacity of the vessels engaged in trade with foreign ports, according to the mode of measurement adopted by the Government.

Hence it is claimed that New York is properly selected as the chief market to which the grain of the country tends, and which fixes the value of grain in all other cities and localities of the country, the value in any locality being determined by the value in New York and the cost of moving it there.

Northern through route.

The northern through route, of which the New York canals are the eastern end, and the Wisconsin and Fox Rivers improvement the western end, leads to the food-producing centers, upon lines shorter and more direct than any others open or proposed. In their rapid yet regular movement westward these centers have already reached the valley of the Upper Mississippi. Their present location and the location of the centers of wealth, intelligence, density of population and foreign population, are most vividly and forcibly presented and illustrated upon the maps published by the United States Census Bureau, accompanying the Census Reports for 1870. Copies of these maps, presenting these facts so much more clearly and forcibly than words can express them, are hereto annexed.

It appears that the center of the surplus product of wheat of the country is grown north of and near to the point at which the Wisconsin River improvement enters the Mississippi; that the center of the surplus product of corn is only a short distance south of that point, and that the centers of the surplus products of oats, rye, barley, hay, &c., are in part considerably north, and all closely contiguous to the same point upon the Mississippi, while the locations of density of population, foreign population, wealth, and intelligence all lie upon the line of that route. When it is remembered that a portion of the surplus product of corn and nearly the whole of the surplus product of wheat and of other crops are moved eastward, and largely to the sea-board, that at least five-eighths of the surplus product are for distribution within the country, the balance being quite sufficient to supply foreign demand, that the channels of distribution emanating in all directions from all parts of this northern through line, permeate the centers of density of population, of foreign population, of wealth, and intelligence, and into those agricultural districts the least of all devoted to the raising of cereals, and necessarily having the largest deficits, the necessity for making this channel, as against all other proposed channels, open, clear, and unobstructed, does not seem to admit of question. It is parallel to the lines upon which the railway business of the country is done. It connects upon the shortest water-lines the terminal points of all of the proposed routes. Opening other routes will not diminish the necessity for this. The great importance of improving the Mississippi River cannot be denied, and yet the improvement of the Mississippi will not in any way diminish the necessity for the improvement of the northern route. When the centers of the density of population, of the working population, of that energy begotten of a temperate climate, of intelligence and wealth, shall have moved well down the valley of the Mississippi, then, and not till then, will the importance of the northern route become diminished, and the city of New Orleans perhaps become the chief market and have control of the exports of the country.

COMPARED WITH RAILWAYS.

The following table is designed to represent the northern route via the Wisconsin and Fox Rivers improvement in comparison with railways. Dubuque is selected as an initial point with reference to its central position in the Northwest and upon the Mississippi.

TABLE No. 4.—*Showing the northern route via the Wisconsin and Fox Rivers to New York, in comparison with railway routes.*

Distances.	Route.	Number of miles.					Average rate per ton per mile, in mills.		Average rate per ton to New York, (excluding transshipments.)		Average rate of charges per bushel of wheat to New York, (excluding transshipments.)	Percentage in favor of water-route.
		Place to place.	Lakes.	Canal and improvement.	River.	Total.	Cost.	Receipts or charges.	Cost.	Receipts or charges.		
DUBUQUE TO NEW YORK.											*Cents.*	
Dubuque to Prairie du Chien	River	60										About 67 per cent.
Prairie du Chien to Green Bay	Improvement	278										
Green Bay to Buffalo	Lakes	875	875				1½	*2 to 4				
Buffalo to Albany	Canal	350		628			4	8 to 11				
Albany to New York	River	150			210		2	3 to 5				
Total distance by water						1, 713			$4 24	$9 43	28½	
Dubuque to Chicago	G. & C. U. R. R	188										
Chicago to Dunkirk	M. S. & L. S. R. R.	497										
Dunkirk to New York	N. Y. & E. R. R.	460										
Total distance by railroad						1, 145	15 to 18	† 20 to 30	18 00	28 62	† 86	
SAINT PAUL TO NEW YORK.												
Saint Paul to Prairie du Chien	River	250										About 72 per cent.
Prairie du Chien to Green Bay	Improvement	278										
Green Bay to Buffalo	Lakes	875	875				1½	*2 to 4				
Buffalo to Albany	Canal	350		628			4	8 to 11				
Albany to New York	River	150			400		2	3 to 5				
Total distance by water						1, 903			4 62	10 19	31	
Saint Paul to Milwaukee	M. & St. P. R. R	408										
Milwaukee to Chicago	C. & N. W. R. R	84										
Chicago to New York	See above	957										
Total distance by railroad						1, 449	15 to 18	20 to 30	23 90	36 23	† 109	

* Milwaukee Board of Trade Report for the year 1868.

† By the Red Line, or through freight line, rates are reduced to 17 mills, or 1.7 cents per ton per mile. If extended to Dubuque, the rate per bushel for wheat might be reduced to 59 cents, and if to Saint Paul, might be reduced to 75 cents.

From this table it appears that while Dubuque, by railway, is 568 miles nearer to New York than by water, the cost (excluding transshipment) is by water $4.24 per ton, and by rail $18; the charges by water $9.43, and by rail $28.62; and the percentage in favor of water 67 per cent. With Saint Paul as the initial point, the percentage is 72 per cent. To transport a bushel of wheat from Dubuque to New York the charges (not the cost) excluding transshipment, are by water 28½ cents, and by rail 86 cents; and from Saint Paul to New York, by water, 31 cents, and by rail $1.09. The lowest rates by the "through freight" line from Chicago to New York ($1\frac{7}{10}$ cents per ton per mile) would, if extended to Dubuque, amount to 59 cents, and to Saint Paul 75 cents. To compete successfully with water-ways (when open) it will be necessary for railways to carry freight at less than one-half of the actual cost as here given.

It is true that from Chicago to New York rail-rates at different times have been reduced considerably below those indicated, which might seem to impeach the accuracy of the foregoing table; but it is believed, from the fact that water-rates as given can be greatly if not correspondingly reduced, and the reduction in rail-rates was occasioned largely, if not wholly, by water competition, that quite or nearly the full percentage of saving claimed is fairly attributable to the opening of water-routes.

From a table appearing in the memorial of the Union Merchants' Exchange of Saint Louis to the Forty-third Congress of the United States, and purporting to have been calculated from the official reports of different roads, and from which table the following extract is taken, it appears that the rates per ton per mile on railways are not less than those stated in the foregoing table; that the average rates for the ten years from 1863 to 1872, inclusive, were, on the New York Central Railway, $23\frac{8}{10}$ mills per ton per mile, and on the Chicago, Burlington and Quincy Railroad, $29\frac{1}{10}$ mills; and that the rates, on the through lines east from Chicago are considerably less than those on lines west of Chicago, showing, it is claimed, unmistakably, the effect of water competition.

Extract from table in memorial of Union Merchants' Exchange of Saint Louis, above referred to:

Railroads.	1863.	1864.	1865.	1866.	1867.	1868.	1869.	1870.	1871.	1872.
New York Central.	.240	.275	.331	.292	.253	.259	.220	.186	.165	.159
Erie	.209	.231	.276	.245	.204	.192	.160	.137	.147	.150
Chicago, Burlington and Quincy..	.235	.255	.364	.369	.288	.318	.324	.306	.239	.210

Averge, New York Central, 23 8-10 mills, and Chicago, Burlington and Quincy, 29 1-10 mills.

The effect of water competition is not only shown in the low rates on the New York Central for all classes of freights which obtained in 1872, being $15\frac{9}{10}$ mills per ton per mile, but more especially in the rates for wheat and other grain, which are the chief articles for eastward transport by water. The rates on wheat from Chicago to New York, by the New York Central and connecting lines, for about one-half of the year 1872, were $13 per ton, being 65 cents per hundred, and about 14½ mills per ton per mile; while the average rates on wheat for the whole year were $11.60 per ton, being 58 cents per hundred, and about 13 mills per ton per mile, and while for about 19 days of that year even the average rates fell off fully twenty-two per centum.

It is also true practically, however it may be theoretically, that the rate of movement by rail is but little, if any, greater than by water.

Cost of railways.

The average cost of constructing the railways of the United States exceeds $41,000 per mile. (Census 1860.) The estimate for the improvement of the Wisconsin and Fox Rivers, including the moneys already expended, would not build much over one-third of the same number of miles of railway. There had been expended for railways in Wisconsin, as far back as 1871, (see Table No. 9,) more than 24 times the estimated sum required for the improvement, and in the five States of Wisconsin, Minnesota, Iowa, Illinois, and Missouri, more than 168 times the sum required. The increase in the number of miles of completed railway since 1871, has been as great as for any corresponding period prior thereto.

In every fourteen days of profound peace there is now expended by the War and Navy Departments of the United States a sum greater than the estimated cost of improvement.

DISTANCE THAT GRAIN WILL BEAR TRANSPORTATION.

The following note and table are taken from the pamphlet compiled by the president and directors of the James River and Kanawha Company. The table does not purport to show how far grain may be carried by river or lake, but unquestionably that distance is not less than twice the distance it can be carried by canal.

"The respective distances for which canals, railroads and ordinary highways command trade is approximately exhibited by the following table. It takes no account of charges other than for freight, (actual cost,) and is made out for wheat at $1.50 per bushel, or $49.50 per ton, of 33 bushels, and corn at 75 cents per bushel, or $24.75 per ton. It assumes the cost of carriage at 5 mills per ton per mile on canals, fifteen mills on railroads, and fifteen cents on ordinary highways.

"The charges on produce, other than for carriage proper, would materially curtail the distances indicated by the following table. The exhibit is valuable, however, as showing by contrast, for how much greater distances navigation commands trade than overland methods of transit. At 330 miles, the cost of carriage on *common roads* consumes the whole value of wheat, leaving nothing at all for the farmer. At 1,980 miles the freight on railroads leaves but 60 cents per bushel (the actual cost of production) for the grower; and at 3,300 miles sweeps off the total value. But on *canals* the cost of carriage does not trench upon the cost of production (of 60 cents per bushel) until the wheat has been carried 5,940 miles; nor is the value wholly exhausted within a distance of 9,900.

Statement showing the value of a ton of wheat and one of corn at a given distance from market, as affected by cost of transportation respectively by canal, by railroad, and over the ordinary highway.

	Canal carriage.		Railway carriage.		Common-road carriage.	
	Wheat.	Corn.	Wheat.	Corn.	Wheat.	Corn.
Value at market	$49 50	$24 75	$49 50	$24 75	$49 50	$24 75
10 miles from market	49 45	24 70	49 35	24 60	48 00	23 25
20 miles from market	49 40	24 65	49 20	24 45	46 50	21 75
30 miles from market	49 35	24 60	49 05	24 30	45 00	20 25
40 miles from market	49 30	24 55	48 90	24 15	43 50	18 75
50 miles from market	49 25	24 50	48 75	24 00	42 00	17 25
60 miles from market	49 20	24 45	48 60	23 85	40 50	15 75
70 miles from market	49 15	24 40	48 45	23 70	39 00	14 75
80 miles from market	49 10	24 35	48 30	23 55	37 50	14 25
90 miles from market	48 05	24 30	48 15	23 30	36 00	11 25
100 miles from market	48 00	24 25	48 00	23 25	34 50	9 75
110 miles from market	47 95	24 20	47 85	23 10	33 00	8 25
120 miles from market	47 90	24 15	47 70	22 95	31 50	6 75
130 miles from market	47 85	24 10	47 55	22 80	30 00	5 25
140 miles from market	47 80	24 05	47 40	22 65	28 50	3 75
150 miles from market	47 75	24 00	47 25	22 50	27 00	2 25
160 miles from market	47 70	23 95	47 10	22 35	25 50	75
170 miles from market	47 65	23 90	46 95	22 20	24 00	....
320 miles from market	46 90	23 20	44 70	19 95	1 50	....
330 miles from market	46 85	23 15	44 55	19 80	....	....
340 miles from market	46 80	23 10	44 40	19 65	....	....
350 miles from market	46 75	23 05	44 25	19 50	....	....
1,000 miles from market	44 50	19 75	34 50	9 75	....	....
1,650 miles from market	41 25	16 50	24 75	....	....	....
1,980 miles from market	39 60	14 85	19 80	....	....	....
3,300 miles from market	33 00	8 25	....	....	....	....
4,950 miles from market	24 75	....	....	....	....	....
5,940 miles from market	19 80	....	....	....	....	....
9,900 miles from market	....	....	....	....	....	....

CREATIVE POWER OF WATER TRANSPORTATION.

The creative power of water transportation is not restricted to the increase of existing values, but extends to the creation of values where otherwise none would exist. Certain articles of commerce, such as stone, brick, gravel, fire-wood, earth, &c., become articles of commerce, almost exclusively from its operation. It is by some asserted that its benefits in the creation of new values are greater and in every way more important than its benefits in the enhancement of existing values.

SAVING.

Will enough be saved to justify the expenditure?

It will save by reducing the freight-charges upon every ton of coarse freight moved from the Mississippi, eastward, or from Lake Michigan, westward, by water or by rail.

The following table shows the comparative cost and receipts upon railroads, canals, rivers, bays, and sea-borne:

Classification.	Per ton per mile, cost.	Per ton per mile, receipts.
	Mills.	*Mills.*
Transportation by railroads	17. 90	29. 80
Transportation by canals, including deduction, lockage, &c	6. 40	11. 40
Transportation by Erie Canal, including deduction, lockage, &c	4. 05	....
Transportation by rivers, steam-towage	2. 26	2. 90
Transportation by bays	2. 27	3. 73
Transportation by ocean	1. 26	2. 50

NOTE.—See Hon. W. J. McAlpine's table, New York Produce Exchange Report, 1872–'73, p. 246.

From this statement it appears that the receipts and cost of transportation by rail are each about *three times as great* as by canal, and about *eight times as great* as by river.

From the auditor's report for 1866, it appears that the tons moved one mile in New York, on the Central and Erie Railroads, for that year were 809,561,319, and on the canals 1,012,448,034, yet the railroad receipts amounted to $20,282,943, and the canal receipts to only $10,160,651, making the charges by rail nearly *three times* as great as by canal.

In the *ten* years, 1855 to 1864 inclusive, the total number of tons moved one mile by the Central Railroad was 2,132,073,612, by the Erie Railroad 2,587,274,914, and by the New York canals 8,175,803,065; and the average charges of the Central were 2 6-10, the Erie 2 22-100, and the canals 91-100 cents per ton per mile, making the average charges by rail nearly *three times* (2 2-3) as great as by canal.

Had the freights which were carried by canal for the ten years referred to been carried by rail, the *additional* freight charges would have amounted to $122,637,045.97; add to this that portion of canal receipts which was applied to the extinguishment of the canal debt—a sum which, it will be remembered, is quite three-fourths of the total receipts from tolls, and which, after paying the full cost of repairs and management, is $73,184,640, and of which sum it is estimated that $56,000,000 was paid in the ten years referred to—and it then follows that, in addition to the reduction of railroad freights, a benefit, probably the greatest rendered, and in addition to the appreciation of real estate on the line of the canals, at New York City, and at the West, the canals have in the ten years referred to, saved to the public $178,637,045.97, or $17,850,000 annually.

It was estimated by Senator (then Governor) Fenton and the State engineer of New York that, by adapting the Erie or New York Canals to the use of steam, the cost of transportation will be reduced at least fifty per centum.

The improvement of the Wisconsin and Fox Rivers partakes more of the nature of a river improvement than a canal, having in all only six miles of canal. The motive-power upon the Erie Canal is horse-power, and upon the river steam; and the rate of movement upon the river is at least four times as great as upon the canal. It is safe to say that the cost of transportation and receipts per ton per mile will be less than one-fourth of the same by rail; and will be still less, and not exceed three mills per ton per mile, if the Government shall collect tolls only sufficient to pay the cost of repairs and management.

BUSINESS ALREADY DEVELOPED.

Is the business of the country sufficiently developed to demand this outlet?

The statistics upon this subject, most carefully compiled, were in different reports submitted to the canal conventions which met at Chicago June 2, 1863, Dubuque February 14, 1866, and at Saint Louis February 12, 1867, and are embraced in numerous memorials, papers, and reports which have been presented to, and are now before, Congress, to which reference is made.

The commerce of thirteen States and four Territories, in greater or less degree, stands in present need of this water channel at its eastern outlet.

It is impracticable to present in this paper a statement of the nature and extent of the productions of the thirteen States and Territories, or even of the entire productions of a single State.

The States of Illinois, Missouri, Iowa, Wisconsin and Minnesota, known as the five most productive of the famous eight food-producing States, are more deeply and immediately in need of this outlet.

The following statement of the increase and extent of the grain-crop of these States will furnish a fair sample of the increase and extent of the entire productions of each and all of the States and Territories referred to.

TABLE No. 5.—*Statement showing the increase and extent of the grain-crop of five of the "food-producing" States, for the years* 1849–'50, 1859–'60, 1869–'70.

[The figures for 1850, 1860, and 1870 were obtained from the United States census, and for 1866 were obtained from the report of the Commissioner of Agriculture.]

States.	Population.			Wheat.			Corn.			Total grain, including wheat, corn, rye, &c.		
	1849–'50.	1859–'60.	1869–'70.	1849–'50.	1859–'60.	1869–'70.	1849–'50.	1859–'60.	1869–'70.	1849–'50.	1859–'60.	1869–'70.
				Bushels.	*Bushels.*	*Bushels.*	*Bushels.*	*Bushels.*	*Bushels.*	*Bushels.*	*Bushels.*	*Bushels.*
Illinois	851, 470	1, 711, 951	2, 539, 891	9, 414, 575	24, 159, 500	30, 128, 405	57, 646, 984	115, 296, 779	129, 921, 395	77, 527, 563	157, 294, 393	207, 936, 491
Missouri	682, 044	1, 182, 012	1, 721, 295	2, 981, 652	4, 227, 586	15, 315, 926	36, 214, 537	72, 892, 157	66, 034, 075	44, 551, 808	81, 504, 669	97, 793, 338
Iowa	192, 214	674, 918	1, 194, 020	1, 530, 581	8, 433, 205	29, 435, 692	8, 656, 799	41, 116, 994	68, 935, 065	11, 809, 550	56, 276, 547	121, 951, 917
Wisconsin	305, 391	775, 881	1, 054, 670	4, 286, 131	15, 812, 625	25, 606, 344	1, 988, 979	7, 565, 290	15, 033, 998	10, 060, 605	30, 172, 333	64, 199, 568
Minnesota	6, 077	172, 123	439, 706	1, 401	2, 195, 812	18, 866, 073	16, 725	2, 987, 570	4, 743, 117	50, 564	7, 662, 498	35, 450, 001
Total of five States	2, 037, 196	4, 516, 885	6, 949, 582	18, 214, 340	54, 828, 728	119, 352, 440	104, 524, 024	240, 858, 790	284, 667, 650	143, 400, 000	332, 610, 440	527, 331, 315

1869–'70.	Population.	Wheat.	Corn.	Grain, including wheat, corn, rye, &c.
		Bushels.	*Bushels.*	*Bushels.*
Total of all the United States	38, 558, 371	287, 655, 626	760, 944, 549	1, 387, 209, 153
Proportion crop of 1869–'70—five States to United States	About one-sixth.	About one-half.	More than one-third.	More than one-third.
Value of grain-crop of United States, 1865–'66, estimated by Commissioner of Agriculture				$1, 118, 904, 376
Value of crop of five States			About one-third.	$391, 596, 000

From this statement (Table No. 5) it appears that a population of little more than two millions in 1850, has increased to four and a half millions in 1860, and to nearly seven millions in 1870; that the product of wheat, eighteen million bushels in 1850, has increased to nearly fifty-five millions in 1860, and to one hundred and nineteen millions in 1870; and that the product of grain, including wheat, &c., one hundred and fifty-three million bushels in 1850, has increased to three hundred and thirty-two and a half millions in 1860, and to five hundred and twenty-seven millions in 1870.

It also appears that about one-sixth part of the population of the United States has raised about one-half of the wheat, more than one-third of the corn, and more than one-third of the grain, including wheat and corn, which in the year 1870 was produced in all the States and Territories of the United States.

The total value of the grain-crop of the United States for the year 1865 was, by the Commissioner of Agriculture, estimated at $1,118,904,376, in which estimate the crop of the five States referred to was put down at nearly one-third of the whole—$391,596,000.

The following table is designed to show the quantities of wheat, and flour reduced to wheat, which were actually shipped eastward from Lake Michigan ports alone in and prior to 1866:

TABLE No. 6.—*Statement designed to show the actual shipments of grain from Lake Michigan ports.*

[The following table, in the main, has been compiled from the reports of the Boards of Trade of Milwaukee and Chicago.]

Ports.	Wheat.	Flour.	Wheat and flour, reduced to bushels.	Corn.	Total grain, including wheat, flour, &c.	Total shipments	Shipments by lake.	Shipments by railroad and Illinois Canal, east and west.	Shipments by railroad, east.	Proportion shipments by railroad east to total shipments east.	Shipments by lake.	Total shipments by lake, railroad, and canal.
	Bushels.	*Barrels.*	*Bushels.*	*Bushels.*	*Bushels.*	*Bushels.*	*Bushels.*	*Bushels.*	*Bushels.*	*Bushels.*	*Tons.*	*Tons.*
1862.												
Chicago	13, 808, 898	1, 739, 849		29, 452, 610	56, 484, 110							
Milwaukee	14, 915, 680	711, 405		9, 489	18, 832, 489							
Other ports, (estimated)	1, 300, 000	245, 000	43, 505, 848	1, 000	2, 551, 000	77, 767, 599	*74, 487, 674	*3, 279, 925	(†)			
				29, 463, 099								
1863.												
Chicago	10, 389, 381	1, 536, 690		24, 906, 930	54, 741, 839							
Milwaukee	12, 887, 620	603, 526		88, 989	16, 993, 335							
Other ports, (estimated)	1, 789, 489	176, 029	36, 597, 715	10, 000	2, 729, 634	74, 464, 808	*68, 042, 456	*6, 422, 352	(†)			
				25, 005, 919								
1864.												
Chicago	10, 249, 330	1, 287, 545		12, 740, 543	47, 124, 494							
Milwaukee	8, 992, 479	414, 833		146, 786	12, 084, 079							
Other ports, (estimated)	1, 500, 000	200, 000	39, 253, 699	200, 000	2, 700, 000	61, 909, 073	54, 848, 179	7, 060, 894	4, 909, 489	8 per cent.	*1, 441, 076	*1, 589, 065
				13, 087, 329								
1865.												
Chicago	8, 098, 968	1, 523, 876		25, 228, 526	53, 212, 224							
Milwaukee	10, 479, 777	567, 576		371, 130	13, 803, 359							
Other ports, (estimated)	1, 543, 997	100, 671	31, 082, 347	89, 050	2, 327, 139	69, 342, 722	59, 123, 060	10, 219, 662	7, 156, 717	10 per cent.	*1, 620, 851	*1, 892, 974
				25, 688, 706								
1866.												
Chicago	10, 341, 549	2, 197, 787		32, 953, 530	66, 736, 660							
Milwaukee	11, 634, 749	720, 365		480, 408	17, 627, 994							
Other ports, (estimated)	1, 128, 423	114, 747	38, 269, 216	591, 125	1, 157, 007	87, 421, 681	67, 671, 010	19, 750, 671	15, 474, 456	18½ per ct.	*1, 869, 239	*2, 421, 001
				34, 025, 063								

* Approximate. † Could not be conveniently ascertained.

It appears that the quantity actually shipped from the ports upon Lake Michigan was as follows:

Year.	Wheat and flour.	Grain, including wheat and flour.
	Bushels.	*Bushels.*
In 1862	43, 595, 848	77, 767, 509
In 1863	36, 597, 715	74, 464, 808
In 1864	30, 253, 699	61, 969, 073
In 1865	31, 082, 357	69, 342, 752
In 1866	38, 269, 216	87, 421, 681

The shipments have been largely increased since 1866.

While it is true that a quantity of grain is raised upon the immediate shore of Lake Michigan, and does not require transportation across the State, it is equally true that a quantity of the grain-crop of the five States referred to is shipped to the West and South, and another quantity to the East, by channels other than the ports of Lake Michigan. With water-channels opened and freights reduced, thereby stimulating shipments, it is thought the yearly crop is now, and possibly as far back as 1866, was sufficiently large to make the shipments eastward from points west of Lake Michigan not less than 50,000,000 bushels of wheat, and of grain, including wheat, not less than 100,000,000 bushels.

This quantity in weight, estimating for the different kinds of grains, is about 2,500,000 tons. The average distance from the Mississippi River to Lake Michigan by rail is at least 170 miles, and by the Wisconsin and Fox Rivers, 271 miles. To the distance by rail must be added the average distance to the head of Lake Michigan, opposite Green Bay, estimated at 150 miles. The charges for transportation over 170 miles of railway, at thirty mills per ton per mile, and over 150 miles of lake, at three mills per ton per mile, amount to $5.55 per ton, and with the cost of transshipment at the Mississippi added, to $6.21 per ton; while the charges over 271 miles of river, at seven mills per ton per mile, amount to $1.90 per ton. The saving of $4.31 per ton upon the whole quantity for shipment, would amount to $10,775,000, a sum more than twice the estimated cost of the proposed work, to be saved upon the movement eastward of a single grain-crop.

It may be said that railway charges will be less than 30 mills per ton per mile, and may ultimately be as low as 20, or even 15 mills per ton per mile; but it will be observed that the charges by water are put as high as seven mills, when it is expected that ultimately they will be as low as three mills per ton per mile. The reduction from railway charges can never be proportionately greater than the reduction from water-route charges as given above.

It may be said that this great product would not go all by water. Be that as it may, whether moved by rail or water, it must go at approximate water-rates. The saving to the public is equally certain, whether effected by light tolls or light rail-rates.

It is, however, by no means certain that water-routes cannot successfully compete with railways. It appears (table No. 6,) that from the ports of Lake Michigan the shipments were nearly all to the East, and were made by water, excepting that in 1864 8 *per cent.*, and in 1865 11 *per cent.*, and in 1866 18½ *per cent.*, were made by rail.

The following statement is designed to show what proportion of the shipments by rail to the East were carried in the five winter months.

TABLE NO. 7.—*Statement designed to show the proportion of shipments East by rail in the five winter months.*

[Compiled from the Board of Trade reports of Chicago, for the years 1865, 1866, and 1867. Shipments by railroad from Milwaukee not given, because included in the Chicago shipments.)

Railroads and years.		Shipments of wheat flour, (reduced to bushels,) corn, and oats, in the 7 months of April, May, June, July, August, September, and October.	Shipments of wheat, flour, (reduced to bushels,) corn, and oats, in the 5 months of November, December, January, February and March.	Proportion of shipments in five winter months to total shipments of year.
		Bushels.	*Bushels.*	
Pittsburg, Fort Wayne and Chicago..... Michigan Southern and Northern Indiana Michigan Central.................... Chicago and Great Eastern..............	1864................	2, 002, 949	2, 830, 040	58½
	1865................	3, 534, 170	3, 303, 020	......
	1864–'5............	5, 537, 110	6, 133, 060	52½
	1866................	9, 591, 082	5, 314, 498	......
	1864–'5–'6..........	15, 128, 192	11, 447, 558	43

From this it appears that of the shipments East by rail there were carried, in the five winter months of the year 1864, 58½ per centum; of the years 1864 and 1865, 52½ per centum; and of the years 1864, 1865, and 1866, 43 per centum. Deducting from the shipments carried in the summer months the quantity discharged at points not reached by water, and it follows that during the seven months of navigation while the water-channel was open and in competition with the four great lines of railway leading from Chicago to the East, there *were shipped by rail not much over 5 per centum of the gross shipments East.*

The opening of a water-route will stimulate the export of corn. It appears that from a product of 273,000,000 bushels in 1865, only 25,000,000 bushels (according to table No. 6) were shipped eastward from all the ports on Lake Michigan—less than one bushel in ten. These tables show, says the Commissioner of Agriculture, in his report for 1865, p. 62, "how excessive charges for transportation are eating out the substance of the West, reducing home prices and farmers' profits, and consigning corn to the grate or furnace. It should teach the West to diversify its industry, and divert labor from wheat-growing to industries which make light products."

Having spoken so freely of the grain-crop, it is impracticable to do more than refer to the other varied and great productions of the territory tributary to this route seeking an eastern outlet by water. It is thought that upon the Wisconsin and Fox Rivers improvement the western freights will approximate in amount to the eastern freights. The opening of this route will furnish a western market for the great lumber districts of Michigan and Eastern Wisconsin, for the coal and salt districts of the East, for Lake Superior iron, and for general merchandise.

The following is a statement of the lumber trade of the two ports of Milwaukee and Chicago for 1866:

TABLE No. 8.—*Statement of receipts and shipments of lumber and coal at the two ports of Milwaukee and Chicago.*

Locality.	1860.	1866.				
	Lumber.	Lumber.				Coal.
	Total receipts.	Total receipts.	Receipts by lake.	Receipts by railroad, canal, &c.	Shipped by railroad and canal.	Total rec'ts.
	Feet.	*Feet.*	*Feet.*	*Feet.*	*Feet.*	*Tons.*
Milwaukee	30, 124, 000	*58, 808, 000	56, 846, 000	1, 962, 090	21, 906, 156	66, 617
Chicago	225, 372, 340	730, 057, 168	687. 851, 000	42, 206. 168	422, 087, 266	496, 193
Total	255, 496, 340	788, 865, 168	744, 697, 000	44, 168, 168	443, 993, 422	562, 810

Estimated product of lumber in Wisconsin for 1866	†800, 000, 000 feet.
Estimated product of lumber in Michigan for 1866	‡1, 125, 000, 000 feet.
Total	1, 925, 600, 000 feet.

* Not estimating lath, shingles, posts, ties, bolts, cord-wood, &c.
† Estimate secretary Wisconsin State Agricultural Society's report, gathered from reports of boards of trade.
‡ Estimate of Commissioner General Land-Office, report of 1867.

To move by rail the quantity actually received, (788,865,168 feet,) allowing for each car 7,000 feet, and for each train fifteen cars, will require 7,513 trains of cars, or one for every hour, day and night, in the year Sundays excepted; and to move the quantity actually shipped (443,993,422 feet,) will require 4,228 trains, or about fourteen trains for every day in the year, Sundays excepted.

At Chicago alone there was received in 1871 over 1,000,000,000 feet of lumber.

Should the western freights amount to not more than one-half of eastern grain-freights, they would swell the aggregate of the saving to $16,162,500 per annum.

BUSINESS WHICH WILL BE DEVELOPED.

However great in quantity and value the productions of the five States referred to now are, under the stimulus of cheap transportation they will grow into quantities and values vast and immeasurable. However great may be the development indicated by the miles of completed railway therein, it has not reached nor approached its limit.

The following statement is designed to show the number of miles of railway completed in these States, and the number of acres of improved land, as compared with the total area.

TABLE No. 9.—*Statement designed to show the number of miles of completed railway in the five States referred to, and the number of acres of improved land as compared with the total area.*

[Compiled from the reports of the Commissioner on Agriculture, the report for 1867 of the Commissioner of the General Land-Office, &c.]

STATES.	LANDS, (ACRES.)										RAILROADS, (MILES COMPLETED.)		
	FARMS.						Not in farms in 1869-'70.	Total in farms and out.	Proportion of improved lands to whole in 1870.	Lands unsold, title in United States, in 1867.	1849-'50.	1859-'60.	1871.
	1849-'50.		1859-'60.		1869-'70.								
	Improved.	Unimpr'd.	Improved.	Unimpr'd.	Improved.	Unimpr'd.							
Illinois	5, 039, 545	6, 997, 867	13, 096, 374	7, 815, 615	19, 329, 952	6, 552, 909	9, 579, 539	35, 462, 400	22 per cent.—about 1 acre in 5.	2, 000	110	2, 868	4, 823
Missouri	2, 938, 425	6, 794, 245	6, 246, 871	13, 737, 939	9, 130, 615	12, 576, 605	20, 116, 780	41, 824, 000		1, 835, 893	......	817	2, 000
Iowa	824, 682	1, 911, 382	3, 792, 792	6, 277, 115	9, 396, 467	6, 145, 326	19, 687, 007	35, 228, 800		3, 113, 464	......	680	2, 683
Wisconsin	1, 045, 499	1, 931, 159	3, 746, 167	4, 147, 420	5, 899, 343	5, 815, 978	22, 796, 039	34, 511, 360		10, 016, 701	20	923	1, 730
Minnesota	5, 035	23, 846	556, 250	2, 155, 718	2, 322, 102	4, 161, 726	46, 976, 012	53, 459, 840		36, 776, 171	......	......	1, 072
Total	......	......	......	......	46, 078, 479	......	......	200, 486, 400		......	130	5, 288	*12, 308
United States											8, 590	30, 794	53, 399
Proportion of above five States to United States											......	......	Over 1-5
Six New England States											......	......	4, 494
Six Middle States, including New York and Pennsylvania											......	......	12, 476

* The increase since 1871 has been as great as for any corresponding number of years prior thereto.

It appears from this statement that in 1850, in the States referred to, there were 130 miles of completed continuous railway, while in 1871, only twenty-one years later, there were 12,308 miles, and more in process of construction. The total number of miles of completed and continuous railway in the United States was 8,590 in 1850, and 53,399 in 1871. These five newly-created States contained in that year about as many miles as the six older "Middle States," nearly three times as many as the six "New England States," much more than one-fifth as many as the United States, and more than one-fifth as many as all the rest of the world. They contained in 1871 nearly 50 per cent. more miles than all of the United States in 1850, and the increase since 1871 has been as great as for any corresponding period prior thereto.

It also appears that the total area of these States embraces more than two hundred millions of acres of land, a surface as great as that of forty States as large as Massachusetts; and that the quantity actually improved but little exceeds forty-six million acres—one acre in five.

The valley of the Mississippi, which, by the opening of water-routes, will become connected with the valley of the Saint Lawrence, and tributary to the commerce of the lakes, contains 768,000,000 acres "of the finest lands on the face of the globe—enough to make more than one hundred and fifty States as large as Massachusetts. More territory than the areas of Great Britain, France, Spain, Austria, Prussia, European Turkey, and the Italian Peninsula combined. If peopled as Massachusetts is, it would contain five times the present population of the United States; and as France is, it would hold as many people as the whole area of Europe contains; and as Belgium and the Netherlands are, with not the same danger of famine, it would contain four hundred millions of souls, largely more than one-third of the entire population of the world."

With the valleys of the Mississippi and the Saint Lawrence so connected there would be an uninterrupted lake, river, and canal navigation from New York to Fort Benton, at the falls of the Missouri, a distance, east and west, of nearly five thousand miles. Barges loaded at Green Bay might be discharged of their cargoes in Montana. The distance on the Mississippi navigable by steamboats from Saint Louis north to the Falls of Saint Anthony, and thence on the Dakota, is about 1,300 miles, and south from Saint Louis to New Orleans, 1,200 miles. Steamers go loaded with freight to be delivered at the heads of navigation upon the rivers which run through Illinois, Ohio, Arkansas, Louisiana, Tennessee, Mississippi, and Alabama, and to Pittsburgh, in Pennsylvania. Steamers of a large class go from Saint Louis to Fort Benton, a distance of 3,100 miles. It is stated that in the spring of 1868 sixty boats were advertised to leave for the Rocky Mountain region, and that the gold-dust which came by steamers in 1866 was estimated at $16,000,000.

About the year 1820, soon after the Erie Canal was projected, Gouverneur Morris, who, with James Hawley, shares the honor of its conception, writing to a friend in Europe said:

"Hundreds of large ships will, in no distant period, bound on the billows of these inland seas. Shall I lead your astonishment up to the verge of incredulity? Know, then, that one-third part of the expense borne by Britain in the late campaign would enable ships to sail from London through the Hudson River into Lake Erie."

Nearly two thousand ships now "bound on the billows of these inland seas," and upon the Mississippi and its tributaries quite two thousand more. And no man can *now* fix the limit at which the extension of the water-route then conceived, and the development of the country then inaugurated, shall stop. A water communication extending from New York over one-half of the length—and possibly the entire length—of the Pacific Railroad, will furnish the only reliable check against extortionate charges for transportation.

THE WORK IS NATIONAL IN CHARACTER.

The work is national in character, and is not one for the State of Wisconsin. It cannot be undertaken without a change in the organic law of the State. If completed, it would benefit other States equally or more than the State of Wisconsin. By the ordinance of 1787, the navigable waters leading into the Mississippi and the Saint Lawrence, and the carrying places between the same, were declared to be public highways, forever free to the inhabitants of every State. The control over them was retained by the General Government, and was substantially excluded from the States to be thereafter formed out of the territory northwest of the Ohio. A similar provision was embodied in the law of Congress organizing the Territory of Wisconsin, and in the law of Congress admitting the State of Wisconsin into the Union. Not only by virtue of special legislation, but from the character itself of the Fox and Wisconsin Rivers, they fall within the class of waters over which the General Government has retained control, and to improve which it has long been its policy to make appropriations.

A work which affects the interests of every locality, which reaches out and touches many States, and binds together all by the ligaments of commerce, and develops avenues of intercourse into bonds of unity, can be no less national in character than that which guards against outward foes.

Its importance is declared in the resolutions of nearly all of the commercial, freight, and river-improvement conventions which have been held in the northwest, including the conventions held at Chicago in 1863, at Dubuque in 1866, at Saint Louis in 1867, and at Keokuk and Louisville in 1869, and in nearly all of the political conventions of all parties and classes which for many years, and especially of late years, have been there held. It has been called to the attention of the legislatures of several of the States in the messages of their respective governors nearly every year for the several years last past, and in 1870 in the messages of the governors of Missouri, New York, Wisconsin, Iowa, and Minnesota. It is urged upon Congress in repeated memorials from the legislatures of Iowa, Illinois, Minnesota, and Wisconsin, wherein it is suggested "that this work should be undertaken at this time because the public debt is great. Its accomplishment will increase the wealth of the country, out of which the debt is to be paid, and will enlarge the incomes of consumer and producer, by whom it is to be paid. At any cost its early accomplishment is dictated by true economy."

The prayer is submitted that soon it may be said of this work, as it was said of the Erie Canal: "The great work has advanced to completion, giving to the world a practical example of the proverb 'there is that scattereth and yet increaseth.'"

I am, sir, your obedient servant,

B. J. STEVENS.

Hon. WILLIAM WINDOM,
Chairman of the Committee of the United States Senate on Transportation-Routes to the Seaboard.

LETTER OF HON. JOHN YOUNG, OF MONTREAL, IN REPLY TO THE REPORT OF HON. WILLIAM J. McALPINE, TO THE OSWEGO BOARD OF TRADE.

MONTREAL, *November* 13, 1873.

SIR: Having, at your request, sent you several statements embracing my views as to the route of the Saint Lawrence via Lake Champlain being the cheapest and quickest from the Western States to the Eastern States and New York, when the Caughnawaga Canal is constructed, I feel myself compelled again to address you in defense of my opinions, in consequence of a pamphlet which has been published by the Oswego Board of Trade, containing a report of the route, by William McAlpine, civil engineer to that board, on the subject of "Transportation Routes from the West to the Seaboard."

Mr. McWharter, the secretary of the Oswego Board of Trade, says, on 1st September last, that "it is with much gratification I am enabled to state that, as will appear by reference to the report, Mr. McAlpine decides in favor of the Oswego route, and shows most conclusively that a ton of freight or bushel of grain can be transported from Chicago via the enlarged Welland Canal, or the projected Niagara Ship-Canal, Lake Ontario, the Oswego route via Oneida Lake, the improved Erie Canal, from the Oneida Lake Junction to Troy or Albany, and the Hudson River to New York, *much more cheaply and quickly* than by the Erie Canal route via Buffalo, *or the Saint Lawrence and Lake Champlain routes were either of these routes improved to their best capacity.*"

The committee of the Oswego Board of Trade in addressing you state further:

"1st. That the Oneida Lake route is the oldest route.

"2d. The Oneida Lake route is the shortest between the lakes and the Hudson.

"3d. The Oneida Lake route, properly improved, is the cheapest.

"4th. The Oneida Lake route is the best, for other considerations, as compared with the Saint Lawrence and Champlain route.

"1. It has the advantage of being entirely within our own territory, except the Welland Canal. The use of that canal is secured to us by the treaty of Washington, which also secures to the people of Canada very important privileges, including, among others, the navigation of Lake Michigan and the use of the Saint Clair Flats Canal, and should the treaty be infringed or applied in a hostile manner by the Canadian authorities, we can withhold privileges equally important to them. But the true remedy; and one which should long since have been applied, we have in our own hands, in the construction of the *Niagara Ship-Canal.*

"The treaty of Washington also protects us in the use of the canals and rapids of the Saint Lawrence, forming part of the Champlain route. But this protection does not extend to the proposed Caughnawaga Canal; and unfriendly legislation or action as to this canal, intended to advance the interests of Montreal at the expense of American ports, could not be claimed as an infringement of the letter or spirit of the treaty.

"Besides, if our Government adopt the Champlain route, what probability is there of the construction of the Caughnawaga Canal? Our own Government will not expend its money on a foreign soil.

"2. Our route has the advantage of two weeks earlier navigation in the spring and two weeks later in the fall, and that at the time when the pressure of freights for movement is the greatest.

"3. It escapes the fogs of the Saint Lawrence, which any one acquainted with the navigation of that river knows to be a serious inconvenience, especially in autumn."

Such are the opinions expressed by the Oswego Board of Trade, said to be based on the report of their engineer, the Hon. Wm. McAlpine.

Before I enter upon the consideration of Mr. McAlpine's facts and figures by which he has arrived at the conclusion that the Oneida Lake route via Oswego, through the Welland Canal to New York, is the "cheapest and quickest" for the transport of Western States' produce, I must place before you a contradiction of this opinion by Mr. McAlpine himself.

In November, 1857, the harbor commissioners of Montreal, having come to the conclusion that very extensive enlargement of the harbor was necessary, they formed a commission of American engineers, consisting of Mr. McAlpine, James P. Kirkwood, of Brooklyn, N. Y., and the late Capt. John Chalde, of Springfield, Mass.

That you may fully understand the very important subject thus committed to Mr. McAlpine and his colleagues by the commissioners, it is necessary I should give a few extracts of their instructions:

"The commissioners desire to direct your attention to the fact that, although the magnificent canals on the Saint Lawrence are in perfect order, and have been in operation since 1849, with a system of railways also in operation for the two past years, running from Quebec and connecting with all points south and west, yet up to the close of 1856 the Saint Lawrence route has only succeeded in attracting 15 per cent. of the western Canadian and western United States trade, 85 per cent. of that trade passing through the Erie Canal and over the railways of the State of New York. Should you, on examination, find that, with the improvements now going forward on the Erie Canal, the routes from the West via Buffalo and Oswego are likely to continue to be the best and cheapest to the Eastern States, New York, and Europe, then this opinion must guide you as to the extent of Montreal Harbor improvements.

"The harbor commissioners have been of opinion that the Saint Lawrence route, as a means of transport between Europe, the Eastern States, New York, and the Western States and Western Canada, has not yet been fully developed; that if the Welland Canal was enlarged so as to admit the passage of vessels of 850 tons, and a canal constructed to connect the Saint Lawrence with Lake Champlain of the same size, and suitable facilities created in this port whereby the cost of handling property should be reduced to the lowest possible rate, a vast increase of trade would thus be attracted to the Saint Lawrence route, to the great advantage not only of this port, but to the general public interests; and to these points your attention is specially directed."

On the 24th March, 1858, Mr. McAlpine, with his associates, sent me, as chairman of the harbor commissioners of Montreal, their report, in which the following references are made to the route via the Saint Lawrence into Lake Champlain, and to the Erie and Oswego Canal routes:

"The determination of the question of the best route for the water-borne trade is, therefore, reduced to a comparison between the routes through the State of New York and that along the Saint Lawrence. For the present purpose each of these routes will be examined as if they already had been improved and completed upon the most advantageous plans which the anticipated extent of the trade through them would warrant.

"With this view, the cost of transport on the Erie and Oswego Canals will be taken as if they were enlarged throughout. The Caughnawaga Canal, from the Saint Lawrence to Lake Champlain, will be considered as completed on the same scale as the Saint Lawrence Canal, and the Champlain Canal will be regarded as also enlarged to the same dimensions.

"The locks on the Welland Canal will be considered as enlarged to the same capacity as those on the Saint Lawrence Canal. In comparing the routes through the State of New York with each other and the Saint Lawrence, *it is necessary to observe that by the way of Buffalo and Oswego a transshipment must be made from the lake-vessels to the canal-boats, and that the extra cost of canal transport and heavy tolls must be added to those routes, while by the way of Lake Champlain to New York, and by the Saint Lawrence to Montreal, no transshipment is required, and the extra cost of the movement on the canal and of tolls is very much reduced.*

"The Welland Canal locks enlarged to the same size as those on the Saint Lawrence Canal (with some additional length,) and those on the Saint Lawrence Canal also lengthened, will allow vessels of 850 tons burden to pass through, while the advantage of the use of such large vessels making such long voyages will so reduce the cost of transport as to divert a large portion through the Welland Canal, and to New York and Montreal.

"From the computations we have made it will be seen that the cost of transport to New York by the way of the proposed Caughnawaga and enlarged Champlain Canals, in ordinary vessels, *is less than by the way of Oswego.*

"The Champlain route thus improved will have the further advantage of the more economic use of vessels of the *largest class proceeding* from any port on the lakes, without breaking bulk, direct to New York, and also the diminished length of canal-navigation by that route. The construction of the Caughnawaga Canal will enable such vessels to land and receive cargo at Burlington and Whitehall, from whence western freights can be carried to and from Boston by railways *cheaper than by any other route to that city.*

"This Caughnawaga Canal into Lake Champlain would thus open a large portion of New England to this route, and add largely to the revenues of the Welland and Saint Lawrence Canals, and give value to the railways of Western New England, which terminate at Lake Champlain. The Caughnawaga Canal built, the State of New York would not long hesitate in the enlargement of the Champlain Canal, so as to allow the vessel of 850 tons to sail from the interior lakes to New York direct without breaking bulk.

"The following table of the cost of transport by the several routes is made up from Chicago, as a starting point common to all, from which vessels of 850 tons will perform the duty as far eastward as they can be navigated on each route. The routes through the Erie Canal, both by the way of Buffalo and of Oswego, will require the voyage of the large vessels to terminate at these ports, and the cargo to be transferred into canal-boats of 250 tons.

TABLE.

First. From Chicago to New York, by the way of the lake to Buffalo, the Erie Canal, and the Hudson River to New York.

	By sailing-vessels.	By steam-vessels.
From Chicago to Buffalo, 914 miles lake navigation, at 2 and 3½ mills per ton per mile	$1 83	$3 20
From Buffalo to West Troy, 353 miles canal navigation, at 8 mills	2 82	2 82
From West Troy to New York, 151 miles river navigation, at 3 and 5 mills	45	76
Transferring cargo at Buffalo	20	20
1,418 miles, per ton	5 30	6 98

Second. From Chicago to New York, by the way of the lakes and Welland Canal to Oswego, and thence by the Oswego and Erie Canals and the Hudson River to New York.

	By sailing-vessels.	By steam-vessels.
From Chicago to Oswego, 1,057 miles lake navigation, at 2 and 3½ mills	$2 11	$3 70
Additional expenses on Welland Canal, 28 miles, at 3 mills	08	08
Oswego to Troy, 202 miles canal navigation, at 8 mills	1 62	1 62
West Troy to New York, 151 miles river navigation, at 3 and 5 mills	45	76
Transferring cargo at Oswego	20	20
1,410 miles	4 46	6 36

Third. From Chicago to New York, by the way of the lakes, Welland Canal, Saint Lawrence, Caughnawaga, and Champlain Canals, and Hudson River to New York.

	By sailing-vessels.	By steam-vessels.
From Chicago to New York, 1,632 miles, at 2 and 3½ mills per ton	$3 26	$5 71
Additional expenses on the Saint Lawrence, Welland, Caughnawaga, and Champlain Canals, 167 miles, at 3 mills	50	50
1,632 miles	3 76	6 21

These are the figures of the cost of transport on the routes referred to, given by Mr. McAlpine to the harbor commissioners of Montreal, in March, 1858, and indorsed by Messrs. Kirkwood & Childe. The summary is as follows:

	Miles.	Vessels.	Steam.
From Chicago to New York via Buffalo	1,418	$5 30	$6 98
via Oswego	1,410	4 46	6 36
via Lake Champlain	1,632	3 76	6 21

Showing that, in the opinion of these engineers, the Lake Champlain route was superior to every other in cheapness, both as regards sailing and steam vessels. There was no estimate then made of the time required on each route, and the result of the computation was based on the vessels being 850 tons measurement by the Champlain and Saint Lawrence route, and 250 tons from Oswego. Messrs. McAlpine, Kirkwood, and Childe concluded their report by stating that "the construction of the proposed Caughnawaga Canal, from the Saint Lawrence, opposite Lachine, to Lake Champlain, will allow the large lake-vessels to continue their voyage to Whitehall, (two hundred and ten miles from New York,) at 20 cents per ton less cost, even if the Champlain Canal should not be enlarged to allow the vessels to go to New York, and the economy of time and transport by the Lake Champlain route could not fail to attract to it a large share of the trade between the Western States, New England, and New York."

Mr. McAlpine in his late report to the Oswego Board of Trade reverses the conclusion which he, in 1858, with Messrs. Kirkwood and Childe, arrived at, and now declares *that the route via Oswego, the Oneida Lake, and the Erie Canal to Troy is the cheapest, quickest, and best,* and superior to the Champlain or any other route from the West to the East. Differing with Mr. McAlpine in this conclusion, and having expressed to you a contrary opinion, it becomes necessary for me to point out several important errors in Mr. McAlpine's calculations. He leaves out in the comparison the route from Buffalo through the Erie Canal, and confines the rivalry of routes to those from Oswego via the Oneida Lake and Erie Canal to Troy, with that down the Saint Lawrence and through Lake Champlain to Troy. In this, I think, he is correct, but it is all-important that the facts should be correctly stated as regards the natural capacity of both routes.

Mr. McAlpine describes "the Caughnawaga Canal route" as follows:

	Miles.
From point on Lake Ontario opposite Oswego, to Saint Lawrence River, at Kingston	22
Saint Lawrence River navigation	134
Saint Lawrence Canal navigation	35½
Caughnawaga Canal	34½
Richelieu River	23
Lake Champlain	111
Champlain Ship-Canal	25
Hudson River to Troy	40
Total	425

This statement is not correct. In the downward trip from Kingston to Caughnawaga, the canals on the Saint Lawrence will not be used, so that the river navigation will be 169½ miles instead of 134. There is no Richelieu River above Saint John's, and from that point to Whitehall the whole distance is equal to lake navigation, making the lake 134 instead of 111. These changes will make considerable difference in the character of the two routes.

	Lake.	River.	Canal.
Mr. McAlpine makes	133	197	95 =425
Mr. Young makes	156	199½	59½=425

Mr. McAlpine says that by the Oswego-Oneida route the distance to Troy is 191⅘ miles, in which there are 68 locks and 609 feet lockage. By the Caughnawaga route, he says as above, the distance is 425 miles, with 44 locks and 390 feet of lockage. Here is a serious mistake. Mr. McAlpine includes in this statement 22 locks and 162 feet lockage on the Saint Lawrence River Canals, when he is well aware that on the downward trip these canals are not now navigated by steamers, and that the whole river is to be improved for vessels drawing 12 feet water; so that instead of 44 locks, 390 feet lockage, there are 22 locks and 229 feet lockage, against the Oswego-Oneida route of 68 locks and 609 feet lockage, or a difference of 380 feet of lockage in favor of the Champlain route.

Mr. McAlpine says that engineers compute one lock to be equal to one mile of canal, and as the difference in distance is 233 miles in favor of the Oswego route, yet, there being only 44 locks instead of 68 via Oswego, the difference is thus reduced to 209 miles. The fact, however, is, there are 22 locks on the Champlain and Saint Lawrence route, hence the distance is reduced from 209 miles to 187.

Mr. McAlpine's table of the lockage of the route.

	Locks.	Lockage.
Saint Lawrence River Canal	22	162
Caughnawaga Canal	3	29
Champlain Canal	8	84
Hudson River improvement	11	116
	44	391
Deduct Saint Lawrence Canal	22	162
	22	229
Against Oswego route	68	609
Difference in favor of Champlain route	46	380

Mr. McAlpine, in his report to the Oswego Board of Trade, states that on the Oswego route, the lockage—

	Feet.
Ascending eastward, is	182
Descending eastward, is	427
Total	609

And by the Champlain route, should be—

	Locks.	Lockage.
Ascending eastward	79	79
Descending eastward	312	150
	390	229

Mr. McAlpine states that Mr. John B. Jarvis first surveyed the Caughnawaga Canal. This is a mistake, as the late John B. Mills first surveyed it in 1849; then Messrs. Clarke & Gample; in 1855 Mr. Jarvis, and in 1859 Colonel Swift, of Massachusetts.

The enlarged canals now being built will have locks throughout of 270 feet in length by 45 feet in width, with 12 feet of water. The Caughnawaga will be of the same dimensions; but there is now an agitation to have the locks at least 300 feet in length. This size of locks will accommodate a propeller of 1,000 or 1,200 tons measurement, of a carrying capacity of 50,000 bushels.

I shall now refer to the question of speed on the lakes and river, discussed by Mr. McAlpine on page 9 of his report to the Oswego Board of Trade. He says it will not be found economical to exceed 8 miles an hour on lakes and 6 miles on rivers. On canals he thinks 4 miles can be maintained, but he bases his calculations on 3½ miles and that 15 minutes will be required for each lockage.

On this basis Mr. McAlpine gives the following table of the time which will be occupied on the Champlain and Saint Lawrence route:

	Hours.
From point as stated to Kingston, lake	2.75
From Kingston to Caughnawaga, river	22.33
From Kingston to Cauhnawaga, canal	14.00
From Caughnawaga to Saint John's, canal	9.04
From Saint John's to Rouse's Point, river	3.83
From Rouse's Point to Whitehall, lake	13.87
From Whitehall to Fort Edward, canal	9.00
From Fort Edward, to Troy river	9.41
	48.33

Or 3.52 days.

Such is Mr. McAlpine's estimate; but he should have added 15 minutes for each lockage, which would be, with 22 locks 5.30

Or, in all 90.00

Before correcting this statement I beg to say that the propellers now running to this port from the upper lakes, and which pass through the Welland Canal, of 400 tons, have a speed of 10 miles per hour on the lakes, and on the river below Kingston of 12 miles an hour on the down trip. If such vessels have this speed it is not too much to say that with vessels of greater power and 1,000 tons measurement their speed will be at least equal to those now in use. The only river to be traversed in coming from the West to Troy is the Saint Lawrence, and the speed on the downward voyage must, in the nature of things, be more rapid than on the upper lakes. In making the following table I shall therefore assume the speed on lake and river at 10 miles per hour and 3½ miles on canal, and apply these figures to what I know to be the actual distances on the route.

	Miles.	Hours.
From point opposite Oswego, as stated, to Kingston	22, lake	2.20
From Kingston to Caughnawaga	169½, river	16.09
From Caughnawaga to Saint John's	24½, canal	9.25
From Saint John's to Whitehall	134, lake	13.40
From Whitehall to Hudson River	25, canal	7.14
From Hudson River to Troy, 6 miles per hour	40 miles, river	7.00
Twenty-two locks, at 15 minutes		5.30
Total		60.38

Or a difference with Mr. McAlpine's report to the Oswego Board of Trade of 30 hours

Then, on page 11, comes Mr. McAlpine's comparison of the time by the Oswego-Oneida Lake route.

	Hours.
From Oswego to Phœnix Canal	8.50
From Phœnix to Oneida Lake	3.75
Through Oneida Lake	3.83
Through Oneida Canal	3.25
Higginsville to Troy	43.50
Total	62.83

If to this time are added 15 minutes for each of the 68 locks, we have 17 hours; add Mr. McAlpine's time, 62.83, we have 79.83 hours. But this is not all. Mr. McAlpine admits that when the Welland Canal is improved, vessels of at least 1,000 tons measurement will be employed, and that such vessels will carry 50,000 bushels of grain to Oswego. This cargo he proposes to transship into steam-barges of 500 tons measurement, or 25,000 bushels capacity. Now, how is it that Mr. McAlpine, in making out his table of time, has not referred to the time required for transshipment of this cargo of 50,000 bushels from the lake into the canal-vessel? Taking 4,000 bushels per hour as good average work for an elevator, we have thus 12½ hours, and allowing two hours more for berthing, we have 14½ hours, which, added to the 79.83 hours, makes 94.33 hours by the Oswego-Oneida route, against 60.38 hours by the Saint Lawrence and Champlain route, or two and a half days.

This saving in time by this route is an important item in the annual saving of interest on the enormous commerce which now passes from the West to the East; nor have I included the item of insurance, which would also be necessary in the transfer of cargo from the ship into the elevator at Chicago.

As Messrs. McAlpine, Childe, and Kirkwood said in 1858, to the Montreal harbor commissioners, "By way of Oswego a transshipment must be made from the lake-vessel to canal-boats, and the extra cost of canal transport and tolls must be added to that route, while by way of Lake Champlain to New York no transshipment is required;" and again, "The Champlain route thus improved will have the further advantage of the more economic use of vessels of the largest class, proceeding from any port on the lakes directly to New York, without breaking bulk, and also the diminished length of canal navigation by that route. On the whole the economy of time and transport by the Lake Champlain route could not fail to attract to it a very large share of the trade between the Western States, New England, and New York."

I shall now advert to the comparative cost of transport by the two routes. Messrs. McAlpine, Kirkwood, and Childe, in the report alluded to, fixed the cost of transport at 3½ mills per ton per mile on large ship-canals, and at 2 mills per ton on lakes. Mr. McAlpine in his late report to the Oswego Board of Trade changes this to 1½ mills per ton per mile on lakes and to a fraction less than 3½ mills on canals, rates which I shall apply to both routes.

First—From Chicago to Troy, (via Caughnaawga.)

	Miles.		
Lake navigation to Kingston from Chicago	1,077		
Lake Champlain	134		
	1,211	at $1\frac{1}{2}$ mills	$1 82
River from Kingston	169	at $1\frac{1}{2}$ mills	25
River from Hudson to Troy	40	at $1\frac{1}{2}$ mills	8

Canal navigation.

	Miles.		
Welland Canal	28		
Caughnawaga	34		
Champlain	25		
	87	at $3\frac{1}{2}$ mills	30
			2 45

Second—From Chicago to Troy, (via Oneida Lake.)

	Miles.		
Chicago to Oswego	1,077		
Oneida Lake	23		
	1,100	at $1\frac{1}{2}$ mills	$1 82

Oswego to Troy.

	Miles.		
Oswego Canal	21		
Canal to Oneida Lake	$13\frac{1}{2}$		
Oneida Canal	6		
Erie Canal to Troy	128		
	169	at $3\frac{1}{2}$ mills	59
Cost of transshipment at Oswego			25
			2 66

Besides any cost for insurance, showing a difference of 20 cents per ton in favor of the route on which there is no transshipment of cargo—where the time is 30 hours less, and on a route which would be beneficial to the whole of the Eastern States as well as to New York. If the route from Oswego to Troy should be adopted as the route between the West and the East, then Troy or Albany is the nearest point from whence the products of the West can be distributed to Northern New York, Vermont, New Hampshire, Connecticut, and Maine, while all of these States could be reached at a much cheaper cost of transport by the route through Lake Champlain; and while it would also be the cheapest and quickest to New York, it would also open up for all of these States a direct communication with the great timber regions of the Ottawa Valley.

The secretary of the board of trade of Oswego states that the distance from—

	Miles.
Chicago to Albany by the Saint Lawrence route is	1,495
Chicago to Albany by Buffalo and Erie Canal	1,277
Chicago to Albany by Oswego and Oneida Lake	1,260

and "that these distances are each made up of lake, river, and canal navigation, and the difference between them will best be shown by reducing the distance to equivalents of one of these methods of navigation." Taking $1\frac{1}{2}$ mills per ton as the cost per mile on the lakes, 2 mills on the river, 4 mills on ship-canals, and 6 mills on the Erie Canal, we derive the following distances of navigation by ship-canals equivalent to each of the above routes:

		Miles.
Chicago to Albany, ship-canal navigation by Erie Canal		874
Chicago to Albany, by enlarged ship-canal navigation		698
Chicago to Albany, by Oswego and Oneida Lake ship-canal navigation		597
Chicago to Albany, by Albany and Lake Champlain—		
1,173 miles lake navigation	440	
165 miles ship-canal navigation	165	
157 miles river ship-canal navigation	78	
		683

From this statement the Oswego and Oneida route stands better than all the other routes by this mode of comparison; but the statement is incorrect; there is not, as I have shown, 165 miles of canal on the Saint Lawrence route below Oswego, but only 34½ miles from Caughnawaga, and 25 miles from Whitehall to Fort Edward, or 59½ miles of canal in all on the downward voyage. The 40 miles from Fort Edward to Troy is more a river navigation than a canal. The Saint Lawrence River below Kingston has all the equivalents of lake navigation in speed and freedom. The comparison will stand as follows:

	Miles.
1,173 } 169 } miles = 1,342 miles lake and river navigation	503
59½ miles ship-canal	59½
40 miles river ship-canal	20
	582½

Thus placing the Champlain route, even by this mode of calculation, as the best.

Another objection by the Board of Trade of Oswego is, that the Oneida route has the advantage of two weeks' earlier navigation in the spring and two weeks later in the fall, while the facts prove that Lake Champlain is open as soon and as late as the Erie Canal. Then, again, the Oneida route "escapes the fogs of the Saint Lawrence." We have all heard of fogs in the Gulf of the Saint Lawrence; but I have never heard of fogs on the Saint Lawrence above Lachine. The Oswego board make a point in claiming the route via Oswego as the oldest route. This I also must dispute, for I find in the "Vermont Centinel" of the 14th of February, 1802, a letter from Gen. Ira Allen, dated Colchester, 3d February, in which he declares: "In the year 1784 I applied to General Haldemand, then governor and commander-in-chief of the province of Quebec, for license to open up a ship-canal by the Sorel River into Lake Champlain. This work is of the first importance, not to our neighbors in Canada, but to us. When in London, in January, 1796, I had an interview with the Duke of Portland on the subject of said canal, when, after several interviews at his grace's office concerning said canal, it was agreed to defer its consideration till after the close of the European war, and His Majesty's ministers then agreed that charter privileges would be granted for its construction. Every mercantile man, farmer, and even every citizen contiguous to Lake Champlain are more or less interested in the success of said canal." This was written more than eighty years ago by a distinguished citizen of Vermont, and, although the location is not that which I suggested from Caughnawaga, yet the present Chambly Canal, from the Richelieu River into Lake Champlain, is the same as that originally suggested by General Allen.

But it perhaps was unnecessary for me to enter so minutely into this discussion, nor would I have done so but from my belief of its great importance to the people of both the United States and Canada. The great fact is acknowledged by Mr. McAlpine, and is not contradicted by the Oswego Board of Trade, that it is impossible to take the vessel from Chicago or other Western lake-ports, carrying 1,500 tons, through from Oswego to Troy without breaking bulk and transferring cargo into barges carrying 750 tons. While this is the fact, it is acknowledged by all that there is no difficulty, by the Saint Lawrence and Champlain route, in this vessel going through and on to Lake Champlain, and discharging her cargo at Burlington for Boston or elsewhere, or to New York, without transfer of cargo or breaking bulk. This is conceded by every engineer who has examined the subject. Is it not, then, evident, from the time and cost of transferring cargo at Oswego, and the greater cheapness of moving freight by large than by small vessels, that the Saint Lawrence is the great natural route to New York and to the Eastern States. The Board of Trade of Oswego state that the Washington treaty "does not protect nor extend to the Caughnawaga Canal," and that "the United States Government cannot expend its money on foreign soil."

Canadians do not wish the United States to spend money in Canada, but they are anxious to have such a good understanding with their kindred people in the United States that all will have a feeling of entire confidence with each other in choosing and using any route of transport, either by canal or railway, no matter whether part of such route may be in the territory of the United States or of Canada, especially when the effect of using such route is to lessen the cost of transport from any one point to another.

It is of the very highest importance in the interests of both countries to cherish and promote the most liberal principles of trade between each; and having some experience of the feeling in Canada, I am sure everything will be done to guarantee every reciprocal advantage that may be demanded in the way of transport.

In conclusion, I have only to say that the cost of the improved works by the Oswego and Oneida Lake route is estimated at twenty-five millions of dollars by Mr. McAlpine, while the late Mr. Mills, a civil engineer of great experience, estimated the cost of the

Champlain Canal improvement at six and one-half millions, on a line which Messrs. McAlpine, Kirkwood, and Childe declared to be "a better line, one of greater capacity, and of quicker transit."

I have the honor to be, sir, your obedient servant,

JOHN YOUNG.

To Hon. WILLIAM WINDOM,
Chairman of Senate Committee on Cheap Transportation and Water-Routes from the West to the Seaboard.

Without expressing any opinion in regard to the following enterprises, the committee submit them merely as evidence in regard to the cost of building a freight-railroad between the Ohio River and the seaboard:

POTOMAC AND OHIO RAILROAD.

To the United States Senate Committee on Transportation, and the Committee on Railways and Canals, House of Representatives:

GENTLEMEN: I respectfully submit to your honorable committees, for consideration, the following exhibit of the proposed line of a double-track freight-railway between the Potomac and Ohio Rivers, showing its length, location, grade, and curvature, cost of construction, amount of through and local tonnage and comparative cost of transportation over the line of railway, in connection with barges on the Mississippi and Ohio Rivers, with lake and canal transportation to New York, and river and sea transportation via New Orleans to Liverpool, and river, rail, and sea transportation via Potomac; and all rail from Saint Louis and Chicago to New York, Philadelphia, and Boston.

The western termination of the Potomac and Ohio Railway will be between the mouths of the Guyandotte and Great Kanawha. From said terminus to Dayton, Ohio, the distance would be 150 miles, Dayton being a radiating railway point to Chicago, Toledo, and all points north and west. The distance by river from terminus to Cincinnati is 151 miles; the flow of water in Ohio River below this termination, giving much better navigation than can be had above it. There will also be a connection south, by the Lexington and Big Sandy Railway, with Louisville, Lexington, Nashville, and Memphis, and entire southwest. The distance from its western terminus on the Ohio River to its eastern terminus on the Potomac River is 265 miles in direct line, and from examinations of surveys already made, the 7 per cent. for curvature will be ample, which would make the railway distance 283 miles. To place the length of railway beyond question, call it 300 miles.

LOCATION, GRADE, AND TUNNELING.

A due east line from the Ohio River terminus to the crossing of Great Kanawha, at or below Charlestown, admits of low grades and slight curvature. The Great Kanawha from this crossing to its junction with the Ohio River admits of as good navigation as does the Ohio above this junction, and all freight received and delivered at this crossing, by steamboats or barges, reduces the railway transit from the Ohio to the Potomac terminus to 243 miles. The location of line from said crossing would follow up the valley of the Elk River, on the north slope of the divide between Elk and Gauley Rivers, and the distance from said crossing to head of Elk and Gauley would be 108 miles. The elevation of Kanawha crossing is 593 feet, and at head of Elk and Gauley is 1,800 feet above tide-water, giving an average rise of $11\frac{17}{100}$ feet per mile going east. A short tunnel would be necessary to overcome the summit elevation between head of Elk and Gauley, and the valley of the Greenbrier River; the grade from this tunnel going east will be a descending one. The elevation of the crossing of the Greenbrier will be about 1,400 feet above tide-water. The ascending grade east out of valley of Greenbrier will be about 40 feet per mile; to overcome the summit east of said valley, a short tunnel of about 3,200 feet will be required, and this will bring the line to the table-lands and at an elevation of about 2,300 feet, or 360 feet below summit level of Baltimore and Ohio Railway; it will then follow these table-lands until it reaches the North Mountains, which is the dividing ridge from the valley of Virginia, and here a tunnel of 1,800 to 2,000 feet will be required to bring the line into the valley of Virginia at an elevation of 1,100 feet with descending grade east. To leave this valley at Swift Run Gap requires an ascending grade of 30 feet per mile for 10 miles, and in order to keep at this grade a tunnel at this gap of 1,600 feet will be necessary; the elevation of east end of tunnel will be about 1,400 feet, and the distance therefrom to Potomac, about 68 miles, with an average descending grade of 20 feet per mile, brings the line to Potomac, a point at tide-water on the Potomac River in the State of Virginia, 38 miles below and 14½ miles west of Washington.

The Potomac River at this point is 8,000 feet in width, and the channel reaches from shore to shore; the depth of water from this point to the ocean will admit vessels drawing 26 feet at mean tide. The distance to Cape Henry is 144 miles.

ESTIMATED COST.

From a careful examination of the line, the estimated cost of constructing the road for a double track, with 65 pound steel rails, would be $75,000 per mile exclusive of tunnels. The estimated length of tunnels is 15,000 feet, at a cost of $150 per linear foot for 7,500 feet, and $225 per linear foot for 7,500 feet. The maximum grade not to exceed 60 feet to the mile, and maximum curvature of 1,000 feet radius; that only on level grade.

The grade and curvature admits of the passage of freight-trains carrying 200 tons. At ten miles per hour would make the time between the Ohio and Potomac River thirty-three hours.

The capacity of the road at this rate of speed would be as follows:

Trains 200 tons of freight each:

	Tons each way.
Space, 2 miles between trains; yearly freight capacity	7,008,000
Space, 1 mile between trains; yearly freight capacity	14,016,000
Space, half mile between trains; yearly freight capacity	28,032,000

Estimated cost of Potomac and Ohio Railway, exclusive of tunnels and bridges across Ohio River:

300 miles of double track, at $75,000 per mile	$22,500,000
15,000 linear feet of tunnels, at $150 and $225 per foot	2,812,500
Cost of double-track bridge across Ohio River	1,500,000
Wharves and docks	350,000
Total	27,162,500

ESTIMATED YEARLY RECEIPTS AND EXPENSES.

3,500,000 tons of easterly-bound through freight at a toll of 2 mills per ton per mile, equal to 60 cents per ton	$2,100,000
500,000 tons of westerly-bound through freight, at 60 cents per ton	300,000
2,000,000 tons of coal, at 50 cents per ton	1,000,000
500,000 tons of iron, at 50 cents per ton	250,000
100,000 tons local freight, at 30 cents per ton	30,000
Yearly income	3,680,900

YEARLY EXPENDITURE.

Maintenance of roadway and taxes, $5,000 per mile	$1,500,000
6 per cent. interest on $17,500,000	1,050,000
8 per cent. dividend on 9,662,500	773,000
	3,323,000

Surplus fund, $357,000.

MINERAL RESOURCES.

Coal and iron will be the two principal resources for intermediate freighting. The coal-beds on Elk River and head of Gauley consist of cannel, splint, and gas coal, and are unequaled as to quality and virtually inexhaustible in quantity, and the average distance of the beds from tide-water will be 170 miles for coal going east and for that going west; the distance to the Kanawha, where the coal would be discharged, would be about 60 miles; consequently, the superior coal of Elk and Gauley could be delivered at Potomac in 170 miles against 196 miles for the Cumberland coals.

During 1873 the Baltimore and Ohio Railway transported to Baltimore from Cumberland over 2,500,000 tons of Cumberland coal, and the Chesapeake and Ohio Canal brought in 1,300,000 tons, making 3,800,000 tons. The coal of Elk and Gauley being of higher grade than the Cumberland coal, they would not necessarily come in competition. Heretofore, all our cannel-coal has been imported from England, and sold at $16 to $22 per ton, and with a large consumption even at that high price. By the completion of the Potomac and Ohio Railway the same quality of coal could be delivered at tide-water and afford ample remuneration at from $6 to $7 per ton. The same grade of gas-coal, now imported and worth $12 to $14 per ton, could be afforded from the Elk and Gauley beds at from $5 to $7 per ton. The most valuable coal from this region is what is called the splint-coal; this coal possesses all the properties for making iron that charcoal does, and by tests at Ironton, on the Ohio River, and elsewhere, 2¼ tons of this coal makes 1 ton of pig-iron.

IRON-ORE BEDS ON LINE OF ROAD.

Magnetic iron-ore formations extend northeast and southwest along the eastern foothills of the Blue Ridge, and of high grade and inexhaustible quantities; on the western slope of the Blue Ridge the brown hematite comes in, and the quality is of the highest grade, and the quantity also inexhaustible. On the table-lands of Virginia are large deposits of specular iron, and, from examinations made, is of very high grade.

Iron can undoubtedly be manufactured at suitable points on the line of this road as cheaply as at any place in the world, for the following reasons:

First. For all eastern or sea-board demand, or foreign exportation, furnaces could be located in the valley of Virginia and on the eastern slopes of the Blue Ridge, giving short haulage from the beds of magnetic and brown hematite to furnace.

Second. For western demand and the valley of the Mississippi furnaces should be located in the coal formation of the Elk; consequently, to supply the furnaces in the valley of Virginia and eastern slope of the Blue Ridge, coal would have to be hauled from the coal deposits of Elk and same cars take the iron-ore back to the furnaces of Elk, thus giving freight both ways. Consequently the coal and iron could be transported at very low rates, the amount of coal and ore to make pig-iron being about equal, two tons of ore and two and a quarter tons of coal.

It is estimated that the intermediate tonnage of the road would be 2,500,000 tons annually, and when it is taken into consideration that the coals of the Elk are of higher grade and do not come into competition with the coals of the Baltimore and Ohio Railway, and the great facilities for manufacturing the iron, it must be conceded that the above estimate of local tonnage is not at all in excess.

In regard to through transportation the quantity must, of course, depend in a measure on the cheapness of transferring from the Ohio River to the sea-board. Allowing the greater distance, three hundred miles from the Ohio to the Potomac, at one cent per ton per mile for tolls and transportation, taking the lesser distance from the crossing of the Kanawha to Potomac, two hundred and forty-three miles, it would be at the same rate, $2.43 per ton. No existing line can compete with these prices; consequently the route would command all the freight that belongs to the Ohio and Middle and Upper Mississippi Rivers that could reach its western terminus. It is, therefore, believed that 3,500,000 tons yearly is not an overestimate for eastern-bound through-freight and 500,000 tons for western-bound through-freight.

Comparative cost of this line with other through double-track lines.

Name of company.	Length in miles.	Cost.	Earnings on hand and invested in stock and improvements.	Stock of.	Bond of.	Total stock and bond liability.	Value of stock.
New York Central and Hudson River, double track.	441	$63, 772, 031	....	$89, 428, 300	$16, 196, 002	$105, 624, 302	$0 98
New York and Erie, double track.	459	97, 048, 084	....	86, 636, 910	26, 398, 800	113, 035, 710	46
Pennsylvania Central, double track.	354	43, 280, 396	....	51, 271, 937	35, 072, 300	86, 344, 237	93
Baltimore and Ohio, double track.	379	31, 171, 756	$29, 000, 000	16, 740, 762	12, 466, 639	29, 207, 401	1 53
Potomac and Ohio, estimated	300	27, 162, 500	....	9, 662, 500	17, 500, 000	27, 162, 500	.....

Comparative grades—

	Feet per mile.
Maximum grades of New York Central and Hudson River Railroad	91
Maximum grades of New York and Erie Railroad	90
Maximum grades of Pennsylvania Central Railroad	98
Maximum grades of Baltimore and Ohio Railroad	116
Maximum grades of Potomac and Ohio Railroad	60

IMPORTANT RAILWAY CROSSINGS AND CONNECTIONS BETWEEN POTOMAC AND THE OHIO RIVER.

Potomac is now connected with the North and East by the Pennsylvania Central Railroad to Washington and Baltimore, and south by the Richmond, Fredericksburgh, and Potomac Railroad via Richmond to Wilmington, Charleston, Savannah, &c., and at a point 38 miles west the line would cross the Washington City, Virginia Midland and Great Southern Railroad, running from Washington via Gordonsville, Lynchburgh, Danville, &c., to the South and Southwest. In the valley of Virginia it crosses first the Pennsylvania Central running from the north via Front Royal and Luray to Fishersville on the Chesapeake and Ohio Railroad, and at a short distance beyond this crossing of the Pennsylvania Central, the line crosses the Baltimore and Ohio Railroad, running from Martinsburgh via Strasburgh and Harrisonburgh to Staunton on the Chesapeake and Ohio Railroad, and thence south to Salem on the Atlantic, Mississippi and Ohio Railroad, which connects via Knoxville, Atlanta and Chattanooga with New Orleans and the Southwest. At or in the vicinity of Charlestown, West Virginia, the line will connect with the Chesapeake and Ohio Railroad, and thence with the Lexington and Big Sandy Railroad to Lexington, Louisville, Nashville, Memphis, and entire southern line of the Mississippi.

The terminus of the Potomac and Ohio Railroad is on latitude 4 miles south of Saint Louis, and directly east of the great northern bend of the Ohio River. The general course of the Ohio River from the western terminus of the road to its mouth, 700 miles, is south of west.

The cost of transportation, including tolls, 2 mills per ton per mile, for the use of the road-bed should not exceed 1 cent per ton per mile, allowing 3 mills per ton for river transportation, the cost of moving a ton of freight from Saint Louis to Potomac, Virginia, via the Mississippi and Ohio River and the Potomac and Ohio Railroad, would be as follows:

903 miles river transportation, at 3 mills per ton per mile, and 10 cents for transfer	$2 31
300 miles railroad transportation on Potomac and Ohio Railroad, at 1 cent per ton per mile	3 00
	5 81

Equal to 17 cents and 4 mills per bushel of wheat, allowing 1 cent for transfer, would be 18 cents and 4 mills for transporting a bushel of wheat from Saint Louis to Potomac.

Cincinnati and Potomac:

Cincinnati to western terminus of Potomac and Ohio Railroad, 156 miles river, at 3 mills per ton per mile	$0 47
300 miles over Potomac and Ohio Railroad, at 1 cent per ton per mile	3 00
	3 47

Equal to 11 cents and 4 mills, allowing 1 cent for transfer, for transporting a bushel of wheat from Cincinnati to Potomac.

IN REGARD TO THE ADVANTAGES OF THE PORT OF POTOMAC FOR FOREIGN COMMERCE.

1st. It is the most westerly deep-water harbor on the Atlantic coast.

2d. Vessels drawing 26 feet of water can load at the wharves, and proceed to sea, distance one hundred and forty-four miles.

3d. Cumberland coal can be procured from $2 to $2.50 per ton cheaper than at New York or Boston, thus making a difference of 50 cents per ton on all outward-bound freights by steamer, equal to 1½ mills per ton per mile, to three hundred and forty miles in distance, about equalizing ocean freights, between New York and Potomac.

4th. As our exports to Europe are now mostly carried in iron steamers, it is very desirable that they should lie in fresh water while in port. The river-water at Potomac is perfectly fresh.

5th. The Chesapeake Bay and Potomac River below the port of Potomac is never seriously obstructed by ice.

6th. Inland navigation now exists between Potomac, Baltimore, Philadelphia, New York, and Providence, R. I., for vessels of 350 tons.

By the provisions of the proposed contract between the Secretary of the Interior and the Potomac and Ohio Railway Company, the railway is to be open to free competition in transportation. Any company or individual privileged to run over the road by paying tolls therefor, and conforming to the established regulations.

A moderate and uniform rate of speed to be adopted for all trains, such speed to be graduated with reference to economy in fuel, and the preservation of the road and rolling-stock, probably from eight to ten miles per hour.

FREIGHT CAPACITY.

The Erie Canal is opened on an average two hundred days, and has a freight-carriage capacity of 3,900,000 tons each way, total of 7,800,000 tons.

On a speed of ten miles per hour, and two miles space between trains, the Potomac and Ohio Railroad can carry from the Ohio River to the Potomac River, three hundred miles, 7,008,000 tons each way yearly, about twice the present capacity of the Erie Canal.

In all the above statements and comparisons as to cost of transportation, it has been assumed that 1 cent per ton per mile is a fair compensation for railway transportation, but in order to illustrate what it can and should be done for on the Potomac and Ohio Railway, estimating the average cost to the Ohio River, at $84,375 per mile, to be used as a freight road only, the actual cost per mile, affording a fair remuneration for cars, motive-power and road-bed, can be made up as follows:

	Mills.
For use of freight-car per ton per mile	$1\frac{1}{4}$
For use of motive-power per ton per mile	$2\frac{1}{2}$
For use of road-bed per ton per mile	2
	$5\frac{3}{4}$

which would be per ton from the Ohio River to Potomac, 300 miles, $1.73.

And to demonstrate that the above is a fair compensation, we will allow a freight-car to average 100 miles per day, for 300 days, and that it is loaded only one way, and it would earn $375 per year, on a purchase expenditure of say $650, and allow four years for its existence, it would earn $1,500, or twice its cost. We have loaded it but one way, while it would earn enough by freight going the other way to pay its repair.

Allowing $2\frac{1}{2}$ mills per ton for motive-power, which moves freight-trains of 200 tons, an engine would earn 50 cents per mile, and its average work is 80 miles per day, for 300 days, and the actual cost of running the engine, including everything, is 20 cents per mile, leaving a profit of 30 cents per mile for through-freight, and allowing $12\frac{1}{2}$ cents on her back freight of, say 50 tons, makes her gross earnings, $62\frac{1}{2}$ cents per mile,

or total of	$187 50
and cost of running each way	120 00
Gives net per trip	67 50

or $22\frac{1}{2}$ cents per mile; and at 80 miles per day for 300 days, or 2,400 miles, her net earnings would be $5,400 per year.

In the exhibit of cost of construction of the Potomac and Ohio Railway, and amount of tonnage required to pay the interest on its bonded debt, and a dividend of 8 per centum, it is shown that a toll of two mills per ton per mile is sufficient, and leave a yearly surplus of $357,000. Thus proving that a ton of freight can be moved at a profit from the Ohio River to the Potomac for $5\frac{3}{4}$ mills per ton per mile, being for the 300 miles $1.57 per ton, and extending the line to Chicago, a distance of 700 miles, $4.02½ per ton; to Cincinnati, 456 miles, $2.62 per ton; to Saint Louis, 769 miles, $4.57 per ton; to Memphis, 834 miles, $4.79 per ton.

Estimate of yearly receipts, at 1 cent per mile per ton:

3,500,000 tons of easterly-bound through-freight carried 300 miles, at $3 per ton		$10,500,000
500,000 tons westerly-bound through-freight, at $3 per ton		1,500,000
2,000,000 tons coal carried 200 miles, at 1 cent per ton per mile		4,000,000
500,000 tons iron ore carried 100 miles, at $1 per ton		500,000
100,000 tons local freight carried 100 miles, at $1 per ton		100,000
		16,600,000
Allowing $57\frac{1}{2}$ per cent. on gross receipts, as above, for maintenance and use of way, and all expenses of transportation, amounts to		9,545,000
		7,055,000
Cost of constructing double-track road-bed	$27,162,500	
Equipment	10,000,000	
	37,162,500	
Surplus earnings at above rate of transportation, viz, 1 cent per ton per mile, amounts to		7,055,000

Be it understood that the proposed construction of the Potomac and Ohio Railway under the provisions of the bill has been honestly devised, with an eye to financial economy to construction and the fullest popular advantage in management.

In order to avoid imposition on the public, Congress, according to the provisions of the bill, has a power to control, and the right to regulate the tolls to be paid to the owners of the road-bed, and also to regulate and fix the tariff of charges by the carriers.

The Government also has the power to appoint a commissioner with full power to institute examinations and make report to Congress; his duty being to see that justice is maintained between the proprietorship of the road-beds, the carriers engaged in transporting over it, and the *people*. It is proposed *for once* to make the *people* a party.

The bill also provides and establishes a sinking fund from the receipt of tolls, which is paid into the Treasury of the United States, being 1 per cent. yearly on the bonded debt of the company, so that in time the tolls can be reduced to a sum sufficient to pay a dividend on the individual stock and maintenance of road-bed.

The Erie and Champlain Canals, 460 miles in length, is an illustration of the policy of providing a sinking fund. In forty-two years their improvements have paid for themselves, principal and interest, all costs of enlargement, superintendence, repairs, and salaries, and a clear surplus of $23,108,000 into the treasury of the State of New York; thus showing that the road-bed of the Potomac and Ohio Railway could be dedicated to the free use of the public in thirty-five years, except for superintendence and repairs.

ANSON BANGS,
President.

OFFICE OF POTOMAC AND OHIO RAILWAY,
Potomac, Va., January 28, 1874.

WASHINGTON AND OHIO RAILROAD.

Washington and Ohio Railroad in Virginia and West Virginia.

Distances by said road, as follows:

	Miles.
Washington City to Alexandria	6
Washington City to Leesburgh, Va	43½
Washington City to Winchester, Va	80
Washington City to Capon Springs, W. Va	101
Washington City to Moorefield, Va	137
Washington City to summit of Alleghanies	172
Washington City to Coal Fields, Red Creek	178
Washington City to Buckhannan	228
Washington City to Ravenswood, Ohio River	326
Washington City to Point Pleasant, Ohio River	331

The counties through which the road will run, are:

Alexandria, Fairfax, Loudoun, Clarke, Frederick, Virginia; Hardy, Grant, Tucker, Randolph, Barbour, Upshur, Lewis, Gilmer, Calhoun, Roane, Jackson, Mason, West Virginia.

The maximum grades of the road are:

Coming east, 52.8 per mile.

Going west, 79.2 per mile.

The total estimated cost of the road, from Hamilton, Loudoun County, Virginia, 50 miles from Washington, including second track, tunneling, &c., a distance of 275 miles, is $20,809,362. This estimate is based upon a careful preliminary survey of the entire line.

The estimated cost to the coal-beds of Red Creek, Randolph County, West Virginia, is $11,906,162.

The gauge of the road being the same as that of Baltimore and Ohio Road, its capacity would also be the same, with an equal number of tracks, or greater, as the grades are much less.

The connections of the road at Winchester will give a very direct line to New York via Martinsburgh, Williamsport, Hagerstown, Chambersburgh, Harrisburgh, Lebanon, Reading, &c., as may be seen by a glance at the map of the United States; also with the railroads running south and southwest to New Orleans, Memphis, &c.

The country traversed by our line is rich in agricultural products, in minerals, and in timber. The growth of valuable timbers, in West Virginia especially, is not surpassed in the world for variety and abundance, except, perhaps, in the tropics. The principal kinds are the oaks, hickory, pine, poplar, black-walnut, and many others.

Going west from Washington City the first mineral deposit reached is the iron ore of Clarke County, Virginia, which extends along both sides of the Shenandoah River, in immense quantity. The pamphlet herewith (A) is referred to as giving all necessary and reliable information in relation to these ores. Their distance from navigation on the Potomac is 67 miles. The next large deposit of this ore is found near Capon Springs, in Hardy County, West Virginia, and at Keller's, near Wardensville, where it has been yielding a first-class iron for years past. It exists in quantity along the eastern base of the Alleghanies at several other points already well known, in Hardy and Grant Counties. These ores may be said to be inexhaustible in quantity, and of great richness in the yield of pure metal. So far as known it is all of the brown hematite variety.

The coal-beds begin at Red Creek, in Tucker County, West Virginia, on the western slope of the Alleghanies, and extend along the road all the way to the Ohio River. There are two varieties, known as the Cumberland and the Pittsburgh coals. The latter is an excellent gas-coal.

The distance of gas-coal from Washington by this road is 204 miles, 98 miles shorter than by the Baltimore and Ohio Railroad. The Cumberland coal is reached at the distance of 172 miles west of Washington by this line, and at 206 miles by the Baltimore and Ohio Road, or, by the Point of Rocks branch, 179 miles.

The Washington and Ohio Road is finished and in operation 45 miles, and will be completed 2½ miles farther in a few days. This distance is not embraced in the foregoing estimates of cost.

Respectfully submitted.

LEWIS McKENZIE,
President.

ALEXANDRIA, VA., *February* 23, 1874.

STATEMENT IN REGARD TO THE PULLMAN PALACE-CAR COMPANY.

OFFICE OF PULLMAN'S PALACE-CAR COMPANY,
Chicago, February 6, 1874.

SIR: I have received your letter requesting me to furnish such information in reference to the relations of Pullman's Palace-Car Company to the railway companies, and the system under which its cars are operated, as may be of service to your committee in its investigation of the general subject of transportation.

In replying, it seems requisite to allude briefly to the condition of things that existed prior to the organization of this company, and which pointed to such an organization as its remedy, together with such details of the system as show the advantages to the public derived therefrom, as well as the existing relations to the railway companies.

About the year 1858, sleeping-cars were adopted by a few of the leading railways of the country. The cars then used were for the most part crude and unsatisfactory in their arrangement and appointments. They were constructed under a variety of patents, and employed various devices which had not been perfected by experience, and, in many instances, ordinary passenger-cars were utilized. They served, however, to educate the traveling public to the existing want, and demonstrated the necessity of something better.

These cars were, moreover, confined to the roads of the railway companies owning them, and were unsuited to the necessities of the travel on long lines. They were chiefly used to accommodate local travel, and then only in case the road was of sufficient length to occupy an entire night in the transportation of its passengers.

It soon became apparent that a class of cars that would furnish accommodations adequate to the wants of both night and day travel, together with a system that should afford continuous and unbroken communication between far-distant points, over several distinct lines of railway, would supply a growing want of the traveling public, and probably largely increase the passenger-traffic.

It was not easy or, indeed, possible for fifty or more independent railway companies to unite upon a uniform pattern of car, to perfect uniform arrangements, or to utilize the many different inventions and devices which, combined, make up the comfort and convenience of the Pullman car.

Even had any general plan been suggested by one or more companies for acting in concert, some companies would not, perhaps, have found it convenient, at any given time, to furnish their proportion of cars; nor would it have been easy to decide, without experience, what in such a case equity between the roads would demand.

It is obvious that the constant provision of abundant supplies of bedding and changes of linen, and the necessary laundry arrangements, as well as the selection of suitable devices for heating, ventilating, constructing, and running cars with special reference to their use as sleeping apartments, is of the very essence of a successful sleeping-car system; yet this was foreign to the regular business of railway companies, and less likely to receive their careful attention than that of a company especially organized for the purpose.

Hence the necessity for a separate organization which should be able to make arrangements of a uniform character with the different railway companies on such reasonable terms as would appeal to their interests.

The organization of such a company, which should be charged with the duty of providing the accommodations required by an intelligent public, presented questions of much magnitude and importance.

The problem was, to build cars which should embrace inventions and improvements perfected by the best ingenuity and skill of the country, and thus meet the just demands of the traveler, and at the same time secure the railways a fair equivalent for their service and provide a reasonable return upon the capital invested.

The following are the principal features of existing contracts with the railway companies whereby it is sought to accomplish this end.

The Pullman Company contracts to furnish its cars to railway companies for a period of fifteen years, and gives each company the option, if exercised within a reasonable time, to purchase a one-half interest in the cars assigned to its road at their cost, with no charge for the use of patents, and to share equally with the Pullman Company in the results of the business. The Pullman Company agrees to provide such number and kind of cars as may be required by the railway companies to meet the demand of the traveling public; it furnishes the employés, who are subject to the rules and regulations provided by the railway companies for the government of their own employés. The railway companies control the movement of the cars, and use them the same as if they were their own, carrying their passengers in them, and receiving the whole of the railway-fares, thus saving the amount of capital which they would otherwise have to invest in building cars of their own. The Pullman Company derives revenue from the rental of berths and seats as its compensation for furnishing the cars and attendance.

As the railway companies receive the service of the cars for the transportation of their passengers, free of cost, they agree to maintain them the same as they would have to maintain their own, with the exception of the carpets, upholstery, and bedding, which constitute that portion of the equipment pertaining to the sleeping accommodations, which require frequent renewals, and are maintained by the Pullman Company.

More than sixty railway companies in the United States and Canada have already entered into such contracts.

Some of these companies have become participants in the entire business by subscribing to the stock of the Pullman Company, at its par value, and receiving the usual dividends; others by associations, in which they are joint owners with the Pullman Company in the cars assigned to their respective lines, providing half the capital and sharing equally in the results.

The prosecution of this enterprise in every step of its progress has demonstrated the paramount importance of constructing cars which shall, as far as practicable, meet every want of the traveling public, combining convenience of arrangement and elegance of finish with such undoubted strength as will guarantee, so far as is attainable, safety to the passenger, and such durability as insures to the railway companies the minimum of ordinary repairs, and at the same time avoid overloading the trains with excessive weight.

These objects have been steadily pursued without faltering at the expense and labor involved, until, as it is believed, reasonable success has been attained in the present standard sleeping-car, the weight of which is twenty-eight tons.

This only exceeds the weight of the ordinary twelve-wheel, first-class passenger-cars used on leading western roads by about two and one-half tons, the excess being in consequence of bedding and partitions essential to the sleeping arrangements.

The Pullman cars are now used on over thirty thousand miles of railroad in this country alone, and the advantages of the system have so recommended it that it has already been introduced in Europe. These facts present the best evidence of the great importance of the conveniences which the Pullman cars and the system under which they are operated afford the public and the railway companies who have adopted them.

The Pullman Company claims to have rendered the traveling public substantial benefits in organizing and perfecting a system by which its cars are not only run through without change between far-distant points, and over a number of distinct lines of railway, in charge of responsible through agents, to whom ladies, children, and invalids can be, and constantly are, safely intrusted, but it has, by a number of ingenious devices, very greatly improved the comfort, safety, and healthfulness of railway passenger-cars, lessening the fatigue of travel and making night-journeys convenient and easy.

By its system the traveler is also enabled to avoid anxiety and loss of time by securing specific accommodations in advance for the entire journey, thus saving, especially to ladies and traveling parties, constant annoyance and discomfort.

It will be seen by your honorable committee, from the above statement, that the Pullman Company aims to do a work for the public, in connection with the railway companies, which they separately could not so well perform.

An organization was therefore needed to amicably unite all the different interests for the better service of the public, and to combine, in one class of car and one system, as only a single company could, all the improvements which ingenuity has contrived for the convenience, safety, and comfort of the traveler, so as to enable the public to use the different railway lines as though they were all under one management.

It is believed that the public will never consent to return to the old plan of frequent changes of cars and broken travel, but, instead of taking any step backward, will demand even further improvements. These, so far as attainable, this company has no doubt it can furnish, if its efforts to meet the public wants shall be as thoroughly seconded by the railway interests of the country in the future as they have been in the past.

Inclosed will be found a copy of the form of contract, and a map showing the lines on which the company's cars are operated in the United States and Canadas.

With respect,

GEO. M. PULLMAN,
President.

Hon. WM. WINDOM,
Chairman Senate Committee on Transportation, Washington, D. C.

The following letter in regard to the latest results of the efforts being made to introduce steam propulsion on the Erie Canal has been referred to this committee by Hon. F. A. Alberger, of Buffalo, N. Y.:

STEAM ON THE ERIE CANAL.

STATE OF NEW YORK, DIVISION ENGINEER'S OFFICE,
NEW YORK STATE CANALS,
Albany, February 10, 1874.

DEAR SIR: Your note of the 28th ultimo, requesting answers to three questions proposed by the Hon. William Windom, chairman of the United States Senate Committee on Transportation Routes to the Seaboard, is received.

In reply I have to say:

1. That the results of our last year's experience with steam upon the Erie Canal are very satisfactory. As was to have been expected, the number of competing boats has been very much reduced. Those boats and devices, which were so obviously without merit that even their owners could not fail to discover the fact, have gradually disappeared; so that, during the season of 1873, our attention has been called to only six boats which were actually in operation upon the canal.

There have been several other boats upon the canal during the season; but their performances were not such as to encourage their owners to invite an inspection when under steam.

On the 15th and 16th of October, 1873, a trial was had between Syracuse and Utica, under the supervision of the commission. Five boats were entered for the trial; but while all of these boats succeeded in making the required speed of three miles per hour, while running with the current from Rome to Utica—15 miles—only one boat (the Baxter) averaged three miles per hour for the entire distance run.

After the trial a second boat, the Newman, was so altered and improved that she has since averaged over three miles on the canal, from Utica to Troy, running east with a cargo of 200 tons, and running west over the entire canal from West Troy to Buffalo with a cargo of 121 tons.

During her last trip west the Newman made the following speeds, (121 tons cargo:)

	Miles per hour.
Average speed, including all detentions	2.98
Average speed, exclusive of 10 hours for lockage	3.26
Average speed, exclusive of detentions other than lockages	3.78
Average spead, exclusive of all detentions	4.24
	Pounds.
Average coal consumption per mile	35

As indicating the improvement made during the season of 1873, I may say that the Baxter has maintained her speed of 1872, (3 miles,) and has reduced her coal consumption from 31 pounds per mile to less than 20 pounds per mile; and that the Newman has increased her speed from an average of 2.72 miles per hour, with a coal consumption of 65 pounds per mile, in 1872, to over 4 miles per hour, on a consumption of 35 pounds per mile, in 1873.

These two boats alone, in the opinion of the commission, have met the requirements of the law so far as speed and economy are concerned. Their models, however, being somewhat different from those of the ordinary horse-boats, I am inclined to think that the commission will not be satisfied that the requirement of "ready and easy adaptation of the devices to existing boats" has been met. My own impression, however, is that there is no difficulty whatever in the application of steam to the present boats. Of course somewhat larger power will be required, and a correspondingly increased coal consumption will be involved. I am also of opinion that, under no circumstances likely to arise, will steamboats be introduced upon the canals more rapidly than the horse-boats will die out; and hence, that the introduction of steam will not involve loss or inconvenience to the owners of present boats, except so far as they may ultimately affect the rates of freight between Buffalo and New York.

Without assuming to speak for the commission, I do not hesitate to say that, in my judgment, the question of the practicability of substituting steam for animal power on the Erie Canal is substantially settled in the affirmative, and that better results will be attained in the future than have ever yet been attained.

2. The average speed of horse-boats moving east, loaded, and including all detentions other than at locks, is very nearly 1½ miles per hour. The speed of such boats while in motion varies from 1¾ to 2 miles per hour, depending upon the speed of the current and the ability of the animals. Running west, with cargoes of 100 tons, against the current, the speed is about the same as that east with 230 tons. Light boats moving west average, perhaps, 2 miles per hour, exclusive of lockages. It should be understood that the prevailing current is eastward, and that this current averages at least ½ mile per hour. There is a westward current only from Rome to Syracuse, 41 miles, and for a short distance west of Syracuse, as will be seen by reference to profiles of the Erie Canal accompanying reports of Canal department.

3. Should steam be generally adopted upon the Erie Canal, the speed between locks should not exceed 5 miles per hour in the wider and deeper portions of the canal, or 4½ miles in the canal proper.

I doubt very much whether rates of speed so high would be found profitable. I have written in much haste, but have endeavored to fully answer Senator Windom's inquiries.

Trusting that the foregoing may be satisfactory to yourself,

I am, sir, very respectfully,

D. M. GREENE,
Engineer of Commission.

Hon. F. A. ALBERGER.

The committee submit the statements here made simply as evidence in regard to the practicability of a double-track freight-railroad from the West to the seaboard:

THE CONTINENTAL RAILWAY COMPANY.

THE CONTINENTAL RAILWAY COMPANY,
OFFICE NO. 20 NASSAU STREET,
New York, March, 1874.

SIR: In compliance with your request, I have the honor to hand you herewith a brief statement of the status of the Continental Railway Company, giving the amount of work done, the time required to construct the entire road, and the results to be obtained by its operation under the auspices of the General Government, as suggested therein.

I am authorized to state, in addition, that legislation by Congress binding the company to a low schedule of freight-rates, which shall give the necessary recognition and aid, will be accepted.

I have the honor to be, your obedient servant,

WM. C. KIBBE,
On behalf of the Continental Railway Company.

Hon. WILLIAM WINDOM,
Chairman Senate Committee on Transportation to the Seaboard.

Impressed with the importance of connecting the Mississippi Valley and the harbor of New York by the shortest and best railway route, the projectors of the Continental

Railway employed engineers to examine the intervening country for a road between New York Bay and Council Bluffs, and report whether a practicable air-line route could be found. The survey disclosed a line from New York Bay to Council Bluffs with only 96 miles consumed in curvature, reducing the rail-distance between these two points, so that the entire distance will be 1,224 miles between New York and Omaha, 786 miles between New York and Chicago, and 969 miles between New York and Saint Louis, shortening the distance to Chicago 128 miles.*

Subsequent surveys have demonstrated the certainty that the maximum grades will not exceed 30 feet to the mile going east, and 40 feet to the mile going west, the maximum curves being four degrees on a radius of 1,433 feet. The uniformity of low grades and easy curves will contribute largely to the ability of the company to transport freights at low prices, and will be found of equal importance with the saving in distance, in reducing the cost of moving loaded trains. The company having secured the best route between the points named, is preparing to build a first-class double-track railway, over every part of which, when completed, a 33-ton locomotive will haul a train of 40 ten-ton loaded cars, at a speed of ten miles the hour without interruption from steep grades or short curves. The road is to be laid with steel rails, weighing 68 lbs. to the yard, and iron bridges of approved strength and durability, with the necessary turnouts and side-tracks to utilize it to its fullest capacity.

A double-track railway thus constructed and equipped, operated exclusively for freight, with a uniform speed of ten miles the hour, and all the necessary appliances, turnouts, signals, &c., can accommodate 250 trains, according to the experience of English roads, moving each way daily, with a capacity of 200,000 tons.†

The company has obtained charters with ample powers from the several States through which the road is to run. ‡

It has full reconnaissances of the entire line—two surveys across the Alleghany Mountains—surveys and location of line for over 450 miles. It has graded and constructed bridges for 100 miles of double-track, and has secured upward of 900 miles of right-of-way. For this work the company had expended to November 1, 1873, $1,806,498.88. The road can be finished from New York to Chicago and Saint Louis in three years, and to Council Bluffs in five years. It will require an expenditure of $50,000,000 for equipment adapted to the business of the road.

The rates of freight must depend largely upon the ability of the company to raise money for its completion, at low rates of interest, and without the payment of any bonus to stock or bondholders.

If such funds can be obtained, the company will establish the rates of freight upon cereals and breadstuffs at six mills per ton per mile for through-freight in summer, and seven mills in winter, and at such equitable rates upon other classes of freight as shall be fixed by a board of commissioners.

It is believed that, in consideration of the prompt construction of the road, and the assurance of low rates, it would be for the interest of the country to have Congress guarantee payment of interest at five per cent. gold per annum upon the first-mortgage bonds of this company to the amount of one-half of the cost of construction, including the necessary lands, buildings, and appurtenances required for its successful operation.

The railway company, on its part, to furnish an amount in cash equal to the said bonds by the issue and sale of its stock, in addition to the cost of the necessary equipment of 1,400 engines and 15,000 freight-cars at the estimated cost of $50,000,000.

A commission to be appointed, in such manner as Congress may direct, whose duty it shall be to regulate the rates of freight from time to time, and adjust the rates to be paid over connecting roads. The company will also agree that they will not increase the rates upon cereals and breadstuffs, and that the regulation of rates shall continue under the control of the Government commission referred to, and whenever the net earnings of the road shall exceed 8 per cent. per annum upon the capital stock, an equitable reduction of all rates shall be made.

The company, before proposing to move freights at these rates, made a careful analysis of the expenditures and receipts, and believe a profit can be made at these prices. That they are very low will appear by contrasting them with the present prices, (February, 1874, 36 cents per bushel from Chicago, and 47 4-10 cents from Saint Louis to New York,) viz: the proposed price for carrying wheat from Chicago to New York is 15 cents per bushel; from Saint Louis to New York 18 cents per bushel; from Council Bluffs to New York 24 cents per bushel.

None of the lines of railway between New York and Chicago, as at present constructed and operated, can carry freights at the rates proposed. The cost per ton depends upon the tonnage moved as well as upon distance, gradients, curvature, and the character of business. Neither of them has a double-track for the whole distance; all

* See distance-table annexed. † See Appendix B. ‡ See Appendix C.

do a mixed passenger and freight business, and a larger local than through business.* The capacity of any of these lines for through-business is limited to the capacity of a single track, doing a mixed business. These roads all run six classes of trains—express, ordinary, and local passenger, through, fast, and local freight-trains—averaging only forty trains a day each way, while if trains were run at a uniform rate six times as many as are now run could be operated with certainty. The result of doing a mixed passenger and freight business involves high freight-charges and a longer trip, as the capacity of the road is greatly lessened and the detention is always placed upon freight-trains. None of these lines have the advantages of short distance, easy grades, and curves of the Continental, all of which elements enter largely into the cost of moving freight.

Even this road cannot carry freights at the low prices named without a large business. A careful estimate has been made, and it is believed that sufficient freight can be obtained to warrant its success, and that, ultimately, its capacity will be taxed to its utmost extent.

It is believed that we can control the business of supplying Great Britain with the low rates of transportation fixed herein.†

The gauge adopted is 4 feet 8½ inches to meet the requirements of the western railways, of which the Continental will become the great highway.

---

*Tonnage of Pennsylvania Central, 1872, 8,459,535; eastward through, 791,504 tons, or less than 10 per cent.

Tonnage of Erie, 9 months ending June, 1873, 4,295,431; eastward through, 730,514, or 17 per cent.

Total freight earnings of Baltimore and Ohio $8,959,318.41; east and west through-tonnage, 557,609.

So insignificant, therefore, in comparison is the amount of cereals carried by these lines, and so small is the dependence upon them for this service, that grain-shippers paid last year 15 cents per bushel for its shipment from Chicago to Buffalo by the lakes.

†See Appendix F. †See Appendix E.

APPENDIX A.

Comparison of distances between New York City and prominent points by existing lines with those by the Continental Railway.

From—	To—	By what line.	Distance.	Distance by Continental.	Saving.
			Miles.	*Miles.*	*Miles.*
New York	Pittsburgh, Pa	Pennsylvania Central	446	382	64
Do	Cleveland, Ohio	New York Central and Lake Shore	623	463	160
Do	do	Pennsylvania Central and connections	596		133
Do	do	Erie, via Leavittsburgh	605		142
Do	Sandusky, Ohio	New York Central and Lake Shore	693	520	173
Do	do	Baltimore and Ohio, via Lake Erie Division	790		270
Do	Toledo, Ohio	New York Central and Lake Shore	736	558	178
Do	do	Erie and Lake Shore	718		160
Do	do	Pennsylvania Central and connections	708		150
Do	Columbus, Ohio	do. do.	639	571	68
Do	do	Baltimore and Ohio and connections	705		134
Do	Cincinnati, Ohio	Erie and Atlantic and Great Western	860	695	165
Do	do	Pennsylvania Central and connections	759		64
Do	do	Baltimore and Ohio and connections	778		83
Do	Akron, Ohio	Erie and Atlantic and Great Western	615	432	183
Do	do	Pennsylvania Central and connections	575		143
Do	Fort Wayne, Ind	New York Central, Lake Shore, and T., W. and W	830	631	199
Do	do	Pennsylvania Central and connections	766		135
Do	Indianapolis, Ind	do. do.	827	640	187
Do	do	Baltimore and Ohio and connections	893		253
Do	do	New York Central, Lake Shore, and C. C. C. and I.	905		265
Do	do	Erie, Atlantic and Great Western and connections	849		209
Do	Louisville, Ky	Pennsylvania Central and connections	896	748	148
Do	do	Erie and connections	997		249
Do	do	Baltimore and Ohio and connections	886		138
Do	Chicago, Ill	Pennsylvania Central and connections	914	786	128
Do	do	New York Central and Lake Shore	980		194
Do	do	New York Central, Great Western of Canada, and Michigan Central	961		175
Do	do	Erie and connections	961		175
Do	Cairo, Ill	Pennsylvania Central and connections	1,132	1,051	81
Do	do	Baltimore and Ohio and connections	1,173		122
Do	do	Erie and connections	1,255		204
Do	do	New York Central and connections	1,309		258
Do	Saint Louis, Mo	Pennsylvania Central and connections	1,064	969	95
Do	do	Erie and connections	1,200		231
Do	do	New York Central and connections	1,168		199
Do	do	Baltimore and Ohio and connections, via Cincinnati	1,118		149

Comparison of distances between New York City and prominent points by existing lines with those of the Continental Railway—Continued.

From—	To—	By what line.	Distance.	Distance by Continental.	Saving.
			Miles.	*Miles.*	*Miles.*
New York	Rock Island, Ill	Pennsylvania Central and connections	1, 041		116
Do	do	Pennsylvania Central, via Chicago	1, 096	925	171
Do	do	New York Central and Lake Shore, via Chicago	1, 162		237
Do	Muscatine, Iowa	Pennsylvania Central and connections	1, 074		123
Do	do	Pennsylvania Central, via Chicago	1, 129	951	178
Do	do	New York Central, via Chicago	1, 195		244
Do	Saint Paul, Minn., via Chicago	Pennsylvania Central and connections	1, 320		128
Do	do	New York Central and connections	1, 386	1, 192	194
Do	do	Erie and connections	1, 367		175
Do	do	Michigan Central and connections	1, 367		175
Do	Council Bluffs	Pennsylvania Central, shortest line	1, 347		123
Do	do	Pennsylvania Central, via Chicago	1, 402		178
Do	do	Erie, via Chicago	1, 449	1, 224	225
Do	do	New York Central, via Chicago	1, 468		244
Do	do	Michigan Central, via Chicago	1, 449		225

APPENDIX B.

The capacity of a double-track freight-railway, operated at a uniform rate of speed of 10 miles an hour, or 200 miles run in 24 hours, maximum grade 40 feet to the mile; maximum curves 4 degrees on radius of 1,433 feet, may be stated as follows:

Trains carrying 300 tons; each starting from a given point, in either direction.

Daily trains carrying 300 *tons.*

No. of trains.	In miles.	Daily tonnage each way.	Annual tonnage each way.
250	Distance between trains 4-5	75, 000	27, 375, 000
200	Distance between trains 1 1-5	60, 000	21, 900, 000
150	Distance between trains 1 3-5	45, 000	16, 425, 000
100	Distance between trains 2 2-5	30, 000	10, 950, 000
80	Distance between trains 4 4-5	24, 000	8, 760, 000

NOTE.—In 1872 the tonnage of the London and Northwestern Railway, England, operating 1,539 miles of road, doing a mixed business, was 22,831,000 tons of freight moved, and 38,006,014 passengers carried, equivalent to 200 trains of 312 tons each per day for freight movement, and for passenger movement 347 trains of 300 passengers each, daily, or equivalent to 273½ trains each way daily.

At this rate the Continental would carry annually 39,931,000 tons eastward, or, reduced to bushels of wheat, 1,197,930,000 bushels. The London and Northwestern was operated for fast and slow trains, and thus its capacity was diminished.

Railway-trains are operated on English roads at intervals of three minutes, and at distances of one-half mile and upward, under the block system, by which the capacity of a road can be greatly increased.*

Extracts from report of the royal parliamentary commission, of 1873.

[Mr. Fenton, superintendent Metropolitan Railway; 20 miles long.]

"We run 1,000 trains daily over our entire system." What is the average time between trains?—Answer. "The average time is about 5 minutes, the longest interval 10 minutes; shortest, 2 minutes; lowest rate of speed, 15 miles the hour; highest, 35 miles the hour."

The road carried 41,392,665 passengers, and 951,501 tons freight in 1872, or an average of 2,600 tons freight, and 113,000 passengers daily.*

NOTE.—*Explanation.*—The block-system referred to herein is maintained in order to preserve a proper distance between trains running in same direction, on same track; and the proximity of stations indicates the number of trains run.

[E. Moore Needham, superintendent Midland Railroad, trackage 773 miles double; 251 miles single.]

"Distance of block stations, longest less than 4 miles, shortest ½ mile, average under 2 miles."

In 1872, passengers, 21,308,369; freight, 17,000,000 tons.

[J. Robertson, superintendent Great Eastern, 840 miles.]

"We ran in 1872, 406,800 trains. On the Blacknell line, for 2 miles, we run 246 trains daily in one direction.

Passengers, 25,606.744; freight, 4,500,000 tons.

*If this road, doing mainly a passenger business, can operate its trains every two minutes, or 1,000 trains per day, at rates of speed varying from 15 to 35 miles the hour, surely a road operating at a uniform rate of speed can run as many trains.

P. S. The maximum number given in this calculation is only one-half this number.

*On the 27th of February, 1873, Col. William Yolland, inspector of railways in England, testified before the select committee of the House of Lords that the Metropolitan lines of railway run trains only two and three minutes apart; on the Great Northern Line, 3¾ minutes apart. Corroborated by Col. C. S. Hutchinson, also inspector of railways, in same examination. At intervals of 4 minutes the number of trains in twenty-four hours would be 360, by our trains tonnage, 108,000. 100 train movement gives 14 4-10 minutes between trains.

The Philadelphia and Reading Railway, doing a mixed business, the main freighting being in one direction only, carried an equivalent in 1873 of 12,000,000 tons. No doubt, therefore, can exist of the capacity of the Continental to carry twice as much, if full loads both ways can be obtained by a daily movement of 250 trains.

APPENDIX C.

Opinion of Judge B. R. Curtis and others.

SIR: In compliance with your request, we express our opinion upon the interrogatories submitted to us by you, viz:

"Is the Continental Railway Company, formed by the consolidation of five several companies, organized under and by authority of the laws of Iowa, Illinois, Indiana, Ohio, and Pennsylvania, and consolidated under and by authority contained in the laws of said several States, a valid body-corporate, legally organized, and possessing the legal capacity to construct or complete the constrution of a railway from the easterly boundary-line of the State of Pennsylvania to the western line of the State of Iowa?"

In answer, we say that, after an examination of the laws of each of said States, we are of opinion that authority is contained therein for the organization and incorporation of each of said companies, and that the organization and incorporation thereof were authorized by and in accordance with the laws of said several States, and, therefore, that each of said corporations was legally organized.

We are of the opinion that the laws of said several States authorizing the consolidation of railway corporations organized for the construction of continuous lines of railway have been duly complied with by said companies, and that each and all of said consolidations resulting in the formation of "The Continental Railway Company," have been made in the manner required by the laws of said several States, and that each of said companies, at the time of said several consolidations, had legal capacity so to do.

Our opinion, therefore, is that the Continental Railway Company is duly organized, and has a legal existence, with authority to construct, maintain, and operate a railroad from the easterly line of Pennsylvania to the city of Council Bluffs, in the State of Iowa, and is vested with the right and powers necessary therefor.

B. R. CURTIS.
E. W. STOUGHTON.

Dated June 13, 1872.

EDWARD DODGE, Esq.,
President of the Continental Railway Company, New York.

On the 18th day of January, 1873, the Continental Railway Company purchased and consolidated with the New Jersey Tube Transportation Company, making a continuous line of railway from Council Bluffs to the Hudson River or New York Bay; and on the 20th of March, 1873, an act to legalize the consolidation of the New Jersey Tube Transportation Company with the Continental Railway Company, for the purpose of constructing and operating a railroad across the State of New Jersey as part of a continuous line of railway from Council Bluffs, on the Missouri River, to the waters of the Hudson River, opposite New York, or New York Harbor, in New Jersey, was passed by the legislature of New Jersey.

Organizations of companies, and their legal consolidation with each other, and with the Continental Railway Company, have been made in Indiana and Illinois for the construction of a line of railway from Rensselaer, Ind., to the city of Chicago.

APPENDIX D.

EXPENSES AND EARNINGS COMPARED.

Interest-account.

Estimated cost of road, including stations, grounds, equipment, machine-shops, water-tanks, and all property and appliances appurtenant, $225,000,000.

5 per cent. interest on $87,500,000 first-mortgage bonds	$4,375,000
8 per cent. dividend on $87,500,000 capital stock	7,000,000
7 per cent. interest on $50,000,000, cost of equipment	3,500,000
To annual sinking fund	1,000,000
Total interest, dividend, and sinking-fund account	15,875,000

This would be a daily expense of $43,496, and divided among 800 trains would amount to $54.37 per train per day.

NOTE.—The above calculation is on the basis of starting, on the average, eighty trains each way from a given point, on first 1,000 miles from the sea-board, and forty trains each way upon the western division of the road daily, which would give on whole road 800 trains moving in both directions at all times. The number of trains per day will vary with the demands of business. This estimate gives the average for the entire year. The equipment will consist of 1,400 engines, and 55,000 cars.

The company, by the construction of its freight-cars, will, while preserving the requisite strength, capacity, and durability, greatly reduce their weight, saving thereby largely in dead-weight to be hauled over those now in use for similar purposes by other roads.

Labor-account.

We compute labor of all classes, officers, agents, skilled and unskilled labor, required in all departments for operating, replacement, maintenance of way, of rolling-stock, &c., at ten men per mile of single track, at the average wages of $2.50 per day, making a total aggregate of 35,000 men, at $2.50 per day, equal to a daily cost of $87,500. On this basis the labor account per train per day would amount to $109.37.

The number of men employed in all capacities on the New York Central and the Philadelphia and Reading railroads is ten per mile, and the average wages paid is about $2 per day.

ROLLING-STOCK.

Material-account, other than labor.

The cost of material for repairs of engines and tenders on the Philadelphia and Reading Railroad is $2\frac{1}{2}$ cents per mile run, which, upon the basis of operation given for this road, would be as follows:

Cost of repairs for engines and tenders per train per day, (200 miles, at $2\frac{1}{2}$ cents per mile)	$5 00
The same company gives the cost of repairs and reconstruction of coal and freight-cars at $19\frac{7}{10}$ cents each per day, which would give for train of 30 cars	5 91
Total cost of material for repairs per train per day	10 91

The Pennsylvania Central Railroad gives the cost of repairs of engines and tenders for 1871 at $6\frac{8}{10}$ cents per mile run, or at above comparison $2\frac{9}{10}$ cents for materials, and $3\frac{9}{10}$ cents for labor, which for a run of 200 miles would be as follows:

Cost of material used for repair of engines and tenders per train per day	$5 80

The average cost for repairs of each freight-car is $18\frac{3}{10}$ cents per day, which for 30 cars would give as follows:

Cost of materials used for repairs of freight-cars per train per day	5 49
Total cost of material per train per day by Pennsylvania Central	11 29

We estimate cost of materials used for repairs, with rolling-stock adapted to the road, at the highest of these estimates, $11.29.

ROADWAY.

Material-account, other than labor.

The Baltimore and Ohio Railroad Company give the annual cost of material for maintenance of way, $666.30 per mile; which on Continental Road, at above basis per train per day, would amount to $6.39.

The Pennsylvania Central Railroad Company give the annual cost for material and labor for maintenance of way, $2,330 per mile, which, after deducting the cost of labor, would give as the cost of materials used on roadway-account, for the Continental Road, at the same rate, as follows:

Cost of materials per train per day	$9 77
We give the estimate in this calculation per train per day	10 70

N. B.—Both of the above roads are substituting steel rails for iron as rapidly as possible, and when this substitution is completed it will result in a large reduction of the cost of material for maintenance of roadway.

We estimate the cost of material for maintenance of way with steel rails, 107 tons per mile, at $120 per ton, lasting fifteen years, which would give per train per day	$8 21
Ties, 2,600 to the mile, cost 60 cents each, and to last six years, would give per train per day	2 49
Total	10 70

Experience has demonstrated the fact that steel rails are much the cheapest that can be laid down. The chief engineer of the Philadelphia and Reading Railroad, in his report of January 1, 1873, says: "Of the 3,350 tons of solid steel rails laid down on that road since 1867, less than fifteen tons have been moved from the track, and these have been taken from places where the life of iron rails had been found not to exceed four months."

Train-supplies.

Coal per day (or for 200 train miles)	$21 20
Oil and waste per day	5 00
Water per day	1 00
	27 20

NOTE.—The average cost of fuel to the Pennsylvania Central and Lake Shore and Michigan Southern Railroad, running through the same section of country was, in 1872, 10.6 cents per train-mile, which for 200 miles is $21.20.

Recapitulation.

1. Interest-account per train per day	$54 37	
2. Labor-account per train per day	109 37	
3. Material for maintenance of rolling-stock per train per day	11 29	
4. Material for maintenance of roadway per train per day	10 70	
5. Train-supplies per train per day	27 20	
Total expenses per train per day carrying 300 tons 200 miles		$212 93

based on a movement of 80 trains daily each way.

The Philadelphia and Reading Railroad Company give as the cost of running a train carrying 520 tons a round trip of 190 miles (empty cars one way) at $157.55. If it should cost us just as much to run a train of 300 tons 200 miles, the total cost would be as follows, viz:

Running expenses, including maintenance of rolling-stock	$157 55	
Interest	54 37	
Maintenance of roadway	10 70	
Total		223 62
Or 4½ mills per ton per mile		212 93
Difference in the two statements		10 69

NOTE.—It is evident that a train of 300 tons can be moved at considerable less expense than one of 520, and that this comparison is largely in our favor.

All the items for operating and replacements given above are believed to be greatly in excess of what will be the actual cost for this road.

Earnings.

The earnings of a train of thirty cars carrying 300 tons 200 miles per day, at 6½ mills per ton per mile, is $390.

Cost of running a train, including all expenses of the road, is, according to the above estimate, $212.93 per day.

The bulk of the freight, however, upon an east and west trunk-road being from west to east, it will be necessary to compute earnings in both directions, taking two trains, one moving east, the other west:

	Tons.
The Erie Railway Company, for 1872, gives their eastward through-freight tonnage at	675,285
Westward	274 846

At this ratio on the Continental Road the train-earnings would be as follows:

For eastward train	$390 00
For westward train	158 74
Total for earnings of two trains per day	548 74
Cost of running two trains per day, including interest and dividends	425 86
Surplus profits	122 88
Per train	61 44

The Pennsylvania Central Railroad Company give as their tonnage 1,000 tons eastward to 286 tons westward, which would give on Continental Road—

Surplus per train per day	$37 84

This calculation is based on trains of thirty cars of ten tons each, capable of carrying 300 tons, but the loads can be reduced to an average of 164 tons, having over 45 per cent. empty space, most of which will be in the westward-bound cars, and yet afford sufficient profit to pay all expenses, dividend and sinking-fund.

The engines will have ample power to haul forty cars, or 400 tons, over all parts of the road at the low and uniform rate of speed adopted. Three hundred tons is the daily average, to be increased or diminished with the business.

APPENDIX E.

If there is business enough to load eighty trains daily upon this road, as per Appendix D, the problem of cheap transportation will be solved. That there *will* be, we shall attempt to prove. The gross amount to be earned to cover all expenses is $67,898,760 per annum, viz:*

Annual interest-account	$15,875,000
Annual labor-account	31,937,500
Annual cost of material, rolling-stock	4,063,080
Annual cost of material, roadway	3,124,400
Cost of train-supplies	7,942,400
Damages, taxes, and contingencies	4,956,380
Total	67,898,760

To be derived from the following sources, viz:

From cereals, carried an average of 1,000 miles, $30,000,000, equal to 154,000,000 bushels, 4,620,000 tons, or 15,426 train-loads, which would occupy one track 192½ days.

Live stock and their products, $7,544,307,† estimated at one-ninth of the whole tonnage, employing for the year 3,326 trains, would occupy one track 40½ days.

Coal, eastward, 3,000,000 tons, at $1.25, $3,750,000, occupying 66⅔ days, and requiring 6,666 trains. Coal, westward, 2,000,000 tons, at $5, $10,000,000. These estimates are for hard coal east and west, and for bituminous coal from Ohio, Indiana, Illinois, and Iowa, both east and west; 1,500,000 tons hard coal are annually imported into Chicago. The line of the road runs directly through the heart of the anthracite coal region and will give the shortest line to tide-water at New York as well as to Chicago.

Westward movements of general merchandise, by existing trunk-railways, amount of a little more than 25 per cent. of the total tonnage. We estimate it at 20 per cent. to the total tonnage, or $13,579,752, leaving for miscellaneous freights east, petroleum, lumber, dairy products, &c., $1,250,000, the receipts from carrying which will be largely in excess of that amount.

While there is no reasonable doubt that the business required for a 100-train movement will be realized within six months after the road is in operation, we assume a basis of 80 trains a day for a commencement as certain to be obtained. We compute rates at 6 mills per ton per mile for summer and 7 mills per ton per mile for winter traffic, requiring the movement annually of 154,000,000 bushels of cereals, which will be a moderate calculation for 1877, considering that Great Britain consumes 215,000,000 bushels of

* The total earnings of the Pennsylvania Central Railroad, between Jersey City and Pittsburgh, 448 miles, was, in 1872, $28,277,085.60, tonnage 8,500,000. At this ratio the Continental would earn per annum the sum of $106,885,778.56.

† One-ninth of the entire tonnage of the principal trunk-lines is live stock and their products. In 1872 there was carried to the four principal sea-board cities 6,506,678 head of live stock, and this movement is increasing at the rate of 1,000,000 head annually.

mported grain annually now, (the quantity having increased from 28 per cent. of consumption in 1868 to 40 per cent. in 1872,) and that the consumption in the east is rapidly increasing. By this computation the cost of carrying cereals is 15 cents per bushel from Chicago, 18 from Saint Louis, and 24 from Council Bluffs to New York. We propose, therefore, to commence with the rates at 6 and 7 mills, and to reduce them to 5 and 6 mills per ton per mile, simsultaneously with the payment of the first dividend upon the capital stock.

The calculation, at 6 and 7 mills per ton per mile, would yield the earnings given below:

Earnings on cereals, 154,000,000 bushels, or 4,620,000 tons	$30, 000, 000
Earnings on live stock and their products	7, 544, 307
Earnings on coal, eastward	3, 750, 000
Earnings on petroleum	500, 000
Earnings on iron	1, 500, 000
Earnings on dairy products	250, 000
Earnings on lumber	500, 000
Earnings on miscellaneous	274, 701
Earnings on coal, 2,000,000 tons, westward	10, 000, 000
Westward movement	13, 579, 652
Total	67, 878, 760

This amount of business will require less than an 80-train daily movement.

Can it be obtained?

This is the important question; and in answer it may be said that there is in the United States area 3,000,000 square miles, 900,000 of which are embraced in the Atlantic slope and 1,350,000 in the Mississippi and Lake Valleys. Between these sections is conducted the larger portion of our internal commerce, for the service of which this road is especially designed.

The New England and Middle States on the one hand, and the Western States on the other, have large commercial transactions with each other. The centers of these sections are a thousand miles apart. Each contains a population exceeding 13,000,000, dependent each upon the other for the necessaries of life—food, clothing, dry-goods and manufactures, fuel, &c.

To illustrate the importance of this commerce it may be stated that the State of Illinois raised, of cereals, in 1872, 280,000,000 bushels, equal to 110 bushels per capita, while Massachusetts raised only one and a half pints of wheat per capita, but produced in manufactured articles the value of $554,000,000. The State of New York manufactured articles to the value of $785,000,000, and consumed 50,000,000 bushels of western grain.

The eight States of Ohio, Indiana, Illinois, Missouri, Iowa, Minnesota, Wisconsin, and Michigan raised, of cereals, in 1850, 310,384,775; in 1860, (with less than one-sixth of the land under cultivation,) 557,551,811; and in 1870, 920,000,000 bushels; the population in those years being, respectively, 5,403,595 in 1850, 8,955,962 in 1860, and 12,477,304 in 1870. At this ratio of increase these States will produce, in 1877, (the time fixed for the completion of this road,) 1,518,000,000 bushels of grain, and will have a population of 15,000,000 souls.

It will be observed that the surplus productions have increased in a ratio exceeding that of the population. Of the products of 1877, which will amount to more than 100 bushels *per capita* for these States, at least one-half will be surplus or marketable, and 750,000,000 bushels will require to be transported; of this the South will require, say, 100,000,000 bushels.

The cotton-product east of the Mississippi River is 3,200,000 bales. We will compute it at 5,000,000 bales in 1877. It requires for its production the consumption of 15 bushels of grain to the bale, equal to 75,000,000 bushels annually; then 100,000,000 bushels will be sufficient, with the home-production, for the South.

Allowing to the present trunk-railways and canals, including the Canadian lines, twice their present grain-tonnage, which will be 372,906,220 bushels, and there will be left for the Continental over 322,000,000 bushels of grain to carry to market, or 185,406,220 bushels more than is called for by this computation.

Then there is an area, double in extent of that occupied by the States named, still farther west, comprising States and Territories, portions of which are already settled, having extensive mineral deposits, a salubrious climate, and a productive soil, capable of sustaining an immense population, approached by this road at a central point, giving to its products a direct outlet to the sea-board. The rates of carrying will have a potent influence in inviting population and business to this road, as well as in stimulating the production of grain, which requires the cheapest medium of transportation which can be devised. The product in the States named was over 1,000,000,000 bushels in 1872, only about one-fourth of which was marketed, owing largely to high freight-charges and the lack of facilities.

The average cost of carrying wheat from Chicago to New York, by water, for the last six years, has been 20 9-10 cents per bushel; the average cost from point of production, in States west of Illinois, to Chicago is about 20 cents per bushel, or 44 cents per bushel from point of production to New York, via Chicago, by water, including the charges for storage, transfer, insurance, &c., and 53 cents by all rail, exclusive of these charges. There was received at New York, in 1872, of western grain by inland routes, 86,853,989 bushels:

53,711,100 by water, via Chicago, cost	$24,632,884 00
33,142,889 all rail, via Chicago, cost	17,565,731 17
86,853,939 cost	42,198,615 17

Same quantity carried a distance of 1,200 miles (which exceeds the average rail-distance from the point of production by the Continental and connecting roads) would cost at the prices herein named $18,240,325.19, saving in transportation $23,958,389.19. At this rate the saving in transportation on the entire cereal-crop marketed would have been nearly eighty millions of dollars. There can be no doubt, therefore, that the quantity of grain required for the earnings of this road will be obtained and transported by it. An important item for consideration in this connection is the time required by existing routes for the transportation of grain and flour from the Mississippi Valley to the sea-board, or the New England and Middle States. Rail-routes require the shortest time, and they take an average of 25 days for the transportation of grain and flour from Saint Louis, and nearly that from Chicago. This line would require from 5 to 7 days' average time only between the points named.

The animal-food for the older States will be more and more drawn from the remote Western and Southwestern States, while the requirements for the Middle, Sea-board, and Gulf States will be augmented in proportion to their growth in population. The increased demand of the four principal sea-board cities is now equal to 1,000,000 head of live stock per annum.

The business, therefore, of carrying live stock and their products may be safely anticipated to exceed the amount required by this calculation.

Coal.—Our coal-area exceeds that of any other country. Our consumption of coal for 1864 was 21,000,000 tons; for 1872, 41,785,609 tons; if it continues to increase in this ratio, we shall consume in 1877 62,000,000 tons. The coal-tonnage herein given is, therefore, largely below that which is sure to be realized, considering that this road passes through the very heart of the anthracite region, and traverses 300 miles or more of bituminous coal-fields in four States, while it saves largely in distance to both the eastward and westward tonnage.

This road passes through the very center of iron-production, and the transportation of the ore, the coal, limestone, iron, and its multifarious products will require large facilities.

It crosses fifty-one railways between New York and Council Bluffs, and will shorten the distance to forty-five of these roads over 100 miles.

While the products named are rapidly increasing in quantity, so is the demand, and were cheap rates of transportation inaugurated it would stimulate to increased activity all the industries of the country, and give the ability to equalize our import and export trade.

If further proof was needed of the sufficiency of business for this road, reference might be had to the population, wealth, and product of the counties traversed by it and the adjacent counties.

These counties had in 1870 a population of 2,500,672; personal and real estate valued at $2,149,619,985; they raised of corn, over 58,000,000 bushels; wheat, over 22,000 bushels; rye, over 3,000,000 bushels; oats, over 26,000,000 bushels; barley, over 2,250,000 bushels; buckwheat, over 2,000,000 bushels; making a grand total of 115,000,000 bushels of grain; potatoes, over 10,000,000 bushels; hay, 3,000,000 tons.

They raised 400,000 horses, 1,000,000 head of cattle, the same number of hogs, and 1,125,000 sheep. Produced the value of $500,000 in stone, $1,500,000 in iron ore, and $1,500,000 in petroleum; mined 15,000,000 tons anthracite, and 1,500,000 tons bituminous coal.

There were 14,850 manufacturing establishments with $145,000,000 capital; wages paid, $42,000,000; material used, $179,000,000, and products of the value of $282,955,561.

The adjacent counties produce 95,000,000 bushels of cereals, 9,000,000 bushels potatoes; bituminous coal to the value of $10,000,000; 1,000,000 tons anthracite coal, and manufactured products to the value of over $100,000,000.

We have a population of 44,000,000 of people, who pay $800,000,000 per annum for transportation; every man, woman, and child pay tribute to the railroads in some form for what they eat, drink, or wear. Complete and operate this road upon the basis herein named, and the saving to the country in a single year on its tonnage will nearly equal its total cost, while the results will add to the general prosperity, and command the admiration of the Old World, alluring hither its wealth and its industrious citizens in greater proportion than at any period hitherto, to aid in the further development of the resources of our new and wonderful country.

All admit that the road will pay from the day of completion. Should Government pay interest on the first-mortgage bonds during construction, the amount paid would be $7,500,000, for which advance the security of a first lien upon property worth $175,000,000 would be held.

APPENDIX F.

In proof of the assertion that the inauguration of a cheap system of transportation would enable us to control the supply of breadstuffs to Great Britain, it is simply necessary to state that the wheat-lands of England are worth about $500, are rented at $25, and yield 25 to 30 bushels of wheat to the acre. So that the English farmer cannot produce wheat at less than $2 per bushel. The wheat-lands of Europe, from which the main grain imports to the United Kingdom have been drawn, are worth from $100 to $300 per acre, and are generally rented to the farmer at a high price. The average price of wheat at Odessa for the past five years has been $1.70; freight to Liverpool $23\frac{8}{10}$ cents, or $\$1.93\frac{8}{10}$ gold per bushel landed there. Konigsburg, Prussia, ships largely of wheat, both of home-production and of the product of Russia and Poland. The average price at Konigsburg has been, for same period, $1.67, and freight to Liverpool 18 cents, making $1.85. The average price at Berlin, the chief wheat-market in Germany, has been $\$1.74\frac{6}{10}$. In the other countries contributing to the supply of Great Britain the price approximates closely to those above given. So that the supply of Great Britain with breadstuffs and of some of the countries of the Continent by us depends only upon cheap transportation.

If we can bring our cereals from the productive valleys to the sea-board at or near the prices named in Appendix D, we can supply those markets to the exclusion of all other countries and of the home-production in Great Britain, at least.

The import demand of the United Kingdom for 1873 was 99,000,000 bushels of wheat, or 40 per cent. of the consumption, but of this amount the United States furnished only one-fifth, and of other cereals, 38,000,000 bushels of corn, 46,000,000 bushels of oats, and 19,000,000 bushels of barley, 4,000,000 bushels of peas and 9,000,000 bushels of beans.

With the certainty of a supply from the United States, at such prices as we could afford to deliver the products, the demand would be largely increased, as an additional acreage is needed each year in Great Britain for grazing, causing a gradual withdrawal from cultivation of the wheat and barley lands of the country, while the seasons are too cold for corn.

Russia is fully awake to the importance of securing the trade of Great Britain, and has very recently, by virtue of a ukase from the Emperor, changed her policy by authorizing German railway companies to construct lines into her wheat regions, and also by subsidizing her own lines to enable them to carry grain to the ports of the Baltic and Black Sea at the lowest rates.

By this means she hopes to retain thecontrol of the English markets and the price of the grain product of America; and although we are much the largest consumers of the manufactures of Great Britain, and therefore entitled, in a commercial point of view, to the privilege of supplying her with breadstuffs, we shall not be able to do so without providing the means for cheap transportation.

TERMINAL FACILITIES.

The company has secured the ground necessary for its terminal facilities on a scale commensurate with the capacity of its great railway, and upon plans which will permit the business of receiving and distributing the immense products of the country to be done at low cost and with the utmost dispatch.

These facilities are embraced in two systems, one upon the west bank of the Hudson River and the other on the bay below. That upon the river occupies an area of nearly 300 acres, and is capable of being developed to give 6,000 linear feet of piers, and more than 12,000 linear feet of dock-front, with side-tracks sufficient for loading and unloading 40 trains in 24 hours, allowing 6 hours to a train. The piers to be covered by warehouses and elevators. Each story added will give double the storage capacity and largely increase the trackage.

I. The system upon the bay is on a more comprehensive scale. It is 11,250 feet long from the upland to deep water, the total length of which can be occupied with docks and piers.

There are between six and seven hundred acres, with capacity for 63 piers of 50 feet in width and 1,365 feet in length, with an aggregate surface of 4,299,760 square feet, and a length of 85,995 linear feet. These piers are constructed with a solid filling on either side of 200 feet and 400 feet, respectively, and a grand canal in the center 400 feet in width.*

Six piers at the east end, (three on either side of the grand canal and perpendicular to the inner piers,) each 150 feet wide, with an aggregate length of 9,750 feet, (see Appendix G,) containing 1,405,500 square feet of land. Therefore the system gives an area of piers in the grand aggregate of 5,705,250 square feet, or equal to 131 acres, and a grand aggregate of dock-front equal to 190,730 linear feet. (See Appendix H.)

The water-ways between the six outer piers are 250 feet in width, and are entirely independent of the grand canal.

II. The aggregate number of piers being 69, if one train was handled on each pier it would provide for that number of trains at one time.

The aggregate net length of the piers is 95,365 feet, which is equal to 18 miles of single-track railway.

The length of the solid filling on either side is 11,250 feet. On the north filling, which is 200 feet wide, there is room for 16 tracks, and on the south filling, which is 400 feet wide, 32 tracks, or, in all, 48 tracks of 11,250 feet each, 540,000 linear feet of single-track railway, to which add 85,365 linear feet on piers, and we have 635,365 linear feet or 120 miles of track, or enough to accommodate 500 trains at one time by allowing 1,270 feet to the train. (See Appendix J.)

III. The gross linear feet of dock-front, less bulk-heads, pier-heads, and waste, is, for all purposes of commerce, 190,730 linear feet, and as on an average it requires 400 feet for all classes of vessels, there will be berth-room furnished for nearly 500 ships.

The aggregate length of the six outer or eastern piers is 9,370 feet, and width 150 feet. These six piers are entirely disconnected from the grand canal, and vessels lying by the said piers would not be disturbed by the in and out passage of vessels to reach the inner piers. Therefore they are pre-eminently fitted for the location of grain-elevators.

Their capacity, if properly utilized by the erection of elevators, would be at least equal to 70,000,000 bushels of grain in storage, and would provide for the handling and shipping in twelve months of ten times that amount, or 700,000,000 bushels per annum.

There can be at least eight tracks placed upon each pier, which would provide for the simultaneous handling and discharging of 48 trains loaded with grain; but admitting that it would take six hours to back in, discharge, and pull out a train on each track, it would then give track-capacity for 192 trains in 24 hours, and if each train was composed of 30 cars, carrying 333⅓ bushels each, it would equal 300 tons per train, or 57,600 tons per day of 24 hours, or, in other words, each train would carry 10,000 bushels, which would be an average of 1,920,000 bushels in each 24 hours, or, for a year of 300 days, 17,280,000 tons, or 576,000,000 bushels of wheat or corn.

With a dock-front of 190,730 linear feet, capable of giving berth-room to 500 vessels at one time, with an average of two weeks to discharge and receive cargo, it would furnish ample facilities for 13,000 bottoms a year. If the vessels averaged 1,000 tons, it would give a tonnage-capacity of 13,000,000 tons per annum. If this was represented by wheat or corn it would provide for the shipment of more than 433,000,000 bushels.

As a proper elevator system on the six outer piers is capable of receiving in one day 1,920,000 bushels, and in one year of 300 days 576,000,000 bushels, (see Appendix G,) and the dock-room on six piers is 9,370 linear feet, it would give room for not less than 23 vessels at one time, each one of which could be loaded at the rate of 1,000 tons† in 4 hours, or, allowing 12 hours per vessel, would load 46 vessels per day, or 46,000 tons in 24 hours, which would, in 300 days, give 13,800,000 tons of grain from those piers alone.

One thousand two hundred and seventy feet will accommodate a freight train of 40 cars with locomotive and tender.

Observe that each of the 63 piers (50 feet wide) is capable of accommodating a double track, which would give a trackage on the said piers of 171,990 feet.

Observe that the six outer piers are capable of containing eight tracks each, with a trackage of 65,550 linear feet, to which add 171,990 feet as above, and it would give a track capacity on piers of 237,540 feet, to which add the solid filling, and we have a gross aggregate of 777,540 feet of track, or more than 147 miles of single-track railway.

Observe that, to increase the storage capacity, any or all the piers may be furnished with elevators and be used for that purpose.

Observe that, if the road can do a business of 400 trains per day each way, of 40 cars each, in this system there is an abundance of room.

---

* The slips or water-ways between these piers are 150 feet in width.

† In Milwaukee and Chicago that amount of grain is loaded in less than four hours, and no doubt a proper elevator system could be increased 50 per cent. in its discharging capacity over the above figures.

CONTRAST.

The Erie Railway Company has in Jersey City and Weehawken for terminal purposes, in daily use, less than 13,000 lineal feet of dock-room (which includes both bulkheads and pier-heads) for their general freighting business, including grain, oil, coal, general merchandise, and live stock, as well as their passenger business.

Observe, finally, that Manhatten Island, or New York City, now the nation's commercial banking-house and counting-room, (which, with the proposed facilities for moving cheaply and expeditiously the rapidly-increasing and valuable products of the country,) so soon destined to become the great money center of the world, is circumscribed in territory, and cannot be utilized as the national store-house. The great bulk of western freights naturally seek the west side of the Hudson, and it is equally convenient to have return freights for the West stored upon that side of the River. Therefore these systems go further, by providing ample facilities for all purposes, (store-houses, warehouses, elevators, and even bonded warehouses,) to solve the question of cheap termini than any heretofere attempted.

Statement of average rate per ton per mile charged on shipments of flour and grain from Pittsburgh to Philadelphia and New York during the years 1871, 1872, *and to October*, 1873.

[Compiled for the use of the Senate Committee on Transportation Routes.]

	To Philadelphia.			To New York.		
	1871.	1872.	1873.	1871.	1872.	1873.
January	.0138	.0138	.0138	.015	.015	.015
February	.0138	.0138	.0138	.015	.015	.015
March	.0128	.0128	.0136	.0147	.0147	.0147
April	.0089	.01	.0130	.011	.0119	.0147
May	.01	.01	.01	.0114	.0114	.0117
June	.0091	.0091	.0091	.0106	.0106	.0106
July	.01	.0091	.0091	.0123	.0106	.0106
August	.01	.0091	.0091	.0119	.0106	.0106
September	.0091	.0091	.0091	.011	.0106	.0106
October	.0122	.0128	.0117	.0141	.0145	.0123
November	.0144	.0138	....	.015	.015	....
December	.0144	.0128	....	.0147	.0145	....

Average annual lake freights on wheat and corn from Chicago to New York, 1861 *to* 1872 *inclusive.*

Year.	Wheat per bushel.	Corn per bushel.	Year.	Wheat per bushel.	Corn per bushel.
	Cents.	*Cents.*		*Cents.*	*Cents.*
1861	11.5	10.6	1867	6.7	5.4
1862	10.5	9.6	1868	7.1	6.0
1863	7.5	6.6	1869	6.8	6.3
1864	9.6	8.9	1870	5.9	5.4
1865	9.8	9.1	1871	7.6	7.1
1866	13.4	11.5	1872	11.1	10.3

Annual report of the auditor of the canal department of the State of New York for 1872.

Year.	UP-FREIGHT PER TON FROM ALBANY TO BUFFALO.			DOWN-FREIGHT PER TON FROM BUFFALO TO ALBANY.		
	Average per year.	Tolls deducted.	Leaving freight.	Average per year.	Tolls deducted.	Leaving freight.
1830	$20 00	$10 22	$9 78	$9 07	$5 11	$3 96
1831	10 80	10 22	9 58	8 89	5 11	3 78
1832	20 00	10 22	9 78	9 26	5 11	4 15
1833	14 80	8 76	6 04	8 15	3 65	4 50
1834	16 40	6 57	9 83	7 68	3 28	4 40
1835	16 00	6 57	9 43	6 29	3 28	3 01
1836	21 00	6 57	14 43	7 13	3 28	3 85
1837	18 00	6 57	12 03	7 50	3 28	4 22
Annual average from 1830 to 1837, 8 years	18 32	8 21	10 11	8 00	4 01	3 99
1838	17 80	6 57	11 23	6 76	3 28	3 48
1839	17 80	6 57	11 23	6 94	3 28	3 62
1840	16 60	6 57	10 03	7 50	3 28	4 22
1841	12 20	6 57	5 63	6 57	3 28	3 29
1842	13 20	6 57	6 63	6 02	3 28	2 74
1843	11 20	6 57	4 63	5 56	3 28	2 28
1844	13 00	6 57	6 43	5 56	3 28	2 28
1845	9 60	6 57	3 03	6 57	3 28	3 29
Annual average from 1838 to 1845, 8 years	13 92	6 57	7 35	6 43	3 28	3 15
1846	8 00	4 80	3 20	5 92	2 92	3 00
1847	7 80	4 80	3 00	7 13	2 92	4 21
1848	7 80	4 80	3 00	5 37	2 92	2 45
1849	7 80	4 80	3 00	5 18	2 92	2 26
1850	7 20	4 80	2 40	5 48	2 92	2 56
1851	6 20	4 40	1 80	4 71	2 19	2 52
1852	5 20	2 92	2 28	4 90	2 19	2 71
1853	5 60	2 92	2 68	5 18	2 19	2 99
Annual average from 1846 to 1853, 8 years	6 95	4 28	2 67	5 48	2 64	2 84
1854	5 00	2 92	2 08	4 81	2 19	2 62
1855	5 00	2 92	2 08	4 81	2 19	2 62
1856	5 40	2 92	2 48	5 56	2 19	3 37
1857	4 80	2 92	1 88	4 26	2 19	2 07
1858	2 80	1 46	1 34	3 14	1 46	1 68
1859	2 40	70	1 70	2 87	1 41	1 46
1860	2 40	1 40	1 00	3 88	1 41	2 47
1861	2 20	1 40	80	4 26	1 76	2 50
Annual average from 1854 to 1861, 8 years	3 75	2 08	1 67	4 20	1 85	2 35
1862	2 50	1 40	1 10	4 42	2 11	2 31
1863	2 50	1 40	1 10	4 17	2 11	2 06
1864	2 60	1 05	1 55	5 32	2 11	3 21
1865	2 50	1 05	1 45	4 72	2 11	2 61
1866	2 60	1 05	1 55	4 82	2 11	2 71
1867	2 60	1 05	1 55	4 44	2 11	2 33
1868	2 60	1 05	1 55	4 44	2 11	2 33
1869	2 60	1 05	1 55	4 72	2 11	2 61
1870	2 60	1 05	1 55	3 06	1 05	2 01
1871	2 60	1 05	1 55	3 70	1 05	2 65
1872	2 60	1 05	1 55	3 70	1 05	2 65
Annual average from 1862 to 1872, 11 years	2 57	1 12	1 45	4 38	1 90	2 48
Annual average from 1830 to 1872, 43 years	8 79	4 29	4 50	5 63	2 69	2 94
Average from 1830 to 1833, 4 years	18 65	9 85	8 80	8 84	4 74	4 10
Average from 1834 to 1837, 4 years	18 00	6 57	11 43	7 15	3 28	3 87
Average from 1838 to 1841, 4 years	16 10	6 57	9 53	6 94	3 28	3 66
Average from 1842 to 1845, 4 years	11 75	6 57	5 18	5 93	3 28	2 65
Average from 1846 to 1849, 4 years	7 85	4 80	3 05	5 90	2 92	2 98
Average from 1850 to 1853, 4 years	6 05	3 76	2 29	5 07	2 37	2 70
Average from 1854 to 1857, 4 years	5 05	2 92	2 13	4 86	2 19	2 67
Average from 1858 to 1861, 4 years	2 45	1 24	1 21	3 54	1 51	2 03
Average from 1862 to 1865, 4 years	2 52	1 22	1 30	4 66	2 11	2 55
Average from 1866 to 1872, 7 years	2 60	1 05	1 55	4 13	1 80	2 33

STATEMENT IN REGARD TO THE EXPORTATION OF GRAIN, PREPARED FOR THE SENATE COMMITTEE ON TRANSPORTATION BY MESSRS. HUGH McLENNAN AND THOMAS RIMMER, OF MONTREAL, CANADA.

The general use of the Atlantic cable has greatly changed the trade in breadstuffs in some important respects. The Associated Press of New York receives and publishes quotations of the Liverpool market three times daily; quotations are also received each day from London. These quotations, particularly those from Liverpool, are transmitted by telegraph to every market on this continent, and have considerable influence on daily prices. Our markets are, therefore, more strongly affected by European fluctuations than formerly. With these and other quotations, and the rates of freight and insurance before them, exporting merchants can make offers by cable at a gross price, including cost, freight, and insurance, to their correspondents in Europe.

One firm in Montreal ships in this way between three and four million bushels of grain annually, consisting chiefly of wheat and Indian corn. Between 80 and 90 per cent. of that aggregate is the produce of the United States, the remainder being the produce of Canada. This business takes that firm to Chicago and Milwaukee as purchasers to that extent; for, as a rule, no Western States grain is consigned to Montreal. It will thus be readily understood that the business of the leading houses here with the West is, at times, very extensive. It will also be evident that, in making offers by cable, Canadian merchants must keep in view the state of the New York market; for their correspondents, having quotations as well from that quarter, will naturally give the order to the lowest bid. Thus Montreal furnishes a very important outlet for Western States produce, not only in consequence of her merchants being large purchasers in the western markets, but in that it is their interest to get the grain to this point as cheaply as possible; thus offering a wholesome competition as a second port of export. It is, therefore, very much to the advantage of the producer in the Western States that the route eastward to the sea-board via the Saint Lawrence should be developed to the utmost, because ocean-freights are sometimes low from Montreal, and favor shipment hence rather than from New York.

It is to be observed that while 95 per cent. of the corn, and probably 85 per cent. of the wheat, raised east of the Rocky Mountains, is consumed in the United States—leaving 5 per cent. of the former and 15 per cent. of the latter for export—this smaller quantity that is exported controls the price of the whole crop. Cheapness and facility of transport to the sea-board, combined with moderate rates of ocean-freight, being what affect the price which the exporting merchant can afford to pay for the grain, these are obviously the conditions that rule the price to the producer of the entire crop. It must also be borne in mind that the price which the English purchaser can pay is regulated by the price of wheat in other countries. There are enormous quantities of wheat and corn shipped from the Black Sea ports, and American grain has to compete with these in English markets. This point calls for very close attention on the part of the trade here. The following remarks will illustrate this:

The improvements effected in the navigation of the Danube, and in the port of Sulina at its entrance to the Black Sea, have opened up this river for large inland craft, and ocean-steamers can now load to a draught of 19 feet or more. The practicable draught ten years ago was 10 or 12 feet. This river drains a territory of over 300,000 square miles, adapted to the raising of corn and wheat; labor is cheap, and rates of freight are moderate. Daunbian corn is, as to quality, preferred to Northwestern, and can be delivered in the English markets at an equally low price, generally speaking; while there are seasons when it can be delivered some shillings a quarter below the price of corn from the United States.

The great extension of railways in Russia has opened up an enormous wheat-growing country, and the shipments of Ghirka wheat at Odessa are very large, and are increasing annually. This wheat comes into close competition with No. 2 western spring, being of the same class, although the latter always commands a preference, if at same price. It is noticeable that while Odessa-Ghirka is produced and shipped at a constantly decreasing rate of cost, owing to increasing facilities, the contrary is the case with American wheat; and western spring appears to be increasing in price rather than declining. Improved cultivation and housing has caused a marked improvement in the quality and condition of the Russian wheat—and this reduction in cost and improvement in quality appear to be continuous. Details of prices for a series of years are not presently at hand; but it may be mentioned that Odessa-Ghirka sells at about 1*s.* to 2*s.* per quarter below the price of No. 2 Milwaukee spring in the English markets. If, therefore, the wheat-growing States in the West and Northwest would keep their foreign grain-trade, they must largely increase the facilities for reaching the sea-board; and it seems to be of especial importance that they encourage the Saint Lawrence route, thereby securing a second sea-port, (Montreal,) and a healthy competition in ocean-freights.

In seasons when the condition of grain is a little doubtful, the Saint Lawrence route seems to offer an especial advantage.

In further illustration of the circumstances and conditions with which the American grain-exporter has to contend it may be remarked that the area from which Great Britain draws supplies of wheat becomes enlarged in proportion to the advance in prices in the English markets. During the early part of the present year (1873) when wheat was 60*s.* a quarter, orders were sent to the East Indies, the Cape of Good Hope, South America, Oregon, Adelaide, in South Australia, and other distant places, the high price permitting importers to pay the rates of freight that would command sail-and-steam tonnage. But at 50*s.* a quarter importers cannot afford to pay the necessary rates of freight, and consequently draw supplies from a more contracted circle. San Francisco, although distant, may continue to ship wheat even when prices rule low in England, but the places before mentioned will cease to export to Great Britain.

When wheat is brought to England from very remote places, such as those above referred to, the effect is to increase rates of ocean-freight, even on short voyages. American wheat now going into England is subject to unusually high freights, and is met on the markets with wheat shipped from distant ports in January and February last. When prices in England are low importations can only be profitably made from near ports, which economize charges of freight, interest, and insurance. The length of voyage by freight-steamer from Bordeaux and Nantes to London is three days; the rate of freight 2*s.* 6*d.* per quarter. From Saint Petersburg the voyage occupies eight days, and the rate of freight is 4*s.* 6*d.* and 5*s.* per quarter. Thus, from French ports the time occupied by the voyage and the rates of freight are about one-fourth, and from Northern Russia about one-half, of the corresponding items from the Atlantic ports of North America.

Against such formidable competition the position of the export grain-trade of the United States and of this Dominion is not satisfactory. Producers must be content to accept lower prices, or means must speedily be devised for the reduction of internal charges.

The rate of insurance upon grain-cargoes from Chicago or Milwaukee to Montreal, via Kingston, by water, by steam-propeller or schooner, is 90 cents to $1 per $100. This includes risk by barge if transshipped at Kingston; also the risk while at Kingston. This is the summer rate, increasing as the season advances, in same proportion as other lake-routes. No insurance is paid on shipments by rail, the Grand Trunk Railroad Company (like other lines) being responsible for delivery.

Marine insurance on produce shipped by steamers from Montreal to Europe is ½ to ⅝ of 1 per cent. in summer, increasing to 2½ per cent. at close of navigation. By first-class sailing-vessel the summer rate of insurance is ⅞ of one per cent., increasing to 3 or 4 per cent. at the close of navigation. The rate on vessels of a lower class is difficult to quote; it depends upon the ship and is generally high.

The summer rate rules during the months of May, June, July, and August, the gradual advance commencing in September.

The annual report of the secretary of the Montreal Board of Trade and Corn Exchange Association for the year 1872 contains a comprehensive table, (see p. 54,) which indicates the progress and variations of the grain-trade of Montreal during a period of twenty-eight years. The figures given there for the years 1860 to 1864 show a large increase of business, resulting from abundant crops and the disarrangement caused by the war. A decrease followed, the lowest point in receipts of wheat being touched in 1866; the crop in that year being a comparatively light one. In 1867 the corn-crop of the United States yielded less than an average, and Great Britain was supplied, to a large extent, from Hungary.

It will be observed that for many years, in fact since the completion of the Saint Lawrence canals, the grain-export trade via the port of Montreal has, with slight variations, risen in about the same ratio as that of New York.

From the nature of the grain-trade, the opinion does not seem to be entertained in Montreal that contracts through from Chicago to Liverpool can be conveniently undertaken, as a rule, by any line, owing to the difficulty of making prompt connection at Montreal between inland and ocean craft, a few hours either way being of serious consequence to owners of steamers. It is, moreover, found to be more convenient to depend here upon the supply of freight offering in the market. No such through connection has hitherto been made, except by rail in the winter season, by proprietors of steamship-lines. All things considered, there is no good reason to doubt that Montreal and New York merchants will continue to be the connecting link between the western merchants and the Liverpool ones.

During the winter season, in the absence of a constant flow of trade, railway-lines have arrangements to divide through rates via Baltimore and Portland, to provide return freights for the few steamers leaving these ports. The small trade done in that way, at least in the case of the Portland steamers, is on account of Montreal merchants.

In brief, the problem of eastward transportation for the products of the Western and Northwestern States will be solved by the replies to the following questions:

1. How can sufficient mechanical water-way be provided for exit from the West to a port of export to Europe?

2. How far, in constructing such an outlet, can the option of competing ports or markets be advantageously held open to the owner of grain in transit?

3. At what point does the interest of the producer cease?

4. What are the usual agencies and participators in the transfer of grain from the accumulating ports at the West to the consuming ports in Europe, speculatively and financially considered?

5. With Chicago and New York City as the objective points, what canal-route would be the most economical for transportation of grain?

LETTER ADDRESSED THE CHAIRMAN BY HON. HUGH McLENNAN, OF MONTREAL.

OFFICE BOARD OF TRADE,
Montreal, November 1, 1873.

DEAR SIR: In response to yours of 21st ultimo, Mr. Patterson has prepared the figures giving the rates of freight, so far as procurable, during the last five years between Chicago and Montreal. Your letter would indicate the probable termination of the correspondence at this point, and I feel called upon in behalf of our Canadian interests to express our appreciation of the comprehensive range your committee has taken from the time you entered upon the special duty intrusted to you, knowing, as we do, the character and extent of investigation necessary to enable you to form an opinion upon the most practicable manner of affording relief to the producer and consumer of breadstuffs, now stultified by inadequate and over-costly modes of transportation. While we were fully sensible of the probable advantages to us of being included in the estimate of possible resources toward obtaining the relief required, and were desirous of giving every information at our disposal, we find that in the process of the inquiry we observed principles governing our relations with the United States hitherto not so fully comprehended, and perhaps, by the experience, gained some facility in the ability to gather up points more concisely having reference to trade and the hinderances to its greater increase in the past, while seeing changes that would call forth a more rapid development in the future.

The documents placed before you, largely in reply to your inquiries, give you the following points:

The dependence of the great grain-growing countries of the world upon Great Britain for the establishment of current prices; that any local diminution of quantity produced in one country ordinarily furnishing part of her supply, does not generally carry the price *upward;* that the country or locality affected drops out of the general market for the time being, and prices only attain to such advance as her own requirements will sustain; that when the demand and price have to take in the wider circuit, as California and Australia, or disproportionately from America, in order to complete the supply, the rate of freight on account of the additional service required by distance is proportionately increased on the whole supply; that to compete favorably, the internal lines of navigation on our continent must be improved at least as rapidly as those of other countries competing for the supply of Great Britain, otherwise the producer of the West will continue to be at such a disadvantage under our ordinary range of prices as to give him a very small return for his labor, notwithstanding the advantages of soil and climate with which he is favored.

The Canadian branch of commerce, which we may be assumed to represent in the present inquiries, does not pretend to offer a solution of your difficulties such as will obviate the necessity of fostering every other available avenue of transportation that can economize the cost; our progress must stimulate other routes in the competition which has hitherto existed. The Welland and Saint Lawrence Canals made the enlargement of the Erie Canal a necessity in former times, and the increase in the size of lake vessels beyond the present dimensions of the Welland returns the necessity upon us, which we are now prepared again to overcome, while each route will, no doubt, continue to contend, in fair and honorable effort, for the trade of the interior with Europe. But owing to the existence of many other influences, such as the amount of tonnage giving preference to different Atlantic and Saint Lawrence ports on account of the import trade, ownership, financial facilities, speculative enterprise on the part of dealers in grain, and a multitude of causes, *no one port can increase its grain-trade largely out of proportion to the other business of the port;* any large increase enhances the *cost of ocean freight* and other charges to a point that will give some rival port the next opportunity. The Atlantic cable and the European merchant act as ready regulators between the competing ports.

We are now enlarging our canals; not from lack of capacity for even a ten-fold trade, but because, for reasons stated, we find we cannot bring grain to Kingston at *a rate proportionate to that obtainable to Buffalo,* and hence our disadvantage in competition with that route.

The service of transportation via the Saint Lawrence, taking Great Britain as the destination from the lake ports, is largely divided *into three interests.* About *three-fourths of the lake craft carrying grain to Kingston* are of *American ownership,* partly owing, I believe, to the increasing wealth produced by that branch of industry, and which, as is commonly the case in all businesses, is returned in additional craft, to repeat the same result, while the trade is sustained by the adaptability of a large class of the population of the lake cities for that particular service. Moreover, the disadvantages under which ship-building in the United States has been stated to suffer have been largely over-estimated; so long as they are not subjected to the competition that would arise from the right of purchase of foreign vessels, I believe that the lake trade, not only to Buffalo and Oswego, but to Kingston as well, will continue to be conveyed principally *in American craft.*

At Kingston our barge service commences, and our French Canadian population are peculiarly adapted for this service, and this portion of the route is easily supplemented to provide for even a sudden increase. A civil engineer of the highest repute, (Walter Shanley, esq.,) who has studied the subject of Canadian internal navigation in all its phases, has expressed the opinion that transportation from Kingston to Montreal can be much more expeditiously and economically accomplished by barge service, practically making that port the lower limit of lake navigation.

Assuming that the cheapest mode of transporting grain is by sail from the lake ports to Buffalo, Oswego, and Kingston, (and in the increase of the trade, sailing crafts continue to compete successfully with steam,) the enlargement of the Welland Canal will admit of the larger vessels coming to Lake Ontario, reducing the difference of freight now existing between Buffalo and Lake Ontario ports 40 to 50 per cent., and enable the Canadian grain-purchaser, for export, to compete more successfully with the Atlantic ports.

The limit of trade has, in the past, not been owing to a lack of lake craft. The extreme rates paid on different occasions, and sounded as the note of alarm, have, as during a few weeks this season, been a reaction from a very low rate of lake freight, that had driven the tonnage to other employment. Our river-barge capacity has likewise kept pace with the requirements of trade at a uniform rate of 4 cents, with the exception of this season, under an advance in labor, increased to 4½ cents.

The ocean tonnage that could be secured for the grain trade from the Saint Lawrence *has, therefore, been the measure of our imports of grain from the West in the past.* Your facilities of transportation have been overtasked from *two causes:* the abrogation of the reciprocity treaty, putting a prohibitory duty upon coarse grains, cut off the supply from the province of Quebec for New England and forced that section to draw from the West, to the disadvantage of every interest concerned. Under the reciprocity treaty Quebec supplied oats produced in this climate, of better quality than in the West; and under a liberal interpretation of the revenue laws, corn and wheat, the products of the Western States, were admitted from Montreal into New England.

While we expect much advantage from the enlargement of the canals, in competing for the portion of your surplus products exported, yet the amount of ocean tonnage under existing regulations must continue to be the limit of our trade with the West. The privilege of selling grain or flour, the products of the Western States, to New England, without hinderance or charge, would, even with our present canal facilities, enable us to import largely from the West; not only to obtain that additional trade, but with that as an alternative for surplus, our export-trade by sea would assume larger proportions. The vessel-owner or charterer now acts with caution, fearing that the tonnage may exceed the volume of freight offering. The grain operator, if he now orders in excess of the tonnage, has no alternative but to store until relieved by additional arrival of vessels. Last season we had a surplus of grain of over one million bushels, which had to be held in store until this summer, to the serious embarrassment of all parties concerned. During last month (October) our lake and river craft could conveniently have brought an additional million bushels had they not been over-cautious. With the privilege of the New England trade we would supply part of it with great advantage, particularly as a winter depot, and would probably double our export trade; all thus tending to the relief of the West. With this trade open to us the Dominion government would, do doubt, construct the Caughnawaga Canal, making it a portion of the Saint Lawrence canal system; but to do so now would be out of the question, as, after its construction, Canadians would practically be excluded from the use of it.

A consideration of international relations, having in view the interests of both countries, would include the improvement of the channel in rivers owned in common (as the Detroit River, and navigation between Lakes Erie and Huron,) the common use of the lakes and canals, under the same rules, and a specified maximum of charge on the latter. Also the construction of the Caughnawaga Canal, and the right, in return, of Canadian craft to navigate Lake Champlain and the Hudson River and con necting canals, with the re-entry of western grain from Canadian vessels, as free from restrictions as if being conveyed by American craft; giving New England and New York the advantage of cheap water-communication, and affording a mode of relief to our trade from excessive importations of grain from the West. Further, giving American craft all corresponding privileges obtained for Canadian, which would enable the former to load coal at Pictou, or other Dominion ports, for the Saint Lawrence, thus utilizing a large amount of tonnage that now comes from Atlantic ports to Montreal in ballast, to procure cargoes of lumber for South America. The shipments of lumber this season are about 60,000,000, while our coal has averaged this season $3 per ton, the proposed amendment to the law being likely to not only prove profitable to the vessels, but a great advantage to the commerce of the dominion.

I have the honor to be, dear sir, your obedient servant,

HUGH McLENNAN,
President Board of Trade.

Hon. WILLIAM WINDOM,
Chairman of the United States Senate Committee on Transportation-Routes,
Washington, D. C.

ANSWERS TO INQUIRIES IN REGARD TO THE ECONOMY OF TRANSPORT BY RAIL, BY COL. JOSEPH D. POTTS, PRESIDENT OF THE EMPIRE TRANSPORTATION COMPANY.

Queries of Hon. Wm. Windom, chairman Senate Transportation Committee, and the replies thereto:

Query 1. What is the speed of maximum profits of freight-trains, fourth-class freights?

Reply 1. No definite reply is possible. The same tracks are used for passenger-trains, for repair-trains, and for trains moving other freight than fourth class. No one can define the exact proportion which each of these different varieties of service is chargeable with in respect to the work of any worn-out rail, of any decayed tie, of any snow-blockade, of any damage by flood or fire. The cost of engines can be proportioned with reasonable accuracy, as can also the repairs to cars and train-hand expenses, but track-repairs, general expenses, and many other joint items of cost can only be divided arbitrarily, and therefore with only an approximation to accuracy. The same may be said with regard to the degree of increase in cost resulting from an increase of speed. There are no actual reliable data obtainable on this point, except in regard to a very few items of cost, for the reason that no attempt has ever been made to operate any one road at one uniform rate of speed in comparison with another under precisely similar conditions, operated at a different but uniform rate of speed. The best that can be done, with facts now known to transporters, is to make a reasonably accurate guess, and it will probably be found that no two will guess precisely alike. Very slow speeds result in so limited a service of track and rolling-stock that a greatly-increased investment in both these particulars is necessary to accomplish a given amount of work, and it is quite evident a point can easily be reached where the interest on this increased investment would exceed the economy in expense. It is also evident that while a very high speed would produce greater gross earnings from a given investment, a point can easily be reached where the enlarged cost of operations would exceed the amount of interest saved.

Again, on a single-track road with a very large traffic and numerous trains, the speed prescribed by the time-card is by no means the speed actually made. Many delays in waiting for opposing or higher class trains so reduce the actual running-time that the speed of freight-trains between waiting points, especially where the train-hands can escape supervision, frequently reaches the rate made by an express passenger-train. My own judgment in the matter is that on the existing trunk lines between the northern Atlantic ports (Baltimore being the most southerly referred to) a time-card speed for through-freight traffic of fifteen miles per hour would be found to give the largest net results.

Query 2. Taking the actual freights moved in both directions on the Grand Trunk roads from the West to the sea-board, namely, the New York Central, Erie, Pennsylvania, and Baltimore and Ohio roads, what proportion does the actual tonnage of freights transported bear to the actual weight of the trains themselves, including cars and locomotives?

Reply 2. I have not immediate access to very late data from several of the roads you name, but from investigations previously made I believe the percentage that the actual tonnage subject to transportation charges will be found not to range higher than from 40 to 45 per cent. of the total average weight of trains moved, including in this the weight of cars, locomotives, and tenders.

Query 3. Assuming two roads, one of them transporting three-quarters of its entire tonnage within the space of three months and one-quarter during the remaining nine months of the year, the second road transporting an equal amount of freight equally distributed throughout the year, all things else being equal, how much more would it cost per ton to move freights on the first road than on the second?

Reply 3. A road which does three-fourths of its trade in three months must have the capacity in roadway, depots, and equipments sufficient to do the same amount per month throughout the year. Whatever is a fair monthly compensation, therefore, for the capital and risks involved in furnishing these three items is for nine months properly chargeable to the remaining fourth of the business to be done in that time. The only saving in expense possible will be in the labor and material consumed; but to operate a railway safely and economically the bulk of the force engaged must be trained and disciplined, and hence, in practice, a force of this character could only be secured by its retention on pay throughout the year. Economy in labor, therefore, could not be effected in proportion to the reduction in tonnage. In respect to material, also, so far as its renewal was made necessary by decay and not by wear, the expense would be alike, whether the business done was great or small. For a very rough estimate, however, it may not be amiss to assume that the expense of labor and material can be reduced as the business is lessened. It might also roughly be assumed that, under present conditions, from 30 to 35 per cent. of the gross earnings of a road with fair trade, distributed throughout the year about as at present, will be requisite to pay a fair return upon the cost of roadway, depots, and equipment.

If, on this basis, it is assumed that one road moves 1,200,000 tons in a year at the rate of 100,000 tons per month, and earns $1 per ton therefrom, and that another road of like capacity moves, in the first three months, 100,000 tons per month, or 300,000 tons in all, and in the remaining nine months but 100,000 tons, earning on both items the same price, *i. e.*, $1 per ton, the difference in cost would be as follows:

First road.

1,200,000 tons at $1		$1,200,000 gross earnings.
Expense, 65 per cent	$780,000	
Profit required on capital, 35 per cent	420,000	
		1,200,000

Second road.

300,000 tons at $1	300,000	
100,000 tons at $1	100,000	
		400,000 gross earnings.
Expenses, 65 per cent	260,000	
Profit required on capital, (35 per cent. of $1,200,000)	420,000	
		680,000
Loss		280,000

That is, on the second road the earnings must be $680,000 on 400,000 tons, or $1.70 per ton, an increase of 70 per cent.

It must be observed that, so far as I know, the foregoing conditions of tonnage-movement do not actually exist anywhere, and that the actual difference in cost would doubtless be considerably increased because of the inability to save in labor and material to a degree corresponding with the reduction in traffic.

Query 4. Assuming two roads again, one of which transports all its freight in one direction, and the other of which transports its freight equally in both directions, all things else being equal, how much more would it cost per ton to transport in the one case than in the other?

Reply 4. If, in the case you propose, it is assumed that the gradients of the road are such that the average weight of a train which the standard engine can haul is substantially the same in both directions, (as, after taking into account all the assistant power required over the heavy points, is practically the case on the Pennsylvania road between Philadelphia and Pittsburgh,) then, if the total expenses of the freight-traffic for any given period are divided by the number of miles run by freight-engines in the same time, so that these expenses are expressed as amounting to a certain price per mile per freight-engine, it is plain that if these expenses per engine-mile in both directions are borne in the one case only by traffic in one direction, and in the other case by twice the volume of tonnage equally divided between the two directions, the cost in the latter case for moving a ton one mile will be just one-half that in the former This will be slightly modified by the cost of loading and discharging the additional freight, and also, probably, by a slight increase in the cost of fuel for moving the same. In practice I think it would be found that firemen would use substantially as much coal whether the train they hauled consisted of empty or full cars.

Query 5. What is the relative cost of moving a light freight train and a loaded train?

Reply 5. I presume your question is intended to ascertain whether the cost of moving a full freight-train, of fully loaded cars, differs materially from moving the same train of cars without loading. I think in practice the difference in cost would be found very trifling, except so far as the expense of procuring, loading, and discharging of the lading is concerned.

Query 6. What is the most economical number of cars (stating weight and length of each car) which can be employed upon a road of favorable alignment and maximum grades of forty feet? What gradient, in your opinion, would reduce the train to three-fourths of that weight; what grade would reduce it to one-half, and what grade to one-fourth of the weight transported upon a maximum gradient of forty feet to the mile?

Reply 6. I am not sure I understand the purport of this question, except as to the characteristics of freight-cars. Any number of cars can be used on a road of any gradient, if tracks and engines are sufficiently increased, and can be so used economically to the extent they are required by profitable traffic. But, perhaps, the query was intended to ascertain the most economical number of cars per train on any given road. I will answer it on this latter supposition.

The average weight of an eight-wheel box-car may be placed at about 20,000 pounds, and its length at twenty-seven to thirty feet. Its ordinary lading may be placed at 20,000 pounds, or ten net tons. The maximum curvature of our leading roads may be placed at 8 degrees, in view of the curves used in passing onto and off sidings. In respect to resistances from other causes than curvature and gravity, it will probably not be much out of the way to place them (at ordinary speeds) at a total of eight pounds per net ton of the weight of train. Placing the weight of the engine to be used at sixty net tons when fully equipped with its tender, water, and fuel, and assuming that the weight upon its drivers is 50,000 pounds, then upon such a road, with cars weighing and loaded as above, the following would be the results: With maximum gradient at 40 feet per mile the load would be *twenty cars*, if the gradient is 60 feet it would be *fifteen cars*, if 95 feet *ten cars*, if 174 feet *five cars*. In these calculations fractions are disregarded.

Query 7. In your opinion what degree of curvature would cause the length of freight-trains to be reduced to one-half the length which could be practically employed upon a road of very favorable alignment, supposing all things else to be equal?

Reply 7. Using the data set forth in the sixth reply, but, assuming that the roadway is level, it would require a curvature of about 31 degrees or a radius of 185 feet to reduce the size of a freight-train one-half. There are other elements, however, which enter into the problem that would considerably change this result, and that would also make such a curvature on any road intended to compete with existing lines entirely out of the question.

Query 8. What is the practical proportion of the tractive power to weight of loco motives upon their driving wheels?

Reply 8. In an ordinary condition of rail and weather about one-fourth of the weight resting upon the driving-wheels of an engine represents its practical tractive power that is, the number of pounds resistance it will overcome without help at starting or at times when the rail is somewhat wetted.

JOSEPH D. POTTS.

LETTER IN REGARD TO THE ECONOMY OF TRANSPORT FROM THE WEST TO NEW YORK, BY WATER AND BY RAIL, BY FRANKLIN EDSON, ESQ PRESIDENT NEW YORK PRODUCE EXCHANGE.

NEW YORK PRODUCE EXCHANGE,
New York, December 6, 1873.

MY DEAR SIR: Your favor of the 2d instant, received on the 4th instant, states: "That you are informed by an intelligent correspondent, who seems to have had some experience in the business of transportation—

"First. That the time for the transportation of freight from Chicago to New York varies from ten to twenty days.

"Second. That no means have yet been provided whereby freight contracts can be procured requiring the delivery within a specified reasonable time by railway for long distances.

"Third. That frequent delays occur during the fall and winter months of from one to two months in the transportation of merchandise from interior western points to New York."

You ask for my opinion as to the correctness of these statements, and also for such general information as I may be able to furnish to the committee in regard to the average time of transportation by rail from Chicago to New York, and the commercial difficulties which are encountered by merchants and others, arising from delays and uncertainty as to the time required for the delivery of goods at New York. In answer to your queries in their order:

First. The time that goods are in transit from Chicago to New York by railway is from eight to ten days, and from that to fifteen and thirty days. If thirty thousand bushels of grain are shipped from Chicago on any one day, destined for this city, a considerable portion, say the larger, will be delivered in New York in eight to ten days, and the remaining portion may be anywhere from twelve to thirty days in the delivery at destination.

Second. Time contracts for the transportation of property by rail are exceptional, and are as a general rule declined by the railway companies.

Third. Delays of property in transit by rail are frequent, and especially so during the fall and winter months when there is a pressure of business consequent upon the close of the water-lines by frost, and portions of shipments are not unfrequently a month or more in time of transit for a long distances from interior points to this city.

The time of the transit of property by rail from Buffalo to New York ranges from four to twenty days, when transported in the company's cars. Shipments of grain from Buffalo, to the extent of fifty cars, or less, by one shipper, at one time, will most of it come through in four to five days, and the remaining portion will be from eight, ten, twelve, fifteen, and twenty days. Shipments without this irregularity in time are the exception. The general rule is irregularity in transit, ranging, when transported in the cars of the railway companies, from four to twenty, and even thirty days from Buffalo to New York. The larger portion of any one shipment from Buffalo is usually delivered in New York in the minimum time of four to five days, and the remaining portion of any one shipment of from twenty-five to fifty cars irregularly in from eight to thirty days. The average time is approximately six to seven days, taking the whole of any one shipment of from twenty-five to fifty cars of freight.

The railway companies all issue shipping-bills or bills of lading, "more or less," for grain, and do not in any case guarantee quantity. A car will generally carry ten tons of grain, or about 333 bushels of wheat. If this is short from ten to one hundred bushels when arrived at destination, the railway companies do not pay for shortage. Shipments made by lake vessels, if short at Buffalo, are made good by the vessels carrying the grain, paying for it at the market price, or receiving pay at the market price if more than the bill of lading calls for. The canal barge also pays for any deficiency there may be on delivery in New York if less than the bill of lading of shipment from Buffalo calls for, and receives pay at the market value in New York if there is an excess over and above what the bill of lading calls for. The margins of the New York acceptor of the western merchant's draft for property shipped are protected when the shipments are made by the water-lines, but may be entirely used up if shipped by rail by the shortage at place of delivery, in consequence of the railway companies' non-guaranty of quantity. This, in and of itself, is a serious objection to the shipment of grain by railway. Railways, as common carriers, should be required to guarantee quantity, to protect the interests of the shipper in the West and the pockets of the receivers at the sea-board.

The irregularity of railway transportation in time of transit for either long or short distances subjects receivers and exporters at sea-board ports to onerous burdens. A receiver sells a shipper, say, one hundred thousand bushels of grain, to arrive by rail; the shipper makes his contract for the freight of this quantity of grain and sells his sterling bills to pay for it on its arrival from the West. If only part of it arrives in time, the shipper cannot fill his freight engagement without going into the market and purchasing sufficient wheat or grain to make good the deficiency that is caused by the delay in the transit by railway, and frequently has to pay several cents per bushel on the amount of the deficiency to fill his freight engagement, and then take the chance of selling that amount deficient from the railway company's delay, making in the two transactions frequently a loss of several cents per bushel. In transportation by the water-lines, when not closed by frost, the quantity of grain is always guarantied, both on lake and canal shipments, while on shipments by rail no such guaranty at present exists.

The water-lines may be so improved that during seven and one-half months of the year the time of transit from Chicago and Milwaukee to New York need not be more than ten to eleven days, at a cost of about three dollars to three dollars and a half per ton, including all charges, and quantity always guarantied.

The rail charge, in summer, from Chicago to New York cannot be less than eight dollars per ton, to pay actual expenses, and no dividends; and in order to pay dividends there has to be an advance of about four dollars per ton for five-twelfths of the year in the railway freight-charges, which advance is uniformly made every year on the close of the water-lines by frost.

This presupposes the use of all large-class vessels on the lakes, the enlargement of the Erie Canal for barges of six hundred tons, and the application of steam as a motor on both the lakes and the Erie Canal; all of which is respectfully submitted for the consideration of your Committee on Transportation from the Interior to the Seaboard.

Very respectfully, yours,

FRANKLIN EDSON,
President New York Produce Exchange.

Hon. WILLIAM WINDOM,
Chairman of the U. S. Senate Committee on Transportation Routes to the Seaboard.

LETTER IN REGARD TO THE CANALS OF SWEDEN, ADDRESSED TO THE CHAIRMAN OF THIS COMMITTEE BY HON. C. C. ANDREWS, UNITED STATES MINISTER RESIDENT AT STOCKHOLM.

LEGATION OF THE UNITED STATES,
Stockholm, October 24, 1873.

DEAR SIR: In reply to your letter of August 6, I now have the honor to send you such information as I have been able to procure relative to the canal-system of Sweden.

A short time before the receipt of your letter I had addressed some inquiries on the subject to Colonel Modig, chief of the bureau of public roads and canals, with a view of collecting information for a report thereon to the Department of State; and on getting your letter I hastened to lay before him your inquiries respecting the Swedish canals, and also, in person, handed to him the blank which you inclosed, and which you desired should be filled. Colonel Modig in due time kindly forwarded to me answers to many of your inquiries, also short statements with tables, in Swedish, separately as to each of eight of the principal canals. But while this information was being collected his office was moved to other apartments, and I regret to say that your blank was mislaid and cannot, therefore, be returned to you. From a rough copy, however, which I made of it, I have prepared another, retaining such columns as can now be filled and adding some others, and which I now beg to transmit herewith as fully filled as I am able at the present time to make it.

In this blank, or table, the eight principal canals are put down in alphabetical order, namely, Dalsland, Forshaga, Göta, Hjelmar, Kinda, Seffle, Strömsholm, and Trolhætte.

In addition to these are Väddö, Akers, Eshilstuna, Dragets, Södertelge, Vestervids, Snäcke, and some other canals or canalized routes.

In stating the length of the canals I have given the length of the particular navigable route or line of communication which the canal and its intermediate lakes or rivers make; and in another column state the length of the "actually excavated canal." For example, the Göta Canal may be said to begin at the Baltic Sea and end at Lake Venern, and the distance between those two points, along its course, is 119½ miles, of which 54 miles are of actual canal, and the balance navigable lakes. The Trolhætte Canal begins at the south end of Lake Venern, (the largest lake in Sweden, and with the exception of a couple in Russia, the largest in Europe,) and after passing the celebrated Trolhætte Falls, connects with the Göta River, which is navigable to Gothenburg and the Cattegat. The two canals, the Göta and Trolhætte, with the intermediate natural navigation, constitute a very advantageous and popular line of water communication directly across the country from east to west. In going to Gothenburg or intermediate points from Stockholm over this route steamers reach the Baltic by first passing up the Malar lake (westwardly) and then turning south through the canal at Södertelge.

The Trolhætte Canal was begun early in the seventeenth century, during the reign of the youngest of Gustaf Vasa's sons, Charles IX, when a piece called "Charles's Grave" was done. But the work soon ceased, and was not resumed again till Swedenborg, a century afterward, directed the attention of Charles XII to it. By him it was committed to Polhem, who undertook to complete it in five years; but the King's death caused its suspension, and it was not resumed till 1742. In 1753 a lock was built in "Charles's Grave," so that sailing-vessels could pass; and under the direction of an engineer named Wirnan work was continued along the falls till 1755, when his so-called master-piece, the Float Rock Dam, was destroyed, causing a failure of the plan and the confidence it had before enjoyed. Finally, in 1793, a company was formed for building the canal after the plan of Capt. Erik Nordewall, and it was opened August 14, 1800.

The Göta Canal was originated by Baltazar Von Platen, who called to his assistance the English engineer, Thomas Telford. The canal company was formed April 11, 1810. The first lock, on the west line, was ready for sailing-vessels September 23, 1822:

and the whole canal, notwithstanding many and great obstacles, was completed and opened September 26, 1832.

The last-mentioned canal being larger than the Trolhætte, as finished in 1800, it became necessary to enlarge the Trolhætte to equal dimensions, which was done from 1837 to 1844; and the Swedish canal-system for steamers may be said to date from about that period.

I will now endeavor to answer your inquiries in the order in which they are put.

1st. The number of days of navigation on the canals in Sweden during the last ten years have been on an average 225 each year.

2d. The cost of transporting oats by canal, allowing 24 pounds of oats to the bushel, and 2,240 pounds to the ton, is, on the route from Stockholm to Gothenburg, the entire distance of 383 miles, *one cent seven mills and a half per ton* per mile; or one-tenth of a mill and $\frac{90}{100}$ of a mill per bushel per mile. This would be the charge in summer, when the days are quite long. It would be about 30 per cent. higher in the autumn or winter months. Oats and all other kinds of grain are shipped in Sweden in sacks, and not in bulk as with us. The rate stated is on the assumption that they are shipped in sacks. This is the case equally in vessels or in cars. The sacks are always returned free of charge. The rate just stated covers all charges. The route includes the short canal at Södertelge, and the two main canals of Göta and Trolhætte; in all, 69 locks and 5 half locks, and the whole time consumed 52 hours.

On the route from Stockholm to Jönhoping, at the south end of Lake Vettern, requiring 36 hours by steamer at this season, the freight-charge for grain is exactly the same as on the through-route from Stockholm to Gothenburg.

On the route from Stockholm to Gefle by steamer through the short Vaddo Canal and thence northerly on the Baltic, a distance of 175 miles, the whole freight-charges in summer are *two cents three mills and two-tenths of a mill per ton per mile*, for grain; or two-tenths of a mill and $\frac{51}{100}$ of a mill per bushel per mile; English miles, of course, being meant. In calculating the charge per ton I have allowed 92 bushels of oats to a ton, leaving off one bushel and a fraction to balance the supposed weight of the sacks.

Probably 2 cents a ton per mile would be the average charge for transporting grain by canal.

3d. Assuming "light commodities" to be such goods as are conveyed on express-trains, the answer will be as follows: The freight-charges on *bulky* goods by express-train is 58 cents (coin always *being understood*) *per* 100 *pounds per* 100 *miles*, and 91 cents for 200 miles. For goods not bulky the charge per 100 miles per 100 pounds is 46 cents, and increases at the rate of one öre (3.76 öre = to 1 cent) for every one-tenth of a Swedish mile; a Swedish mile being equal to 6$\frac{2}{3}$ English miles.

For grain of all sorts, in sacks, the usual way of transporting, the charge through from Stockholm to Malmö, 457 miles, is at the rate of one cent two mills and nine-tenths of a mill per ton per mile; or say 5$\frac{1}{4}$ cents per bushel for oats the whole distance, which is at the rate of 12 cents a bushel for 1,000 miles. The charges for wheat, allowing 60 pounds to a bushel, would be 13 cents per bushel for the whole distance of 457 miles. From all stations below Stockholm as far as to Palsboda, which is 125 miles below Stockholm in the direction of Malmö, the freight-charges for such goods are the same as from Stockholm. For a first-class passenger-ticket on the express-train from Stockholm to Malmö the charge is 54$\frac{20}{100}$ riksdalers, or $14.41.

4th. Competing railways have not caused the abandonment of any canal. On the contrary, the business of canals has increased with the increase of railways and the general development of the industries of the country.

5th. The principal part of the canal-work of Sweden has been accomplished during the present century, and has cost a little over $8,000,000. Such work would now cost thirty per cent. more than it did ten years ago.

6th. None of the canals are undergoing enlargement. It is expected, however, that a proposition will be submitted at the next session of the Diet to authorize a company, already formed, to canalize a certain passage the depth of seven feet below lowest low-water mark.

7th. Steam-power was first introduced on the canals in Sweden in 1838, and its use since then has steadily and successfully increased. The number of different Swedish steamers belonging to private persons or companies which navigated the canals in Sweden in 1871 was 419, of, in all, 12,735 horse-power, and an aggregate tonnage of 26,223 tons.

8th. At first side-wheels were used; but of late years propellers have been the most in use and are the most preferred.

9th. The business of the canals as a whole is increasing at the rate of about four per cent. a year.

10th. There are no statistics that show the number of tons of freight moved on the canals each year during the last ten years. From the report of the state board of trade, "or college of commerce," for 1871, it appears that out of 65,186 boats and vessels, of, in all, 3,927,270 tons, which passed on the canals that year, 42,243 of such boats and vessels were freighted. It is to be remarked that a good deal of timber is also floated over some of the canals.

11th. The canals have all been constructed by private companies, which, in some cases, as specified in the accompanying table, have received aid from the State.

12th. The canals are all operated or administered by the companies owning them. However, the president of the board of direction of the Göta Canal receives his appointment, for a term of four years, from the government; the second member of the board is chosen by the deputies of the National Bank and of the Public Debt Office; and the third member is chosen by the company. The president of the Trolhætte Canal Company is also appointed, for similar term, by the government.

13th. The government not being the owner of any, has made no sale of any canal.

14th. In regard to the system of canal-*tolls* it may be said that *the government fixes the tolls*, after receiving the propositions of the companies, for a certain number of years, and the tariff-rates are published in pamphlet form, as is the case with railroad-tariffs, and can be purchased at any book-store, so that people know what to depend on in regard to the cost of transportation for a period of a few years together, at least. With respect to tolls on the Göta and Trolhætte Canals, and probably most of the other canals, owners of steamers at the first trip of the season declare their purpose either to pay by the trip, which will be the same sum each trip, according to the tonnage of the vessel, and without regard to the freight it may have on board, or to pay according to the freight the steamer has at each trip; and the plan, whichever it be, must be adhered to for such steamer or vessel during the season. In case of payment, according to the freight the steamer has on board, the tolls are separately for the vessel and for the cargo. When payment is by the trip the canal-tolls are 1 riksdaler and 32 öre (35 cents) per 100 cubic feet of the vessel to the Göta Canal. The Trolhætte Canal (this is assuming the vessel makes the through-trip) has one-third as much, or 11½ cents, and in all 46 cents per 100 cubic feet of the vessel for one trip. Payment by the trip is the most common practice, as it saves much time and trouble. Where vessels pay toll, according to their freight, the charges on the Göta Canal are 43 and $\frac{2}{10}$ öre per 10 cubic feet of oats, or about one cent and a half a bushel; and twice as much for wheat. This, for interior transportation. For so-called "transito passage" of goods going to or coming from a foreign country the toll on oats would be but 4.5 öre (one cent. and two mills) per 10 cubic feet of oats; this low tariff having been fixed with a view of drawing freight away from the Danish Sound when tolls were charged there.

15th. It is not the policy of the Government that the canals shall yield any further revenue than is sufficient for their maintenance, and for a fair interest on the private capital actually invested in them.

In regard to the *speed* of steamers on canals it may be remarked that generally the rules of the companies do not allow steamers to make greater speed on the canals proper than 2,000 feet in five minutes, or, say, 4½ miles an hour. It is claimed, however, by steamboat-owners that when a vessel is lightly freighted a greater speed can be made without any injury to the canal. Owing to the amount of natural navigation on the route between Stockholm and Gothenburg, steamers going by the canals in summer average 7⅓ miles an hour on the entire route.

I shall take the liberty to send you one or two maps of Sweden showing, among other things, the lines of canals. And referring for further details to the accompanying table, I beg to assure you that it will afford me a satisfaction to communicate any additional information you may wish on the subject that it is in my power to procure.

I am, sir, very respectfully, yours,

C. C. ANDREWS.

Hon. WILLIAM WINDOM,
Chairman Committee on Transportation-Routes, &c., United States Senate, Washington, D. C.

P. S.—I would state that Mr. S. B. Ruggles, of New York, who is intimate with the canals of that State, personally examined some of the Swedish canals, including the Trolhætte, in 1869.

Table of eight of the principal canals of Sweden.

Names of canals.	Length of each canal-route, in English miles.	Length of actual canal-work, in English miles.	Year when built.	Cost, (in United States gold.)	Amount contributed by state.	Dimensions of canal.		Highest elevation, or "lift," in feet.	Locks.			Average lift to each lock.	Size of largest steamers navigating.			Capacity of largest steamers navigating, tons of 2,240 pounds.	Steam or horse power used, or both.	Average number of minutes consumed in each lockage.	Speed of steamers in motion, per hour, not including lockage-stops.	Average number of months navigable each year.	Number of movable bridges over.	Yearly receipts, (in United States gold.)	Yearly expenditures.	Percentage of income on capital.	Remarks.
						Breadth of bottom, in feet.	Depth, in feet.		Number of complete, 2 gates to each.	Length, in feet.	Breadth, in feet.		Length in feet.	Breadth in feet.	Depth, in feet.										
Dalsland	157	5	1865–1868	$382, 782	(*)	15½	6½	230	28	100	14	10–14	77	13. 8	5½	67	Both	10–15	4½	7½	....	$6, 000	$3, 528	1. 56	Affords communication with southeastern part of Norway.
Forshaga	21	(†)	1870	55, 811	‡40 000	......	.....	.....	1	130	26	12	....	....	....	....	Both	10–15	4½	6¾	....	4, 220	704	7. 56	Along Klar River, north of Venern Lake, on Carlstad.
Göta	119½	54	1810–1832	4, 172, 900	....	44–48	10	308	§53	120	24. 5	9	110	24	9½	117	Both	10–15	4½	9	34	76, 555	27, 343	1. 01	One of the largest; and with Trollhätte affords water-communication directly across country from east to west.
Hjelmar	8¾	5½	1819–1823	400, 000	....	25–36	7	77	‖9	120	24	.....	.....	.....	.....	.....	Both	10–15	4½	7	....	4, 000	3, 482	0. 126	Affords communication between Stockholm and Örebro via Mälar Lake.
Kinda	50	5	1865–1871	344, 101	....	18–32	6	176. 9	15	98	16. 5	.....	.....	.....	.....	.....	Both	10–15	4½	8½	15	6, 130	3, 167	0. 9	From Lake Roxen, near Linköhing south, to Åsunden Lake.
Seffle	58½	1	1835–1837	100, 000	50, 000	......	7–10	.....	1	125	26	2–5	.....	.....	.....	.....	Both	10–15	4½	....	....	5, 079	1, 414	0. 515	From Lake Venern to Arvika.
Strömsholm	64	7¾	1842–1860	849, 308	....	18–20	5	336. 4	§25	70–86	18	.....	.....	.....	.....	.....	Both	10–15	4½	6½	16	29, 140	29, 140	....	North from Lake Mälar; regular steamers between Stockholm and Smedjebaken; center of a rich iron district.
Trollhätte	22	4	1837–1844	¶835, 464	....	24–40	10	143	**15	120	24. 5	10	110	24	9½	117	Both	10–15	4½	8½	....	93, 300	38, 415	6. 4	From south end of Lake Venern to Göta River,

* $358.22?, in loan; $66,422, in grant. † 1,540 feet. ‡ Grant. § Also 5 half-locks. ‖ 2 half-locks. ¶ That is, the new canal. ** Also 1 double.

LETTER IN REGARD TO THE CANALS OF NORWAY, FROM HON. C. C. ANDREWS, MINISTER RESIDENT AT STOCKHOLM.

LEGATION OF THE UNITED STATES,
Stockholm, November 29, 1873.

SIR: Referring to my letter to you of the 24th ultimo on the canals of Sweden, I now beg to inclose to you herewith four brief statements relative to the canals of Norway, which I have to-day had the honor to recei·e from Mr. J. Vogt, acting director of canals in Norway. It will be seen that the canals in Norway have all been constructed since 1850 at a cost of about $400,000.

I am, sir, very respectfully yours,

C. C. ANDREWS.

Hon. WILLIAM WINDOM,
Chairman Committee Transportation Routes to the Sea, U. S. Senate, Washington.

Respecting canals made in Norway, (with three documents relating thereto.)

There are but few canals in Norway. The nature of the country offers but few localities where there can be a question as to the construction of long, continuous canals. The canals that are constructed are, therefore, detached short pieces, by which navigable lakes or navigable pieces of rivers are mutually connected or connected with the sea. Until 1850 there were only a few private canals constructed in the country, which were principally made for floating timber through them. The construction of canals in Norway is accomplished by contributions from the state, the parishes, and private people. They are managed by directors, and are subject to the control of the director of canals in case of a question on technical alterations, &c.

By the accompanying list of the canals which have been made since 1850 by the Norwegian canal department, it will be seen that there are only five canals supplied with locks. The other twelve canalizations on the list are regulations and deepenings, partly in fresh, partly in salt water. The list of the goods that pass through the canals relates only to the Skien Canal, and, as regards the Fredrickshall Canal, only of the number of pieces of timber and the number of planks that have passed through; the quantity of other goods passing through this canal is but trifling. On none of the canals are horses used for drawing, but steamboats are employed.

With regard to the five first-mentioned canals on the accompanying list it may be noticed—

1. The Friedrickshall Canal, in the Smaalehnen Amt—by four separate canals with, respectively, three, one, four, and four locks. There are five lakes connected together in the Friedrickshall water-course, by which a navigable water-communication of the length of forty-five English miles is formed. The lowest lake is situated three English miles from the sea and two hundred and fifty feet over its level. Two steamers are employed on this canal in the transport of timber.

2. The Skien Canal, in Bratsberg Amt, comprises two canals, separated from each other by a distance of four English miles, with, respectively, four and two locks. By the Skien Canal the Lake Nordsjö is connected with the Skien Fjord, (the sea.) At present there are six steamers running on this canal. The Lake Nordsjö lies forty-eight feet above the level of the sea.

3. The Eidsvold-Sundpas Canal in Aggershuus Amt. A large dam, constructed above a water-fall at this place in order to regulate the height of the water in the Aljósen, (the largest lake in Norway,) necessitated the construction of this canal; the principal object of which was to prevent the stoppage of the comparatively unimportant boat-traffic between the Aljösen and a short piece of a river lying below the lake.

4. The Storstrómmen Canal, in Nedenaes Amt, with one lock, connects two large lakes in Seatersdalen, by which there is made a continuous water-communication of twenty-two English miles. One steamer is employed here.

5. By the Vraadals Canal, with one lock, Vraadalsvand (Vand, a small lake) is connected with Nisservand, in Bratsberg Amt. One steamboat is employed on this sailing-line, of which there is a length of thirty-two miles opened.

At present there is an idea of making two new canals in Norway: one to form a continuation of the Friedrickshall Canal, which would thus be lengthened fifteen English miles; the other, a canal between Fyrrisvand and Dranysvand, in Bratsberg Amt. Here will be made two locks. The length of the sailing-line on both the lakes opened by this canal will be twenty English miles.

List of the canals made by the Norwegian canal department from the year 1850.

	Names of the canals.	The situation of the canals.	Canals.					Locks.				The dimensions of largest vessels that can pass through the canals.			Tonnage and horse-power of steamers going through the canals.		Number of times that the locks are opened.
			Length.	Breadth.	Depth.	Cost, (specie-daler.)	Opened.	Number.	Total fall.	Length.	Breadth.	Length.	Breadth.	Depth.	Tonnage.	Horse-power.	
				Feet.	*Feet.*				*Feet.*	*Feet.*	*Feet.*	*Feet.*	*Feet.*	*Feet.*			
1	Friedrickshall Canal*	Smaalehnen Amt	45 miles	30.9	7.21	54,500	1860	12	127.72	113.30	20.60	92.70	19.60	5.665	35 tons	12	
2	Skien Canal	Bradsberg Amt	40 miles	30.9	11.3	225,600	1861	6	49.44	123.60	20.60	103.00	19.60	‡{8.24 / 9.78}	88 tons	20	8,944
3	Eidsvold-Sundpas Canal	Aggershuus Amt	Aljósen	(†)	(†)	32,000	1857	1	{Until 8.24}	113.30	20.60	92.70	19.60	5.15			1,212
4	Storstrómmen Canal	Nedenaes Amt	22 miles	(†)	(†)	6,500	1869	1	{Until 8.24}	87.55	14.42	77.20	12.36	3.35	530 cwt	8	
5	Vraadals Canal	Bratsberg Amt	32 miles	15.45	5.15	6,270	1868	1		103.00	15.45	92.70	14.42	4.63	195 cwt	12	
	The canalization of—																
6	Aadalselven	Buskerud Amt	35 miles	36.05	{L. W., 15.45 / H. W., 20.60}	28,700	1869	No lock	(§)			87.55	14.94	4.12	1,500 cwt	15	
7	Hódnebókilen	Nedeneas Amt	309 feet	14.42	4.12	600	1867	do									
8	Rüsorsand	do	515 feet	10.30	4.12	1,100	1864	do									
9	Laugestróm	do	1,030 feet	24.72	6.18	2,700	1864	do									
10	Raanene	do	3,090 feet	6.18	4.64	1,600	1869	do									
11	Strómmestróm	do	515 feet	15.45	5.667	1,000	1866	do									
12	Hisóstróm	do	618 feet	26.78	9.27	5,660	1869	do									
13	Heloigsstróm	Lister and Mandals Amt	2,266 feet	4.12	2.06	260	1853	do									
14	Lógerne	do	5,150 feet	6.18	3.09	1,700	1852	do									
15	Skjoldsstróm	Stovangers Amt	1,030 feet	41.20	8.24	4,500	1872	do									
16	Rőksund	Sóndre Bergenhuus Amt	4,635 feet	12.36	4.12	1,370	1859	do									
17	Kulleseid Canal	do	1,433 feet	18.54	10.3	1,630	1856	do									

OBSERVATION.—All the feet and inches are given in English measure.

* At present the lower part of this canal is under repair, it having been damaged some years ago.
† The short upper and lower canals have the same dimensions as the locks at this place.
‡ At the lower division vessels of 1.54 greater depth can pass.
§ The total fall varying between 15.5 and 20.5 feet.

List of the goods transported through the Skien Canal in the year 1872.

Goods.	Upper division of the canal.	Lower division of the canal.
Round and square timber	574,257 logs	392,519 logs.
Sawer timber	569,263 planks or boards	631,813 planks or boards.
Fire-wood, split wood, and slabs	123,683.3 cubic feet	103,600 cubic feet.
Corn and potatoes	26,384¾ tönder*	2,654¼ tönder.
Herrings	1,130¾ tönder	600½ tönder.
Salt	4,396¾ tönder	1,990½ tönder.
Tar	180½ tönder	39¾ tönder.
Lime	398½ tönder	15 tönder.
Ore	11,148½ tönder	11,147 tönder.
Coals	528¼ tönder	20,309 tönder.
Cinders	6,546 tönder	6,546 tönder.
Iron	1,327.6 tons	1,281.2 tons.
Pig-iron and old iron	684.3 tons	704.8 tons.
Raw copper	232.3 tons	232.3 tons.
Coffee	2,456 bags	970½ bags.
Beer	132,150 bottles	132,150 bottles.
Fat goods	145 tons	15.9 tons.
Mackerel	2,050	2,000.
Apples	12 tönder	
Bones	61.1 tons	38.8 tons.
Bricks	7,858	4,200.
Teles	25,570	49,500.
Draining-pipes	45,150	24,000.
Whetstones	174,800	174,800.
Grinding-stones	196	27.
Millstones	10 pairs	1 pair.
Hay and straw	4 tons	4 tons.
Live animals	20 horses	
Do	360 cows	
Do	4 calves	
Do	183 sheep	
Do	33 dogs	
Do	31 pigs	
Ice		1,660 tons.
Sundry goods	17,212 tönder	4,797 tönder.

*A tönde is equal to four bushels or a half quarter.

List of the timber and planks transported through the Friederickshall Canal from 1863 *to* 1872.

Year.	Number of logs.	Number of planks.
1863	658, 692	27, 480
1864	728, 004	108, 060
1865	767, 076	53, 463
1866	531, 516	33, 156
1867	651, 960	44, 232
1868	537, 336	52, 092
1869	747, 456	81, 608
1870	968, 028	73, 968
1871	526, 068	31, 764
1872	533, 472	61, 884

STATEMENTS IN REGARD TO APPROPRIATIONS MADE BY THE GOVERNMENT OF THE UNITED STATES IN AID OF PUBLIC IMPOVEMENTS.

Statement showing the amount of money expended by the Government of the United States in the erection of permanent public buildings in the District of Columbia, from the time the seat of government was located at Washington to the close of the fiscal year ending June 30, 1873.

Capitol, about	$12,000,000
Treasury, about	6,000,000
Interior, about	4,000,000
Post-Office, about	2,000,000
President's House	300,000
Agricultural Department	200,000
New State Department	1,300,000
Total	25,800,000

Statement showing the amount of money expended by the Government of the United States in each State and Territory of the Union for custom-houses, post-offices, and court-houses, from the adoption of the Constitution to June 30, 1873.

Maine	$1,961,595
New Hampshire	173,671
Vermont	214,534
Massachusetts	3,602,360
Rhode Island	315,290
Connecticut	240,373
New York	9,634,695
New Jersey	250,263
Pennsylvania	2,583,016
Delaware	41,128
Maryland	1,185,620
Virginia	876,596
North Carolina	217,459
South Carolina	2,767,945
Alabama	493,880
Georgia	283,474
Florida	103,478
Mississippi	24,000
Louisiana	3,806,678
Texas	114,360
Arkansas	103
Missouri	775,223
Kentucky	287,790
Tennessee	317,486
Ohio	682,745
Indiana	456,746
Illinois	2,574,415
Michigan	228,505
Wisconsin	566,592
Iowa	477,393
Minnesota	543,695
Kansas	49,545
California	890,199
Oregon	435,805
Nebraska	299,996
West Virginia	94
Total in States	37,476,747
TERRITORIES.	
New Mexico	99,650
Utah	68,254
Washington	27,650
Colorado	90,728
Idaho	40,240
Montana	41,575
Wyoming	37,455
Total in Territories	405,547
Grand total	37,882,294

Statement showing the amount of money expended by the Government of the United States in each State and Territory of the Union for marine hospitals and light-houses, including beacons and fog-signals, from the adoption of the Constitution to June 30, 1873.

Maine	$766,755
New Hampshire	122,465
Vermont	84,125
Massachusetts	1,535,487
Rhode Island	305,316
Connecticut	467,925
New York	1,580,639
New Jersey	423,071
Pennsylvania	204,865
Delaware	343,843
Maryland	358,314
Virginia	425,416
North Carolina	852,407
South Carolina	278,289
Georgia	279,599
Alabama	298,623
Florida	1,498,488
Mississippi	248,209
Louisiana	1,603,453
Texas	241,005
Arkansas	59,081
Missouri	87,647
Kentucky	135,948
Tennessee	
Ohio	765,961
Indiana	86,892
Illinois	681,989
Michigan	1,879,350
Wisconsin	284,657
Iowa	28,446
Minnesota	14,847
Kansas	
California	628,196
Oregon	212,249
Nebraska	
West Virginia	
Washington Territory	153,558
Total	16,937,115

Statement showing the amount of money expended by the Government of the United States in each State and Territory of the Union for the improvement of rivers and harbors, from the adoption of the Constitution to June 30, 1873.

THE ATLANTIC COAST.

Maine	$746,152
New Hampshire	23,000
Massachusetts	1,621,235
Rhode Island	286,485
Connecticut	563,407
New York	1,249,500
New Jersey	95,963
Pennsylvania	208,894
Delaware	2,653,102
Maryland	522,359
Virginia	424,422
North Carolina	740,377
South Carolina	88,254
Georgia	321,023
Florida	43,000
The Atlantic coast	9,587,173

THE GULF COAST.

Florida	103,730
Alabama	312,476

Mississippi	$30,500
Louisiana	25,000
Texas	108,000
The Gulf coast	579,706

THE PACIFIC COAST.

California	326,500
Oregon	202,314
Washington Territory	109,189
The Pacific coast	638,003

THE NORTHERN LAKES.

Vermont	304,357
New York	3,814,314
Pennsylvania	330,942
Ohio	1,292,794
Michigan	2,213,100
Indiana	320,734
Illinois	821,305
Wisconsin	1,229,612
Minnesota	110,000
The Northern lakes	10,437,158

THE WESTERN RIVERS.

Pennsylvania	
Ohio	
Kentucky	30,000
Tennessee	292,947
Indiana	35,000
Illinois	73,000
Wisconsin	240,000
Minnesota	72,500
Iowa	29,500
Missouri	115,000
Kansas	
Arkansas	256,500
Nebraska	
Mississippi	5,000
West Virginia	5,000
Louisiana	805,847
Texas	20,000
Improvements of rivers chargeable to the several States	9,458,006
The Western rivers	11,438,300

RECAPITULATION.

The Atlantic coast	$9,587,173
The Gulf coast	579,706
The Pacific coast	638,003
The northern lakes	10,437,158
The western rivers	11,438,300
Total	32,680,340

SUMMARY.

Amount expended for improvement of harbors	$21,242,040
Improvement of western rivers	11,438,300
Light-houses (including fog-signals and beacons,) and marine hospitals	16,937,115
Custom-houses, post-offices, and court-houses	37,882,294
Total	87 499 749

SHIPMENTS BY RAIL FROM THE WESTERN STATES TO THE ATLANTIC AND GULF STATES.

Wheat, wheat-flour, corn, oats, barley, and pease delivered at Portland, Me., by the Grand Trunk Railway, each month during the year 1872.

[Prepared for the United States Senate Committee on Transportation.]

Months.	Wheat.	Wheat-flour.	Corn.	Oats.	Barley.	Pease.
	Bushels.	*Barrels.*	*Bushels.*	*Bushels.*	*Bushels.*	*Bushels.*
January	48, 286	36, 192	27, 500	23, 587	23, 336	14, 573
February	69, 182	28, 680	40, 030	24, 840	15, 672	21, 085
March	11, 305	32, 132	15, 360	21, 740	5, 282	22, 700
April	41, 094	48, 749	20, 704	30, 036	6, 526	43, 662
May	22, 398	65, 987	91, 610	35, 640	345	55, 030
June	350	55, 687	129, 003	65, 044	399	330
July	....	26, 050	69, 300	35, 822	385	369
August	42	25, 906	157, 150	22, 806	30	....
September	350	18, 593	184, 575	45, 211	3	353
October	....	38, 690	63, 510	12, 883	1, 465	330
November	21, 429	68, 250	16, 935	15, 460	2, 735	2, 837
December	66, 350	53, 648	5, 775	1, 320	5, 070	6, 780
Total	280, 786	498, 564	821, 452	334, 389	61, 248	168, 049

Total bushels grain 3, 741, 413

Wheat, wheat-flour, oats, barley, and pease imported into the United States, either in bond or by payment of duty, by the Grand Trunk Railway, each month during the year 1872.

[Prepared for the United States Senate Committee on Transportation.]

Months.	Wheat.	Wheat-flour.	Oats.	Barley.	Pease.
	Bushels.	*Barrels.*	*Bushels.*	*Bushels.*	*Bushels.*
January	30, 000	23, 200	20, 400	20, 100	13, 750
February	42, 150	18, 500	15, 200	14, 000	19, 000
March	9, 450	26, 400	2, 600	4, 000	21, 700
April	30, 000	35, 000	7, 800	900	40, 300
May	10, 450	44, 300	10, 200	....	29, 750
June	....	25, 700	11, 400	....	330
July	....	20, 200	10, 800	....	369
August	....	14, 200	7, 200	....	....
September	....	11, 200	7, 500	....	....
October	....	31, 000	6, 600	1, 300	....
November	20, 000	43, 600	....	2, 250	2, 837
December	60, 000	4, 310	600	4, 000	5, 000
Total	202, 050	*1, 339, 245	100, 300	46, 550	134, 036

Total bushels of grain 1, 688, 145

* Bushels.

Statement of wheat, wheat-flour, corn, oats, barley, and rye, received by the Rome, Watertown and Ogdensburgh Railroad, at Cape Vincent, or any other lake or Saint Lawrence River ports, during the year 1872.

[Prepared for the United States Senate Committee on Transportation.]

Months.	Wheat.	Wheat-flour.	Corn.	Oats.	Barley.	Rye.
1872.	*Bushels.*	*Barrels.*	*Bushels.*	*Bushels.*	*Bushels.*	*Bushels.*
January	20, 551	7, 740	34, 815	2, 887	1, 457	400
February	20, 326	8, 400	4, 768	5, 200	15, 174	617
March	15, 373	9, 043	14, 847	1, 878	15, 381	800
April	18, 788	16, 737	11, 102	4, 730	29, 185	....
May	27, 260	12, 957	68, 363	6, 639	14, 205	2, 799
June	33, 038	7, 586	24, 246	3, 333	....	....
July	32, 655	16, 406	1, 561	4, 837	....	....
August	30, 534	13, 297	29, 534	3, 699	72	....
September	8, 719	17, 620	31, 027	1, 744	....	....
October	26, 916	15, 002	18, 485	551	337	....
November	31, 985	14, 373	24, 679	222	4, 805	....
December	23, 084	9, 721	27, 374	1, 463	7, 344	860
Total	289, 229	148, 882	290, 801	37, 183	87, 960	5, 476

Total bushels of grain 1, 380, 618

Wheat, wheat-flour, corn, oats, barley, and rye, shipped eastward from Albany by the Boston and Albany Railroad, each month during the year 1872.

[Prepared for the United States Senate Committee on Transportation.]

Months.	Wheat.	Wheat-flour.	Corn.	Oats.	Barley.	Rye.
1872.	*Bushels.*	*Barrels.*	*Bushels.*	*Bushels.*	*Bushels.*	*Bushels.*
January	14, 150	77, 900	1, 297, 201	271, 674	17, 749	2, 656
February	21, 327	68, 733	877, 640	285, 997	1, 824	491
March	27, 546	89, 948	1, 166, 923	374, 432	4, 151	709
April	34, 984	90, 546	1, 582, 152	367, 553	451	....
May	11, 631	160, 322	1, 007, 137	534, 374	1, 000	167
June	9, 104	101, 553	955, 940	931, 976	....	1, 474
July	32, 767	75, 283	702, 354	334, 246	....	6, 273
August	98, 142	138, 754	1, 031, 733	339, 519	754	3, 215
September	60, 095	213, 509	905, 993	750, 434	10, 668	4, 328
October	78, 514	302, 990	640, 243	713, 661	63, 015	5, 071
November	27, 161	205, 072	596, 532	325, 920	26, 515	4, 042
December	34, 027	143, 630	568, 421	205, 469	6, 495	7, 924
Total	449, 448	1, 668, 240	11, 332, 269	5, 435, 255	132, 622	36, 350

Total bushels of grain 24, 893, 024

Wheat, wheat-flour, corn, oats, barley, and rye, delivered at Boston by the Boston and Albany Railroad, each month during the year 1872.

[Prepared for the United States Senate Committee on Transportation.]

Months.	Wheat.	Wheat-flour.	Corn.	Oats.	Barley.	Rye.
1872.	*Bushels.*	*Barrels.*	*Bushels.*	*Bushels.*	*Bushels.*	*Bushels.*
January	....	2,700	332,473	10,749	9,672	....
	526	33,046	236,566	81,913	5,845	....
February	....	3,000	193,808	20,804	....	....
	....	21,952	123,675	56,113	479	....
March	1,065	4,034	232,306	35,019	1,434	....
	8,747	36,243	91,390	73,277	1,506	....
April	773	8,331	775,926	35,258	....	....
	12,664	25,152	141,259	99,847	....	....
May	....	5,605	177,804	44,845	....	....
	344	82,042	102,591	180,494	....	....
June	....	3,101	196,181	30,706	....	....
	....	60,109	152,568	495,711	....	....
July	4,171	3,845	172,505	10,261	....	....
	15,423	29,085	130,234	81,627	....	3,380
August	73,678	13,480	429,458	13,106	....	....
	333	65,721	131,479	57,826	754	....
September	11,578	22,140	186,852	39,466	....	368
	14,340	105,429	176,665	276,520	10,669	766
October	21,513	50,754	90,883	62,492	1,050	....
	24,863	136,071	70,853	254,250	59,145	....
November	33,861	24,864	94,728	19,181	9,957	374
	9,424	95,103	73,334	85,943	15,665	....
December	....	12,609	140,916	13,147	1,683	422
	12,430	66,708	59,558	58,229	537	1,374
Total	146,639	154,463	3,023,840	332,034	23,796	1,164
	99,094	756,661	1,490,172	1,804,750	94,599	5,520
Grand total	245,733	911,124	4,514,012	2,136,784	118,395	6,684

Total bushels of grain 11,121,666

Wheat, wheat-flour, corn, oats, barley, and rye shipped from Buffalo and Suspension Bridge into New England by rail from the New York Central and Hudson River Railroad Company, each month during the year 1872.

[Prepared for the United States Senate Committee on Transportation.]

Months.	Wheat.	Wheat-flour.	Corn.	Oats.	Barley.	Rye.
	Bushels.	*Barrels.*	*Bushels.*	*Bushels.*	*Bushels.*	*Bushels.*
January	11,142	50,467	1,153,382	256,163	1,722	732
February	12,611	43,539	1,040,014	292,290	1,375	1,157
March	21,654	68,546	1,522,911	270,975	1,712	832
April	27,416	91,780	1,824,367	363,781	....	....
May	6,750	120,737	1,182,218	623,161	....	....
June	7,483	80,442	1,045,640	996,049	....	1,200
July	28,283	43,297	690,476	267,450	450	2,400
August	94,633	110,656	1,153,261	381,737	900	3,600
September	62,073	211,841	867,723	768,912	15,750	5,646
October	72,389	254,201	660,425	792,112	52,104	5,200
November	59,109	186,160	707,806	359,726	9,276	4,517
December	30,263	111,420	594,773	267,085	1,325	4,400
Total	433,806	1,373,086	12,442,996	5,639,441	84,614	29,684

Total number bushels grain 24,809,428
Number bushels in summer months 15,434,462
Number bushels in winter months 9,374,966
Average per month, summer 2,204,923.1
Average per month, winter 1,874,993.2

Wheat, wheat-flour, corn, oats, barley, and rye shipped from Buffalo and Suspension Bridge and delivered at New York by the New York Central and Hudson River Railroad Company, each month during the year 1872.

[Prepared for the United States Senate Committee on Transportation.]

Months.	Wheat.	Wheat-flour.	Corn.	Oats.	Barley.	Rye.
	Bushels.	*Barrels.*	*Bushels.*	*Bushels.*	*Bushels.*	*Bushels.*
January	7, 197	46, 983	218, 992	28, 538	7, 582	....
February	383	22, 584	200, 314	23, 106	4, 333	....
March	....	46, 004	110, 453	18, 694	8, 358	....
April	41, 300	49, 800	155, 307	5, 722	....	....
May	1, 800	70, 648	574, 543	58, 400	2, 854	....
June	50, 710	55, 678	236, 629	232, 800	450	....
July	292, 185	33, 262	139, 355	174, 975	15, 384	....
August	252, 486	46, 274	197, 934	324, 494	4, 500	....
September	308, 613	76, 209	78 125	179, 769	55, 600	....
October	125, 778	86, 991	35, 328	229, 594	50, 362	800
November	238, 028	136, 213	25, 832	203, 537	24, 959	793
December	226, 511	71, 722	78, 194	295, 250	48, 641	....
Total	1, 544, 991	742, 368	2, 051, 006	1, 774, 879	223, 023	1, 593

Total number bushels of grain	8, 936, 148
Number bushels in summer months	6, 390, 355
Number bushels in winter months	2, 545, 793
Average per month, summer	912, 908
Average per month, winter	509, 158

Wheat, wheat-flour, corn, oats, barley, and rye shipped from Buffalo and Suspension Bridge and delivered at Albany, including Schenectady and Troy, by the New York Central and Hudson River Railroad Company, each month during the year 1872.

[Prepared for the United States Senate Committee on Transportation.]

Months.	Wheat.	Wheat-flour.	Corn.	Oats.	Barley.	Rye.
	Bushels.	*Barrels.*	*Bushels.*	*Bushels.*	*Bushels.*	*Bushels.*
January	1, 750	3, 618	67, 745	14, 581	34, 187	....
February	4, 383	3, 214	19, 986	13, 944	45, 829	....
March	5, 640	6, 890	51, 200	20, 250	22, 035	....
April	6, 496	10, 264	73, 396	27, 325	1, 210	....
May	10, 401	12, 450	88, 291	49, 569	3, 052	....
June	4, 833	9, 690	49, 448	82, 487	3, 896	....
July	19, 550	4, 690	20, 003	46, 036	4, 906	....
August	44, 250	8, 940	51, 875	60, 200	2, 662	400
September	68, 856	13, 575	26, 000	95, 112	33, 229	3, 993
October	54, 575	22, 726	29, 117	135, 043	92, 103	4, 000
November	34, 737	14, 429	36, 360	40, 332	66, 160	4, 614
December	10, 366	8, 175	28, 777	82, 587	25, 563	8, 400
Total	265, 837	118, 661	542, 398	667, 466	334, 832	21, 407

Total number bushels grain	2, 365, 914
Number bushels in summer months	1, 655, 339
Number bushels in winter months	710, 575
Average per month, summer	236, 477
Average per month, winter	142, 115

GRAND TOTAL.

Wheat, wheat-flour, corn, oats, barley, and rye shipped east from Buffalo and Suspension Bridge each month by the New York Central and Hudson River Railroad Company during the year 1872, destined to Albany, Troy, Schenectady, New York, and Boston and other New England points.

[Prepared for the United States Senate Committee on Transportation.]

Months.	Wheat.	Wheat-flour.	Corn.	Oats.	Barley.	Rye.
	Bushels.	*Barrels.*	*Bushels.*	*Bushels.*	*Bushels.*	*Bushels.*
January	20, 089	101, 068	1, 440, 119	299, 282	43, 491	732
February	17, 377	69, 337	1, 260, 314	329, 340	51, 537	1, 157
March	27, 294	121, 440	1, 684, 564	309, 919	32, 105	832
April	75, 212	151, 844	2, 053, 270	396, 828	1, 210	....
May	18, 951	203, 835	1, 845, 052	731, 130	5, 906	....
June	63, 026	145, 810	1, 331, 717	1, 311, 336	4, 346	1, 200
July	340, 018	81, 249	849, 834	488, 461	20, 740	2, 400
August	391, 369	165, 870	1, 403, 070	766, 431	8, 062	4, 000
September	439, 542	301, 625	971, 848	1, 043, 793	104, 579	9, 639
October	252, 742	363, 918	724, 870	1, 156, 749	194, 569	10, 000
November	331, 874	336, 802	769, 998	603, 595	100, 395	9, 924
December	267, 140	191, 317	701, 744	644, 922	75, 529	12, 800
Total	2, 244, 634	2, 234, 115	15, 036, 400	8, 081, 786	642, 469	52, 684

Total number bushels grain	36, 111, 490
Number bushels in summer	23, 507, 156
Number bushels in winter	12, 604, 334
Average per month, summer	3, 358, 179
Average per month, winter	2, 520, 866

Wheat, wheat-flour, corn, oats, barley, and rye delivered at New York by the Erie Railway each month during the year 1872.

[Prepared for the United States Senate Committee on Transportation.]

Months.	Wheat.	Wheat-flour.	Corn.	Oats.	Barley.	Rye.
	Bushels.	*Barrels.*	*Bushels.*	*Bushels.*	*Bushels.*	*Bushels.*
January	39, 009	56, 657	887, 937	26, 442	50, 184	....
February	97, 964	34, 189	593, 239	67, 208	119, 473	982
March	70, 277	58, 203	502, 614	987, 679	82, 725	355
April	53, 738	74, 434	280, 225	434, 297	18, 556	....
May	12, 024	102, 989	792, 192	129, 390	....	....
June	57, 327	133, 871	471, 358	437, 560	....	....
July	168, 242	81, 504	274, 632	432, 494	....	....
August	140, 764	81, 594	229, 410	456, 019	....	....
September	295, 601	142, 112	223, 810	630, 508	15, 755	335
October	128, 806	250, 702	89, 736	313, 565	32, 699	803
November	212, 271	220, 747	70, 991	237, 163	6, 221	1, 171
December	262, 684	138, 371	129, 298	363, 404	74, 072	508
Total	1, 538, 707	1, 375, 373	4, 545, 442	4, 515, 729	399, 685	4, 154

Total bushels grain	17, 192, 895
Total bushels summer	10, 421, 683
Total bushels winter	6, 771, 212
Average per month, summer	1, 488, 811. 8
Average per month, winter	1, 354, 242. 4

J. B. HOFFMAN, *Eastward Agent.*

EASTWARD AGENT'S OFFICE,
Foot Duane street, New York.

Wheat, wheat-flour, corn, oats, barley, and rye shipped eastward on the Erie Railway from Salamanca each month of the year 1872.

[Prepared for the United States Senate Committee on Transportation.]

Months.	Wheat.	Wheat-flour.	Corn.	Oats.	Barley.	Rye.
	Bushels.	*Barrels.*	*Bushels.*	*Bushels.*	*Bushels.*	*Bushels.*
January	2, 183	20, 557	244, 300	108, 781	4, 766	....
February	683	14, 821	130, 533	57, 125	5, 709	....
March	....	26, 934	218, 482	113, 000	983	350
April	4, 016	30, 118	137, 749	129, 846	14, 200	....
May	11, 652	34, 540	125, 683	107, 094	25, 649	350
June	2, 916	23, 949	97, 799	124, 621	....	333
July	7, 906	21, 461	51, 666	84, 781	....	....
August	29, 633	39, 906	68, 100	82, 125	....	667
September	24, 883	59, 846	67, 516	131, 375	3, 463	1, 266
October	23, 800	88, 134	120, 132	71, 188	9, 166	1, 116
November	5, 601	77, 358	77, 134	62, 345	2, 100	....
December	14, 100	48, 210	91, 794	119, 875	733	333
Total	127, 373	485, 834	1, 430, 888	1, 192, 156	66, 760	4, 415

Total bushels grain	5, 007, 845
Number of bushels in summer	2, 968, 489
Number of bushels in winter	2, 039, 356
Average per month, summer	424, 070
Average per month, winter	407, 871

Wheat, wheat-flour, corn, oats, barley, and rye shipped eastward on the Erie Railway from Buffalo and Suspension Bridge each month of the year 1872.

[Prepared for the United States Senate Committee on Transportation.]

Months.	Wheat.	Wheat-flour.	Corn.	Oats.	Barley.	Rye.
	Bushels.	*Barrels.*	*Bushels.*	*Bushels.*	*Bushels.*	*Bushels.*
January	38, 767	16, 723	804, 434	104, 601	30, 852	357
February	147, 709	8, 018	567, 683	28, 613	28, 005	....
March	85, 052	28, 979	449, 577	160, 572	49, 728	....
April	47, 317	55, 002	390, 905	262, 461	13, 255	....
May	50, 319	94, 079	1, 030, 146	233, 792	472	....
June	107, 005	107, 559	460, 395	529, 549	....	....
July	137, 080	68, 140	171, 113	372, 677	....	....
August	255, 741	81, 529	459, 848	388, 703	....	34
September	245, 978	124, 314	264, 196	524, 018	27, 074	1, 480
October	227, 445	172, 172	417, 624	429, 280	66, 543	2, 188
November	365, 373	105, 368	187, 803	202 957	135, 885	718
December	155, 517	23, 539	143, 214	208, 951	31, 611	2, 864
Total	1, 863, 303	885, 422	5, 346, 938	3, 446, 174	383, 425	7, 948

	Bushels.
Total number bushels grain	11, 047, 788
Total number barrels flour, 885,422, equal to	3, 984, 399
Total number bushels grain	15, 036, 187
Number bushels in summer	10, 688, 968
Number bushels in winter	4, 347, 219
Average per month, summer	1, 537, 793. 6
Average per month, winter	869, 443. 8

Statement of flour and grain of all kinds delivered at New York by the Pennsylvania Railroad Company during the year 1872.

[Prepared for the United States Senate Committee on Transportation.]

Months.	Flour, pounds.			Grain of all kinds, pounds.		
	From Pittsburgh and way points on Pennsylvania Railroad.	From way points between Philadelphia and New York.	Total.	From Pittsburgh and way points on Pennsylvania Railroad.	From way points between Philadelphia and New York.	Total.
January	6, 157, 513	202, 000	6, 359, 513	28, 584, 437	304, 000	28, 888, 437
February	4, 178, 020	203, 000	4, 381, 020	22, 047, 522	306, 000	22, 353, 522
March	6, 496, 351	201, 414	6, 697, 765	27, 104, 393	305, 236	27, 409, 629
April	8, 717, 546	351, 847	9, 069, 393	37, 679, 792	151, 684	37, 831, 476
May	8, 749, 160	157, 110	8, 906, 270	18, 540, 146	24, 269	18, 564, 415
June	8, 881, 271	116, 835	8, 998, 106	14, 621, 374	1, 500	14, 622, 874
July	5, 303, 758	120, 050	5, 423, 808	7, 019, 524	3, 250	7, 022, 774
August	5, 467, 328	131, 400	5, 598, 728	18, 581, 532	4, 260	18, 585, 792
September	8, 186, 554	96, 910	8, 283, 464	12, 808, 002	4, 694	12, 812, 696
October	9, 797, 962	138, 082	9, 936, 044	3, 314, 619	13, 185	3, 327, 804
November	12, 233, 669	295, 385	12, 529, 054	2, 814, 036	94, 010	2, 908, 046
December	9, 682, 360	1, 148, 924	10, 831, 284	4, 063, 241	104, 236	4, 167, 477
Total	93, 851, 492	3, 162, 957	97, 014, 449	197, 178, 618	1, 316, 324	198, 494, 942

NOTE.—Pennsylvania Railroad records have not been kept to show, in totals, the shipments of different kinds of grain separately.

Statement of flour and grain of all kinds delivered at Philadelphia by the Pennsylvania Railroad Company during the year 1872.

[Prepared for the United States Senate Committee on Transportation.]

Months.	Flour, pounds.			Grain of all kinds, pounds.		
	From Pittsburgh.	From Erie and way points.	Total.	From Pittsburgh.	From Erie and way points.	Total.
January	4, 710, 365	4, 340, 438	9, 050, 803	10, 517, 569	11, 888, 635	22, 406, 204
February	3, 007, 851	4, 578, 069	7, 585, 920	17, 515, 914	16, 518, 111	34, 034, 025
March	2, 749, 431	6, 214, 579	8, 964, 010	14, 001, 664	10, 076, 668	24, 078, 332
April	7, 271, 199	3, 197, 222	10, 468, 421	17, 484, 682	10, 719, 372	28, 204, 054
May	4, 854, 720	5, 146, 082	10, 000, 802	37, 952, 485	14, 620, 993	52, 573, 478
June	3, 749, 759	6, 577, 668	10, 327, 427	49, 219, 348	10, 279, 563	59, 498, 911
July	4, 978, 388	4, 464, 731	9, 443, 119	48, 000, 916	6, 914, 778	54, 915, 694
August	3, 169, 053	4, 170, 934	7, 339, 987	42, 985, 986	9, 617, 979	52, 603, 965
September	3, 264, 805	4, 580, 442	7, 845, 247	46, 937, 694	14, 634, 362	61, 572, 056
October	5, 748, 448	6, 548, 019	12, 296, 467	43, 158, 571	15, 063, 220	58, 221, 791
November	6, 220, 220	6, 016, 580	12, 236, 800	19, 066, 451	15, 210, 715	34, 277, 166
December	4, 331, 885	4, 217, 337	8, 549, 222	12, 416, 566	10, 139, 668	22, 556, 234
Total	54, 056, 124	60, 052, 101	114, 108, 225	359, 257, 846	145, 684, 064	504, 941, 910

NOTE.—Pennsylvania Railroad records have not been kept to show, in totals, the shipments of different kinds of grain separately.

Statement of shipments of flour and grain of all kinds from Pittsburgh and Erie, eastwardly, by the Pennsylvania Railroad Company, during the year 1872.

[Prepared for the United States Senate Committee on Transportation.]

Months.	Flour, pounds.			Grain of all kinds, pounds.		
	From Pittsburgh.	From Erie.	Total.	From Pittsburgh.	From Erie.	Total.
January	12, 887, 887	3, 234, 647	16, 122, 534	43, 175, 358	15, 807, 410	58, 982, 768
February	7, 896, 491	1, 975, 107	9, 871, 598	45, 550, 615	16, 714, 834	62, 265, 449
March	10, 193, 598	2, 616, 217	12, 809, 815	37, 741, 783	11, 768, 910	49, 510, 693
April	18, 735, 146	2, 427, 683	21, 162, 829	61, 701, 153	24, 072, 826	85, 773, 979
May	16, 972, 649	7, 196, 675	24, 169, 324	64, 644, 840	60, 474, 820	125, 119, 660
June	14, 256, 566	9, 177, 967	23, 434, 533	69, 206, 277	35, 010, 098	104, 216, 375
July	12, 038, 381	6, 227, 977	18, 266, 358	63, 794, 706	18, 622, 077	82, 416, 783
August	12, 865, 542	6, 453, 086	19, 318, 628	70, 745, 158	38, 576, 015	109, 321, 173
September	14, 683, 882	6, 745, 963	21, 429, 845	69, 960, 136	37, 608, 278	107, 568, 414
October	18, 863, 131	9, 097, 681	27, 960, 812	57, 892, 108	32, 800, 206	90, 692, 314
November	22, 528, 194	9, 095, 760	31, 623, 954	34, 620, 123	40, 518, 644	75, 138, 767
December	16, 406, 391	7, 586, 169	23, 992, 560	22, 568, 005	31, 206, 585	53, 774, 590
Total.	178, 327, 858	71, 834, 932	250, 162, 790	641, 600, 262	363, 180, 703	1, 004, 780, 965

NOTE.—No records have been kept showing shipments of different kinds of grain separately.

Wheat, wheat-flour, corn, oats, barley, and rye delivered at Baltimore by the Baltimore and Ohio Railroad each month during the year 1872.

[Prepared for the United States Senate Committee on Transportation.]

Months.	Flour.	Wheat.	Corn.	Oats.	Barley.	Rye.
	Barrels.	*Bushels.*	*Bushels.*	*Bushels.*	*Bushels.*	*Bushels.*
January	48, 930	7, 500	466, 681	35, 625	2, 458	4, 500
February	53, 670	11, 167	348, 750	47, 687	....	3, 321
March	52, 793	11, 533	278, 541	22, 375	1, 833	214
April	60, 940	22, 367	195, 000	82, 437	1, 750	786
May	56, 112	11, 167	587, 391	161, 625	83	1, 536
June	48, 458	32, 167	780, 393	226, 750	....	357
July	29, 888	28, 067	443, 107	164, 563	....	2, 268
August	83, 542	48, 133	288, 143	190, 813	....	1, 357
September	103, 664	47, 700	195, 429	198, 000	2, 292	3, 893
October	91, 196	55, 567	304, 678	114, 061	9, 083	1, 107
November	99, 876	69, 667	116, 143	76, 687	3, 750	1, 536
December	57, 482	47, 400	228, 607	55, 250	7, 583	643
Total	786, 551	391, 835	4, 232, 863	1, 375, 872	28, 832	21, 518

Total bushels of grain 9,590,399

Grain and flour delivered at Cairo, Ill., by the Illinois Central Railroad during the years 1872 *and* 1873.

[Prepared for the United States Senate Committee on Transportation.]

Grain.	1872.	1873.	Grain.	1872.	1873.
Wheat..........bushels..	393, 460	432, 340	Rye...........bushels..	21, 620	26, 430
Wheat-flour.....barrels..	258, 127	137, 225	Oats...............do....	1, 998, 670	1, 566, 790
Corn............bushels..	1, 452, 100	1, 747, 360	Barley............do....	2, 000	1, 480

Statement showing amount of flour and grain forwarded from Nashville south—June 30, 1872, to June 30, 1873.

[Prepared for the United States Senate Committee on Transportation.]

Route.	Flour.	Wheat.	Corn.	Other grain.
	Barrels.	*Bushels.*	*Bushels.*	*Bushels.*
Via Louisville and Nashville and Great Southern Railroad, via Decatur.	54, 029	33, 568	785, 342	111, 545
Via Nashville and Chattanooga Railroad:				
From Nashville proper	24, 067	54, 089	568, 941	22, 059
From Louisville and Nashville Railroad	64, 212	32, 639	304, 897	86, 147
From Nashville and Northwestern Railroad	17, 155	35, 333	661, 110	268, 122
From Saint Louis and Iron Mountain Railroad	54, 125	86, 493	507, 952	222, 810
From Saint Louis and Southeastern Railroad	17, 367	36, 370	356, 464	143, 006
Total	230, 955	278, 492	3, 184, 706	853, 689

ALBERT FINK,
Vice-President Louisville and Nashville and Great Southern Railroad.

STATEMENT IN REGARD TO THE CHESAPEAKE AND OHIO CANAL, BY A. P. GORMAN, PRESIDENT.

OFFICE OF CHESAPEAKE AND OHIO CANAL COMPANY,
Annapolis, March 23, 1874.

To the Committee on Transportation-Routes to the Seaboard, United States Senate:

GENTLEMEN: We beg to present to your honorable consideration, the following condensed statement of the advantages possessed by the Chesapeake and Ohio Canal, and the feasibility of its extension to the Ohio River as a *great central water-line* to unite the valley of the Mississippi with the Atlantic sea-board.

The charter of this company was granted in 1824, by the State of Virginia, and ratified by the States of Maryland and Pennsylvania and by the Congress of the United States.

The surveys were made by the engineers of the General Government, under the direction of the United States Board of Internal Improvement.

The original design contemplated a canal of small dimensions, but the board of engineers, considering this to be the great central line of communication between the East and the West, advised its construction on a much larger scale, commensurate with its importance as a national highway.

Enlarged dimensions were also recommended by the committees of Congress, and adopted by the company, controlled as it was by the United States and the District cities, and the legislation of Congress strongly encouraged the company to expect that the national Treasury would supply a due portion of the requisite means for its completion to the Ohio River.

One million dollars was subscribed to the capital stock of the company by the United States, and a like amount by the city of Washington, but the assistance of the General Government was limited to the one subscription.

Notwithstanding the reasonable expectations of the company of further aid from the General Government, the work had so far progressed upon the enlarged plan that the State of Maryland was compelled to furnish the greater part of the sum necessary for its completion to Cumberland, relying, as she always has, that the original design of completing the canal to the Ohio River would be carried out by further subscriptions by Congress.

The board of engineers reported upon the work in three divisions:

First. From the city of Washington to Cumberland, at the foot of the Alleghany slope.

Second. From Cumberland across the Summit to the mouth of Castleman's River.

Third. Thence to Pittsburg, a total distance of 341 miles.

From Pittsburg, Lake Erie may be reached by a canal of 119 miles.

The first division extending from Washington to Cumberland, a distance of 184½ miles, has been constructed upon the enlarged dimensions, at a cost of about $11,000,000, and is now in successful operation.

From Washington to Harper's Ferry the width of water-surface is 60 feet. From that point to Cumberland it is 54 feet, and the depth throughout is 6 feet.

Upon this division there are 74 locks, 100 feet long between the gates and 15 feet wide, admitting boats of 135 tons burden.

The capacity of this canal, with its present dimensions, for a season of navigation of nine months is not less than 4,000,000 tons per annum.

The second or mountain division was surveyed in great detail by the United States engineers in 1824 and '25, who examined and reported upon two routes, one by way of Savage River and Deep Creek, and a second by Wills Creek and Castleman's River.

This latter route, leaving Cumberland by the Valley of Wills Creek ascends that stream 29 miles to the Summit tunnel, 4 miles in length, designed to pierce the main divide between the waters of the Potomac and those of the Ohio at an elevation of 1,972 feet above tide.

The canal emerging from the tunnel into the waters of Castleman's follows that stream to its junction with the Youghiogheny a distance of 35⅝ miles.

The second route reported upon by the United States engineers and called the Deep Creek route, follows from Cumberland the north branch of the Potomac to the mouth of Savage; thence by Savage River and Crabtree Creek to the Summit level, distant 45 miles from Cumberland. The tunnel on this line will be but 1⅛ miles in length, although at an elevation higher by 400 feet than that on the Wills Creek route. The summit-level is 13 miles in length, and from its western end the canal follows Deep Creek and the Youghiogheny to the mouth of Castleman's, a distance of 31 miles. The total distance from Cumberland being 89⅝ miles, or 19⅝ miles longer than the Wills Creek route.

Of these two routes that by Wills Creek alone is estimated, the cost being placed at $10,028,122.

The western division, 85¼ miles in length, reaches from the mouth of Castleman's River to Pittsburgh, and was estimated by General Bernard to cost $4,170,223, making the total estimated cost of the canal from Cumberland to Pittsburgh, $14,198,345.

As these surveys and estimates were made in 1825, and for a canal of 48 feet in width, the cost of constracting a canal of the dimensions of the eastern division would be increased; in addition to which, the construction of a railroad up the valley of Wills Creek renders the construction of a canal upon this route more difficult and expensive.

We should, however, here remark that the estimate of cost and other matters reported upon by the board of United States engineers were found, in the construction of the eastern division, to be remarkably accurate, the actual cost of work not having exceeded the estimate; and with the same conditions we are convinced that their estimate for the remaining portions of the line would be found to be equally reliable.

It is proper, however, to say that since the surveys of 1824–'25, that portion of the western division which extends from Pittsburgh, up the Monongahela, to the mouth of the Youghiogheny, has been made good slack-water navigation, and a company is now incorporated to improve the Youghiogeny by locks and dams as far up as Connellsville, at the mouth of Castleman's River, and even to Ohiopyle Falls, a total distance of sixty-six miles from Pittsburgh, leaving but *ninety* miles of canal to be constructed. In view of these facts, Congress at its last session made a small appropriation, only sufficient to make an examination of an intermediate line to those surveyed in 1824–'25, the survey being in charge of Colonel Sedgwick, under the general direction of Colonel Merrill, of the United States Engineer Corps, who reports that he examined the Savage River route which was explored by instrumental recannaissance in 1873, and is a continuation of the navigable feeder designed to follow the Deep Creek route to the mouth of Savage River. It turns off from that route at the mouth of Crabtree Creek and follows the Savage River, bearing nearly north, for 8 miles, to the mouth of Blue Lick Creek, and thence eastward, 3 miles, to the summit-tunnel level. This tunnel would be 5 miles long, and lead directly into the Castleman's River at Pleacher's Narrows, at the place where the supply reservoir for the Wills Creek route would now be located. This tunnel would have an elevation of 2,100 feet above tide, and be 128 feet higher than the Wills Creek Summit tunnel. Thence the route lies in the valley of Castleman's River for 12 miles to the mouth of Flaugherty Creek, joining on to the main line. This route is longer than the Wills Creek route, but the cost, as compared with the Wills Creek route, is very nearly the same.

The estimated cost of the construction of the canal by the route examined by Colonel Sedgwick, with a tunnel of five miles in length, of sufficient width for the passage of boats in both directions, is $19,900,000, and he reports, as did the board of United States engineers, in 1824–'25, that the water-supply is ample, as the Catchment basin of the Castleman's River above the western end of the Savage Summit tunnel is about twelve miles long and five or six miles wide, equal to, say, sixty square miles. Taking the annual rain-fall as an average of that of record for a long series of years at Carlisle, Gettysburgh, and Pittsburgh, at Marietta and Portsmouth, Ohio, and the higher mountain region should be somewhat greater, we get an annual rain-fall of 38 inches. If but one-third of this rain-fall should be conserved in reservoirs, there would be stored 1,965,632,000 cubic feet of water.

The daily consumption and loss of water by passing 180 boats over the Summit, allowing for loss by filtration and evaporation, as given by the best authorities, would be about 3,500,000 cubic feet, and the annual consumption in a period of ten months, 1,150,000,000 cubic feet, less than 60 per cent. of the quantity saved, or only 20 per cent. of the total rain-fall.

The daily consumption of water is for, say, one hundred boats passing the Summit in twenty-four hours, 2,500,000 cubic feet, equal to 29 cubic feet per second. The average daily supply of the stream at the Pleacher's Narrows, the place where the Savage River line would enter the valley, taken from gauges of March and June, is at the rate of 58 cubic feet per second, or twice the quantity required.

A reservoir-site has been surveyed at this place, Pleacher's Narrows, to store water for the dry months of July, August, and September, during a portion of which time the minimum supply of the stream is about 18 cubic feet per second.

This reservoir has a capacity of 126,333,780 cubic feet. The demands of the canal, including all losses by evaporation and filtration, are, as above, 2,500,000 cubic feet per day, and the daily influx to the reservoir not less than 1,500,000 cubic feet by the minimum gauge of 18 cubic feet per second, leaving to be supplied from the reservoir daily 1,000,000 cubic feet, which would not exhaust the supply in less than 126 days, or four months and six days. There are favorable conditions for another large reservoir at the crossing of the National Road over Castleman's River, near Grantsville, about three miles farther up. The conditions for feeding the summit-level of the Savage River route are particularly favorable in that the tunnel would have its western approach immediately at the site of the reservoir, and at the same level, saving from 300,000 to 400,000 cubic feet of water daily.

The slope of the canal leading down from the Summit would receive feed-water from the Savage River, within three miles of the Summit; and again at the mouth of the Savage River from the main north branch of the Potomac; while on the western slope the canal would descend again to the bed of the stream at the mouth of Piney Run, and receive the full supply of the Castleman's River. Auxiliary reservoirs are quite practicable on Meadow Run and Piney Run, and at convenient intervals in the valley of the Castleman's from the main stream and its tributaries.

THE BENEFITS OF THE EXTENSION.

The extension of this canal by the Wills Creek route would bring it three miles nearer the Cumberland coal-fields, which now produce nearly three millions of tons of coal annually, of which amount about one-third passes over the canal to tide-water, notwithstanding the competition between it and the railroad lines, who control the only means of transportation between the mines and the canal.

The extension by the Wills Creek route would touch within three or four miles of the Salisbury coal-basin, next west of the Cumberland basin, lying in the valley of the Castleman's, together with the coal-fields, mining and manufacturing interests of the Youghiogheny Valley, from which over three millions of tons annually is now shipped.

By the Savage River route, the extension would cut the southern end of the Cumberland coal-basin at Piedmont, twenty-eight miles west from Cumberland, (from which point no shipments of coal to the canal are now made because of railroad discrimination against the canal,) and traverse the Salisbury coal-basin from the summit-level to Myer's Mills, a distance of ten miles, while from the mouth of Savage River to Myer's Mills, a distance of thirty-six miles, the region abounds in coal, fire-clay of the best quality, and fine timber-lands, all of which have no outlet to market. In addition to which, the coal-basin of the Youghiogheny Valley and all the mining and manufacturing interests of this valley to Pittsburgh would be upon the banks of the proposed extension.

If this line were now completed for the sum herein estimated, (including the cost of the one hundred and eighty-four miles constructed and the ninety miles to be completed, and the completion of the slack-water navigation,) the entire cost would not exceed $35,000,000.

TRADE OF THE CANAL.

The annual tonnage of the Chesapeake and Ohio Canal, with its present imperfect connections from only a part of the Cumberland coal-basin, and its entire exclusion from the trade of the southern or Piedmont end of the basin, is one million tons. If extended, as proposed, through the coal-regions heretofore enumerated, the mines of which are now in active operation, and from which there is now being annually shipped over five million tons, at a cost of not less than $5 per ton, it is safe to say that at least three million tons of coal per annum alone would pass over this canal, at a reduction of not less than $2 per ton, thus saving to the consumers $6,000,000 per annum.

In addition to which, a very large tonnage could be reasonably expected from the agricultural and other productions of the West, which would insure from the very day of its completion a tonnage which, at moderate charges for tolls and transportation, would pay the interest upon the cost of the work and its maintenance in proper navigable condition.

As hereinbefore stated, the trade from the mines and products of the West is already created, in part passing through less favorable channels, is sufficient to engage the whole capacity of this canal, but the capacity of that portion now completed can be doubled by the expenditure of not more than one million of dollars, by lengthening its locks so as to admit the passage of two boats at once.

So favorable as are the conditions of this route, and so vast are the results to be attained by its completion at such a moderate cost, when compared with the benefits to be derived by the mining, manufacturing, agricultural, and other industrial interests, that we cannot too strongly urge upon your honorable committee a favorable consideration and recommendation to the Congress of the United States to grant sufficient aid to secure its completion at an early day.

In making this request we beg leave to remind you that the General Government is to some extent committed to this work and a stockholder to the amount of $2,500,000, and has invested large amounts of the Indian trust-funds in its bonds, all of which would be greatly increased in value by the completion of this work.

Respectfully submitted.

A. P. GORMAN,
President Chesapeake and Ohio Canal Company.

Table showing the quantities of wheat, wheat-flour, and corn received at and shipped from Montreal during a period of twenty-eight years.

[From the Report of the Board of Trade of Montreal.]

Years.	Flour.		Wheat.		Corn.	
	Receipts.	Shipments.	Receipts.	Shipments.	Receipts.	Shipments.
	Barrels.	*Barrels.*	*Bushels.*	*Bushels.*	*Bushels.*	*Bushels.*
1845	494, 295	....	344, 890	....	....	....
1846	582, 922	202, 821	439, 177	376, 852	....	....
1847	627, 137	271, 559	540, 957	560, 858	....	....
1848	546, 292	154, 908	482, 645	130, 187	44, 150	....
1849	485, 901	535, 593	357, 900	481, 768	50, 514	....
1850	483, 603	182, 988	345, 272	71, 359	51, 965	5, 719
1851	510, 738	255, 546	443, 477	129, 114	96, 930	26, 912
1852	565, 938	215, 524	724, 056	307, 656	92, 199	300
1853	595, 698	244, 400	906, 989	485, 609	83, 421	....
1854	484, 684	97, 724	531, 785	122, 636	651, 149	146, 748
1855	433, 011	53, 383	634, 317	45, 707	622, 208	28, 629
1856	589, 767	196, 731	1, 340, 705	774, 167	437, 154	158, 234
1857	573, 445	239, 301	1, 667, 724	859, 912	330, 084	28, 631
1858	669, 064	197, 742	1, 774, 464	669, 241	105, 087	14, 967
1859	575, 810	105, 973	635, 424	58, 005	71, 430	3, 015
1860	577, 196	277, 567	2, 622, 602	1, 645, 209	138, 214	24, 387
1861	1, 095, 339	605, 942	7, 738, 084	5, 584, 727	1, 565, 477	1, 477, 114
1862	1, 174, 602	597, 477	8, 534, 172	6, 500, 796	2, 661, 261	1, 774, 546
1863	1, 193, 286	616, 021	5, 509, 143	3, 741, 146	862, 534	638, 281
1864	858, 795	858, 071	4, 194, 217	2, 406, 531	158, 564	21, 974
1865	782, 216	637, 001	2, 648, 674	787, 938	934, 421	734, 849
1866	704, 376	575, 198	773, 208	83, 278	2, 117, 208	1, 870, 223
1867	738, 518	569, 021	2, 939, 295	1, 576, 528	891, 605	681, 708
1868	790, 311	683, 612	2, 426, 869	1, 081, 958	1, 086, 152	782, 497
1869	975, 295	966, 067	7, 462, 033	5, 595, 332	141, 982	108, 018
1870	1, 061, 273	975, 513	6, 508, 315	5, 973, 048	83, 656	6, 043
1871	951, 760	908, 844	8, 224, 805	7, 680, 834	3, 171, 757	2, 870, 998
1872	921, 973	832, 931	4, 665, 314	3, 818, 450	7, 656, 440	7, 546, 390

Statement showing date of the opening and closing of navigation on Lake Champlain, at Rouse's Point, during the years enumerated.

Year.	Opened.	Closed.	No. of days open.	Year.	Opened.	Closed.	No. of days open.
1859	April 5	Dec. 2	242	1867	April 21	Dec. 1	225
1860	April 16	Dec. 5	234	1868	April 7	Dec. 2	240
1861	April 3	Nov. 29	241	1869	April 23	Dec. 3	225
1862	April 24	Dec. 1	222	1870	April 18	Dec. 1	228
1863	April 11	Dec. 6	240	1871	Mar. 28	Nov. 27	244
1864	April 11	Dec. 9	243	1872	April 28	Nov. 30	217
1865	Mar. 31	Dec. 5	250	1873	April 27	....	....
1866	April 19	Dec. 13	239				

HENRY ORVIS,
Deputy Collector.

ROUSE'S POINT, *October* 13, 1873.

ESTIMATED YIELD OF WHEAT, CORN, RYE, OATS, AND BARLEY, FOR THE YEAR 1872, IN THE SEVERAL DIVISIONS OF THE UNITED STATES.

[The following table was prepared for this committee by Mr. J. R. Dodge, statistician of the Department of Agriculture.]

Divisions and States.	Wheat.	Corn.	Rye.	Oats.	Barley.
FIRST DIVISION.	*Bushels.*	*Bushels.*	*Bushels.*	*Bushels.*	*Bushels.*
Ohio	18, 203, 000	99, 351, 000	414, 000	27, 489, 000	1, 752, 000
Michigan	13, 936, 000	16, 987, 000	228, 000	9, 248, 000	554, 000
Indiana	19, 381, 000	85, 541, 000	410, 000	13, 080, 000	323, 000
Illinois	24, 711, 000	217, 628, 000	2, 211, 000	43, 122, 000	2, 073, 000
Wisconsin	22, 307, 000	21, 180, 000	1, 193, 000	16, 546, 000	1, 546, 000
Minnesota	23, 200, 000	7, 988, 000	75, 000	9, 459, 000	979, 000
Iowa	22, 080, 000	101, 989, 000	533, 000	19, 934, 000	2, 194, 000
Missouri	7, 695, 000	105, 741, 000	406, 000	16, 850, 000	251, 000
Kansas	2, 155, 000	29, 631, 000	81, 000	6, 084, 000	111, 000
Nebraska	2, 560, 000	7, 589, 000	12, 300	1, 667, 000	309, 000
Total	156, 228, 000	693, 625, 000	5, 563, 300	163, 479, 000	10, 092, 000
SECOND DIVISION.					
Maine	293, 000	1, 218, 000	30, 600	1, 741, 000	526, 000
New Hampshire	182, 000	1, 374, 000	43, 500	1, 127, 000	93, 000
Vermont	392, 000	1, 921, 000	62, 100	3, 509, 000	100, 000
Massachusetts	32, 000	1, 461, 000	235, 000	716, 000	118, 000
Rhode Island	....	295, 000	19, 300	163, 000	29, 300
Connecticut	37, 100	1, 705, 000	311, 000	1, 063, 000	23, 000
Total	936, 100	7, 974, 000	701, 500	8, 319, 000	889, 300
THIRD DIVISION.					
New York	6, 712, 000	19, 231, 000	1, 872, 000	31, 305, 000	6, 529, 000
New Jersey	1, 680, 000	12, 142, 000	454, 000	3, 076, 000	6, 500
Pennsylvania	11, 603, 000	43, 964, 000	3, 069, 000	31, 545, 000	453, 000
Delaware	550, 000	3, 289, 000	10, 700	318, 000	1, 700
Total	20, 545, 000	78, 626, 000	5, 405, 700	66, 244, 000	6, 990, 200
FOURTH DIVISION.					
Maryland	3, 957, 000	11, 002, 000	287, 000	1, 999, 000	9, 300
Virginia	6, 432, 000	18, 184, 000	443, 000	4, 089, 000	6, 600
North Carolina	3, 289, 000	24, 012, 000	342, 000	2, 860, 000	2, 300
Total	13, 678, 000	53, 198, 000	1, 072, 000	8, 948, 000	18, 200
FIFTH DIVISION.					
South Carolina	662, 000	10, 627, 000	50, 000	494, 000	5, 100
Georgia	3, 109, 000	23, 777, 000	108, 000	1, 814, 000	5, 100
Florida	....	1, 920, 000	....	104, 000	....
Alabama	1, 106, 000	22, 896, 000	22, 000	651, 000	....
Total	4, 877, 000	59, 220, 000	180, 000	3, 063, 000	10, 200

Estimated yield of wheat, corn, rye, oats, and barley, for the year 1872, &c.—Continued.

Divisions and States.	Wheat.	Corn.	Rye.	Oats.	Barley.
SIXTH DIVISION.	*Bushels.*	*Bushels.*	*Bushels.*	*Bushels.*	*Bushels.*
Mississippi	199, 000	21, 816, 000	16, 000	460, 000	....
Louisiana	....	10, 125, 000	....	40, 000	....
Arkansas	701, 000	17, 062, 000	39, 000	702, 000	....
Texas	1, 377, 000	27, 934, 000	54, 000	783, 000	51, 000
Total	2, 277, 000	76, 937, 000	109, 000	1, 985, 000	51, 000
SEVENTH DIVISION.					
Tennessee	10, 298, 000	46, 818, 000	222, 000	5, 103, 000	81, 000
Kentucky	7, 854, 000	63, 534, 000	1, 303, 000	6, 767, 000	243, 000
West Virginia	2, 712, 000	9, 905, 000	278, 000	2, 341, 000	53, 500
Total	20, 864, 000	120, 257, 000	1, 803, 000	14, 211, 000	377, 500
EIGHTH DIVISION.					
California	25, 600, 000	1, 400, 000	36, 000	2, 250, 000	7, 359, 000
Oregon	2, 406, 000	89, 000	3, 800	1, 790, 000	243, 000
Nevada	314, 000	13, 000	....	73, 000	402, 000
The Territories	2, 272, 000	1, 380, 000	14, 300	1, 385, 000	414, 000
Total	30, 592, 000	2, 882, 000	54, 100	5, 498, 000	8, 418, 000
Grand total	249, 997, 100	1, 092, 719, 000	14, 888, 600	271, 747, 000	26, 846, 400

NOTE.—Total number of bushels of grain of all kinds, 1,656,198,100.

J. R. DODGE,
Statistician.

STATISTICAL DIVISION, *May* 27, 1873.

Western States—area.

[Compiled from census.]

States.	Area.	States.	Area.
	Acres.		*Acres.*
Ohio	25, 576, 960	Minnesota	53, 459, 840
Michigan	36, 186, 240	Iowa	35, 228, 800
Indiana	21, 637, 760	Kansas	52, 043, 520
Illinois	35, 462, 400	Nebraska	48, 636, 800
Wisconsin	34, 511, 360	Missouri	41, 824, 000

Western States—population.

[Compiled from census.]

States.	Population.				
	1830.	1840.	1850.	1860.	1870.
Ohio	937, 903	1, 519, 467	1, 980, 329	2, 339, 911	2, 665, 260
Michigan	31, 639	212, 267	397, 654	749, 113	1, 184, 059
Indiana	343, 031	685, 866	988, 416	1, 350, 428	1, 680, 637
Illinois	157, 445	476, 183	851, 470	1, 711, 951	2, 539, 891
Wisconsin	....	30, 945	305, 391	775, 881	1, 054, 670
Minnesota	....	....	6, 077	172, 023	439, 706
Iowa	....	43, 112	192, 214	674, 913	1, 194, 020
Kansas	....	....	....	107, 206	364, 399
Nebraska	....	....	....	28, 841	122, 993
Missouri	140, 455	383, 702	682, 044	1, 182, 012	1, 721, 295
Total	1, 610, 473	3, 351, 542	5, 397, 518	9, 091, 879	12, 926, 930

Western States—improved land.

[Computed from census.]

States.	Improved land.		
	1850.	1860.	1870.
	Acres.	*Acres.*	*Acres.*
Ohio	9, 851, 493	12, 625, 394	14, 469, 113
Michigan	1, 929, 110	3, 476, 296	5, 096, 939
Indiana	5, 046, 543	8, 242, 183	10, 104, 279
Illinois	5, 039, 545	13, 096, 374	19, 329, 952
Wisconsin	1, 045, 499	3, 746, 167	5, 899, 343
Minnesota	5, 035	556, 250	2, 322, 162
Iowa	824, 682	3, 792, 792	9, 396, 467
Kansas	....	405, 468	1, 971, 003
Nebraska	....	118, 789	647, 031
Missouri	2, 938, 425	6, 246, 871	9, 130, 615

Western States—miles of railroad.

[Compiled from census.]

States.	Miles of railroad.				
	1830.	1840.	1850.	1860.	1870.
Ohio	....	36	575	2, 946	3, 538
Michigan	....	138	342	779	1, 638
Indiana	....	....	228	2, 163	3, 177
Illinois	....	22	111	2, 790	4, 823
Wisconsin	....	....	20	905	1, 525
Minnesota	....	....	....	....	1, 072
Iowa	....	....	....	655	2, 683
Kansas	....	....	....	....	1, 501
Nebraska	....	....	....	....	1, 812
Missouri	....	....	....	817	2, 000

Grain produced in Western States, 1830,* 1840, 1850, 1860, *and* 1870.

[Compiled from census.]

States.	1840.					1850.				
	Wheat.	Corn.	Rye.	Oats.	Barley.	Wheat.	Corn.	Rye.	Oats.	Barley.
	Bushels.	*Bushels.*	*Bushels.*	*Bushels.*	*Bushels.*	*Bushels.*	*Bushels.*	*Bushels.*	*Bushels.*	*Bushels.*
Ohio	16, 571, 661	33, 668, 144	814, 205	14, 393, 103	212, 440	14, 487, 351	59, 078, 695	425, 918	13, 472, 742	354, 358
Michigan	2, 157, 108	2, 277, 039	34, 236	2, 114, 051	127, 802	4, 925, 889	5, 641, 420	105, 871	2, 866, 056	75, 249
Indiana	4, 049, 375	28, 155, 887	129, 621	5, 981, 605	28, 015	6, 214, 458	52, 964, 363	78, 792	5, 655, 014	45, 483
Illinois	3, 335, 393	22, 634, 211	88, 197	4, 988, 008	82, 251	9, 414, 575	57, 646, 984	83, 364	10, 087, 241	110, 795
Wisconsin	212, 116	379, 359	1, 965	406, 514	11, 062	4, 286, 131	1, 988, 979	81, 253	3, 414, 672	209, 692
Iowa	154, 693	1, 406, 241	3, 792	216, 385	728	1, 530, 581	8, 656, 799	19, 916	1, 524, 345	25, 093
Minnesota						1, 401	16, 725	125	30, 582	1, 216
Kansas										
Nebraska										
Missouri	1, 037, 386	17, 332, 524	68, 608	2, 234, 947	9, 801	2, 981, 652	36, 214, 537	44, 268	5, 278, 079	9, 631

States.	1860.					1870.				
	Wheat.	Corn.	Rye.	Oats.	Barley.	Wheat.	Corn.	Rye.	Oats.	Barley.
	Bushels.	*Bushels.*	*Bushels.*	*Bushels.*	*Bushels.*	*Bushels.*	*Bushels.*	*Bushels.*	*Bushels.*	*Bushels.*
Ohio	15, 119, 047	73, 543, 190	683, 686	15, 409, 234	1, 663, 868	27, 882, 159	67, 501, 144	846, 890	25, 347, 549	1, 715, 221
Michigan	8, 336, 368	12, 444, 676	514, 129	4, 036, 980	307, 868	16, 265, 773	14, 086, 238	144, 508	8, 954, 466	834, 558
Indiana	16, 848, 267	71, 588, 919	463, 495	5, 317, 831	382, 245	22, 747, 222	51, 094, 538	457, 468	8, 590, 409	356, 262
Illinois	23, 837, 023	115, 174, 777	951, 281	15, 220, 029	1, 036, 338	30, 128, 405	129, 921, 395	2, 456, 578	42, 780, 851	2, 480, 400
Wisconsin	15, 657, 458	7, 517, 300	888, 544	11, 059, 260	707, 307	25, 606, 344	15, 033, 998	1, 325, 294	20, 180, 016	1, 645, 019
Iowa	8, 449, 403	42, 410, 646	183, 022	5, 887, 645	467, 103	29, 435, 692	68, 935, 065	505, 807	21, 005, 142	1, 960, 779
Minnesota	2, 186, 993	2, 941, 952	121, 411	2, 176, 002	109, 668	18, 866, 073	4, 743, 117	78, 088	10, 678, 261	1, 032, 024
Kansas	194, 173	6, 150, 727	3, 833	88, 325	4, 716	2, 391, 198	17, 025, 525	85, 207	4, 097, 925	98, 405
Nebraska	147, 867	1, 482, 080	2, 495	74, 502	1, 108	2, 125, 086	4, 736, 710	13, 532	1, 477, 562	216, 481
Missouri	4, 227, 586	72, 892, 157	293, 262	3, 680, 870	228, 502	14, 315, 926	66, 034, 075	559, 532	16, 578, 318	269, 240

* No data for 1830.

Table showing the time of opening and closing of the Sault Ste. Marie Canal during the last fifteen years.

Year.	Time of opening.	Time of closing.	No. of days open.
1858	April 19	November 20	216
1859	May 3	November 28	210
1860	May 11	December 1	205
1861	May 1	November 14	198
1862	April 27	November 27	215
1863	April 28	November 24	211
1864	May 2	December 4	217
1865	May 1	December 3	217
1866	May 5	December 2	212
1867	May 4	November 28	209
1868	May 2	November 30	213
1869	May 4	November 29	210
1870	April 29	December 1	217
1871	May 8	November 29	206
1872	May 10	November 27	202
Total			3,158

Respectfully submitted.

G. WEITZEL,
Major of Engineers.

Return showing the opening of navigation in the port of Quebec in each year from 1860 *to* 1873, *inclusive; also the date of closing thereof during that period.*

Year.	Arrivals from Montreal, steamers.	Arrivals from sea.	Sailed for sea.	Average time.
1860	April 26	April 28	November 26.	6 months 29 days.
1861	April 26	April 22	November 26.	7 months 5 days.
1862	April 30	April 16	November 29.	7 months.
1863	May 3	May 4	November 27.	6 months 25 days.
1864	April 21	April 27	November 30.	7 months 4 days.
1865	April 21	April 29	November 28.	7 months.
1866	April 26	April 28	December 1.	7 months 4 days.
1867	May 3	April 17	November 29.	7 months 13 days.
1868	April 28	April 23	November 28.	7 months 6 days.
1869	April 30	April 27	November 27.	7 months 1 day.
1870	April 25	April 16	December 2.	7 months 17 days.
1871	April 18	April 22	November 27.	7 months 9 days.
1872	May 6	April 30	November 26.	6 months 27 days.
1873	May 2	April 28		

River-rates of freight on corn from Saint Paul to Saint Louis during each month of the season of navigation, 1870 *to* 1873, *inclusive.*

Year.	Month.							
	April.	May.	June.	July.	Aug.	Sept.	Oct.	Nov.
	Cents per bu.	*Cents per bu.*	*Cents per bu.*	*Cents per bu.*	*Cents per bu.*	*Cents per bu.*	*Cents per bu.*	*Cents per bu.*
1870	14½	14½	16	17½	19	20⅓	23⅓	23⅓
1871	14½	14½	16	17½	19	20⅓	23⅓	23⅓
1872	14½	14½	16	17½	19	20⅓	23⅓	23$\frac{4}{3}$
1873	14½	14½	16	17½	19	20⅓	23⅓	23⅓

River-rates of freight on wheat from Saint Paul to Saint Louis during each month of the season of navigation, 1870 *to* 1873, *inclusive.*

Year.	Month.							
	April.	May.	June.	July.	Aug.	Sept.	Oct.	Nov.
	Cents per bu.	*Cents per bu.*	*Cents per bu.*	*Cents per bu.*	*Cents per bu.*	*Cents per bu.*	*Cents per bu.*	*Cents per bu.*
1870	15	15	16½	18	19½	21	24	24
1871	15	15	16½	18	19½	21	24	24
1872	15	15	16½	18	19½	21	24	24
1873	15	15	16½	18	19½	21	24	24

Average rate of freight on wheat and corn by rail from Saint Paul to Milwaukee each month during the years 1872 *and* 1873.

Month.	Freight on wheat, per bushel.		Freight on corn, per bushel.	
	1872.	1873.	1872.	1873.
	Cents.	*Cents.*	*Cents.*	*Cents.*
January	16	18	13¾	15¾
February	16	18	13¾	15¾
March	16	18	13¾	15¾
April	15	18	13	15¾
May	15	18	13	15¾
June	15	18	13	15¾
July	15	18	13	15¾
August	15	18	13	15¾
September	18	21	15¾	17
October	18	21	15¾	17
November	18	21	15¾	17
December	18	21	15¾	17

Quantity of wheat and corn shipped from Saint Paul to Du Luth each month during the years of 1872 *and* 1873.

Month.	Wheat, bushels.	
	1872.	1873.
January	....	....
February	....	....
March	....	....
April	....	....
May	90, 214	51, 879
June	122, 093	539, 935
July	88, 355	398, 300
August	96, 515	232, 953
September	183, 539	629, 674
October	403, 647	759, 752
November	345, 640	370, 388
December	....	....
Total	1, 330, 003	2, 982, 881

NOTE.—Very little corn shipped from Saint Paul. The freight on wheat from Saint Paul to Du Luth by rail was 15 cents per bushel during the years 1871 and 1872.

LETTER IN REGARD TO THE ERIE CANAL, ADDRESSED TO THE CHAIRMAN OF THE UNITED STATES SENATE COMMITTEE ON TRANSPORTATION, BY HON. F. A. ALBERGER, OF BUFFALO.

BUFFALO, *December*, 1873.

SIR: In accordance with my promise I herewith present my views upon the subject of cheapening transportation between the Great West and the seaboard.

Very respectfully, your obedient servant,

F. A. ALBERGER.

Hon. WM. WINDOM,
Chairman United States Senate Committee on Transportation Routes, &c.

The great interest now awakened in regard to the cost of transporting the productions of the interior to the seaboard promises to be of much value, and, under proper management, may produce very important results.

Complaints of excessive and extravagant rates have been prevailing for the past fifteen years, and have had reference more especially to the cereals of the Great West. The railroad-lines seize upon all articles of trade which are compact and easily handled, such as merchandise, beef, pork, lard, cheese, butter, flour, live stock, &c., leaving to the water-routes the more bulky and less-easily handled articles, as ores, coal, lumber, and grain.

Notwithstanding the rapid creation of new railroad-lines, and the increased facilities afforded by the old lines and in the water-routes, the means of transportation have not kept pace with the increased productions. Consequently, when an active demand arises, the prices of transportation rapidly advance, and very frequently the carrier, not the grower, reaps nearly all the advantage.

Supply and demand are great regulators, and no legislation can compel these elements to hold an equal and proper ratio with each other. When demand is light, the prices of the staples as well as freights are low; with an active demand, prices of both will increase.

The supply is steady, full, and overwhelming; the demand, irregular, uncertain, and though constantly increasing, bears no comparison to the increase of the former.

The importance of delivering to the exporting points the productions of our labor at as low a rate as possible cannot be overrated. If, by reason of cheap and fertile lands and cheap conveyances, we may be able to compete with foreign producers, and export such quantities commensurate with our increase, we shall have the gratifying results of providing satisfactory rewards for labor, and of adding to the permanent wealth of the country.

Our people have relations peculiar to themselves, and an understanding of their needs and necessities is a study of wider research and of greater import than ever demanded the attention and study of the statesmen of any lands.

The emigration from the remainder of the world brings to us all workers, nearly all producers, and this element of political economy—unknown to other countries—is a question worthy of consideration. The enormous and unparalleled additions of nearly half a million people the present year, with the probability that the tide has not yet reached its height, raise the point not only how to provide such labor for them, but also in what way it may best receive proper and adequate compensation.

Our production is far greater than the consumption at home and by exportation, and no system can be devised to increase home-consumption to equal present productions of the laborers now in the country aside from the great mass of immigrants being added thereto.

We must look for relief to the only possible source, the exportation of the products of our surplus labor. And to increase this, it is necessary to reduce the cost. In this effort each State has a duty to perform in the premises, but as each State, by acting in accordance with local demands, must render united action impossible, the needs of the hour will not have requisite attention.

The action of the President in calling the attention of Congress to this subject, the co-operation of the Senate in appointing a committee to examine and investigate the subject of cheap transportation, and the careful, thorough, and the elaborate examination of the committee, have invested this matter with a national indorsement. It is truly a national question, and the whole people are looking for and demanding national action.

For many strong and cogent reasons, the nation ought not to construct, own, or operate any means or lines of communication, it being contrary to its customs and usages, and in contravention of the almost united sentiment of the people, but the Government may lend and has lent its aid by lands and moneys as loans or as subsidies.

It is now believed that congressional action will be taken in this matter. Politics has entered into the arena, and its indorsement will be more effectual in obtaining early action than the necessities of the case or the writings or exertions of the ablest men in the commonwealth would accomplish in a quarter of a century.

This new phase in the question is very agreeable to the pioneers in this great work, who have for years been earnest and persistent in their efforts to solve the problem of cheap transportation. They welcome this new agent, that with invincible power is now marshaling forces to accomplish a great, worthy, and needed reformation.

It is fair and proper to assume that the desire to furnish *immediate relief* will necessarily lead to the improvement of the lines now in use, to add connecting-links when necessary, rather than to create or stimulate the construction of new lines requiring years for their completion. This line of action seems imperative, because it will furnish, at comparatively little cost, the immediate much-desired relief, and will meet with more general approval than the attempt to create new lines, which must be more or less speculative in their character, and which will require greater amounts of money than the people will be willing to give for speculative purposes. Unless there are some great natural advantages, or some most sure and speedy relief to be had, it would be manifestly improper for the Government to aid new routes which, when completed, would interfere with and seriously injure those that have been constructed by public or private enterprise.

Assuming the General Government may provide means for the purpose of cheapening transportation, the question arises, how shall they be best applied to accomplish desirable results?

Can it be done by railroads as cheaply as by water-routes? This proposition is not mooted on short lines, as railroads have absorbed all the trade and travel, and upon through-routes have taken all the light or easily moved articles. It is conceded by railroad experts that, at the present time, there is no profit on roads of heavy grade at a receipt of one cent per ton per mile, and hardly a reasonable profit at that rate on easy grades. This being the case, a bushel of wheat cannot be transported to New York City, Philadelphia, Boston, Portland or Baltimore, by rail, except at what is considered very extravagant rates. Taking Chicago as the central western distributing point, the distance to Baltimore is nine hundred and forty-two miles, (by their connecting-routes.) At the aforesaid rates it is equivalent to twenty-eight and one-quarter cents per bushel of wheat. To Philadelphia, eight hundred and twenty-three miles, equivalent to twenty-four and two-thirds cents per bushel. To Boston, ten hundred and thirty-eight miles, equaling thirty-one and one-quarter cents per bushel. To New York, nine hundred and eighty-five miles, equal to twenty-nine and one-half cents per bushel. To Portland, (via Canadian Grand Trunk Road,) eleven hundred and forty-five miles, equaling thirty-four and one-third cents per bushel.

It therefore seems self-evident that if railways could be required to carry grain at the aforesaid rates, there would be no visible and material assistance to be derived from that source.

Through nearly five months in the year, the water-routes north of Mason and Dixon's line are closed, or rendered practically inoperative by ice, and without some judicious regulations it is then in the power of railroad corporations, under an implied or actual agreement, to establish such rates as they may deem proper.

This point is one of material embarrassment, and presents the novel and difficult question of a controlment of the business of corporations by State or General Government.

The question is not of so great practical importance as generally believed, because unless there should be a very great rise in the values of property, and an active demand during the winter months, (especially in grain,) the owners could not afford to send it in very large quantities by rail; and if the price were greatly enhanced, then there would be no serious complaint of cost of carriage.

During the season of navigation the great bulk of the cereals of the West, and especially those destined for exportation, find their way by the lakes, canals, and rivers to the seaboard.

The rates charged by the carriers, upon this system of transportation, are regulated entirely by the demand for services; the competition is close, necessarily sharp, and not governed by combination, nor from the numerous parties having many adverse interests is it possible to establish any system for the regulation of carrier's charges; it is and must be left entirely under competition.

The question now recurs, can the rates of transportation be reduced upon water-routes?

There are obstructions to navigation upon the lakes, which, if removed, would have a vast influence in this direction.

This could be accomplished by deepening the channel in Lake Saint Clair flats, and also the upper and lower ends of the lake. During the past season, the water upon the flats averaged about fourteen and one-half feet. Removing obstructions known as the "lime-kilns," in Detroit River, and at the mouth of the same off "Bar Point," would also tend to reduce the cost of transportation.

The cost of these improvements would not involve a very large sum of money, and it is not easy to form a fair estimate without maps and surveys. The obstructions named are all that are in the way of improved navigation from Chicago to Buffalo. The harbors on the lakes would require deepening to prepare them for the large vessels.

Good authorities claim that by removing all obstructions, so as to furnish twenty feet of water, vessels from two thousand to twenty-five hundred tons would navigate the lakes and carry grain with a profit at three to three and a half cents per bushel, provided that they should find return-cargoes proportionably as plentiful as they now are.

Mr. Walker, the statistician of the New York Produce Exchange, states that "the rate on the lakes during the six years ending with 1872, averaged, from Chicago to Buffalo, seven $\frac{69}{100}$ cents per sixty pounds."

There cannot be much doubt that herein lies the solution of the problem of cheap transportation on the lakes, and all parties concede that this work is within the legitimate powers and duties of the National Government, and that it is of such great moment and import as to demand prompt attention.

The point known as the Lime Kilns is in Canadian territory. This is not mentioned as being in any respect a barrier to the valuable work proposed to be done. The proposed improvements, when made, will encourage the more general use of large vessels. The larger the vessel the cheaper the cost of carriage. Of course, there is a maximum size beyond which there is neither safety nor profit; but this condition seems not to have been reached, as a very large proportion of the new tonnage is of sail-craft having the greatest carrying capacity yet known in the history of the lakes.

The great mass of the products of the nation finds its way to its commercial center, the city of New York. The breadstuffs of the West are not exempted. In the summer season they are sent through the lakes to the Erie Canal at Buffalo, through the canal and Hudson River to the great emporium. This seems to determine a very important question, that this route is now the cheapest and best adapted for the purpose, for if this were not true the property would not take this direction. The shipper and owner send their goods where it may secure the best pecuniary results, and one-half of one cent per bushel would control the destination of all the grains exported from the country.

An examination of the following tables will show that this route is the *favored* and *most valuable one to the producer and consumer*, and, to fully comprehend the value of the tables, it should be recollected that the canals are open but seven months, and the railroads are active the entire year; further, the tables are made by the auditor of the canal department of the State of New York, and represent the movement of property upon the canals of the State. The tolls collected upon all the canals in the year 1872 were $3,072,411, all of which, with the exception of $323,500, was received from the Erie Canal.

MOVEMENT OF TRADE.

The auditor submits a series of comparative statements of the movements of freight on the two railways connecting New York with Lake Erie, and the State canals, during the last seventeen years, showing the tons carried each year, the total movement or number of tons moved one mile, and the freight and tolls received therefrom.

This statement shows the tons of total movement on the lines named for seventeen years, the freight paid to the roads, and the tolls paid to the State, and carrier's charge on the canals with the tolls:

Railroads and canals.	Year.	Tons moved one mile.	Freight and tolls.	Average per ton for one mile.
New York Central Railroad	1856	145, 733, 678	$4, 328, 041 10	2. 97 cents.
New York and Erie Railroad	1856	183, 458, 046	4, 545, 782 00	2. 48 cents.
Canals	1856	592, 009, 603	6, 573, 225 00	1. 11 cents.
Total	......	921, 201, 327	15, 447, 048 00	1. 67 cents.
New York Central Railroad	1857	145, 773, 791	4, 559, 276 00	3. 13 cents.
New York and Erie Railroad	1857	167, 100, 850	4, 097, 610 00	2. 45 cents.
Canals	1857	484, 750, 864	3, 876, 000 00	7. 99 mills.
Total	......	797, 725, 505	42, 532, 886 00	1. 57 cents.
New York Central Railroad	1858	142, 691, 178	3, 700, 270 44	2. 59 cents.
New York and Erie Railroad	1858	165, 895, 635	3, 843, 310 77	3. 32 cents.
Canals	1858	564, 842, 095	4, 502, 437 00	7. 97 mills.
Total	......	873, 428, 908	12, 046, 018 21	1. 38 cents.
New York Central Railroad	1859	157, 136, 000	3, 337, 148 00	2. 13 cents.
New York and Erie Railroad	1859	147, 127, 039	3, 195, 869 00	2. 17 cents.
Canals	1859	544, 309, 072	3, 665, 806 00	6. 72 mills.
Total	......	848, 572, 111	10, 198, 823 00	1. 19 cents.
New York Central Railroad	1860	199, 231, 392	4, 095, 934 00	2. 06 cents.
New York and Erie Railroad	1860	214, 084, 395	3, 884, 343 00	1. 84 cents.
Canals	1860	809, 524, 596	8, 049, 450 00	9. 94 mills.
Total	......	1, 222, 840, 383	16, 029, 727 00	1. 31 cents.
New York Central Railroad	1861	237, 392, 974	4, 644, 449 00	1. 96 cents.
New York and Erie Railroad	1861	251, 350, 127	4, 351, 464 00	1. 73 cents.
Canals	1861	863, 623, 507	9, 369, 378 00	1. 08 cents.
Total	......	1, 352, 366, 608	18, 365, 291 00	1. 36 cents.
New York Central Railroad	1862	296, 963, 492	6, 607, 331 00	2. 22 cents.
Erie Railway	1862	351, 092, 285	6, 642, 915 00	1. 89 cents.
Canals	1862	1, 123, 548, 430	10, 780, 431 00	9. 59 mills.
Total	......	1, 771, 604, 207	24, 030, 677 00	1. 36 cents.
New York Central Railroad	1863	312, 195, 796	7, 498, 509 00	2. 40 cents.
Erie Railway	1863	403, 670, 861	8, 432, 234 00	2. 09 cents.
Canals	1863	1, 034, 130, 023	9, 065, 005 00	8. 76 mills.
Total	......	1, 719, 996, 680	24, 995, 748 00	1. 45 cents.
New York Central Railroad	1864	314, 081, 410	8, 542, 370 00	2. 75 cents.
Erie Railway	1864	422, 013, 644	9, 855, 087 00	2. 31 cents.
Canals	1864	871, 335, 150	10, 039, 609 00	1. 15 cents.
Total	......	1, 607, 430, 204	28, 438, 066 00	1. 77 cents.
New York Central Railroad	1865	264, 993, 626	8, 776, 028 00	3. 31 cents.
Erie Railway	1865	388, 557, 213	10, 726, 264 00	2. 76 cents.
Canals	1865	843. 915, 779	8, 605, 961 00	1. 10 cents.
Total	......	1, 497, 466, 618	28, 108, 253, 00	1. 85 cents.
New York Central Railroad	1866	331, 075, 547	9, 671, 920 00	2. 92 cents.
Erie Railway	1866	478, 485, 772	11, 611, 023 00	2. 45 cents.
Canals	1866	1, 012, 448, 034	10, 160, 051 00	1. 00 cents.
Total	......	1, 822, 209, 353	31, 442, 994 00	1. 73 cents.
New York Central Railroad	1867	362, 180, 606	9, 151, 750 00	2. 53 cents.
Erie Railway	1867	549, 888, 422	11, 204, 689 00	2. 04 cents.
Canals	1867	958, 362, 953	8, 663, 119 00	. 90 cents.
Total	......	1, 870, 431, 981	29, 019, 558 00	1. 55 cents.
New York Central Railroad	1868	366, 199, 786	9, 491, 427 00	2. 59 cents.
Erie Railway	1868	595, 699, 225	11, 425, 739 00	1. 92 cents.
Canals	1868	1, 033, 751, 258	9, 012, 659 00	. 88 cents.
Total	......	1, 995, 650, 279	29, 929, 825 00	1. 49 cents.

Railroads and canals.	Year.	Tons moved one mile.	Freight and tolls.	Average per ton for one mile.
New York Central Railroad	1869	474, 419, 726	10, 457, 582 00	2. 20 cents.
Erie Railway	1869	817, 829, 190	13, 046, 804 00	1. 60 cents.
Canals	1869	919, 153, 611	8, 492, 131 00	. 92 cents.
Total	......	2, 211, 402, 527	31, 996, 517 00	1. 57 cents.
New York Central Railroad	1870	769, 087, 777	14, 327, 418 00	1. 86 cents.
Erie Railway	1870	898, 862, 718	12, 328, 027 00	1. 37 cents.
Canals	1870	904, 351, 572	7, 552, 988 00	. 83 cents.
Total	......	2, 572, 302, 067	34, 208, 433 00	1. 33 cents.
New York Central Railroad	1871	888, 327, 865	14, 647, 580 00	1. 65 cents.
Erie Railway	1871	897, 446, 728	13, 232, 235 00	1. 47 cents.
Canals	1871	1, 050, 104, 125	10, 779, 887, 00	1. 02 cents.
Total	......	2, 835, 878, 718	38, 659, 702 00	1. 36 cents.
New York Central Railroad	1872	1, 020, 908, 885	16, 259, 647 00	1. 69 cents.
Erie Railway	1872	950, 708, 902	14, 509, 745 00	1. 52 cents.
Canals	1872	1, 048, 575, 911	10, 648, 711 00	1. 02 cents.
Total	......	3, 020, 193, 698	41, 418, 103 00	1. 37 cents.

The following table shows the separate tonnage of the canals and two railroads, and the aggregate of both for twenty years, from 1853 to 1872, inclusive:

Canals and railroads.	Tons.	Tons.
	1853.	1854.
New York canals	4, 247, 853	4, 165, 862
New York Central Railroad	360, 000	549, 804
New York and Erie Railroad	631, 039	743, 250
Total	5, 238, 892	5, 458, 916
	1854.	1855.
New York canals	4, 165, 862	4, 022, 617
New York Central Railroad	549, 804	670, 073
New York and Erie Railroad	743, 250	842, 048
Total	5, 458, 915	5, 534, 738
	1855.	1856.
New York canals	4, 022, 617	4, 116, 084
New York Central Railroad	670, 073	776, 112
New York and Erie Railroad	842, 048	943, 215
Total	5, 545, 738	5, 835, 409
	1856.	1857.
New York canals	4, 116, 082	3, 344, 061
New York Central Railroad	776, 112	838, 791
New York and Erie Railroad	943, 215	978, 066
Total	5, 835, 409	5, 160, 918
	1857.	1858.
New York canals	3, 344, 061	3, 665, 102
New York Central Railroad	838, 791	765, 407
New York and Erie Railroad	978, 066	816, 954
Total	5, 160, 918	5, 247, 553
	1858.	1859.
New York canals	3, 665, 192	3, 781, 684
New York Central Railroad	765, 407	834, 319
New York and Erie Railroad	816, 954	869, 073
Total	5, 247, 553	5, 485, 076
	1859.	1860.
New York canals	3, 781, 684	4, 650, 214
New York Central Railroad	834, 319	1, 028, 183
New York and Erie Railroad	868, 073	1, 139, 554
Total	5, 485, 076	6, 817, 951

Canals and railroads.	Tons.	Tons.
	1860.	1861.
New York canals	4, 650, 214	4, 507, 635
New York Central Railroad	1, 028, 183	1, 167, 302
New York and Erie Railroad	1, 139, 554	1, 263, 418
Total	6, 817, 951	6, 928, 355
	1861.	1862.
New York canals	4, 507, 635	5, 598, 785
New York Central Railroad	1, 167, 302	1, 387, 433
Erie Railway	1, 253, 418	1, 632, 955
Total	6, 928, 355	8, 619, 173
	1862.	1863.
New York canals	5, 598, 785	5, 557, 692
New York Central Railroad	1, 387, 433	1, 449, 604
Erie Railway	1, 632, 955	1, 815, 096
Total	8, 619, 173	8, 822, 392
	1863.	1864.
New York canals	5, 557, 692	4, 852, 941
New York Central Railroad	1, 449, 604	1, 557, 148
Erie Railway	1, 815, 096	2, 170, 798
Total	8, 822, 392	8, 580, 887
	1864.	1865.
New York canals	4, 852, 941	4, 729, 654
New York Central Railroad	1, 557, 148	1, 275, 299
Erie Railway	2, 170, 798	2, 234, 350
Total	8, 580, 887	8, 239, 303
	1865.	1866.
New York canals	4. 729, 654	5, 775, 220
New York Central Railroad	1, 275, 299	1, 602, 197
Erie Railway	2, 234, 350	3, 242, 792
Total	8, 239, 303	10, 620, 209
	1866.	1867.
New York canals	5, 775, 220	5, 688, 325
New York Central Railroad	1, 602, 197	1, 667, 926
Erie Railway	3, 242, 792	3, 484, 546
Total	10, 620, 209	10, 840, 797
	1867.	1868.
New York canals	5, 688, 325	6, 442, 225
New York Central Railroad	1, 667, 926	1, 846, 599
Erie Railway	3, 484, 546	4, 908, 243
Total	10, 840, 797	12, 197, 067
	1868.	1869.
New York canals	6, 442, 225	5, 859, 080
New York Central Railroad	1, 846, 599	2, 281, 885
Erie Railway	3, 908, 243	4, 312, 209
Total	12, 197, 067	12, 453, 174
	1869.	1870.
New York canals	5, 859, 080	6, 173, 769
New York Central Railroad	2, 281, 885	4, 122, 000
Erie Railway	4, 312, 209	4, 852, 505
Total	12, 453, 174	15, 148. 274
	1870.	1871.
New York canals	6, 173, 769	6, 467, 888
New York Central Railroad	4, 122, 000	4, 532, 056
Erie Railway	4, 852, 505	4, 844, 208
Total	15, 148, 274	15, 844, 152
	1871.	1872.
New York canals	6, 467, 888	6, 673, 370
New York Central Railroad	4, 532, 056	4, 393, 965
Erie Railway	4, 844, 208	5, 564, 274
Total	15, 844, 152	16, 631, 609

The charges for delivering wheat from Chicago to New York for a series of years are noted as follows:

Year.	Cents per bushel by lake.	Cents per bushel by canal and river.	Total.
1865	9.78	16.84	26.62
1866	13.04	16.96	30.00
1867	6.67	15.69	22.30
1868	7.14	15.05	22.19
1869	6.81	14.07	20.88
1870	5.83	11.02	16.90
1871	7.62	12.62	20.24
1872	11.15	13.00	24.18

The above includes toll of three cents and one mill per bushel on canal since 1869 The question now arises, can the cost of transportation upon the canal be reduced ?

During the session of the legislature of the State of New York in the year 1863, resolutions were adopted providing for a detailed estimate, to be made by the State engineer, of the cost of constructing one tier of locks 26 feet wide and 225 feet long on the Erie, Oswego, Champlain, Cayuga, and Seneca Canals; also to report if any new feeders would be necessary to bring the enlarged locks in use, and appropriating $25,000 for the expense of the surveys. At the same time the following concurrent resolutions were adopted:

"Whereas the construction of said locks, of the dimensions above specified, will materially promote the interests of the United States, in providing for the common defense, augmenting the national commerce, foreign and domestic, and strengthening the bonds of the national Union; and

"Whereas the General Government may deem it desirable and important to secure without delay the right of perpetual passage through said canals with locks thus enlarged, free from tolls, for the vessels, gun-boats, troops, and munitions, military and naval, of the United States, and to render its fair equivalent to the State by contributing justly to the cost of the work: Therefore,

"*Resolved*, That the governor be, and he is hereby, empowered and requested to invite the President of the United States to select and detail a competent engineer, in behalf and at the expense of the General Government, to consult with the engineers so to be appointed by the canal-board, in respect to the surveys mentioned in the preceding resolution and as to the mode of constructing the work so as most effectually to promote the national interests."

Hon. William B. Taylor, then State engineer, directed the surveys and detailed estimates to be made, and gave the results in his report to the legislature in 1864, noted as assembly document No. 179.

His conclusions were sustained by the opinion of the Hon. Charles B. Stuart, who was appointed consulting engineer by the President of the United States. One of the most interesting features of the report is the statement regarding the supply of water needed for the large locks. In his own words, he says: "No estimates have been made for a further supply on the western division, the present quantity being deemed ample and equal to all the requirements of many years to come. Lake Erie can furnish all that may be needed."

This portion of the canal referred to extends from Buffalo to Clyde, 140 miles. The Clyde or Cayuga marsh level is sixteen miles in length, and is supplied from the first-named section and from the Port Byron level. The Port Byron level is nine miles in length, and is fed by the lockage water from the Jordan level and the Weedsport feeder. On page 121 of aforesaid document the engineer states that Owasco Creek and Owasco Lake reservoir can furnish, with present resources, 2,660 cubic feet more water than will be necessary.

On the Jordan level, fourteen and nine-tenths miles long, fed by the Camillus and Skaneateles Lake feeders, the engineer remarks: "To obtain the needed supply it is proposed to resort to Otisco Lake."

The report also states that for the remainder of the canal, no additional supply will be necessary, except for the levels west of Little Falls, and extending to Syracuse. His calculations show that "between these points it will be necessary to provide for an increased quantity of water, equal to six thousand eight hundred and fifteen cubic feet per minute, and this can be readily obtained from Fish Creek."

The engineer seems to have no doubt as to his conclusions respecting this point, for on page 120 he adds: "This question is one of the most important connected with the construction of the gun-boat locks. Indeed, by many it has been deemed impossible to obtain a supply sufficient for the purposes contemplated. In view of this theory, very careful examinations have been made, in order to cover all contingencies that could possibly arise, and to provide means for securing the desired result."

In discussing the results to be obtained by the proposed canal improvement, he says: "The engineers who fixed, in 1835, the dimensions of the prism and locks, estimated that the enlargement would enable the carrier to reduce the cost of transportation fifty per cent. John B. Jervis went into a thorough investigation of the subject, and reduced it to a mathematical certainty."

He also proved, from valuable compiled tables, that the reduction of cost of carrying by the completed enlarged canal was actually fifty and one half per cent.

Based upon the same theories and calculations, and having the proven results of Mr. Jervis's prophecy before him, the State engineer "finds the enlargement of the Erie Canal, with proposed locks two hundred and twenty feet in length between quoins, and twenty-five feet width of chamber, at water-line of lower level, would reduce the cost of transportation fifty per cent."

On page 134 he acknowledges that "the conclusions arrived at are that by enlarging one tier of the present locks, and constructing a new enlarged lock by the side of present single ones on the Erie Canal, at an expense of $10,380,169.75 (which includes land damages, altering structures, removing bench-walls and deepening canal one foot,) the same results are obtained in cheapening the cost of transportation as by the original enlargement at an expense of $32,008,850.40."

The engineer seems to advise the deepening of the canal one foot, not from any idea of commercial necessity, for, in his own language, he explains that "the cost of deepening the prism of the canal one foot, not including mechanical structures, and of increasing the depth of water to eight feet, although not required by the resolution, is included in the aggregate expen e of the work. The draught of gun-boats of the size contemplated will be six and one-half feet, which leaves a space of only six inches between the keel and canal bottom. As this is insufficient to allow the boats to successfully navigate the channel, the items above mentioned have been inserted."

It therefore seems that the expenditure of $1,789,900 was required for national interests and not for purely commercial purposes.

It is the recorded opinion of the engineer, that the entire work can be completed in two years. There is no doubt that with proper superintendence and management the promise of the engineer would be verified.

Since the date of this report (February, 1864,) a very large amount of money has been used in removing bench-walls, and not more than one-half of the sum then estimated ($1,784,185) would now be required.

Again within a few years fourteen stone locks have been nearly completed, thus making one tier of combined locks on the entire line of the canal. The report contemplated the construction of large new locks where the locks were single, and thus the expense in this respect is very materially decreased.

In advocating the immediate enlargement of the locks upon the Erie Canal, and commenting upon the State engineer's report, the undersigned took occasion to say, (see Canal Commissioner's report, 1866,) "The estimates for the work were made in the summer of 1863, when the value of labor and materials had largely increased, as compared with 1861. Reference is made to Engineer Story's report, incorporated in State engineer's report, (see page 195,) in which it is stated that the estimate made for the enlargement on the western division was fifty per cent. greater than prices paid for work in 1861. Engineer Jenne, of the eastern division, makes a similar statement, (page 169.) Such additions were no doubt proper to be made, as the uncertain condition of national affairs compelled contractors to require advanced prices to protect them against all contingencies. I have no hesitation in expressing the opinion that twenty per cent. reduction from the estimates then made is fully warranted, and that such education is not less than might be proposed, with regard to reputation for prudence and caution.

The aforesaid estimates included every possible expenditure; provision being made for enlarging and improving aqueducts, lengthening bridges and culverts, constructing reservoirs and feeders, widening canal in certain localities, for land damages, and nearly one million being set aside for engineering and contingencies. The probable expense of the entire work at this time, as laid down by the engineer, would not exceed $7,370,000. Of this gross amount the sum of $1,789,000 was intended for deepening the canal one foot. This is not absolutely necessary, and can be dispensed with, not materially interfering with the anticipated successful results of cheapening cost of transportation.

We have thus before us reliable and satisfactory evidence that the Erie Canal can be adapted to the use of a very large class of boats, capable of carrying six hundred and ninety tons of freight; that all the necessary improvements can be perfected within two years, and that the result would be a reduction of fifty per cent. in the cost of carrying property on the canal.

Another method of improving navigation has many advocates, and has much merit. It embraces but three propositions: 1. Extending the locks to admit the passage of three or four boats at one lockage. 2. The removal of the bench-walls. 3. The furnishing of a larger supply of water.

These works could be completed as quickly as those named in the other project. The largest number of the present class of boats now on the canals would be at once, and without delay or new expenditure, adapted to this scheme of navigation. In this respect a material advantage in giving immediate value to the principle of cheapening cost would be found, as all boats and accessories to navigation now in use would be at once utilized. No necessity would then arise for the construction of the larger class of vessels, and the delay consequent on providing the increased number requisite to do the business would be avoided.

Steamboats have been frequently constructed for the purpose of towage upon the canals, combined with the carrying of a small cargo. They have invariably been failures, have proved unprofitable, and the chief reason has been the detentions encountered at the locks. An experienced canal-engineer writes: "This is a serious objection to towing, but it is not the only one. The canal-steamer passes through the canal with a necessary average detention of, say, six minutes at each lock, or seven hours' detention between Buffalo and Troy. The towing-steamer passes a lock as quickly as the former, but after it has passed it must wait for the first and succeeding boats of the tow to be locked through."

Each additional single lockage will require nearly or quite double the time required for the first, on account of the greater difficulty in the management of the towed boats, and of the necessity of waiting for the locks to be "shifted," or for a boat to be locked in the opposite direction. The time of three single lockages is, therefore, required for the passage of the steamer with one boat in tow; but the boats already locked through must still await the slow process of locking the balance of the tow. If there be two boats towed the detention will be increased five times; if three, seven times; four, nine times. Thus the detention of a tow of four boats at each lock would be fifty-four minutes. This, between Buffalo and Troy, would make an aggregate detention of sixty-three hours against the detention of seven hours experienced by the non-towing steamer.

The cost of extending the locks so as to permit the steamer (carrying part of a cargo) with two boats in tow, would be near $3,960,000. Furnishing full supply of water, same as estimated for gun-boats, $393,000; removing bench-walls, $875,000; total, $5,228,000.

To extend the locks so as to pass through three boats with steamer, $1,800,0C0 additional.

This, unquestionably, is the simplest and cheapest project, can be speedily accomplished, and without possible detriment to canal navigation.

That it would cheapen the cost of transportation in as great a ratio as by the other proposed system is not certain, but that it would make a large and useful reduction cannot be doubted.

The calculations made with reference to the 50 per cent. were based upon large boats moving with horse-power, not with steam-propulsion, as would most naturally follow upon such large craft being brought into use; therefore, we may very properly look for better results than anticipated by the engineer, as such a barge moving at once the quantity moved by three first-class boats in half (or nearly) the time at present made, must certainly prove of great economical value.

Practice has demonstrated that upon canal, lock, and river navigation combined, the most economic plan of moving property is by barges, for they cost far less in their construction, proportioned to their carrying capacity, require few hands, and move with less expense, greater ease, and more rapidly than sail-craft. It is a remarkable fact that, upon the Saint Lawrence River, 95 per cent. of all the grain that reaches Kingston by sail-vessel is transferred at that point in barges for Montreal.

It has been difficult to obtain accurate statements of the Canadian vessels navigating the lakes and Saint Lawrence River, but it may be fairly assumed that their steam and sail ratio corresponds with ours. The aggregate of American vessels is 2,090, of which 1,420 are sailing-vessels and 670 steamers.

Experience is a safe guide, and if owners and parties interested in navigation upon the Saint Lawrence route found it more profitable to use lake-vessels, barges would not be in use. This fact is very demonstrative, and elucidates the folly of advocating ship-canals for interior navigation. The barges upon the Saint Lawrence are not propelled by steam, and each carries about four hundred and seventy tons.

Upon this point it is proper to inquire if steam can be profitably employed upon our canals. In the year 1871, the legislature of this State passed a law providing for the payment of $100,000 to the person or persons who in this direction should successfully introduce steam navigation and profitably apply it to the boats now in use upon the canals. A commissioner was appointed to examine and decide upon the merits of the contestants, and in his second annual report (Senate Document No. 71, February 25, 1873,) the engineer of the commission gives the result of several trial trips, a few of which are herewith noted.

Steamer William Newman left Buffalo, August 31, 1872, with a cargo of seven thousand two hundred bushels of wheat, weighing two hundred and ten and six tenths of a ton, reached West Troy 6.45 p. m., September 6, time six days, thirteen hours and fifteen minutes; deducting detentions and lockage, (nineteen hours and thirty-five minutes,) leaves for running-time five days, seventeen hours and forty minutes; average speed, including all detentions, 2 19-100 miles per hour.

The return-trip, with a cargo of one hundred and fourteen tons of iron ore, was made in five days twenty-two hours and twenty minutes; deducting time consumed in lockage and detentions, (nineteen hours and forty-three minutes,) leaves for running-time five days, two hours and thirty-seven minutes; average speed, including all detentions, 2 42-100 miles per hour.

The second trip east commenced on the 21st of September, at 6.40 a. m., with cargo of two hundred and one tons of wheat. The vessel reached West Troy at 7 a. m., on the 28th instant; gross time seven days twenty minutes; detentions, one day, thirteen hours and thirty-five minutes; running-time five days, ten hours and forty-five minutes; a detention of nineteen hours occupied in replacing broken rudder-post.

The return trip, with one hundred and twenty-seven and three-quarter tons of iron ore, was made in six days and thirteen hours; detentions, twenty-three hours; running-time five days, four hours and thirty minutes; average speed, including detentions, 2 34-100 miles per hour.

Third trip east, with cargo of wheat weighing two hundred four and four-tenths of a ton, commenced at Buffalo, at 7 a. m., on the 16th of October, and West Troy was reached on the 22d instant at 11.15 a. m.; time six days, four hours and fifteen minutes; deducting lockage and detention, the running-time was five days, four hours and fifty-five minutes.

Starting from West Troy with a cargo of one hundred and one and nine-tenths tons of merchandise, Buffalo was reached in five days and twenty-one hours; running-time, deducting detentions and lockage, (twenty-one hours and fifty minutes,) four days, three hours and fifty minutes.

In the fall of 1872 the steamer William Baxter made three round trips between Buffalo and West Troy, and on her first trip transported eastward two hundred and one and six-tenths tons of what, and on her second and third trips each two hundred and one tons of wheat. The return cargoes were, first trip, one hundred and two and a quarter tons of plaster; on the second, one hundred and thirteen and one-eighth tons plaster; and on the third, one hundred and fourteen and one-half tons iron ore.

The gross time of the three trips east averaged six days, eighteen hours and thirty-five minutes; running-time averaged four days, eight hours, and forty minutes; average speed, running-time, 3 30-100 miles per hour.

The average gross time consumed in the three return-trips was six days, six hours, and two minutes; average running-time four days, ten hours, and twenty minutes; average speed, running-time, 3 27-100 miles per hour.

On page 108 the engineer acknowledges that, "in order to judge correctly as to the relative capacities and economy of steamers, as compared with horse-boats, it is of course necessary to know the average time of the latter between Buffalo and Troy. For the purpose of ascertaining this time I caused an examination to be made of the clearances of seventy-two boats arriving consecutively at West Troy from Buffalo. The results of this examination are as follows: Average time between Buffalo and West Troy, ten days, two hours, and forty-six minutes; average cargo, two hundred and twenty-seven tons; average speed, 1 42-100 miles per hour. This examination was commenced on the 16th of October, and in only two or three instances was mention made of delay due to sickness of horses. It is assumed, therefore, that the results obtained fairly represent the average performance of the horse-boat between Buffalo and Troy."

These statements exhibit the value of steam thus applied and the perfect adaptability of the Erie Canal to its use, notwithstanding the impediments offered by the small and narrow locks. We find that, under the supervision of an experienced engineer, boats made trips against the current, westward, with cargoes over one hundred tons, at greater speed than was attained by the same boats going eastward with about two hundred tons of cargo. No report has been made for the current year, but it is understood the experiments have proven very satisfactory.

On the downward trip to Albany the current exercises material influence. From Lake Erie to Montezuma there is a continuous descent of 151½ miles, with a lockage of 177½ feet through twenty locks. From Montezuma to the center of the Jordan level the movement of boats may be said to be against the current, and in a distance of 19 miles they have to pass through two locks with 16½ feet lockage; thence descending to the Syracuse level, the distance from the center of the Jordan level is about 14 milest; hence ascending through three locks, rising 26 96-100 feet to the "long level," the level extending 53 miles, and thence continually descending 113 miles through 46 locks with 426 96-100 feet of lockage.

Estimating that on the long level, from the Black and Mohawk River feeders at Rome to Syracuse, a distance of 40 miles, the current is westward, there would be on the whole, 351½ miles of canal, only 59 miles influenced by it, with the exception of the lakes. Is there any natural water-route possessing a tithe of the advantages held by this artificial route, and can any channel be constructed that can equal the Erie Canal in its wonderful utility?

In determining the nature and scope of improvements considered necessary to be made with the design of cheapening cost of transportation, permanent as well as speedy results are required.

During the season of navigation the Erie Canal exercises a strongly marked and unquestioned controlment of carriers' charges upon all routes competing for western trade, and to a considerable extent upon property moving westward. Upon the opening of the Erie Canal the great railroad lines invariably reduce their rates, and as invariably increase them when through-shipments from Chicago can no longer be made by water.

The annexed tables fully establish this fact.

Date.	Charges on all rail, per bushel, of wheat from Chicago to—		
	New York.	Boston and Portland.	Baltimore and Philadelphia.
1871.	*Cents.*	*Cents.*	*Cents.*
January 1 to January 16	36	39	4
January 17 to March 8	33	37	33
March 9 to April 6	30	36	33
April 7 to April 23	27	33	32
April 24 to June 12	27	30	24
June 13 to July 9	24	27	27
July 10 to August 10	27	30	24
August 11 to September 20	30	33	27
September 21 to October 1	33	36	30
October 2 to October 24	36	39	33
October 24 to December 31	39	42	36
1872.			
July 1 to March 24	39	42	36
March 25 to April 30	36	39	33
May 1 to August 11	30	33	27
August 12 to September 1	27	30	24
September 2 to September 8	30	33	27
September 9 to September 15	33	36	30
September 16 to October 13	36	39	33
October 14 to December 31	39	42	36

The increase in the winter-months over the summer and late fall averaging two dollars and seven cents a ton on wheat.

It is apparent that, in the season of navigation, any appliances made for reducing cost of carriage upon the Erie Canal necessarily reduces cost upon all other lines, and this most important and permanent result cannot be obtained upon any other line.

The reason of this conclusion is obvious. The State owns the line, and, therefore, is precluded from the possibility of entering into combinations with corporations to seize upon opportunities to increase their profits. 2d. It is the interest of the State to reduce rather than enhance the cost; and, 3d, it is impossible to combine upon the canals the rolling-stock owned by thousands of individuals, or enter into any arrangement with their natural antagonists, railroad corporations.

Cheapness of transportation upon this route is also assured by advantages not offered by any other, viz, the return-cargoes, whose value is also felt upon the lakes, and although such cargoes on water-routes seldom prove of material profit, they serve to pay expenses, and to that extent reduce the charges on cargoes taken eastward, as well by lakes as by canal.

Buffalo bids fair to be a very great coal emporium, the increase in the trade being very remarkable and worthy of a moment's consideration. In the year 1873, the shippers paid to vessels leaving Buffalo one dollar per ton freight, free on and off vessel. At the port of Erie, 90 miles west from Buffalo, the additional sum of twenty-five cents per ton is paid, both qualities of coal being found there. From Cleveland, 180 miles from Buffalo, the additional sum of twenty-five cents per ton is paid upon the bituminous coal sent westward. The result is inevitable; the coal-trade of Erie is to be directed to Buffalo. This difference of twenty-five cents per ton is occasioned by the fact that vessels have cargoes to Buffalo instead of Erie, and it is worth that amount for vessels to stop on their westward trip from Buffalo to load from these ports. This is another evidence of the superiority of lines having the control of commerce. The vast amount of property imported in the city of New York, and which is to find its way west, gives opportunities for water-craft to find cargoes in that direction, which no other port, save Montreal, possesses, and that to a very limited extent. The productions of the West finding their way eastward from lake ports, for export, also take the same line to the metropolis.

In the following tables are shown the shipments of freight from Buffalo by the Erie Canal; the westward freight, by canal, to the same point, and the ratio of return freights by this route:

Eastward movement, tons freight.

1868	1,476,298
1869	1,281,706
1870	1,[illegible],904
1871	1,742,157
1872	1,774,996

Westward movement, tons freight.

1868	682,916
1869	506,532
1870	633,849
1871	538,593
1872	699,916

The increase in the anthracite coal brought by canal is shown by the following statement:

	1871.	1872.	1873.
Tons	102,185	190,994	254,044

In addition to the tonnage delivered by canal, there have also been received by railway, for the current year, nearly half a million of tons of anthracite coal, most of which is sent westward.

The proportion of return cargoes brought by canal is nearly forty per cent. of the shipment by canal eastward.

In addition, it is the fixed and declared policy of the State to cheapen transportation.

During the last session of the legislature the following article was adopted and directed to be submitted to the people as an amendment to the constitution:

ARTICLE —. The commissioners of the canal-fund shall borrow on the credit of the State such sums as may be necessary for paying the canal and general-fund debts now charged on the canals, as the same shall fall due, by the issue and sale of bonds or certificates of stock, having forty years to run from this date, bearing interest at the rate of five per cent. per annum, payable semi-annually. For the payment of the principal at maturity a sinking-fund of one per cent. per annum shall be established, and the tolls of the canals shall be fixed from time to time by the canal board at rates sufficing, as near as may be, to provide only for said sinking-fund the interest on the debt so created, the expenses of collection, superintendence, and keeping the canals in repair; and the contribution so created for said sinking-fund shall be invested annually; invested by the comptroller in the bonds or certificates of stock authorized by this article, or in the stock or bonds of the State of New York or of the United States, which shall be held for the redemption and payment of the bonds or certificates herein authorized to be issued, and sacredly applied to that purpose. All of said debt and interest shall be paid from the revenues of the canals, and no direct tax shall ever be levied or collected for canal purposes either for current expenses or repairs, ordinary or extraordinary.

Should this proposition become operative, the tolls upon the canal may be reduced nearly twenty per cent. in the year 1875, and with a constant declination upon those rates until they shall be so reduced as to simply provide sufficient for reparation and management.

The policy of the State in this respect has been most liberal, as found in the following statement: The toll-freight on a barrel of flour from Buffalo to Albany in 1830, '31, '32, was 55 cents; carriers' charges average 43 cents; in 1833, 39 cents; carriers' charges average 49 cents; from 1833 to 1846, 35 cents; carriers' charges average $36\frac{3}{4}$ cents; from 1845 to 1851, 31 cents; carriers' charges average $31\frac{2}{5}$ cents; from 1850 to 1858, 23 cents; carriers' charges average $29\frac{4}{7}$ cents; from 1857 to 1861, 15 cents; carriers' charges average $20\frac{1}{3}$ cents; in 1861, 19 cents; carriers' charges average 27 cents; from 1861 to 1870, 23 cents; carriers' charges average 27 cents; from 1869 to 1873, $11\frac{1}{2}$ cents; carriers' charges average $26\frac{83}{100}$ cents.

The following tables exhibit receipts of cereals at various points for a series of years:

Port.	1868.	1869.	1870.	1871.	1872.
	Bushels.	*Bushels.*	*Bushels.*	*Bushels.*	*Bushels.*
Chicago, Milwaukee, Detroit, and Toledo.	112, 144, 800	115, 882, 241	117, 276, 560	141, 458, 061	139, 584, 622
Buffalo*	49, 949, 856	45, 807, 163	46, 613, 096	67, 155, 742	62, 260, 332
Oswego	13, 987, 377	13, 396, 542	12, 273, 498	14, 216, 974	9, 124, 914
Montreal	8, 353, 617	13, 089, 787	12, 230, 093	14, 166, 066	17, 547, 428
Ogdensburgh	3, 828, 826	4, 124, 176	4, 652, 500	4, 952, 259	3, 540, 227
Boston	11, 508, 120	11, 863, 049	13, 047, 905	14, 862, 899	16, 701, 934
Portland	4, 086, 993	2, 611, 349	....	3, 711, 846	4, 071, 792
Baltimore	12, 235, 558	13, 818, 483	13, 819, 101	17, 389, 443	20, 571, 499
Philadelphia	12, 151, 207	14, 679, 515	15, 307, 011	20, 102, 425	24, 117, 150
New York	62, 937, 980	66, 206, 570	69, 418, 732	88, 925, 844	90, 217, 315

* By lake.

Receipts of grain at West Troy and Albany, by the Erie and Champlain Canal.

	Bushels.
1868	50, 086, 800
1869	37, 862, 185
1870	37, 641, 200
1871	54, 695, 930
1872	52, 683, 700

Of the receipts for 1872, as given in the last table, 298,080 bushels of grain came by the Champlain Canal.

Shipments of grain from Oswego by Oswego Canal, and from Buffalo by Erie Canal.

	Buffalo.	Oswego.
1870	37, 641, 200	8, 506, 266
1871	54, 695, 930	10, 442, 880
1872	52, 683, 700	5, 993, 822

The following shows shipments from ocean ports:

Port.	1871.	1872.
Baltimore	5, 356, 575	6, 442, 231
Philadelphia	3, 491, 436	4, 450, 283
Boston	2, 218, 399	2, 913, 559
Montreal	14, 752, 795	16, 196, 474
New York	43, 867, 411	45, 974, 923

These tables are presented to indicate the current of interior and export trade, and to call attention to the fact how nearly the entire receipts of Montreal are exported, and that they are larger than the exports of Boston, Baltimore, and Philadelphia combined.

In the above tables the only foreign exports are given from Philadelphia and New York, but it is most likely that the bulk of the exports from other cities is for foreign ports.

The statistics are also presented for the purpose of calling attention to the consumption of cereals by the great cities, and the consequent importance to their residents of this question of cheap transportation. The quantity retained for consumption in New York, Baltimore, Philadelphia, and Boston, for the year 1872, was 91,826,000 bushels, while the total exports for the four great cities were less than 60,000,000 of bushels.

Thus we find the people of the great cities, as well as the hard-worked farmers on the prairies, are most deeply and vitally interested in this great proposition, and it is the duty of all classes, whether as the laborer, the mechanic, miner artisan, or business class, to use their best exertions to cheapen the great necessaries of life, and thus increase the savings and proportionate value of their labor.

Another point in the exhibit is to show the great preponderance of export from New York, by reason of the unrivaled water-communications connecting that port with the great West.

It is almost impossible to ascertain the amount of cereals moved by rail, but it is very large. The New York Central Railway Company is now constructing two additional tracks between Buffalo and Albany. It has been stated that over seventy per cent. of the entire business received at Buffalo is for the New England States.

A very large proportion of their business is in grain, which is carried, through the system of red, white, and blue lines, throughout New England, and a very large proportion of that grain will always find that manner of conveyance.

For the year 1871 the receipts of grain (flour reduced to wheat included) at Buffalo, by the Lake Shore and Michigan Southern Railway, were 24,801,539 bushels, and for the year 1872, 29,756,700 bushels. All of the last item, except about 250,000 bushels, was taken eastward by rail.

The State of New York cannot, nor will not, assign control of her canals, nor will she allow any governmental management of them; yet will not, or should not, object to the General Government providing means for increased facilities to internal commerce and trade, and for the marked benefit of the people of her sister States.

For the improvement of her present canals, the State has given her consent and acquiescence. For the opening or constructing new routes it is questionable if her permission could be obtained, having been repeatedly and distinctly refused, as in the case of the Niagara ship-canal. The following law is yet upon the statute-books:

Chapter 415, Laws 1862.

AN ACT to adapt the canals of this State to the defense of the northern and northwestern lakes.*

The people of the State of New York, represented in senate and assembly, do enact as follows:

Section 1. Whenever the Government of the United States shall provide the means, either in cash or their six per cent. stocks or bonds, redeemable within twenty years, for defraying the cost of enlarging a single tier of locks or building an additional tier, in whole or in part, upon the Erie and the Oswego Canals, including any necessary alteration of said canals or their structures, to a size sufficient to pass vessels adequate to the defense of the northern and northwestern lakes, the canal board shall without delay put such work under contract in the manner now required by law, to be constructed and completed at the earliest practicable period, without serious interruption to navigation, with power, in the discretion of the canal board, to direct the construction of new and independent locks, when found more advantageous. The said canal board shall, whenever the Government of the United States shall provide the means as aforesaid, construct a canal of requisite dimensions and capacity, from the Erie Canal, at or near the village of Clyde, to some proper point on the Great Sodus Bay or Lake Ontario.

Sec. 2. The canal board are also hereby authorized, in like manner, to enlarge the Champlain Canal, and its locks and other structures, to a size sufficient to pass vessels of like capacity, in case the Government of the United States shall, in like manner, provide the means required for that purpose.

Sec. 3. The dimensions and character of all the work hereinabove mentioned shall be determined by the canal board, subject to the examination and concurrence of the War Department of the Government of the United States. Contracts for any of said work may be made payable in the said six per cent. stock and bonds of the United States, if the commissioners of the canal fund shall so elect.

Sec. 4. On completing the said work on either of the said canals the Government of the United States shall have the perpetual right of passage through the canals thus enlarged or built, free from toll or charge, for its vessels of war, boats, gun-boats, transports, troops, supplies or munitions of war, subject to the general regulations prescribed by the State from time to time for the navigation of its canals.

Sec. 5. Any moneys or other means which may be received from the Government of the United States to pay for any of said work are hereby appropriated to be expended for the purpose hereinabove mentioned.

Sec. 6. But nothing in this act contained shall authorize the contracting or incurring of any debt or liability, directly or indirectly, on the part of the State, or the expenditure of any means or money of the State of New York, for the purposes specified in this act.

That the legislature would make any reasonable modification in the above there can scarcely be any question.

The question of the ability of the Erie Canal to carry the bulk of the productions of the Western States is an important one, yet the proposition is so easily determined that discussion is not necessary.

Its capacity has never been tested, as upon one division (the western) of the canal there has been but one tier of locks. The second tier is nearly completed. The introduction of steam, as a motive power, will greatly add to its efficiency, and the enlargement of the locks will double its present carrying capacity.

In addition, the widening and deepening are perfectly feasible, and thus its capacity can be made to equal all the demands of the future.

F. A. ALLBERGER.

*Passed April 22, 1862; three-fifths being present.

LETTER ADDRESSED TO THE CHAIRMAN OF THIS COMMITTEE BY ISAAC HINCKLEY, PRESIDENT OF PHILADELPHIA, WILMINGTON AND BALTIMORE RAILROAD, IN RELATION TO THE SUBJECT OF RAILWAY COMPETITION.

PHILADELPHIA, WILMINGTON AND BALTIMORE RAILROAD COMPANY,
President's Office, Philadelphia, February 23, 1874.

DEAR SIR: In reply to your question as to the effect of railroad competition upon rates: It is now forty years since Robert Stephenson said, in substance, "railway competition is not possible where consolidation is practicable." Numerous instances occur to me illustrative of the truth of his axiom; while I know that cases where it has not been verified are exceptional. In here speaking of "competition," I do not refer to cases where the business competed for is but a portion of the business of the road, and therefore is not of prime consideration. Thus the great trunk-lines may go on competing indefinitely for the western and seaboard-traffic, because such competition is not destructively exhaustive, in view of the large local traffic which those lines enjoy free from competition. Yet even here the public frequently suffers; as, for instance, when competition has reduced the rates to cost, or even below cost, and the railroad companies, in self-preservation, agree together for a time, forming what we may call a temporary consolidation, under which rates are spasmodically raised.

But, taking the cases where two roads compete practically for their whole business, you will find that compromise or consolidation in some shape has been the result; and the public thereafter pays for the support of two roads when one only was necessary; as a man who keeps two horses to do the work of one must pay for oats for both.

I will instance two or three such cases:

Lowell, Mass., 26 miles from Boston, was connected with that city by the Boston and Lowell Railroad, of which I was a director for fifteen years. We were, in or about 1854, carrying passengers at 60 cents, coal at 75 cents, other freights in proportion. The Salem and Lowell Railroad about that time commenced, in connection with the Boston and Maine Railroad, to compete for the trade. Passenger rates went to 45 cents and coal to 50 cents generally, and once to 30 cents. These rates were injurious to the Boston and Lowell, and insupportable by the Salem and Lowell. Compromise and lease followed. Passenger rates went to 75 cents, then to $1, and now is 75 cents. Coal rate went to $1.25 at once, and subsequently to $1.75; since reduced, I think, to $1.25. Other rates were affected in the same direction, yet the Boston and Lowell Railroad Company, who took the lease, fared no better than it did with low rates before the Salem and Lowell was built.

Similar results followed at Manchester, New Hampshire, on the construction of the Manchester and Lowell Railroad—a competitor of the Connecticut River Railroad. I inclose a copy of a letter received to-day from general manager Boston and Lowell and Nashua and Lowell Railroad Companies, bearing upon these cases.

I also inclose a table of rates on the Connecticut River Railroad, showing that where competition reaches a town, (as in the case of Northampton and Greenfield, Mass.,) it does not fare so well as other towns on the same line of road. The president of that company recently told me that, by the terms of the compromise with the competing road at Greenfield, he is forced to charge $3 per ton for coal to that town, while he carries coal to towns beyond Greenfield for $2.75.

The public do not seem to realize that railroad competition is not similar to stage-coach or steamboat competition, where, if one party be worsted, he can retreat with his capital to a new field. They should know that railroad managers will always, after a longer or shorter trial of strength, terminate a strife which is mutually injurious, and agree in some way to work harmoniously.

Did I not suppose that you had the able reports of the Railroad Commissioners of Massachusetts for past years, which treat of the inexpediency of fixing railroad rates by statute, I should forward them with this.

Please command me at any time.

Very respectfully, your obedient servant,

ISAAC HINCKLEY.

Hon. WILLIAM WINDOM,
Chairman Senate Committee on Transportation, &c., Washington, D. C.

[Copy.]

BOSTON AND LOWELL RAILROAD COMPANY,
Manager's Office, Boston, February 20, 1874.

DEAR SIR: Mr. Winslow has turned over to me an unfinished memorandum in pencil made by you when last in his office, and requested that I would send some statement of the results of the competition between the Boston and Lowell, and the Boston and Maine, and Salem and Lowell Roads, in 1856. Not knowing exactly the purpose of the inquiry, I can only say generally that this competition resulted in combination between the competing parties and an increase of rates above what they were before the Salem Road was built.

Previous to the building of the competing line the Lowell Road had reduced its passage-fare from Lowell to Boston to 50 cents. This was raised to 60 cents, then competition put it down to 45 cents, and, after a compromise, it went immediately up to 75, and remained at that figure until war prices advanced it to one dollar. It has now gone back, in the absence of any competition whatever, to 75 cents again. Coal was carried by the competing roads at 50 cents per ton. After a compromise, it was put up to one dollar and a quarter, or about 25 per cent. above old non-competing rates. Other freights were affected in a similar manner.

The competition at Manchester, N. H., brought about by building the Manchester and Lawrence Road, resulted in precisely the same manner, and the competing road fell into the hands of its established rival in the same way.

I mail with this a copy of an argument made by Colonel George, in 1867, on page 23 of which you will find a table of rates charged by this road for a series of years.

Respectfully yours,

GEO. STARK,
General Manager.

ISAAC HINCKLEY, Esq.

Table showing different freight-tariffs on Connecticut River Railroad since 1858.

Date.	Springfield and Chicopee.*				Springfield and Holyoke.*				Springfield and Northampton.†				Springfield and Greenfield.†			
	1	2	3	4	1	2	3	4	1	2	3	4	1	2	3	4
April 1, 1858	4	3	2^2	....	6	4^2	3^2	....	9	7	6	....	16	13	11	....
June 1, 1864 ‡	5	3^2	3	3	8	6	4^2	4	10	8	6^2	6	17	13	11	10
October 1, 1864	6	4^2	4	3	9	7	5^2	4^2	12	9^2	8	7	22	16	14	12
January 15, 1867	6	4^2	4	3	9	7	5^2	4^2	12	9^2	8	7	22	16	14	12
May 1, 1867	5^2	4	3^2	3	8	6	5	4^2	11	9	8	7	22	16	14	12
December 1, 1867	5^2	4	3^2	3	8	6	5	4^2	11	9	8	7	22	16	14	12
April 1, 1868	5^2	4	3^2	3	8	6	5	4^2	11	9	8	7	22	16	14	12
July 1, 1868	5	4	3	3	8	6	5	4	11	9	8	7	22	16	14	12

Date.	New York and Chicopee.*				New York and Holyoke.*				New York and Northampton.†				New York and Greenfield.†			
	1	2	3	4	1	2	3	4	1	2	3	4	1	2	3	4
April 1, 1858	....	....	....	....	....	....	....	....	32	30	25	....	....	....	....	....
June 1, 1864 ‡	31	27	21^2	....	34	29	23	....	32	30	25	....	42^2	36^2	39	....
October 1, 1864	36	31	26^2	....	39	33^2	28	....	40	35	30	....	46	40	34	....
January 15, 1867	36	31	26^2	....	39	33^2	28	....	40	35	30	....	46	40	34	....
May 1, 1867	33	28	24	23	35	30	26	24^2	40	35	30	27	46	40	36	32
December 1, 1867	33	28	24	23	35	30	26	24^2	40	35	30	27	46	40	34	32
April 1, 1868	28	25	21	20	30	27	23	22	40	34	29	25	46	40	34	30
July 1, 1868	28	25	21	20	30	27	23	22	35	31	27	24	43	38	33	29

* Roads free from competition.
† Roads competing since.
‡ Compare the rates of June 1, 1864, with the rates of July 1, 1868, and bear in mind that Greenfield and Northampton each have two lines of railroad to New York, while Chicopee and Holyoke have but one.

The following letter was furnished to this committee through the Department of State.

ENGLISH RAILWAYS AND CANALS.

LONDON, *December* 10, 1873.

DEAR SIR: I have now the honor to hand you herewith sundry documents, giving as nearly as possible the information required, under date October 11, 1873, by the chairman of the United States Senate Committee on Transportation-Routes to the Seaboard:

A. Statement showing various through-passenger-fares on English railways.

B. Statement showing various through-rates per ton of freight on English railways.

C. Statement showing rates of wages paid by English railway-companies.

D. Statement showing the rates per ton for the transportation of through-freights on English canals.

E. Statement showing tolls levied on English canals.

I send copies of the regulations of the railway clearing-house—an institution by means of which the business, whether in goods or passengers, exchanged between the different railway-companies, is arranged—showing the latest classification of goods adopted.

I send the second report of the royal commission on railways in Ireland, which contains valuable statements in regard to the management of the Belgian state railways, and to the rates charged and the cost of working.

In regard to the comparative accommodation afforded, and to the question of the classification of passengers on English railways, I beg to refer you to the inclosures of my letter of September 30th last, which referred at some length to that subject.

In regard to goods traffic, the rates quoted in Statement B are inclusive of loading and unloading, and collecting and delivering within certain stated limits from the stations. Where goods are taken from the trucks and stored for an indefinite period, a special charge is made for warehousing; but under the ordinary circumstances of business no such charge is made. Class S and M rates are from station to station only; that is to say, sender and consignee have to bring, load, unload, and take away the goods, the company providing only the trucks and haulage. Grain is never carried in bulk on English railways, being loaded in bags or sacks containing about four bushels each. I may add that there are companies who loan sacks on hire to railway companies or shippers at a stated annual rent.

As I have stated above, the whole of the business, both in goods and passengers, exchanged between the different lines, is settled in accordance with the clearing-house rules herewith. Whenever the rolling-stock of one company passes on to the system of another company, the owning company is credited by a mileage-rate, balances being periodically settled by checks issued from the clearing-house. The nearest approach to the co-operative-freight system, in use in the United States, is found in the case of what is known as the East Coast line, where the Great Northern, North Eastern, and North British Railway Companies own rolling-stock jointly, and have an arrangement for the division of its receipts. The Cheshire lines also, constructed by the Midland, Great Northern, and Manchester, Sheffield and Lincolnshire Companies under a joint agreement, are administered, and their receipts ratably divided, by a joint committee of the companies. These, however, are exceptional arrangements, made with a special view to competing traffic.

Statement D, in relation to the carriage of freight by canal, is necessarily limited in scope, as there are but few canals in the country owned by railroad-companies. The canal-companies in themselves are not carriers; they simply provide the water-way and towing-path, and collect a specified toll from the vessels passing the locks. I have thus added a statement, E, showing the tolls levied on various canals. None of the English canals are owned by the state.

The costs per passenger per mile, and per ton of goods per mile, are not calculated in English railway-statistics, it being thought that these figures would have little practical value, as they would vary so much under the changing conditions of the traffic. The receipts and expenditure "per passenger-train mile," and "per goods-train mile" are given yearly in the returns issued by the board of trade.

I am, dear sir, very truly, yours,

JAMES McHENRY.

His Excellency General ROBERT C. SCHENCK,
Envoy Extraordinary and Minister Plenipotentiary of the U. S. of America, London.

Statement showing the railway fares on English railways, for first, second, and third class passengers, from point to point herein mentioned, and the distances by rail between such points.

[Compiled for the United States Senate Committee on Transportation Routes to the Seaboard.]

Journeys.		Dis-tances.	Railway fares.			Remarks.
From—	To—	Miles.	1st class.	2d class.	3d class.	
			£ s. d.	£ s. d.	£ s. d.	
London	Inverness	595	4 10 0	3 10 0	2 2 6	Return-tickets usually 1⅔ fares.
Do	Aberdeen	542	4 0 0	3 0 0	2 0 0	
Do	Glasgow	406	3 10 0	2 11 0	1 13 0	Via London and Northwestern.
Do	Edinburgh	398	3 10 0	2 11 0	1 13 0	Via Great Northern.
Do	Carlisle	299	2 14 9	2 0 0	1 4 2½	
Do	Liverpool	202	1 15 0	1 6 0	0 16 9	
Do	Fleetwood	231	2 0 0	1 10 0	0 19 1	
Do	Holyhead	264	2 6 10	1 15 4	1 1 10½	
Do	Leeds	225	1 13 0	1 4 0	0 15 5½	
Do	Manchester	189	1 12 6	1 4 0	0 15 6	Several competing lines.
Do	Milford	285	2 8 3	1 16 2	1 6 3	
Do	Bristol	118	1 0 10	0 15 8	0 9 10	
Do	Plymouth	247	2 6 6	1 12 10	0 18 8	
Do	Southampton	76	0 15 6	0 11 0	0 6 6	
Do	Brighton	50	0 10 0	0 7 9	0 4 3	No competition; extra fares by special express.
Do	Dover	78	0 18 6	0 13 6	0 6 6	Extra fares by continental express.
Do	Norwich	113½	1 3 9	0 13 0	0 12 3	Government rate by slow trains 3d class, 9*s.* 5½*d.*
Do	Hull	174½	1 10 6	1 3 0	0 13 6	
Manchester	Bristol	191	1 10 6	1 1 6	0 13 7	
Do	Newcastle	158	1 4 9	0 18 7	0 11 9	
Do	Scarborough	117	0 19 0	0 14 3	0 9 0	
Do	Hull	88	0 15 8	0 11 9	0 7 5	
Do	Edinburgh	221	1 17 0	1 6 6	0 18 5½	Via Midland and North British.
Do	Glasgow	225	1 17 0	1 6 6	0 18 6	Do.
Edinburgh	Glasgow	47	0 5 6	0 4 0	0 2 6	Keen competition.
Bristol	Newcastle	301	2 15 0	2 0 6	1 5 6	
Do	Edinburgh	426	3 10 0	2 11 0	1 12 5	
Liverpool	Yarmouth	265	2 8 2	1 17 0	1 2 2	

B.—*Statement showing the rates per ton for the transmission of through-freights on English railways.*

[Compiled for the United States Senate Committee on Transportation Routes to the Seaboard.]

Points between which the rates of freight are stated.		Railways composing the route mentioned.	Double or single track.	Distances.	Rates of freight per ton for the entire distance for commodities of these classes.						
From—	To—				1st class.	2d class.	3d class.	4th class.	5th class.	Class S.	Class M.
				Miles.	*s. d.*	*s. d.*	*s. d.*	*s. d.*	*s. d.*	*s. d.*	*s. d.*
London	Inverness	Great Northern, Northeastern, North British, and Highland.	About 100 miles of single track.	594	48 4	60 0	80 0	115 0	135 0	36 8	36 8
Do	Edinburgh	Great Northern, Northeastern, and North British	Double	398	41 8	51 8	70 0	100 0	120 0	31 8	31 8
Do	Glasgow	do	do	445	41 8	51 8	70 0	100 0	120 0	34 2	34 2
Do	Newcastle	Great Northern, Northeastern	do	274	31 8	35 0	50 0	80 0	100 0	20 0	20 0
Do	Grimsby	Great Northern	do	155	28 4	40 0	50 0	60 0	70 0	18 4	18 0
Do	Carlisle	London and Northwestern	do	298	36 8	41 8	55 0	80 0	100 0	30 0	(*)
Do	Liverpool	do	do	201	27 6	32 6	37 6	50 0	70 0	20 0	15 10
Do	Milford	Great Western	do	285	42 6	47 6	57 6	72 6	107 6	25 0	16 8
Do	Bristol	do	do	118	22 6	27 6	35 0	40 0	50 0	12 6	10 0
Do	Plymouth	do	do	247	32 6	37 6	45 0	60 0	90 0	20 0	16 8
Birmingham	do	do	do	220	28 4	35 0	48 4	60 10	98 4	20 3	20 0
Do	Southampton	London and Southwestern and London and Northwestern.	do	192	25 0	30 0	40 0	50 0	60 0	20 0	(*)
London	Brighton	London, Brighton, and South Coast	do	50	8 4	12 1	16 8	21 3	(*)	6 1	4 10
Do	Dover	London, Chatham and Dover	do	78	10 0	11 3	17 11	26 8	36 8	8 4	(*)
Do	Ramsgate	do	do	79	9 7	11 3	15 5	20 5	32 6	7 6	(*)
Wolverhampton	Yarmouth	Great Eastern, London, and Northwestern	do	214	35 0	43 4	51 8	76 8	110 0	22 6	18 4
Dover	Birmingham	London, Chatham and Dover, Great Western	do	209	33 4	41 8	51 8	70 0	85 0	23 4	(*)
Do	Bristol	do	do	198	36 8	47 6	60 0	72 6	80 0	22 6	(*)
Do	Sheffield	London, Chatham and Dover, Great Northern, and Manchester, Sheffield and Lincolnshire.	do	242	43 4	48 4	62 6	85 0	105 0	25 0	(*)
Bristol	Newcastle	Midland, Northeastern	do	301	37 6	42 6	55 0	83 4	105 0	25 0	(*)
Do	Edinburgh	Midland, Northeastern, North British	do	424	41 8	51 8	70 0	100 0	120 0	31 8	(*)
Liverpool	Dundee	London and Northwestern, Caledonian	do	301	26 8	31 8	40 0	60 0	80 0	24 2	(*)
Do	Edinburgh	do	do	227	25 0	28 4	32 6	60 0	80 0	21 8	(*)
Do	Grimsby	Manchester, Sheffield and Lincolnshire	do	136	23 4	28 4	40 0	50 0	60 0	16 8	15 0
Do	Yarmouth	Manchester, Sheffield and Lincolnshire, Great Eastern	do	265	33 4	41 8	50 0	70 0	90 0	23 4	(*)
Manchester	Glasgow	London and Northwestern, Glasgow and Southwestern	do	249	26 8	30 0	35 0	50 0	80 0	21 8	(*)
Do	Edinburgh	London and Northwestern, North British	do	222	31 8	35 0	40 0	55 0	85 0	25 0	(*)

* Not quoted.

REMARKS.—Where class M rates are not quoted they are usually about the same as class S. In addition, there are a large number of special rates quoted by the companies for special kinds of traffic, and to traders doing a large freight business with the companies.

C.—*Rates of wages paid by English railway companies.*

[Compiled for the United States Senate Committee on Transportation Routes to the Seaboard.]

Rank.	Pay.
Conductors, (first-class guards)	28*s*. to 30*s*. per week.
For long routes, however, and special service, up to	40*s*. per week.
Engine-drivers	5*s* 6*d*. to 8*s*. per day.
Stokers or firemen	3*s*. 6*d*. to 5*s*. 6*d*. per day.
Baggagemen, (second-class guards)	25*s*. to 28*s*. per week.
Brakemen, (occasional guards)	21*s*. to 22*s*. per week.
Signalmen	20*s*. to 30*s*. per week.
Varying greatly with the responsibility of the post.	In special cases, over 30*s*.

D.—*Statement showing the rates per ton for the transportation of "through-freights" on English canals.*

[Compiled for the United States Senate Committee on Transportation-Routes to the Seaboard.]

Points between which the rates of freight are stated.		Canals composing the routes here mentioned.	Distance in miles.	Rates of freight per ton for the entire distance on commodities of these classes.*						Remarks.
From—	To—			S.	1st.	2d.	3d.	4th.	5th.	
				s. d.	*s. d.*	*s. d.*	£ *s. d.*	£ *s. d.*	£ *s. d.*	
Manchester	Macclesfield	Ashton, Peak Forest, and Macclesfield Canals.	26¼	5 10	9 2	10 0	0 10 10	0 15 0	1 0 0	In cases where parties provide their own boats, towage, &c., toll only is charged. The tolls on the different canals vary as under: Per ton per mile. Lime, salt, &c .... ½*d.* to ¾*d.* Coal, coke, &c .... ¾*d.* to 1½*d.* Bricks, iron, stone ... 1*d.* to 1½*d.* Grain, malt, &c ...... ¾*d.* to 1½*d.* Timber, lead, and general goods .... 1 *d.* to 2 *d.* P. S.—These remarks apply only to the canals belonging to the Manchester, Sheffield, and Lincolnshire Railway Company, viz, the Ashton, Peak Forest, and Macclesfield Canals. Rates on canals vary according to the nature of country through which the canals pass, the period at which the parliamentary powers were obtained, and the amount of competition.
Do	Bollington	......do	24¼	6 8	7 6	8 4	0 10 0	0 15 0	1 0 0	
Do	Marple	Ashton and Peak Forest Canals	15	4 2	5 0	6 8	0 7 6	0 10 0	0 15 0	
Do	New Mills	......do	18½	4 2	5 10	6 8	0 7 6	0 8 4	0 12 6	
Do	Whaley Bridge	......do	21	5 0	7 6	8 4	0 9 2	0 13 4	0 15 10	
Do	Chapel-le-Frith	......do	24½	5 0	8 4	9 2	0 10 0	0 15 0	1 0 0	
Do	Hyde	......do	9	3 4	5 0	5 10	0 6 8	0 10 0	0 12 6	
Do	Ashton	Ashton Canal	6½	3 0	5 0	5 10	0 6 8	0 7 6	0 10 0	
Do	Stockport	......do	7½	2 6	5 0	5 0	0 5 10	0 8 4	0 10 0	
Liverpool	Macclesfield	River Mersey, Bridgewater Canal, Rochdale Canal, Ashton, Peak Forest, and Macclesfield Canals.	74½	10 10	14 2	15 10	0 18 4	1 2 6	1 10 0	
Do	Bollington		72½	14 2	15 0	15 10	1 0 0	1 5 0	1 10 0	
Do	Marple	River Mersey, Bridgewater Canal, Rochdale Canal, Ashton and Park Forest Canals.	63¼	10 10	12 6	14 2	0 15 10	0 19 2	1 2 6	
Do	New Mills		66¾							
Do	Whaley Bridge		69¼	12 6	14 2	15 10	0 17 6	1 0 0	1 5 0	
Do	Chapel-le-Frith		72$\frac{5}{4}$	10 0	15 0	17 6	1 0 0	1 5 0	1 13 4	
Do	Hyde		57¼	9 2	10 10	12 6	0 14 2	0 16 8	1 1 8	
Do	Ashton	River Mersey, Bridgewater Canal, Rochdale Canal, and Ashton Canal.	54¾	8 4	10 0	11 8	0 13 4	0 15 10	1 0 0	
Do	Stockport		55¾	7 6	8 4	10 0	0 11 8	0 14 2	0 17 6	

* These rates are per ton of 2,240 pounds.

NOTE.—See classification-book for articles included in each class.

E.

STATEMENT SHOWING TOLLS LEVIED ON ENGLISH CANALS.

COMPILED FOR THE UNITED STATES SENATE COMMITTEE ON TRANSPORTATION-ROUTES TO THE SEABOARD.

Tolls on the Macclesfield Canal.

Coals for burning lime, 1*d.* per ton per mile for 13 miles, then free.

Coal, slack, cannel, coke, culm, and cinders, (except for burning lime,) ¾*d.* per ton per mile.

Limestone, ½*d.* per ton per mile.

Limestone taken as back-carriage in boats which shall have previously brought and paid for at least 5 tons not less than 9 miles on the same voyage, ¼*d.* per ton per mile.

Lime, lime-ashes, and road-stone, ½*d.* per ton per mile.

Salt, ½*d.* per ton per mile.

Malt, ¾*d.* per ton per mile.

Iron, ¾*d.* per ton per mile.

All goods, wares, merchandise, and other articles not mentioned above, 1*d.* per ton per mile.

Tolls on the Peak Forest Canal.

Coal, cannel, slack, and coke navigated above 5 miles, 1*d.* per ton per mile.

Coals, except for burning lime, navigated 5 miles or a shorter distance, 2*d.* per ton per mile.

Coal for burning lime, 1*d.* per ton per mile for 7 miles, then free.

Gritstone, flags, slate, common bricks, dung, sand and gravel, bowlders, engine-ashes, clay, 1*d.* per ton per mile for 12 miles, then free.

Limestone for roads, 1*d.* per ton per mile for 15 miles, then free.

Lime, ashes, street-scrapings, soil, and peat-earth, ½*d.* per ton per mile.

Salt and limestone, ¾*d.* per ton per mile.

Tiles, quarries, earthenware-pipes, fire-bricks, stock-bricks, malt, lead, pig-iron, brass-lumps, scrap-iron, iron-ore, bar-iron, sheet, plate, and hoop-iron, and large iron castings and lime, 1*d.* per ton per mile.

Steel in bars, spar and chirt-bones, and grain, 1½*d.* per ton per mile.

Timber, general goods, &c., 2*d.* per ton per mile.

Tolls on the Ashton Canal.

Coal and cannel, passing locks, 1½*d.* per ton per mile for 8 miles, then free.

Gritstone, flags, slate, iron-ore, coal, cannel, brass-lumps. 1*d.*, (not passing locks.)

Lime, lime-ashes, limestone, sand and gravel, street-scrapings, dung, clay, and marl-salt, ½*d.* per ton per mile and 2*s.* per boat extra.

Stock-bricks and seconds, common bricks, timber, goods, wares, and merchandise, 1¾*d.*, per ton per mile, not passing locks.

Gritstone, flags, slate, brass-lumps, scrap-iron, pig-iron, iron-ore bowlders, 1½*d.* per ton per mile, not passing locks.

Malt and grain, lead, timber, bark, bones, horns, hoofs, and hides, steel, 2*d.* per ton per mile, passing locks.

Fire-bricks, tiles, and unpacked brown earthenware, 1*d.* per ton per mile.

Iron, all kinds, unpacked, 1½*d.* per ton per mile.

Grain and flour from Macclesfield Canal to Manchester, 1*d.* per ton per mile.

All other goods, 2*d.* per ton per mile.

Sheffield Canal.

For coal, culm, charcoal, road materials, manures, lime and limestone, ½*d.* per ton per mile.

For iron, slate, stone, bricks, tiles, and clay, 1*d.* per ton per mile.

For grain, timber, general merchandise, and all other articles not before enumerated, 1*d.* per ton per mile.

Dun Navigation and Deame and Dove Canal.

For coal, culm, and charcoal, ½*d.* per ton per mile.

For road materials, manures, lime, and limestone, ½*d.* per ton per mile.

For iron, slates, stone, bricks, tiles, and clay, 1*d.* per ton per mile.

For grain, timber, general merchandise, and all other articles, 1½*d.* per ton per mile.

Tolls on the Chesterfield Canal.

CLAUSE 265—12 AND 13 VICTORIA, CHAPTER 86.

General merchandise, grain, timber, and iron, 1*d.* per ton per mile.
Coal, 1*d.* per ton per mile, then free.
Coal going into Trent beyond Stockwith, 3*s.* 6*d.* per ton gross.
Drawback of 2*s.* per ton on all coal delivered into Trent.
Drawback of 2*s.* 6*d.* on all coal going coastwise, or beyond seas.
Stone. 1½*d.* per ton per mile for 20 miles, then free.
Manure, ½*d.* per ton per mile.

Stairforth and Keadby Canal.

For coal, culm, charcoal, road-materials, manure, lime, and limestone, ½*d.* per ton per mile.

For iron, slate, stone, bricks, tiles, and clay, 1*d.* per ton per mile.

For grain, timber, general merchandise, and all other articles not before enumerated, 1½*d.* per ton per mile.

The following tables, marked, respectively, A and B, are taken from the second report of the parliamentary commission on Irish railways:

TABLE A.—*Showing the excess of expenditure (including payments to companies and interest on borrowed money) over receipts, or of receipts over expenditure, from* 1835 *to* 1867, *on railways worked by the state in Belgium.*

Year.	Length worked.	Annual excess of expenditure.	Annual excess of receipts.	Year.	Length worked.	Annual excess of expenditure.	Annual excess of receipts.
	Miles.				*Miles.*		
1835	9	£4, 247	....	1852	387	....	£28, 781
1836	22	....	£5, 728	1853	301	....	84, 306
1837	56	34, 518	....	1854	395	....	150, 414
1838	125	27, 486	....	1855	404	....	144, 361
1839	169	49, 071	....	1856	442	....	67, 009
1840	201	93, 331	....	1857	462	....	110, 373
1841	211	239, 530	....	1858	463	....	155, 245
1842	247	131, 548	....	1859	463	....	175, 187
1843	300	141, 725	....	1860	463	....	256, 669
1844	347	65, 383	....	1861	464	....	327, 688
1845	347	43, 246	....	1862	464	....	339, 953
1846	347	34, 581	....	1863	464	....	329, 255
1847	347	84, 692	....	1864	464	....	374, 485
1848	369	151, 146	....	1865	464	....	344, 792
1849	387	65, 628	....	1866	490	....	209, 959
1850	387	82, 218	....	1867	535	....	183, 622
1851	387	12, 915	....	Total			2, 807, 228
Total		1, 261, 265					

TABLE B.—*Showing the reduction on fourth-class goods from the scale of 1856 to the scale of February 1, 1868.*

Distances.	Belgian fourth-class goods.				
	Charge per ton in 1856.	Charge per ton in 1868.	Amount of reduction.	Percentage of reduction.	Charge per ton per mile in 1868, including terminals.
	s. d.	*s. d.*	*s. d.*	*Per ct.*	*d.*
15 miles	1 11	1 7	0 4	17	1.27
31 miles	3 2	2 5	0 9	24	.93
46 miles	4 4	3 2	1 2	27	.83
62 miles	5 7	3 7	2 0	36	.69
77 miles	6 9	3 9	3 0	44	.59
93 miles	8 0	4 0	4 0	50	.51
108 miles	9 2	4 2	5 0	55	.46
124 miles	10 5	4 5	6 0	58	.43
139 miles	11 7	4 7	7 0	60	.40
155 miles	12 10	4 10	8 0	62	.37

LETTER FROM THE UNITED STATES INSPECTORS OF STEAM-VESSELS AT CINCINNATI, IN REGARD TO THE NAVIGATION OF THE OHIO RIVER.

OFFICE OF UNITED STATES LOCAL INSPECTORS OF STEAM-VESSELS,
Cincinnati, Ohio, September 2, 1873.

SIR: In compliance with verbal request made by you on the 26th ultimo, we submit the following in regard to the suspension of navigation on the Ohio River, by both low water and ice.

During the ten years from 1863 to 1872, inclusive, there has been 120 days when the larger class of steamboats could not navigate on account of low water, viz: in the year 1863, 45 days; in 1864, 17 days; in 1867, 24 days; in 1871, 25 days; and in 1872, 9 days, making a total of 120 days. During that period the smaller class of steamers were not compelled to suspend navigation entirely, but they could not be loaded to their capacity while so navigating,

During that period there were 249 days when the water was 4 feet and under in depth; the lowest depth was 2 feet 4 inches; the average depth under 4 feet was 3½ feet; the water was 3 feet and under for a period of 73 days, thus suspending navigation in a great degree.

While navigating at such a stage of water the expense of freight and passage is at least 33 per cent. higher than when there is a great stage of water, say from 6 to 9 feet.

The largest class of steamers have a carrying capacity of from 1,000 to 1,600 tons, and the average draught is as follows: When loaded, 9 feet; when light, 3½ feet.

There is a smaller class of steamers, of capacity between 400 and 600 tons, whose average draught loaded is 6 feet, and when light 2 feet. A still smaller class of vessels of from 200 to 400 tons, whose average draught loaded is 4 feet, and when light, 1½ feet, but the smallest vessels in extreme low water are compelled to tow lighters to facilitate their passage over bars.

During the years 1863 and 1872, inclusive, navigation has been totally suspended by reason of ice for a period of 180 days. During the winter of 1872 and 1873 there was a suspension of about 30 days. There has been an average suspension by ice of about two weeks in each year.

Very respectfully,

H. H. DEVENNY,
C. W. FISHER,
United States Local Inspectors.

R. H. STEPHENSON, Esq.,
Surveyor of Customs, Cincinnati, Ohio.

Shipments from Chicago by lake during the year 1873.

[From the annual report of the Chicago Board of Trade.]

Articles.		January.	February.	March.	April.	May.	June.	July.	August.	September.	October.	November.	December.	Total.
Flour	bbls			80	1, 275	69, 330	69, 585	69, 270	66, 367	56, 663	54, 339	41, 337	75	428, 321
Wheat	bush				192, 084	1, 823, 319	1, 184, 248	1, 119, 941	2, 092, 460	4, 205, 776	3, 263, 902	1, 647, 263		15, 528, 984
Corn	do			200	1, 295, 327	4, 082, 589	4, 566, 847	5, 690, 516	6, 213, 981	3, 641, 945	6, 420, 158	2, 664, 542	2, 906	34, 487, 205
Oats	do			1, 269	7, 407	771, 664	1, 367, 452	1, 088, 278	609, 223	201, 164	1, 507, 094	428, 403	4, 900	5, 985, 954
Rye	do					68, 435	179, 913	47, 644	191, 338	128, 227	103, 443	61, 009		690, 009
Barley	do					300	12, 032	7, 153		150, 063	470, 568	128, 653		768, 769
Corn-meal	bbls				1, 120	3, 300	5, 090	1, 649	2, 055	1, 843	473	1, 133		16, 603
Corn-meal	bags					968	855	630	424	723	360	439		4, 399
Feed	do			214	580	7, 009	8, 195	5, 399	7, 287	7, 862	12, 958	10, 179		59, 683
Seeds	lbs				26, 240	276, 839	49, 060	65, 430	587, 185	1, 981, 295	1, 149, 010	727, 350		4, 862, 400
Broom-corn	bales			65	48	504	247	214	152	855	866	260		3, 211
Beef	bbls			20	56	453	515	309	86	124	1, 271	1, 241	25	4, 100
Pork	do				121	3, 000	3, 825	2, 660	3, 020	4, 214	5, 382	4, 829	77	27, 728
Lard	lbs				1, 500	146, 200	486, 700	200, 700	373, 000	727, 660	918, 650	40, 100		2, 894, 510
Tallow	bbls				6	36	215	16	22	1	33	60		389
Butter	pkgs					53	467	104	150	108	299	131		1, 312
Grease	bbls					51	29	30	48	426	10	104		698
Hams	tierces					168	12	41	66	22	16	16		341
Hides	No	501			4, 463	4, 398	6, 553	5, 198	5, 465	3, 171	3, 726	5, 014		38, 489
Pelts	bales					112	483	873	928	1, 612	212	46		4, 266
Wool	lbs						37, 500		60, 150	8, 000				105, 650
Lumber	feet				1, 000	157, 000	209, 000	335, 000	585, 700	140, 000	120, 000			1, 506, 700
Laths	No					20, 000	15, 000	100, 000		50, 000				185, 000
Shingles	do					900, 000								900, 000
Brick	do				32, 000		40, 500	15, 000	40, 000					127, 500
Anthracite coal	tons				1		1	6	37	98	32	24		199
Bituminous coal	do			36	2	39	6	85	3	30	32	30		254
Liquors and high-wines	pkgs			10	124	1, 052	771	669	685	801	943	586	7	5, 648
Ale and beer	do				170	536	849	796	741	851	402	255		4, 600
Railroad-iron	bars					509	1, 111	930	7, 405	6, 918	564	214	100	17, 751
Hay	bales			93	607	1, 764	968	1, 080	2, 415	2, 382	4, 281	3, 658	195	17, 353
Fish	pkgs						280	31	119	77	47			554
Salt	bbls				155	1, 361	855	1, 174	1, 750	654	778	359		7, 086
Oil-cake	bags				2, 000	3, 359	2, 529	2, 175	2, 000	1, 045	3, 776	1, 877		18, 761
Oil	bbls	180		780	355	922	794	764	689	631	738	429	41	6, 323
Cattle	No				10	439	163	315	308	59	45	55		1, 394
Merchandise	pkgs	199		890	9, 157	30, 800	29, 512	31, 721	36, 853	40, 880	59, 011	22, 426	524	261, 973
Sundries	do	185		832	3, 585	22, 425	19, 693	17, 344	16, 508	9, 969	11, 942	10, 206	457	113, 144

TONNAGE OF THE PRINCIPAL AND OTHER ARTICLES SHIPPED EAST FROM CHICAGO, DURING THE YEAR 1873, ON THE LAKE SHORE AND MICHIGAN SOUTHERN RAILWAY, THE MICHIGAN CENTRAL RAILROAD, THE PITTSBURGH, FORT WAYNE AND CHICAGO RAILWAY, AND THE PITTSBURGH, CINCINNATI AND SAINT LOUIS RAILWAY, COMPUTED FROM DATA IN THE LAST REPORT OF THE CHICAGO BOARD OF TRADE.

Articles.	Quantities.	Tons.
Flour .... barrels..	1, 773, 467	177, 346. 7
Wheat .... bushels..	8, 149, 209	424, 476
Corn .... do....	2, 194, 561	61, 447. 7
Oats .... do....	9, 599, 635	152, 954
Rye .... do....	242, 553	6, 791
Barley .... do....	2, 225, 733	53, 417
Beans .... do....	2, 665	80
Seeds .... pounds..	18, 351, 247	9, 175. 6
Mill-stuff and feed .... do....	37, 191, 284	18, 595. 6
Fresh provisions .... do....	17, 730, 187	8, 865. 1
Beef .... barrels..	28, 939	4, 774. 9
Cured meats .... pounds..	328, 725, 491	164, 362. 7
Pork .... barrels..	128, 610	21, 220. 6
Lard .... pounds..	84, 203, 888	42, 101. 9
Tallow .... do....	11, 148 873	5, 574. 5
Grease .... do....	1, 822, 674	911. 3
Stearine .... do....	695, 068	347. 5
Cheese .... do....	352, 772	176. 3
Butter .... do....	11, 919, 283	5, 959. 6
Dressed hogs .... number..	193, 225	11, 322. 5
Live hogs .... do....	2, 179, 439	196, 199. 5
Cattle .... do....	511, 052	316, 631. 2
Sheep .... do....	105, 812	4, 497
Horses and mules .... do....	17, 715	7, 881. 7
Hides .... pounds..	28, 539, 201	14, 269. 6
High-wines, liquors, ale, and beer .... barrels..	104, 642	18, 808. 5
Alcohol .... do....	20, 408	3, 673
Coal .... tons..	3, 755	3, 755
Iron-ore .... pounds..	2, 465, 662	1, 232. 8
Silver-ore .... do....	8, 211, 955	4, 105. 9
Pig-iron .... do....	3, 618, 000	1, 809
Stone .... cubic yards..	3, 357	6, 797. 5
Lime and cement .... barrels..	1, 456	236. 6
Lead .... pounds..	15, 292, 939	7, 646. 4
Iron and nails .... do....	23, 123, 691	11, 561. 8
Wool .... do....	32, 506, 743	16, 253. 3
Broom-corn .... do....	4, 995, 015	2, 497. 5
Potatoes .... bushels..	177, 252	5, 317. 5
Hay .... tons..	3, 333	3, 333
Hops .... pounds..	452, 348	226. 1
Empty barrels .... number..	15, 016	450. 4
Salt .... barrels..	3, 740	561
Fish .... packages..	7, 851	1, 177. 6
Eggs .... do ...	45, 994	1, 839. 7
Oil-cake .... pounds..	13, 198, 426	6, 599. 2
Oil .... barrels..	8, 796	1, 759. 2
Furs and pelts .... pounds..	313, 849	156. 9
Tobacco .... do....	4, 334, 132	2, 167
Machinery and wagons .... do....	1, 136, 445	568. 2
Green and dried fruits .... packages..	1, 034	93
Sugar and molasses .... do....	5, 053	3, 530
Tea .... pounds..	1, 572, 649	786. 3
Cotton .... do....	21, 310	10. 6
Bullion .... do....	11, 736, 490	5, 868. 2
Lumber .... feet..	52, 823, 900	66, 103. 7
Shingles .... number..	34, 299, 000	6, 002. 3
Laths .... do....	7, 780, 000	778
Staves and headings .... do....	23, 000	57. 5
Merchandise and sundries .... pounds..	318, 549, 153	159, 274. 5
Total tonnage	....	2, 054, 416. 7

Dimensions and capacity of Canadian canals in their present condition, (1871.)

[From the report of the canal commission respecting the improvement of the inland navigation of the Dominion of Canada, dated October 24, 1871.]

Canals.		Date of opening.	Length.	Locks.	Lockage.	Size of lock.	Size of canal.		Size of vessel which can pass.	Tonnage.
							Bottom.	Top W.		
Saint Lawrence Canals	Lachine	1848	8½	5	44¾	2 (200 by 45 by 16) 3 (200 by 45 by 9)	80	120	180 by 44 by 9	700
	Beauharnois	1845	11¼	9	82½	200 by 45 by 9	80	120	180 by 44 by 9	700
	Cornwall	1843	11½	7	48	200 by 55 by 9	100	150	120 by 44 by 9	700
	Farran's Point	1847	0¾	1	4	200 by 45 by 9	50	90	180 by 44 by 9	700
	Rapid Plat	1847	4	2	11½	200 by 45 by 9	50	90	180 by 44 by 9	700
	Galops	1847	7⅝	3	15¾	200 by 45 by 9	50	90	180 by 44 by 9	700
Total, (Saint Lawrence Canals)		......	43⅝	27	206½	200 by 45 by 9	50 80 100	90 120 150	180 by 44 by 9	700
Welland Canal on the main line		1846	26 1-5	27	346	1 (230 by 45 by 12) 24 (150 by 26 1-2 by 10¼) 1 (200 by 45 by 10¼) 1 (200 by 45 by 12)	70 58 50 26	110 (rock) 58 90 66	142 by 26¼ by 10¼	500
Saint Ours Lock		1849	0½	1	5	200 by 45 by 7	....	....	180 by 44 by 7	600
Chambly Canal		1843	12	9	74	118 by 23 by 7	30	60	110 by 23 by 6½	230
Rideau Canal		1832	126¼	47	446¼	134 by 33 by 5	54 60	80	120 by 31½ by 4½	250
Ottawa Canals	Saint Ann's Lock	1843	0⅛	1	3	190 by 45 by 6.7	....	....	170 by 44 by 6	600
	Carillon Canal	1834	2⅛	3	34¾	126 1-2 by 32 1-4 by 6	30	50	117 by 32 by 5½	300
	Chute à Blondeau	1834	0½	1	3¾	130 5-6 by 32 5-6 by 6	30	30	120 by 32 by 5½	300
	Grenville Canal	1834	5¾	7	45¾	4 (128 by 31 5-6 by 6) 3 (107 by 19 by 6)	20 30	25 60	95 by 18½ by 5	100
Saint Peter's Canal, Cape Breton, Bras d'Or Lake		1869	0½	Tidal, 1	9	122 by 26 by 13	26	....	114 by 25¾ by 13	500
AMERICAN CANALS.										
Erie Canal, enlarged		1862	352	72	655	110 by 18 by 7	56	70	102 by 17½ by 6½	210
Champlain Canal		1822	66	20	180	97 by 14 by 4	35	50	89 by 13½ by 3½	70
Sault Ste. Marie Canal		......	1⅛	2	19	350 by 70 by 12	....	....	330 by 69 by 12	2,000

OTTAWA, *February* 24, 1871.

SAMUEL KEEFER,
Secretary Canal Commission.

Statement of the tons of property moved on the Erie, Champlain, and Oswego Canals—1837 to 1872, inclusive.

Years.	Erie.	Champlain.	Oswego.	Years.	Erie.	Champlain.	Oswego.
1837..........	667, 151	261, 659	161, 353	1855..........	2, 202, 463	537, 108	654, 399
1838..........	744, 848	266, 553	222, 697	1856..........	2, 107, 678	611, 610	657, 381
1839..........	845, 007	263, 552	221, 014	1857..........	1, 566, 624	547, 236	605, 218
1840..........	829, 960	245, 229	219, 627	1858..........	1, 767, 004	608, 918	688, 960
1841..........	906, 442	276, 418	135, 689	1859..........	1, 753, 954	751, 046	612, 390
1842..........	712, 310	230, 844	129, 498	1860..........	2, 253, 533	681, 157	1, 080, 076
1843..........	819, 216	262, 212	240, 571	1861..........	2, 500, 782	545, 930	852, 930
1844..........	945, 944	269, 546	326, 607	1862..........	3, 204, 277	647, 318	1, 063, 413
1845..........	1, 038, 700	266, 922	340, 481	1863..........	2, 955, 302	878, 920	992, 173
1846..........	1, 264, 408	280, 480	351, 511	1864..........	2, 535, 792	846, 790	765, 097
1847..........	1, 661, 575	313, 124	441, 096	1865..........	2, 523, 490	815, 311	825, 649
1848..........	1, 599, 965	293, 889	490, 147	1866..........	2, 896, 027	1, 001, 493	990, 809
1849..........	1, 622, 444	321, 345	557, 637	1867..........	2, 920, 578	1, 047, 440	940, 136
1850..........	1, 635, 089	460, 219	583, 346	1868..........	3, 346, 986	1, 120, 585	958, 444
1851..........	1, 955, 265	513, 793	676, 321	1869..........	2, 845, 072	1, 059, 334	934, 638
1852..........	2, 129, 334	531, 001	684, 191	1870..........	3, 083, 132	1, 143, 719	917, 728
1853..........	2, 196, 308	608, 354	761, 276	1871..........	3, 580, 922	1, 099, 995	941, 858
1854..........	2, 224, 008	602, 913	611, 533	1872..........	3, 562, 560	1, 449, 528	832, 490

Table for the reduction of sterling money of Great Britain to United States gold coin, under act approved March 3, 1873, fixing the value of the £ sterling at $4.8665.

[Prepared by the First Comptroller of the Treasury, April 1, 1873.]

	0	1	2	3	4	5	6	7	8	9
1	4. 8665	53. 5315	58. 398	63. 2645	68. 131	72. 9975	77. 864	82. 7305	87. 597	92. 4635
2	9. 733	102. 1965	107. 063	111. 9295	116. 796	121. 6625	126. 529	131. 3955	136. 262	141. 1285
3	14. 5995	150. 8615	155. 728	160. 5945	165. 461	170. 3275	175. 194	180. 0605	184. 927	189. 7935
4	19. 466	199. 5265	204. 393	209. 2595	214. 126	218. 9925	223. 859	228. 7255	233. 592	238. 4585
5	24. 3325	248. 1915	253. 058	257. 9245	262. 791	267. 6575	272. 524	277. 3905	282. 257	287. 1235
6	29. 199	296. 8565	301. 723	306. 5895	311. 456	316. 3225	321. 189	326. 0555	330. 922	335. 7885
7	34. 0655	345. 5215	350. 388	355. 2545	360. 121	364. 9875	369. 854	374. 7205	379. 587	384. 4535
8	38. 932	394. 1865	399. 053	403. 9195	408. 786	413. 6525	418. 519	423. 3855	428. 252	533. 1185
9	43. 7985	442. 8515	447. 718	452. 5845	457. 451	462. 3175	467. 184	472. 0505	476. 917	481. 7835

One shilling equals $24\frac{133}{400}$ cents. One penny equals $2\frac{133}{4800}$ cents.

	0	1	2	3	4	5	6	7	8	9	10	11	12	13	14	15	16	17	18	19
0	....	. 24	. 48	. 73	. 97	1. 21	1. 46	1. 70	1. 94	2. 19	2. 43	2. 67	2. 92	3. 16	3. 40	3. 65	3. 89	4. 13	4. 38	4. 62
1	. 02	. 26	. 50	. 75	. 99	1. 23	1. 48	1. 72	1. 96	2. 21	2. 45	2. 69	2. 94	3. 18	3. 42	3. 67	3. 91	4. 15	4. 40	4. 64
2	. 04	. 28	. 52	. 77	1. 01	1. 25	1. 50	1. 74	1. 98	2. 23	2. 47	2. 71	2. 96	3. 20	3. 44	3. 69	3. 93	4. 17	4. 42	5. 66
3	. 06	. 30	. 54	. 79	1. 03	1. 27	1. 52	1. 76	2. 00	2. 25	2. 49	2. 73	2. 98	3. 22	3. 46	3. 71	3. 95	4. 19	4. 44	4. 68
4	. 08	. 32	. 56	. 81	1. 05	1. 29	1. 54	1. 78	2. 02	2. 27	2. 51	2. 75	3. 00	3. 24	3. 48	3. 73	3. 97	4. 21	4. 46	4. 70
5	. 10	. 34	. 58	. 83	1. 07	1. 31	1. 56	1. 80	2. 04	2. 29	2. 53	2. 77	3. 02	3. 26	3. 50	3. 75	3. 99	4. 23	4. 48	4. 72
6	. 12	. 36	. 60	. 85	1. 09	1. 33	1. 58	1. 82	2. 06	2. 31	2. 55	2. 79	3. 04	3. 28	3. 52	3. 77	4. 01	4. 25	4. 50	4. 74
7	. 14	. 38	. 62	. 87	1. 11	1. 35	1. 60	1. 84	2. 08	2. 33	2. 57	2. 81	3. 06	3. 30	3. 54	3. 79	4. 03	4. 27	4. 52	4. 76
8	. 16	. 40	. 64	. 89	1. 13	1. 37	1. 62	1. 86	2. 10	2. 35	2. 59	2. 83	3. 08	3. 32	3. 56	3. 81	4. 05	4. 29	4. 54	4. 78
9	. 18	. 42	. 66	. 91	1. 15	1. 39	1. 64	1. 88	2. 12	2. 37	2. 61	2. 85	3. 10	3. 34	3. 58	3. 83	4. 07	4. 31	4. 56	4. 80
10	. 20	. 44	. 68	. 93	1. 17	1. 41	1 66	1. 90	2. 14	2. 39	2. 63	2. 87	3. 12	3. 36	3. 60	3. 85	4. 09	4. 33	4. 58	4. 82
11	. 22	. 46	. 70	. 95	1. 19	1. 43	1. 68	1. 92	2. 16	2. 41	2. 65	2. 89	3. 14	3. 38	3. 62	3. 87	4. 11	4. 35	4. 60	4. 84

NOTE.—To find the value of any number of pounds represented by one figure, find the figure in the left-hand margin of the upper table, and its value will appear in the column adjoining, opposite that figure. To find the value when expressed by two figures, look for the *tens* in the left-hand column, and for the *units* in the top margin, and the value will be shown in the place where the two columns meet; thus, the value of 57 £ is $277.3905. To find the value of 576 £, look for 57 as before, and move the decimal point one place to the right, and it shows $2,773.905; then add 6 £ as already shown, $29.199, and it gives the sum of $2,803.104.

The lower table shows the value of every combination of shillings and pence less than 1 £; the upper margin representing the shillings, and the left-hand margin the pence. Thus, to find the value of 17 shillings and 6 pence, follow the column 17 downward until it meets the left-hand column opposite 6, and it shows $4.25. By this method any number of pounds, shillings, and pence can be reduced to United States gold quickly and accurately.

O

www.ingramcontent.com/pod-product-compliance
Lightning Source LLC
LaVergne TN
LVHW020913110826
845150LV00004B/660

9781425555696